PERESTROIKA!

PERESTROIKA!

The Raucous Rebellion
in Political Science

EDITED BY

Kristen Renwick Monroe

YALE UNIVERSITY PRESS

New Haven and London

Designed and typeset by Princeton Editorial Associates, Inc., Scottsdale, Arizona.
Set in ITC Stone Serif.
Printed in the United States of America by Vail-Ballou Press, Kirkwood, New York.

Library of Congress Cataloging-in-Publication Data

Perestroika!: the raucous rebellion in political science / edited by Kristen Renwick Monroe.
     p.   cm.
  Includes bibliographical references and index.
  ISBN 0-300-09981-9 (pb: alk. paper)
     1. Political science—Study and teaching (Higher)—United States.   I. Monroe, Kristen
R., 1946–
JA88.U6P47   2005
320'.071'173—dc22   2004030554

A catalogue record for this book is available from the British Library.

The paper in this book meets the guidelines for permanence and durability of the Committee
on Production Guidelines for Book Longevity of the Council on Library Resources.

10 9 8 7 6 5 4 3 2 1

Contents

Acknowledgments

My thanks to John Kulka at Yale University Press for suggesting I edit a volume on Perestroika, to the anonymous referees for comments on revising the volume, to the contributors and members of the Perestroika list for their suggestions on readings that might be used in courses on scope and methods, and to the intrepid Edna Mejia, Ted Wrigley, Amy Alexander, and Saba Ozyurt for their assistance in pulling together the final manuscript. I am grateful to Perestroika—the anonymous person or group—for allowing me to reprint the original communiqué, and to the American Political Science Association (APSA) for its permission to reproduce both the Jacobson Report (Chapter 17) and the Report of the APSA Task Force on Graduate Education (Chapter 29). Although most chapters were written expressly for this volume, a few appeared in print, occasionally in slightly different form, in prior publications. I thank *Political Theory* for its permission to reprint parts of Chapter 8 (Sanford Schram), *Politics and Society* for use of parts of Chapter 9 (David Laitin), and *PS: Political Science and Politics* for permission to reprint Chapter 32 (Gregory Kasza).

Introduction

Kristen Renwick Monroe

Late in the summer of 2000, a small group of political scientists decided they had had enough. Fed up with what they saw as the narrow parochialism and methodological bias toward the quantitative, behavioral, rational choice, statistical, and formal modeling approaches in American political science and concerned that the American Political Science Association (APSA) system of governance systematically underrepresented critical groups, they established an untraceable e-mail address and issued a call for change. Inspired by Mikhail Gorbachev's 1985 call for reform, they chose the name Perestroika.[1] The Russian name reflected the two ideals central to the Perestroika movement: the commitment to restructuring American political science and the desire to welcome—as a warm house welcomes—new ideas and new participants into the political process.[2] The movement was anonymous because the initial participants feared professional reprisal from an establishment angered at criticism and at attempts to transform the discipline.[3]

The initial Perestroika communiqué was sent to some ten individuals, who then were asked to forward it to anyone they thought might be interested. The movement spread like the proverbial wildfire. Fueled by discontent within the academy, the list of political scientists receiving the Perestroika e-mail messages grew. Perestroika began sponsoring events at the annual APSA and regional meetings in 2001, and within two years the face of political science had changed. A new journal and a qualitative section were established by the APSA. Women were chosen as APSA presidents three years in a row. The APSA established formal task forces or committees to encourage the mentoring of women and minorities and to examine graduate education and APSA governance. Although Perestroika was certainly not the only force campaigning for these changes, it is fair to say that its existence played a critical part in the impetus for reform.

The chapters in this volume describe these events. They attempt to outline the basic arguments by and responses to Perestroika that were offered as the American political science community attempted to deal with change at the turn of the twenty-first century. The contributors are, for the most part, people who entered the debate with Perestroika on one of the topics mentioned in the previous paragraph. Perestroika raised complex issues, and the contributors vary in their positions on some of these issues. As editor, I have done minimal editing, choosing to let the authors convey some of the passion as well as the factual details behind what I shall refer to simply as Perestroika.[4] But I have tried to organize the contributions around a few general themes.

What is Perestroika all about? Why did the movement occur when it did, and in this form? What has it accomplished? What might it have done differently? What remains to be done? And, most important, what can we learn about the issues on which the Perestroika movement has focused our attention: the scientific nature of political science, methodological pluralism and diversity, APSA governance, the community of scholars in political science and how they publish their work, and how ideas are transmitted via graduate education? The book is organized around these themes. Part 1 sets the Perestroika movement in historical and comparative perspectives. The volume then moves to the issue at the heart of the Perestroika movement: the restructuring of the accepted conceptualization and methodology of the scientific study of politics (Part 2). Because methodological issues are related to questions of power and influence, the volume next addresses issues raised by Perestroika concerning APSA governance (Part 3), publication in journals (Part 4), and graduate education (Part 5). The book closes with a range of assessments of the Perestroika movement (Part 6).

Within this framework, I encourage readers to think about the following questions while reading the diverse chapters. Does American political science need to be restructured? Is it inhospitable to certain kinds of work? If so, is this attitude justified? Can we adopt a pluralistic approach to the scientific study of politics, or are there scientific standards in social science that tell us certain kinds of work genuinely are better than others? If not, how are we to assess work when hiring, publishing, and teaching? If so, what are these standards? Are they the standards currently used by editors of the profession's top journals? Are they the ones we use when choosing officers and Council members of the APSA or assigning texts to our students?

Such questions touch on the basic concept of science. How we respond to debate and criticism seems intimately related to our view of science. One troubling aspect of the current discussion surrounding the Perestroika movement has been its occasional emotional intensity, which carries the risk of hardening into intolerance and defensiveness. Such a position seems inimical to the essence of scientific discovery; members of our profession should take science seriously but respect alternate views and not demonize those who disagree. Underlying the essence of good science—however that is defined—is the belief that our work today can show that our work yesterday was wrong. This view has to carry with it the idea that our work today also can be proven wrong tomorrow. I hope readers can bear this humbling caveat in mind as we ask how science is being advanced in our profession. Is scientific progress being made? If so, what do Perestroika's claims tell us about the state of this progress in political science? Or is the Kuhnian model more apt, and does Perestroika simply represent the latest swing in the pendulum of scientific debate?

The authors of this volume offer diverse and varied answers to these questions, as do members of the Perestroika movement itself. The issues raised by Perestroika are important ones central to the teaching of and scholarship about political science. Regardless of what the individual reader eventually decides about any particular issue—from APSA governance to methodological diversity, or even about Perestroika as a political movement within academia— these issues will concern the discipline for many years. I hope this volume will contribute in positive ways to a vital debate.

Notes

1. Occasionally they also used the name Perestroika-glasnost. I should note that I do not know if the original Perestroika is one person or a group. If pressed, I would guess the original Perestroika consists of a group of scholars and includes some graduate students. But this is merely a guess

2. The earliest communiqués used the terms *perestroika* and *perestroika-glasnost,* with the initial communiqué (see Chapter 1) signed "Mr. Perestroika." What was meant by these terms? Since Perestroika is an anonymous entity, we cannot ask them. So what follows is only inferential.

In *Perestroika* (1987), Mikhail Gorbachev addresses this question directly, noting that he used the term *perestroika* to refer to many different phenomena. One definition he gives is "overcoming the stagnation process, breaking down the braking mechanism, creating a dependable and effective mechanism for acceleration of social and economic progress and giving it greater dynamism." Another definition is "mass initiative, . . . the conference of development of democracy, socialist self-government, encouragement of initiative and creative endeavor, . . . criticism and self-criticism in spheres of our society. It is utmost respect for the individual and consideration for personal dignity." Later, Gorbachev defines *perestroika* as "the all-round intensification of the Soviet economy, the revival and development of the principles of democratic centralism in running the national economy, the universal introduction of economic methods, the renunciation of management by injunction and by administrative methods, and the overall encouragement of innovation and socialist enterprise." He also characterizes *perestroika* as a "resolute shift to scientific methods, an ability to provide a solid scientific basis for every new initiative." Later Gorbachev defines *perestroika* as "the combination of the achievements of the scientific and technological revolution with a planned economy." Then he says, "*Perestroika* means priority development of the social sphere aimed at even better satisfaction of the Soviet people's requirements for good living and working conditions, for good rest and recreation, education and health care. It means unceasing concern for cultural and spiritual wealth, for the culture of every individual and society as a whole." And still later he says, "*Perestroika* means the elimination from society of the distortions of socialist ethics, the consistent implementation of the principles of social justice. It means the unity of words and deeds, rights and duties. It is the elevation of honest, highly-qualified labor, the overcoming of leveling tendencies in pay and consumerism." Gorbachev, quoted in

Mark Kishlansky, ed., *Source of the West: Readings in Western Civilization,* 4th ed., vol. 2 (New York: Longman, 2001), p. 322.

Given that the term is defined, by the man most closely associated with it, as referring to everything from "unity of words and deeds" to "unceasing concern for cultural and spiritual wealth," how are we to take this term, and what does *perestroika* signify for the Perestroika movement in political science?

I find two definitions most frequently used in the early Perestoika communiqués issued by the entity identified as Mr. Perestroika or Perestroika: "restructuring" and "warm house." The definition of *perestroika* as "restructuring" comes most directly from translation of the Russian term and refers to Mikhail Gorbachev's attempts, from 1985 to 1991, to transform the sluggish, unproductive command economy of the Soviet Union to a decentralized market-oriented economy. As part of this plan, both industrial managers and local government and party officials were given greater autonomy, and open elections were introduced in order to democratize the Communist Party. Hence the definition of the term *perestroika* as "restructuring" is linked by Gorbachev to the definition of *perestroika* as a "warm house" into which reforms opening new avenues of power would be welcomed to the Soviet system. (Ironically, whatever definition one adopts, by 1991 Gorbachev's *perestroika* was in decline, and, after the failed coup of August 1991, *perestroika* was eclipsed by the dramatic changes in the constitution of the now defunct Soviet Union.)

Throughout this volume, the contributers and I shall use the term Perestroika (without italics) to refer to the Perestroika movement in American political science; We place the term in italics when it refers to the Russian movement. I find two ideals central to the American Perestroika movement: the idea of restructuring American political science and the desire to welcome new ideas and new participants to the political process, as is suggested by the definition "warm house."

I shall refer to Perestroika as "they" because it avoids the awkwardness of "he/she" and because my guess is that Perestroika is a group of people. I repeat my prior disclaimer: I have no knowledge as to Perestroika's identity, and even if I did know who issued the original Perestroika communiqué, I would respect Perestroika's wishes to remain anonymous.

3. Some contributors—including some sympathetic to Perestroika's concerns—have been troubled by Perestroika's anonymity, and their concern raises an interesting issue. The desire to protest while still protecting oneself, especially among the untenured, is understandable. Indeed, some of the most upsetting Perestroika communiqués have been those from young scholars relating that they have lost jobs or faced censure or discrimination because of their positions on methodological issues. Their stories—often told anonymously—make clear why Perestroika felt some secrecy was needed in order to protect the weak and the vulnerable in our profession. Another response to those who criticize Perestroika for remaining anonymous is that so many Perestroikans *have* spoken openly, identifying themselves publicly on the list. While both of these factors provide a context for Perestroikan anonymity, another aspect of this issue is the extent to which Perestroika, as a social movement demanding democratic elections and openness, is itself neither open nor democratic. This topic is discussed in several of the chapters, and I hope Perestroika will see this as an invitation to respond to this issue at some point.

4. I should perhaps note that I do not see this volume as a polemic. Nor do I claim that it speaks as the voice of Perestroika. The volume does contain the origi-

nal communiqué by Perestroika, and I asked Perestroika to write a fuller piece, but they declined. However, it would be presumptuous to claim to speak for them. Nor do I claim that the volume represents Perestroika's views, although many of the contributors to the volume—the majority, in fact—would probably identify themselves as Perestroikans, loosely defined.

Certainly I would identify myself as a Perestroikan, because I share what I believe are the twin pillars at the core of Perestroika: the desire for greater tolerance of methodological diversity and a commitment to openness in the process by which the political science community is governed. But in some communiqués Perestroika speaks of an APSA establishment or power structure and sets itself against that structure, and though I identify with Perestroika in many respects I also would probably be classed as a member of the APSA establishment because I have served on the APSA Council twice, as APSA vice president, as president of an organized APSA section, and on numerous APSA committees and several task forces. Perhaps for this reason, I find the dichotomy between Perestroika and "the establishment" awkward and misleading. Indeed, Theda Skocpol (2002–03 APSA president) and Susanne Rudolph (2003–04 president) could be classified as sympathetic to many—although not all—of Perestroika's aims, even though they headed the APSA establishment or power structure. So while I respect the right of others, including contributors to this volume, to juxtapose Perestroika with the APSA hierarchy, this is not a dichotomy I find useful myself.

Furthermore, as will be evident from the contributions to this volume, many of the contributors themselves disagree with one another over specific issues and with many of the arguments put forward by other Perestroikans on particular issues. (For example, on the issue of APSA governance, several Perestroikans with chapters in this book do not endorse competitive elections, preferring some less competitive electoral system that ensures protection of the hard-won rights of minority groups.) I have tried to preserve the richness of this disagreement in the contributions presented here because I believe many of the issues Perestroika raises are ones on which reasonable people might honestly disagree, and I take as one of Perestroika's premises the desire for tolerance of opposing views within the academy. I hope presenting a wide array of opinions will both encourage and assist the reader in reaching independent judgment on these issues.

History, Background, and Perspectives of Perestroika

Part 1 opens with the original communiqué sent by Perestroika in an untraceable e-mail with the request that recipients circulate it to friends. This is followed by several chapters designed to place the Perestroika movement in comparative, intellectual, and historical perspectives.

Perhaps the best-known Perestroikan and the president of the APSA during much of the discussion that followed the original communiqué, Susanne Hoeber Rudolph, focuses on the central issue that first united Perestroikans: the methodological hegemony of the political science establishment of the time. But Rudolph also notes that the Perestroika movement has evolved into what she describes as a relatively acephalous and loose organizational form for conversation and engagement among the diverse groups within the political science community. Rudolph argues that the conversation has taken this form in part to accommodate the multiple modes of inquiry subsumed under the Perestroika label. For Rudolph, these various modes are united by their opposition to the monopoly claim of the scientific trope in the social sciences. Rudolph finds considerable and consequential heterogeneity as well within the collective "other" targeted by Perestroika adherents. Despite this variety, each side displays internal commonalities that Rudolph summarizes in two clusters of contrasting attributes. Her chapter uses these contrasting features to explore the differences between Perestroikans and their epistemological other.

Catarina Kinnvall provides an important contrast between American and European social science. Her chapter makes the critical point that the methodological hegemony in American political science—a hegemony that stimulated Perestroika in the first place—does not exist in Europe. With no *ancien régime* to topple, there is no need for rebellion. Her chapter begins by elaborating potential differences between Europe and the United States in regard to intellectual tradition. In particular, Kinnvall outlines how political science and international relations might be defined in the American context, and how that definition interacts with the intellectual, cultural, and institutional traditions characteristic of Europe. The second part of Kinnvall's chapter compares the differences between the European and the United States political science

communities in regard to publications, research, curricula, and career opportunities. Highlighted in this section is the higher visibility of political philosophy in teaching and research in European departments, and how the formalized tenure-track system of the United States affects publication patterns
in comparison to those of Europe. The chapter ends by drawing general conclusions about how the absence of a European Perestroika debate impacts the
profession and the academic status of the discipline.

Theodore J. Lowi brings a historical perspective, comparing the current Perestroika movement with the activities of the Caucus for New Political Science,
which was formed in the late 1960s and early 1970s. Lowi argues that we should
let a hundred Perestroikas blossom, but only if Perestroika nurtures a permanent
spirit of *glasnost* (enlightened confession), which will produce *samokritika*
(self-criticism) throughout the profession. Lowi argues that a war over propor-
tionality in the *American Political Science Review* and in the APSA won't accomplish anything because there is no elite dominance or conspiracy to vanquish.
The best method of analysis, he argues, is a "politics of knowledge": the cultivation of an awareness that dominant fashions in the field are a product of
what the state is doing at that time. Building on his 1991 APSA presidential
address, Lowi presents two case studies—of the "behavioral revolution" and of
the importation of economic rationality into political science—to demonstrate how their hegemony was literally produced by state development.

The chapter by Samuel H. Beer—originally written in response to a request
from a graduate student at Berkeley—extends Lowi's historical perspective.
Beer attempts to paint an informal sketch of the methods of research fancied
by Beer and his Harvard colleagues during the past half century. Beer's chapter
might be read as the story of the rise and fall of behavioralism, a pattern contrasted with what Beer concludes is the continued dominance of a historical
approach. The thrust of Beer's argument is that history demands our attention
as the activity of culture-creating (and -destroying) actors. This capacity precludes the possibility of universally valid laws of political behavior. It does not
rule out the discovery of regularities resulting from the impact of situational
structure upon intentional motivation. But such generalizations are limited to
particular historical contexts. Because political scientists also have this cul-
ture-bearing capacity, they can imagine themselves in the positions of their
subjects of study and thereby grasp what they do and why they do it. This historical method is commonly called *Verstehen,* or subjective understanding. To
emphasize that the subject matter is activity, Beer calls it with regard to explanations of the past "imaginative reenactment" and with regard to predictions
"imaginative preenactment." As outstanding examples of political science in
this vein he cites Adam Ulam's studies of Lenin and Stalin, Sam Huntington's
survey of the clash of civilizations, and Sidney Verba's analysis of civic volun-
tarism. This chapter, by a major figure in twentieth-century comparative politics, raises important issues about the nature of science, especially in a comparative context, and provides a lovely segue into the next part of the book, on
methodological issues.

CHAPTER I

The Idea

The Opening of Debate

Perestroika

[Following is a reprint of the initial communiqué from the individual or group self-named Perestroika, as received by Kristen Monroe. The reprint preserves the original spelling, punctuation, and spacing.]

On the irrelelvence of APSA and APSR!
Please Spread this Letter as widely as Possible
Let them know we Exist
To: The Editor of *PS* and *APSR* [*American Political Science Review*]
October 15, 2000
On Globalization of the APSA and *APSR:* A Political Science Manifesto
----
Questions to ponder over:

1) Why do people like Benedict Anderson and James C. Scott find the APSA and the *APSR* irrelevant? These are probably the most famous political scientists in the world. They are equally famous abroad and in other disciplines compared to the "stars" of Political Science. (Hey, Hey, Vee. Look at their classic book on literary methodologies.)

2) Related to above is the question: Why do a majority of political scientists who do comparative politics ignore APSA and *APSR* and go to their regional meetings and read regional association journals, e.g., such as those associated with East Asia, Latin America, Hispanic Studies, etc?

3) Why does a "coterie" of faculty dominate and control APSA and the editorial board of *APSR?* I scratch your back, you scratch mine. I give an award to your student from Harvard and you give mine from Duke or Columbia. In short why do the "East Coast Brahmins" control APSA?

4) Why are a few men who make poor game-theorists and who cannot for the life-of-me compete with a third grade Economics graduate student, WHY are

these men allowed to represent the diversity of methodologies and areas of the world that APSA "purports" to represent?

5) Why are FAILED Africanists and Economists allowed to dominate a discipline which has a rich history of intellectual contributions from the likes of James Scott, Charles Tilly, Aristide Zolberg, Leonard Binder, Benedict Anderson, R. Bendix, Susanne Rudolph, Theda Skocpol, etc.?

6) Have we learned any lesson from the thousands of pages of research that was funded by APSA in the name of political science to examine the former Soviet Union and make "predictive" models? What happened to those models and why did they fail? How is it that those esteemed colleagues failed to predict the collapse of the Soviet Empire while Sovietologists from Korea, Japan, India and one even from Tanzania could predict the fall of the empire? Are we making the same mistake by ignoring diverse knowledge and methodologies present in the study of Politics?

7) Why isn't [an] *APSR* subscription made separate from the APSA membership so that *APSR* becomes truly representative of a "coterie" that rules APSA while the rest of the true political scientists can devote their money to buying the more important regional journals? Either reform the *APSR* board and have more political historians, area specialists, political-sociologists, and constructivists on the board or let the market decide. You will find a sharp drop in *APSR*'s subscription as soon as *APSR* is delinked from the membership of APSA.

8) Why are the overwhelming majority of Presidents of APSA or editorial board members of APSR WHITE and MALE? Where are the African-Americans, Hispanics, Women, Gays, Asians—in short, where is the diversity of United States and the world that APSA "pretends" to study—is somebody afraid that APSA will slip out of their hands???

9) Why are all the articles of *APSR* from the same methodology—statistics or game theory—with a "symbolic" article in Political Theory that is often a piece that has been rejected by the journal *Political Theory*. Where is political history, international history, political sociology, interpretive methodology, constructivists, area studies, critical theory and last but not the least—post modernism? Why can't you have 5 per cent of the articles in *APSR* allocated under the category: incomprehensible. Then just go ahead and publish game theory, statistics and post-modernism under the category.

10) At a time when the free market models of economics are being challenged in IMF [International Monetary Fund] and World Bank, discredited in much of Asia, and protested by numerous groups, why are simple, baby-stuff models of political science being propagated in our discipline? If these pseudo-economists know their math so well, let them present at the University of Chicago's Eco-

nomics Workshop. I assure you every single political science article will be trashed and thrown into the dustbin. Then why are these people allowed to throw their weight around based on undergrad math and stats—an Econ 101. We are in the business of Political Science and not failed Economics.

Lastly,

11) When are you going to offer the APSA presidentship to Benedict Anderson or Charles Tilly or Richard Falk or Susanne Rudolph or Ari Zolberg or James C. Scott or Theda Skocpol, who are more representative of our discipline then the "coterie" that runs APSA?

I hope this anonymous letter leads to a dismantling of the Orwellian system that we have in APSA and that we will see a true Persetroika in the discipline.

Mr. Persetroika

CHAPTER 2

Perestroika and Its Other

Susanne Hoeber Rudolph

On October 15, 2000, an anonymous political scientist calling himself, herself, or themselves Mr. Perestroika sent an immoderate e-mail message to a small set of colleagues. It excoriated the APSA and its flagship journal, the *American Political Science Review* (*APSR*), for irrelevance, technicism, statistical obsession, third-class economics, domination by East Coast white males, and oligarchical practices: "Why are all the articles from APSR from the same methodology—statistics or game theory—with a 'symbolic' article in political theory. . . . Where is political history, international history, political sociology, interpretive methodology, constructiv[ism], area studies, critical theory and last but not least—post modernism?"[1]

This e-mail message evoked an astonishing response in a profession in which prudence and gravitas are admired. The message seemed to articulate the suppressed dissatisfactions of a significant portion of the profession. Much of the early e-mail that inundated the apparently astonished sender came from senior faculty who enthusiastically embraced one or another part of the message, and encouraged moves to send challenging letters to *PS: Political Science and Politics*. But the seniors of our profession also set about cleaning up the message's syntax and leaching out its angry tone. Soon they signed on to more sober versions of Mr. Perestroika's critique[2] in order to mobilize a large constituency. A widely signed letter to *PS* by Rogers Smith, a theorist then at Yale, supported the manifesto: "Why do the *APSR* and other professional fora seem so intensively focused on technical methods, at the expense of the great, substantive political questions that actually intrigue many APSA members, as well as broader intellectual audiences? Though some recipients may have felt uncomfortable with the anonymous authorship and the highly polemical tone of this post, nevertheless an astonishing number of scholars, from all ranks of the profession, felt impelled to announce that they, too, shared these profound dissatisfactions with the status quo."[3] Richard Betts, a professor of international relations at Columbia, concurred: "The work published in the journal comes almost exclusively from those who do quantitative research and formal modeling, and very disproportionately from just one of the four principal subfields of the discipline (American Politics)." The Perestroika list serve grew into a casual community of discontent, a horizontal acephalous gathering of like-minded people. Critics asked, Who are you? Whom do you represent? To whom are you accountable? The attempts by some Perestroikans to turn the list serve into a formal organization were resisted. It remained as it had begun, a forum for loosely structured conversation.

The nature of the discontents that surfaced was by no means homogeneous. Perestroika came to include theorists of very different stripes. Some feared for the death of norms at the hands of a militant positivism; others resisted the monopoly claims of scientifically certified objective truth. The Perestroika conversation harbored liberal arts faculty and teachers of undergraduates who sought vivid, engaging texts that address large social and political questions. The parsimonious abstractions of the formalists struck them as devoid of meaning. The conversation spoke for a problem-driven rather than a method-driven discipline and deplored the tendency to reward technical virtuosity for its own sake. Political ethnographers and (old) institutionalists who thought that context mattered protested the one-size-fits-all claim of rational choicers. Communitarians damned the possessive individualism of methodological individualists. Bombs-and-bullets international relations practitioners defended case studies; interpretivists defended participant observation and semiotics; historical institutionalists and area scholars defended variety and difference in face of the homogeneity claims of large n studies.

The anonymity of the original Perestroika, who continued to manage the list serve, was a source of controversy. Did it not compromise the transparency and accountability of the enterprise? Or should the choice of anonymity be read as indicative of the chances a young political scientist took when he or she spoke truth to epistemic power? Perestroika's continued anonymity turned Perestroika into a kind of Rorschach test, amenable to varied interpretations by the many streams of dissent. Anonymity prevented the identity of any particular Mr. or Ms. Perestroika from defining the movement.

Despite the disparate streams constituting Perestroika, there was agreement that the *APSR* had been hijacked and monopolized by practitioners of rational choice and formal modelers using statistical tests and mathematical proofs. The dissidents saw political science as an open-ended category, not an objective one independent of history, ideology, or culture. They saw the discipline's form as the result of a social process in which living agents constituted meanings and models and standards. Lead actors in this social process were the *APSR* and the four regional political science journals, not faceless entities but living organisms motivated by editors and their collaborators. The journals were seen as abusing their certifying role, their capacity to decide for the profession what constituted quality political science, by drawing the boundaries too parochially. Their role as gatekeepers for the profession had consequences for the quality and orientation of teaching and research. When an editor under the spell of the scientific paradigm wrote a would-be contributor, "I'm returning your ms. because it is unsuitable for a political science journal," she was disclosing not a self-evident truth but a socially constructed, contestable judgment. Homogeneous, narrow journals reduce the space in which political scientists can ask questions, pursue knowledge, find and retain jobs, and get promoted. The dissidents wanted a more inclusive view of what counts as political science.

Perestroika did not write on a blank slate. The pervasive presentism of political science obscures the fact that challenges to a prevailing behaviorist hegemony had already been raised in the late 1960s by the Caucus for a New Political Science. However, the crucial issues for the APSA dissidents of 1968–69 had been different from the issues Perestroikans raised at the turn of the millennium. The revolt of the late 1960s had merged the questions of *demographic* representation (race and gender) with questions of *political* representation (opposition to the Vietnam War). The movement that started in 2000 is more about what we might call *epistemological* representation.

The dissidents of 1968–69 felt that American political scientists had been too slow in recognizing the failings of the Johnson administration in the Vietnam War. Resistance to the war fueled resistance to racism and sexism. "Mississippi summer," student activists, and civil rights protests and freedom marches helped radicalize women. Race and gender moved to the top of the country's and the APSA's agendas. The movement of 1968–69 had more of what Robert Jervis, in his chapter in this volume, indicts Perestroika for not having—ideological concern and commitment. It is striking that the prospect of a war against Iraq, not much more popular in academia than the Vietnam War (but without the incendiary stimulant of the draft), played no significant role in the Perestroika movement. Participants in the conversation accepted one of Perestroika's rare personal interventions, a decision not to let objections to the Iraq war crosscut the resistance to epistemological hegemony.

The movement of 1968–69 did have a recessive epistemological dimension. Its spokespersons, like those of 2000, felt that political science had become indifferent to the great social issues of the day. It was increasingly fixated on technique and methodological precision. David Easton's 1968 APSA presidential speech called for an end to the so-called behavioral revolution and for the profession to address the pressing issues of the era, such as race, poverty, and gender: "Substance must precede technique. If one must be sacrificed for the other—and this need not always be so—it is more important to be relevant and meaningful for contemporary urgent social problems than to be sophisticated in the tools of investigation. For the aphorism of science, that it is better to be wrong than vague, post-behavioralism would substitute a new dictum, that it is better to be vague than non-relevantly precise."[4]

While the epistemological discontents of the mid- to late 1960s were directed against empiricism and those of 2000 were directed against formalism, they converged in their protest against technicism and impersonality in the pursuit of knowledge. Both opposed the dehumanization that accompanied academic Fordism. The Berkeley students made the warning on the eighty-column, thirteen-row IBM punchcard—Do Not Fold, Staple, or Mutilate—

their battle cry. The card was central to the rationalization of university proce-dures as well as to the methodologies of the behavioral revolution. This student battle cry expressed alienation from the normative anesthesia of academic objectivity, even while protesting institutional surveillance and regimentation. There are echoes of such alienation in the Perestroika e-mail conversation's repudiation of uncontextualized inquiry and formalistic methodology.

As Brian Caterino points out elsewhere in this volume, there is a long genealogy of such epistemological conflicts, many of which were fought out in the *Methoden Streit* that preoccupied German academics at the end of the nineteenth century. Max Weber's essays on methodology represented an attempt to reconcile the claims of the *Natur Wissenschaften* and the *Geistes Wissenschaften,* an opposition renewed and lamented after World War II by the novelist and scientist C. P. Snow in his *Two Cultures.* Weber conceded that the social sciences, like the natural, could be construed as subject to regularity if not law, a view staunchly resisted by those who imagined that the human sciences grasped only the unique and the particular. Contrary to the *Geistes Wissenschaftler,* who asserted that a lawful universe had to be firmly rejected because it was a determined universe (foreshadowing the structure versus agency argument of the 1990s), Weber argued for the compatibility of regular-ity with agency. The implicit determinism of a lawful universe could be modi-fied by the responsible, choosing individual precisely because he or she under-stood its regularities.

The heterogeneity of the constituency for Perestroika has its counterpart on the opposite side. The unabashedly nonempirical nature of formal modelers who invoke mathematical proofs is in marked contrast with the empiricism of many statistical approaches. But when methodological disputation breaks out, advocates of these tendencies can unite. They fancy they have common objectives because they have common opponents. Can we specify the attri-butes respectively of Perestroikans and their epistemological "other"? I've made myself two lists, each of which represents an ideal type of one of the contend-ing perspectives. It is an ideal type in the conventional sense that while all the attributes that characterize the ideal type do not appear in real world instanti-ation, the ideal type provides criteria that help us analyze and distinguish real world complexity. My categories are not strictly isomorphic. But even when they overlap, each provides a contrasting formulation.

"Scientific" Mode of Inquiry	"Interpretive" Mode of Inquiry
certainty	skepticism; contingency
parsimony	thick description
cumulative knowledge	nonlinear succession of paradigms
causality	meaning
singularity of truth	multiplicity of truth
universal/homogeneous	contextual/heterogeneous
objective knowledge	subjective knowledge

The left-hand list, which I label "Scientific," unites what I have noted are rather disparate tendencies, the deductive formalism of rational choice with the more inductive empiricism of statistical approaches. It is the model of science that unites them even when their practice divides them. The heterogeneity of the right-hand list, which I label good "Interpretive," was summed up in an introductory paragraph of this chapter. The disparate tendencies are united by a lack of enthusiasm for the monopoly claims of the scientific trope.[5]

The first dichotomy, certainty versus skepticism/contingency, reflects the fact that the world and its phenomena appear with varying degrees of clarity and reality to different observers, yielding fluctuating levels of confidence that truth can be ascertained. Descartes and Montaigne had different ontological needs. For optimists about truth attainment the enabling forces are methodologies and research rules drawn from the sciences (replicability, statistical adequacy, impersonality of the observer), whose sharpening is meant to conquer the contextualized subjectivities that are said to bias observers and/or to solve puzzles and assess interrelationships that are said to be too complex to handle with ordinary language. The interpretivist, by contrast, is likely, Rashomon-like, to present multiple takes on the truth or to make more modest claims about the level of confidence with which something can be known. Views differ more sharply among interpretivists than among scientists on what counts as evidence or what constitutes a valid argument. The interpretivist, like the scientist, lives among demanding research conventions designed to discipline the researcher's subjectivity. But while the disciplining of the subjectivity of the scientist lies in the correct selection and processing of evidence or in the theoretical adequacy of formal representation, the disciplining of the interpretivist's subjectivity arises from self-consciousness and reflexivity reinforced by the epistemic community. The interpretivist is invited to apply a sociology of knowledge to her own case, to consider how power or social status or cultural categories shape her vision. Instead of invoking a veil of ignorance to erase those characteristics that mark her existence, she summons a magnifying glass to reveal them more clearly.

The dichotomy between parsimony and thick description highlights the fact that communicative styles and form play different roles for the two sides. Parsimony is the correlate of a deductive mode of inquiry unencumbered by mere facticities. It is a feature more of formal modeling than of quantitative investigations. When the scholar as scientist can assume motivations, he is released from the burden of investigating them. With the benefit of making allegedly self-evident initial assumptions, he is released from the challenging task of convincing his readers of the validity of the warrants that enable him to reason deductively about how the world works. Thick description stands in the service of inductive social science. But Clifford Geertz's suggestive phrase evokes something more than an accumulation of facticities. Through his metaphors and narratives the scholar advances a theory as well as constructing a reality.

Another dichotomy contrasts a vision of a cumulative social science to a vision of a nonlinear series of distinctive paradigms, what Stephen J. Gould calls punctuated equilibria. Historians and philosophers of science differ as to whether knowledge is cumulative. Cumulation is a proposition not only born of the optimism of scientists but nurtured by the enlightenment rationalism that imagined a continuously improving human condition. Thomas Kuhn's nonlinear, nonprogressive view of the scientific enterprise holds that successive paradigms displace each other when researchers pile up enough anomalies to discredit a regnant paradigm and generate a better theory.

The theory of cumulative knowledge in political science poses special problems for the field of political theory. The notion that a recent "breakthrough" renders previous knowledge obsolete doesn't carry much conviction in a field that takes ancient thinkers as seriously as or more seriously than contemporary ones. Those who enroll under the banner of such organized sections of the APSA as Normative Theory, History of Political Thought, and Political Philosophy and Theory treat as valid knowledge texts whose provenance well predates the rise of modern science in the seventeenth century.

Political theory is a field ready to entertain the thought that many good ideas have cycled through once or twice before. Jürgen Habermas is not necessarily thought to represent the product of a cumulative process that goes beyond Plato or Georg Wilhelm Friedrich Hegel, rendering them obsolete or irrelevant. Such cumulation of knowledge as exists among theorists leads to a redefinition of problems in light of new historical situations, refinement of arguments, and clarification and systematization of known positions. But it cannot resolve disputes arising from heterogeneous priors. It is difficult to find good reasons or valid grounds for eliminating players. For example, the theory of natural law, often dismissed, has a way of circling back, as the preoccupation with human rights makes clear. In a chapter in this volume David Laitin insists, "If theoretical logic or scientific evidence finds a theory or procedure to be fallacious, that procedure's flowerbed should no longer be cultivated within the discipline. . . . There can be no hope of cumulation if we insist that all methods, and all procedures, must be protected." Such a judgment relies on the possibility of consensus about what is valid knowledge or "best practice," a consensus that is nowhere in sight. That doesn't mean we live in a standardless universe. It means that different epistemes, different communities of inquiry, develop different standards by which to judge "validity."

The arguments on the two sides of the next dichotomy, causality versus meaning, are not very neatly distributed between the sides. Political scientists on both sides of the line are concerned with explaining outcomes—what determines the advantage incumbents enjoy in congressional races, what moves God to treat the just unjustly, what enabled England to defeat Spain, what makes citizens obey. Even as the interpretivists do not ignore cause, the team for science often finds it revealing to address questions of cause via inquiring into meaning structures.

Despite the overlap, different modes of inquiry produce different types of knowledge. She who has a knack for mathematical reasoning, has training in statistical methods, and is committed to a neo-Newtonian episteme is likely to focus on the objectivist outer world of cause rather than the subjectivist world of meaning. She will look for projects that nurture and employ her special capacities, and find the episteme that focuses on cause. By contrast, he who has mastered Tamil and Hegel will look for projects that use the human capital he has come to possess. Language is a tool that reveals the way the people of a culture perceive it and construct it; it leans to the side of meaning. Hence the alleged trend toward requiring "methods" courses more and language courses less is consequential for the balance between cause and meaning as intellectual goals of our profession.

The next dichotomy, singularity of truth versus multiplicity of truths, is a relative of the dichotomy certainty versus contingency. It functions sluggishly in distinguishing the scientists from the interpretivists. Theory and international relations scholars who have participated in the Perestroika conversation include spirits for whom multiplicity of truth is an unacceptable possibility, a child of relativism, postmodernism, and other undesirable tendencies. Nevertheless, the category has a certain viability. Interpretivists are more likely to imagine a world of multiple truths. Their preference for difference, distinctions, heterogeneity—to be explored later in this chapter—disposes them more favorably toward multiple truths.

The dichotomy universal versus contextual runs parallel with the dichotomy homogeneous versus heterogeneous. Scientists reaching for lawlike generalizations formulate commonalities. Political scientists under the influence of economic models tend to posit a common motivation driving all action, uninflected by historical, cultural, or moral variation. Interpretivists like to emphasize distinguishing features. Their modes of inquiry privilege difference and heterogeneity not only as a principle of observation but also as an aesthetic and a value.

The concept of globalization provides a vehicle for observing these dichotomies in practice. While globalization can claim expounders on both the scientific and the interpretivist sides of the line, the concept resides most comfortably with universalizing/homogenizing phenomena. Globalization is, among other things, a theory of history, a theory that features convergence and the erasure of difference. It has in common with its predecessor, modernization theory, the not-so-hidden implication that convergence entails cultural, economic, and political assimilation of the other to the Atlantic world as mediated by the Washington consensus.

On the homogeneity-heterogeneity continuum the logical academic counterplayers to globalization are area studies.[6] Area studies were crafted during the cold war to stockpile area experts who could guide American policy makers through the exotic linguistic and cultural byways of the other. But the unofficial ideology of area studies was always more subversive. It provided an arena in which difference could be not only explored but celebrated. Area studies worked within an episteme that was more Burkean than Lockean, an episteme in which the heterogeneity that was erased by Lockean liberal universalism was valued. And area studies were unabashedly interdisciplinary against the prevailing currents that held the division of academic labor and specialization in high esteem. Unlike American studies, a species of area studies that could build on students' familiarity with their own language, history, and culture, area studies had to provide a wide array of foundational knowledge in order to lay the groundwork for theoretically and empirically informed interpretation. They had to be interdisciplinary.

The debate on globalization is one way the dichotomy between universal and particular has played itself out. Another way is via the debate, especially heated in comparative politics, between large n studies and case studies. Those committed to the scientific trope tend to argue that large n studies are the only way to do comparative politics. As David Laitin notes in a chapter in this volume, "Theoretical work going back to Harry Eckstein sets constraints on what a particular case study can show," or, more provocatively, "Comparativists who do qualitative case studies have no claim to disciplinary recognition by virtue of the fact that examination of a single case is a time-honored procedure in their field."

Large n studies and single case studies contribute differently to knowledge. Large n studies adopt the rhetorical conventions of science by formulating their findings in terms of general laws.[7] But, as Max Weber reminded us, the more general the law, the less likely is it to explain a particular case.[8] Yet the social sciences often want to explain particular cases rather than universal trends. Exploring why Vichy France supported the Nazis is a different but not inferior project to exploring the general social or historical variables that correlate with authoritarian rule. The deliberately unparsimonious case study provides a more complex and multifaceted image of causality than the large n generalization that has been thinned out to fit the commonalities of multiple cases. Large n studies can generate hypotheses for comparative inquiry by suggesting probable associations—for example, that democracy is most likely to persist in wealthy countries with per capita incomes above a certain threshold and less likely to persist as income falls.[9] The case study, by contrast, can be especially valuable when it deviates from the regnant generalizations by providing a conspicuous and generative anomaly. For example, democracy in India persists despite one of the lowest per capita incomes in the world. Why? The deviant case requires a new line of explanation.

Finally, the dichotomy objectivity versus subjectivity highlights the fact that *who* writes political science is relevant to *what* is written. Scholars who view themselves as scientists believe they can produce objective knowledge because they are unmarked by their location in culture and history. Scientists speak as omniscient observers. The trope of science obscures the situated nature of the knowledge they produce. History's winners and losers affirm different truths. Nationalist histories record popular mobilization differently than do imperial histories. Colonial subjects understand the world differently than do colonial masters. Their subjective knowledge distinguishes their scholarship, not only what they select but also how they interpret.

The schema I have presented sums up some of the differences that distinguish Perestroikans from their imagined other. The debate is not new, and is not likely to be resolved soon. The contrasts provide parameters within which social scientists can fashion the different identities that suit their passions and their skills. Consistent with the skeptical perspective I assign to Perestroikans, I can hardly claim the absolute validity of one side of the schema, but I can and do claim a preference for those modes of inquiry that suit the problems I deal with and the skills I deploy. A comprehensive political science will be a self-conscious discipline, a discipline that recognizes and accepts the role difference plays in scholarship but whose reflexivity helps its differently situated members to see common ground.

Notes

This chapter is based on a paper prepared for Panel 7-1, "Perestroika: Undisciplined, Unpunished," at the American Political Science Association annual meeting on August 31, 2001, in San Francisco.

1. Mr. Perestroika, e-mail titled "To the Editor, *PS* and *APSR*, On Globalization of the APSA: A Political Science Manifesto," posted on the Perestroika list serve, October 26, 2000.

2. Richard Betts, e-mail posted on the Perestroika list serve, October 27, 2000. Letters were written by Greg Kasza, Richard Betts, David Pion-Berlin, and Rogers Smith. Perestroikans signed on to one or another of the letters.

3. Rogers Smith to Robert Hauck, deputy director, American Political Science Association. Circulated on the Perestroika list serve on October 30, 2000.

4. *American Political Science Review,* January 1969.

5. A debate about the appropriate language to designate these categories attended David Collier's initiative to form a new organized section of the APSA on qualitative methods, with some scholars arguing that "interpretive methods" was a stronger formulation. David Collier, personal communication to the author, December 30, 2002.

6. For a recent discussion see Ali Mirsepassi, Amrita Basu, and Frederick Weaver, eds., *Localizing Knowledge in a Globalizing World: Recasting the Area Studies Debate* (Syracuse, NY: Syracuse University Press, 2003).

7. For a sympathetic discussion of large *n* studies in comparative politics see Barbara Geddes, "The Great Transformation in the Study of Politics in Developing Countries," in *Political Science: The State of the Discipline,* ed. Ira Katznelson and Helen V. Milner (New York: W. W. Norton, 2002) 342–70.

8. Max Weber, "'Objectivity' in Social Science and Social Policy," in *Max Weber on the Methodology of the Social Sciences,* trans. and ed. Edward Shils and Henry A. Finch (Glencoe, IL: Free Press, 1949) 49–112.

9. Adam Przeworski, Michael E. Alvarez, Jose Antonio Cheibub, and Fernando Limongi, *Democracy and Development: Political Institutions and Wellbeing in the World, 1950–1990* (Cambridge: Cambridge University Press, 2000).

CHAPTER 3

Not Here, Not Now!

The Absence of a European Perestroika Movement

Catarina Kinnvall

The Perestroika movement has a European precedent in the "post-autistic economics" movement that erupted in June 2000 at the Sorbonne in Paris. This "post-autistic" movement was soon to spread across much of continental Europe as well as making inroads into the United Kingdom with the publishing of an open letter by twenty-seven Cambridge University economics Ph.D. students.[1] The movement was a reaction against the mathematicization of economics as a discipline, which, it was argued, had resulted in an "autistic science with no relation to real life."[2] The attack concentrated on the extent to which a derivative of neoclassical economics—rational choice—had taken on a hegemonic role in research, publication, and teaching, constituting the main obstacle to greater plurality in the field. However, despite this post-autistic economics movement, there has largely been an absence of a European Perestroika debate in the fields of political science and international relations (IR).[3] This is not to say that there has been a lack of debates concerning the development of the discipline and the social sciences in general. Rather it is to argue that such debates have been devoid of most of the components characterizing the American debate, as there has been no overarching hegemonic perspective to rebel against. This absence of hegemony has affected the kinds of debates taking place in Europe as compared to the United States, as without a hegemonic perspective there has been little cause for revolution. In this chapter I discuss some reasons why this may be the case.

First, I elaborate some potential differences in intellectual tradition. Early American social scientists defined their intellectual projects in a society without rigidly structured scientific institutions and without strong and deeply rooted traditions of sociophilosophical discourse. In comparison, their European contemporaries tended to be much more deeply rooted in the institutional structures of science and society. I show how intellectual, institutional, and political relations in Europe were characterized by partly similar and partly different problems than those facing the United States, one of which has been their particular preoccupation with the state. Included in this overview is a general discussion of what may constitute an American definition of political science and IR, and what happens to this definition when it enters other intellectual, cultural, and institutional traditions such as those characteristic of Europe. The focus is on the development of political science and IR in Germany, France, Italy, Scandinavia, and the United Kingdom in contrast to that of the United States. To be fair to this debate, however, I briefly problematize the unified view with which we sometimes regard the American social sciences. This involves a discussion of the ways in which different radical ideas in the United States have emerged within a number of academic fields to challenge the predominance of the rational choice approach.

Second, I examine the differences in intellectual tradition in regard to publications, pointing out that a number of highly regarded American journals are predisposed to publishing formal and quantitative approaches to research, while in contrast, most European journals tend to have a preference for qualitative and theoretical work. This has been one of the most contentious issues in the American Perestroika debate, with the *American Political Science Review* accused of intense preference for technical methods at the expense of more substantive political questions. To this can be added the differences in research, curricula, and career opportunities in many European settings as compared to the United States. Here I will particularly highlight the extent to which political philosophy tends to be more visibly included in teaching and research in European departments and how the lack of a formalized tenure track system affects publication patterns in comparison to the United States.

I end the chapter by drawing together some general conclusions about the absence of a European Perestroika debate in terms of the impact such an absence may have on the profession, on the academic status of the discipline, and on its future relevance. This involves a brief discussion of the extent to which this absence in Europe may actually provide helpful incentives for an American Perestroika movement in search of a more pluralistic discipline that is characterized by less hegemony and more flexibility in research opportunities, curricula, and career opportunities.

Comparing Europe and the United States: Are There Differences in Intellectual Traditions?

As Peter Wagner has written, "A comparative analysis of social science developments can demonstrate that the cognitive orientations of social science discourses are shaped in complex interplays of intellectual traditions, on the one side, and [in] the impact of political structures, on the other, meeting and being mediated in scientific institutions as the societal locus of legitimate discourse."[4] It will be difficult to appreciate the differences in intellectual thought in the United States and Europe unless we contextualize the development of political science as a field in the United States as compared to that in Europe. An interesting starting point is John G. Gunnell's 2002 overview of the development of political science. Gunnell insists that those studying this development have concentrated more on the rise of the American discipline and profession than on situating modern political science in its appropriate historical context. As evidence of this process he points to the various handbooks of political science that have been published to account for the growth of political science as a field. Starting with the eight-volume *Handbook of Political Science* (1975) edited by Fred I. Greenstein and Nelson Polsby, he notes that this was indeed a handbook of American political science by virtue of the absence of material by authors outside the United States or even references to such authors. Indeed, he argues, this handbook reflected the recent history of the discipline in the United States. This reluctance to seriously consider the intellectual history of political science and the practice of the discipline was once again evident in *A New Handbook of Political Science* edited by Robert E. Goodin and Hans-Dieter Klingeman.[5] The authors were almost exclusively beholden to the American formulation of political inquiry, and the editors' attempts to specify "the classic texts" of the discipline accounted purely for works of an American origin.

It is possible to distinguish in very general terms three approaches that have characterized American political science since its inception: behavioralism, functionalism, and economism. Behavioralism emerged out of the "old institutionalism" of the 1920s and 1930s and took as its goal the "observation and measurement of actual political behavior by discrete individuals and groups with the objective of generalizing from this basis in order to create a policy-relevant branch of scientific knowledge."[6] While behavioralism took its lead from the natural sciences, functionalism became the focus of comparativists who more or less followed in the footsteps of Talcott Parsons, who developed a systems theory. In comparison, economism has taken two forms in American political science—that of a "helper" for existing political science theory and that of an alternative. In the former case it found its closest ally in modernization theory, as exemplified by Dankwart Rustow's "stages of economic growth theory," while in the latter case it became the progenitor of rational choice theory. A transitional moment took place between the mid-1970s and the mid-1980s, when a number of fields, such as rational choice, a new Marxism, state-centered approaches, social movement theory, and resource mobilization all competed for attention. Rational choice went off in one direction, while the others (some of them after brief encounters with dependency theory) ended up combining in an American version of state theory, which later became historical institutionalism. Contemporary rational choice theory grew out of three bodies of scholarship: the public choice literature in economics; Mancur Olson's *Logic of Collective Action,* a forerunner to new institutionalism that attacked behavioralism and pluralism; and the literature of game theory in IR.[7]

The development of the field of IR in the United States is a little more complex and contested, but it is relatively undisputed that at its core it consists of classical realism, neo-realism, and neo-liberalism. Classical realism, as developed in the 1930s and 1940s, was fashioned as a direct response to the idealism that had followed the Great War. Similar to rational choice theory, it derived its notion of the instrumental rationality of the sovereign state and the anarchical character of a world system from essential Hobbesian assumptions of human nature. Neo-realism, which emerged in the 1970s, was an attempt to further develop and refine a more rigorous and structural account of world politics. In comparison to realism's insistence on the universalist (aggressive) assumptions of human nature, neo-realism assumed only that states as unified actors were in the pursuit of relative rather than absolute gains and that, given the structure of the international environment (anarchy), their behavior was entirely predictable. Neo-liberals continued the rationalist tradition, but the origins of that tradition lie in the idealism rejected by E. H. Carr (1939) and others. In contrast to neo-realism, neo-liberalism emphasizes the capacity of human agents to achieve cooperation for mutual advantage and proclaims that states are not the only important actors of the international system.[8]

Added to these traditional approaches can be more recent ones, such as IR constructivism and poststructuralism or postmodernism. Constructivism in its IR variant, like historical institutionalism in political science, rejects the rationalism inherent in neo-realism and focuses on the perceptions of interests and on culture, ideas, and identity more than on material interests per se. However, as Steve Smith has repeatedly argued, this mainly North American variant of constructivism remains very close to the neo-realist wing of the rationalist paradigm.[9] In this sense, the challenge posed by poststructuralism and postmodernism is more fundamental, as both call into question the entire enterprise of IR as well as political analysis and social science more generally. The claim is that all theories are partisan and partial despite their attempts to assert universality, neutrality, and scientific status.[10]

This is obviously a rather crude outline. However, what is important is the extent to which American definitions of political science and IR have affected, or been unable to affect, the understanding of where political science (and IR) as a field stands today. A useful starting point for analysis is offered by Ole Waever's (1998) article on the differences between American and European IR. In this article he argues that the last few years have witnessed a de-Europeanization in the United States as specialization around rational choice approaches has increased in a way that shifts IR back toward the mainstream of U.S. political science but is alien to most European scholars. Waever attributes the explanations for this to the interaction of three sets of issues: the nature of the society and polity (including the intellectual style, traditions of political thought, state-society relations, and foreign policy); the state of the social sciences (the general conditions and definitions of social science, and the pattern of academic disciplines); and the intellectual activities within IR (the social and intellectual structure of the discipline, and its theoretical traditions).[11] He then goes on to explore how these sets of issues have differed in Germany, France, the United Kingdom, and the United States.

In this section I refer to Waever's discussion to account for differences in intellectual traditions between Europe and the United States. As space is limited, only certain European societies are highlighted and contrasted to that of the United States, such as those of Germany, France, Italy, Scandinavia, and the United Kingdom. As there are different quantities of sources and problems with language barriers, this is not, however, always done in an entirely consistent fashion. As a result, some political science communities, like that of the United Kingdom, will receive more attention than others. Rather than giving an exhaustive analysis, this overview should be viewed as a general attempt to understand that the particular European intellectual traditions in political science and IR have lacked a hegemonic perspective to rebel against and why, as a result, there has been no European Perestroika debate. As the Perestroika debate tells us, within contemporary American political science rational choice has come to represent the most advanced level of acknowledged scholarly achievement. The result has been that other approaches often have assumed a secondary status or even been squeezed out of the political science departments. As Knud Erik Jørgensen has noted, this has certainly not been the case in Europe,[12] especially not on the continent.[13] Despite the presence of this tendency among certain sectors of the research community, it has remained far from what is generally considered to be a valuable approach. The following account is meant to highlight why this may be the case.

Waever emphasizes that when the modern social sciences developed in the mid–nineteenth century, it was in the context of two important institutional transformations. One was the dramatic change in the nation-state that occurred with national unification in Germany and Italy, modernization in France, and the beginning of state building in the United States. The other was the extensive reform of the universities, which were moving toward the modern research-oriented university. In addition there was another transformation that had to do with the end of unquestioned religious authority, with the bourgeois revolution, and with the emergence of a philosophy of the subject, all of which preceded industrialization and urbanization.[14] This latter point is important, as it directs attention to the relation of social science to other contemporary philosophies that are used to interpret the societal situation. As Peter Wagner has noted, this is also significant from a comparative perspective, as it points to the particular relations of continental European social science to philosophy. On the continent, social thought dealt with these processes of change and transformation in terms of major ruptures and reorientations. In comparison, social thought developed more gradually in English society, while in America social thought was directed mainly toward itself and not toward other authorities.[15]

The Development of Political Science and IR in Europe

Germany In continental Europe, political science approaches were confronted by entrenched institutional legal theorizing about the state, which in Germany meant the existence of a dual system of thinking that left little room for a political science focused on political institutions. On the one hand, political thinking in Germany took a unified historical, legal, and political approach that lacked an analytical focus on the state, while on the other hand, it consisted of legal scholars' developing a legal theory of the state in which all political aspects were reduced to constitutional aspects as formulated in legal positivism. The legal theory of the state relied upon neoclassical economics and became the dominant approach used to discuss the state, thus excluding other discourses from legitimate debate.[16] This particular development had a number of lasting consequences. One was the weak status of political science and the establishment of a hierarchical structure within departments. The other had to do with the separation between political science and professional training, by which the latter has mainly remained within the law departments.[17] The development of IR as a field also took place within this dualist tension of idealism and a strong concept of the state. However, rather than turning toward realism (which had become an impossibility after the Second World War), much of German IR took place within peace research. Flirtation with American behavioralism during the 1960s soon became disappointing due to the lack of results, and German scholars increasingly turned toward traditionalism or Critical Theory.[18]

France   In comparison to German social science, with its dual structure, French social science took a more tripartite form during the eighteenth and nineteenth centuries. Different areas of social theory developed within the human sciences, and in the nineteenth century areas such as psychology and sociology came to constitute one area. Economics became incorporated into the faculty of law, while in 1871 political science found a home in the form of a professional school (the Ecole libre) for training upper-level civil servants. At the same time as the French humanities achieved wide freedom, French politics remained a state monopoly, and a number of fields that in other countries have been classified as part of political science went to economics and sociology instead. As a result, French political science has continued to be torn between public administration and the humanities, in comparison to the emphasis on economics and the natural sciences found in the field in the United States.[19] French policy research thus continues to take place mostly within the framework of newly created governmental research institutions (originally the Ecole libre des sciences politiques, its successor being the Institut d'études politiques).[20]

Within the field of IR, French scholars have generally remained outside the "great debates" that have characterized the Anglo-Saxon IR community (i.e., idealism-realism and traditionalism-behavioralism), and it was only in the late 1990s that French scholars decided to found a professional IR association.[21] Though the French IR community remains on the margins of the Anglo-American mainstream, one noticeable trend in that community deserves to be mentioned: the search for a sociology of IR inspired by Raymond Aron's work. This can be seen as one of the most characteristic features of the French IR community and has constituted a specifically French answer to the Anglo-American quest for general theory.[22]

Italy   Political science in Italy faced an uphill battle before being accepted as a discipline.[23] The intellectual movement for a social science included two separate strands, one sociological and one political. The former was stronger in methodological terms than the latter, providing opposition to the methodological individualism and rational orientation of political economy. The latter, comprised of would-be political scientists, focused on political institutions and elites and their relation to society.[24] Much as in Germany, pure legal theorizing of the state became dominant in the late nineteenth century. However, in contrast to the situation in Germany, such theorizing developed as a clear alternative to administrative and political science, which by now had become a broad social movement. Between 1890 and 1910, Italian economics gained a stronghold, with the social sciences achieving "a degree of formal reasoning and cognitive closure which they had never possessed before and would not reach again until the present."[25]

This predominance changed as a result of the First and the Second World Wars, which made obvious the failure of classical sociology and classical-neoclassical economics to explain current economic, social, and political changes in Italy and elsewhere on the continent. As a result, recourse was taken to earlier intellectual and institutional traditions, with an increased focus on the state and its responsibilities.[26] This was characterized by renewed attention to legal and historical approaches rather than to political science, and by an intense division along ideological-cultural lines. Even today Italian academic debates frequently take the form of political-ideological clashes.[27] If political science has had problems in shaping an identity, the field of IR has encountered even larger obstacles, as it has had to fight both the political science battle and its own battle for legitimacy. As a consequence, in Italy IR appears to have fared worse than in comparable countries, such as France. At the same time, however, it can be noted that, in comparison to the Anglo-Saxons, Italian IR scholars have a pronounced skepticism toward most things "neo" and have generally stayed away from the modernist-postmodernist debate in favor of tradition and a continued lack of theoretical innovation.[28]

Scandinavia   In Sweden political science has a uniquely long history as an independent university discipline, having begun in a formal sense as early as 1622, when a chair in Discourse and Politics was established at Uppsala University. However, it was not until 1860 that the field itself developed in Sweden with a concentration on constitutional history and constitutional law.[29] With this exception, however, political science is a relatively new discipline in Scandinavia, and its intellectual tradition has to a large extent been shaped by "puppet programs" as opposed to the "liberal constructor programs" typical of the American tradition.[30] This implies that even at times when the individual has been made the basic unit of analysis, as in the American discipline, the main emphasis in Scandinavian political science has been on factors conditioning, constraining, and structuring the individual's behavior. Such structural cleavages have been of various kinds, including psychological factors, norms, institutions, or other similar factors.

These general differences may explain why rational choice has not received a prominent position in Scandinavia, despite the region's tendency to follow the American traditions in political science and IR. Work has been done in a rationalist tradition, especially in Sweden, such as studies by Leif Lewin on self-interest and public choice and Jan-Erik Lane's focus on the interplay between public choice and political economy, but this work has not assumed anything close to a hegemonic status. Indeed, as Nannestad notes, it is difficult to decide whether the status of rational choice is that of a paradigm, a school, or a sect in Scandinavia.[31]

The situation in the field of IR is not that much different. IR in Scandinavia has never been a separate discipline, but has developed within political science. Much as in Germany, it was peace research that became the established separate discipline with its own university departments and research institutes. The strong Scandinavian focus on negotiation, mediation, and international cooperation can probably be related to this strong prevalence of peace research. Instead of being a separate subject discipline, the field of IR (or international politics, as it is referred to locally) has been characterized as a diffuse borderline between domestic and international politics, often challenging conventional theories of national democracy and international anarchy. The result has been a larger focus on "middle-range" theories than on "grand" theorizing.[32] Scandinavia's predominant egalitarian political culture and moralistic visions of world politics (characteristic of its lack of war studies departments) reflect a predominantly liberal-minded IR community and a relatively strong peace research community.[33] This, in turn, has made IR less of a focus of the "great debates" in Scandinavia than it has been in the United Kingdom and America.

The United Kingdom   The United Kingdom lies somewhere between the United States and the continent in the development of political science with its combination of "very American" political science and an extensive intellectual pluralism.[34] This lack of theoretical orthodoxy in the U.K. profession is, according to Steve Smith, one of the major differences between the American field and the British.[35] Viewed historically, in the nineteenth century British universities were less concerned with transmitting knowledge than with producing for the empire a homogenous governing class, an elite culture that in many ways was reproduced and modified in academic institutions. As a consequence, political science remained focused on political philosophy until the mid–twentieth century.

The end of the Second World War changed this pattern, especially at the newer universities, where a shift occurred away from law and history and toward sociology, economics, and psychology. However, the close relationship between history and political philosophy continued at the older universities, which in the 1950s were still concentrated on political theory and the history of political ideas together with that of public administration.[36] Within the newer universities, behavioralist assumptions became a dominant theme at the same time as a diffuse but pervasive Whig tradition remained a powerful normative influence on what J. Hayward, B. Barry, and A. Brown name the "distinctive British" approach.[37] This consisted of a commitment to agency, hostility to scientism and grand theory, and sensitivity to history and contingency.[38] The fact that Britain lacks any political *science* departments—they are all departments of politics or some variant of this label—is quite significant in this regard. A number of suggestions have been made as to why this "distinctive" approach differs from that of the United States.

Mark Blyth and Robin Varghese, for instance, suggest that in comparison to the United States, British political science took a different turn after 1945, as its concerns were domestic rather than international.[39] In yielding its status as a hegemonic power, Britain, in comparison to the United States, felt less of a need to explain and plan for the development of the rest of the world. In contrast, at that time American political science, with its close relationship to political objectives, felt more of this need, and thus developed in a way that had little to do with "pure research." The extent to which this explains the hostility to scientism and grand theory in Britain can of course be debated. Here I find Blyth and Varghese's second point more relevant, a point that is also in line with Hayward, Barry, and Brown, as they argue that British political science has always had a different set of progenitors than American political science. From Karl Marx to Max Weber and Emile Durkheim, British social and political thought had been concentrated on either structure or norms as something supraindividual for explaining the complexity and contingency of behavior. This, they argue, has resulted in a focus on "structure" and "agency" missing from the American tradition.[40] Attempts to create a British counter-hegemonic research culture have in many ways been related to such a "distinctive British" approach and were behind much of the effort to initiate and build up the European Consortium of Political Science.

Whether or not political science has accounted for a distinctive tradition in Britain, a number of British IR scholars would persistently argue that this has been the case in the field of IR. British IR has a much more independent status than U.S. IR in relation to political science due to its continuous linkages to the fields of history, international law, political philosophy, and sociology. The reluctance to be part of a political science tradition is especially noticeable in one of the "grand theories" of British IR, the English School or the "international society tradition,"[41] which argued that IR should be studied as a society in its own right.[42] However, only a small section of British IR has been involved in this debate. Instead British IR continues to coexist with other intellectual disciplines, together with an increased focus on political theory and normative theory.[43] The hard scientific approaches have not found many British followers, and rational choice has remained at the margins of the field. The explanation, Waever argues, has to do with the embeddedness of IR in liberal education and its relationship to history and philosophy.[44]

The Absence of One *European Debate: The United States Revisited*

It is clear from this brief outline of British and continental political science and IR that in European societies these fields have had anything but a uniform development and that their historical, cultural, and institutional contexts have differed from that of the United States. The tendency to present the development of political science and IR in a universal mode disregards such fundamental differences among cultural and institutional contexts. As John G. Gunnell has noted in relation to overviews of the development of political science in a number of handbooks, such tendencies assume that there was an actual historically identifiable tradition of political thought from Plato to NATO.[45] To assume such a linear development fails to situate modern political science in its appropriate historical context. A similar tendency can be distinguished in the inclination to talk about *an* "IR theory" with the addition of words such as "contemporary," "today," "state-of-the-art," or "rethinking."[46] As in the case of political thought, such a description fails to acknowledge the many debates that have characterized continental IR theory as influenced by their specific cultural and institutional contexts.

This is also the place to point to differences in the American political science and IR traditions that remain hidden in much mainstream literature on the development of the field. In an earlier note I mentioned the criticism of Hayward, Barry, and Brown's unified view of British political science. In a similar way we may need to complicate the American context by pointing to a number of diverse trends in American social sciences that present a much less unified picture than that provided earlier. As Thomas Bender and Carl E. Schorske (1997) suggest in their volume *American Academic Culture in Transformation,* different American disciplines reacted very differently to the social and political upheavals of the 1960s.[47] The response in economics and philosophy was largely unnoticeable, while English changed dramatically as a result of its debates on feminism, gender, race, and ethnicity. The emergence of cultural studies as an almost metadiscipline was also clearly related to the events of this time. Political science, and perhaps especially IR, did not remain untouched by these processes. The existence of a Perestroika debate today certainly shows a broader pluralism and diversity than the hegemonic position of the rational choice approach may lead us to believe.

The events of the 1960s, with their emphasis on culture and community, made a number of scholars within the U.S. social sciences look to continental European philosophy for ways to address the new agenda, thus establishing a transdisciplinary intellectual discourse.[48] The critical turn in IR and other fields can therefore partly be explained by the import of ideas from the continent, such as those of Jürgen Habermas, Michel Foucault, Jacques Derrida, and Jean-François Lyotard. As Ira Katznelson has noted, a different U.S. academic community was to emerge in the 1960s across a number of disciplines, a community that was more tolerant, eclectic, and pluralistic and thus more open to alternative ideas.[49] The influence from the continent during the 1970s and the

1980s supplied such alternative forms of radical political and epistemological opposition to the perceived liberal orthodoxies of the late cold war period. These, Gerard Holden argues, relied primarily on cultural rather than economic analyses.[50] This indicates a greater pluralism in the U.S. social sciences than described earlier at the same time as it complicates the tendency to see intellectual migration as originating solely in America.

Publications, Course Requirements, and Career Opportunities in Europe and the United States

At the same time, however, it would be difficult to disregard the hegemonic role played by hard scientific approaches, as evidenced by the Perestroika debate. The argument made by one of its initiators, Gregory Kasza, that "the hard scientists have corrupted decision-making on hiring, promotion, curriculum and publication" in the United States,[51] suggests the existence of a hegemonic project. Even in this regard we see some major differences between the American context and the European.

Publication Patterns in Europe and the United States

An early study by Ivor Crew and Pippa Norris, which compares British and American journal evaluation in political science, confirms such differences.[52] Crew and Norris show that three of the journals that are more highly regarded in the United States than in Britain (*Administrative Studies Quarterly, Comparative Political Studies,* and the *Journal of Conflict Resolution*) tend to publish formal, mathematical, and quantitative approaches to research, whereas three of the journals regarded much more highly in Britain than in the United States (*Daedalus, Political Science Quarterly,* and *Politics and Society*) tend to publish qualitative, reflective, and theoretical work.

Crew and Norris also found a striking difference in familiarity with different journals between American and British political science scholars. This they attribute to three factors: associational sponsorship, subject coverage, and national provenance. The journals with which the large majority of American political scientists were familiar, but that were unfamiliar to a large majority of British scholars, included *PS: Political Science and Politics* (87 percent as against 11 percent), *Western Political Quarterly* (78 percent as against 13 percent), and *Journal of Politics* (91 percent as against 11 percent). In the British case, the journal with which the large majority of British political scientists (75 percent) were familiar, *Political Studies* (the journal of the U.K. Political Studies Association) was familiar to only 25 percent of American scholars. Unsurprisingly, journals devoted to domestic politics were more familiar to political scientists in each of their respective countries. The survey also suggested that American political scientists were less insular than their British counterparts, as the proportion of American political scientists reading U.K.-based journals was almost two and a half times that of British political scientists reading U.S.-based journals. Finally, the survey found that four journals that appeared in the British "top ten," were not even included in the American "top twenty"—*Political Studies, Government and Opposition, International Affairs,* and *Political Theory.* The first three are U.K.-based, while the familiarity of the fourth, *Political Theory,* may reflect the greater prominence of political theory in Britain compared with the United States, as argued by Crew and Norris. As a whole, these results show that although there is a certain agreement about the quality of many journals among British and American political science scholars, the scholars in the two countries tend to be familiar with different types of literature, theoretical discourse, and research agenda.

A more recent survey of IR journals confirms this trend. Ole Waever looked at eight leading IR journals (four U.S.-based and four Europe-based) from 1970 through 1995, and found that 88.1 percent of the total number of authors in the U.S.-based journals were American-based, while the authors in European journals were more balanced, with around 40 percent American-based and 40 percent Europe-based.[53] Also, the figures for the *American Political Science Review* and the *American Journal of Political Science* were particularly striking (97 percent and 96.8 percent American-based scholars, respectively). Waever also studied the contents of the journals, coding them into six categories, three "rationalist," two "reflectivist," and one "other," and found that the three rationalist categories accounted for 77.9 percent of the articles in *International Studies Quarterly* and 63.9 percent in *International Organization* compared to 42.3 percent in the *European Journal of International Relations* and only 17.4 percent in the *Review of International Studies.* The two forms of "reflectivist" work accounted for 7.8 percent and 25 percent of the articles in the two American journals, respectively, while they constituted 40.6 percent of the articles in the *Review of International Studies* and 40.4 percent in the *European Journal of International Studies.* The percentages of articles in these journals reflecting postmodern, Marxist, and feminist approaches were 2.6, 4.2, 15.4, and 18.8 percent, respectively. This clearly confirms Norris and Crew's findings that the British community is characterized by a different research agenda than is the American one.

The national diversity is even greater when we visit the political science literature of the continent. One of the most significant changes in European contexts has been the appearance of new journals as a result of the changed political landscape in Europe after 1989. For illustrative purposes, five of these are mentioned. In Russia a new bimonthly political science journal was launched in 1991: *Polis: Politicheskie issledovania* (Polis: Political research), in Lithuania the quarterly *Politologija* (Political science) began publication in 1989, and in Bulgaria the quarterly journal *Politicheski izledvanija* (Political studies) was launched in 1992. The same year saw the emergence of the quarterly *Politikatudomanyi szemle* (Political science review) in Poland, while the Czech quarterly *Politologicka revue* (Political science review) appeared in 1994. These journals reflect the particular political, cultural, and institutional developments in these countries. More significant than the emergence of new journals in Europe is the difference in content in the various countries. In the countries discussed in the previous section, some trends may be discerned, as accounted for by John Coakley and John Doyle (1998) in their comparison of the content of a number of journals during 1997.

Traditional concern with political institutions was clear in a number of cases. Various aspects of government formation and institutional reform were addressed in the *Revue française de science politique, Political Studies,* and the Finnish *Politiikka,* while aspects of corporatism attracted a great deal of interest in Italy and Germany (in *Rivista italiana di scienza politica* and *Politische Vierteljahresschrift,* respectively). The focus on the welfare state and its ramifications received much attention in both Italy and Germany as well as in Scandinavia (*Scandinavian Political Studies*) and the United Kingdom (*Political Studies*). This widespread focus on the welfare state reflects a major difference between European and American political science departments as discussed in the section on Scandinavia. As David McKay has noted:

> In no European country is the business of politics infused with the liberal individualism so intimately associated with the USA. Instead, European democracies are a complex melange of liberalism, corporatism, consociationalism, elitism, populism, statism and socialism. European political science reflects this in just the same way as American political science—which is primarily concerned with the study of the USA—reflects the individualism of American politics.[54]

Political parties and electoral behavior constituted another focus in Germany, France, and Scandinavia. However, more important in comparison to the United States is the general concern with the transformations in Russia and Central and Eastern Europe and with issues related to the European Union.[55] *Politiikka, Revue française de science politique,* the *Rivista italiana di sciena politica,* and *Political Studies* all published studies on various aspects of the European Union, and it constitutes one of the fastest-growing areas of political science research and publication in Sweden.[56] In line with the argument made earlier, political theory and political philosophy received much attention in *Political Studies,* and there was a strong theoretical component in Finnish *Politiikka,* with articles on Louis Althusser and Hannah Arendt, but in the rest of the journals investigated there was a clear absence of this kind of work. Instead, there tended to be a distinct reflection of national perspectives in most of the journals; all of the journals had a certain focus on the domestic politics of their own countries.

Research, Curricula, and Career Opportunities in Europe and the United States

Does this mean that there are no or few aspects of continental philosophy that have actually influenced continental political science and IR? Jørgensen makes an interesting point in this regard when he argues that basic ideas within certain currents of continental IR theory, such as conceptions of what theory is and what it can do, were provided by the Vienna Circle's philosophy of science.[57] Continental IR theory also seems to have been underpinned by the philosophy and social theory represented by scholars such as Norbero Bobbio, Carl Schmitt, Norbert Elias, Niklas Luhmann, and Jürgen Habermas, all of whose ideas are widely taught at the university level. However, as noted earlier, there seems to be a reluctance in much continental IR to import new theoretical constructs; it appears that continental IR theory never seriously went "on the 'detour'—away from normative theory, and back."[58] Tradition is still the rule in much continental IR. However, tradition tends to encompass a broad spectrum and is, according to Frederick H. Gareau, philosophically based in the sense that philosophy provides a worldview that illuminates such aspects of life as politics.[59] In comparison to the Americans, Gareau argues, most continentals tend to be less behavioral; to make less use of figures, tables, and statistics; and to be less methodology oriented and instead tend to be more concerned with normative issues, with legalistic methodology, and with political theory. The British, he adds, "are at worst hybrids."[60]

However, as the publication records suggest, British political science and IR have retained a strong emphasis on political theory and political philosophy. The interface between political theory and IR is especially noticeable in "normative international theory" and "international ethics," two fields in which British scholars have a comparative advantage in comparison to North America–based scholars.[61] This renewed marriage between political theory and IR has provided space "both for developing normative international theory and for linking international theory with similar debates in other disciplines, particularly moral philosophy, and social and political theory."[62]

As Chris Brown has indicated,[63] this linkage may be closely related to the nature of graduate education in IR in the United Kingdom, which, in contrast to the situation in the United States, is less concerned with the techniques of the behavioral sciences and more positive toward speculative theory.[64] To this can be added the Economic and Social Research Council's general guidelines for political science graduate education in the United Kingdom, which emphasize the need for a thorough understanding of the major theoretical and epistemological debates in the social sciences together with the acquisition or further development of a second international language.[65] The need to understand the differences between positivist, realist, and other accounts of social science from perspectives including feminism, postmodernism, and critical theory is a main focus of these guidelines.[66]

The tendency to replace much of this broad graduate training with formal methodology in the United States has, according to Kasza, slighted such basic normative and epistemological questions, with the result that graduate students enter political science as if "boarding a spaceship in midflight."[67] The fact that the American journals are mainly defined, structured, and to some extent controlled by theorists implies that scholars gain top positions not so much by publishing in their own subfield, but by making it into the top all-round journals located at the center of the discipline.[68] In this sense the disciplines of political science and IR are much more united in the United States than in Europe. The presence of a unified discipline makes it possible in the United States to debate and compete for the whole field, while in Europe it is easier to maintain local peculiarities. The existence of one big national "job market" also means that strategic dependence is higher in the United States than in Europe.[69] In comparison, it is only recently that political science and IR in Europe have started to break free of the very local career opportunities that have hitherto existed, such as single-university employment and the impact of informal personal power structures, by heading for less national areas or for language-defined areas (e.g., Scandinavia or French-speaking or German-speaking areas) in search of employment.[70] A job market with clearly defined ground rules and career patterns is, however, far from a reality in Europe.

Internationally, the predominance of rational methodology and research design reflects the sheer size and dominance of the American political science and IR communities, where certain kinds of insights, theories, paradigms, and data sets dominate the literature. Hayward Alker and Thomas Biersteker's 1984 survey of seventeen reading lists from major U.S. universities in the field of IR confirmed this. These researchers found that 70 percent of the literature was behavioral, 20 percent was traditional, and less than 10 percent was dialectical. In methodological terms, the survey showed that 72 percent was neo-realist and that 82 percent of the traditional literature was realist.[71] The effect, according to Smith, is a discipline skewed even today toward the policy concerns of the United States to ensure that the theories used fit the U.S. definition of "proper" social science.[72] A more recent example of this can be found in Svante Ersson's description of the lack of "cutting-edge" political science research in Sweden; Ersson argues that *only one* Swedish political scientist has been able to publish an article in the *American Political Science Review*.[73] Perhaps even more telling, however, is the 2002 evaluation of Swedish research in political science, in which the reviewers deplore the fact that they found Swedish political scientists more concerned about values such as legitimacy and broad participation than about effectiveness and efficiency. Only by focusing on these latter issues, they believe, would Swedish departments "stimulate the development of a theoretical base for applied research,"[74] thus reducing theory to its "proper" place, meaning hard scientific approaches.

Such "proper" science is often equated with increased production based on more and better knowledge from which we can come closer to the truth about political phenomena. As Keith Schimko argues, "Implicit in such an account is a view of social science as being divorced from broader contextual forces such as interests, values, and cultural predispositions: social theorizing is seen as a purely 'scientific' enterprise rather than a social process."[75] If the continental situation tells us anything, it is how problematic such a view is, as it entirely disregards cultural context. Hence, it is important to emphasize the extent to which different university systems, different disciplinary configurations, and

organizational structures create differences in career paths and incentive structures. As Jørgensen asks in his rhetorically posed questions:

> Why should a Continental PhD student attend an academic job market—
> read conferences like the APSA or ISA [International Studies Association]
> annual conventions—when there is no equivalent European market for
> academics? Why do German-speaking IR scholars tend to "disappear" from
> the surface of the earth during the (long) period they write their Habilita-
> tionsschrift, i.e. spending time on an obsolete institution, if the habilitation
> did not constitute a precondition for the next step of their career?[76]

The career possibilities in Germany hence depend more on a person's relationship to the local professor or local faculty for the acceptance of the Habil-
itationsschrift than it depends on national competition, as in the United
States. Until very recently, in Germany power largely rested with professors,
and there have been no clear benefits to publishing internationally, although
this is starting to change.[77] One of the most significant areas in which German
scholars are becoming heard is within European politics. This is related to
certain European political developments in the 1990s, such as Sweden's and
Finland's joining the European Union in 1995. The emergence of Scandinavian scholars in the field of European politics brought in English, rather than
French, as the main language for publication, and German scholars, from perhaps the most "Europeanized" society,[78] soon started to use this increasingly
common language of communication.[79] Thus in the 1990s German IR seems
to have developed more independent theory and to have oriented this toward
an international audience. Here it can be noted that until the introduction of
the German IR journal *ZIB* (*Zeitschrift für Internationale Beziehungen*) in 1994,
there was no peer-reviewed journal in this field. However, the fact that comprehensive training in social theory has pervaded German curricula has made it
relatively easy for a number of German scholars to relate to the Anglo-American
debate of the 1980s and 1990s. As Ole Waever has argued, "One has a Habermas at hand (in the original language). Therefore the whole discussion about
rational choice, which at first looks like the US debate, is couched in different terms because the alternative to strategic rationality is not mainly norm-
regulated but communicative rationality."[80]

The fact that more Germans have entered the English-language literature
does not, however, reduce the linguistic gap that exists between Anglo-American
knowledge production and that of the continent (which is less pronounced in
Scandinavia and in the Netherlands). In Italy, for example, the introduction of
English as a means of widespread communication and production of culture
is rather new, and until recently French was the most widely used foreign language. Most Italian undergraduate students read only Italian texts and encounter English only as they reach the graduate level, which means that they
are not trained in reading and studying foreign literature. Nor are they often
encouraged to attend international conferences and events. As a consequence,

very few Italian political science and IR scholars publish internationally, which makes their work less visible abroad. A general dissatisfaction with the Anglo-Saxon, and especially the American, rational turn in the 1980s is also prevalent among Italian scholars. A common complaint is that the Anglo-Saxon tradition is too detached from the rich tradition of European political and philosophical thought.[81] To this can be added the reluctance by mainstream Anglo-Saxon political science and IR communities to incorporate theoretical inputs from other cultural (and linguistic) traditions. The fact that books can be difficult to get ahold of because they are published and marketed by largely unknown publishers "who have never dreamt of renting a booth at a major international conference" plays an important role in this regard.[82]

Another significant feature in relation to Italy but also in regard to Scandinavia is the general tendency of university textbooks to provide as broad and comprehensive a picture as possible.[83] Christer Jönsson, for instance, notes that the U.S. academic culture encourages specialists and that the academic reward structure, as well as the university educational system, provides strong incentives for life-long specialization.[84] He argues that the Scandinavian academic culture is different, as university courses are designed to give general overviews of broad subfields of political science and there is a premium on versatility in academic appointments. To this can be added the fact that in most of Scandinavia it is necessary to have broad teaching experience to qualify as a lecturer. Such teaching experience is often given more weight than research qualifications in the appointment of lecturers. Furthermore, in comparison to the American context, which tends to categorize scholars according to certain approaches (game theorists, deconstructivists, institutionalists), the Scandinavian context tends to be less prone to conflict between different schools of thought. This may have to do with a number of factors, such as the fairly consensual atmosphere prevalent in Scandinavian academia, but may also, especially in Sweden, be related to the hierarchical structure there, with only a few persons holding chairs that have long characterized the political science discipline.[85]

The constant positioning vis-à-vis one general debate is even less significant in France, and French scholars are likely to have felt the American hegemony over the discipline much less than German and Scandinavian scholars. As Waever has noted, where the Germans have been preoccupied with measuring up to the standards of the Americans, the French have not shown much interest in comparing themselves to anyone.[86] Instead, most French scholars do empirical or policy work without feeling the need to locate themselves theoretically or by justifying their work according to different theoretical traditions. According to Waever, "What counts in both theory and policy work is firm conceptualization and a proper use of the concepts."[87] The use of French as the main language for writing and teaching also implies an atmosphere in which less emphasis is put on international English language–based work. In relation to this, however, we should emphasize the strength of French area studies, with its close relationship to sociology, philosophy, and anthropology.

Furthermore, as Klaus-Gerd Giesen has argued, even when the French scholarly community cultivates global approaches such as game theory, they tend
to give them a certain twist that counters pure copying.[88] Overall, however,
general theory does not have the same status as it does in the United States.
This may have something to do with the fact that the French academic world
is quite hierarchical, with the hierarchies related to specialization, which
means that "general theory does not play the role of prioritizing and system-
atizing these different specialties."[89] This lack of general theory is evident in
graduate training, in which more sociological inquiry continues to inform
specialization. At the same time, it should be noted that career opportunities
are often confined to special research centers with their policy-oriented research
focus. The combination of these fields is reflected in much recent research on
identity and security, in which scholars draw intensively on sociological,
philosophical, and anthropological literature at the same time that they often
stay close to policy concerns.[90]

Conclusion

In sum, then, we are able to distinguish certain features characterizing the
European context of political science and IR in comparison to that of the
United States. First of all we should reemphasize that in European societies
these fields have had anything but a uniform development and that their
diverse historical, cultural, and institutional contexts have been different in
Europe than they have in the United States. Far from following a path parallel
to that of the modernization of the European societies, the development of the
social sciences has been a very complex process with various national outcomes.
One of the major concerns that have characterized the situation, particularly
in Germany, France, and Italy, has been the role, function, and stability of the
state. Social thought has, as a consequence, been marked more by disruptions
and transformations than by the more even development that we have seen in
the United Kingdom and in Scandinavia. Hence it is not surprising that these
latter societies have more readily assimilated parts of the American political
science and IR discourses. However, the lack of rationalist approaches in these
societies has also been significant and is related to their particular historical
context. The lesser emphasis on "grand" theory and on formal reasoning and
methodology in favor of more pluralistic approaches that tend to privilege
social theory and philosophy have implied the existence of different research
agendas in Europe as compared to the United States.

   To this can be added the differences in publication patterns, curricula, and
career opportunities, which in Europe have been characterized by the lack of
a unified theoretical core against which scholars constantly need to position
themselves. The lack of a clear hierarchy of journals, especially of theoretically
centered journals, has also created different incentives in regard to publication
in Europe as compared to the United States. Linguistic barriers, the emphasis
on subfields, and the existence of local and often national academic commu-

nities in Europe have implied different reward structures in regard to publications and career possibilities. The fact that European departments are marked by differences in languages and cultures, lower mobility, and stronger institutional affiliation thus constitutes a powerful explanation for the differences that are seen between the continents. Together these differences take us a long way toward understanding and accounting for the absence of a European Perestroika debate, and provide good reasons for believing that such a debate may never occur.

This may not be a bad thing, however. Instead the diversity of the profession in Europe may give rise to more original work affecting the academic status of the discipline and its future relevance. As Steve Smith has argued in relation to the situation in the United Kingdom, "The very pluralism of the UK community, the very lack of one overriding theoretical model, the lower pressure towards intellectual conformity means that the UK community is much more likely to be able to respond to demands and pressures of globalization than will be the case in the US."[91] The recent American establishment of a more transdisciplinary intellectual discourse through the importation of certain European theoretical perspectives may, however, be an initial step in that direction in the United States. But this effort will require some larger incentives for the English-speaking community to read articles or books in other languages. Establishing foreign language requirements in the graduate curricula may be one step in that direction, together with more thorough training in regard to social theory. The absence of a European debate may thus provide helpful incentives for an American Perestroika movement in search of a more pluralistic discipline. If nothing else, it may serve as a healthy dose of pessimism in regard to the constant search for grand unified theories of politics, as such theories repeatedly seem to fail to acknowledge human, cultural, political, and institutional diversity.

Notes

1. See the "Post-Autistic Economics Network" Web site: http://www.paecon.net.

2. *Guardian,* April 3, 2001.

3. Considering the diversity of Europe and European political science departments, it is of course problematic to claim to speak for such a diverse area. However, I believe there are certain diverse patterns that can be said to characterize the development of the disciplines in Europe as compared to the United States.

4. Wagner, 1989, 510.

5. Gunnell, 2002.

6. Blyth and Varghese, 1999.

7. Blyth and Varghese, 1999; Gunnell, 2002; Hay and Wincot, 1998.

8. Hay, 2002.

9. Smith, 2000 and 2000b.

10. Hay, 2002; Walker, 1993; Weber, 2001.

11. Waever, 1998; see also Smith, 2000b.

12. Jørgensen, 2000.

13. Similar to Jørgensen, 2000, I use the term "continent" to largely refer to Western Europe outside the Anglo-American tradition. This means that I treat the United Kingdom as a separate case and make only some brief references to political science in Russia and the former "Eastern bloc," and then only in regard to publications.

14. Wagner, 1989.

15. Ibid., 512.

16. Ibid.

17. Waever, 1998.

18. Jørgensen, 2000; Gareau, 1981.

19. Waever, 1998.

20. Wagner, 1989.

21. Jørgensen, 2000.

22. Friedrichs, 2001.

23. Lucarelli and Menotti, 2000; Morlino, 2000.

24. Wagner, 1989.

25. Quoted in ibid., 517.

26. Ibid.

27. Lucarelli and Menotti, 2002.

28. Ibid; Jørgensen, 2000.

29. Olof Ruin, in Hydén, Immergut, and Underdal, 2002.

30. Nannestad, 1993.

31. Ibid.

32. Jönsson, 1993; Hansson and Stenelo, 1990.

33. Jørgensen, 2000.

34. Also in political terms, the United Kingdom is often described as existing between the United States and the European Union. See Blair, 2002.

35. Smith, 2000b.

36. Waever, 1998.

37. Hayward and Brown, 1999.

38. This unitary description of the development of political science in Britain has been disputed by, among others, Mark Bevir. See Bevir, 2001.

39. Blyth and Varghese, 1999.

40. See also Hay and Wincot, 1998. It should be noted, however, that the rational choice approach also has strong supporters in Britain. Todd Landman, for instance, challenges the initiators of the Perestroika movement, arguing that they provide research with an unscientific focus that is damaging to the social sciences. See Landman, 2002.

41. Bull, 1977.

42. Waever, 1998; Smith, 2000b.

43. Schmidt, 2002; Brown, 2000.

44. Waever, 1998, 711.

45. Gunnell, 2002.

46. Jørgensen, 2000.

47. Bender and Schorske, 1997.

48. Holden, 2002.

49. Katznelson, 1997.

50. Holden, 2002, 269.

51. Kasza, 2000.

52. Crew and Norris, 1991.

53. Waever, 1998.

54. McKay, 1991.

55. Morlino, 2000.

56. Coakley and Doyle, 1998; Hydén, Immergut, and Underdal, 2002.

57. Jørgensen, 2000.

58. Smith in ibid., 20.

59. Gareau, 1981.

60. Gareau, 1981, 783–84; c.f. Jørgensen, 2000, 27.

61. Brown, 2000.

62. Smith, 1995.

63. Brown, 2000.

64. See also Schmidt, 2002.

65. Economic and Social Research Council, 2000.

66. In contrast to these guidelines, however, it is interesting to note a recent review of textbooks in the field of British politics in which the author complains that these do not measure up to the expected standards as they are largely institutional and treat the political system as hermetically sealed, paying little attention to the outside world. They also tend to be descriptive rather than analytical. See Smith, 1999.

67. Quoted in Kasza, 2000.

68. For a recent attempt to clearly define such a "center" of political science around which *one* political science discipline can emerge, see Laitin, 1998.

69. Waever, 1998.

70. Ibid.

71. Alker and Biersteker, 1984, 129–30; c.f. Smith, 2000b.

72. Smith, 2000b, 394.

73. Ersson, 2002.

74. Hydén, Immergut, and Underdal, 2002, 137.

75. Schimko, 1992, 296; c.f. Jørgensen, 2000.

76. Jørgensen, 2000.

77. Ibid.; Waever, 1998.

78. Waever, 1998.

79. Manners, and Whitman, 2000.

80. Waever, 1998, 705–6; see also Risse, 2000.

81. Lucarelli and Menotti, 2002.

82. Jørgensen, 2000.

83. Lucarelli and Menotti, 2002; Jönsson 1993.

84. Jönsson, 1993.

85. Ruin, 2002; Jönsson, 1993.

86. Waever, 1998.

87. Ibid., 709.

88. Giesen, 1995; c.f. Jørgensen, 2000.

89. Waever, 1998, 719.

90. Waever, 1998.

91. Smith, 2000b, 398.

References

Alker, Hayward and Biersteker, Thomas (1984). "The Dialectics of World Order: Notes for a future archeologist of international savoir faire." *International Studies Quarterly*, Vol. 28: 121–42.

Bender, Thomas, and Schorske, Carl, E., eds. (1997). *American Academia in Transformation: Fifty Years, Four Disciplines*. Princeton, NJ: Princeton University Press.

Bevir, Mark (2001). "Prisoners of Professionalism: On the Construction and Responsibility of Political Studies: A Review Article." *Public Administration*, Vol. 79, No. 2: 469–509.

Blair, Alasdair (2002). "Bridging the Gap: The UK between the US and the EU." *European Political Science*, Vol. 2, No. 1 (Autumn): 11–19.

Blyth, Mark, and Varghese, Robin (1999). "The State of the Discipline in American Political Science: Be Careful What You Wish For?" *British Journal of Politics and International Relations*, Vol. 1, No. 3 (October): 345–65.

Brown, Chris (2000). "International Political Theory—A British Social Science?" *British Journal of Politics and International Relations*, Vol. 2, No. 1 (April): 114–23.

Bull, Hedley (1977). *The Anarchical Society: A Study of Order in World Politics*. Basingstoke, England: Macmillan.

Carr, E. H. (1939). *The Twenty Years' Crisis*. New York: Harper & Row.

Coakley, John, and Doyle, John (1998). "Developments in European Political Science Journal and Electronic Literature during 1997." *European Journal of Political Research*, Vol. 33: 525–47.

Crew, Ivor, and Norris, Pippa (1991). "British and American Journal Evaluation: Divergence or Convergence?" *PS: Political Science and Politics*, Vol. 24, No. 3 (September): 524–31.

Economic and Social Research Council, Quality Assurance Agency for Higher Education (2000). *Politics and International Relations*. Gloucester, England: Kall Kwik.

Ersson, Svante (2002). "Political Science in Sweden." *European Political Science*, Vol. 1, No. 2 (Spring): 45–52.

Friedrichs, J. (2001). "International Relations Theory in France." *Journal of International Relations and Development*, Vol. 4, No. 2 (June): 118–37.

Gareau, Frederick H. (1981). "The Discipline of International Relations: A Multi-National Perspective." *Journal of Politics*, No. 43: 779–802.

Giesen, Klaus-Gerd (1995). "French Cancan zwischen Positivismus, Enzylopädismus and Historismus." *Zeitschrift fur Internationale Beziehungen*, Vol. 2, No. 1: 141–70.

Gunnell, John G. (2002). "Handbook and History: Is It Still the American Science of Politics?" *International Political Science Review*, Vol. 23, No. 4: 339–54.

Hansson, Göte, and Stenelo, Lars-Göran, eds. (1990). *Makt och Internationalisering*. Stockholm: Carlssons.

Hay, Colin (2002). *Political Analysis: A Critical Introduction*. Basingstoke, England: Palgrave.

Hay, Colin, and Wincot, Daniel (1998). "Structure, Agency and Historical Institutionalism." *Political Studies*, Vol. 46: 951–57.

Hayward, J., Barry, B., and Brown, A., eds. (1999). *The British Study of Politics in the Twentieth Century*. Oxford: Oxford University Press.

Holden, Gerard (2002). "Who Contextualizes the Contextualizers? Disciplinary History and the Discourse about IR Discourse." *Review of International Studies,* Vol. 28, No. 2 (April): 253–70.

Hydén, G., Immergut, E., and Underdal, A. (2002). *Swedish Research in Political Science: An evaluation.* Uppsala, Sweden: Ord & Form.

Jönsson, Christer (1993). "International Politics: Scandinavian Identity Amidst American Hegemony?" *Scandinavian Political Studies,* Vol. 16, No. 2: 149–66.

Jørgensen, Knud Erik (2000). "Continental IR Theory: The Best Kept Secret." *European Journal of International Relations,* Vol. 6, No. 1: 9–42.

Kasza, Gregory (2000). "Perestroika: For an Ecumenical Science of Politics." *PS Online,* Special Edition (December). http://www.apsanet.org/PS/.

Katznelson, Ira (1997). "From the Street to the Lecture Hall: The 1960s." In Bender, Thomas, and Carl, E. Schorske, eds., *American Academic Culture in Transformation: Fifty Years, Four Disciplines.* Princeton, NJ: Princeton University Press, pp. 331–52.

Laitin, David, D. (1998). "Toward a Political Science Discipline: Authority Patterns Revisited." *Comparative Political Studies,* Vol. 31, No. 4 (August): 423–43.

Landman, Todd (2002). *Rebutting "Perestroika": Method and Substance in Political Science.* privatewww.essex.ac.uk/-todd.

Lucarelli, Sonia, and Menotti, Roberto (2000). "IR Theory in Italy in the 1990s." Paper presented at the European Consortium of Political Science, 28th Joint Sessions of Workshops, Copenhagen, April 14–19, 2000.

Manners, Ian, and Whitman, Richard, eds. (2000). *The Foreign Policies of European Member States.* Manchester, England: Manchester University Press.

McKay, David (1991). "Is European Political Science Inferior to or Different from American Political Science?" *European Journal of Political Research,* Vol. 20, Nos. 3–4: 459–79.

Morlino, Leonardo (2000). "How We Are, or Who We Say That We Are: The Post-War Comparative Politics of Hans Daadler and Others." *European Journal of Political Research,* Vol. 37: 497–516.

Nannestad, Peter (1993). "Paradigm, School or Sect? Some Reflections on the Status of Rational Choice Theory in Contemporary Scandinavian Political Science." *Scandinavian Political Studies,* Vol. 16, No. 2: 127–48.

Risse, Tomas (2000). "'Let's Argue!' Communicative Action in World Politics." *International Organization,* Vol. 54, No. 1 (Winter): 1–40.

Ruin, Olof (2002). "The Development of Swedish Political Science." In Hydén, G., Immergut, E., and Underdal, A., eds., *Swedish Research in Political Science: An Evaluation.* Uppsala, Sweden: Ord & Form, pp. 27–44.

Schimko, Keith (1992). "Realism, Neorealism, and American Liberalism." *Review of Politics,* Vol. 54: 281–301.

Schmidt, Brian, C. (2002). "Together Again: Reuniting Political Theory and International Relations Theory." *British Journal of Politics and International Relations,* Vol. 4, No. 1 (April): 115–40.

Smith, Martin, J. (1999). "Instituionalising the 'Eternal Return': Textbooks and the Study of British Politics." *British Journal of Politics and International Relations,* Vol. 1, No. 1 (April): 106–18.

Smith, Steve (1995). "The Self-Images of a Discipline: A Genealogy of International Relations Theory." In Booth, Ken, and Smith, Steve, eds. *International Relations Theory Today.* Cambridge: Cambridge University Press, pp. 1–37.

Smith, Steve (2000a). "Wendt's World." *Review of International Studies,* Vol. 26, No. 1 (January): 151–63.

Smith, Steve (2000b). "The Discipline of International Relations: Still an American Social Science?" *British Journal of Politics and International Relations,* Vol. 2, No. 3 (October): 374–402.

Waever, Ole (1998). "The Sociology of a Not So International Discipline: American and European Developments in International Relations." *International Organization,* Vol. 52, No. 4 (Autumn): 687–729.

Wagner, Peter (1989). "Social Science and the State in Continental Western Europe: The Political Structuration of Disciplinary Discourse." *International Social Science Journal,* Vol. 41, No. 4 (November): 509–28.

Walker, R. B. J. (1993). *Inside/Outside: International Relations as Political Theory.* Cambridge: Cambridge University Press.

Weber, Cynthia (2001). *International Relations Theory: A Critical Introduction.* London: Routledge.

CHAPTER 4

Every Poet His Own Aristotle

Theodore J. Lowi

If ever I should condescend to prose,
I'll write poetical commandments, which
Shall supercede beyond all doubt all those
That went before. . . .
I'll call the work "Longinus o'er a Bottle,
Or every poet his own Aristotle."

       —Lord Byron, *Don Juan*

At the risk of alienating the entire Perestroika movement, I must say at the outset that there is a lot of justice in the APSA, justice that can reward passion and individuality just as it can reward lockstep loyalty to the canons of method, evidence, theory, and paradigm. If I have had one consistent beef against my profession, it is that there is not enough love of subject—or, worse if true, that the love of subject is there, but the passion is suppressed by graduate training. For that reason alone, I embrace Perestroika with the hope that it is a genuine intellectual rebellion that will bring passion back in, with or without bringing the state back in. Although the APSA is not a Stalinist dictatorship, it is an oligarchy, and all oligarchy, especially academic oligarchy, needs the sustained spirit of *perestroika,* because *perestroika* as a principle produces *glasnost,* a kind of confession that sheds light. And as long as we are Sovietizing our vocabulary, let's go all the way with *samokritika,* self-criticism. But one Perestroika will never be enough; so let's bring in the spirit of Mao Tse-tung with "Let a hundred Perestroikas blossom." These inspirational appeals for a "cultural revolution" gave me a chance to make use of a favorite line of mine, adapted from my title and epigram: "Every *politist* his own Aristotle."

At my advanced age, I am able to say, "This is where I came in." My critique of pluralism in my 1969 book *The End of Liberalism* produced an invitation from the perestroikans of the 1960s to become a charter member of the Caucus for a New Political Science. For a while, I was a vigorous participant in the caucus. There was not a single ideology—and how could there be, considering that the luminaries ranged from Daniel Patrick Moynihan and Hans Morgenthau to Dankwart Rustow and Christian Bay? But there was a shared commitment to making political science more intellectual, more relevant, more critical, and above all, independent of prevailing governmental, corporate, partisan, ideological, and disciplinary commitments. I was also sympathetic to the caucus's agitation against the emergent orthodoxy of behavioralism as well as knee-jerk pluralism. But after a year or so I resigned from the caucus in a huff, and became an ardent critic as it transformed itself from an intellectual rebellion into an organized reform movement with the goal of organization takeover. I even published my swan song in one of the early issues of what was then simply *PS*. I did not know it then, but that was my first experience with Perestroika: I did not in fact want a Perestroika. What I wanted was *glasnost,* and the only way to get *glasnost* was, to quote Mao again, "let a hundred flowers blossom."

Having cut myself off from the Yale pluralist school and the caucus, and having no inclination to study institutions behaviorally, I was free to found my own school of thought, which I proceeded *not* to do. I can say without fear of contradiction that of all the many graduate students I have worked with, only two or three have done anywhere near the kind of work I do, and even they use my stuff in their own way, usually with a critique of separation before they get under way. That to me is a measure of my success as a teacher. If together they all took one thing from me, it was a sensitivity to the inarticulated major premises lurking behind every method, every approach, every school of thought or organized subdiscipline. Political scientists, above all others, must be able to engage constantly in a political analysis of their own situation. (Again, *samokritika.*) And that requires that we do a "politics of knowledge"— which is even more important than a sociology of knowledge—of all leading or currently fashionable folkways, mores, or thoughtways of the profession. I barely made a ripple with this argument in my 1991 APSA presidential address, "The State in Political Science: How We Become What We Study." I would like to think that my effort here will strengthen my earlier statement, that we cannot tolerate just one Perestroika in political science, because one Perestroika is one restructuring, which can simply become the next orthodoxy.

Since the principal focus of Perestroika seems to be the *American Political Science Review* (*APSR*), I will also focus on that, using behavioralism and rational choice as my two cases in point. But I have to begin with another statement of my recognition of the justice in the APSA as an organization. Managing editors and their administrations are beset by the flow of article submission. And in my nearly fifty years in the APSA, I have the distinct impression that a vigorously conscientious effort has always been made to circulate every submission to standard peer review, with reviewers drawn conscientiously from scholars identified by their qualifications in the relevant subfield. It is difficult to ask for more than that; and I think far fewer fundamental errors have been made by this procedure than have been made by juries of peers in capital murder cases. But why, then, is there such a gap between that which is now paraded in the *APSR* as political science and that which is of interest to most political scientists in the association? Or, to put the question another way, where the hell is the mainstream?

The first place to look for an explanation of the disparity between a just process and such unjust outcomes is *critical mass*. According to a recent survey (described in the chapter of this book by David Pion-Berlin and Dan Cleary, especially in their first table), nearly 75 percent of all articles submitted to the *APSR* in the decade between 1991 and 2000 were in the two categories labeled "Stats" and "Math Modeling" (MM). The other two categories of articles were those labeled "Theory" and "Qualitative." According to these authors' count, 4,250 articles were submitted during that decade, of which 3,130 were in the first two categories, with 2,250 Stats articles and 880 MM articles. The remaining 1,120 submissions were in the category of Theory (1,070) and Qualitative (50) and I would guess that a substantial number of those were on game theory, rational choice theory, or other types of nontraditional formal theory. Although no one can be precise about this, all I can say is that there has to be a "tipping point" somewhere in a distribution like this.

That leads to a second aspect of critical mass, the psychological impact of such a distribution. The overwhelming presence of Stats, MM, and formal theory acceptances creates a dynamic with which we are all familiar, the self-fulfilling prophecy. When scholars in traditional political theory or American political development or other "soft" subjects have an article to submit for publication, they turn away from the *APSR* on the assumption that they will be turned down. Thus, in what appears to be a "hostile environment," these scholars are turning *themselves* down. I have a personal stake in this matter. Back in the 1960s, I did pretty well for a softy, with hits in the *APSR* in 1963, 1964, and 1967. After that, I didn't publish an article in the *APSR* again until 1992, when the full text of my 1991 presidential address was published. And that was merely ex officio, automatic, the one "perk" one gets from being APSA president. In any case, between 1967 and 1992, my record was one submission and one turn-down. Meanwhile, I was sending articles to *PSQ, PAR, Daedalus, Review of Politics, National Political Science Review, Administration & Society,* various policy study reviews, and *PS: Political Science and Politics.* We cannot blame the self-negating psychology some believe is at play here on the *APSR* or the APSA: we softies must overcome our fear of failure and submit, submit, submit.

For further explanation of the disparity between just process and unjust outcomes, I turn now to my first substantive case, that of the so-called behavioral revolution. And it will be in the form of a politics of knowledge to understand where this particular critical mass came from. As far as I am concerned, the most important factor was neither a natural and spontaneous "revolution" nor a conspiracy but rather a deliberate and open imposition *by public policy*. I repeat, public policy created the "behavioral revolution" in political science. In the 1950s, political scientists were already beginning to imitate psychology; there was going to be a political behavior subdiscipline within political science arising out of imitation alone. But the kick-off for hothouse growth came with the creation of the National Science Foundation (NSF), followed by a number of private foundations. Many leading scholars—including Charles Merriam at Chicago; Robert Dahl, Harold Lasswell, and Robert Lane at Yale; V. O. Key at Yale, then Harvard; David Truman at Columbia; David Easton at Chicago; and so on and so on—all jumped on board with articles "in praise of" the coming movement, typified by creation of a Committee on Political Behavior at the Social Science Research Council.[1] Most of that founding group abandoned this commitment almost as quickly as they had embraced it,[2] but by the end of the 1950s they were not needed. They had helped get political science accepted *as a science* by the NSF. APSA Executive Director Evron Kirkpatrick proclaimed more than once that that was the greatest triumph of his long service. Science, which now included political science, was no longer defined classically as the objective pursuit of knowledge; it was now officially defined as laboratory science, with white coats and measurements down to the fourth or fifth decimal point, and with all inquiry driven by hypotheses about cause and effect, as though all politics is determined by simple, operationally defined variables.

Hothouse cultivation produced tremendous growth, and growth legitimizes choice. Just check the footnotes of behavioral articles and see how many of them acknowledge their NSF-numbered grants. And, of course, like amateurs investing in the stock market, the foundations followed suit, with additional support for behavioral research, which was becoming more and more expensive. But that also meant that it had to become more collaborative, and that meant the production of a torrential flow of research results in the form of articles. And once those articles met the canons of evidence, the peer review process had no choice but to accept those articles for publication.

For purposes of my politics of knowledge, the principal product of this growth was a consensus that Heinz Eulau was to term "the behavioral persuasion." The behavioral persuasion requires consensus around at least two types of criteria. One is consensus about how to harden inherently soft attitudinal items to a point where they can qualify as indexes, then be elevated to an acceptable level of measurement for those unobservables called "behavior." Second, there has to be consensus about what constitutes acceptable quantification. Simple enumeration is far from enough. The data collected, drawn almost entirely from questionnaires, must constitute absolutely uniform items (such as peas or fruit flies) and be properly designed samples in a known statistical universe or population. That can satisfy the mathematical requirement of probability, such that observed distributions, especially relationships between two distributions, cannot have occurred by chance alone.

I put all this in boringly commonplace terms because it is these very elementary things that reveal the "soft underbelly" (excuse me, Churchill) of behavioral science in politics. Once the items in the samples are all unitized and made absolutely uniform, and once the population base for the samples is agreed upon, and once the concepts for which these indexes are supposed to be measures have been properly operationalized, the math part is damned easy—especially because it is mainly cookbook stuff that produces immediate printouts.

I used to enjoy an old, cynical quip (given me by Ray Wolfinger) that "the plural of anecdote is data." But I no longer can smile about it, because it sets a standard that behavioral science cannot meet. First of all, each behavioral datum becomes an index for a concept that behavioralists insist on calling a measurement. An index is nothing more than the best available approximation of a phenomenon that the observer is truly interested in but cannot directly measure. Thus, an index is already a compromise, which so many behavioral scientists take as truth. Second, and more to the point here, each response taken from the questionnaire or interview is in itself an anecdote with different meanings and different contexts. Granted, recent surveys have a very good record of forecasting election outcomes, but the elections that are forecastable are the simple yea-nay choices that eliminate all the slippage in the unrelated anecdotes—such as, for instance, the relatively poorer record of forecasts in primary elections, multiple-party elections, referendum-type elections, and so on. Nor are these items, these anecdotes, rendered any harder as data by the mathematics we associate with superior science.

This elementary and commonplace treatment is intended to support one simple point: the steps and outcomes that appear to make a superior science constitute something we softer scientists have understood for many years— that behavioral science can be understood as a *sociopolitical decision-making process.* Consensus about measurement is reached through talk, mutual persuasion, compromise, and then agreement on "the best way available to get the job done." That is far from "the one best way." And there is a whole series of decision points on which this sociopolitical process of reaching consensus is required—from data and indexes to testing—and all of these decision points are artifacts of training in concept development, questionnaire technology, quantification methods, and cookbook testing formulae. This is quite familiar to people who have studied bureaucracies and other task-oriented organizations, because they try their best and are usually successful in inducting members into the "fact premises" and "value premises" of the organization so that consistent and coordinated decisions can be made even when the functionaries are located far apart from one another.

In sum, the behavioral revolution was a triumph of consensus. Science did not produce the consensus; *consensus produced the science.* And the production of that consensus was as complicated a political process as the production of legislation in an assembly.

This kind of institutionalization made behavioral science particularly attractive to government-supported science because it provided a solution of sorts to a larger political problem, that social science eventually has to ask some questions that are thought to be taboo. There is a tacit social contract here: keep it academic, keep it neutral, keep it lofty and abstract. This is all part of what Karl Mannheim had in mind in his concept, dating back to 1929, of "bureaucratic conservatism," which he defined as the "tendency . . . to turn all problems of politics into problems of administration" such that "irrational factors are overlooked, and when these nevertheless force themselves to the fore, they are treated as 'routine matters of state.'"[3]

This leads directly to my second case, that of the importation of economics and economic rationality into political science as rational choice theory. Fortunately, it is not necessary to delve into the particulars here, because when rational choice turns from theory to empirical science, it is joined at the hip with behavioralism and a similar sociopolitical decision-making process for producing consensus. This has all been hardened with math and modeling, but the indexes involved are so institutionalized that many of them go all the way back, unchanged, to Anthony Downs in the 1950s. But rational choice advances well beyond that, to situate its science not in a tournament of jousting hypotheses but in a system with its own inherent, orderly tendencies, that has come all the way down from the "invisible hand" of Adam Smith.

However, I can leave the substantive critiques of rational choice in order to get back to my original question: how and why did it succeed and become virtually hegemonic in political science, political science departments, and political science journals?[4] A political, or politics-of-knowledge, understanding of the success of rational choice can be fostered by recognizing that it was a mini–social movement. And, as is the case in all other social movements, the members share, rather intensely, an ideology—basically classical economics. The only comparable phenomenon I can think of in political science is Straussianism, because it, like rational choice, took on many of the characteristics of a cult. One anecdote can illustrate the cultish nature of rational choice. In the mid-1980s, William Riker was appointed a member of the membership committee of the American Academy of Arts and Sciences. Within no more than three years, virtually every visible rational choice practitioner had been inducted. This is to question not their qualifications but only the timing, the circumstances, and the average age of the inductees. I noticed this because I was partly responsible, having been a member of the nominating committee responsible for the appointment of Riker to that selection committee. Bill Riker was one of the most unpolitical persons I have known in this profession. It is inconceivable that he would have been party to the organization of a social movement or a cult. What happened requires a Darwinian, not a Marxian, sociology or politics of knowledge. Of all the ideas and methods circulating in political science in the late 1970s, those in the environment of the emerging Republican regime were most hospitable to rational choice. First, they satisfied the needs of government-supported science. Moving from the general toward the particular, an immensely important feature of the environment was the emergence as the hegemonic theory of liberal, laissez-faire economic theory, which won out over its predecessor, Keynesianism. As I said in my presidential address nearly fourteen years ago, political scientists enjoy the primitive wisdom of the proverbial Mr. Dooley, especially his proposition that "no matter whether th' Constitution follows th' flag or not, th' Supreme Court follows th' iliction returns." A more dignified, academic Dooley would observe that "the APSA follows Leviathan." As the distinguished economic philosopher Joan Robinson put it, "Economics . . . has always been partly a vehicle for the ruling ideology of each period as well as partly a method of scientific investigation."[5] As Milton Friedman was replacing John Maynard Keynes, rational choice was becoming hegemonic in the regime of academic political science. We are here confronting *not* political opportunism but environmental consonance—that is to say, a symbiotic relationship between the regime and the discipline of political science.

To be even more sophisticated within the Darwinian spirit, we could say that a still larger environment was hospitable both to the new regime and to the newly hegemonic economic theory. That larger environment is globalization. Vigorous and vast expansion of world trade required a more laissez-faire national government, which in turn strongly favored replacement of the Democratic Party with a newly hegemonic Republican Party and its commitment to liberal, laissez-faire economic theory. In the process, rational choice as political thought grew and prospered far beyond anything its founders could have imagined. I do not think it is an insult, nor is insult intended, to observe that rational choice (like behaviorism) has become hegemonic not because of the superiority of its science but because of its affinity or consonance with the regime of the 1980s and beyond. It will not disappear if and when the American regime changes again, but it will be far less in demand as the next regime creates an intellectual environment more hospitable to some other school of political thought. Alexis de Tocqueville was speaking to all epochs and not only his own when he asserted that "a new science of politics is needed for a new world."[6]

Meanwhile, I must urge again, as I did in 1991, that we cultivate an ongoing political analysis of our own situation. Rebellions like Perestroika are good, but they are wasted if they focus on conspiracy instead of critical mass. And rebellion against the APSA becomes virtually counterproductive if it focuses merely on reform of the organization by such means as replacing the managing editor or proportionalizing the editorial board or the distribution of article acceptances. The rebellion should be focused on the articles themselves, on expanded criticism of clusters of related articles, and, of utmost importance, on a vast increase in the number of traditional articles that are in fact submitted to the *APSR* for publication. No more self-fulfilling prophesy. Every poet his own Perestroika.

These efforts could lead to the higher goal of changing the *APSR* itself. Willingness to respond to criticism is indicated in the APSA's decision to establish the new journal *Perspectives on Politics*. It is to be welcomed; I hope to publish there one of these days myself. However, it is not an adequate response; in fact, it could be another Tale of a Tub, a diversionary tactic to take pressure off the *APSR*.

In that spirit, I will conclude with an anecdote I hope will provide supporting data for another assault on the *APSR*. Way back in the 1970s, when I first sat on the APSA Administrative Committee, I made a modest proposal that the APSA adopt for the *APSR* an editorial policy of publishing only articles of merit that were theoretical in nature, that attempted to synthesize sets of findings or to sustain arguments of criticism or theory construction that were aimed at joining the political discourse extending back over the past two thousand-plus years. Articles that were of merit but were reports based on research findings or specific applications of a method and so on would be referred to the more specialized journals. My motion was voted down by a vote of something like 18 to 2, and my only success was that I alienated the then-managing editor, who took my motion as a personal affront. Maybe times have changed. Although I won't ever be on the Administrative Committee again, this anecdote may inspire some other member to make a similar but improved motion. If any such motion carried the day, it would be a great victory for political science as it starts its second century.

Notes

1. See especially *ITEMS* 5 (1951) of the Social Science Research Council; Robert Dahl, "The Behavioral Approach to Political Science: An Epitaph for a Monument to a Successful Protest," *APSR* 55 (1961): 763–72; and Raymond Seidelman with Edward Harpham, *Disenchanted Realists: Political Science and the American Crisis, 1884–1984* (Albany: SUNY Press, 1985), Chapter 5.

2. See, for example, Robert Dahl, "The Behavioral Approach to Political Science"; the one inferior book published by V. O. Key was his behavioral effort, *Public Opinion and American Democracy* (New York: Knopf, 1961); and David Truman's behavioral study of Congress was virtually a dead end despite the flourishing of congressional research in the 1960s. Truman, *The Congressional Party* (New York: John Wiley, 1959). Truman's last major contribution to the political science literature before becoming a college dean, vice president, and provost was to organize and edit what became an important book of essays by several of America's leading non-behavioral students of Congress: David Truman, ed., *The Congress and America's Future* (Englewood Cliffs, NJ: Prentice-Hall, 1965).

3. Karl Mannheim, *Ideology and Utopia* (New York: Harcourt/Harvest Book, 1936), 118–19.

4. The best source of critiques from a variety of points of view will be found in the symposium "Rational Choice Theory," *Critical Review* 9 (Winter–Spring 1995): entire volume.

5. Joan Robinson, *Economic Philosophy* (New York: Doubleday Anchor, 1962), 1.

6. Alexis de Tocqueville, "Author's Introduction," *Democracy in America* (New York: Knopf, Vintage Edition, 1945), 7.

CHAPTER 5

Letter to a Graduate Student

Samuel H. Beer

Dear Student,

You ask, What was the role of history in the study of politics at Harvard in the 1950s and 1960s?[1] You are right in suspecting that during those years the members of this department typically made wide use of data from the past. Although we were, of course, aware of the introduction of behavioralism in other places, especially at Yale, it did not make an appearance here until the arrival of V. O. Key, whom we seduced from Yale. The historical dimension was a crucial feature of his splendid book on Southern politics, and later on I learned that he had taken a great interest in history in his earlier years. As a colleague here, however, he was distinctly hostile to a historical approach. I did a lot with history, especially in a big course called Western Thought and Institutions in the then-flourishing General Education program. When V. O. asked me the use of all that history, I said that, for one thing, the contrast with the past brought out basic features of the present. He replied, Why not get at these features of the different societies of different periods simply by using other social sciences, such as anthropology? His approach at that time was much like that set out in Gabriel Almond's APSA presidential address in 1965, in which, making use of Kuhn's model of revolutions in natural science, he presented "behavioralism" as providing "a new, more surely scientific paradigm" for the study of politics.

At Harvard Key produced some brilliant students. I think of Walter Dean Burnham, David R. Mayhew, and Milton C. Cummings. But his approach remained in the minority. After his premature death in 1963, one of his brightest products, Doug Price, although an assistant professor, felt so isolated at Harvard that, while on leave for a term at Berkeley, he wrote an angry letter to Art Maass, our chairman, saying that he would not return. Maass solved the problem by successfully putting through the promotion of Price to tenure, saying, "Doug is our new V. O. Key." Although a superb teacher and wonderful colleague, however, Doug published very little. Our stream of graduate students, a brilliant, creative crowd who flocked into political science after the war—Henry Kissinger, Zbigniew Brzezinski, Melvin Richter, Louis Hartz, Stanley Hoffmann, Herbert McCloskey, Judith Shklar, Samuel Huntington, Adam Ulam, and others—went on to fame (and sometimes fortune) in political science, all making major use of historical materials in one way or another. New concerns, such as "modernization" and "development," have forced the discipline to devote ever more serious attention to the past, both near and distant. In our department today, the historical approach is still strongly represented. You must, for example, see what Peter Hall says about the uses of history in his recent paper on ontology and methodology in comparative research.[2] In my time the most successful and sophisticated behavioralist was Sid Verba. But he was not a pupil of Key, and, as I recall, he came here in the 1970s from Yale, having concentrated in history and literature as an undergrad at Harvard and having taken his PhD at Princeton.

Already in the early 1960s, Bob Dahl had pointed out that much work in the behavioral mode had neglected both theory and history. In the 1970s there was, at Harvard as elsewhere, a shift away from behavioralism. This was forcefully reflected in Gabriel Almond's 1977 reassessment of "the now dominant 'behavioral tradition'" in *World Politics* on the grounds that it mistakenly attempted to apply "a hard science strategy" drawn from the natural sciences to "human subject matters." We must, Almond argued, "give up the notion that there is some analogy in the social sciences to basic research in physical science." Finding that "the interplay of imagination and induction" is in no way inferior to "mathematical and statistical analysis," Almond concluded: "The blinding attraction of powerful science has begun to fade as our efforts *fall short of our aspirations*" (my emphasis).

Scientism, Behaviorism, and Math

This rough sketch suggests that there has been a rise and fall of behavioralism in contrast with a historical approach. But to see what has happened in our methodology, we need to be clear about the meaning of the two big terms. In political science *behavioralism* has meant various things, and *history* has similarly been seen and used in more than one way.

In *behavioralism* I find three meanings that can be thought of and used in combination or separately. The first is "scientism," that is, the belief that the study of politics can produce laws of political process that have a validity comparable to that of the laws of natural science. These are statements of the sequence of events that are universal in that they hold *semper et ubique,* as do the laws of theoretical physics. Quoting Karl Popper and Carl Hempel, I once examined this view in an essay titled "Political Science and History."[3] Both men see nomological universality as required if a statement is to be a "scientific" causal explanation. If we follow David Hume, *causality* means "universality," that is, invariable sequence, and nothing more. A notable logician and a friend of mine, Willard Van Orman Quine, disabused me of this dogma of universality, as I recalled in that essay, where I also noted that the findings of the best comparative studies I knew did not pretend to universality, but were confined to some time-space context; in short, as I say there, they were "limited generalizations." From time to time, I would ask colleagues and graduate students who believed in scientism whether, after all this labor, anyone had yet discovered a universal law of political behavior—with nil results. This general failure of an essential premise of scientism was obviously one reason for Almond's severe reassessment.

There's nothing new in this cycle of hope and failure in the history of social methodology. As Isaiah Berlin recalled in an essay titled "The Concept of Scientific History" in the first issue of the journal *History and Theory* in 1960, "All seemed ready, particularly in the nineteenth century, for the formulation of this new, powerful, and illuminating discipline. All was ready, but virtually nothing came forth. No general laws were formulated . . . from which historians could deduce (together with knowledge of the initial conditions) either what would happen next, or what had happened in the past." Indeed, the hope for social science goes back as far as Francis Bacon, who, in his *New Atlantis* (1627), contemptuously dismissing Aristotle's teleological method, displayed an even greater expectation for an empirical science of society than for an empirical science. of nature. The nonappearance of the former in comparison with the immense progress of the latter in the course of three centuries must surely suggest that there is something about the substance of social studies that makes it unsuitable to study by the methods of the hard sciences.

The peculiarity of this substance is that it consists of entities that not only behave, but also think about their behavior, and this thinking affects that behavior. This capacity "to live in their heads," as a brilliant anthropologist puts it,[4] is a capacity that arose in the evolution of mankind from its prehuman hominid ancestors and that anthropologists with a bent for deep history are learning to date. From it comes the problem of "social self-knowledge,"[5] which I discuss in the concluding pages of the 1970 essay. Knowledge is not a mirror, but enters into a process of thinking and doing. Knowledge of the effects of what we do affects what we choose to do. New knowledge is intrinsically unpredictable; so also, therefore, are its effects. As a noted methodologist observes, well-established generalizations will be rendered invalid if and when they are made public and people alter their behavior in the light of this new knowledge.[6] Continually threatening the advances of social science with such obsolescence, this kind of freedom, which is uniquely characteristic of human behavior, may also function as an agent of reform, innovation, and historical development. Social self-awareness is one reason why human beings have a history.

Behaviorism and Its Troubles

A response to this devastating criticism of hard-science behavioralism must deny the premise of that criticism, that knowledge can affect behavior, that ideas can be causes. This would be the argument of the rugged behaviorist. The great exemplar is B. F. Skinner. I recall a hilarious, but not entirely pointless, argument with a friend that boiled down to the question What caused Jack and Jill to go up the hill? I said the cause was that they wanted to get a pail of water. My friend said, No, it was the "initial conditions" leading to such a sequence, as formulated in some pattern of observed regularity of behavior into which this incident fit. Coming down to the specifics of the argument, a behaviorist might focus on the problem of testing. He could contend, as some students of method do, that whether or not an idea was a cause cannot be confirmed or discon-firmed, because this is a subjective event that one cannot observe empirically, but can only surmise by a kind of "guesswork," which will differ from one to another observer, making it impossible to test a hypothesis. The substance of one's study ultimately must remain only externally observed behaviors. For behavioristic methodology thinking, in its various forms—cognitive, norma-tive, affectual, and expressive—is simply "spooks" or "soul stuff."[7]

The trouble with trying to confine the study of politics to observable behav-ior is that human behavior always comes with meaning, with intentions and purposes. That is to say, the way others see and react to what we do is power-fully affected by what they think we mean, what we are trying to do and why. So if the social scientist wants to describe the sequence of the interaction, he cannot omit what it means to the actors. He studies not just behavior but action. I recall during the disorders of the 1960s a recurring discussion with some junior colleagues of the meaning of violence, a common concern in those days. Knocking a man down can be a crime, an accident, an applauded play in football. Sheer behavior is ambiguous. *Volenti non fit iniuria.*

Social theory, as Talcott Parsons taught, is theory of action. That means behavior oriented by culture—in our field, political culture, to use the term given currency by Almond. Participants may be wrong about the purposes they impute to others. A common culture narrows the chances of such failures of communication. Similarly, the scientific observer of the politics of some group will prepare himself by getting acquainted with the beliefs, values, and affectual life of the people he is studying. Here we are again led to appreciate the role of ideas and the need for subjective understanding. With some fudging, the champions of behavioralism recognized these facts, and, as the syllable *al* in the name they chose for their movement indicates, they resisted the temp-tations of hard science implied by behaviorism *strictu sensu.*

In contrast with a strictly behavioristic approach, a more forbidding and also more instructive denial of a causal role for thinking comes in the Marxist package. (For a quick summary of my critique of Marxism, you can look at the introduction to the edition of *The Communist Manifesto* that I wrote for the Crofts Classics in 1955.) Here ideas have great immediate power as ideology, but in the Marxist view ideology is only a "reflection" or "echo" of economic structure, which alone causes change from age to age according to the laws of its objective development revealed in the theory of dialectical materialism. While Marxism can in this manner be seen as a variety of behavioralism, it surely does not exclude the study of history. On the contrary, its conception of how the "laws" of social behavior will change from stage to stage—for example, from feudalism to capitalism—is a formidable and instructive challenge to the social scientist blinkered by his parochial concern with only the data of here and now.

Indeed, the eye-opening experience of such a revelation may lead the neophyte in social science to explore whether those powerful ruling ideas of an age may well have a non-Marxian origin. Conceivably, they may themselves be the dynamic force in development, as presumed in the Hegelian scheme, which Marx turned upside down. At the same time, the Marxian emphasis on structure, on the compulsions of the situation, great or small, is an indispensable supplement to the cultural approach. It certainly encouraged me to look for the situational as well as the intentional, the structural as well as cultural aspects of the political process. Combining the two approaches, I worked up what I called a cultural/structural method, which I developed and used in my *Modern British Politics* (1965; reprinted 1982) and also explained there, especially, on. pp. 403–9 in chapters titled "Latent Function and Operative Ideal" and "The Laws of Political Concentration." See also the introduction to my *Britain against Itself* (1982), pp. 3–5, and also Chapter 4, pp. 107–10.

What I did owed something to Robert Merton, but is especially indebted to Talcott Parsons and Max Weber.[8] It was not structural/functional, however. That was the rationale of the Social Science Research Council series in which Richard Rose did an admirable volume on Britain. But the series did not last. Generally, the authors of the separate volumes paid little attention to the model. Just what are the functions of any political system? And how do they manage to exert causal force in the political process? In the third edition of *Patterns of Government* (1973), I tried my hand at this sort of modeling with a framework of functions based on Dewey's means-ends continuum plus political culture. It served to organize that book, but as far as I know was adopted by no one else. Again I advise you to look at Peter Hall's treatment, in particular his method of "systematic process analysis."

Quantification

The third aspect of behavioralism is its mathematical techniques. I am referring to the practice of stating hypotheses in such a way that they can be confirmed or disconfirmed by quantification, which lends itself to stating results with different degrees of probability. This was surely the innovation of behavioralism most evident to the naked eye. And I should say it is that element which has survived and prospered most successfully. Peter Hall concedes as much in his reference to "the standard regression model" of behavioral analysis. The procedures are limited to data that are sufficiently numerous and similar for such analysis, and the techniques can vary in complexity and subtlety.

But quantification is not all that recent an addition to our field. In 1902 Professor A. L. Lowell, then a professor of government within the Department of History at Harvard, used a very simple definition of "party voting" to measure the influence of party on legislation in England and America. The resulting study was an immense piece of work, sheer drudgery covering several sessions of the Commons, the Congress, and the legislatures of several states. But it decisively gave the lie to a common and important misconception of that time, viz., that political parties had much greater influence on public policy in the United States than in Britain. I used the same type of measurement, adding a coefficient of cohesion taken from Stuart Rice's work on sampling, to show a trend toward what I termed the "collectivist age" in *Modern British Politics*.[9]

There was no hostility to history in these efforts. The far greater abundance of quantified data in very recent times, however, does tend to slant the use of relevant techniques to this time period and its problems and processes. Public opinion surveys, for instance, have provided the right sort of data for hardly more than the last fifty years, but they comprise a large portion of such studies of intentional behavior. They do show the importance of political culture. For instance, an understanding of what voting means to the voters beyond the sheer physical act of casting a ballot is indispensable if variations in arithmetical outcomes are to be compared and understood. The interviews on which surveys are based, therefore, need to be adjusted to the emerging significance of the research, as Bob Putnam showed when he relaxed and broadened his perspective and questions as he went forward with the interviews on which he based the excellent book *Making Democracy Work: Civic Traditions in Modern Italy*. Again I make these points to emphasize how the demands of subjective understanding keep popping up.

In summary: The shift with regard to behavioralism had negative and positive aspects. The sharp rejection of scientism was the most prominent feature. It was accompanied by a clearer recognition of the inadequacy of behaviorism. Yet these withdrawals also gave rise to a more realistic view of structural explanations that, examined with more sophisticated mathematical and statistical techniques, spelled progress in causal analysis. At the same time, the appreciation of the role of ideas and subjective understanding as specified in the concept of political culture made great strides. In these ways, the growing recognition of both the cultural and the structural aspects of the political process was bringing about a rapprochement between the methods of *Naturwissenschaft* and *Geisteswissenschaft*, the two old enemies (the materialists and the idealists) of the nineteenth-century *Methodenstreit*. My discussion of the papers by Michael Walzer and Charles Tilly,[10] in the symposium published in *History and Theory* in 1963, was such an effort to integrate the two approaches of causal explanation and imaginative enactment.

A voice from down the academic corridor rings out: Where do you put rational choice? Has this methodology contributed to the decline of behavioralism, or is it a variety of behavioralism? I should say, the answer to both questions is Yes. The central role of motivation and calculation puts it in the idealist camp. Preferences are central to this explanation of choice. As one political scientist has remarked, "The theory of games is . . . directed to the question: What would I reasonably do if I were in the other fellow's shoes?"[11]

At the same time, the structure of the situation faced by the chooser can be powerfully influential (decisive among an array of egoists), as in the self-defeating pluralism of the n-persons prisoners' dilemma presented in Garrett Hardin's celebrated "tragedy of the commons." The narrow view of the choosing mind as necessarily a self-interested calculator, however, severely limits the method's power of explanation. It simply is not in accord with obvious facts. Other-regarding behavior as well as self-regarding behavior is common in human interaction. Concern for the interests of others ranges through a variety of different cultural outlooks. I have even found it helpful to refer to the Nazis as "altruists with teeth." It takes no great knowledge of history to shatter the narrow dogmas of self-interested rationalism.

Culture as Mover and Shaker

But what does all this talk of meaning, culture, and imagination have to do with history? It depends on what one means by *history,* and that varies. Peter Hall brings out the use of two different conceptions of pastness. Sometimes it is simply a larger collection of data, as in that strong bit of advice Tilly gave to his fellow sociologists when he reminded them that "all history is past social behavior." My classification of history as "duration" means that we must take a longer view of time, or we may miss some overarching condition, material or ideal, that makes itself known only on distant occasions. Classifying history as "development" introduces the central insight. Walzer identifies it in his analysis of the rise of the Puritan purpose. After recognizing in a broad and perceptive survey the many structural changes that had some influence on the Puritan state of mind, he finally concedes, or rather reveals, what he calls "the creative moment," when the culture of Puritanism emerged as a new vision of man and society. Clifford Geertz has similarly brought home to social science the importance of such moments in his emphasis on "the autonomous process of symbol formulation." The sociological and psychological background of new ideas is, of course, relevant. But it cannot explain away the contribution of man, the "'agent of his own realization,' who through the construction of schematic images of social order . . . makes himself for better or worse a political animal."[12] Here an ancient insight is being assimilated and put to work by modern social science. Shelley had celebrated in his *Defense of Poetry* (1821) "the imaginative and creative faculty" that makes "poets . . . the unacknowledged legislators of the world." Purposes can be causes. Ideas have consequences, as their designs reshape our worlds, great and small. When we look back in time, we can explain these moments by imaginative reenactment. When we look forward, the same capacity opens the possibility of prediction by imaginative preenactment. Such moments of transformation, creative and destructive, make history in this mode a central area of study in political science.

I thank you for occasioning this look back, and trust it may be of some help to you in exploiting and expanding the rich resources of our discipline.

Sam Beer

Notes

1. A couple of years ago, a former student of mine, now a political science professor, had a brilliant student who was much interested in methodology, especially the role of history. So she suggested that he ask me directly about the Harvard experience. I have kept the informality of a letter in this slightly elaborated version of my reply.

2. "Aligning Ontology and Methodology in Comparative Research," in James Mahoney and Dietrich Ruescheneyer, eds., *Comparative Historical Research* (New York: Cambridge University Press, 2002).

3. Chapter 1 in Melvin Richter, ed., *Essays in Theory and History: An Approach to the Social Sciences* (Cambridge, MA: Harvard University Press, 1970).

4. Professor Alison Brooks, Department of Anthropology, George Washington University.

5. I owe this term to Dankwart Rustow, *A World of Nations: Problems of Modernization* (Washington, DC: Brookings Institution, 1967).

6. Ernest Nagel, *The Structure of Science: Problems in the Logic of Scientific Explanation* (New York: Harcourt, Brace and World, 1961), 468.

7. Arthur F. Bentley, *The Process of Government* (Chicago: 1908).

8. Robert K. Merton, *Social Theory and Social Structure* (New York: 1968); Talcott Parsons, *The Structure of Social Action* (New York: 1937); Max Weber, *The Theory of Social and Economic Organization,* trans. Parsons and Henderson (New York: 1947).

9. A long footnote on p. 122 of that book discusses the methods.

10. "Puritanism as a Revolutionary Ideology" and "The Analysis of a Counter-Revolution," respectively.

11. Richard C. Snyder, "Game Theory and the Analysis of Political Behavior," in Nelson Polsby et al., eds., *Politics and Social Life* (Boston: Houghton Mifflin, 1963), 132.

12. Clifford Geertz, *The Interpretation of Cultures: Selected Essays* (New York: Basic Books, 1973).

PART 2

Methodological Concerns

At the heart of the Perestroika movement is a concern for the scientific nature of political science. Can methodological diversity and pluralism exist? Should they?

Ian Shapiro begins by posing a fundamental question: how should students of politics deal with the reality that there are always multiple true descriptions of any given political phenomenon? Shapiro rejects the reductionist impulse always to select one type of description as apt. This leaves us with the difficulty of selecting among potential competing descriptions of what is to be accounted for in politics. Shapiro considers the possibility that the capacity to generate successful predictions is the appropriate sorting criterion. In some circumstances, he argues, that is the case, yet he also finds that too much preoccupation with prediction entails the risk of trapping researchers into forlorn attempts to refine predictive instruments at the expense of illuminating political reality. For Shapiro, insisting on the capacity to predict as the criterion for problem selection risks predisposing political science to the study of trivial, if tractable, problems. In light of prediction's limitations, Shapiro considers other ways in which the aptness of competing accounts can be assessed. He argues that political scientists must identify, criticize, and suggest plausible alternatives to theoretical assumptions, challenge interpretations of political conditions, and reconceptualize the assumptions underlying prevailing empirical accounts and research programs so that new, promising, problem-driven research agendas can be created.

Stuart J. Kaufman takes a slightly different tack. He begins by noting that while some scholars have called for making rational institutional analysis the foundation of all subfields of political science, Perestroikans view this project as profoundly unwise, even dangerous to the future of the field, portending the exclusion or marginalization of approaches other than formal modeling and quantitative research. In the study of international and ethnic conflict, Kaufman argues, such a move would be especially unwise, because rationalist theories and models, whether based on quantitative data or not, are currently inferior to their competitors. Prominent formal models are frequently based on demonstrably false premises, and they focus analytical attention on less important factors while obscuring more important ones. Existing alternatives —realist, institutionalist, and liberal explanations of international war, and the symbolic politics theory of ethnic war—better explain the phenomena in question. Kaufman concludes by arguing that symbolic politics theory is also useful for understanding the Perestroika controversy within political science, and for developing options for managing the conflict.

Sanford F. Schram finds justification for a Perestroika-inspired alternative political science in two important recently published books: Bent Flyvbjerg's *Making Social Science Matter* and Stephen Toulmin's *Return to Reason*. Schram takes from these volumes the thought that the concerns expressed by Perestroika reach beyond political science to broader movements that are roiling each of the human and social sciences. Further, these works provide important philosophical justification for Schram's own Perestroika-inspired alternative to conventional political science: a "post-paradigmatic political science" that deemphasizes any single dominant approach to the study of politics in order to dedicate itself to enhancing the critical capacity of people to practice politics. If this political science were to do this to enhance the capacity to challenge power from below, it would be all the more to the good. Such a new political science, Schram argues, would be not just more politically efficacious but also more intelligent, offering more robust forms of political knowledge.

David D. Laitin disagrees. He takes strong exception to the Perestroikan challenge to the hegemony of formal and statistical analysis in the discipline, and focuses on the Flyvbjerg arguments that interest Schram. Laitin believes that Flyvbjerg makes the best case for a renewed dominance for qualitative and case study work throughout the social sciences. Laitin's chapter challenges Flyvbjerg's call for a *phronetic* as opposed to an *epistemic* discipline. It challenges as well the unqualified call for pluralism advocated by many in the Perestroika movement, offering instead what Laitin believes is an integrated tripartite method in which narrative, statistics, and formal modeling fill in a scientific frame.

In sharp contrast to Laitin, Brian Caterino touches on a major complaint among Perestroikans: that rational choice theorists believe they can fully incorporate dimensions of social and political order and integrate aspects of interpretative social inquiry into their models. Caterino addresses this charge by examining representatives of two major branches of this approach: neo-institutionalism and the analytic narratives school. Caterino finds neo-institutionalists acknowledging that the genesis and maintenance of modern social institutions (such as the market) rely on a normative infrastructure, which provides binding force. This approach grasps the insufficiency of core institutions in providing a basis for establishing social order, but it remains wedded to the micro foundational project, which sees markets as core structures. In contrast, Caterino argues that the analytic narrative approaches attempt to explain the genesis and transformation of social life by combining "thick descriptions" of culturally embedded meanings with game-theoretical structures. These thick descriptions suggest a model that goes beyond what neo-institutionalism can offer by showing that acts of expression—in which symbolic meanings are publicly manipulated—can provide motivational power to mobilize subjects embedded in these cultural meanings for action. Caterino concludes that this move away from strategic to interpretive models is insufficient; he suggests that the real transformational power of narratives can be modeled only by seeing them as embedded in episodes, that is, as linked sequences of events that retain a sense of historic development.

Cecelia Lynch also discusses narrative, but does so by turning the discussion to a critical concept in political science: rigor. The "r" word in both its nominal and adjectival forms is extremely powerful in assessing the quality of research in political science. Peer reviews judge articles by the "rigor" of their methodology, and political science departments judge candidates for recruitment and promotion in terms of whether their work is sufficiently "rigorous." The "r" word, however, has become a trope, a prop used by some to support certain methods over others, and by others—even qualitative and interpretivist scholars—to "mark" their own research as valid. Lynch's chapter discusses rigor in the context of current debates about method in the subfield of international relations, and relates these debates to recent controversies about the use of narratives. Lynch finds that an overly great concern for rigor results in misunderstanding by some interpretivists as well as proponents of "analytical narratives." She argues that a discussion of the narrative controversy should help us dispense with the "r" word or, at the very least, find more fruitful standards for quality research. However, a discussion of the forms of narrative also leads us to raise questions about the methods-politics dichotomy engineered by Perestroika itself. Perestroika wishes to focus on the problem of exclusivity of methods in the field, and to distinguish this problem from other forms of political debate in the field. This choice, however, results in a potentially irresolvable tension between the need to include a critique of "meta-narratives" in world politics in any serious discussion of method in the discipline, and the perceived needs of Perestroika as a social movement.

Elizabeth Sanders also addresses a critical methodological issue of concern to Perestroika: the negative consequences of quantifying social sciences. She argues that what is most objectionable about the trend in methodologies requisite for publication in political science journals is not quantification per se. Indeed, there are many important propositions that Sanders finds are best addressed by systematic counting. The problem with quantification lies in the need for highly technical statistics, and the abandonment of simpler, more accessible methods for presenting count data in lieu of, or in addition to, tables of coefficients. The trend toward more technical and esoteric statistics has drastically limited the interpretability and accessibility of political science journal literature and has implied a misleading precision, glossing over questions about the operation of the statistical methods and their assumptions about and suitability to the data. Sanders argues that a focus on arcane methods often replaces needed attention to assumptions, facts, definition or operationalization of concepts, and the adequacy of data. Valuable new descriptive work also has been marginalized in favor of technical analyses of existing data sets. Sanders concludes that, far from making our discipline more "scientific," this trend limits inquiry in a way not characteristic of the "hard" sciences.

Kamal Sadiq addresses an important political aspect of methodological work: the difficulties involved in doing comparative research and work in cultures where data sources are often misleading. Sadiq argues that when states count, monitor, and otherwise make available data about society and politics they use this process as a tool to control and maintain order. Almost all statistics require the acknowledgement, or encouragement, of the states involved. Sadiq examines the theoretical and methodological challenges presented by our dependence on the state for data. He does this by considering two related questions. First, how does one study political phenomena using data that the state has a strong interest in manipulating or suppressing? Sadiq finds the visibility and legibility of many political phenomena are often dependent on the political or ideological form of the state—authoritarian, monarchical, totalitarian, or democratic—or on its ideology. The second question is this: how can we study political and economic phenomena over which the state has no control, and for which it has little of no reliable data? Here Sadiq argues that developing states cannot, with the resources currently available, acquire effective data on terrorist networks, "black" economies, trafficking in women, illegal international financial flows, and undocumented immigration flows. The state's inability to control and monitor key processes becomes a methodological issue to be considered. Sadiq concludes by arguing that greater emphasis must be placed on the quality of data and the validity of the operationalizations applied in the study of such political phenomena. This calls for a new breed of "qualitative" and "interpretive" methodologists. Such people will have the local know-how necessary to carefully assess the reliability and validity of statistics being used for the phenomena being studied.

Dvora Yanow argues that underlying many of the Perestroikan contentions concerning the narrowness of American political science is an argument about the ways in which research and theorizing are imbricated with methodological issues. Her chapter explores the ways in which methods have been separated from methodology, thereby enabling a narrow focus on tools and techniques at the expense of research questions and their ontological and epistemological presuppositions. This chapter examines the common taxonomy for research methods, locates it in a historical context, notes the ambiguity of "qualitative" as a category, and suggests another possible taxonomy. Yanow argues that one of the consequences of the hegemonizing equation of methods with statistics is the narrowing of the realm of researchable questions to those which can be stated explicitly; as an example, she points to the study of public policy and administrative issues, which so often entail that which is known—and communicated—tacitly. Yanow concludes by considering the idea that the implicit rationale underlying the positivist hegemony is the denigration of local "knowledge" and its associated constructionist-interpretive methodology. She suggests that the discipline should proceed with more passionate humility.

Dorian T. Warren's chapter raises important issues about race and methodology, focusing on whether Perestroikans have failed to allow adequately for the methodological bias involved in doing work on race and ethnicity within the political science discipline. Warren notes that critiques of method-driven research have been offered by many scholars of color and students of race and ethnic politics, who have pointed out the limitations of mainstream and dominant methodologies for understanding racialized politics. Yet few of these scholars have played a significant role in this most recent disciplinary insurgency. Warren further notes that there is a resistance toward challenging these methodological tools within the race and ethnic politics subfield, because these tools have given scholarship in the subfield an unparalleled degree of legitimacy.

The last chapter in this section is by Lloyd I. Rudolph and addresses several important Perestroika claims. First is the assumption that there is something called science whose meaning and method are self-evident and transparent. Second is the belief that political scientists—and social scientists more generally—agree that science is the only form of knowledge or truth. The poverty of these two assumptions runs like a leitmotif throughout the Perestroika debate. Equally troubling for Perestroikans involved in the comparative enterprise, Rudolph argues, is the obliviousness of many political scientists to the conundrum of large n studies and the fact that most independent and dependent variables don't travel well across culture, language, and circumstance, much less time.

CHAPTER 6

Problems, Methods, and Theories in the Study of Politics

Or, What's Wrong with Political Science and What to Do about It

Ian Shapiro

Donald Green and I have previously criticized contemporary political science for being too method-driven, not sufficiently problem-driven.[1] In various ways, many have responded that our critique fails to take full account of how inevitably theory-laden empirical research is. In this chapter I agree with many of these basic claims, but I argue that they do not weaken the contention that empirical research and explanatory theories should be problem-driven. Rather, they suggest that one central task for political scientists should be to identify, criticize, and suggest plausible alternatives to the theoretical assumptions, interpretations of political conditions, and above all the specifications of problems that underlie prevailing empirical accounts and research programs, and to do it in ways that can spark novel and promising problem-driven research agendas.

My procedure will be to develop and extend our arguments for problem-driven over method-driven approaches to the study of politics. Green and I made the case for starting with a problem in the world, next coming to grips with previous attempts that have been made to study it, and then defining the research task by reference to the value added. We argued that method-driven research leads to self-serving construction of problems, misuse of data in various ways, and related pathologies summed up in the old adage that if the only tool you have is a hammer, everything around you starts to look like a nail. Examples include collective action problems such as free riding that appear mysteriously to have been "solved" when perhaps it never occurred to anyone to free ride to begin with in many circumstances, or the concoction of elaborate explanations of why people "irrationally" vote, when perhaps it never occurred to most of them to think about the individual costs and benefits of the voting act. The nub of our argument was that more attention to the problem and less to vindicating some pet approach would be less likely to send people on esoteric goose chases that contribute little to the advancement of knowledge.

What we dubbed "method-driven" work in fact conflated theory-driven and method-driven work. These can be quite different things, though in the literature they often morph into one another, as when rational choice is said to be an "approach" rather than a theory. From the point of view elaborated here, the critical fact is that neither is problem-driven, where this is understood to require specification of the problem under study in ways that are not mere artifacts of the theories and methods that are deployed to study it. Theory-drivenness and method-drivenness undermine problem-driven scholarship in different ways that are attended to here, necessitating different responses. This is not to say that problem selection is, or should be, uninfluenced by theories and methods, but I will contend that there are more ways than one of bringing theory to bear on the selection of problems, and that some are better than others.

Some resisted our earlier argument on the grounds that refinement of theoretical models and methodological tools is a good gamble in the advancement of science as part of a division of labor. It is sometimes noted, for instance, that when John Nash came up with his equilibrium concept (an equilibrium from which no one has an incentive to defect) he could not think of an application, yet it has since become widely used in political science.[2] We registered skepticism at this approach in our book, partly because the ratio of successes to failures is so low, and partly because our instinct is that better models are likely to be developed in applied contexts, in closer proximity to the data.

I do not want to rehearse those arguments here. Rather, my goal is to take up some weaknesses in our previous discussion of the contrast between problem-drivenness and method- and theory-drivenness, and explore their implications for the study of politics. Our original formulation was open to two related objections: that the distinction we were attempting to draw is a distinction without a difference, and that there is no theory-independent way of characterizing problems. These are important objections, necessitating more elaborate responses than Green and I offered. My response to them in sections A and B of this chapter leads to a discussion in section C of the reality that there are always multiple true descriptions of any given piece of social reality, where I argue against the reductionist impulse always to select one type of description as apt. This leaves us with the difficulty of selecting among potential competing descriptions of what is to be accounted for in politics, taken up in section D. There I explore the notion that the capacity to generate successful predictions is the appropriate criterion. In some circumstances this is the right answer, but it runs the risk of atrophying into a kind of method-drivenness that traps researchers into forlorn attempts to refine predictive instruments. Moreover, insisting on the capacity to generate predictions as the criterion for problem-selection risks predisposing the political science enterprise to the study of trivial, if tractable, problems. In light of prediction's limitations, I turn in part V to other ways in which the aptness of competing accounts can be assessed. There I argue that political scientists have an important role to play in scrutinizing accepted accounts of political reality: exhibiting their presuppositions, both empirical and normative, and posing alternatives. Just because observation is inescapably theory-laden, this is bound to be an ongoing task. Political scientists have a particular responsibility to take it on when accepted depictions of political reality are both faulty and widely influential outside the academy.

A. A Distinction without a Difference?

The claim that the distinction between problem- and theory-driven research is a distinction without a difference turns on the observation that even the kind of work that Green and I characterized as theory-driven in fact posits a problem to study. This can be seen by reflecting on some manifestly theory-driven accounts.

Consider, for instance, a paper sent to me for review by the *American Political Science Review* on the probability of successful negotiated transitions to democracy in South Africa and elsewhere. It contended, inter alia, that as the relative size of the dispossessed majority grows, the probability of a settlement decreases for the following reason: members of the dispossessed majority, as individual utility maximizers, confront a choice between working and fomenting revolution. Each one realizes that, as their numbers grow, the individual returns from revolution will decline, assuming that the expropriated proceeds of revolution will be equally divided among the expropriators. Accordingly, as their relative numbers grow they will be more likely to devote their energy to work than to fomenting revolution, and because the wealthy minority realizes this, its members will be less inclined to negotiate a settlement as their numbers diminish because the threat of revolution is receding.

One has only to describe the model for its absurdity to be plain. Even if one thought dwindling minorities are likely to become increasingly recalcitrant, it is hard to imagine anyone coming up with this reasoning as part of the explanation. In any event, the model seems so obtuse with respect to what drives the dispossessed to revolt and fails so obviously to take manifestly relevant factors into account (such as the changing likelihood of revolutionary success as the relative numbers change) that it is impossible to take it seriously. In all likelihood it is a model that was designed for some other purpose, and the person promoting it is trying to adapt it to the study of democratic transitions. One can concede that even such manifestly theory-driven work posits problems, yet nonetheless insist that such specification is contrived. It is an artifact of the theoretical model in question.

Or consider the neo-Malthusian theory put forward by Charles Murray to the effect that poor women have children in response to the perverse incentives created by Aid to Families with Dependent Children and related benefits.[3] Critics such as Michael B. Katz pointed out that on this theory it is difficult to account for the steady increase in the numbers of children born into poverty since the early 1970s, because the real value of such benefits has been stagnant or declining.[4] Murray's response (in support of which he cited no evidence) has only to be stated for its absurdity to be plain: "In the late 1970s, social scientists knew that the real value of the welfare benefit was declining, but the young woman in the street probably did not."[5] This is clearly self-serving for the neo-Malthusian account, even if in a palpably implausible way. Again, the point to stress here is not that no problem is specified; Murray is interested in explaining why poor women have children. But the fact that he holds onto his construction of it as an attempt by poor women to maximize their income from the government even in the face of confounding evidence suggests that he is more interested in vindicating his theory than in understanding the problem.

Notice that I am not raising an objection to modeling. To see this, compare these examples to John Roemer's account of the relative dearth of redistributive policies advocated by either political party in a two-party democracy with substantial *ex ante* inequality.[6] He develops a model that shows that if voters' preferences are arrayed along more than one dimension—such as "values" as well as "distributive" dimensions—the median voter will not necessarily vote for downward redistribution as he would if there were only a single distributive dimension. Roemer's model seems to me worth taking seriously (leaving aside for present purposes how well it might do in systematic empirical testing), because the characterization of the problem that motivates it is not forced, as was the case in the earlier examples. Therefore, trying to develop the kind of model Roemer proposes to account for it seems worthwhile.[7]

In light of these examples we can say that the objection that theory-driven research in fact posits problems is telling in a trivial sense only. If the problems posited are idiosyncratic artifacts of the researcher's theoretical priors, they will seem tendentious, if not downright misleading, to everyone except those who are wedded to her priors. Put differently, if a phenomenon is characterized as it is so as to vindicate a particular theory rather than to illuminate a problem that is specified independently of the theory, it is unlikely that the specification will gain much purchase on what is actually going on in the world. Rather, it will appear to be what it is: a strained and unconvincing specification driven by the impulse to vindicate a particular theoretical outlook. It makes better sense to start with the problem, perhaps asking what conditions make transitions to democracy more or less likely, or what influences the fertility rates of poor women, next to see what previous attempts to account for the phenomenon have turned up, and only then to look at the possibility of whether a different theory will do better. To be sure, one's perception of what problems should be studied might be influenced by prevailing theories, as when the theory of evolution leads generations of researchers to study different forms of speciation. But the theory should not blind the researcher to the independent existence of the phenomenon under study. When that happens, appropriate theoretical influence has atrophied into theory-drivenness.

B. Is All Observation Theory-Laden?

It might be objected that the preceding discussion fails to come to grips with the reality that there is no theory-independent way to specify a problem. This claim is sometimes summed up with the epithet that "all observation is theory-laden." Even when problems are thought to be specified independently of the theories that are deployed to account for them, in fact they always make implicit reference to some theory. From this perspective, the objection would be reformulated as the claim that the contrast between problem-driven and theory-driven research assumes there is some pre-theoretical way of demarcating the problem. But we have known since the later Ludwig Wittgenstein, J. L. Austin, and Thomas Kuhn that there is not. After all, in the example just mentioned, Roemer's specification of the problem is an artifact of the median voter theorem and a number of assumptions about voter preferences. The relative dearth of redistributive policies is in tension with that specification, and it is this tension that seems to call for an explanation. Such considerations buttress the insistence that there simply is no pre-theoretical account of "the facts" to be given.

A possible response at this juncture would be to grant that all description is theory-laden but retort that some descriptions are more theory-laden than others. Going back to my initial examples of democratic transitions and welfare mothers, we might say that tendentious or contrived theory-laden descriptions fail on their own terms: one doesn't need to challenge the theory that leads to them to challenge them. Indeed, the only point of referring to the theory at all is to explain how anyone might come to believe them. The failure stems from the fact that, taken on its own terms, the depiction of the problem does not compute. We have no good reason to suppose that revolutionaries will become less militant as their relative numbers increase or that poor women have increasing numbers of babies in order to get decreasingly valuable welfare checks. Convincing as these suppositions might be as response to the examples given, it does not quite come to grips with what is at stake for social research in the claim that all description is theory-laden.

Consider theory-laden descriptions of institutions and practices that are problematic even though they do not fail on their own terms, such as Kathleen Bawn's claim that an ideology is a blueprint around which a group maintains a coalition[8] or Russell Hardin's claim that constitutions exist to solve coordination problems.[9] Here the difficulty is that, although it is arguable that ideologies and constitutions serve the designated purposes, they serve many other purposes as well. Moreover, it is far from clear that any serious investigation of how particular ideologies and constitutions came to be created or have been subsequently sustained would reveal that the theorist's stipulated purpose has much to do with either. They are "just so" stories, debatably plausible conjectures about the creation or operation of these phenomena.[10]

The difficulty here is not that Bawn's and Hardin's are functional explanations. Difficult as it is to test functional explanations empirically, they may sometimes be true. Rather, the worry is that these descriptions might be of the form "Trees exist for dogs to pee on." Even when a sufficient account is not manifestly at odds with the facts, there is no reason to suppose that it will ever get us closer to reality unless it is put up against other plausible conjectures in such a way that there can be decisive adjudication among them. Otherwise we have "Well, in that case, what are lampposts for?" Ideologies may be blueprints for maintaining coalitions, but they also give meaning and purpose to people's lives, mobilize masses, reduce information costs, contribute to social solidarity, and facilitate the demonization of "out-groups"—to name some common candidates. Constitutions might help solve coordination problems, but they are also often charters to protect minority rights, legitimating statements of collective purpose, instruments to distinguish the rules of the game from the conflicts of the day, compromise agreements to end or avoid civil wars, and so on. Nor are these characterizations necessarily competing: ideologies and constitutions might well perform several such functions simultaneously. Selecting any one over others implies a theoretical commitment. This is one thing people may have in mind when asserting that all observation is theory-laden.

One can concede the point without abandoning the distinction between problem-driven and theory-driven, however. The theory-driven scholar commits to a sufficient account of a phenomenon, developing a "just so" story that might seem convincing to partisans of her theoretical priors. Others will see no more reason to believe it than a host of other "just so" stories that might have been developed to vindicate different theoretical priors. By contrast, the problem-driven scholar asks, "Why are constitutions enacted?" or "Why do they survive?" and "Why do ideologies develop?" and "Why do people adhere to them?" She then looks to previous theories that have been put forward to account for these phenomena, tries to see how they are lacking, and whether some alternative might do better. She need not deny that embracing one account rather than another implies different theoretical commitments, and she may even hope that one theoretical outcome will prevail. But she recognizes that she should be more concerned to discover which explanation works best than to vindicate any priors she may have. As with the distinction-without-a-difference objection, then, this version of the theory-ladenness objection turns out, on inspection, at best to be trivially true.

C. Multiple True Descriptions and Aptness

There is a subtler sense in which observation is theory-laden, untouched by the preceding discussion though implicit in it. The claim that all observation is theory-laden scratches the surface of a larger set of issues having to do with the reality that all phenomena admit of multiple true descriptions. Consider possible descriptions of a woman who says "I do" in a conventional marriage ceremony. She could be

- Expressing authentic love.
- Doing (or failing to do) what her father has told her to do.
- Playing her expected part in a social ritual.
- Unconsciously reproducing the patriarchal family order.

- Landing the richest husband she can.
- Maximizing the chances of reproducing her genes.

Each description is theory-laden in the sense that it leads to the search for a different type of explanation. This can be seen if in each case we ask the question "Why?" and see what type of explanation is called forth.

- "Why does she love him?" predisposes us to look for an explanation in terms of the woman's personal biography.
- "Why does she obey (or disobey) her father?" predisposes us to look for a psychological explanation.
- "Why does she play her part in the social ritual?" predisposes us to look for an anthropological explanation.
- "Why does she unconsciously reproduce patriarchy?" predisposes us to look for an explanation in terms of ideology and power relations.
- "Why does she do as well as she can in the marriage market?" predisposes us to look for an interest-based rational choice explanation.
- "Why does she maximize the odds of reproducing her genes?" predisposes us to look for a sociobiological explanation.

The claim that all description is theory-laden illustrated here is a claim that there is no "raw" description of "the facts" or "the data." There are always multiple possible true descriptions of a given action or phenomenon, and the challenge is to decide which is most apt. Indeed, the idea of a complete description of any phenomenon is chimerical. We could describe the activity in the bride's brain when she says "I do," the movements of her vocal chords, or any number of other aspects of the phenomenon.[11]

From this perspective, theory-driven work is part of a reductionist program. It dictates always opting for the description that calls for the explanation that flows from the preferred model or theory. So the narrative historian who believes that every event is unique will reach for the bride's personal biography, the psychological reductionist will turn to the psychological determinants of her choice, the anthropologist will see the constitutive role of the social ritual as the relevant description, the feminist will focus on the action as reproducing patriarchy; the rational choice theorist will see the explanation in terms of maximizing success in the marriage market, and for the sociobiologist it will be evolutionary selection at the level of gene reproduction.

Why do this? Why plump for any reductionist program that is invariably going to load the dice in favor of one type of description? I hesitate to say "level" here, since that prejudges the question I want to highlight: whether some descriptions are invariably more basic that others. Perhaps one is, but to presume that this is the case is to make the theory-driven move. Why do it?

The common answer rests, I think, on the belief that it is necessary for the program of social science. In many minds this enterprise is concerned with the search for general explanations. How is one going to come up with general explanations if one cannot characterize the classes of phenomena one studies in similar terms? This view misunderstands the enterprise of science, provoking three responses, one skeptical, one ontological, and one occupational.

The skeptical response is that whether there are general explanations for classes of phenomena is a question for social-scientific inquiry, not one to be answered before conducting that inquiry. At stake here is a variant of the debate between deductivists and inductivists. The deductivist starts from the preferred theory or model and then opts for the type of description that will vindicate the general claims implied by the model, whereas the inductivist begins by trying to account for particular phenomena or classes of phenomena, and then sees under what conditions, if any, such accounts might apply more generally. This enterprise might, as often happens, be theory-influenced for the reasons discussed in sections A and B, but is less likely to be theory-driven than the pure deductivist's, because the inductivist is not determined to arrive at any particular theoretical destination. The inductivist pursues general accounts, but she regards it as an open question whether they are out there waiting to be discovered.

The ontological response is that although science is in the second instance concerned with developing general knowledge claims, it must in the first instance be concerned with developing valid knowledge claims. It seems to be an endemic obsession of political scientists to believe that there must be general explanations of all political phenomena, indeed to subsume them into a single theoretical program. Theory-drivenness kicks in when the pursuit of generality comes at the expense of the pursuit of empirical validity. "Positive" theorists sometimes assert that it is an appropriate division of labor for them to pursue generality while others worry about validity. This leads to the various pathologies Green and I wrote about, but the one we did not mention that I emphasize here is that it invites tendentious characterizations of the phenomena under study, because the selection of one description rather than another is driven by the impulse to vindicate a particular theoretical outlook.

The occupational response is that political scientists are pushed in the direction of theory-driven work as a result of their perceived need to differentiate themselves from others, such as journalists, who also write about political phenomena for a living, but without the job security and prestige of the professoriate. This aspiration to do better than journalists is laudable, but it should be unpacked in a Lakatosian fashion. When tackling a problem we should come to grips with the previous attempts to study it, by journalists as well as scholars in all disciplines who have studied it, and then try to come up with an account that explains what was known before—and then some. Too often the aspiration to do better than journalists is cashed out as manufacturing esoteric discourses with high entry costs for outsiders. All the better if they involve inside-the-cranium exercises that never require one to leave one's computer screen.

D. Prediction as a Sorting Criterion?

A possible response to what has been said thus far is that prediction should be the arbiter. Perhaps my skepticism is misplaced, and some reductionist program is right. If so, it will lead to correct predictions, whereas those operating with explanations that focus on other types of description will fail. Theory-driven or not, the predictive account should triumph as the one that shows that interest maximization, or gene preservation, or the oppression of women, or the domination of the father figure, or whatever else might be the case, is "really going on." On this instrumentalist view we would say, with Milton Friedman: deploy whatever theory-laden description you like, but lay it on the line and see how it does in predicting outcomes; if you can predict from your preferred cut, you win.[12]

This instrumental response is adequate up to a point. Part of what is wrong with many theory-driven enterprises, after all, is that their predictions can never be decisively falsified. From Jeremy Bentham through Karl Marx, Sigmund Freud, functionalism, and much modern rational choice theory, too often the difficulty has been that the theory is articulated in such a capacious manner that some version of it is consistent with every conceivable outcome. In effect the theory predicts everything, so it can never be shown to be false. This is why people say that a theory that predicts everything explains nothing. If a theory can never be put to a decisive predictive test, there seems little reason to take it seriously.

Theories of everything to one side, venturing down this path raises the difficulty that prediction is a tough test that is seldom met in political science. This difficulty calls to mind the job applicant who said in an interview that he would begin a course on comparative political institutions with a summary of the field's well-tested empirical findings, but then had nothing to say when asked what he would teach for the remaining twelve weeks of the semester. Requiring the capacity to predict is in many cases a matter of requiring more than can be delivered, so if political science is held to this standard there would have to be a proliferation of exceedingly short courses. Does this reality suggest that we should give up on prediction as our sorting criterion?

Some, such as Alasdair MacIntyre, have objected to prediction as inherently unattainable in the study of human affairs due to the existence of free will.[13] Such claims are not convincing, however. Whether human beings have free will is an empirical question. Even if we do, probabilistic generalizations might still be developed about the conditions under which we are more likely to behave in one way rather than another. To be sure, this assumes that people are likely to behave in similar ways in similar circumstances, which may or may not be true, but the possibility of its being true does not depend on denying the existence of free will. To say that someone will probably make choice x in circumstance q does not mean that he cannot choose not-x in that circumstance or that, if he does choose not-x, it was not more likely *ex ante* that he would have chosen x. In any event, most successful science does not proceed by making point predictions. It predicts patterns of outcomes. There will always be outliers and error terms; the best theory minimizes them vis-à-vis the going alternatives.

A more general version of this objection is to insist that prediction is unlikely to be possible in politics because of the decisive role played by contingent events in most political outcomes. This, too, seems overstated unless one assumes in advance—with the narrative historian—that everything is contingent. A more epistemologically open approach is to assume that some things are contingent, others not, and try to develop predictive generalizations about the latter. For instance, Courtney Jung and I developed a theory of the conditions that make negotiated settlements to civil wars possible, involving such factors as whether government reformers and opposition moderates can combine to marginalize reactionaries and revolutionary militants on their flanks. We also developed a theory of the conditions that are more and less likely to make reformers and moderates conclude that trying to do this is better for them than the going alternatives.[14] Assuming we are right, contingent triggers will nonetheless be critical as to whether such agreements are successfully concluded, as can be seen by reflecting on how things might have developed differently in South Africa and the Middle East had F. W. DeKlerk been assassinated in 1992 or Yitzhak Rabin not been assassinated in 1995. The decisive role of contingent events rules out *ex ante* prediction of success, but the theory might correctly predict failure—as might be the case if a moderate Irish Republican Army leader such as Jerry Adams emerges but the other necessary pieces are not in place, or if Yassir Arafat is offered a deal by Ehud Barak at a time when he is too weak to outflank Hamas and Islamic Jihad. Successful prediction of failure over a range of such cases would suggest that we have indeed taken the right descriptive cut at the problem.[15]

There are other types of circumstance in which capacity to predict will support one descriptive cut at a problem over others. For instance, Adam Przeworski and associates have shown that although level of economic development does not predict the installation of democracy, there is a strong relationship between level of per capita income and the survival of democratic regimes. Wealthy democracies appear never to die, whereas poor democracies are fragile, exceedingly so when per capita income falls below $2,000 (in 1975 dollars). When per capita income falls below this threshold, democracies have a one in ten chance of collapsing within a year. When per capita incomes are between $2,001 and $5,000, this ratio falls to one in sixteen. When per capita income is above $6,055 annually, democracies, once established, appear to last indefinitely. Moreover, poor democracies are more likely to survive when governments succeed in generating development and avoiding economic crises.[16] If Przeworski and his colleagues are right, as it presently seems that they are, level of economic development is more important than institutional arrangements, cultural beliefs, presence or absence of a certain religion, or other variables for predicting democratic stability. For this problem the political economist's cut seems to be the right sorting criterion.[17]

These examples suggest that prediction can sometimes help, but we should nonetheless be wary of making it the criterion for problem selection in political science. For one thing, this can divert us away from the study of important political phenomena about which knowledge can advance even though prediction turns out not to be possible. For instance, generations of scholars have theorized about the conditions that give rise to democracy (as distinct from the conditions that make it more or less likely to survive once instituted, just discussed). Alexis de Tocqueville alleged that democracy is the product of egalitarian mores.[18] Seymour Martin Lipsett saw it as a byproduct of modernization.[19] Barrington Moore identified the emergence of a bourgeoisie as critical, while Dietrich Rueschemeyer, Evelyne Huber Stephens, and John D. Stephens held that the presence of an organized working class is decisive.[20] We now know that there is no single path to democracy, and therefore no generalization is to be had about which conditions give rise to democratic transitions. Democracy can result from decades of gradual evolution (as in Britain and the United States), imitation (India), cascades (much of Eastern Europe in 1989), collapses (Russia after 1991), imposition from above (Spain and Brazil), revolutions (Portugal and Argentina), negotiated settlements (Bolivia, Nicaragua, and South Africa), or external imposition (Japan and West Germany).[21]

In retrospect, this is not surprising. Once someone invents a toaster, there is no good reason to suppose that others must go through the same invention processes. Perhaps some will, but some may copy the original toaster, some may buy it, some may receive it as a gift, and so on. Perhaps there is no cut at this problem that yields a serviceable generalization, and as a result no possibility of successful prediction. Political scientists tend to think they must have general theories of everything, as we have seen, but looking for a general theory of what gives rise to democracy may be like looking for a general theory of holes.[22] Yet we would surely be making an error if our inability to predict in this area inclined us not to study it. It would prevent our discovering a great deal about democracy that is important to know, not least that there is no general theory of what gives rise to it to be had. Such knowledge would also be important for evaluating claims by defenders of authoritarianism who contend that democracy cannot be instituted in their countries because they have not gone through the requisite path-dependent evolution.

Reflecting on this example raises the possibility I want to consider next: that making a fetish of prediction can undermine problem-driven research via wag-the-dog scenarios in which we elect to study phenomena because they seem to admit the possibility of prediction rather than because we have independent reasons for thinking it worthwhile to study them. This is what I mean by method-drivenness, as distinct from theory-drivenness. It gains impetus from a number of sources, perhaps the most important of which is the lack of uncontroversial data concerning many political phenomena. Predictions about whether constitutional courts protect civil rights run into disagreements over which rights are to count and how to measure their protection. Predictions about the incidence of war run into objections about how to measure and count the relevant conflicts. In principle it sounds right to say, "Let's test the model against the data." In reality there are few uncontroversial data sets in political science.

A related difficulty is that it is usually impossible to disentangle the complex interacting causal processes that operate in the actual world. We will always find political economists on both sides of the question whether cutting taxes leads to increases or decreases in government revenue, and predictive tests will not settle their disagreements. Isolating the effects of tax cuts from the other changing factors that influence government revenues is just too difficult to do in ways that are likely to convince a skeptic. Likewise, political economists have been arguing at least since Bentham's time over whether trickle-down policies benefit the poor more than do government transfers, and it seems unlikely that the key variables will ever be isolated in ways that can settle this question decisively.

An understandable response is to suggest that we should tackle questions about which good data are readily available. But taking this tack courts the danger of self-defeating method-drivenness, because there is no reason to suppose that the phenomena about which uncontroversial data are available are those about which valid generalizations are possible. My point here is not one about curve-fitting—running regression after regression on the same data set until one finds the mix of explanatory variables that passes most closely through all the points to be explained. Leaving the well-known difficulties with this kind of data-mining to one side, I worry that working with uncontroversial data because of the ease of getting it can lead to endless quests for a holy grail that may be nowhere to be found.

The difficulty here is related to my earlier discussion of contingency, to wit, that many phenomena about which political scientists try to generalize may exhibit secular changes that will always defy their explanatory theories. For instance, trying to predict election outcomes from various mixes of macro political and economic variables has been a growth industry in political science for more than a generation. But perhaps the factors that caused people to vote as they did in the 1950s differ from those that are influential forty or fifty years later. After all, predicting election outcomes is not an activity with much of a track record of success in political science. We saw this dramatically in the 2000 U.S. election, in which all of the standard models predicted a decisive Gore victory.[23] Despite endless post hoc tinkering with the models after elections in which they have fared poorly, this is not an enterprise that appears to be advancing. Political scientists will never get these predictions right if my conjecture about secular change is correct.

It might be replied that if that is really so, either political scientists will come up with historically nuanced models that do a better job or universities and funding agencies will pull the plug on them. But this ignores an occupational factor that might be dubbed the Morton Thiokol phenomenon. When the *Challenger* blew up in 1986, there was much blame to go around, but it became clear that Morton Thiokol, manufacturer of the faulty O-ring seals, shouldered a huge part of the responsibility. A naïve observer might have thought that this would mean the end of that company's contract with the National Aeronautics and Space Administration, but of course this was not so. The combination of high entry costs to others, the dependence of the space program on Morton Thiokol, and the company's access to those who control resources has meant that they continue to make O-ring seals for the space shuttle. Likewise with those who work on general models of election forecasting. Established scholars with an investment in the activity have the protections of tenure and legitimacy, as well as privileged access to those who control research resources. Moreover, high methodological entry costs are likely to self-select new generations of researchers who are predisposed to believe that the grail is there to be found. Even if their figurative space shuttles will never fly, it is far from clear that they will ever have the incentive to stop building them.

To this it might be objected that it is not as if others are building successful shuttles in this area. Perhaps not, but this observation misses my point here: that the main impetus for the exercise appears to be the ready availability of data that sustain a coterie of scholars who are likely to continue to try to generalize on the basis of these data until the end of time. Unless one provides an account that, like the others on offer, purports to retrodict past elections and predict the next one, one cannot aspire be a player in this game at which everyone is failing. If there is no such account to be found, however, perhaps some other game should be played. For instance, we might learn more about why people vote in the ways they do by asking them. Proceeding instead with the macro models risks becoming a matter of endlessly refining the predictive instrument as an end in itself—even in the face of continual failure and the absence of an argument as to why we should expect it to be successful. Discovering where generalization is possible is a taxing empirical task. Perhaps it should proceed on the basis of trial and error, perhaps on the basis of theoretical argument, perhaps on the basis of some combination. What should *not* drive it, however, is the ready availability of data and technique.

A more promising response to the difficulties of bad data and of disentangling complex causal processes in the "open systems" of the actual world is to do experimental work where parameters can be controlled and key variables more easily isolated.[24] There is some history of this in political science and political psychology, but the main problem has been that of external validity. Even when subjects are randomly selected and control groups are included in the experiments (which often is not done), it is far from clear that results produced under lab conditions will be replicated outside the lab.

To deal with these problems Donald Green and Alan Gerber have revived the practice of field experiments, in which subjects can be randomized, experimental controls can be introduced, and questions about external validity disappear.[25] Prediction can operate once more, and when it is successful there are good reasons for supposing that the researcher has taken the right cut at the problem. In some ways this is an exciting development. It yields decisive answers to questions such as which forms of mobilizing voters are most effective in increasing turnout, or what are the best ways for partisans to get their grass-roots supporters to the polls without also mobilizing their opponents.

Granting that this is an enterprise that leads to increments in knowledge, I want nonetheless to suggest that it carries risks of falling into a kind of method-drivenness that threatens to diminish the field-experiment research program unless they are confronted. The potential difficulties arise from the fact that field experiments are limited to studying comparatively small questions in well-defined settings where it is possible to intervene in ways that allow for experimental controls. Usually this means designing or piggy-backing on interventions in the world, such as get-out-the vote efforts or attempts at partisan mobilization. Green and Gerber have shown that such efforts can be adapted to incorporate field experiments.

To be sure, the relative smallness of questions is to some extent in the eye of the beholder. But consider a list of phenomena that political scientists have sought to study, and those drawn to political science often want to understand, that are not likely to lend themselves to field experiments:

- The effects of regime type on the economy, and vice versa
- The determinants of peace, war, and revolution
- The causes and consequences of the trend toward creating independent central banks
- The causes and consequences of the growth in transnational political and economic institutions
- The relative merits of alternative policies for achieving racial integration, such as those related to mandatory busing, magnet schools, and voluntary desegregation plans
- The importance of constitutional courts in protecting civil liberties and property rights and in limiting the power of legislatures
- The effects of other institutional arrangements, such as parliamentarism versus presidentialism, unicameralism versus bicameralism, and federalism versus centralism, on such things as the distribution of income and wealth, the effectiveness of macroeconomic policies, and the types of social policies that are enacted
- The dynamics of political negotiations necessary to institute democracy

I could go on, but you get the point.

This is not to denigrate field experiments. One of the worst features of methodological disagreement in political science is the propensity of protagonists to compare the inadequacies of one method with the adequacies of a second, and then declare the first to be wanting.[26] Because all methods have limitations and none should be expected to be serviceable for all purposes, this is little more than a shell game. If a method can do some things well that are worth doing, that is sufficient justification for investing some research resources in it. With methods as with people, if you focus only on their limitations you will always be disappointed.

Field experiments lend themselves to the study of behavioral variation in settings where the institutional context is relatively fixed, and where the stakes are comparatively low so that the kinds of interventions required do not violate accepted ethical criteria for experimentation on human subjects. They do not obviously lend themselves to the study of life-or-death and other high-stakes politics, war and civil war, institutional variation, the macro-political economy, or the determinants of regime stability and change. This still leaves a great deal to study that is worth studying, and creative use of the method might render it deployable in a wider array of areas than I have noted here. But it must be conceded that it also leaves out a great deal that draws people to political science, so if susceptibility to study via field experiment becomes the criterion for problem selection, it risks degenerating into method-drivenness.

This is an important caution. I would conjecture that part of the disaffection with 1960s behaviorism in the study of American politics that spawned the model mania of the 1990s was due to the fact that the behaviorists became so mindlessly preoccupied with demonstrating propositions of the order that "Catholics in Detroit vote Democrat."[27] As a result, the mainstream of political science that they came to define seemed to others both utterly devoid of theoretical ambition and detached from consequential questions of politics—that is, frankly boring. To paraphrase Immanuel Kant, theoretical ambition without empirical research may well be vacuous, but empirical research without theoretical ambition will be blind.

E. Undervaluing Critical Reappraisal of What Is to Be Explained

The emphasis on prediction can lead to method-drivenness in another way: it can lead us to undervalue critical reappraisals of accepted descriptions of reality. To see why this is so, one must realize that much commentary on politics, both lay and professional, takes for granted depictions of political reality that closer critical scrutiny would reveal as problematic. Particularly, though not only, when prediction is not going to supply the sorting device to get us the right cut, political scientists have an important role to play in exhibiting what is at stake in taking one cut rather than another, and in proposing alternatives. Consider some examples.

For over a generation, in debates about American exceptionalism the United States was contrasted with Europe as a world of relative social and legal equality deriving from its lack of a feudal past. This notion began with Alexis de Tocqueville, but it has been endlessly repeated and became conventional wisdom, if not a mantra, when restated by Louis Hartz in *The Liberal Tradition in America*. But as Rogers Smith showed decisively in *Civic Ideals,* it is highly misleading as a descriptive matter.[28] Throughout American history the law has recognized explicit hierarchies based on race and gender whose effects are still very much with us. Smith's book advances no well-specified predictive model, let alone tests one, but it displaces a highly influential orthodoxy that has long been taken for granted in debates about pluralism and cross-cutting cleavages, the absence of socialism in America, arguments about the so-called end of ideology, and the ideological neutrality of the liberal tradition.[29] Important causal questions are yet to be asked and answered about these matters, but my point here is that what was thought to stand in need of explanation was so mis-specified that the right causal questions were not even on the table.

Likewise with the debate about the determinants of industrial policy in capitalist democracies. In the 1970s it occurred to students of this subject to focus less on politicians' voting records and campaign statements and to look at who actually writes the legislation. This led to the discovery that significant chunks of it were actually written by organized business and organized labor, with government (usually in the form of the relevant minister or ministry) in a mediating role. The reality was more of a "liberal corporatist" one, and less of a pluralist one, than most commentators who had not focused on this had realized.[30] The questions that then motivated the next generation of research became "Under what conditions do we get liberal corporatism, and what are its effects on industrial relations and industrial policy?" As with the Tocqueville-Hartz orthodoxy, the causal questions had to be reframed because of the ascendancy of a different depiction of the reality.[31]

In one respect the Tocqueville-Hartz and pluralist accounts debunked by Smith and the liberal corporatists are more like those of democratic transitions and the fertility rates of welfare mothers discussed in section A than like the multiple descriptions problem discussed in section C. The difficulty is not how to choose one rather than another true description, but rather that the Tocqueville-Hartz and pluralist descriptions fail on their own terms. By focusing so myopically on the absence of feudalism and the activities of politicians, their proponents ignored other sources of social hierarchy and decision making that are undeniably relevant once they have been called to attention. The main difference is that the democratic transition and welfare mother examples are not as widely accepted as the Tocqueville-Hartz and pluralist orthodoxies were before the debunkers came along. This should serve as a salutary reminder that orthodox views can be highly misleading, and that an important ongoing task for political scientists is to subject them to critical scrutiny. This involves exhibiting their presuppositions, assessing their plausibility, and proposing alternatives when they are found wanting. This is particularly important when the defective account is widely accepted outside the academy. If political science has a role to play in social betterment, it must surely include debunking myths and misunderstandings that shape political practice.[32]

Notice that descriptions are theory-laden not only in calling for a particular empirical story, but often also in implying a normative theory that may or may not be evident unless this is made explicit. Compare the following two descriptions:

- The Westphalian system is based on the norm of national sovereignty.
- The Westphalian system is based on the norm of global apartheid.

Both are arguably accurate descriptions, but, depending which of the two we adopt, we will be prompted to ask exceedingly different questions about justification as well as causation. Consider another instance:

- When substantial majorities in both parties support legislation, we have bipartisan agreement.
- When substantial majorities in both parties support legislation, we have collusion in restraint of democracy.

The first draws on a view of democracy in which deliberation and agreement are assumed to be unproblematic, even desirable, goals in a democracy. The second, antitrust-framed, formulation calls to mind John Stuart Mill's emphasis on the centrality of argument and contestation, and the Schumpeterian impulse to think of well-functioning democracy as requiring competition for power.[33]

Both *global apartheid* and *collusion in restraint of democracy* are instances of problematizing redescriptions. Just as Smith's depiction of American public law called the Tocqueville-Hartz consensus into question, and the liberal corporatist description of industrial legislation called then-conventional assumptions about pluralist decision making into question, so do these. But they do it not so much by questioning the veracity of the accepted descriptions as by throwing their undernoticed benign normative assumptions into sharp relief. Describing the Westphalian system as based on a norm of global apartheid, or political agreement among the major players in a democracy as collusion in restraint of democracy, shifts the focus to underattended features of reality, placing different empirical and justificatory questions on the table.

But are they the right questions?

To answer this by saying that one needs a theory of politics would be to turn once more to theory-drivenness. I want to suggest a more complex answer, one that sustains problematizing redescription as a problem-driven enterprise. It is a two-step venture that starts when one shows that the accepted way of characterizing a piece of political reality fails to capture an important feature of what stands in need of explanation or justification. One then offers a recharacterization that speaks to the inadequacies in the prior account.

When convincingly done, prior adherents to the old view will be unable to ignore the recharacterization and remain credible. This is vital, because of course it will usually be true that the problematizing redescription is itself a theory-influenced, if not a theory-laden, endeavor. But if the problematizing redescription assumes a theory that seems convincing only to partisans, or is validated only by reference to evidence that is projected from partisans' alternative theory, it will be judged tendentious to the rest of the scholarly community for the reasons I set out in sections A and B of this chapter. It is important, therefore, to devote considerable effort to making a case that will persuade a skeptic of the superiority of the proffered redescription over the accepted one. One of the significant failings of many of the rational choice theories Green and I discussed is that their proponents failed to do this. They offered problematizing redescriptions that were sometimes arrestingly radical, but their failure to take the second step made their redescriptions unconvincing to all except those who had agreed with them in advance.

F. Concluding Comments

The recent emphases in political science on modeling for its own sake and on decisive predictive tests both give short shrift to the value of problematizing redescription in the study of politics. It is intrinsically worthwhile to unmask an accepted depiction as inadequate, and to make a convincing case for an alternative as more apt. Just because observation is inescapably theory-laden for the reasons explored in this chapter, political scientists have an ongoing role to play in exhibiting what is at stake in accepted depictions of reality, and reinterpreting what is known so as to put new problems on the research agenda. This is important for scientific reasons when accepted descriptions are both faulty and influential in the conduct of social science. It is important for political reasons when the faulty understandings shape politics outside the academy.

If the problems thus placed on the agenda are difficult to study by means of theories and methods that are currently in vogue, an additional task arises that is no less important: to keep them there and challenge the ingenuity of scholars who are sufficiently open-minded to devise creative ways of grappling with them. It is important for political scientists to throw their weight against the powerful forces that entice scholars to embroider fashionable theories and massage methods in which they are professionally invested while failing to illuminate the world of politics. They should remind each generation of scholars that unless problems are identified in ways that are both theoretically illuminating and convincingly intelligible to outsiders, nothing that they say about them is likely to persuade anyone who stands in need of persuasion. Perhaps they will enjoy professional success of a sort, but at the price of trivializing their discipline and what one hopes is their vocation.

Notes

An earlier version of this chapter was published in *Political Theory*, Vol. 30, No. 4 (August 2002): 588–611.

1. See Donald Green and Ian Shapiro, *Pathologies of Rational Choice Theory: A Critique of Applications in Political Science* (New Haven, CT: Yale University Press,

1994), and Green and Shapiro, "Pathologies Revisited: Reflections on Our critics," in Jeffrey Friedman, ed., *The Rational Choice Controversy: Economic Models of Politics Reconsidered* (New Haven, CT: Yale University Press, 1996), 235–76.

2. John Nash, "The Bargaining Problem," *Econometrica,* Vol. 18 (1950): 155–62. For explication see John Harsanyi, "Advances in Understanding Rational Behavior," in Jon Elster, ed., *Rational Choice* (New York: New York University Press, 1986), 92–94.

3. See Charles Murray, *Losing Ground—American Social Policy, 1950–1980* (New York: Basic Books, 1984).

4. Michael B. Katz, *The Undeserving Poor: From the War on Poverty to the War on Welfare* (New York: Pantheon, 1989), 151–56.

5. Charles Murray, "Does Welfare Bring More Babies?" *Public Interest,* Spring (1994): 25.

6. John Roemer, "Does Democracy Engender Justice?" in Ian Shapiro and Casiano Hacker-Cordón, eds., *Democracy's Value* (Cambridge: Cambridge University Press, 1999), 56–68.

7. It should be noted, however, that the median voter theorem is eminently debatable empirically. For discussion see Green and Shapiro, *Pathologies,* 146–78.

8. Kathleen Bawn, "Constructing 'Us': Ideology, Coalition Politics and False Consciousness," *American Journal of Political Science,* Vol. 43, No. 2 (1999): 303–34.

9. Russell Hardin, *Liberalism, Constitutionalism, and Democracy* (Oxford: Oxford University Press, 2000), 35, 86–88, 106, 114, 144, 285.

10. I leave aside, for present purposes, discussion of how convincing the debatable conjectures are. Consider the great difficulties Republican candidates face in forging winning coalitions in American politics that keep both social and libertarian conservatives on board. If one were to set out to define a blueprint for putting together a winning coalition, trying to fashion it out of these conflicting elements scarcely seems like a logical place to start. Likewise, with constitutions viewed as coordinating devices, the many veto points in the American constitutional system could just as arguably be said to be obstacles to coordination. See George Tsebelis, *Veto Players: How Political Institutions Work* (Princeton, NJ: Princeton University Press, 2002). This might not seem problematic if one takes the view, as Hardin does, that the central purpose of the U.S. constitution is to facilitate commerce. In such a view institutional sclerosis might arguably be an advantage, limiting government's capacity to interfere with the economy. The difficulty with going that route is that we then have a theory for all seasons: constitutions lacking multiple veto points facilitate political coordination, while those containing them facilitate coordination in realms that might otherwise be interfered with by politicians. Certainly nothing in Hardin's argument accounts for why some constitutions facilitate more coordination of a particular kind than do others.

11. Recognizing that there can never be a complete description of any phenomenon does not, however, commit us to relativism. Any particular description, while incomplete, is nonetheless true or false in virtue of some state of affairs that either holds or does not hold in the world. See Bernard Williams, *Truth and Truthfulness: An Essay in Genealogy* (Princeton, NJ: Princeton University Press, 2002).

12. Milton Friedman, "The Methodology of Positive Economics," in Friedman, *Essays in Positive Economics* (Chicago: University of Chicago Press, 1953), 3–43.

13. Alasdair MacIntyre, *After Virtue* (Notre Dame, IN: University of Notre Dame Press, 1984), 88–108.

14. See Courtney Jung and Ian Shapiro, "South Africa's Negotiated Transition: Democracy, Opposition, and the New Constitutional Order," *Politics and Society*, Vol. 23 (1995): 269-308.

15. What is necessary in the context of one problem may, of course, be contingent in another. When we postulate that it was necessary that Yasser Arafat be strong enough to marginalize the radicals on his flank if he was to make an agreement with Ehud Barak, we do not mean to deny that his relative strength in this regard was dependent on many contingent factors. For further discussion see Courtney Jung, Ellen Lust-Okar, and Ian Shapiro, "Problems and Prospects for Democratic Transitions: South Africa as a Model for the Middle East and Northern Ireland?" mimeo, Yale University, 2002. In some ultimate—if uninteresting—sense, everything social scientists study is contingent on various factors, for instance, that the possibility of life on earth not be destroyed due to a collision with a giant meteor. To be intelligible, the search for lawlike generalizations must be couched in "if . . . then" statements that make reference, however implicitly, to the problem under study.

16. Adam Przeworski, Michael Alvarez, Jose Cheibub, and Fernando Limongi, *Democracy and Development: Political Institutions and Well-Being in the World, 1950-1990* (Cambridge: Cambridge University Press, 2000), pp. 106-117.

17. For discussion of other explanatory variables by Przeworski et al., see ibid., 122-37.

18. Alexis de Tocqueville, *Democracy in America,* ed. J. P. Mayer, trans. George Lawrence (New York: Harper Perennial, 1966 [1832]).

19. Seymour Martin Lipset, "Some Social Requisites of Democracy: Economic Development and Political Legitimacy," *American Political Science Review,* Vol. 53 (1959): 69-105.

20. Barrington Moore, *The Social Origins of Dictatorship and Democracy: Lord and Peasant in the Making of the Modern World* (Boston: Beacon Press, 1966), 413-32, and Dietrich Rueschemeyer, Evelyne Huber Stephens, and John D. Stephens, *Capitalist Development and Democracy* (Oxford: Polity Press, 1992).

21. See Adam Przeworski, *Democracy and the Market* (Cambridge: Cambridge University Press, 1991), ix-xii, 1-9, 51-99; Przeworski et al., *Democracy and Development,* 78-106; Samuel P. Huntington, *The Third Wave: Democratization in the Late Twentieth Century* (Norman: University of Oklahoma Press, 1991), 3-18; and Ian Shapiro, *Democracy's Place* (Ithaca, NY: Cornell University Press, 1996), 79-108.

22. Perhaps one could develop such a theory, but only of an exceedingly general kind such as "Holes are created when something takes material content out of something else." This would not be of much help in understanding or predicting anything worth knowing about holes.

23. See the various postmortem papers in the March 2001 issue of *PS: Political Science and Politics,* Vol. 34, No. 1, 9-58.

24. For discussion of the difficulties with prediction in open systems, see Roy Bhaskar, *A Realist Theory of Science* (Sussex, England: Harvester Wheatsheaf, 1975), 63-142, and *The Possibility of Naturalism* (Sussex, England: Harvester Wheatsheaf, 1979), 158-69.

25. Alan Gerber and Donald Green, "Do Phone Calls Increase Voter Turnout? A Field Experiment," *Public Opinion Quarterly,* Vol. 65 (2000): 75-85, and "Reclaiming the Experimental Tradition in Political Science," in Ira Katznelson and Helen

Milner, eds., *Political Science: The State of the Discipline,* 3rd edition (New York: W. W. Norton, 2002).

26. For discussion of an analogous phenomenon that plagues normative debates in political theory, see my "Gross Concepts in Political Argument," *Political Theory,* Vol. 17, No. 1 (February 1989): 51–76.

27. Charles Taylor, "Neutrality in Political Science," in Taylor, *Philosophical Papers II: Philosophy and the Human Sciences* (Cambridge: Cambridge University Press, 1985), 90.

28. See Louis Hartz, *The Liberal Tradition in America* (New York: Harcourt Brace, 1955), and Rogers Smith, *Civic Ideals: Changing Conceptions of Citizenship in US Law* (New Haven, CT: Yale University Press, 1995).

29. Indeed, Smith's argument turns out to be the tip of an iceberg in debunking misleading orthodoxy about American exceptionalism. Eric Foner has shown that its assumptions about Europe are no less questionable than its assumptions about the United States. See Foner, "Why Is There No Socialism in the United States?" *History Workshop Journal,* Vol. 17 (1984): 57–80.

30. Philippe Schmitter, "Still the Century of Corporatism?" *Review of Politics,* Vol. 36, No. 1 (January 1974): 85–121, and Leo Panitch, "The Development of Corporatism in Liberal Democracies," *Comparative Political Studies* (April 1977): 61–90.

31. It turns out that joint legislation-writing is a small part of the story. What often matters more is ongoing tripartite consultation about public policy and mutual adjustment of legislation or macroeconomic policy and "private" but quasi-public policy (e.g., wage increases or multiemployer pension and health plans). There is also the formalized inclusion of representatives of private interest in the administration and implementation process, where de facto legislation and common law–like adjudication takes place. The extent of their influence in the political process varies from country to country and even from industry to industry, but the overall picture is a far cry from the standard pluralist account.

32. For a discussion of the dangers of convergent thinking, see Charles E. Lindblom, *Inquiry and Change: The Troubled Attempt to Understand and Shape Society* (New Haven, CT: Yale University Press, 1990), pp. 118–32.

33. For discussion of differences between these models, see my chapter "The State of Democratic Theory," in Katznelson and Milner, eds., *Political Science.*

CHAPTER 7

Rational Choice, Symbolic Politics, and Pluralism in the Study of Violent Conflict

Stuart J. Kaufman

The recent calls for synthesis of most of political science's previously autonomous subfields are in some ways attractive: the subfields certainly have much to learn from each other. The particular approach promoted by some advocates of synthesis is, however, dubious: "Rational institutional analysis," Helen Milner (1998) writes, is the basis of "the emerging synthesis in the study of American, comparative, and international politics" (786). Other theorists are even more specific: David Lake (2002), for example, has pointed to James Fearon's (1995) formal approach to rational bargaining theory as the foundation for such a synthesis.

Perestroikans consider this vision unwise, and the hegemonism implicit in it profoundly dangerous to the future of the field of political science. The idea of unifying these three subfields within the ambit of formal rational choice theory unmistakably implies the subordination if not the exclusion of other modes of studying politics. The concern about methodological or theoretical hegemony is not exaggerated. The subfield of American politics is already so dominated by quantitative methods that important questions best addressed by other methods are rarely even posed, while the earlier traditions that did address those issues have been pushed to the margins of the field. For example, regarding the critical question of who wins presidential elections and why, the state of the art has improved little since Jay Greene's (1993) assessment that "existing quantitative models are not useful predictors of presidential races" (17): they certainly did not do very well in 2000. One reason for the weakness is that because the effects of campaigning are difficult to study quantitatively, they are rarely studied at all; the mainstream assumption is that campaigns do not matter. Most politicians and journalists would beg to differ.

If the process of theory building throughout political science is replaced by formal modeling, and theory testing is done overwhelmingly quantitatively, there will be little room left for attention to the issues of context, nuance, history, or nonrational behavior that many scholars believe are decisive for understanding most if not all of politics—including, for example, election campaigns. Worse, it will allow the field to create a self-referential universe in which deductive theory and quantitative data are tested only against each other, allowing the field to drift further and further from the reality is it supposed to be explaining as data that might challenge the dominant approach is excluded a priori (on what would be lost, see, e.g., McKeown 1999).

The rationalist ideal for social science is economics, the mainstream of which consists overwhelmingly of formal models tested with quantitative methods, leaving very little room for alternatives. Perestroikans reject this vision, based as it is on an inappropriate equation of quantitative and formal methods with social science. Instead, Perestroikans argue that political science must draw more broadly from methods and theoretical traditions across the social sciences broadly construed, including psychology, anthropology, sociology, history, and post-structural social theory. Our view is that a primary focus on rationalist theory and quantitative and formal methods is simply inadequate for explaining politics.

The simplest objection to the newest rationalism, as Jeffrey Legro (1996) has pointed out, is that it does only half of the analytical job. While rationalist analysis is a "two-step," requiring first specification of preferences and then analysis of the resulting strategic interaction, the new rationalist hegemonists generally specify preferences by assumption and focus only on analyzing strategic interaction. For those situations that are driven by the parties' preferences, this approach detracts more than it adds: it diverts attention from the key question and to an ancillary one. And rationalist analysis offers no guidelines on how to identify these preferences; all it does is to constrain the analyst by specifying what qualities the preferences must show in order to be amenable to formal analysis.

A second, broader set of objections argues that, even if preferences are specified in a reasonably accurate way, the rationalist hegemonists' approach still ignores the most important factors in most political phenomena. The rationalist hegemonists insist on perfect rather than bounded rationality, for example, so in cases in which cognitive limitations play an important role (Jervis 1976), that decisive factor is excluded a priori. Recent scholarship in political psychology (Marcus, Neuman, and Mackuen 2000) shows that emotional factors also play a critical role in shaping attitudes and preferences, so the assumption of stable, transitive preferences is simply wrong, and a focus on the emotional sources of attitudes indispensable. From this point of view, any form of rationalism is inaccurate.

Finally, there is a range of even more basic epistemological and ontological objections to rationalism. Constructivists protest that the causal analysis employed by rationalists is inappropriate for circumstances in which mutual constitution, rather than causality, is the crucial relationship (Wendt 1999). Critical and feminist theorists argue that rationalist assumptions conceal a conservative, capitalist, or sexist agenda that needs to be identified and analyzed (Cox 1986; Ashley 1986; Enloe 1990). Hermeneutical theory questions even the possibility of real comparative scholarship, as the fundamental meaning of political and social behavior is so culture-bound that Geertz-style (1973) "thick description" is the best that can be done.

What Perestroikans see at stake in the debate over the new rationalist hegemonism is the bare possibility of continuing these research programs in political science. Rationalist hegemonists and their quantitatively inclined allies protest that they do not oppose alternate modes of analysis, but revealed preferences suggest otherwise: departments controlled by rationalist-quantitativist alliances often seem to discriminate systematically in hiring, consistently favoring rationalist scholars over all competitors. Rationalists' protests that they support intellectual pluralism thus seem suspiciously like cheap talk. The quality of the work also seems secondary, as rationalist analysis has become the latest fad. Thus complicated formal proofs of obvious propositions are hailed as major theoretical advances, less for what they say than for their methodological sophistication. What is neglected is concern with substantive issues of politics.

While I agree with much of the Perestroikan critique I have just outlined, I believe that the debate at this general level is ultimately irresolvable. For those political scientists who accept the Lakatosian positivist epistemology, as I do, the ultimate question is explanatory power. The purpose of this chapter is to show, expanding on the analysis of Stephen M. Walt (1999), that on the issue of ethnic civil war the most prominent rationalist theories are inferior in explanatory power to existing alternatives. Rationalist theories of war, as exemplified by the James Fearon article of that name (1995), offer no new explanatory power and suggest unproductive directions for further research. In the area of explaining ethnic civil war, the better rationalist theories are inferior to the alternative symbolic politics theory. Symbolic politics theory, based on new psychological research on the effects of emotion, also has the virtue of applicability to a broad range of mass political activities that are poorly explained by rationalism.

Before continuing, I need to say a word about what I mean by "rationalism" and "rationalist hegemonists." Rationalist hegemonists are scholars who make three claims. Theoretically, they argue that political science theorizing should begin from the assumption that political actors are unitary and rational. Methodologically, they argue that theorizing should proceed using the methods of formal or "positive" theory. And academically, they argue that these approaches should become the paradigm for political science analysis, marginalizing or subordinating other modes of analysis. It must be emphasized that these three positions are not identical. Most realists and many neoliberal institutionalists are rationalists in their theoretical assumptions, while eschewing formal theory. Some who employ rationalist assumptions and formal methods are also champions of intellectual pluralism. In this chapter I take issue with all three positions, but I focus my criticism on examples of scholarship in my field of study that employ the style of formal theory, whether or not they employ mathematical equations. My purpose is to defend the position that neither rationalist theoretical assumptions nor formal methods should be hegemonic in political analysis.

My argument proceeds as follows. I begin with an analysis of Fearon's "Rationalist Theories of War," since it is often held up as foundational for the would-be rationalist paradigm. I argue that Fearon's analysis is not, in the end, very useful in explaining the causes of war, displaying more the limits than the promise of strict rationalist analysis. I then turn to an application of Fearon's theory to ethnic civil war developed by David Lake and Donald Rothchild, arguing that while the argument is theoretically coherent, it is wrong empirically for many if not most prominent cases. As an example of how prominent theorists can go badly wrong, I then turn to a paper co-authored by former Stanford department chair Barry Weingast, which depends on assumptions that are prima facie absurd and factually unsupported. I then offer as an alternative a brief outline of symbolic politics theory, which provides a more accurate explanation of key cases of ethnic war. I conclude the chapter with a symbolic politics analysis of the current conflict in the political science discipline, offering some suggestions for its resolution.

Rational Choice and Ethnic War

Fearon's Deductive Theory

Because rationalists point to James Fearon's "Rationalist Explanations for War" (1995) as a seminal contribution that provides a basis for their hegemonic project, it makes sense to start with an analysis of this article. Fearon begins with three assumptions: that states know there is some true probability that one side will win a war between them, that states are risk-averse or risk-neutral, and that issues in dispute are perfectly divisible. Building on an insight of Geoffrey Blainey (1973), Fearon argues that if these assumptions hold, there is always some bargain that both states in a dispute would prefer to a war. For example, if Belgium knows that Germany would defeat it in war, it should rationally concede Germany's demands and avoid the devastation of fighting. Fearon's conclusion is that such bargains sometimes are not reached, and war results, only because states have incentives to misrepresent "private information" about their capabilities and willingness to fight, or because they cannot credibly commit to abide by an agreement that both might prefer to war.

The keystone of the argument about "private information" is John Harsanyi's assumption that "if two rational agents have the same information about an uncertain event, then they should have the same beliefs about its likely outcome" (Fearon 1995, 392). Therefore, the only possible rational cause of disagreement about the likely outcome of a future war, Fearon argues, is states' incentives to lie about their power and willingness to fight in order to get a better deal.

This argument, however, overlooks or conflates numerous other sources of uncertainty other than intentionally withheld "private information." Indeed, there are many reasons that reasonable people might disagree about the likely outcome of a war. First, a vast array of variables that affect the outcome of war simply cannot be known beforehand. How will men and equipment hold up in unforeseen circumstances? Will the weaker side really fight to the last? How will tactics and strategy on both sides interact with weather, the fog of war, and the quality of training and leadership in key battles? What stance will neutrals and allies take? Whose intelligence will better penetrate the enemy's deceptions and the fog of war, and whose command and control system will better survive the other's attacks? Even if leaders on both sides could share every scrap of information both sides had on these subjects, they would still frequently reach different conclusions about the likely outcome. In real life, neither side can know how its own morale and resolve will stand up in war, let alone the enemy's. For instance, who predicted that North Vietnam would prove "stronger" than the United States?

The rationalist assumption is that rational agents should, given the same information, assess these uncertainties the same way. But for this to be true, "the same information" would have to include not only information about the current situation, but the vast array of past education and experiences that is part of the professional judgment of military leaders. This is an important point. Rationalists tend to invest the idea of "information" with near-magical qualities: give everyone full and complete information, they suggest, and all problems will be solved. But this is impossible and cannot be approximated: people's past experience colors their judgment, and that experience cannot be communicated. Therefore, private information, defined as information that could be communicated but is voluntarily withheld, is not necessary for leaders to make different rational calculations.

Furthermore, the calculations are not in fact fully rational. Personality differences make it likely that different people will assess risks differently. Additionally, military leaders tend to have not only cognitive but also motivated biases; specifically, they tend to want to believe that their preferred strategies and doctrines—or their own troops—are best (Snyder 1984).

Fearon's response is that the argument about differing judgments under complexity "is entirely plausible, but it is a bounded rationality explanation rather than a fully rationalist one" (393). He therefore discards the idea with little further comment. There are two possible ways of interpreting this move. Fearon concedes in his conclusion that "once the distinction is made clear, bounded rationality may appear a more important cause of disagreements about relative power than private information about military capabilities" (409). But he takes back this concession on the next page, claiming that if his argument is not accepted, "the central puzzle posed by war, its costs, has not been addressed" (410).

The truth is that with his concession about bounded rationality, Fearon has given the game away. His concept of "commitment problems" represents no real advance over previous analyses of anarchy: the inability of one side to commit not to exploit the other in the future has long been understood as a central problem of international relations (Walt 1999); it was simply referred to as lack of trust. The argument that "private information" leads to disagreements over the likely outcome of war is Fearon's one real innovation; conceding that such disagreements are best explained by bounded rationality renders the whole exercise pointless. "Private information" is not the reason states disagree about relative power.

Fearon's argument is further weakened by his dismissal of the third factor he concedes might explain war, indivisibility of the issues at stake. Territory is historically a common stake in war, and territorial integrity, especially under current international law, is considered inviolable, so territory is often indivisible. This explains, inter alia, why conflicts such as that in Kashmir have dragged on decade after futile decade. The identity principles at stake in that conflict—India's secular identity versus Pakistan's Muslim one—merely reinforce the point: many international conflicts involve stakes that are conceived as indivisible, and for nonrational reasons. Understanding these conflicts, therefore, requires understanding the framing of the issue—which, of course, requires an interpretivist rather than a rational modeling methodology.

In sum, previous understandings are superior to the strict rationalist approach for explaining the "puzzle" of war. Because the stakes in international conflicts are often considered indivisible, historically and sociologically based work such as that of Evan Luard (1986), which focuses on the issues at stake in war, points the way forward for understanding the phenomenon. Because human rationality is bounded, state leaders frequently disagree about the likely outcome of war, so the relevant approaches would follow on the seminal work of Robert Jervis (1976) on perception and cognition, or on analyses of ideologies (Van Evera 1990–91) or culture (Katzenstein 1996), which help explain different states' assessments of the costs of war. The commitment problem is nothing more than anarchy in a different guise, and its effects are better analyzed in the mainstream realist-liberal institutionalist-constructivist debate. Upon analysis, the only factors relevant to Fearon's analysis that vary—issue divisibility, attitudes toward war and risk, cognitive effects, and so on—are the ones he excludes. Thus, far from identifying a useful path for improved understanding of war, what Fearon's work really does is to show the limitations of the rationalist approach, and the superiority of its competitors.

The Lake-Rothchild Theory

David Lake and Donald Rothchild's (1998) application of Fearon's theory to ethnic civil war seems one of the more promising applications of Fearon's approach. Unlike in cases of international war, in civil war anarchy represents a change, so it might theoretically be useful to think about ethnic civil war as being caused by information failures, commitment problems, and security dilemmas caused by the breakdown of governing institutions. The overall logic is internally consistent and not implausible. When governments break down, ethnic groups may be uncertain of each other's intentions, and majorities may be unable to commit not to oppress minorities in the future. As Barry Posen (1993; cf. Kaufmann 1996) had previously pointed out, ethnically mixed settlement patterns may then lead to security dilemmas in which the side that attacks first has important military advantages.

The trouble with this story is that I know of no case in which it is true. The critical underlying assumption is that there is some compromise solution that all sides would prefer to war. Because the outcome of civil war is particularly unknowable, it is reasonable that the sides might differ in their assessment of its likely outcome. If the sides have strongly held and irreconcilable goals— which is what I have invariably found—the explanation for war would be found not in commitment problems or private information, but in the sources of the irreconcilable preferences. Following are examples from two different regions that have shown this pattern.

Karabagh   The outbreak of the conflict between Armenians and Azerbaijanis over the mountainous Karabagh region clearly demonstrates the problems with the Lake-Rothchild theory. First, large-scale violence began in February 1988, well before there was evidence that the Soviet Union was collapsing—in short, well before the situation looked at all anarchic. Second, preferences from the beginning were irreconcilable, with the Armenians demanding that Karabagh be transferred from the Azerbaijani Soviet Socialist Republic (SSR) to the Armenian SSR, and the Azerbaijanis adamantly refusing that demand. There were no information problems (other than the unknowability of the war's outcome): both sides' demands were crystal clear. And there is little reason to believe that either side misunderstood the other's intentions. The commitment problem was also irrelevant, as it is unlikely that there was anything the Azerbaijanis could have committed to that would have satisfied the Armenians, short of totally giving up control over Karabagh, which was unacceptable to Azerbaijan (Kaufman 2001).

Sudan   In 1972, Sudanese President Jaafar el-Nimeiri signed with southern Sudanese rebels a peace agreement granting to Sudan's Christian and animist south a regional government autonomous from the Muslim-dominated state. In 1983, however, the civil war resumed. Why? Again, the answer is irreconcilable preferences, not information failures or commitment problems (Kaufman 2001b). While there was always ambiguity in the degree of Nimeiri's commitment to the peace agreement, it fell apart only in 1983, when he unambiguously abrogated its key provisions—revoking the south's autonomy, breaking it into three provinces, imposing Islamic law (Shari'a) nationwide, and attempting to transfer southern troops to the north. Southern troops then mutinied, fled to the bush, and renewed the civil war. In short, the war was caused by clear communication of information about intentions and by unambiguous revocation of commitments. The southerners did nothing to provoke these moves.

Manipulative Leaders and the Followership Problem

A key problem with any rationalist account of ethnic war has to do with why people follow extremist leaders in such a costly endeavor as ethnic war. Rui de Figueiredo and Barry Weingast laudably identify this problem and attempt to resolve it in a work entitled "The Rationality of Fear" (1999). Their argument is that leaders who fear losing power "gamble for resurrection," following a high-risk strategy of trying to hold onto or regain power by provoking ethnic violence, and exploiting their followers' ethnic fears while hiding their own role in provoking the violence so it can be blamed on the ethnic enemy. The hoped-for effect is a "rallying 'round the flag" that will keep the endangered leaders in power.

De Figueiredo and Weingast admit that most of this argument is not new (see, e.g., Gagnon 1995); their central contribution concerns "causal ambiguity" —the claim that followers support extremist leaders because they do not know the leaders are the ones provoking the violence. The authors attempt to support this argument with brief case studies of Croatia and Rwanda. Both case studies, however, seriously distort history. In the model of the conflict in Croatia, the argument is that pivotal Serbs had to choose, after witnessing the breakdown of negotiations over Yugoslavia's future, whether to support Serbian leader Slobodan Milosevic or his reformist rival. The trouble is that Milosevic was reelected president of Serbia in December 1990, whereas negotiations did not break down until the following spring (see Cohen 1995). This model thus cannot work, because it has the timing wrong: pivotal Serbs had to decide whom to support *before* negotiations broke down (cf. Kaufman 2001a).

For the Rwanda case, the argument is based on the following key assumption: "Extremist Hutu leaders initiated genocide because they were losing power. The genocide's diabolic, political purpose was to undermine the stability of the new RPF [Rwandan Popular Front] regime [by killing its likely supporters]. This would allow the extremist Hutus a chance to regroup and, later, to challenge the RPF" (283). This assumption, however, flies in the face of existing evidence. Most experts (e.g., Prunier 1995) argue that the extremist Hutu leadership, the *akazu,* carried out the genocide in order to keep power, not to give it up and hope to regain it. De Figueiredo and Weingast offer not a shred of evidence for their contrary assertion that the *akazu* planned all along to flee Rwanda and then stage a comeback.

On the other hand, the genocide makes little rational sense without this bizarre assumption, either. To implement the genocide, the *akazu* scattered their army across the country to coerce ordinary Hutu into participating in the murders. This allowed their ethnic rivals in the Tutsi-led RPF to conquer most of the country unopposed (Des Forges 1999). If the *akazu* had cared only about keeping power, they had a much more promising alternative. Instead of scattering their army to help implement the genocide, they could have concentrated the army against the RPF, and limited the killings only to key moderate politicians to stymie the peace process. De Figueiredo and Weingast offer no explanation for what most needs explaining in this case: why genocide was a thinkable option at all, why the army and Hutu militias were prepared to carry it out, and why the *akazu* preferred genocide to more sane ways of trying to keep power.

The Symbolic Politics Explanation

One common-sense problem with the rationalist approach to ethnic war is summed up by the oxymoron of de Figueiredo and Weingast's title "The Rationality of Fear." Fear, of course, is an emotion, and while it may be compatible with a rational effort to save one's skin or possessions, either can occur without the other: one can be prudent without being fearful, or fearful without being prudent. Rationalists' recognition that the issue is fear, not prudence, logically demands that any adequate theory of ethnic violence grapple with the emotions inherent in such conflicts. There is, in fact, a growing literature on the role of emotions in political judgment (see, e.g., Marcus, Neuman, and Mackuen 2000), some of which has been applied to ethnic violence (Kaufman 2001a; Peterson 2002). Rationalists marginalize this literature by assumption.

I argue that an explanation based on emotional symbolic politics (Kaufman 2001b) provides a more accurate account of ethnic war than does any rationalist model. The symbolist account begins with Anthony Smith's (1986) insight that the core of any ethnic identity is a "myth-symbol complex" that defines the group, its history, the meaning of membership, and so on. These myths and symbols provide the raw materials that ethnic leaders draw on to gain power. And because the myths and symbols are emotionally loaded, the process of symbolic choice is not rational but emotional. Symbolic appeals that also provoke ethnic fears (promoted by the group's mythology) provide a way of short-circuiting rational calculations of tradeoffs by convincing people emotionally to support an ethnic program. The emotional nature of ethnic appeals also explains why people participate in group action (i.e., how the rational collective action problem is overcome), why they may mobilize along ethnic lines, and why they sometimes follow extremist leaders when they do.

Symbolist theory does not suggest that myths justifying hostility are sufficient conditions for ethnic violence; it suggests only that they are necessary. Also necessary are fears that the ethnic group faces extinction, along with the political opportunity for ethnic mobilization. The stronger the hostile myths and existential fears, and the greater the opportunity for ethnic mobilization, the more probable is ethnic violence. Given all three conditions, violence is still not inevitable, as ethnic leaders can find ways to cooperate and keep ethnic agendas moderate. Only when ethnic groups begin mobilizing around hostile agendas, and defining their existential needs in mutually incompatible ways, thereby creating a security dilemma, does violence become highly likely.

The Karabagh example illustrates how this process works (Kaufman 2001a). Armenian national mythology centers on the genocide committed against Armenians by the Turks during World War I; Azerbaijanis are closely related to

Turks, and were also involved in massacres of Armenians in the early twentieth century. The genocide thus became the central symbol of Armenian nationhood, and Armenian mythology conflated Azerbaijanis and Turks, so that any repression by Azerbaijanis was labeled by Armenians as tantamount to genocide. This mythology explains the inflexible, all-or-nothing demands of the Armenians in that conflict; a complementary anti-Armenian mythology among Azerbaijanis, in turn, explains the volatility of relations among ordinary Armenians and Azerbaijanis. Once Mikhail Gorbachev's policy of glasnost created the opportunity for ethnic mobilization, previously marginal agitators quickly managed to mobilize huge numbers of people around extreme nationalist agendas, quickly sparking violence and creating a security dilemma.

Such emotionally fueled volatility also explains the dilemma of costs identified by de Figueiredo and Weingast: why do people embark on so costly an enterprise as ethnic war? Because they do not think rationally about tradeoffs, but rather are convinced emotionally by appeals to symbolism to support the value evoked by the symbol in the way the symbol suggests—in this case, "protecting" the security of the ethnic group by confronting the group's "enemy." In an environment polarized by such nationalist ideologies, preferences are naturally deadlocked. Indeed, when attitudes are this extreme, very little leadership is needed to achieve ethnic mobilization. In Armenia and Azerbaijan, the incumbent Communist leaderships strongly opposed the rise of nationalist sentiment—which they fully recognized represented a threat to them—but the violence broke out in spite of their efforts at repression, and they were eventually swept aside by a groundswell of popular enthusiasm for the new nationalist counterelite.

Similar logic explains the dilemmas faced by rationalist explanations of other ethnic conflicts. For example, in Sudan in 1983, why did Nimeiri openly abrogate the agreement that he himself had negotiated a decade before? Because the symbolism of Islam was the only political tool left to him to use to try to remain in power after the economy turned sour, and he hoped to harness it by imposing *shari'a* on the whole country. If that required provoking a new ethnic war with the south, that was acceptable—and, indeed, perhaps it was useful as a way of producing a rally-'round-the-flag effect. But again, the key is to explain not only Nimeiri's use of those symbols, but why the symbols have such power. Only a focus on their roots in nationalist mythology and their evocation of emotions that short-circuit tradeoff decisions explains why people support extremist nationalist projects that are predictably costly (Kaufman 2001b).

Finally, the puzzle of the Rwandan genocide is also best explained in terms of symbolic politics. What makes the genocide explicable, if not comprehensible, is the vicious racial ideology promoted by the Hutu regime in Rwanda, first in the 1960s, and then again in the early 1990s (Prunier 1995; Kaufman 2001b). This ideology mythologized Tutsis as threatening outside invaders who wanted to dominate and kill Hutu, while at the same time dehumanizing Tutsis as "cockroaches" who should be exterminated. Killings and atrocities by Tutsi in neighboring Burundi and by the Tutsi-dominated RPF in Rwanda stoked fears that a new Tutsi repression might indeed be coming. In this context, as Gerard Prunier puts it, Rwanda's leaders "cracked up and went genocidally mad," choosing a course of action that ensured the destruction of their own regime as well as the massacre of hundreds of thousands of innocent civilians.

A virtue of these symbolist explanations is their parsimony: behavior is explained by reference to basic (culturally defined) popular values without the need to refer to complicated formal models. Another advantage of the symbolic politics approach is that it is useful for explaining a range of other phenomena involving mass-elite interaction. For example, a symbolic politics theory of election campaigns would be useful for explaining why voters often respond to candidates' manipulation of symbols such as flags, Ronald Reagan's "welfare queens," or George H. W. Bush's "Willie Horton"—and why they vote at all. Comparative study of political mythology and symbolism might also help explain the variation in social welfare policies among advanced industrial democracies. Murray Edelman (1971) proposed the venerable suggestion that even concrete policies should be understood as intended to serve more symbolic than concrete purposes. Finally, symbolic politics is appropriate for studying social movements more generally.

The Contribution of Rationalist Approaches

Though I have argued here that the best account of ethnic war is the symbolic politics theory, rationalist theory also can make important contributions. The realist analyses of Posen (1993) and Kaufmann (1996) are based on a kind of informal rationalism, and were seminal contributions to the discussion. Timur Kuran's (1998) and David Laitin's (1998) related analyses of tipping games illuminate important dynamics of ethnic politics, for example, and Barbara Walter (1997) usefully applies Fearon's (1998) commitment problem idea to develop a liberal rationalist approach to the problem of settling ethnic wars, though all exaggerate the importance of their findings. Rationalist analyses of the intraethnic politics of interethnic conflict are also useful. Stephen Saideman (2001), for example, shows that external support for ethnic movements is typically motivated by the internal ethnic politics of the external power (though I would argue that the reason for that link is, again, the symbolic politics of ethnicity). Similarly, the rationalist focus on tangible interests is useful for explaining the timing of violent outbreaks, typically in times of economic hardship. And rational institutional theory is highly relevant to the problem of designing institutions for maintaining ethnic peace. While rationalism fails as a master narrative, it remains a valid source of insights.

Conclusion: The Symbolic Politics of Disciplinary War

The pretensions of its partisans to make rational choice theory the dominant paradigm, and formal modeling the central methodology in political science, are not justified. Rationalist theories of international relations and of ethnic violence are not the best or the most promising theories. Rationalism merely provides one among many useful lenses for explaining politics, with a place alongside but not above its alternatives. Claims that it represents *"the* emerging synthesis" of the field are undeserved.

The trouble, Perestroikans believe, is that rational choice modeling may come to dominate anyway. Rationalists and their statistically minded allies already have power in the discipline amounting to dominance in certain areas—in some granting agencies, in the editorship of prestigious journals (especially the "general" ones such as the *American Journal of Political Science*), and in decision making on hiring and tenure in many major departments. Still smarting from what they see as the undeserved scale of their predecessors' defeat by the number crunchers in the 1960s, Perestroikans—including scholars doing virtually every kind of work other than formal theory or statistical analysis—fear that in the long run they will be driven from the field by a coalition of statistically oriented and rationalist scholars who do not value other brands of research.

Analytically, this situation looks much like the symbolic politics of ethnic conflict. Rationalists and quantitatively inclined scholars raise the banners (symbols) of Science and Progress, or at least Cumulativity; they mythologize their opponents as unscientific (though most are actually positivist social scientists); and they fear, in one vivid formulation, a "Return of the Luddites" (Niou and Ordeshook 1999). They are naturally networked—that is, mobilized—through shared school ties as well as common conferences and APSA sections, and some indeed do not see much value in other sorts of work. Some have constructed departments that virtually exclude work other than theirs.[1] So we see myths, fears, and extremist mobilization; opportunity to extend dominance is obviously present; and the goal of dominance has been proposed by some leaders.

Perestroikans, on their side, are motivated by the fears of extinction engendered by the hegemonists' goal of dominance (and possibly exclusion), and are united at least tacitly by the myth of the Lost Battle against the Behaviorists. As with most such social myths, there is some truth in this one: while the addition of quantitative methods undeniably improved the field, the marginalization of other methods across wide swaths of the field—and quantitative scholars' ignorance of work done using other methods in some areas—has equally undeniably impoverished it. The growing fears of extinction evoked by these trends have motivated the mobilization of the Perestroika network to fight the hegemonists, yielding some rather extreme rhetoric.

Rationalists might see the problem as primarily information failures ("We don't really want to drive you out of the field") and problems of credible commitment ("Unfortunately, there is no way we can prove our commitment to tolerance"). This assumption, of course, overlooks the attitudinal sources of the problem, which lie in the myths on both sides, and in the accompanying tendency to exaggerate both the hostility and the cohesion of the opposing group. The problem is particularly acute on the side of the more powerful group—the rationalist-quantitativist axis—whose members see themselves as representing Science against the Luddites, so that the extremists among them do indeed want to cleanse the field of squishy-headed constructivists, critical theorists, feminists, interpretivists, political psychologists, and others who oppose their view of the best path to intellectual progress. While this statement may sound exaggerated, it is not. I have heard rationalists refer to qualitative researchers as "squish-heads," not entirely in jest, and dismiss constructivism out of hand. I have heard quantitative researchers state that there is no need for normative theorists in political science. Critical theorists and postmodernists (including most feminists) are widely regarded as troublemakers for their attacks on positivism. The result of logrolling departmental politics among these different biases is often to exclude representatives of any of the schools of thought mentioned here—an outcome not undesirable to many who hold these prejudices.

Taking into account this limitation—that attitudes are critically important—the rationalist diagnosis is still useful as a partial policy prescription. Thinking about the nature of the dispute in terms of information failures and problems of commitment might indeed point the way forward out of the low-level disciplinary civil war that now threatens to escalate. The rationalist axiom is that there is always some bargain that both sides prefer to open conflict, and that the problem is the lack of accurate information, especially about intentions. If rationalists and quantitative scholars are indeed committed to diversity, this could be demonstrated in part by the adoption of official departmental and APSA documents enshrining this value—documents to which scholars of all stripes can refer in justifying specific hiring and promotion decisions. This would suffice for a truce.

What commitments should these documents embody? My own view is that all departments large enough to maintain a graduate program should commit to maintaining the fullest possible range of intellectual diversity among the major active strains of thought in the discipline, because they are responsible for exposing their students to all of these alternatives. All should, of course, include some who do mainstream quantitative American politics and public policy. All should also have normative theorists and offer graduate courses in normative theory. All should include comparativists specializing in most key regions of the world—especially non-Western ones—and using a mix of methodologies, including cultural or interpretivist ones, with language skills a sine qua non for most of them, as well as cross-regional comparativists. Finally, all should include international relations scholars employing a mix of theories and methodologies. Across all subfields (not necessarily within each one), there should also be ideological and theoretical diversity, including the range from rationalists though constructivists, critical theorists, and other postpositivists.

This commitment to ideological, theoretical, methodological, and substantive diversity should be equal in priority to commitments to racial and gender diversity—and should indeed reinforce them, as racial minorities and women often cluster in "nonmainstream" research areas. Such a commitment may be taken as excluding the possibility that departments might specialize in a particular theoretical or methodological approach. It does not. Departments, especially larger ones, could easily choose to specialize, as long as the relative prominence of one particular approach did not mean the exclusion of most others.

A symbolic politics approach to conflict resolution would follow up on the insight that the real problem in these disciplinary fights is not so much information failure as simple intolerance. From this point of view, the value of establishing in writing the norm of tolerance of multiple approaches is to try to institutionalize that norm in disciplinary practice—which should in turn lead scholars to internalize it more. Explicit efforts within the discipline to promote tolerance and mutual respect, and to promote dialogue across methodological and theoretical boundaries, can also help. If and when attitudes begin to change, the values proclaimed in the documents will be securely put into practice.

There is no magic solution to the current methodological and epistemological war in political science, but it is time to start the dialogue toward a modus vivendi.

Note

1. An example is Binghamton University's department, which announces on its Web site its "conviction . . . that in the next generation all the social sciences, including political science, will rely increasingly on systematic evidence and quantitative analysis." Given the opportunity to thoroughly revamp their department after the departure of most faculty members, their decision was to focus on comparative politics, and to hire almost exclusively scholars quantitative or formal analysis with no regional focus and, a fortiori, no attention to cultural variables.

References

Ashley, Richard K. 1986. "The Poverty of Neorealism." In *Neorealism and its Critics,* ed. Robert O. Keohane: 255–300. New York: Columbia University Press.

Blainey, Geoffrey. 1973. *The Causes of War.* New York: Free Press.

Cohen, Lenard J. 1995. *Broken Bonds: Yugoslavia's Disintegration and Balkan Politics in Transition.* Boulder, CO: Westview Press.

Cox, Robert W. 1986. "Social Forces, States, and World Orders: Beyond International Relations Theory." In *Neorealism and Its Critics,* ed. Robert O. Keohane: 204–54. New York: Columbia University Press.

De Figueiredo, Rui, and Barry R. Weingast. 1999. "The Rationality of Fear: Political Opportunism and Ethnic Conflict." In *Civil Wars, Insecurity and Intervention,* ed. Barbara F. Walter and Jack Snyder: 261–302. New York: Columbia University Press.

Des Forges, Allison. 1999. *Leave None to Tell the Story: Genocide in Rwanda.* New York: Human Rights Watch.

Edelman, Murray. 1971. *Politics as Symbolic Action: Mass Arousal and Quiescence.* New York: Academic Press.

Enloe, Cynthia. 1990. *Bananas, Beaches, and Bases: Making Feminist Sense of International Politics.* Berkeley: University of California Press.

Fearon, James D. 1995. "Rationalist Explanations for War." *International Organization* 49 (Summer): 379–414.

Fearon, James D. 1998. "Commitment Problems and the Spread of Ethnic Conflict." In *The International Spread of Ethnic Conflict: Fear, Diffusion and Escalation,* ed. David A. Lake and Donald Rothchild: 107–26. Princeton, NJ: Princeton University Press.

Gagnon, V. P. 1995. "Ethnic Nationalism and International Conflict: The Case of Serbia." *International Security* 19 (Winter): 130–66.

Geertz, Clifford. 1973. *The Interpretation of Cultures.* New York: Basic Books.

Greene, Jay P. 1993. "Forewarned before Forecast: Presidential Election Forecasting Models and the 1992 Election." *PS: Political Science and Politics* 26 (1): 17–21.

Jervis, Robert. 1976. *Perception and Misperception in International Politics.* Princeton, NJ: Princeton University Press.

Katzenstein, Peter J. 1996 *Cultural Norms and National Security: Police and Military in Postwar Japan.* Ithaca, NY: Cornell University Press.

Kaufman, Stuart J. 1995. "The Irresistible Force and the Imperceptible Object: The Yugoslav Breakup and Western Policy." *Security Studies* 4 (Winter 1994-95): 281–329.

Kaufman, Stuart J. 2001a. *Modern Hatreds: The Symbolic Politics of Ethnic War.* Ithaca, NY: Cornell University Press.

Kaufman, Stuart J. 2001b. "Ethnic Violence, Symbolic Politics, and the Security Dilemma." Paper presented at the American Political Science Association Annual Meeting, San Francisco, September.

Kaufmann, Chaim. 1996. "Possible and Impossible Solutions to Ethnic Civil Wars." *International Security* 20 (Spring):136–75.

Kuran, Timur. 1998. "Ethnic Dissimilation and Its International Diffusion." In *The International Spread of Ethnic Conflict: Fear, Diffusion and Escalation,* ed. David A. Lake and Donald Rothchild: 35–60. Princeton, NJ: Princeton University Press.

Laitin, David D. 1998. *Identity in Formation: The Russian-Speaking Populations in the Near Abroad.* Ithaca, NY: Cornell University Press.

Lake, David. 2002. "Roundtable on Using IR Theory to Understand Ethnic Conflict: Insightful or Irrelevant?" Conference presentation, International Studies Association Annual Meeting, March 26, New Orleans.

Lake, David A., and Donald Rothchild, eds. 1998. *The International Spread of Ethnic Conflict: Fear, Diffusion and Escalation.* Princeton, NJ: Princeton University Press.

Legro, Jeffrey W. 1996. "Culture and Preferences in the International Cooperation Two-Step." *American Political Science Review* 90 (March): 118–37.

Luard, Evan. 1986. *War in International Society: A Study in International Sociology.* London: I. B. Tauris.

Marcus, George E., W. Russell Neuman, and Michael Mackuen. 2000. *Affective Intelligence and Political Judgment.* Chicago: University of Chicago Press.

McKeown, Timothy J. 1999. "Case Studies and the Statistical Worldview." *International Organization* 53 (Winter): 161–90.

Milner, Helen V. 1998. "Rationalizing Politics: The Emerging Synthesis of International, American and Comparative Politics." *International Organization* 52 (Autumn): 759–86.

Niou, Emerson M. S., and Peter C. Ordeshook. 1999. "Return of the Luddites." *International Security* 24 (Fall): 84–96.

Peterson, Roger D. 2002. *Understanding Ethnic Violence: Fear, Hatred and Resentment in Twentieth-Century Eastern Europe.* Cambridge: Cambridge University Press.

Posen, Barry. 1993. "The Security Dilemma and Ethnic Conflict." *Survival* 35 (1): 27–47.

Prunier, Gerard. 1995. *The Rwanda Crisis: History of a Genocide.* New York: Columbia University Press.

Saideman, Stephen M. 2001. *The Ties That Divide: Ethnic Politics, Foreign Policy, and International Conflict.* New York: Columbia University Press.

Smith, Anthony D. 1986. *The Ethnic Origins of Nations.* Oxford: Basil Blackwell.

Snyder, Jack. 1984. *The Ideology of the Offensive.* Ithaca, NY: Cornell University Press.

Van Evera, Stephen. 1990–91. "Primed for Peace: Europe after the Cold War." *International Security* 15 (Winter): 7–57.

Walt, Stephen M. 1999. "Rigor or Rigor Mortis? Rational Choice and Security Studies." *International Security* 23 (Spring): 5–48.

Walter, Barbara F. 1997. "The Critical Barrier to Civil War Settlement." *International Organization* 51 (Summer): 335–64.

Wendt, Alexander. 1999. *Social Theory of International Politics.* Cambridge: Cambridge University Press.

CHAPTER 8

A Return to Politics

Perestroika, Phronesis, and
Postparadigmatic Political Science

Sanford F. Schram

Political science is receiving increased critical scrutiny as a discipline these days, and much of that scrutiny is coming from within its own ranks. A growing number of political scientists have signed on to a movement to challenge the dominance of positivistic research, particularly research that assumes political behavior can be predicted according to theories of rationality and that such predictions underwrite cumulative explanations that constitute the growth of political knowledge. The movement to question such thinking is most dramatically represented in the eponymous network of scholars that has developed in response to a letter signed "Mr. Perestroika," which raised this challenge in poignant terms when it first circulated over the Internet back in October of 2000.

A loose collection of political scientists, from graduate students to senior scholars, Perestroikans do not always themselves agree on which features of the dominant approach they want to critique; some focus on the overly abstract nature of much of the research done today, some on the lack of nuance in decontextualized, large-sample empirical studies, others on the inhumaneness of thinking about social relations in causal terms, and still others on the ways in which contemporary social science all too often fails to produce the kind of knowledge that can meaningfully inform social life. As a group, however, the Perestroikans have championed methodological pluralism, charging that exclusionary practices have made graduate education less hospitable to historical and field research, qualitative case studies, interpretive and critical analysis, and a variety of context-sensitive approaches to the study of politics. The major journals of the field, Perestroikans argue, have become preoccupied with publishing research that conforms to overly restrictive scientistic assumptions about what constitutes contributions to political knowledge. Perestroika is a healthy development for political science and all other social sciences as well, opening for reconsideration these very questionable assumptions about what constitutes political knowledge in particular and social knowledge in general.

From the vantage point of many Perestroikans, the dominant paradigm in the field operates according to the following hierarchy of assumptions: (1) political science exists to help promote understanding of the truth about politics; (2) political science research contributes to this quest by adding to the accumulation of an expanding base of objective knowledge about politics; (3) the growth of this knowledge base is contingent on the building of theory that offers explanations of politics; (4) the building of theory is dependent on the development of universal generalizations regarding the behavior of political actors; (5) the development of a growing body of generalizations is accomplished by testing falsifiable, causal hypotheses that demonstrate their success in making predictions; (6) the accumulation of a growing body of predictions about political behavior comes from the study of variables in samples involving large numbers of cases; and (7) this growing body of objective, causal knowledge can be put in the service of society, particularly by influencing public policy makers and the stewards of the state.

This paradigm excludes much valuable research. For instance, it assumes that a study of a single case is "unscientific," provides no basis for generalizing, does not build theory, cannot contribute to the growth of political knowledge, and, as a result, is not even to be considered for publication in the leading journals and is to be discouraged as a legitimate doctoral dissertation project.[1] While there have always been dissenters from the drift toward "large n," quantitative research in service of objective, decontextualized, and universally generalizable truth about politics, there is a good case to be made that the dissenters have increasingly been marginalized as the center of gravity of the discipline has drifted more and more toward reflecting these core assumptions about political knowledge.

Perestroika has, at a minimum, provided an opportunity to halt this drift in political science by questioning these assumptions and posing alternatives. At its best, the Perestroikan impulse creates the possibility of questioning the idea that political science research exists as a unitary enterprise dedicated to the accumulation of an expanding knowledge base of universal, decontextualized generalizations about politics. In its place, Perestroika would put a more pluralistic emphasis on allowing for the blossoming of more contextual, contingent, and multiple political truths that involve a greater tie between theory and practice and a greater connection between thought and action in specific settings. Perestroika lays open the possibility that political science could actually be a very different sort of discipline, one less obsessed with proving that it is a "science" and one more connected to providing delimited, contextualized, even local knowledges that might serve people within specific contexts.

Such a political science would therefore have very different standards as to what counts as meaningful political knowledge. It would, for instance, be less interested in studying such things as "development" or "modernization" in the abstract as objects of inquiry on their own, as when economics becomes the study of "the market" as opposed to the examination of the variety of markets. Instead of focusing solely on "development" or "modernization" per se, political science would be more about studying change in particular countries or using concepts such as development or modernization in contextually sensitive ways to compare change in different countries.

This alternative political science would also be less preoccupied with perfecting method or pursuing research strictly for knowledge's own sake. As Rogers Smith has underscored, "knowledge does not have a sake"; all knowledge is tied to serving particular values.[2] Therefore, this new political science would not be one that is dedicated to replacing one method with another. Instead, such a discipline, if that word is still appropriate, would encourage scholars to draw on a wide variety of methods from a diversity of theoretical perspectives, combining theory and empirical work in different and creative ways, all in dialogue with political actors in specific contexts. Problem-driven research would replace method-driven research.[3]

My own version of Perestroika would build on this problem-driven, contextually sensitive approach to enable people on the bottom to work in dialogue with social researchers to challenge power. My Perestroika-inspired political science would be open to allowing ongoing political struggle to serve as the context for deciding what methods will be used in what ways to address which problems. This new dialogic political science would not find its standards for credible scholarship in arcane vocabularies and insular methods that are removed from local contexts and seem objective but are not without their own agendas. Instead, my political science would find its standards of knowledge in asking whether scholarship can demonstrate its contributions to enriching political discourse in contextualized settings.

Such a new political science, however, would at the same time recognize the risks associated with connecting to ongoing politics. It would guard against losing its critical capacity for the sake of achieving relevance. It would retain its critical capacity while in dialogue with ongoing political struggle, therefore providing a powerful "critical connectedness"—what Charles Lemert has called "global methods."[4] It would, however, be less interested than the old political science in serving the state with objective knowledge. It would forgo the dream of scientific grandeur that aims to produce socially useful, decontextualized, objective knowledge independent of politics.

A political science that forgoes the dream of a science of politics in order to dedicate itself to enhancing the critical capacity of people to practice a politics is, for me, an exciting prospect. A political science that does this to enhance the capacity to challenge power from below is all the more exciting. I would argue that the new political science would be not just more politically efficacious but also more intelligent, offering more robust forms of political knowledge.

I want to provide some justification for a Perestroika-inspired alternative political science by discussing two important, recently published books. For me, these works indicate that the concerns of Perestroika have a serious intellectual grounding and are tied to broader movements for change that are roiling the human sciences across the board. These works also provide important philosophical justification for my Perestroika-inspired alternative to political science.

One important source is Stephen Toulmin's *Return to Reason.*[5] Toulmin builds on his life's work in the philosophy of science, ordinary language philosophy, rhetoric, and the analysis of practical arts to offer a historically informed analysis of the problem of scientism in the social sciences. His primary argument is that since René Descartes, and especially since Immanuel Kant, Western philosophical thought has been increasingly enchanted with the dream of realizing universal rationality as the highest form of knowledge and the basis for truth. Yet Toulmin stresses that it was only relatively recently, in the twentieth century, that this dream came to be ascendant as the hegemonic ideal for organizing knowledge practices in the academy in general and in the social sciences in particular. The dream of universal rationality as the gold standard for objective knowledge of truth became ascendant with the rise of modern science and the growing influence of the argument that science, as best represented by particular natural sciences, was the best route toward achieving universal rationality, objective knowledge, truth with a capital T. In the wake of this new emphasis, the modern university was built, and then increasingly compartmentalized into the multiversity, with growing numbers of specialized disciplines, each increasingly preoccupied with perfecting its own methodological prowess as to how to best arrive at truth.

Toulmin's main argument is that this derangement was a long time coming and involved arduous work as part of a campaign that achieved hegemonic status only in the twentieth century. Toulmin believes that much of the history of modern Western philosophy before then can be understood in terms of striking a balance between universal rationality and contextual reason. The campaigners had to confront time and again the problem that what is universally rational may not be reasonable in particular situations. For centuries, the dream of universal rationality was counterbalanced by the practice of everyday reason. Humans experienced their lives and made sense of them between these poles. Yet the rise of modern science increased the emphasis on the production of objective knowledge in the most abstract and generalizable terms possible. Theory was everything, and practice was subordinated to it. Theory-driven modern science's preferred discourse was mathematics, which since Descartes had come to be seen as the ideal idiom for expressing in abstract and generalizable terms the objective knowledge of universal rationality. Sciences began to be ranked by the degree to which they could produce universal rationality as expressed in mathematical terms. Physics envy spread. Then again, in the twentieth century science in general became ascendant as the best way to produce objective knowledge. The fact that "science as use" was conflated with "science as truth" helped greatly in catapulting science to the forefront as the supposed superior road to truth, as dramatic developments in technology were increasingly showcased as proof positive that science not only could do things but also knew the truth of what it was doing.[6]

The idea that there is a distinctive scientific method that all sciences share began to gain greater currency, and all other means of knowledge production came to be seen as inferior to the degree that they failed to conform to the dictates of the scientific method. Physics envy morphed into science envy, with the social sciences increasingly miming what was seen as the methods of the natural sciences in order to stake their own claim to scientific legitimacy. At this point, the precarious balance between emphasizing abstract rationality and emphasizing everyday reason was seriously upset, and universal rationality in service of abstract generalizable knowledge and stated in mathematical terms was seen as the only real form of truth worth taking seriously. The wisdom of everyday reason was increasingly relegated to the status of folklore or to applied fields and started to become a popular area of study in itself, not so much for the truths it afforded but as an object of inquiry that could be used to provide data with which to test various hypotheses about which types of people, in what cultures, tended to think in what ways, and why. That the science of wisdom, as it were, was being studied, whether in anthropology or philosophy, was a sure sign that rationality had triumphed over reason.

Toulmin effectively illuminates the rise of universal rationality first in philosophy, from Descartes on, then in the sciences, but also in the social sciences and in applied fields as well. He highlights how a consistent bias in favor of abstract knowledge of universal rationality continued to work its way across disparate realms of knowledge production. Toulmin is not a social scientist, and in the past he has written about almost everything but. Yet in *Return to Reason* he demonstrates a real feel for how the social sciences rose in the shadow of the preoccupation with the abstract knowledge of universal rationality and how that played out in selected fields. This is a wide-ranging book, written in a very inviting conversational style, from an Olympian vantage point; however, it is no mere dilettante rumination on the misguided project John Dewey called the "quest for certainty."

My favorite example in the entire book is that of Lancelot Brown, the famous nineteenth-century landscaper, who was also popularly known as "Capability" Brown because he developed the designs for his quintessentially British gardens out of the available landscape rather than, as in the French style, imposing an idealized image of a garden on the landscape and forcing the landscape to conform to that ideal. Toulmin uses Capability Brown to demonstrate how British empiricism, in contrast to French idealism, very pragmatically offers a way to "play it as it lays" and work with what is available within any particular context rather than trying to impose abstract, universal ideals on situations. In Toulmin's hands, Capability Brown effectively illustrates the value of a return to reason as a counter-balance to the excessive emphasis on abstract knowledge of universal rationality.

Toulmin is most convincing when he notes that for the social sciences the scientistic preoccupation with universal rationality was a particularly troubling turn. His primary case in point is the popular one, economics. He calls it the "physics that never was." Toulmin effectively shows that the history of the development of economics as a discipline involved the progressive elimination of historical and social considerations, increasingly decontextualizing its subject matter and expressing its findings in ever more abstract and mathematical terms to produce its own universal rationality of market-related behavior. The application of abstract economic models to problems of public policy increasingly became the vogue. Theory dictated practice in often ruthless terms, particularly when First World lending institutions prescribed "structural adjustment" or "shock therapy" policies that required nation-states to retrofit their economies to conform to the models' requirements.

The central problem here for Toulmin, as for so many others, is that these sorts of applications all too often mistook contextually specific understandings of predictable market behavior as universally applicable, abstracted them from those contexts, and imposed them in social settings, cultures, and political systems where they make very little sense at all, and did so all too often at great cost to the well-being of the people who were supposed to be helped by such "development" schemes. Toulmin counters these disasters of "top-down," theory-driven economic practice with the example of Muhammad Yunus, who works from the "bottom up" in his Grameen Bank, which provides small loans in over fifty thousand Bangladeshi villages so that local people can develop "appropriate" enterprises fitted to their communities, values, and local practices. Yunus, a professional economist, is quoted by Toulmin as saying: "If Economics [as it stands] were a social science, economists would have discovered what a powerful socio-economic weapon credit is. . . . If we can redesign economics as a genuine social science, we will be firmly on our way to creating a poverty-free world" (65). Toulmin ends his tale of the disenchantment of economics by saying: "This message does not, of course, affect Economics alone: similar traditions in the other human sciences have led to similar misunderstandings and errors of practical judgment" (66).

Toulmin believes that the antidote to the twentieth-century hegemony of universal rationalism is respect for everyday reason, as practiced in contextualized settings, in ways that cannot be legislated by theory from the top down and are open to living with the uncertainty that such situated knowledges must accept as the ineliminable contingency of what Toulmin calls the "clinical arts." The social sciences are, for Toulmin, more akin to "applied sciences," but "applied" mischaracterizes the situation, suggesting that theory is applied in practice—an idea most significantly popularized by the reports Abraham Flexner wrote on professional medical education in 1913 and on social work in 1915. Instead, drawing on the work of Donald Schon and others, Toulmin wants us to learn that social theory is better seen as growing out of practice, as an intensification of those meditative moments in social practice.[7]

Toulmin sees the need for the social sciences, operating ever more beyond disciplinary boundaries, to be more about teaching practical wisdom—*phronesis,* as Aristotle termed it—as something that grows out of an intimate familiarity with the contingencies and uncertainties of various forms of social practice embedded in complex social settings. Therefore, we need to revise the standards for acceptable research methodologies, reincorporating context-sensitive research such as case studies, not to dictate what is to be done but more to inventory infinitely unique cases from which social actors can learn to appreciate the complexities of social relations and thus can practice various social crafts all the more effectively. If practiced in this way, social science would be more like bioethics than like moral philosophy, basing itself on the insight that Toulmin provides when he notes that bioethics owes very little to moral philosophy, which, as theory, is incapable of specifying from the top down most bioethical decisions, which instead grow from the bottom up, in unlegislated form, varying with contexts, negotiating ambiguity, living with uncertainty, and still doing the necessary work of determining life and death every day. For bioethicists and many others, case study research, often conducted in dialogical and collaborative relations with the people being studied, can help enable social actors to use knowledge to address their problems. Toulmin believes that such participatory action research would be more fitting for a real social science that better understood its relationship to its contingent, contextual, and ever so thoroughly social subjects. For Toulmin, the return to reason will best be evidenced in the social sciences when wisdom of this sort is taught not as an object of scientific scrutiny, as evidence of cultural variation, but as the very goal of knowledge production itself.

In his introduction Toulmin cites another recent book as a sign that some social scientists are tapping into the themes he emphasizes. That book is *Making Social Science Matter: Why Social Inquiry Fails and How It Can Succeed Again,* by Bent Flyvbjerg.[8] It, too, is a remarkable book that adds fuel to the idea that perhaps Perestroikans are part of broader academic currents. Flyvbjerg's book takes us one step further down the road that Toulmin has laid out for us, and it does so eloquently with its own impassioned argument, which not only demonstrates what is wrong with the social sciences today but provides a detailed list of examples of how a phronetic social science is already possible and already happening here and there amid the detritus of contemporary social science.

Flyvbjerg's book is a breath of fresh air; he creatively uses Aristotle, as well as Friedrich Nietzsche, Michel Foucault, Pierre Bourdieu, and others to make many of the same points as Toulmin, but in his own distinctive way. He fuses an Aristotelian concern for phronesis with a Marxist concern for praxis, adding a Foucauldian critique of Jürgen Habermas's preoccupation with consensus to demonstrate that a phronetic social science that can offer a praxis worth pursuing is one that would work within any contextualized setting to challenge power, especially as it is articulated in discourse. Flyvbjerg's phronetic social science would be open to using a plurality of research methods to help people challenge power more effectively.

Flyvbjerg begins where Toulmin left us, in the present, with social science hopelessly lost, seeking to emulate the natural sciences with a quest for theory-driven abstract knowledge of universal rationality. Flyvbjerg adds a compelling critique that convincingly demonstrates that there is no symmetry between natural and social science in that natural science's interpretive problems are compounded by what Anthony Giddens called the "double hermeneutic" of the social sciences. By virtue of the distinctively human subject matter of their field, the social scientists inevitably are people who offer interpretations of other people's interpretations. And the people being studied always have the potential to include the social scientists' interpretations in theirs, creating an ever-changing subject matter and requiring a dialogic relationship between the people doing the studying and the people being studied. Flyvbjerg believes that this situation unavoidably means that there can be no theory for social science in the sense that social science needs to forgo the dream that it can create time-tested theories of a static social reality.

As a result, Flyvbjerg argues, the social sciences should not seek to emulate the natural sciences. In comparison with the natural sciences, the social sciences will always fare very poorly, being seen as inferiors incapable of producing knowledge based on tested theories that can evince prediction of the worlds they study. Instead, Flyvbjerg feels that the social sciences are better equipped to produce a different kind of knowledge—phronesis, practical wisdom—that grows out of intimate familiarity with practice in contextualized settings. Take local knowledges, even tacit knowledges, that cannot be taught a priori, grown from the bottom up, emerging out of practice, forgoing the hubris of seeking claims to a decontextualized universal rationality stated in abstract terms of false precision. Add a sense of praxis, seeking the ability to push for change, leaven it with an appreciation of the ineliminable presence of power, and this phronetic social science can help people in ongoing political struggle question the relationships between knowledge and power and thereby work to change things in ways they might find more agreeable and even satisfying. Such a phronetic social science can contribute to what I have called "radical incrementalism," or the idea that praxis involves promoting change for the least advantaged by exploiting the possibilities in current political arrangements.[9]

Yet what is most exciting is that Flyvbjerg not only goes beyond critique to offer a positive program; he demonstrates it in detail, pointing to a rich variety of contemporary work, from that of Bourdieu, to that of Robert Bellah, to his own work. Flyvbjerg's research spanned fifteen years and focused on a major redevelopment project initiated by the Danish city of Aalborg, where Flyvbjerg continues to teach urban planning. His research on the project evolved over time, quickly becoming more phronetic as he came to appreciate how social science could make real contributions to the ongoing dialogue over the city's redevelopment efforts once his research was retrofitted to the specific context in which the issues of development were being debated. At first, Flyvbjerg was put off that decision makers rejected the relevance of studies about education done elsewhere, and he came to be concerned with power. Without saying so, he evidently took to heart the idea that he had to work harder to produce research that, even while it challenged power, demonstrated its sensitivity to the Aalborg context. In the process, power relations were challenged in a very public way, the development agenda was successfully revised to include more grass-roots concerns, an ongoing dialogue with participants in the redevelopment process was richly elaborated, and social science research that gave up an interest in proving grand theories became critical to a very robust discourse on urban planning. As a result, the Aalborg planning project gained increased visibility as a successful project that went out of its way to democratize its decision making, in part by allowing social science research to help keep it honest, open, and collaborative.

Phronetic social science such as this would be very different from the social science that predominates today. Yet I wonder whether it would be constructive to say that this would represent a new paradigm. This is because I am increasingly convinced that social science is ideally better seen as postparadigmatic rather than as organized by one paradigm or another. For me, the idea of paradigm has no relevance to social science except as its own form of mimicry. Paradigmatic research is what natural scientists do. Yet for the reasons provided in this chapter, social science ideally should not be seen as amenable to being organized paradigmatically in any strict sense of the term.

The strict sense of the term *paradigm* is of course subject to intense debate, starting with its author, Thomas Kuhn. Paradigm started to become a critical idea for thinking about scientific knowledge in Kuhn's *The Structure of Scientific Revolutions* and served as the linchpin for his theory that, in any one field, "normal" science is periodically punctuated by "revolutionary" science that induces a conceptual transformation of the subject matter and initiates new ways of studying it.[10] From the beginning Kuhn struggled to respond to critics by relying in particular on two additional concepts—those of the exemplar and the disciplinary matrix.[11] An exemplar is an exemplary example, usually in the form of an innovative experiment or analytical treatment, that by its very success implies a particular way to understand and study the subject in question. To the extent that they are contingent upon exemplars, Kuhn's paradigms are therefore to a great degree implicit in the very act of "learning by doing" in a contextually sensitive fashion, making them in their own way forms of phronetic reasoning, learned and elaborated through situated practice.[12] A disciplinary matrix is the social, institutional, and organizational side of the process by which cohorts of scientists were introduced to the paradigm and encouraged to practice normal science according to how they were socialized by the disciplinary matrix. It is therefore as if paradigms have both material and symbolic dimensions. Through learning to practice exemplars, graduate students became normal scientists. Natural science was its own form of phronesis, if only so as to practice natural scientific reasoning in the context of actually doing it.

Once a new exemplar arises that is seen as providing a preferred understanding of the subject matter in ways that the prevailing paradigm cannot, scientists have to learn the new rules for study implied by the new exemplar. Translation into the old system of study is not possible, because the paradigms are, in Kuhn's mind, to an ineliminable degree and by definition, incommensurable. Each paradigm's evidence is of such a nature that it always has to be evaluated by its own standards, in its own context, making it impossible to use evidence to decide if one paradigm is better than another. Kuhn believes that knowledge does not grow cumulatively, with one paradigm building on another. We should never say that we now know more or better; we should say only that, with a paradigm change, we know differently.

What was most radical about Kuhn's notion of paradigm was that it un-masked the fiction that the twentieth-century metastory of science tells us about the growth of objective knowledge. This Kuhnian claim led critics to charge him with relativism on the grounds that Kuhn seemed to be implying that one paradigm might be as true or right as another. Kuhn spent much of the rest of his life responding to critics with clarifications that more often than not moved him away from the relativistic implications of his work. Yet I agree with Richard Rorty that when someone calls you a relativist, one of the better responses is to say, "Thank you" for highlighting your well-founded commit-ment to challenging the illegitimacy of the master narrative of science.[13]

Kuhn, however, left to the side whether paradigm is relevant to under-standing the social sciences. Given the subject matter of the field, there ideally should be no normal science in any one of the social sciences. Regardless of the fact that both the natural and the social sciences are forms of learning in context that produce value-laden facts, social life, as opposed to the objects of natural scientific inquiry, involves multiple interpretive lenses offering a disharmonious array of competing perspectives emanating from its origins in conscious, thinking human beings. Under these conditions, no one form of disciplined study of social life should be organized paradigmatically to exclude the consideration of multiple perspectives.

Ironically, the objectivists in the social sciences themselves most often resist the application of Kuhn's idea of paradigm to their fields because it implies that their scientific work was value-laden. I agree with them about resisting its application to the social sciences, but for a different reason, that multiple perspectives are inherent in the subject matter. It is a sad irony that even though the objectivists resist paradigm, the methodological hegemony of objectivists is the reality today in social sciences such as political science and economics. This is a doleful reminder that paradigms involve the very human power struggles of a disciplinary matrix as much as they do the practices of inquiry demonstrated in exemplars. Paradigms can be imposed socially even where they are most inappropriate intellectually.

Regardless of the roots of paradigm in learning from examples, to talk of a new "paradigm" in the context of the social sciences risks reinscribing the very foundationalism that a Perestroika-inspired phronetic social science seeks to challenge. To replace one paradigm with another simply encourages social sci-entists to privilege theory as some legislating and authorizing activity, which it is not. Such foundationalism reflects a lingering commitment to universal rationality and fails to appreciate the contextualism that Toulmin and Flyv-bjerg emphasize as central to understanding and contributing to social and political life.

A better response would be to approach phronetic social science as post-paradigmatic research. Such a body of work would involve theory as something that grows out of the social practices in specific contexts while still working to achieve a critical distance in developing prevailing understandings of those practices. This would be the beginning of research that could better help people challenge power.

In conclusion, I would like to emphasize that phronetic social science is more than a dream; it already exists. It is just not organized, recognized or named as such, existing here and there where scholars come to it on their own; it has multiple sources of intellectual sustenance that have provided resources for challenging the orthodoxy of scientistic social science. One set of resources over the last few decades has come from what came to be called "interpretive social science."[14] Yet there are others, as the "interpretive turn" in the social sciences was overtaken by the subsequent linguistic turn, and a series of other related turns that followed, all contributing to the growing resistance to the hegemony of scientistic social science. Phronetic social science is but a pathway that comes from all these different turns. Yet while the interpretive and subsequent turns helped provide resources for developing the phronetic research that already is among us, these prior turns do not by themselves constitute phronetic social science. A Perestroika-inspired phronetic social science involves taking more turns along the lines I have suggested in the foregoing pages, and perhaps taking turns along other lines as well. Yet the future is not as predictable as the hegemons might suggest it is. Will the road ahead take more turns in a phronetic direction? That will depend to a large extent on the plays of power in the academy, the government, the think tanks, and anywhere else knowledge and power are being "disciplined."

Notes

1. The Perestroika list serve is replete with examples of dissertation advisors and journal editors who as a rule will not consider case studies. The archives of the list serve can be accessed by e-mail to perestroika_glasnost_warmhome@yahoo.com.

2. See Rogers M. Smith, "Should We Make Political Science More of a Science or More about Politics? *PS: Political Science and Politics* 35 (2002): 199–201.

3. See Ian Shapiro's chapter in this volume.

4. Charles Lemert, *Social Things* (Lanham, MD: Rowman & Littlefield, 2001), 176–206.

5. Stephen Toulmin, *Return to Reason* (Berkeley: University of California Press, 2002).

6. "Science as use" versus "science as truth" is from Jacqueline Stevens, "Symbolic Matter: DNA and Other Linguistic Stuff," *Social Text* 20 (Spring 2002): 105–36.

7. See Donald Schon, *The Reflective Practitioner* (New York: Basic Books, 1983).

8. Bent Flyvbjerg, *Making Social Science Matter: Why Social Inquiry Fails and How It Can Succeed Again* (New York: Cambridge University Press, 2001).

9. See Sanford F. Schram, *Praxis for the Poor: Piven and Cloward and the Future of Social Science in Social Welfare* (New York: New York University Press, 2002).

10. Thomas S. Kuhn, *The Structure of Scientific Revolutions* (Chicago: University of Chicago Press, 1970).

11. On Kuhn's use of "exemplar" and "disciplinary matrix," See Erich von Dietze, Paradigms Explained: Rethinking Thomas Kuhn's Philosophy of Science (Westport, CT: Praeger, 2001).

12. Etymologically, *paradigm* is from the Greek *paradeiknunai:* literally, "to show beside," from *para,* "alongside," and *deiknunai,* "to show," implying learning by imitating an example.

13. Richard Rorty, "Thomas Kuhn, Rocks, and the Laws of Physics," *Common Knowledge* 6 (1997): 6–16, and John G. Gunnell, "Relativism: The Return of the Repressed," *Political Theory* 21 (1993): 563–84.

14. For a collection of essays on the "interpretative turn" from a conference celebrating the twenty-fifth anniversary of the founding of the School of Social Science at the Institute for Advanced Study, see Joan W. Scott and Debra Keates, eds., Schools of Thought: Twenty-five Years of Interpretive Social Science (Princeton, NJ: Princeton University Press, 2001). It is telling that in order to mount its challenge to orthodoxy phronetic social science had to declare its independence from the supposedly independent ivory tower of the university, further complicating the issue of what it takes for social science to challenge power.

CHAPTER 9

The Perestroikan Challenge to Social Science

David D. Laitin

The specter of an insurgency haunts political science. Under the leadership of a "Mr. Perestroika," a broad group of political scientists has abandoned the project of a scientific discipline.[1] It would indeed be convenient to write off this quasi-coordinated attack on the scientific turn in the study of society, calling its proponents Luddites. Indeed, their abhorrence of all things mathematical —and their typical but useless conflation of statistical and formal reasoning— reveals a fear of the modern. It would be equally convenient to write off this attack due to lack of any manifesto offering an alternative view of the discipline. Mostly we hear a desire for pluralism rather than a defense of best practices. But I think it would be prudent to respond, to defend what may well be a Sisyphean project in seeking a science of social life.

While there is no intellectual manifesto that lays down the gauntlet, a recently published book by Bent Flyvbjerg captures many of the core themes of Mr. Perestroika's insurgency.[2] And thus this book, *Making Social Science Matter: Why Social Inquiry Fails and How It Can Succeed Again,* offers an intellectual target for those who wish to confront the Perestroikan challenge intellectually.[3] For in this clever, succinct, and readable book Flyvbjerg portrays the quest for a social science as quixotic at best and self-defeating at worst. The social world, he argues, is sufficiently different from the natural world that any hopes for a Galilean conquest of the unknown in social science will forever remain unrealized.[4] Social scientists, in order to sidestep the scorn that is regularly heaped on them by natural scientists who recognize the scientific limits to the study of humans, should cultivate their own turf by making reasonable judgments about the social world based on a realistic view of power and a sensitivity as to how that power is exerted. Relying on Aristotle's categorization, Flyvbjerg dubs this methodology "phronesis." Social scientists can succeed doing phronesis, Flyvbjerg confidently asserts, because we write and read careful case studies that provide us with an expert's feel for how, in a particular context, our political interventions can bring social betterment.

This is a viewpoint to be taken seriously. Flyvbjerg has conducted well-conceived fieldwork in Denmark and has long been an astute commentator on urban planning and popular participation in social planning. Furthermore, *Making Social Science Matter* has received excellent notices from some of the leading social scientists in the world, including Pierre Bourdieu, Clifford Geertz, and Steven Lukes. Finally, the arguments in the book resonate with parallel points articulated by political science Perestroikans, who have yet to be seriously confronted with intellectual arguments.

My response to Flyvbjerg and the challenge he presents to the scientific aspirations of many political scientists proceeds in stages. First, I challenge Flyvbjerg's stylized facts purportedly showing the failure of what he calls "epistemic" social science. Because Flyvbjerg presents these facts to motivate his study, it is important to establish that the premise of the book—constructed from these stylized facts—stands on weak foundations. Second, I challenge Flyvbjerg's portrayals of both context (which he claims is not subject to analysis) and science (for which he sets a standard that many research programs in the natural sciences could not meet). It is important to challenge these views because Flyvbjerg argues that the irreducibility of social context makes a predictive science of the social impossible. I can then show that Flyvbjerg's claims for the greater intellectual payoff of phronesis need to be radically circumscribed because of his mistaken views on context and science. Third, I describe phronesis at work, first in a discussion of Flyvbjerg's use of that method in his field research on urban planning in Aalborg, Denmark, and then in a discussion of the work by Stanley Tambiah on ethnic war in Sri Lanka. In both cases, I argue, the work would have much greater scientific value if placed within what I have dubbed the tripartite method of comparative research—a method that integrates narrative (much of what Flyvbjerg calls phronesis), statistics, and formal modeling.[5] Fourth, I discuss the contributions that phronesis makes in scientific explanation, showing why it has a stature equal to that of statistics and formal modeling in the tripartite method. Finally, in the conclusion I discuss (in defense of the tripartite method as a standard and in reference to claims by one of Mr. Perestroika's defenders) the limits of methodological pluralism.

The Premise of Flyvbjerg's Book

Flyvbjerg introduces his brief with three examples. Astonishingly, they all work to undermine his entire argument. The opening example is that of the now infamous contribution by New York University physicist Alan Sokal to the journal *Social Text*. Sokal's "contribution" was a hoax. He purposefully submitted what he conceived of as postmodern gobbledygook. Yet it sailed through *Social Text*'s peer review as a serious critique of science. Flyvbjerg offers this example, and the controversy that occurred in the wake of Sokal's publication, as, inter alia, an "exposé of . . . social science." But why, the reader might ask, would social science get implicated in this scandal? *Social Text* has no pretensions to science. More important, in large part because of a cult of science in leading social science journals such as the *American Political Science*

Review, Econometrica, and the *American Journal of Sociology,* it is doubtful that a physicist could get an article of that sort past the peer reviewers of those journals. Reviewers would want to assure themselves that the data set was available and subject to review, the theory was clearly articulated, and the findings were linked closely to the theory and data. Sokal chose *Social Text* precisely because members of its editorial board had ridiculed the notion of scientific objectivity.

The second example, immediately on the heels of the presentation of the Sokal hoax, concerns the study of human sexual practices conducted by scholars working at the National Opinion Research Center (NORC). Flyvbjerg delights in quoting the *Economist*'s humorous put-down of this study (and later he uses an equally clever one-liner from the *Economist* to write off the entire profession of economics). Flyvbjerg also cites a more serious attack on the statistical methods employed in this study, written by a population geneticist, and a rather limp defense of those methods by the authors in response. Flyvbjerg sees this as evidence that natural scientists hold social scientists in contempt. Social scientists, he concludes, should not even try to imitate the scientific method by producing fancy statistics and impressive regressions. Rather, if they sang a tune that they in fact could hold, they would no longer have opprobrium heaped on them by their natural science colleagues.

This example also works against Flyvbjerg's argument. The inference that social science in general is held in low esteem, based on a single review of a particular work in social science, is unjustified. Making an inference from a single case, an ambiguous one at that, is logically unjustified. This suggests that Flyvbjerg has little concern for valid inference, something that should make supporters of his phronetic alternative nervous. His inference is not only invalid; it is wrong, and on two counts. First, Flyvbjerg ignores the intriguing collaborations between biologists and social-scientific game theorists in the past two decades that have created new knowledge in fields closely related to that of the scientific critic of the NORC study.[6] Natural scientists who have worked in productive collaboration with social scientists would hardly hold social scientists as a species in contempt as did the reviewer of the NORC book.

Flyvbjerg's inference is wrong on a second count. The NORC book appeared when the AIDS epidemic was first spreading. Many in the press were reporting linear and ghastly projections of the spread of the disease based on briefings from medical professionals. The NORC team, relying on its scientific finding that there are in America, especially among homosexuals, closed networks of sexual practice, predicted that the growth curve would flatten, and the disease would continue to eat away at people within segmented sexual communities. The NORC researchers could not offer a precise prediction of how many would incur AIDS, but their research on sexual practice entailed an observable implication, which turned out to be true. This does not prove that their methods were impeccable. Indeed, one could well point to the methodological problem not only in the NORC study but also in the entire genre of studies that postulate causal sequences from cross-sectional survey data. But the NORC team's correct analysis that AIDS would not spread through the American population in general gives confidence that they were accurately portraying American sexual networks.[7] In sum, Flyvbjerg's use of the NORC example as evidence that natural scientists ridicule all forms of scientific activity in the study of the social world is unconvincing.

Flyvbjerg's third example, a model of human learning developed by Hubert and Stuart Dreyfus, serves as a leitmotif for his entire book. The Dreyfuses reported on an experiment in which subjects were asked to observe videotapes and then evaluate the competence of paramedics, including one expert and five novices, who were all engaged in giving cardiopulmonary resuscitation (CPR) to victims of heart failure. The experimental subjects included people with three levels of expertise: experienced paramedics, students learning to become paramedics, and lifesaving instructors. The experimental results showed that experienced paramedics, but not the other two sets of observers, could consistently and correctly pick out the expert practitioner of CPR. According to Flyvbjerg's interpretation, those subjects who were novices were attuned to the matter of who was best following the rules of CPR. Meanwhile, the expert subjects were less interested in the rules; they were looking for the single practitioner who had an eye for context and knew which rules could be waived to save the largest number of victims.

One of the interpreters (Stuart Dreyfus) offered the following insight to make sense of the finding. He was a mathematician and a chess aficionado. For a long time, he believed that if he could solve all the necessary algorithms, he would become a chess master. To his chagrin, mathematical logic took him only so far. Those with an expert's "feel" for chess were able to defeat him, and very often these people had no education in higher mathematics. Consequently, Stuart Dreyfus observed, only those with a feel for chess (often honed by playing "fast chess" rather than studying algorithms) could become masters. The lesson for social science that Flyvbjerg draws from the experiment and from the chess anecdote is that, in the complex world of human beings, no algorithm will correctly predict action; rather, an expert's feel for the context will give him or her a better grasp of what is likely to occur. Only experts who have worked and lived in the social world (like chess players who have developed skills through practice) would know how best, in the experimental case, to choose a paramedic if they were in need of one.

One could criticize the chess analogy (and by implication the inference) by pointing out that it is increasingly dated, as supercomputers are becoming chess masters using rule-based algorithms. But there are two far more disconcerting things about the use of the Dreyfuses' model as a justification for the use of phronesis. First, there is another interpretation of this study, never considered, that undermines the thesis of the book. From what was presented (as Flyvbjerg admits),[8] the Dreyfuses used a rather standard scientific procedure common in experimental psychology to make a discovery concerning human cognition. The experimenters learned from their controlled environment (certainly not from a case study!) that there are different levels of competence in the human learning process, with implications for what it entails to become an expert. This seems to me an advertisement for the scientific method as a way of gaining new psychological knowledge rather than an invitation to jump the scientific ship. Second, there is overwhelming support for the notion that in controlled experiments statistical models outperform expert clinical intuitions in diagnosing human disease.[9] Here is a case in which natural scientists would subject Flyvbjerg to ridicule for not examining whether a finding he liked was sufficiently robust to work in other experimental settings.

In sum, looking at the Sokal example, the NORC sex study, and the Dreyfuses' model as compelling reasons to abjure the scientific method in social science, one can see that Flyvbjerg's attempt to create a sense of scientific failure through the use of telling examples is manifestly unsuccessful.

Three Misunderstandings

Flyvbjerg is adamant that methodological admonitions urging students to study society scientifically are mired in misunderstandings about the social world. But he is guilty of some grievous misunderstandings himself.

What Is Context?

"Context" plays a leading role in many tracts purporting to show the limitations of scientific procedures for the study of society, and in Flyvbjerg's book as well.[10] But Flyvbjerg never actually defines it. His method, we are told, is sensitive to context, whereas science is not. Humans are always sensitive to context, but computers are not. Therefore, people are better judges of complex situations that are heavily influenced by context than are computers. This judgment rests on a grievous overstatement. *Context* comes to us from the Latin *contextus,* meaning "a connection of words." In English this has come to mean, among other related things, "the parts of discourse that surround a word or passage and throw light on its meaning" (*Webster's Ninth New Collegiate Dictionary*). If this is what *context* means, surely computers have been programmed to use surrounding words to throw light on a particular word's meaning. Search engines allow us, in our investigation of a particular concept, to specify words before and after this concept. This procedure helps throw light on a particular concept's meaning.

Of course, Flyvbjerg sees *context* as meaning more than word connections. Indeed, *contextus* is closely related to the Latin *contexere,* "to weave." Here *context* implies a skein of interwoven factors. But to say that humans are good at capturing context is hardly a justification for the use of phronesis. For one purpose of social science is to disentangle such skeins in order to trace the effects of its separate strands, or to examine the impact of particular interactions among strands. Arguing that we must be sensitive to context is merely to say that we have not yet discovered the various factors or the interaction of factors that have produced outcomes of significance. Science is sensitive to context if sensitivity means the desire to analyze it, to break it down to its separate strands, and to hypothesize how the interwoven strands influence the course of social events. Ultimately one's hypotheses about the implications of various contextual strands will demand statistical verification using interaction terms and flexible functional forms. Arguing that we must be sensitive to context is therefore a cop-out; analyzing it and verifying our analytical judgments about it are what social scientists ought to be doing.

What Is Science?

Flyvbjerg believes that science must meet an ideal or else it is not science. He portrays it as the activity that can "generate ultimate, unequivocally verified knowledge," yielding some "final truth."[11] Hardly anyone in the natural sciences would hold such a view. Nor would mathematicians, who mostly rearrange symbols consistent with axioms rather than pursue a final truth. Most scientists see their findings as provisional, contingent, and subject to replication and rejection.

Oddly, of the several criteria for science elucidated in *Making Social Science Matter,* the only one Flyvbjerg insists social scientists cannot achieve is prediction. Yet this is the only criterion for which Flyvbjerg provides no "philosophy of science" citations. He just asserts that it is a necessary component of science.

This criterion is the most demanding of all, and many fields that are widely respected as scientific (e.g., population biology, evolution, and geology) would quickly fail this test. But if what is meant by prediction is the ability of scholars in the field to make reasonably good probability estimates of individual behavior under laboratory conditions or in well-defined activities (e.g., voting), several branches of social science can meet such criteria. Social scientists, for example, have long been able to make reasonable predictions of how any individual will vote knowing a few facts about his or her socioeconomic background, age, and education.

Stating ideal criteria for science—and writing off those fields that do not meet these criteria as a breeding ground for phronesis—represents a bimodal approach to scientific categorization. It is better to evaluate research environments as a continuous variable, measuring the extent to which they approach commonly accepted scientific standards, with the notion that doing better in meeting such criteria is better than doing worse. Instead of setting some unreachable ideal as the criterion of science, I propose the notion of a scientific frame. To the extent to which a community of scholars is concerned about such things as uncertain (ex ante) conclusions, public procedures, careful measurement, rules of inference, and rewards for replication, that community has adopted a scientific frame.

I also propose that within the scientific frame the best defense we have against error and the surest hope for valid inference is a tripartite methodology that includes narrative (the essential component of phronesis) as well as formal and statistical analyses. To the extent that a community has adopted a scientific frame and relies on a tripartite method, that community will be in a condition to make good judgments. The problem with saying that good judgment rests on only one leg of the tripartite method (exemplified by Flyvbjerg's rendition of phronesis) is that it is hard to know if one's judgment is wrong. The scientific frame, buttressed with the tripartite method—as I will illustrate in a subsequent section—has ample procedures for figuring out if our best judgments are misplaced.

For What Is Phronesis Valuable?

Flyvbjerg is ambiguous about the goals to be maximized in social science. He seems to move the goalpost. On one hand, he points to social scientists seeking to make valid causal inferences about the social world. He criticizes them for the inevitability of their failures. But in his alternative model, that of phronesis, his goal is to give students in professional schools useful knowledge, helping them to make a better world. Here I am sympathetic with Flyvbjerg's brief. For professional training of policy analysts and politicians, it would seem useful to focus on normative questions (What kind of life do we want to lead?), experience to give them a feel for the practical, and case studies (What kind of world did my predecessors face, and how well did they do?), with somewhat less emphasis on making valid causal inferences about how certain outcomes were reached. For PhD training, the balance would need to be reversed. But the point here is that while Flyvbjerg's notion of phronesis may have some important role to play in the professionalization of social practitioners, it must be combined with statistical and formal analysis if the goal is achieving valid social knowledge.

Phronesis at Work

Flyvbjerg summarizes his politically engaged and ultimately successful research on city planning in Aalborg, Denmark as an example of the potential of phronesis. He reports that a city planning initiative in Aalborg was captured by downtown businessmen who had a vision of super profits to be derived from shoppers who arrived from long distances in their automobiles. They sacrificed the interests of local pedestrians and bicyclists, whose interests were subverted in the plan to build roadways into the downtown center. Leaving the ivory tower of intellectual debate, Flyvbjerg confronted local power with phronetic knowledge acquired through painstaking penetration of the particularities of a single city. Armed with a deep understanding of all backroom deals, he made several public appearances at which he parried the slander heaped on him. More important, he presented his data in such a way that the public could appreciate it. He was thus able to turn the tide away from business control of planning and back toward the interests of the pedestrians and bicyclists. The citizens of Aalborg were rewarded with democratic debate based on phronetic intervention and with an outcome closer to their own preferences.

The smoking gun in Flyvbjerg's investigation was the Aalborg Chamber of Industry and Commerce's preferred access to the technical committee of the City Council. Through this preferred access, the chamber's point of view, in which the only route to commercial survival was attracting customers from far away arriving by car, came to be seen as the "rational" one in terms of how the future was to be determined. Flyvbjerg sees this as confirming the "basic Nietzschean insight [that] 'interpretation is itself a means of becoming master of something.'" Flyvbjerg concludes, now basing his notion of power on an extended analysis not only of Aristotle and Nietzsche but also of Jürgen Habermas, Pierre Bourdieu, and Michel Foucault, that "the interpretation which has the stronger power base [namely, that of the Chamber of Industry and Commerce] becomes Aalborg's truth."[12]

There appears to be something tautological about this finding. The only way one can know the strength of the chamber's power base is to observe the degree to which it was able to make its position hegemonic. This is hardly a finding about the effects of power on the setting of interpretive frames.[13] For that we would need to know what resources translate most efficiently into the victory of hegemonic interpretations. We would further need to know the mechanisms (bribes, implicit or explicit threats to leave Aalborg and move to other cities, campaign contributions) by which certain resources are expended to secure preferred interpretations. We would also need to know how far people can be moved from their ideal points on a policy spectrum by power such as that held by the chamber. And if power is being exerted merely because those who are without it are afraid to defy those with it (and therefore, the exertion of power is not directly observable), we would need to know about the off-the-path beliefs of those without power so that we could know how they could be induced to be quiescent. Pointing out that power rules hardly explains its influence, and the two chapters of Flyvbjerg's book on power give us little handle on its prospects and merits under different contextual conditions.

To be sure, Flyvbjerg wants phronesis to answer a range of questions. The question of how power is used to create rationality is but one. He also wants social science to answer normative questions about what is desirable and what ought to be done.[14] And he wants social science to help prepare professional students "to help them achieve real practical experience."[15] I have no quarrel at all with the promotion of normative and professional pursuits, but the promotion and quality of such pursuits stand outside of the question of whether for a certain range of questions the scientific frame is appropriate for study of the social. Furthermore, in his discussion of power Flyvbjerg trespasses into the zone of science (seeking to identify the causes of the chamber's influence) without playing by its rules. This is phronesis inappropriately applied.

The Danger of Isolated Phronesis

Nothing calls out more strongly for "social science that matters" than do civil wars in the post–World War II world. In the course of the past half century, there has been a slow, steady, incessant outbreak of new civil wars throughout the world. New wars break out at a faster rate than they get settled, such that the number of active civil wars and the percentage of countries experiencing civil wars increased steadily from 1945 to 1993. In the last half century, there have been more than twelve million deaths as a result of 112 distinct civil wars. Many of these wars have cost the lives of far more than one thousand people, the minimum necessary to be included in Michigan-inspired data sets. In this category stands Sri Lanka, where more than sixty thousand people have been killed in a war pitting Tamil separatists against the majority Sinhalese government. A social science that could help reduce the devastation of civil wars would matter a great deal.

Stanley Tambiah, a world authority on Buddhism, has sought to understand the sources of violence in Sri Lanka from a perspective that Flyvbjerg would clearly agree is phronetic. Tambiah was impelled to study this conflict from a deep normative desire to make his homeland once again an island of peace. He accumulated materials related to the conflict and wrote scholarly books on it and on a related set of deadly conflicts. But he was continuously engaged with authorities in Sri Lanka; with the international press, which all too often systematically misrepresented the conflict; and with Sri Lankans around the world who were equally interested in ending a human tragedy. He examined the particular cultural and historical context of the dispute, and all his writings exhibit deep understanding of the local situation, a full recognition of the sources of local power, and a clear desire to alter the terrible curse of interethnic relations that seems to be Sri Lanka's fate.

Tambiah was at first revolted by but not engaged in Sri Lanka's troubles. In 1956 he had taken a student team with him to investigate a peasant resettlement program in the country's Eastern Province. But the project was interrupted by the first ethnic riots to take place since independence in 1948. These riots occurred when an oppressive language law was being debated in parliament. The majority Sinhalese population had been from the time of independence pressing for their language to become the medium of instruction, ultimately through the university curriculum. The language law of 1956, popularly known as the "Sinhala Only Act," promised to make Sinhalese the sole official language of the island within twenty-four hours. Tambiah, then teaching at the University of Ceylon, was immediately disenchanted and felt that he must emigrate. He felt he could not advance professionally if he were compelled to teach in Sinhalese (he is a native Tamil speaker, and English was the medium of instruction throughout his education). Furthermore, the quality of university education would, in his judgment, plummet were it to be cut off from Western scientific literature, a likely prospect were the medium of instruction to become Sinhalese. With ethnic tensions already evident on his home island, he moved his research site to Thailand.[16]

It was twenty-seven years later that Tambiah felt "compelled to take up the issues in Sri Lanka concerning ethnic conflict, ethnonationalism, and political violence."[17] A pogrom in 1983, leveled against the middle-class Tamil community in Colombo, in which ministers of the state were implicated, in his words "fractured two halves of [his] identity as a Sri Lankan and as a Tamil." He wrote *Sri Lanka: Ethnic Fratricide and the Dismantling of Democracy* to find his "way out of a depression and to cope with a personal need to make some sense of that tragedy, which was the beginning of worse things to come."[18] In the preface to that book, he acknowledges that it is not a "distanced academic treatise" but more an "engaged political tract." His goal, he writes, is "not only to understand the Sri Lankan problem but also to change it; [the book] intends to be a historical and sociological reading which necessarily suggests a course of political action."[19] One might say that the 1983 pogrom moved Tambiah from epistemic to phronetic social science.

In his subsequent work on Sri Lanka, Tambiah was never far from contemporary politics, asking such phronetic questions (ones asked by Flyvbjerg)[20] as "Where are we going, and what should be done?" He used his theoretical work on Buddhism (conducted in Thailand) to address a compelling concern of all those interested in a peaceful Sri Lanka: how could a religion that advocates nonviolence become the breeding ground for anti-Tamil pogroms? That his answer, published as *Buddhism Betrayed?*[21] was banned in Sri Lanka (and its author accused of being a terrorist) showed that he was speaking truth to power.[22]

Tambiah's accounts of the sources of the Sri Lankan civil war reflect deep concern and careful judgment. He weaves together the social, economic, religious, and political themes in a way that shows mastery of the material. He puts special emphasis on the Sinhala Only Act. "That," he has noted, was "the beginning of the feeling among Tamils that they were discriminated against by the majority."[23] Tambiah recognizes that those Tamil youths who were planning for professional employment and therefore most threatened by the language policy were not themselves involved in the riots subsequent to the language act. The worst violence occurred in the peasant-populated settlements in the Eastern Province. Tambiah therefore provides a holistic contextual account and writes, "If one wonders what could be the relationship between the official language controversy and the ethnic violence . . . the answer is . . . the language issue was also becoming interwoven with the government's policy of peasant resettlement."[24]

Sensitive to the same phronetic concern as is Flyvbjerg, that researchers address the issue in regard to any policy of "Who gains, and who loses, by which mechanisms of power?"[25] Tambiah analyzes the winning coalition. Politicized Buddhists who espoused racialist doctrines calling for the extermination of Tamils had organized this coalition. These Buddhists were able to attract into their program rural elites, teachers, indigenous doctors, traders, merchants, and all those educated in Sinhalese who were threatened by the English-speaking elites in the capital. As for the 1983 riots in which up to two thousand people were killed, Tambiah writes, "Those who stood to gain [the] most were, firstly, middle-level Sinhala entrepreneurs, businessmen, and white-collar workers, and secondly, the urban poor, mainly through looting."[26]

Tambiah's analysis is fair-minded and judicious. But what kind of truth comes from his phronetic engagement, one not combined with the statistical and formal methods? Consider first some statistical data that put a wrinkle in Tambiah's account. A cross-sectional analysis with "civil war" as the dependent variable shows that high levels of linguistic grievance are not predictors of civil war. In fact, controlling for gross domestic product, in most model specifications there is a negative sign, suggesting that higher levels of linguistic grievance are associated with a lower susceptibility to civil war. Although the idea is counterintuitive, the statistical models open the possibility that the oppressive Sinhalese language laws might have ameliorated the violence (triggered by the settlement schemes) rather than exacerbated it.[27]

The first-cut statistical test of the effects of interethnic oppression on the linguistic front raises a host of new questions, previously unasked.[28] Why, if Tamils were most threatened by the language policy, did the Sinhalese initiate most of the rioting in Colombo in both 1956 and 1958, with virtually no Tamil violence aimed at Sinhalese until 1975? Why should there have been riots after passage of the language law that were initiated by Sinhalese, inasmuch as they got the law they wanted? Why did the most horrifyingly fatal riots (those of 1981 and 1983) and the consequent full-scale Tamil rebellion occur after Tamil was accorded a status nearly equal to that of Sinhalese in Sri Lankan law? And finally, why did the language issue disappear from public debate in inverse proportion to the level of escalation of violence on the island?

The tripartite method helps to address these questions. The cross-sectional statistical data show that the holistic context of an interwoven linguistic and settlement grievance was not like two final straws on a camel's back. Rather, these two issues could well have had polar opposite impacts on the Tamil community.[29] To analyze why, it is useful to model linguistic grievances and to show what would have been each party's best response to the probable action of others. From such a model, taking into account the preferences of the parties over a range of possible outcomes, it turns out that those most aggrieved by the language act were students and teachers. The aggrieved, given their payoff schedule, would gain more from bureaucratic bargaining than they would from guerrilla attacks. From this model one can comprehend the logic by which the language laws temporarily concentrated Tamil opposition onto the bureaucratic field and politicized rather than militarized the ethnic conflict.

This same model gains plausibility because it helps us make sense of another conundrum, namely, that while the Sinhala Only Act had broad public support, its implementation was almost nonexistent. In fact, Sinhala civil servants had every interest in undermining the implementation of a law that would diminish the value of the primary skill—competence in English—that had earned them their positions. These bureaucrats wrote careful annual reports on the efforts to implement Sinhala hegemony, and in so doing perpetually delayed its fulfillment.

In this research statistical results put previous narratives under critical scrutiny. A formal model captured the strategic core of the politics of language in Sri Lanka. Thus, through a combination of statistics and formal modeling, one is now compelled to rethink the relationship of the Sinhala Only Act to the Sri Lankan civil war. But explanation does not stop there. There is a third component to scientific explanation. Complementing the statistical and formal approaches is a return to narrative to see if the truth of the case would be illuminated rather than obscured by the statistical and formal models.[30] Suppose it were the case that a return to narrative showed again that language grievances drove Tamils into guerrilla camps and into violent confrontation with the state. This knowledge would compel the statistical analyst to specify anew the interaction terms that seemed important in the narrative. If this approach should turn out to be successful, the Sri Lankan narrative would have helped yield a more powerful general statistical model. Similarly, formalists would be compelled to rethink the preferences of the actors or the structure of their interactions. Again, the goal would be the development of a general model of language grievance that could capture the effects of oppressive language laws for political action and violence.

In this case, however, the statistical and formal models helped construct a new and more coherent narrative, one that has not (according to my search through the literature) elsewhere been told. Facts that had been obscure in the Tambiah narrative can now be highlighted. For one, those educated Tamils who did not emigrate (as did Tambiah) mostly appealed their cases in the various governmental ministries to ensure their professional advance and the security of their civil service appointments. Second, as noted, the law was consistently subverted by Sinhalese government bureaucrats. More stunning is the fact that previous narratives ignored the crucial sequencing of the violence that had erupted in 1956 in response to the passage of the Sinhala Only Act. It was the Sinhalese who struck first in a violent manner, not the Tamils. A more coherent narrative (one that shows that the Tamils did not respond to the act with violence) can be told when there is knowledge that the coefficient relating language grievance to violence is negative! That this narrative has not yet been constructed is in part due to the hegemonic vision among experts that the language issue played at least some role in driving ethnic conflict into ethnic warfare.

The methodological lesson here is that social analysis requires a scientific frame, and this frame encompasses all three elements of the tripartite method. Sensitive observers saw oppression in the 1950s and civil war in the 1980s and naturally linked the two in a causal chain. In the absence of a data set including many countries, some with linguistic oppression but most without, it is impossible to ascertain whether one particular factor was ameliorating or exacerbating. Tambiah imagined a positive coefficient linking levels of linguistic grievance to the likelihood of ethnic fratricide, and he therefore viewed Sri Lanka as a case confirming his theory of ethnic warfare. But if he had pictured a negative coefficient as his model, he would have been pushed to ask why Sri Lanka was the exception, with both language grievance and violence. The narrative demands of the question "How did the linguistic grievance play into the set of grievances that led to ethnic war?" are quite different from those of the question "Why, despite linguistic grievances, Sri Lanka experienced a civil war?" In some cases, a powerful narrative would force a respecification of statistical models that had initially challenged the narrative's causal chain. Here the statistical findings induced a narrative that shed new light on an old case.

As this example of civil war violence in Sri Lanka shows, it is the interaction of statistical, formal, and narrative work that fills the scientific frame. It helps illustrate why Flyvbjerg's attempt to separate out phronesis (as a kind of narrative) from its statistical and formal complements is radically incomplete and subject to uncontrolled bias. The stark distinction that Flyvbjerg draws between phronesis and the epistemic obscures the productive complementarity of narrative, statistics, and formal analysis in social science.

The Tripartite Method in Practice

But what, it might be asked, especially by those who accept Flyvbjerg's plea for phronesis, is the positive scientific role of narrative within a tripartite method? Is my tripartite method merely giving lip service to narrative while the technological giants of formal and statistical models wash away all its value? My answer is No. I see narrative as coequal to the statistical and formal elements of the tripartite method, playing three roles. First, narrative provides plausibility tests of all formal models, helping us to assess whether a game-theoretical model actually represents a set of real-world cases. Connecting a plausible narrative with a formal model is a difficult and subtle task; doing it successfully adds plausibility to a formal model.

An exemplary use of this narrative tool is that of Robert Bates, who applied a reputation model (based on the chain-store paradox) to account for the dynamics of the rise and fall of the coffee cartel. It is often the case that formal models, absent narratives, lead researchers astray. The chain-store paradox is no exception. This formal model explains the rationality of large stores' cultivating reputations for underpricing new competition, even if it means selling at a loss until the upstart store goes bankrupt. The model can be appropriated elegantly to show how large countries leading primary product cartels can drive out of the international market those smaller countries that are seeking to lower prices to gain market share. In applying this model to the coffee cartel, Bates found that although the model was internally consistent and powerful, he could not narrate the historical sequencing of the cartel based on the moves of the reputation game because Brazil was insufficiently powerful to serve as a chain-store leader. Thus the narrative compelled him to rethink the strategic logic and to apply a different analytic tool. It turned out that a spatial model of coalition formation within the largest purchasing country (the United States)—in which a cold war logic provided American support for high-priced imports—explained how a dispersed set of sellers could maintain an oligopoly price as long as they did and why it fell apart when the cold war waned. The narrative did not prove the reputation model wrong; rather, it showed that it was an inappropriate representation of the strategic situation that faced the coffee-exporting countries.[31] Elegant formal models standing alone are inadequate; they need to be supplemented by narrative to show that the real world is represented in the models. Thus narrative adds plausibility to formal models.

The second role of narrative is to provide mechanisms linking independent and dependent variables in statistical analyses. It is quite common in social science to find explanatory power in macro variables such as gross domestic product (GDP) per capita, or democracy, or ethnic linguistic fractionization (a dispersion index giving the probability that an individual randomly matched with another in his or her country will be of the same ethnic group). The problem is that such social facts as GDP are more likely facilitating conditions rather than causal forces. They do not have the capacity to alter the values of a dependent variable. It is therefore difficult to assess what it means for GDP to be causal for some outcome, such as democracy or civil war. As Elster has taught us, we need to link independent and dependent variables with mechanisms, basically showing how conditions that are favorable from a statistical standpoint translate into outcomes.[32]

For example, Adam Przeworski and associates show the statistical link between parliamentary rule and stable democracy (with everything else held to mean value). This means that parliamentary democracies are more robust against economic shocks than are presidential systems.[33] But this finding requires a mechanism to give it causal weight. This has led Przeworski (and other collaborators) to examine exogenous shocks in a narrative mode to figure out which of the scores of mechanisms listed in the literature are actually causal. One early conjecture was that in parliamentary systems governments face no-confidence votes and are likely to fall. But here the government, not the democracy, is challenged. Because presidents have fixed terms and there is no institution with the constitutional authority to vote the president out of office for weak performance, in a presidential system an exogenous shock is likely to invite the army to compel the president to leave office. When this occurs, not only the government but also the democratic regime falls. So in this example the no-confidence weapon is the mechanism (found through narrative but then complemented with a formal model and statistical tests) that gives the original statistical finding causal weight. This conjecture remains provisional. Although one of the papers to emerge from this search for mechanisms emphasizes statistical tests and formal proofs,[34] the narrative mode was the source of insight into the relevant mechanisms.

In providing plausibility to formal models and mechanisms for statistical models, it is sometimes the case that the role of narrative is obscured in the final presentation of scientific work. Consider an exemplary model of the use of the tripartite method, Randall Stone's *Lending Credibility*.[35] This study assesses the impact of International Monetary Fund (IMF) conditionality programs on economic performance in the former Soviet states. Numerous earlier studies found only mixed results. Sometimes the IMF impact was positive, and other times negative, bolstering the accepted view that the IMF was no nostrum for structural maladjustment. Through careful (one might say phronetic) investigations Stone figured out that the IMF succeeded only where its threats (to cut a country off from further loans) were credible. For large countries of great strategic value to the United States, however, such threats were not credible, as these countries knew that the United States would bail them out if they defaulted. Stone therefore created a model of credibility that predicted where the IMF would have success, and his statistical tests confirmed the observable implications of the theory. As expected, strategically important countries were punished more often, but the periods of their punishment were shorter. Also, they were less likely to keep inflation under control and less likely to attract foreign investment.

Stone's narratives helped him develop the formal model that was then put to statistical test. The very success of the model meant, however, that there were few surprises or new causal conjectures in the chapters that included narratives of particular countries that received IMF support. One might say that the findings of the narratives had already been eaten up by the formal model and statistical tests. The four chapters narrating how the model worked in the cases of Russia, Ukraine, Poland, and Bulgaria therefore fell flat. This was not because narrative was not important; rather, it was because the findings from the narratives fit the specifications for a statistical model such that there was little new to add in the ultimate telling of the country-level stories.

As Stone's work illustrates, mechanisms are in some cases no more than underspecified intervening variables. To the extent that a narrative provides the appropriate mechanism, it is incumbent on the researcher to specify the values of that mechanism and run the statistical model again with a new variable. If the mechanism turned variable fails in a significance test, it should give us pause as to whether it really was the causal link between the independent and the dependent variables. But if it proves significant statistically, and it gets built into a formal model, adding it to the narrative will make it appear that the narrative is secondary. In fact, the narrative was the source of the correctly specified causal mechanism.

Suppose, however, that there are several mechanisms linking a set of values of right-hand-side variables to a specific value of a dependent variable. The favorable right-hand-side conditions might be thought of as opening a set of separate pathways toward the same value of the dependent variable. In such cases, all of the mechanisms could fail statistical tests even if properly specified, because none could account for more than a small subset of the observations.[36] A statistician might respond by saying that the mechanisms were not properly specified because the conditions under which they were conjectured to operate ("a small subset of the observations") were not adequately operationalized in the statistical model via interactions, nonlinearities, and so on. Even if there were not enough data for signal to overwhelm noise at conventional levels of statistical significance, Bayesians have developed methods to squeeze significance even when faced with problems of "degrees of freedom." But as pathways multiply, these techniques become increasingly tenuous. Under such conditions, narrative would need to stand alone, and rules of narrative coherence and completeness would help to decide whether the causal structure was as theorized. Here narrative would be providing a more apparent value added than in the case in which there was a single mechanism that linked right- and left-hand-side variables.

But even in a case in which there is a single mechanism, one that holds up to statistical scrutiny, narrative plays a third role through the analysis of residuals. Never in social science is all variance explained, and even if powerful models are used, the amount that we are able to explain is often paltry. Narrative, by giving a more complete picture of a social process, fills in the picture when statistical and formal models have left it incomplete. In the case of Stone's narratives, we learn that in Poland Finance Minister Leszek Balcerowicz was more committed to showing the credibility of Poland's reform to international capital than was the IMF. In the narrative, part of the causal weight goes to the charismatic and technical mastery of Balcerowicz over politicians on both the left and the right sides of the political spectrum. We have few tools that enable us to model formally or test statistically the role of charismatic leadership in fostering reform. Yet in this case it may well have had causal weight, especially because Stone reveals that Poland was quite important strategically to the West, and this should have made its leaders more likely to defy the IMF and to inflate the currency.[37] Examination of the residuals through narratives plants the seeds for future work that can better specify and model causal factors that carried weight in the narratives but were absent from the statistical and formal models.

Thus three scientific roles are entrusted to narratives in social science. First, they provide plausibility tests of formal models. Second, they provide mechanisms that link statistically significant facilitating conditions to outcomes. And third, through the plotting of residuals they plant the seeds for future specifications of variables that have not yet been successfully modeled. In no sense is the phronetic part of the scientific enterprise a marginal one.

The Aristotelian division between episteme and phronesis, as applied by Flyvbjerg, maps well onto recent methodological debates within political science, as evidenced in Mr. Perestroika's assault on the disciplinary hegemons, between rational choice and qualitative research. Like Flyvbjerg in regard to epistemic science, supporters of qualitative research equivocate about the long-term prospects of rational choice modeling in the social sciences. But, at a minimum, Mr. Perestroika's acolytes call for methodological pluralism.[38] The approach taken to science in this chapter, while carrying no brief against pluralism, entails a caution against a pluralism that sees formal and statistical research as only two of a thousand flowers that should be permitted to bloom.

The caution is to insist that if theoretical logic or scientific evidence finds a theory or procedure fallacious, that procedure's flowerbed should no longer be cultivated within the discipline in which it was originally seeded. There can be no hope of cumulation if we insist that all methods, and all procedures, must be protected. A few examples of unjustified pluralism follow. Consider first the method of case selection used in comparative politics. The community of comparativists once considered it a useful exercise to choose a set of cases that had the same interesting outcome (for example, modernization breakdowns) to learn what causes it. Subsequent work in the methods field called this procedure "selecting on the dependent variable" and showed why it ultimately leads to faulty inferences about causation.[39]

Similarly, many statistically oriented scholars in the field of international relations relied on logistic regressions to analyze binary time-series data on whether there was an outbreak of war in a given year. This procedure was found to lead, at least in some cases, to invalid inferences. The authors who reported the bias showed that this problem can be corrected by using a set of dummy variables tapping unmeasured serial dependence in the data (e.g., the longer a spell of peace, the less likely a war, ceteris paribus).[40] It would be a scientific travesty should one group of international relations specialists demand that statistical modelers who do not correct for serial dependence have a right to continue what they were doing simply because there is a long tradition in cross-sectional work that has in the past ignored problems of time dependence.

A final example: comparativists who do qualitative case studies have no claim to disciplinary recognition by virtue of the fact that examination of a single case is a time-honored procedure in their field. Theoretical work going back to Harry Eckstein sets constraints on what a particular case can show.[41] More recent methodological work, exemplified in the text by Gary King, Robert Keohane, and Sidney Verba, provides a road map showing how a study of a single country can be transformed into a large n research design, thereby increasing the study's scientific leverage.[42] There can be no argument based on tradition justifying the minimization of leverage. If new work in comparative politics is to gain respect in the wider discipline, it must adjust methodologically to take into account scientific advances. Pluralism without updating is not science.

This point is doubly important when fields come to be defined by positions in grand debates and are protected by tradition. It would warp the scientific frame if we built into the charter of any department of political science that there had to be an expert in "realism," or in "South Asia," or in "democracy," or in "qualitative methods." Of course advertising jobs by area of specialization is crucial, especially if a department seeks broad disciplinary coverage. But institutionalizing slots for particular specialties is a threat to scientific progress. Consider a document from seventeenth-century Spain in which the University of Barcelona appealed to the king's audience for the right to sidestep interference in its affairs by the Council of Castile, which had stipulated that the department of philosophy was to have three professors who held to Thomist views and three who did not.[43] Three centuries later, it appears quaint that a philosophy department should be divided along those lines. But the implications of such royal charters are dangerous. When any academic field consecrates a debate by giving interlocutors on both sides permanent representation, the result can only be resistance to innovation. A scientific frame would lead us to expect that certain fields will become defunct, certain debates dead, and certain methods antiquated. A pluralism that shelters defunct practitioners cannot be scientifically justified.

Flyvbjerg at his most generous is calling for pluralism but giving pride of place to an alternate methodology for the social sciences, going back to Aristotle's recommendations. But rather than accepting an alternate methodology, in this chapter I ask that we all work inside a scientific frame. Within that frame, we ought to maximize inter alia openness of procedures, internal coherence of argument, good measurement of variables, increasing attempts to unravel context, assiduous concern for valid causal inferences, and rewards for replication. Along with formal and statistical analysis, narratively based case studies (one element of the procedures Flyvbjerg recommends as phronesis) play a crucial role in filling in this frame;[44] but there is nothing to be gained in advertising a program that does not insist on the best approximation to science that the data and our abilities will allow.

Notes

An earlier version of this chapter appeared in *Politics and Society,* Vol. 31, No. 1 (March 2003): 163–83, © 2003 Sage Publications, reprinted by permission of Sage Publications. The author thanks Nathaniel Beck, Kanchan Chandra, Jon Elster, Simon Jackman, Steven Lukes, Sidney Tarrow, and Charles Tilly for comments on an earlier draft of this chapter.

1. "Mr. Perestroika" is the pen name of an anonymous insurgent or group within the political science discipline. This volume is a testimony to the success of this individual or group in raising issues of professional and intellectual concern.

2. Bent Flyvbjerg, *Making Social Science Matter: Why Social Inquiry Fails and How It Can Succeed Again* (Cambridge: Cambridge University Press, 2001).

3. In his review of this book for the *American Political Science Review* (March 2002), Stephen White emphasizes that Flyvbjerg's book ought to serve as the foil for a fully articulated negative response to "Mr. Perestroika."

4. Flyvbjerg equivocates throughout the book on the question of whether scientific work has any merit in the study of the social world. On one hand, he writes, "it is . . . not meaningful to speak of 'theory' in the study of social phenomena, at least not in the sense that 'theory' is used in natural science" (25). On the other hand, he acknowledges the value of "attempts at formal generalization, for such attempts are essential and effective means of scientific development" (76). Despite these occasional nods to the value of a social science (see also formulations on pp. 49 and 87), his major theme is that "we must drop the fruitless efforts to emulate natural science's success in producing cumulative and predictive theory" (166). He does not provide evidence on the degree to which natural science research meets his standards.

5. The tripartite approach recommended here is more fully developed in David D. Laitin, "Comparative Politics: The State of the Subdiscipline," in *The State*

of the Discipline, ed. Ira Katznelson and Helen Milner (New York: Norton, 2002). In a critique of the tripartite approach that I recommend, Sanford Schram argues in "Beyond Paradigm: Resisting the Assimiliation of Phronetic Social Science" (*Politics and Society,* September 2004) that it is a "top-down perspective" insouciant as to what can be learned from ethnography. Not only is this claim a grievous misreading of my position, but it also ignores the fundamental challenge my position offers to those who hold that statistical or formal analysis is sufficient for making valid inferences about the social world.

6. I know of three prominent contributions along these lines. Robert Axelrod (political science) has collaborated with William D. Hamilton (biology) in "The Evolution of Cooperation," *Science,* New Series, Vol. 211, No. 4489 (March 27, 1981): 1390–96; Reinhard Selten (economics) has collaborated with Peter Hammerstein (biology) in "Game Theory and Evolutionary Biology," in *Handbook of Game Theory,* ed. Robert J. Aumann and Sergiu Hart (Amsterdam: Elsevier, 1994), Vol. 2, 929–93; and Robert Boyd (anthropology) has collaborated with Peter J. Richerson (ecology) in *Culture and the Evolutionary Process* (Chicago: University of Chicago Press, 1985).

7. See a summary discussion on this matter at http://www.cdc.gov/mmwr/preview/mmwrhtml/00001277.htm. While acknowledging validity problems due to the sensitivity of the questions, the team reported that "most Americans appear to be at relatively low risk of infection with HIV-1 and other STDs from sexual exposures." See also Edward O. Laumann, John H. Gagnon, Robert T. Michael, and Stuart Michaels, *The Social Organization of Sexuality* (Chicago: University of Chicago Press, 1994), 546–47.

8. Flyvbjerg, *Making Social Science Matter,* p. 22, where he implies that the model is insufficiently phronetic.

9. For an extensive review of this literature, see Robyn M. Dawes, David Faust, and Paul E. Meehl, "Clinical versus Actuarial Judgment," *Science,* New Series, Vol. 243, No. 4899 (March 31, 1989): 1668–74.

10. "Context is central to understanding what social science is and can be" (Flyvbjerg, *Making Social Science Matter,* 9). There are nineteen other references to this term in the index. Chapter 4 is called "Context Counts."

11. Flyvbjerg, *Making Social Science Matter,* 139.

12. Ibid., 153.

13. In fairness to Flyvbjerg, there is more explicit attention to mechanisms in his full study, *Rationality and Power: Democracy in Practice* (Chicago: University of Chicago Press, 1998).

14. Flyvbjerg, *Making Social Science Matter,* 145.

15. Ibid., 72.

16. Stanley Tambiah, "Continuity, Integration and Expanding Horizons" (an interview with Mariza Peirano), *Série Antropologia,* No. 230, Departamento de Antropologia, Universidade de Brasília, 1997, 8–10.

17. Ibid., 14.

18. Ibid., 26.

19. Stanley Tambiah, *Sri Lanka: Ethnic Fratricide and the Dismantling of Democracy* (Chicago: University of Chicago Press, 1986), ix.

20. Flyvbjerg, *Making Social Science Matter,* 145.

21. Stanley Tambiah, *Buddhism Betrayed?* (Chicago: University of Chicago Press, 1992).

22. Tambiah, "Continuity," 26–27.

23. Ibid., 9.

24. Tambiah, *Buddhism Betrayed?* 57 and 47.

25. Flyvbjerg, *Making Social Science Matter,* 145.

26. Tambiah, *Sri Lanka,* 20–27; Stanley Tambiah, *Leveling Crowds* (Berkeley: University of California Press, 1996), 100.

27. These points are developed in David D. Laitin, "Language Conflict and Violence," *Archives Européennes de Sociologie,* Vol. 41, No. 1 (1997): 97–137. The subsequent discussion draws on that article, without use of quotation marks.

28. The results would be more compelling if the magnitudes of the effects were properly analyzed so that something could be said about substantive significance of the negative relationship between language oppression and violence. The point here, however, is not to infer a negative relationship supported by the data but to wonder why there was no strong positive relationship, as standard theories of grievance had led us to expect there would be.

29. James Fearon and I address the issue of why settlement schemes more likely yield guerrilla action in "Sons of the Soil," an unpublished manuscript (for the most current version, go to www.stanford.edu/~dlaitin).

30. Many in the narrative tradition claim that narratives ought to be formalized. It may well be that both game trees and narrative are formal models but perform complementary tasks in scientific explanation. If this were the case, the terms referring to the tripartite agenda would require adjustment.

31. Robert Bates, "The International Coffee Organization: An International Institution," in *Analytic Narratives,* ed. Robert Bates, Avner Grief, Margaret Levi, et al. (Princeton, NJ: Princeton University Press, 1998). The references for the chain-store paradox are Reinhard Selten, "The Chain-Store Paradox," *Theory and Decision,* Vol. 9 (1978): 127–59, and David Kreps and Robert Wilson, "Reputation and Imperfect Information," *Journal of Economic Theory,* Vol. 27 (1982): 253–79.

32. Jon Elster, "A Plea for Mechanisms," in *Social Mechanisms: An Analytical Approach to Social Theory,* ed. Peter Hedstrøm and Richard Swedberg (Cambridge: Cambridge University Press, 1998), 45–73. Techniques to assess causal mechanisms without the use of narrative include experiments and recently developed random-matching models in statistics. See Judea Pearl, *Causality* (Cambridge: Cambridge University Press, 2000), for explications of these techniques. I remain skeptical that either the experimental or the statistical innovations will supplant narrative in helping to uncover the causal mechanisms linking values of independent variables to values of dependent variables.

33. Adam Przeworski, Michael Alvarez, José Antonio Cheibub, and Fernando Limong, *Democracy and Development: Political Institutions and Well-Being in the World 1950–1990* (Cambridge: Cambridge University Press, 2000). Random-matching techniques (see Pearl, *Causality*) allow us to avoid the unrealistic assumption that other independent variables have comparable values in parliamentary and presidential regimes.

34. José Antonio Cheibub, Adam Przeworski, and Sebastian Saiegh, "Government Coalitions and Legislative Effectiveness under Presidentialism and Parliamentarism," unpublished paper, 2002, subsequently published in the *British Journal of Political Science,* Vol. 34 (2004): 565–87.

35. Randall Stone, *Lending Credibility* (Princeton, NJ: Princeton University Press, 2002).

36. I believe this is at least part of what Elster is suggesting with his view that mechanisms will almost never reveal statistically significant relationships.

37. Stone, *Lending Credibility*, 99.

38. See John J. Mearsheimer, "Methodological Parochialism vs. Methodological Pluralism," paper presented for Panel 7-1, "Perestroika: Undisciplined, Unpunished," APSA meetings, San Francisco, August 31, 2001.

39. Barbara Geddes, "How the Cases You Choose Affect the Answers You Get: Selection Bias in Comparative Politics," *Political Analysis*, Vol. 2 (1990): 131–50.

40. Nathaniel Beck, Jonathan N. Katz, and Richard Tucker, "Taking Time Seriously: Time-Series Cross-Section Analysis with a Binary Dependent Variable," *American Journal of Political Science*, Vol. 42, No. 4 (1998): 1260–88.

41. Harry Eckstein, "Case Study and Theory in Political Science," in *Handbook of Political Science*, Vol. 1, ed. Fred Greenstein and Nelson Polsby (Reading, MA: Addison-Wesley, 1975).

42. Gary King, Robert Keohane, and Sidney Verba, *Designing Social Inquiry* (Princeton, NJ: Princeton University Press, 1994).

43. Case number 064, from the year 1681, from a data set of 617 documents from seventeenth- and eighteenth-century Spain housed in the Rare Book Division of the Princeton University Library.

44. This argument applies to my promotion of the tripartite method. In response to a critic of their article cited earlier, Dawes, Faust, and Meehl point out that although the results are not conclusive, clinical predictions appear to be better if researchers rely on statistical models only and ignore clinical judgments by experts. See Benjamin Kleinmuntz, David Faust, Paul E. Meehl, and Robyn M. Douglas, *Science*, New Series, Vol. 247, No. 4939 (1990): 146–47. Should it be demonstrated that narrative judgments add no explanatory or predictive value in political science (which I doubt would occur), it would be in defiance of the scientific frame to continue insisting on use of the tripartite method.

CHAPTER 10

Interpretation and Institution

Rational Choice and the Problem of Social Action

Brian Caterino

From of the last third of the nineteenth century until the start of the First World War, German philosophers and social scientists engaged in a contentious dispute about the nature and aims of social inquiry.[1] This methodological controversy (*Methodenstreit*) had two major dimensions. The first took place between marginal utility theorists and the historical school of economics. It focused on the foundations of social-scientific analysis. Could theory be founded, as classical economic theory claimed, on a fixed and a historical concept of rationally self-interested economic man, or did it require a historically oriented theory of economic development that treats cultural contexts as a source of unique significance? The second was the philosophical controversy that arose in post-Hegelian philosophy between positivism and its opponents. These disputes questioned whether the social sciences were to model themselves after the more successful natural sciences, which followed the covering law model of explanation, or whether they should employ a unique method of study for social and cultural phenomena. Whereas the deductive nomological model aimed at explanation of events through general laws, the interpretive model of the human sciences held that the primary goal of the human sciences is the interpretation and explication of the meaning of the symbolic expressions of culture.

For interpretive social theorists, who drew on the insights of hermeneutics, understanding was fundamentally distinguished from explanation because the former was concerned with the way that cultural expressions and "objectifications" reflect inner processes, while explanation draws on strictly "external" connections. In contrast to the external observer or third person perspective, proponents of the *Geisteswissenschaften* conceptualized understanding in opposition to what they saw as the methodological solipsism of modern thought. Understanding, on this line of reasoning, takes place in the context of a preexisting ethical community. As Johann Droysen argued: "Historical research does not intend to explain i.e. to derive the later from the earlier, or to derive phenomena from laws in terms of which they can be seen to be necessary, to be mere effects or developments. If the logical necessity of the later lay in the earlier, there would be an analogue to the eternal matter and material processes, not the ethical world. If historical life were the reproduction of what always remains the same, it would be without ethical content, hence only organic matter."[2] Individuals have access to this world through their position as participants in the social world, and they have access to the world thought these interpretations. The importance of the issues of interpretative access to the world through the participants' perspective remains central to the debates today.

Following a (postbehavioral) period of diffuseness, a new round of methodological disputes arose in political science and sociology.[3] By incorporating elements of interpretive social theory, such as contextually situated values and expectations, into explanatory frameworks, proponents of rational choice institutionalism argue they can now account for elements of genesis and historical development that have traditionally been the domain of comparative and historical theories. Some versions have rejected the covering law model and claim to explain singular historical constellations rather than to subsume events under general laws.[4] Rational choice theorists have attempted to incorporate elements of the "horizon of expectations" employed by interpretive analysis.

I want to examine two versions of rational choice theory, neo-institutionalism and analytic narratives, which have modified rational choice theory in order to address the issues of history genesis and social order raised by interpretive social theory. I will argue that the encounter is at best incomplete. Modification leads to a tension between retained elements of the strong version of rational choice theory and the requirements of interpretive theory. As a result, interpretive elements are subordinated to rational choice explanations. A broader integration of interpretive theory is needed.

Questions of historical understanding, such as those developed in the interpretive approach, lead us to consider the capacity of individuals to critically assess and appropriate the understanding of their times. In this way interpretive theories bear a relation, not always fully developed, to critical theories of society. It is the nature of this critical and reflective capacity that has traditionally been at issue between partisans in the dispute. The neo-institutional approach, in spite of some merits, cannot incorporate this critical dimension.

Rational Choice Fundamentalism: The Foundational Project

In Jon Elster's formulation, rational choice is a micro-foundational project.[5] Like the successful natural sciences (physics, chemistry, biology), rational choice theory seeks to find the most elementary unit of analysis, in this case the self-interested individual who seeks to maximize his or her benefit, and build up a theory that can explain social phenomena. This elementary unit, in Elster's view, corresponds with the assumptions of methodological individualism. The explanation of social and political phenomena can dispense with holistic or "dialectical" premises and proceed from the initial condition of individual behavior to construct complex models of social behavior. Rational choice did not always adopt the methods of logical positivism, but it certainly displayed a positivist temper. It employed the positivist and scientific conception of theory as an integrated body of propositions governed by the covering law model. William Riker saw theory as "a body of related and verified generalizations, which describe occurrences accurate enough to be of use for prediction."[6] For Riker, science was empirical. Its data were confined to those statements that "objectively" described states of affairs and were free of value judgments and presuppositions.[7] While Riker recognized that the actions of participants are value-relevant, he adhered to the idea that there is a gap between the observing theorist and the participant. This "strong version" of rational choice was fundamentalist: it sought a universal and comprehensive foundation of the science of social behavior.

In the fundamentalist version of rational choice, theory is linked to instrumental reason. Theory generates the type of knowledge that enhances our effectiveness in achieving desired outcomes through prediction and control. Peter Ordeshook illustrated this view when he distinguished between theorists (scientists), who discover fundamental laws of political life, and engineers, who apply them.[8] Practice is a matter of technique. The flaws in this conception of the relation of knowledge to practical activity are obvious. When social policy is the value-free application of laws like those of nature to social life, it bypasses reference to the normative conceptions of the good or the just. Yet the consent of participants seems a necessary feature of legitimacy. Policy must ask the question "Who decides what is a desirable state of affairs, and why it is desirable?"

From its inception, however, rational choice fundamentalism employed an ambiguous conception of action. Was rational choice a theory of behavior or a theory of social action? Action is meaningful behavior interpreted by participants, and it cannot be redescribed in neutral language. Riker again illustrates this dilemma. Following David Easton's definition of politics as the authoritative allocation of values, Riker notes that authority requires deliberate choices (intentional action). Still he fails to grasp the tension inherent in the fact that political authority is subjectively meaningful action. Legitimacy must be grasped from the standpoint of a participant who finds a law or form of political authority legitimate.

Rational Choice and Social Action: Modifications, Round 1

In response to criticism, most proponents of rational choice theory now interpret it as a theory of normative analytic social action. This reading of rational choice theory rejects the assumptions that theory is value-free. Rational choice is a *prescriptive* theory that tells us what we ought to do if we want to achieve an outcome in which our preferences are optimized. In a polemical exchange with Theodore Lowi, Randall Calvert argues that a postpositivist version of rational choice avoids the pitfalls of its predecessors. He believes that critics of rational choice have mistaken the relation between "politics, ideology and science."[9] Rational choice theories are normative. They can "generate endogenous institutions, social norms, cultural elements, socially induced habits or rules of thumb, and other factors that can override individual calculations of myopic selfish gain."[10]

Rational choice theorists believe that they have avoided the atomism of Thomas Hobbes's position. Although they begin analysis of action from Hobbesian notions of the initial conditions of social action—with the situation of the individual subject who acts under conditions of scarcity to maximize the satisfaction of desires—they distinguish strategic social action from purely purposive rational action. In the ideal type of purposive rational action, an individual can act on nature (as a singular subject) in order to obtain an outcome or achieve a goal. In strategic action, outcomes always involve the preferences of others. Social action, as Max Weber defined it, is any action in which individuals affect or are affected by the action of others.[11] For Peter Ordeshook, game theory models individual decision making when people's fates are interdependent and "when people are aware of their interdependence."[12] Strategic actors must *take into account the preferences of others* if they are to maximize their own return. The object of rational choice theory is forms of collective social action or, more precisely, questions of aggregation.

It is not immediately clear that the notion of aggregation avoids the problem of atomism. After all, an aggregation is not a group with a common identity or a common orientation. The problem stems from a one-dimensional reduction of social action to strategic action. The latter is defined as a type of action oriented to success. Actors assess action according to its effectiveness in influencing the decisions of others in order to achieve optimal results. Consistent with the utilitarian roots of this concept of action, norms are hypothetical imperatives; they prescribe the courses of action that are necessary to achieve a goal. Rational choice theory is not seen as empirical social science aimed at prediction, but as a formal model of normative social action. It tells us what we would do if we acted in a purely strategic fashion given certain initial conditions. To be sure, rational choice theory still seeks the causal explanation of social action. It has to take a different route to that goal. Here games are like ideal types. They serve as pure models of strategic rationality from which to gauge actions. Ironically, the more formal account of strategic action opens the way to historical-genetic accounts. Models are essentially synchronic. To have explanatory power they have be interpreted diachronically, in space and time.

Interaction is expressible though a series of moves between strategically rational actors in a "game." The problem of coordinating social action is "solved" by establishing equilibrium among outcomes or preferences. Preferences are stabilized, and order is created (as in the case of Nash equilibrium), when no participant has an incentive to change preferences. The achievement of order is a form of self-organization without reference to consent or legitimacy. Social order has force because no alternatives seem better. Coordination is achieved through the outcomes of action.

The goal of modeling the binding character of action as a function of self-sustaining strategic action has proved elusive. In many cases, optimal equilibrium solutions do not exist for every problem. In other cases, equilibrium solutions are suboptimal. In still others, a number of different equilibria can "solve" a problem. This has led to analyses of political institutions as either irrational (as in the case of voting studies) or simply incapable of generating a self-sustaining order. The classical example of this problem is found in William Riker's work on democracy.[13]

The normative analytic version of rational choice represents a first set of modifications to the strong version. Rejecting positivism, it looks to meaningful social action to solve questions of method and social order. There are, however, some serious questions as to whether this set of modifications meets the requirements of interpretive theory. The first question is whether the foundational project can provide a model of interpretive access to the social world. The strategic actor *takes account of others;* the interpretive participant *is accountable to others.* At best, strategic action is an incomplete account of intersubjectivity. It is doubtful, then (turning to the second question), whether any modification of strategic action can model the forms of identification required to analyze questions of our ties to others. Rational choice theories often yield implausible results, not simply because of an exclusive methodological focus, but because of an inadequate conception of social action.[14] Democratic institutions and practices, for example, can be adequately understood not as outcomes of strategic actions, but only as modes of mutual understanding and mutual accountability. Democracy is a way of conducting our political relations with each other.

Neo-Institutionalism and Social Action: Modifications, Round 2

The second modification of rational choice theory involves the introduction of values and norms as genetic features of social order. Kenneth Shepsle, generally considered the originator of rational choice institutionalism, proposed to modify rational choice theory by finding an alternative basis for social order. In spite of the emphasis of "classical" rational choice theories on the aggregation of social action, Shepsle argues, these theories remain atomistic and undersocialized. "Rationality based theories," he maintains, "worry hardly at all about the sources of preferences and beliefs."[15] "Classical" rational choice theories are based on market models. The idea is that equilibrium rests in the core—that is, with the self-sustaining order generated by unbounded aggregate choices. For Shepsle, however, the failure of rational choice theories to fulfill this goal indicates that the "glue," the binding force of social or political relations, lies elsewhere. Against core models of equilibrium, Shepsle proposes a model of structure-induced equilibrium in order to explain the ways in which institutional rules of order rather than core games can underlie equilibrium. Such rules represent background conditions of order that influence or select out equilibrium in less than optimal conditions.

Shepsle introduces a diachronic, historical dimension into his analysis. He argues that institutions are examples of sequential games. These differ from standard games because they have a temporal and social order dependent on prior conditions. Individuals in such games are particulars, that is, named individuals rather than general and anonymous, and they act in an order that is dictated by social role, status, and authority.

Randall Calvert endorses the institutional turn in rational choice theory, but notes the ambiguous status of common values and expectations. He develops a theory of institutions that is more consistent with the methodological individualism of rational choice theory.[16] Calvert agrees with Shepsle that neo-classical theories are ill suited to analysis of the emergence of or transition to well-formed intuitional systems.[17] Neo-classical theories assume a well-functioning if imperfect market system, and they also assume widespread acceptance or compliance with the market system. They also assume that basic structures of economic and political life, such as property rights, are stable and that media of exchange are intact.

In focusing on just those questions that neoclassicists have taken for granted, the establishment of market conditions and institutions, rational choice theorists address questions of the genesis and change of institutional design. Under these conditions, questions of cooperation and coordination of action are central. Neo-institutionalism aims to explain how institutions lead actors to work together and why there are stable sets of rules. For neo-institutionalists these are *normative* questions. Focus on the coordination of action connects them to the problems of traditional moral theory and to the sociological questions of the rise of normative structures. Jack Knight and Itai Sened note: "The key to understanding the importance of social institutions lies in the role they play in the formation of expectations and beliefs. The problem here is one of establishing expectations about the actions of either players in the game; the formation of such expectations is a prerequisite for making a rational choice."[18]

The problem with Shepsle's approach, according to Calvert, is its implicitly holistic character. Like Emile Durkheim, some proponents of institutionalism employ an overly socialized account of institutions in which the "social" represents a distinctive level of analysis, logically and analytically separate from individual behavior. Durkheim's model of functional explanation is circular. It presupposes what needs to be explained: the binding power of social actions. Shepsle, who understands institutional rules as constraints, partially avoids Durkheim's problem but still takes for granted a well-functioning set of constraints. He assumes that constraints cannot be violated. For Calvert, however, the only account consistent with rational choice explains why individuals obey: they are motivated by self-interest. The institutions-as-constraint model fails to address the question of why institutions succeed or fail in "constraining individual behavior in some circumstances and not in others." It fails to explain why individuals change their preferences.[19] Institutions must be composed of individual actions or, more specifically, of preferences. Calvert defines institutions as "behavior patterns of individuals and their expectations about the behavior of others."[20]

Issues of social action unavoidably involve the coordination of action plans. For Calvert these are problems encountered by several individuals or more in situations in which they must act together to reach a goal. Coordination problems arise from imperfect communication or disagreement about which action is best. We cannot, in fact, plan or choose from alternatives without a sense of the plans of others. Institutions then require some level of coordination of action plans among social actors.

Given his commitment to individualism, Calvert seeks to understand the features of mutual expectations primarily as an aspect of equilibrium. Calvert argues: "An institution is equilibrium in the underlying game and different institutional structures correspond to the different equilibria that remain constant. The institutions as equilibrium model suggests that we define an institution within a group of individuals as an equilibrium in which individuals are dependent on the past actions of many others, or upon expectations about the future reactions of many others to one's present actions."[21]

For neo-institutionalists, then, institutions represent "structures" of rules within which individuals act to attain their goal and maximize their outcomes but also act within normative constraints.

Calvert is correct to point to the limits in Shepsle's account of the overly socialized conception of the binding force of social action, but he fails to recognize the force in Shepsle's critique of the latent atomism of rational choice theory. The seeming aporias of social action generated by the primacy of strategic action suggest that the foundational project has limits.

Calvert does not take this path. He retains the foundational aim of the strong version and views the structure-building force of social action through the aggregation of strategic action. While norms and expectations may provide the mortar of social action, strategic action remains the bricks. Institutions are essentially structured as markets are— as arrangements of aggregate choices guided by rules and expectations. Calvert remains attached to the initial conditions set out by rational choice theory: the need for singular individuals to cooperate in forming social order. "In the absence of any inherent motivation for it," he asks, "why do people cooperate sometime?"[22]

A more apt analogy, however, would be to consider social life a dense web of relations of mutual accountability that link members of a community. There is no distinction between bricks and mortar. The web is the structure and the binding force. Social and political institutions are media through which individuals create and renew their relations with others; they come to be what they are through commitments and projects in which they take a position on their common world. The structure-building power of institutions lies in communicative rather than strategic action.

Strategic Misinterpretations: Modal Overload

As long as the neo-institutionalist program is still committed to a foundational project, it must account for noninstrumental action such as values, expectations, and norms in terms of strategic action. Calvert takes a broad view of strategic action; for him it is not egocentric action, but any action that influences the pursuit of a goal in the social context. He treats alternative forms of social action as *modalities* of strategic action. Consider two examples: cooperation and expressive action.

Cooperation is not a type of action motivated by immediate self-interest, but a type of action in which short-term goals are sacrificed for long-term benefit. Actions that are not immediately egocentric can serve long-term success in action.[23] Similarly, Garrett Hardin argues that ethnic identities are constructed from forms of self-interest; that is, as a modality of action in which benefit derives from collective action: "Ethnic identification is an equilibrium that requires members to contribute to the group's collective action; it also requires that each member engage in symbolic expression indicating that he or she upholds the prescribed behaviors, and requires that members follow prescribed ways of interacting with others to facilitate pairwise and small-group co-operation."[24]

Through this collective identification, however, ethnic groups are able to mobilize resources to achieve outcomes. In this respect, identities are elements of political processes, not simply social psychological ones. They are elements in a political conception of power as seen in coordination relationships; power "involves that ability to direct the concerted behavior of numerous people."[25] Here "power" is basically a strategic inducement to act as a form of power over others.[26] In surveying recent work on voting behavior, for example, Calvert contends that an expressive public regarding behavior such as honesty can be related to the strategic aim of establishing a reputation. The latter is strategic in the sense that it "creates expectations that one will act in a certain way." It "engenders behavior in an agent's principals that benefits the agent."[27]

Reputation is an element of "expressive action" that signals one's own intentions or preferences. To identify with a group would mean to share and express expectations with members of that group that prescribe how specific forms of behavior will be rewarded through the "values" of the group.[28]

Overloading the modalities of strategic action provides no remedy for the limits of a one-sided account of action. Ultimately these other "modes" assert their stubborn independence. Calvert admits this in more recent work: Rational choice theory "requires supplementation in order to give a full account of identity and expressive phenomena."[29] Even a perfect model of rational choice cannot predict how individuals will behave without additional assumptions about mutual expectations. Still Calvert remains tied to the mast of fundamentalism Admitting for now the need for independent factors, he still looks to the development of a unified theory of equilibrium at some later point.

James Johnson takes a further step, arguing for the independence of strategic and communicative action.[30] Yet this move still proves illusory. Johnson sees all action as goal-directed; thus he ends up subordinating understanding to strategy.[31] In their joint work Calvert and Johnson approach problems of constitution formation in Eastern Europe from the angle of transition and institution making. The latter presents a situation of genesis in which there are no fixed institutional rules, a situation that poses new and unanticipated problems. Under unsettled conditions, basic principles are up for grabs, and social actors find it difficult to articulate these interests, to express and form preferences.[32] Social actors have few resources on which to draw to make sense of new situations. Transitions illustrate something basic about the "political" nature of interpretation: it is contested and strategic.

For a liberal cosmopolitan, "Europe" has one meaning, while for a conservative nationalist it has another connotation altogether. This indicates an essentially contested terrain. Actors pursue strategies to impose their interpretations on others. Here Calvert and Johnson suspend the relation of meaning to validity. They claim the primary goal of interpretation is to achieve success in action, that is, to achieve hegemony for one's own interpretation.

Oddly, Calvert and Johnson emphasize the role of deliberation. Introducing questions of deliberation could have taken analyses of the rationality of action in a different direction. In dialogue and deliberation, participants take account of others not simply as choosers who affect their own choices, but as participants who are accountable to them as they are to these others. Rational choice theories, however, do not take seriously enough the distinction between the market and the forum suggested by Elster. They bypass the formative power of mutual understanding in favor of outcomes. Here, according to Calvert and Johnson, "the incentive to advocate and bargain over constitutional prescriptions is based purely on the outcomes those prescriptions will yields on average, if followed."[33] Calvert and Johnson add, however, that the deliberative processes can also serve to gain the support of other individuals for future outcomes and also for possible future uses of the argument in other contexts. These outcomes serve as rules or precedents for later arguments. In this way, such stable arguments serve a coordinating role. They facilitate the formation of derived preferences. In setting up stable institutional structures, constitutional rules act to coordinate because they "transform situations of possible social conflict and confusion into derived coordination problems that are easier to solve."[34] Once individuals are confronted with a stable institutional structure in which they can predict behavior, they can then "derive" preferences. Discursively achieved understanding, however, cannot be explained through outcomes.

Communicative action loses its supposed independence. While Johnson recognizes that communicative action with its discursive orientation relies on a model of action coordination distinct from that of strategic action, he ends up subordinating it to strategic "power" aims. Power, however, is not simply strategic. Communicative power binds us to one another as members of a community or society in which there are shared political aims.

Interpreting Interpretation: Rethinking the Problem of Order

The permutations of rational choice theory I have discussed share a common flaw: each employs a limited conception of social action. This limits their ability to encounter interpretive methods on their own terms. In spite of its modifications, rational choice theory still sees the structure of the world made up of success-oriented action.

Consider trust as a counter-example. Trust cannot adequately be understood as a type of success-oriented action. It is one dimension of our accountability to each other in social life. Trust between participants holds even in the face of undesirable results. I may well act responsibly and faithfully without ever achieving a desired goal, yet still be considered trustworthy. Trust is not a strategic relation between social actors who seek to maximize return, but rather a form of understanding among participants. We bring into being and transform our social world *and ourselves* primarily though such communicative actions.

Communicative action is a form of action oriented to mutual understanding. However, social order, while it may rest on a rough background consensus, by no means requires complete agreement.[35] Participants in everyday social action are linked to others through forms of accountability to others. They are interested not just in the effects of others' decisions not just on their action, but also in the necessity of maintaining the common fabric of social life. They can account for their actions when needed in order to reestablish an ongoing consensual order. This requires a certain amount of trust in the sincerity of the participants to maintain interaction and discourse and to engage in the discursive repair of social relations when required.

Communicative action requires reflexivity. Social actors, in Anthony Giddens' felicitous phraseology, engage in reflexive monitoring of action—though Giddens is fuzzy regarding the role of communicative action. They must know what they are doing in the course of doing it.[36] As Anthony Giddens says, "Actors—also routinely and for the most part without fuss—maintain a continuing 'theoretical understanding' of the grounds of their activity."[37] Social actors have to be able to recognize situations as relevant to types of actions or to problems that arise in the course of interaction. They also must be able to know what is the right thing to do in a situation and what to expect from others. However, reflexivity also implies that participants are self-interpreting beings who have to take up the norms in their own way so as to accept, reject, or modify the norms they are given. In so doing, they draw upon not just simply the resources of the society but their own interpretive capacities, which allow them to critically evaluate social practices.

Rational choice theory presupposes that actors are reflexive. They know they are engaged in a certain type of game to which they respond in certain ways.[38] For a rational choice theory that grasps action nomologically, however, these elements serve primarily to introduce a notion of indeterminacy into the analysis of social action. Individuals may employ differing and incompatible interpretations of the world. Here reflexivity extends neither beyond the participants' awareness of effects on others, nor to the creation of a common world. The problem of indeterminacy is not rich enough to account for all the aspects of the participant's perspective, which entails a mode of self-interpretation.

Strategic action represents only one, incomplete, dimension of communicative actions. If we begin from the situation of a strategic actor who seeks to maximize outcomes, it is impossible to derive the full range of understanding-oriented action. Rather than seeing communicative action as the adjunct to rational choice explanation, communicative action is the broader and prior conceptual structure. Strategic action is derivative.

The priority of communicative action has further implications for normative social action. Calvert mistakes hypothetical imperatives for moral ones. While there is a class of practical imperatives that employ an if-then structure, moral norms are relations of mutual accountability among participants. Individuals must recognize the rightness of the norms that are proposed or instituted. We come to be what we are though our participation in institutions of communicative action, such as the appropriation of the traditions we live in, the social groups we belong to, and our individual socialization. Individuals however, are not simply recipients of communicative action; they are also initiators. They have to take up these traditions and social experiences on their own terms, as part of a life history.

The theory of communicative action provides a more adequate notion of bounded rationality. Typically critics argue that "neo-classical" rational choice theorists have assumed complete knowledge and fully formed institutions. In actual situations, individuals choose with only limited knowledge. Interpretive theory radicalizes this idea. All understanding, however, complete or incomplete, is bounded or situated. It is the basic condition of understanding. Seen in this way, any genuine encounter between rational choice and interpretive theory would undermine the foundationalist versions of rational choice.

The Nature of Interpretive Access

Once the social theorist admits expectations and values into her analysis, she is no longer concerned solely with outcomes of action but with the intersubjective relation of social actors. She must encounter others she studies through interpretive access to the social world. Questions of interpretation enter into the framework of theory in two distinct ways: the social inquirer has to employ meanings in the course of theory construction, that is, in the symbolic apparatus needed to make scientific statements, and the subjects of inquiry are other humans whose actions are already meaningful and who themselves interpret the world. Here the inquirer encounters the "double hermeneutic" of social inquiry.[39] More than a supplement to strategic action, interpretation is generic to all social interaction.[40] Participants in the social world do not relate to each other primarily or fundamentally through strategic action, but as participants in a communicative form of interaction. Expectations, for example, are not just the property of singular individuals who confront a world of strategically acting others; they are mutual expectations formed in a context of communicative interaction with others.

Social order is achieved and renewed through the interpretive accomplishments of actors.[41] The social scientist can never fully abstract from this context of interpretive understanding, but has to draw on her abilities as a participant in social life. In the traditional model of scientific observation, the observer is like a third person, a pure observer detached from the object of study. In social inquiry, however, the scientist must draw on the nonobjectivating participants' perspective. We can understand other participants only from a position internal to the participants.

The basic starting point of social inquiry for interpretive theory differs from that postulated by rational choice. We do not begin with a singular ego, which seeks to achieve success in action. There, the problem of order becomes the coordination of action of individuals who at first share no common relationships. Despite many efforts, this problem cannot be solved. It is generated by the conditions of a particular type of social order, namely, a market situation. However, the basic problems of social order revolve not around market situations but around questions of our relation to others through mutual understanding. Ego and Alter have to come to an understanding about something in the world.

Each of the rational choice theorists I examined subordinates communication to strategy. They claim that rational choice, suitably modified, is still potentially a comprehensive theory for the explanation social action.[42] If the position I have outlined is valid, however, both the micro-foundational project and rational choice fundamentalism are unworkable. Because rational choice theory presupposes prior expectations of actors about the social world that it cannot acknowledge, presuppositions that are essentially holistic, it cannot build from the simplest assumptions to a theory of institutions.

Interpretive theory has a distinctive notion of social science. Rather than depending on a connected set of propositions that construct the world from the theorist's perspective, social theory is more dependent upon the participants' perspectives for the "data" of inquiry. Its conceptual apparatus remains on the same level as those of participants. Explanation takes the form of an explication. The theorist reconstructs the concepts of ordinary actors who make sense in the course of their actions. Still, explication is not pure description or recapitulation. It adds something new. It rests on evaluative structures and typologies of action that articulate standards of knowledge and validity. In each case, however, these evaluative standards have to be ones that participants could agree to in a free and equal discussion. In social inquiry, the subjects are incapable of mutual criticism of those who study them.

The theory of communicative action provides a rereading of the classical concerns of the *Geisteswissenschaften* without surrendering to a one-sided reading of causality. In the communicative model institutions are not states of equilibrium, but enduring social structures for the constitution and reconstitution of social life. While the notion of equilibrium may approximate the workings of the pure market, this model does not suffice to explain the salient features of communicative action. In this latter respect, institutions are a primary medium through which we achieve and maintain our identities and through which we achieve mutual understanding.

Analytic Narratives: Overcoming Fundamentalism?

A more extensive response to the limits of classical rational choice models is the analytic narratives approach of Robert Bates and his associates.[43] Like neo-institutionalism, analytic narratives theory contends that rational choice theories have been most effective in analyzing political and economic processes in well-developed Western nations. The analytic narratives approach proposes a weaker version of rational choice. In the first instance, this entails a weaker explanatory program; in the second, it requires the further integration of symbolic elements to explain the achievement or transformation of social order. Analytic narrative theorists believe that they can best account for processes of institutional transformation using a combination of interpretive and analytic tools. Analytic narrative theory is ideographic rather than nomothetic.[44] It seeks to explain singular phenomena or processes that have unique historical properties and cannot be subsumed under a covering law. Here grasping the forces at work in a particular situation calls for interpretation, a detailed "political anthropology" that requires detailed knowledge of the values of individuals, of the expectations that individuals have of each other's actions and reactions, and of the ways in which these expectations have been shaped by history.

The elements of interpretation and analysis are used in distinctive ways. Narrative elements pay "close attention to stories, accounts, contexts" and construct the context of beliefs, traditions, and orientations within which decisions are made. These contexts have an important effect on the way that alternatives are defined and expectations shaped. In contrast, analysis extracts formal lines of reasoning that facilitate explanation and exposition.[45] Analysis explains the kinds of game matrices and the reasons they are stable or coherent aspects of order. Following John Ferejohn's conceptualization, analytic narrative theory contends that cultural theories represent "thick descriptions" of cultural traditions, while rational choice theories represent thin descriptions of basic forms of action.[46]

A prime example of the analytic narrative approach is Bates's discussion of political protest and change in Zambia. Bates tries to incorporate more fully the nature of expressive action. After it achieved independence, Zambia was primarily a one-party socialist state governed by they United National Independence Party (UNIP), which governed through large majorities that discouraged opposition. Popular protest arose over economic issues such as the need to maintain the purchasing power of the urban poor and the rural peasantry, but the protest turned against the government and led to the inception of contested elections in which UNIP was defeated. What is of interest in popular political protest is its expressive dimension.[47]

Like neo-institutionalists, analytic narrative theorists link expressive and strategic action. However, they grant the symbolic and self-presentational aspects of expressive action a greater autonomy and independent power. They are not linked to maximizing strategies. Drawing on the work of Erving Goffman and Murray Edelman,[48] symbolic interaction is considered largely a kind of expressive self-presentation through which the actor hopes to influence her audience. In this way, the expressive or strategic use of symbols is a kind of theatrical performance. Analytic narrative theory considers protest a form of this theatrical power, which in "transforming public festivals into political theatre" infuse "day-to day life with 'hidden transcripts' of public dissent."[49] Expressive performances have the power to mobilize and motivate individuals to act in accord with new preferences.[50]

Explaining Transformation

In order to explain processes of transformation, analytic narrative theory draws on Aristede Zolberg's discussion of "moments of madness." Here transformation is read though an expressivist theory in which values and symbols "express" the preferences of groups.[51] The power of emotional feeling and preferences and its motivating force then can build to the point at which seemingly unexpected and radical transformations occur. In this view, symbols take on a kind of free-floating motivating power that can attach itself to discontent at will without regard to truth or validity.[52]

Though the analytic narrative approach takes us further in the direction of interpretation, it still falls short of a true integration. While it does take into account interpretive claims, it does so by reducing them to an adjunct of "analytic" explanation. While history shapes choices, the latter still have the primary structure-building capacity. The relation between analytic and interpretive elements, which are seen as far from complementary, is understood in a one-sided manner. Thin descriptions are still the structure-forming components of social action. Interpretation is given a restrictive interpretation as a type of strategic manipulation of symbols.

In addition, analytic narrative theory still employs an impoverished notion of symbolic action. More than a free-floating motivational power, emotions are never pre-rational motivations but are rather elements of our symbolic relation to the world. What we fear and what we hope for are elements of our understanding of the world. They are forms of symbolic interaction in which the self relates to the world and to the audience. We may be cynical about authority or celebrate it. In either case, we give an account of the world that is open to evaluation and criticism based on standards that are worthy or shallow. In each of these cases, it is a matter of recognition of the worth of the ideal. It is the character of our evaluation of these expressive performances that gives them motivating power.

I think there are two major aspects of political transformation that cannot be reduced to strategic considerations or subordinated to them. The first is the change in the participants' sense of legitimacy. More than just an expression of preferences, in times of radical political change political actors seek new justifications and new reasons for acting. They have to form new conceptions of justice or now conceptions of the good. Of course forms of mutual accountability do not simply develop in the abstract. They come to the fore as conflicts arise within a society. In the case of Zambia, participants do more than simply express a "preference" for open elections; they find new reasons for action.

The second aspect is the linkage of these discursive forms of accountability to the life histories and political identities of participants. By life history I mean a practical reflection on one's own past that also critically appropriates that past for the present. This way of understanding identity becomes relevant to political change when it enters into the sense of the good: how one wants the political world to be. For example, one's sense of distrust of an authority is not simply brute data or pure feeling but reflects a judgment of the accounts given by an authority. Emotions that give expression to our situation and our sense of the world are not entirely detached from forms of understanding. Therefore, radical change also means a change we make in our identities by taking up our own life histories in a new way.

It would be more effective to think of transformative process along the model of an episode.[53] This essentially narrative device also can incorporate some of the structural dimensions of change. An episode is a linked sequence of events with a beginning and an end. The episodic nature of action retains reference to the participants' perspective of historical actor. For an episode always requires the framework of the meaning of action.

The social scientist's account of an episode, however, is in some ways an explication rather than an explanation. It draws out and interprets the formation of the elements of mutual accountability and the new life histories that motivate actors. The mobilization of resources for change requires that these interpretive components move to center stage. If we follow this line of argument, the focus also shifts from causal explanation to interpretive explanation.[54]

Narratives bear a relation to critical reflection. While critical theories draw upon the structural features of communicative action in order to unearth the basic features of mutual understanding, they also draw upon the narrative features of episodes in order to form narratives of emancipation in which forms of domination are transformed. Such narratives are not just symbolic patterns. They are linked to the transformation of our commitments as participants. They may always entail not the end of domination or the realization of complete freedom, but rather the history of struggles against unnecessary constraint.

Notes

1. For the *Methodenstreit* see Anthony Oberschall (1965), *Empirical Social Research in Germany 1840–1914* (The Hague: Mouton); Fritz Ringer (1969), *The Rise of the German Mandarins* (Cambridge, MA: Harvard University Press); Thomas Wiley (1978), *Back to Kant* (Detroit: Wayne State University Press); Thomas Burger (1967), *Max Weber's Theory of Concept Formation* (Durham, NC: Duke University Press); Fritz Ringer (2000), *Max Weber's Methodology: The Unification of the Cultural and Social Sciences* (Cambridge, MA: Harvard University Press); Jürgen Habermas (1988), *The Logic of the Social Sciences* (Cambridge, MA: MIT Press).

2. J. G. Droysen, "Grundrisse der Historik," cited in K. O. Apel (1984), *Understanding and Explanation: A Transcendental-Pragmatic Perspective* (Cambridge, MA: MIT Press), 3. A brief but useful discussion of historicism in relation to hermeneutics can be fond in Georgia Warnke (1987), *Gadamer: Hermeneutics Tradition and Reason* (Stanford, CA: Stanford University Press).

3. See the essays in James Farr, John Dryzek, and Stephen Leonard, eds. (1995), *Political Science and History* (Cambridge, MA: Cambridge University Press).

4. Rational choice institutionalism sees a convergence with a version of historical institutionalism that has taken up use of quantitative methods and the search for more rigorous explanatory models. See Theda Skocpol (1995), "Why I Am an Historical Institutionalist," *Polity* 28 (1), and Morris Fiorina's (1995) reply, "Rational Choice and the New(?) Institutionalism," in the same issue. See also Theda Skocpol and Margaret Somers (1980), "The Uses of Comparative History in Macrosociological Inquiry," *Comparative Studies in Society and History* 22 (2): 174–97. A fuller discussion of historical institutionalism is, however, beyond the scope of this chapter.

5. Jon Elster (1982), "Marx, Marxism, Functionalism, and Game Theory: The Case for Methodological Individualism," *Theory and Society* 12: 111–20, 453–82; Elster (1985), "The Nature and Scope of Rational-Choice Explanations," in Ernest LePore and Brian P. McLaughlin, eds., *Actions and Events: Perspectives on the Philosophy of Donald Davidson* (Oxford: Blackwell 60–72); on the overextension of rational choice theory, cf. Elster (1986), "The Market and the Forum: Three Varieties of Political Theory," in Elster, *Foundations of Rational Choice Theory* (Cambridge: Cambridge University Press).

6. William Riker (1962), *Theory of Political Coalitions* (New Haven, CT: Yale University Press), 3.

7. Riker (1962), 5–6.

8. Peter C. Ordeshook (1992), *A Political Theory Primer* (New York: Routledge), 5.

9. Randall Calvert (1993), "Lowi's Critique of Political Science: A Response," *PS: Political Science and Politics* 26 (2): 196. Calvert is responding to Theodore Lowi's inaugural address to the APSA, published as "The State in Political Science: How We Become What We Study" *American Political Science Review* 86: 1–7.

10. Calvert (1993), 197.

11. Max Weber (1978), *Economy and Society: An Outline of Interpretive Sociology* (Berkeley: University of California Press).

12. Ordeshook (1992), 9.

13. See Riker (1998), *Liberalism against Populism: A Confrontation between the Theory of Democracy and the Theory of Social Choice* (Long Grove, IL: Waveland Press).

14. The distinction between method-driven and problem-driven social science is often cited by Perestroikans. For a defense see Bent Flyvbjerg (2001), *Making Social Science Matter: Why Social Inquiry Fails and How It Can Succeed Again* (Cambridge: Cambridge University Press).

15. Kenneth A. Shepsle (1995), "Studying Institutions: Some Lessons from the Rational Choice Approach," in Farr, Dyrzek and Leonard, *Political Science and History*.

16. Randall Calvert (1995a), "The Rational Choice Theory of Social Institutions: Cooperation, Co-ordination and Communication," in Jeffrey S. Banks and Eric A. Hanushek, eds., *Modern Political Economy: Old Topics, New Directions* (Cambridge: Cambridge University Press), 222.

17. Calvert (1995a): 222–23.

18. Jack Knight and Itai Sened (1995), "Introduction," in Knight and Sened, *Explaining Social Institutions* (Ann Arbor: University of Michigan Press), 10.

19. Randall Calvert (1995b), "Rational Actors, Equilibrium and Social Institutions," in Knight and Sened, *Explaining Social Institutions*. Cf. Debra Satz and John Ferejohn (1994), "Rational Choice and Social Theory," *Journal of Philosophy* 91: 71–87.

20. Calvert (1995b), 59.

21. Calvert (1995b), 59–60.

22. Calvert (1995a), 224.

23. Calvert (1995a), 224.

24. Randall Calvert (2000), "Rational Choice Models of Group Identity," paper presented at the APSA Annual Meetings, Washington, DC, 2000, 45.

25. Calvert (2000), 45.

26. In contrast to the power to command power with others is the consensual power that is generated when individuals act together through understanding. See, for example, Hannah Arendt (1970), *On Violence* (New York: Harcourt Brace), esp. 44–45, and Jürgen Habermas (1977), "Hannah Arendt's Communications Concept of Power," in *Social Research* 44 (1): 3–24.

27. Calvert (2000), 15.

28. Calvert (2000), 15.

29. Calvert (2000), 55.

30. James Johnson (1991a), "Habermas on Strategic and Communicative Action," *Political Theory* 19: 181–210; Johnson (1993), "Is Talk Really Cheap? Prompting Conversation between Critical Theory and Rational Choice," *American Political Science Review* 87 (1): 74–86; Johnson (1991b), "Rational Choice as Reconstructive Theory," in Kristen Renwick Monroe (1991), ed., *The Economic Approach to Politics: A Critical Reassessment of Rational Action* (New York: Harper Collins), 113–42.

31. Brian Caterino (2003), "Marketing Critical Theory," *New Political Science* 25 (3): 435–49.

32. Randall Calvert and James Johnson (1998), "Interpretation and Co-ordination in Constitutional Politics: Working Paper No. 15, W. Allen Wallis Institute of Political Economy, 5.

33. Calvert and Johnson (1998), 28.

34. Calvert and Johnson (1998), 29.

35. Like rational choice theories, agreement is an ideal type of communicative action.

36. Anthony Giddens (1986), *The Constitution of Society: Outline of a Theory of Structuration* (Berkeley: University of California Press).

37. Giddens (1986), 5.

38. Calvert (2000).

39. Anthony Giddens (1976), *New Rules of the Sociological Method* (London: Hutchinson).

40. Giddens (1976), 52.

41. A good example of the employment of this type of analysis is Peter Grahame (1998), "Criticalness, Pragmatics and Everyday Life: Consumer Literacy as Critical Practice," in John Forester, ed., *Critical Theory and Public Life* (Cambridge, MA: MIT Press), 147–74.

42. Kenneth A. Shepsle (1996), "Statistical Political Philosophy and Positive Political Theory," in Jeffrey Friedman, ed., *The Rational Choice Controversy* (New Haven, CT: Yale University Press), 213–23, and, in the same volume, Morris Fiorina (1996), "Rational Choice, Empirical Contributions and the Scientific Enterprise," 85–94, and John Ferejohn and Debra Satz (1996), "Unification Universalism and Rational Choice Theory," 71–84.

43. See Robert Bates, Avner Greif, Margaret Levi, Jean-Laurent Rosenthal, and Barry S. Weingast (1998a), *Analytic Narratives* (Princeton, NJ: Princeton University Press); Robert Bates, Rui J. P. de Figueiredo, and Barry S. Weingast (1998b), "The Politics of Interpretation, Rationality Culture and Transition," *Politics and Society* 26 (4): 603–42.

44. Bates et al. (1998a).

45. Bates et al. (1998a), 10.

46. John Ferejohn (1991), "Rationality and Interpretation: Parliamentary Elections in Early Stuart England," in Monroe (1991), *The Economic Approach to Politics.*

47. Bates et al. (1998b).

48. Erving Goffman (1959), *The Presentation of the Self in Everyday Life* (Garden City, NJ: Doubleday), and Murray Edelman (1967), *The Symbolic Uses of Politics* (Urbana: University of Illinois Press).

49. Bates et al. (1998b).

50. Bates et al. (1998b).

51. Bates et al. (1998b).

52. Bates et al. (1998b).

53. This dimension is discussed in Giddens (1986), 244–45.

54. I am thinking here primarily of work that follows in the wake of Max Weber. See Ringer (2000).

CHAPTER 11

The "R" Word, Narrative, and Perestroika

A Critique of Language and Method

Cecelia Lynch

This chapter examines three significant and interrelated types of language used in political science. First, the concept of methodological rigor—the "r" word—represents a standard bar that quality scholarship in political science must pass to be acceptable for publication in peer-reviewed journals or university press books. Many of us have also heard the term applied (or applied it ourselves) to candidates for recruitment and promotion in assessing their worth. However, the "r" word has become a trope that is used by authors themselves to demonstrate the worth of their manuscripts, as well as by peer reviewers for some journals to elevate particular types of usually quantitative methods over others. Ironically, however, qualitative scholars also employ this trope to assess their own work. The "r" word thus conveys muscular academic credentials, but its overuse and the misunderstanding of the boundaries of quality research have rendered it, paradoxically, both discriminatory and meaningless.

The first part of this chapter discusses the types of scholarship and methods the "r" word promotes. Scholars frequently apply the term to mathematical modeling and large n quantitative studies, but small n qualitative research can also meet alleged "r" word criteria. As Dvora Yanow points out in her contribution to this volume, one of the major differences in political science methodology is not between quantitative and qualitative research, but rather between positivist and constructionist-hermeneutic methods. However, these latter interpretive methods are generally considered out of luck in meeting "r" word standards. This is of small importance in the subfield of political theory, but of much greater importance for work in American politics, comparative politics, and especially international relations, where some proponents of interpretive research still strive for acceptance according to these standards.

The subfield of international relations (IR), however, has increasingly turned to interpretive research, largely through the use of constructivist and other poststructural approaches. This is not to say that behavioralist and rational choice research is unimportant, but rather that the methodological playing field is strongly contested. Interpretive methods include discourse analysis, genealogy, and narrative, among others. In this chapter I focus on the fact that increasing numbers of international relations theorists are recognizing the importance of narrative, including its construction, method, and meaning (Alker 1996). A number of recent IR books have cast their arguments in terms of alternative narratives, including Latham 1997, Barnett 1998, Lynch 1999, and Suganami 1996). To their credit, some scholars on each side of the methodological spectrum have also attempted to cross methodological and epistemological boundaries. In IR, this has taken the form of game theorists who acknowledge the importance of culture and interpretivists who acknowledge the value of comparison across cases. A group of comparative politics scholars has also made a widely debated effort to bridge the divide through the concept of "analytic narratives" (Bates, Greif, Levi, Rosenthal, and Weingast 1998).

The next part of the chapter examines more closely this second type of political science language usage: the concept of narrative. In particular, it focuses on the method of "analytic" narrative in the context of the "r" word and relates it to interpretive work being done in IR and history. Analytic narratives, according to their proponents, are more systematic, analytical, and "logically rigorous" than much other narrative scholarship (Bates et al. 1998, 12). Yet such a claim is unhelpful. The term "logically rigorous" is only one of several that Robert Bates and associates employ, and they do not insist on its primacy over other "analytic" criteria. Yet not only are all of the criteria advocated by the promoters of analytic narratives already being met by historians and interpretive international relations scholars who employ narrative methods, but the understanding of interpretive philosophy of science also adds critical features that the concept of analytic narratives lacks. This section examines these features and relates them to aspects of international politics. Specifically, some interpretive analyses in IR demonstrate that we must also understand the "meta-narratives," or dominant narratives (Lynch 1999) that structure both our understanding of events in world politics and the way we undertake research to study them. Most interpretive IR scholars who employ narrative methods recognize the importance of meta-narratives in methodological debates, but Bates and associates dismiss them too lightly, and many of their critics do not address them.

The third part of the chapter turns to an analysis of the Perestroika movement's treatment to date of meta-narratives and method. Perestroika has developed a linguistic practice (the third type of language usage addressed in this chapter) of attempting to separate "method" from "politics." Yet our politics rest on meta-narratives, or understandings of how the world works, that are shaped by the ways we are constituted as both subjects and agents. The same goes for our methods, which are also constituted of meta-narratives. Especially in the world of IR, politics and academics traditionally intersect and constitute each other in significant ways (Oren 2003). We therefore cannot separate "practice," or real-world politics, from "method," especially when both practice and method concern constitutive meta-narratives. Perestroika, therefore, effectively has made a choice, which is to focus on, discuss, and debate (and hence, provide a critique of) *most* methods. It has chosen to leave out others, especially the method of meta-narrative construction in the political world and its effects on academia, in the interests of movement coherence. This choice, made by "Mr. Perestroika" and approved by many others, has resulted in truncated discussions, if not censorship, of postings on hot political issues such as the wars in Afghanistan and Iraq. But the problems inherent in separating method and politics keep creeping into other Perestroika discussions, including those on academic freedom, the history of the Caucus for a New Political Science versus the history of Perestroika, and the worth of area studies. I argue that the choice to separate method and politics is arbitrary. This separation can have benefits, but it also entails costs. The costs, ironically, may include reinforcing the problems inherent in applying "rigor" as a rhetorical standard to work in political science. I summarize these issues in the chapter's conclusion.

The "R" Word, Interpretation, and International Relations

Lively debate about methods has marked the subfield of IR for the past two decades, taking off with the publication in 1986 of Friedrich Kratochwil and John Ruggie's *IO* piece "The State of the Art on an Art of the State." Kratochwil and Ruggie articulated the problems associated with attempts to employ positivist methodologies to resolve interpretive questions about "regimes," the term used to describe the confluence of norms and rules governing particular issue areas such as money, trade, and the environment. The study of regimes in IR, according to Kratochwil and Ruggie's argument, posited a relational ontology, but tried unsuccessfully to superimpose on it a positivist epistemology. Since that time, an increasing number of scholars and students of IR have employed social constructionist approaches to study substantive as well as meta-theoretical issues in world politics, and debate about appropriate methods and ontological or epistemological "fit" remains rife. However, in the midst of these debates, the "r" word ironically continues to resurface as a vague standard for assessing quality work.

For example, prompted by Robert Keohane's (1988) critiques of "reflectivists," John Ruggie asserts that what he calls "neo-utlitarianism," which is akin to Robert Cox's "problem-solving theory" (Cox 1996), "permits a degree of analytical rigor, and in neoliberal institutionalism's case . . . rigor and specificity are desirable on intellectual grounds because they make cumulative findings more likely, and on policy grounds because they raise the probability that predicted effects will actually materialize. At the same time, neo-utilitarianism's major weakness lies in the foundations of its axiomatic structure, its ontology, which for some purposes is seriously flawed and leads to an incomplete or distorted view of international reality." Conversely, reflectivism, including what has become known in IR as social constructivism, "rests on a deeper and broader ontology, thereby providing a richer understanding of some phenomena and shedding light on other aspects of international life that, quite literally, do not exist within the neo-utilitarian rendering of the world polity. At the same time, it lacks rigor and specification" (Ruggie 1998, 36–37). Ruggie concludes that "neo-utilitarians should strive to expand their analytical foundations, and constructivists should strive for greater analytical rigor and specification" (39).

Likewise, Jennifer Milliken titles an otherwise brilliantly argued article on appropriate methods for discourse analysis "Discourse Study: Bringing Rigor to Critical Theory" (Milliken 2001). Milliken criticizes the tendency of some interpretivists in IR to reject "the elaboration of methods and the setting of research standards, debate about research design, or evaluation of substantive research," because "it puts discourse analysts and their critics essentially on the same side with respect to social science standards . . . , in the sense that both conclude that discourse study is not fundamentally about doing rigorous empirical research or developing better theories" (137). Milliken makes a critical point in reminding discourse analysts not to cede the social-scientific methodological high ground.

Similarly, interpretivists outside of IR also employ the term "rigor" in objecting to the charge that their research does not employ high standards. Dvora Yanow argues, "Even though interpretive methods emphasize the centrality of human interpretation and, hence, subjective meaning—that is, meaning to the 'subject,' the actor or the researcher—they are, nonetheless, methods: systematic, rigorous, methodical" (Yanow 2000, ix).

Nevertheless, I argue that rigor is the wrong word and the wrong standard for judgment of scholarly work in IR and in political science as a whole. *Rigor,* according to the *Oxford English Dictionary (OED)*, refers to "severity in dealing with a person or persons; extreme strictness; harshness . . . , the strict application or enforcement of a law, rule, etc., . . . strictness of discipline etc.; austerity of life; puritanical severity or strictness . . . extreme distress or hardship." These definitions are pretty much self-explanatory with regard to the problematic nature of using rigor as a standard for good scholarship, and many of us have experienced personally the puritanical nature and severity of witchhunts against those performing "nonrigorous," interpretive research. Perhaps more tellingly, a second set of definitions of *rigor* refers to "a sudden feeling of chill, accompanied by a bout of shivering, marking a rise in body temperature, as at the onset or the height of a fever," and, of course, this in reference to rigor carried to the extreme: "in full *rigor mortis,* the stiffening of the joints and muscles of a body a few hours after death" (*OED* 1993, 2601). Several aspects of these definitions are worth pointing out in more detail.

First, greater clarity and specificity and sharper insights are laudable goals for all scholarship. As Peter Katzenstein puts it, we should strive for "the diminishing of sloppy logic, flabby prose, circularity in reasoning, and vacuousness of insight" (Katzenstein 1996, 1). But rigor is not a sufficient or proper means to accomplish these goals. For example, we should not impose on research specificity and rigor in the same breath; being more specific regarding the objects of analysis and the interplay of interpretive factors that produce actions may at first glance necessitate a "stiffening of the joints" in the sense of

holding static important variables, but if we treat this as more than a temporary heuristic device, the end result is not merely a robotic subject, but the
death of insightful analysis.

Second, as Ruggie acknowledges, "improvements" in constructivist work
(towards analytical rigor and specificity) are both inevitable and inherently
limited, "given the nature of the beast" (Ruggie 1998, 37). Yet he does not
explain how, if neo-utilitarianism results in seriously flawed, incomplete, or
distorted views of international reality, we can have any reasonable amount of
confidence in its predicted policy or cumulative theoretical findings. Of course
this is a criticism often leveled at positivist work in general, and treated amply
elsewhere in this volume. But it again begs the question of why "rigor" should
be considered a standard for serious scholarship in IR or political science in
general.

Third, Milliken's argument that interpretivists should take seriously questions of research design and method is apt. But certainly it adds nothing of
value to conduct these tasks with "extreme strictness," "harshness," or "puritanical severity." As Joel Migdal states, "Fashionable rigor may force-feed
overly constraining hypotheses on readers by searching for one-way causality
that starts at a key moment." Migdal also opposes rigor to narrative: "Existing
understanding of rigor may divert the observer from the continuing dynamic
. . . called narrative—the unexpected, the unstable, the reactive to daily life"
(Migdal 2001, 24).

Ruggie and most interpretivists agree that our standards should be based on
practical, not aesthetic, grounds. Given the criterion of usefulness, I now turn
to a comparison of the standards advocated by the authors of "analytic narratives" with accepted standards for using narrative methods in IR and history.

Narratives, Analysis, and "Analytic Narratives"

A narrative is, simply put, a story. A narrative explanation or interpretation is
one that seeks to explain or interpret by constructing from the available evidence a story about an event or series of events or about an actor or group of
actors. Unlike a nomological or nomothetical explanation, it does not employ
covering laws à la Carl Hempel to tell us why things are the way they are and
not some other way (Ruggie 1998; Gerth and Mills 1946/58). Political scientists,
and especially scholars in IR, use narrative methods frequently, but, in the
United States at least, some express frustration with narrative explanation
because of concerns about how we know when the narrative is "right," or how
to distinguish a good narrative from a bad one. Moreover, narratives can be
extremely powerful in influencing the way we think about the world, because
they tend to embody either explicit or implicit moral judgments about the
way things were, are, and should be. For some scholars, again especially in the
United States, the goal of positivist social science renders such moral judgments
problematic and requires them to be excised from "objective" analysis.

In the late 1990s, a group of comparative politics scholars made a bold attempt to bridge paradigmatic divides by attempting to apply rational choice insights to narrative methods of research. The resulting book, *Analytic Narratives* (Bates et al. 1998), represented both a response to critiques of rational choice, especially that by Green and Shapiro (1994), and the beginning of a new phase in the rationalist-interpretivist (and also intrarationalist) debates. The book's premises, assertions, cases, and success in attaining its goals were discussed and debated at some length, especially in the *American Political Science Review* (*APSR*) and in *Social Science History*.

Bates and associates stated, for example, that their book on "analytic narratives" provided an answer to Green and Shapiro's criticisms of rational choice theory; it also represented a departure from Riker's use of rational choice as the means of attaining "a universal approach to the social sciences, capable of yielding general laws of political behavior" (Bates et al. 1998, 11). Green and Shapiro asserted that the preoccupation with universal theories resulted in research that was "theory driven rather than problem driven." Even worse, the very purpose of much research had become "to save or vindicate some variant of rational choice theory, rather than to account for . . . political phenomena" (Green and Shapiro 1994, 6). Bates and associates responded to these critiques in their book, but in so doing they engendered a new controversy that played out in the pages of the *APSR,* among other venues. While much of the controversy surrounding this book has seemingly died down, it is worthwhile to recapitulate several important points of debate for our discussion of rigor, narrative, and interpretive methods.

In *Analytic Narratives* Bates and associates initially responded to Green and Shapiro as follows: "Clearly the chapters in [our] book are problem driven, not theory driven; they are motivated by a desire to account for particular events or outcomes. They are devoted to the exploration of cases, not to the elaboration of theory. In these ways, they counter the charges raised by Green and Shapiro. By the same token, neither do the chapters conform to Riker's vision of the role of theory. Although informed by deductive reasoning, the chapters themselves seek no universal laws of human behavior" (Bates et al. 1998, 11).

But why a focus on narrative? Bates and associates recognized the relationship of narrative to "the historical turn in the social sciences," and they asserted the importance of empirical as opposed to ahistorical theoretical work. In both instances, they implicitly acknowledged the power of narrative forms. Narratives, by contextualizing explanations in broader stories about the way in which the world works, can add rationality and common sense to social-scientific conclusions. However, the more context is provided for a particular story, the more difficult it becomes to justify applying its "lessons" to other situations. Therefore, as they stated in the last sentence of the preceding quote, Bates and associates relinquished claims to universal theorizing. In so doing, they engaged in a laudable attempt, from the rationalist side, to bridge paradigmatic gaps between historical and "analytic" research.

Yet Bates and associates' explanation of how they evaluate the success of analytic narratives is problematic. Four of the five questions they pose (14–18) to assess and test their explanations—whether the assumptions fit the known facts, whether conclusions follow logically from the premises, whether the data confirm the implications, whether the explanation stands up well in comparison to alternatives—represent analytical tasks already performed by narrative historians and interpretivists in IR. As Theda Skocpol says in her review of the book, "On the methodological front, there is actually little here that is new" (Skocpol 2000, 669).

Interpretive narrative analysis is centrally concerned with coherence, logic, fit, and full and appropriate evidence. Again, Skocpol's review asserts, "These perfectly sensible principles could have come from any good methods textbook" (Skocpol 2000, 671). Scholars who employ narrative strive to obtain the fullest evidence through archival and other documentary work, interviews where possible, participant observation techniques, and reexamination of secondary sources. Much historical debate focuses on the "fit" of these types of evidence with previously held assumptions and with the logic of existing narratives. When scholars uncover new evidence, as in the annual January rush of historians to the Public Record Office near London to be the first to see just-released British government papers or when scholars make successful appeals for documents through the U.S. Freedom of Information Act, they sift through this new evidence carefully to see if it alters existing explanations. Narratives can be altered when the new evidence relates to a "gap" in a previously existing story, causing the analyst to reevaluate the whole. For example, realist IR theorists and diplomatic historians made assumptions about the role of peace movements between World Wars I and II that were colored by selective governmental archival evidence because the researchers didn't also make use of peace movement archives. Putting together evidence from peace movement archives, the League of Nations, and governmental sources has resulted in new interpretations that challenge the purportedly strong linkages between peace movements and appeasement or isolationism (Lynch 1999).

Nevertheless, while obtaining complete evidence remains a goal, most narrative scholars remain sophisticated enough about debates over the philosophy of science to understand that "the evidence" is never overdetermined. Rather, the problem is that the evidence is never complete, for narrative construction or for any other method of social analysis (Hesse 1974).

Thus, if there is a difference between the perspective presented in *Analytic Narratives* and that of the narrative interpretivist, it is more in the degree of sophistication the latter brings to the problem of bias in interpreting evidence than it is in research design or measures of validity. The interpretation must "make sense of" the data or the evidence, but the term *make sense of* is one that itself is liable to a variety of interpretations. This leads to awareness of the "hermeneutic circle" by most scholars of narrative. As Sunita Parikh points out, other disciplines in the social sciences have "become much more aware of the biases that arise in the narrative form, no matter how high the quality of the scholar and the research effort." Parikh names three sources of bias: "the structure of the data from which the narrative is drawn, the biases of the researcher constructing the narrative, and the biases the reader brings to the interpretation of the finished work" (Parikh 2000, 682–83). Indeed some, such as Hayden White, go so far as to find all narrative histories problematic, not on rationalist grounds but on interpretivist ones. According to Keith Jenkins, White asserts that narrative discourses, such as history, "combine known or found parts (facts) with ultimately unknown and thus imagined/invented wholes," and thus "the past in all its sublimity can never be grasped fully in narrative form" (Jenkins 1995, 134–35). We are all caught in meta-narratives that suggest stories about the past based on our present ideological frameworks.

The fifth question, whether the conclusions are generalizable, is problematic for Bates and associates given that they have already disallowed the goal of universal theorizing in their response to Green and Shapiro. If one extends generalizability to "lessons learned" that may be set against other contests for comparative purposes, then again there is no difference between this question or criterion and those of historians and interpretivists (see May 1985). Some of the contributors to *Analytic Narratives,* however, do in fact construct models for generalizing their conclusions, but at least some prominent readers have found these less than persuasive on the basis of the available evidence. Jon Elster, for example, writes in the *APSR* that in one chapter the logic of constructed preferences can be questioned, and in another the model's fit is "very artificial" (Elster 2000, 687).

In short, there is nothing inherent in the method espoused by Bates and associates, where narratives are concerned, that provides any additional clarity, specificity, logic, or analytical purchase than the method already practiced by the historian or the poststructural interpretivist. (Whether or not their method, or any method, provides additional "rigor"—in the sense of undue severity, puritanism, or deathly stiffening, as defined by the *OED*—is perhaps a matter of perspective.) Moreover, most interpretivist IR scholars who employ narrative methods explicitly recognize the problem of narrative embeddedness in larger meta-narratives, as well as the fact that the scholar works within and between various theoretical and political meta-narratives. This recognition of embeddedness is critical to the narrative project, both theoretically and empirically. This is because such an awareness forces us to confront not only the reasons particular narratives become dominant in any given place or time, but also the conditions that enable our alternative narratives to develop and gain an audience. The IR rationalist's attempt to explain behavior through the prism of neoliberal motivation and the critical theorist's critique of hegemonic power both emanate from meta-narratives that are part and parcel of contemporary debates about the worth and value of progress, science, and capitalism.

Bates and associates acknowledge that they "may unwittingly be participating in a meta-narrative, be it of the extension of rationality or the scientific method." But they insist that they can escape this problem, "through vigilance and self-awareness" (p. 13, n. 14). Such an assertion is problematic, however, because it assumes that we can become sufficiently self-aware to eliminate all forms of bias.

In IR, a perhaps more powerful motive force encouraged a return to the narrative form: the failure of (formerly) dominant paradigms in the discipline to help us understand, let alone explain, the enormous changes in world politics since 1991. This failure resulted in challenges both to the methodological meta-narrative, which asserted that structuralism explained everything of importance in world politics, and the ideological meta-narrative, which gave primacy to realpolitik as the necessary lens for understanding international events. As Peter Katzenstein asserts, "One observer has likened the embarrassment that the end of the Cold War caused us as scholars of international relations and national security to the effects the sinking of the *Titanic* had on the profession of naval engineers" (Katzenstein 1996, xi). Thus a special 1994 symposium of *IO* was devoted to several different narratives of the Cold War's demise (Gross Stein, Risse-Kappen, Koslowski and Kratochwil, and Lebow 1994). These analyses were also marked by mutual complementarity; each highlighted portions of the story of the decline of the Soviet Union and the end of bipolarity left relatively unilluminated by the others, yet none insisted on mutually exclusive explanations. Taken together, these articles provided a coherent set of stories about the role of political leaders (Mikhail Gorbachev), domestic and transnational actors, and historical changes in Eastern Europe (Ottomanization, Finlandization, Austrianization, and beyond) to explain the disintegration of the bipolar world. The end of the cold war also led to debate about the relative value of nomological versus historical methods in security studies, represented in a 1996 APSA panel and later a special issue of *International Security*.

After 1991, the collapse of Yugoslavia and the Soviet Union into warring ethnic groups heightened scholars' concern about the relationship between identity and narrative in international politics. Nationalist identities, based on narratives that are socially constructed and promote some actions over others, became a potent object of study (Campbell 1998; Anderson 1991). The fact that narratives were constructed and successfully deployed to found and reinforce nationalist claims, wars, and even "ethnic cleansing" and genocide in such places as Rwanda, Bosnia, Kosovo, and Chechnya brought into stark relief the contingent nature of identity and begged the question of how nationalists and idealogues could alter such constructions of self and other. Here the stories to be recounted by scholars concerned the way in which participants constructed their own narratives of events that privileged some historical "facts" over others, that is, the way in which some individuals and sectors of society reinterpreted history, race, ethnicity, religious beliefs, and threats into coherent nationalist narratives that gained broader acceptance and legitimized conflict. Some scholars also asked how these narratives became reified and exacerbated by external actors such as the United States, nongovernmental organizations, the North Atlantic Treaty Organization, and theorists of IR (see Campbell 1998).

Today the selective construction of security narratives in IR continues apace with the war on terror. IR scholars continue to participate on policy as well as scholarly levels in these debates. Although we cannot achieve complete objectivity in relation to world events, we can become more aware of the meta-narratives within which our positions on terror, the wars in Afghanistan and Iraq, security, democracy, and human rights are embedded.

Perestroika, Method, and Meta-Narrative

I am someone who advocated including in the Perestroika debates discussions of issues related to Afghanistan and Iraq along with the meta-narratives in which foreign policy is embedded. These issues include the construction of "terrorism" before and during the war in Afghanistan as well as the legitimacy of the U.S. war against Iraq in the context of a "war on terror." Most on the list serve, however, have successfully argued in favor of restricting the challenge posed by Perestroika to one of "methods."

Two main arguments underpin the desire for restriction. One argument is that including "political" concerns will split the movement; I address this concern later. The second argument is that Perestroika's purpose is to reopen the discipline of political science to the full panoply of methods practiced by social scientists, especially qualitative ones. According to this argument, political postings simply do not belong on the Perestroika site.

I find this second argument particularly problematic. This is because enacting a principle based on this argument in effect restricts us, as political scientists, from examining too closely many of our own assumptions, which cannot always be classified as exclusively "methodological" or "political." Thus how we look at politics remains outside of our critical lens. Many methodological perspectives are based largely or in part on political or ideological predispositions. Just as the medieval period and the Enlightenment promoted related political and methodological agendas, so it is impossible to disassociate rational choice from certain types of liberalism, or structuralisms from either neo-realism or neo-Marxisms of various kinds. Moreover, because of the often symbiotic relationship between method and politics, the Perestroika policy has also been implemented somewhat selectively: some political postings get through, while I know from personal experience that others do not. It must be difficult for Peretroika to discern precisely which postings are political and which are methodological.

After September 11, 2001, political debate in the United States was severely restricted; it has been rejuvenated only as a result of the increasingly obvious problems with the war in Iraq. I believe we need to ask ourselves how and why this is so, and we should not avoid the obvious relationship between meta-narratives of what constitutes security and threats and the politics or methods they embody. For example, scholars have posted on the Perestroika list serve their worries concerning the constraints imposed on in-depth ethnographic work on Muslim-majority societies. Simply employing ethnographic methods can lay one open to charges of being too sympathetic to state enemies.

As a scholar of social movements in world politics, I understand that including debates about the meta-narratives employed in the war on terror could split the Perestroika movement. After all, the movement includes neo-realists who oppose the U.S. war in Iraq but not necessarily the war on terror. It also includes critics of U.S. economic, political, and cultural hegemony, as well as area studies specialists who warn against attempts to ignore the backlashes against that hegemony. Therefore it is understandable that Perestroika attempts to limit political (or "ideological") debate, however difficult it may prove to do so in practice.

Nevertheless, there are several dangers associated with Perestroika's presumptive stance in favor of restricting the Perestroika discussions to "methods." First, from the point of view of social movements, such a restriction does not guarantee the coherence of the movement and might indeed provoke a split of another kind. Such a split would be akin to the Democrats' move to the center during the 1990s, which shut out discussion of critical issues about poverty, labor, and social welfare. A significant chunk of the electorate decided to vote for Ralph Nader instead of the Democratic candidate in 2000, thus costing the Democratic Party the election in the eyes of some. For the moment, however, such a split in Perestroika does not seem likely; there remains too much work to do in advocating inclusiveness in political science departments and journals, and this work continues to unify the movement. Still, we do not know how many on the Perestroika list, other than myself, have fallen silent because of the movement's exclusion of the politics and method of meta-narrative construction.

The second danger, therefore, and one more important for the goals of Perestroika, is that such a restriction on debate results in an effective prohibition on discussing methods that allow us to probe and understand dominant narratives. Thus, from the point of view of the use of narrative as a method, Perestroika does not provide a forum for examining—or, in "r" word terminology, "testing"—meta-narratives against each other or against ontological and epistemological perspectives that attempt to reject meta-narratives altogether. We have not been able to have a good discussion of the problems with the George W. Bush administration's national security meta-narrative, for example, and the degree of its relationship (if any; this could be debated) to broader theoretical trends and practices in IR. Thus, whether one employs the "r" word or what this author considers less muscular but more valid terminology such as "historic reliability," "persuasiveness," or "systematicity," the elimination of the construction of meta-narratives and discussion of their impact from Perestroika also limits our effectiveness in opening the movement to all valid social-scientific methods.

Conclusion: Insurmountable Divisions or Further Openings?
Suggestions on How to Proceed

I have argued that the language we use in assessing our methods is related to which methods are deemed acceptable, and moreover that both are related to our understanding of politics. Yet I am ambivalent about my conclusions. I do not believe that Perestroika will open itself to discussion of the methodological and political worth of various meta-narratives any time soon, and I also understand that it is precisely the politically chaotic consequences of international politics today that increases the contentiousness of undertaking the self-examinations necessary for such discussions to occur.

However, we can still allow more discussion of how the allegedly "political" meta-narratives of the recent past have contributed to the conditions of methodological hegemony within which we find ourselves today. We can also go back to Bates and associates' promotion of "self-awareness" and take it one step further to encourage constant self-criticism. If we do not adopt these minimal steps, it seems to me that we are in danger of applying the negative aspects of rigor and becoming too rigid, puritanically uninteresting, and prone to alternate chills and fevers rather than advancing our abilities to understand nuance and complexity in politicomethodological relationships.

References

Alker, Hayward R. 1996. *Rediscoveries and Reformulations: Humanistic Methods for International Studies.* Cambridge: Cambridge University Press.

Anderson, Benedict. 1991. *Imagined Communities: Reflections on the Origin and Spread of Nationalism.* London and New York: Verso.

Barnett, Michael N. 1998. *Dialogues in Arab Politics: Negotiations in Regional Order.* New York: Columbia University Press.

Bates, Robert H., Avner Greif, Margaret Levi, Jean-Laurent Rosenthal, and Barry Weingast. 1998. *Analytic Narratives.* Princeton, NJ: Princeton University Press.

Campbell, D. 1998. *National Deconstruction: Violence, Identity, and Justice in Bosnia.* Minneapolis: University of Minnesota Press.

Cox, Robert, with Timothy J. Sinclair. 1996. *Approaches to World Order.* Cambridge: Cambridge University Press.

Elster, Jon. 2000. "Rational Choice History: A Case of Excessive Ambition." *American Political Science Review* 94 (3): 685–95.

Gerth, H. H., and C. Wright Mills, eds. 1946/58. *From Max Weber: Essays in Sociology.* New York: Oxford University Press.

Green, Donald, and Ian Shapiro. 1994. *Pathologies of Rational Choice.* New Haven, CT, and London: Yale University Press.

Hesse, Mary B. 1974. *The Structure of Scientific Inference.* Berkeley, CA: University of California Press.

Jenkins, Keith. 1995. *On "What Is History?": From Carr and Elton to Rorty and White.* London and New York: Routledge.

Katzenstein, Peter, ed. 1996. "Preface." *The Culture of National Security: Norms and Identity in World Politics.* New York: Columbia University Press.

Keohane, Robert O. 1988. "International Institutions: Two Approaches." *International Studies Quarterly* 32 (4): 379–96.

Kratochwil, Friedrich, and John Gerard Ruggie. 1986. "International Organization: A State of the Art on an Art of the State." *IO* 40 (4): 753–75.

Latham, Robert. 1997. *The Liberal Moment: Modernity, Security, and the Making of Postwar International Order.* New York: Columbia University Press.

Lynch, Cecelia. 1999. *Beyond Appeasement: Interpreting Interwar Peace Movements in World Politics.* Ithaca, NY, and London: Cornell University Press.

May, Ernest R. 1985. *"Lessons" of the Past: The Use and Misuse of History in American Foreign Policy.* Oxford: Oxford University Press.

Migdal, Joel S. 2001. *State in Society: Studying How States and Societies Transform and Constitute One Another.* Cambridge: Cambridge University Press.

Milliken, Jennifer. 2001. "Bringing Rigor to Critical Theory." In Karin M. Fierke and Knud Erik Jørgensen, eds. *Constructing International Relations: The Next Generation.* Armonk, NY, and London: M. E. Sharpe.

Oren, Ido. 2003. *Our Enemies and Us: America's Rivalries and the Making of Political Science.* Ithaca, NY, and London: Cornell University Press.

Parikh, Sunita. 2000. "The Strategic Value of *Analytic Narratives.*" *Social Science History* 24 (4): 677–84.

Ruggie, John Gerard. 1998. *Constructing the World Polity: Essays on International Institutionalization.* London and New York: Routledge.

Skocpol, Theda. 2000. "Commentary: Theory Tackles History." *Social Science History* 24 (4): 669–76.

Stein, Janice Gross, Thomas Risse-Kappen, Rey Koslowski and Friedrich V. Kratochwil, and Richard Ned Lebow. 1994. "Symposium: The End of the Cold War and Theories of International Relations." *IO* 48 (2): 155–277.

Suganami, Hidemi. 1996. *On the Causes of War.* Oxford, England: Clarendon Press.

Yanow, Dvora. 2000. *Conducting Interpretive Policy Analysis.* Thousand Oaks, CA: Sage Publications.

CHAPTER 12

Work That Counts

Elizabeth Sanders

The tendency of our discipline, the Perestroika movement included, to adopt polar categories ("quantitative" and "qualitative") to describe our methods is an unfortunate distraction. "Quantitative" has come to mean only work that employs highly technical statistics, and "qualitative," work that contains only "interpretive" text. What we lose in these categories is a large body of valuable work that has the advantage of systematically counting and categorizing observed phenomena in the service of hypothesis testing; work that provides rigorously empirical and comprehensive, theoretically informed description; and work that employs *both* systematic counting *and* description or interpretation.

We have learned so much from this work. It is wonderfully interpretable, straightforward, and accessible to a broad audience. Yet in the past decades we have gradually pushed such work out of our leading journals. Fortunately the books get published, and win prizes and the recognition of citation and inclusion on syllabi. But what does it say of our discipline that our leading journals adopt such a narrow view of "science" that only arcane statistical analysis counts as systematic, "scientific" analysis? I think it is the insistence on a particular, highly technical form of empirical analysis that has raised so many objections to the quantitative analysis favored by the *American Political Science Review* (*APSR*), the *American Journal of Political Science,* and other journals, not a general objection to systematic counting.

Let me give some examples of important work in American politics that do not rely (or at least not solely) on advanced statistics for the systematic analysis of data. One is V. O. Key's *Southern Politics,*[1] one of the most influential political science books of the twentieth century, which used maps and tables of election statistics and roll call votes to explore the nature of party, race, region, and ideology within the South. For an example of Key's tables, see Table 12.1.

In a similar vein, Michael Rogin's *The Intellectuals and McCarthy*[2] set out to debunk Richard Hofstadter's widely accepted interpretation of the American Populist and Progressive movements as dangerously atavistic forerunners of McCarthism and spiritual cousins of fascism. Rogin demolished those

Table 12.1 Relative Solidarity of Southern and Non-Southern House Democrats When Majorities of Each Group Opposed Majorities of Republicans, 1933–1945

Congress: Session, Year	Total Roll Calls	Southern Democratic (SD) and Non-Southern Democratic (NSD) Majorities against Majorities of Republican		
		Number	With Higher SD Cohesion	With Higher NSD Cohesion
73:1 1933	56	44	38	6
75:1 1937	77	41	27	14
77:1 1941	67	39	36	3
79:1 1945	75	40	24	16
Total	275	164	125	39

Source: Key, *Southern Politics,* Table 45, p. 377.

Table 12.2 McCarthy, Proxmire, and the Progressive Past, 1904–1957 [Correlations between Pairs of Candidates in Wisconsin Counties]

	1952 McCarthy	1957 Steinle (Proxmire's Opponent)	1950 Republican Governor
1904 La Follette	–10	–33	–28
1904 T. Roosevelt	–03	–21	–18
1904 Direct primary [in favor]	–23	–42	–31
1914 Philipp (anti-Progressive)	00	18	13
1916 Republican president	30	13	27
1918 Thompson [Republican]	19	32	37
1922 La Follette	–15	–37	–20
1930 P. La Follette primary	22	–25	–11
1930 P. La Follette general	–02	–39	–29
1932 Hoover	–03	26	01
1934 Progressive governor	–15	–37	–31
1934 Republican governor	13	35	23
1936 Progressive governor	–41	–63	–63
1938 Progressive governor	–48	–64	–68
1940 Progressive senator	–58	–64	–74
1950 Schmitt [progressive Republican]	–07	–53	–29

Source: Rogin, *The Intellectuals and McCarthy,* Table 3.5, p. 88.

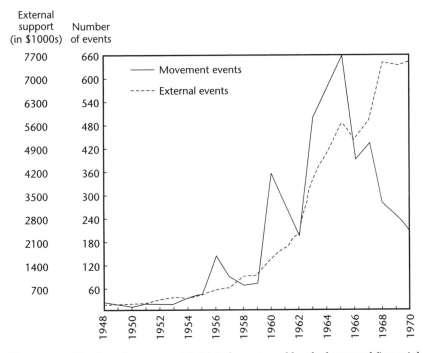

Figure 12.1   Number of movement-initiated events and level of external financial support, 1948–1970.
Sources: McAdam, *Political Process,* Figure 6.2, p. 123. For the number of movement-initiated events, McAdam referred to the annual *New York Times Index;* for financial data, see Appendix 3 of his book.

arguments with a tour de force of empirical analysis, most of it in the form of maps, graphs, charts, and simple correlations—all situated in extensive historical description. For an example of Rogin's tables, see Table 12.2.

Doug McAdam's seminal *Political Process and the Development of Black Insurgency*[3] employed some path coefficients, but mostly relied on simple tables and graphs like that in Figure 12.1, which addresses the question of whether outside support triggered or responded to grass-roots protest.

More recently, John Gerring's *Party Ideologies in America*[4] demonstrates how rigorous and systematic the analysis of discourse can be. Gerring counted the verbal formulations in (all) party platforms from 1828 to 1992 inclusive, grouped the party platforms within temporal and ideological categories, and summarized data in graphs and charts that are easily intelligible. For an example, see Figure 12.2.

Frederick Wirt's *"We Ain't What We Was"*[5] is a highly readable, even lyrical, exploration of attitude and behavior change in the Deep South. Wirt uses a variety of accessible count data, from interviews, surveys, newspaper articles,

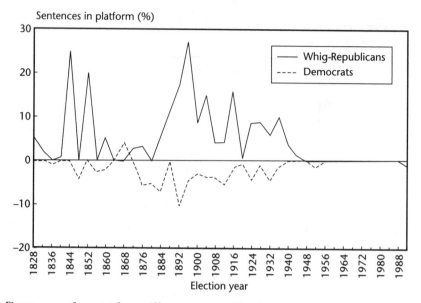

Figure 12.2   Support for tariffs, as measured by the percentage of sentences in Whig-Republican and Democratic Party platforms proposing protection minus the percentage of sentences in opposition to tariffs, tariffs for revenue only, and so forth.

Source: Gerring, *Party Ideologies in America,* Figure 1, p. 69.

precinct vote divisions, public and private employment breakdowns, school achievement patterns, and so on, to draw a richly complex and nuanced portrait of change in Mississippi racial politics after 1965. For an example of one of Wirt's tables, see Table 12.3.

Stephen Skowronek's highly influential book *The Politics Presidents Make,*[6] a pathbreaking theoretical work on the presidency, creates an inclusive four-fold typology of presidents, based on easily observable regime affiliations, to predict the advantages, challenges, and chances of success faced by presidents in each group. The typology was derived inductively from a close comparative reading of administration histories.

Richard Bensel's *The Political Economy of American Industrialization*[7] analyzes a massive amount of quantitative data in tables that use simple statistics, such as the analysis of the relationship between an index of economic development and party competition found in Table 12.4.

Recent books by Eric Schickler (*Disjointed Pluralism*),[8] Sarah Binder (*Minority Rights, Majority Rule*),[9] and Charles Cameron (*Veto Bargaining*)[10] employ some "sophisticated" statistics or model relationships in equations, but do not present information in that way only. The meat of their arguments is presented in graphs, charts, and tables made up of prose and simple percentages that we can all follow. (For an example of Schickler's tables, see Table 12.5, and for an example of Cameron's, see Table 12.6.) Their prose is clear, abundant (featuring a high word-to-number ratio) and mercifully free of stilted jargon; their historical explanations and examples are extensive. We don't learn just about specified variable relationships in these books; we learn about broad historical trends in institutional development, party conflict, and presidential-congressional competition.

Even less reliant on "sophisticated" statistics but critical to an understanding of two major policy arenas are Daniel Tichenor's *Dividing Lines,*[11] an analytical description of immigration policy and politics from the first years of the republic to the present, and Jacob Hacker's comprehensive historical-institutional analysis of the development of public and private health care systems, *The Divided Welfare State.*[12] (For an example of Tichenor's tables, see Table 12.7.) A few years ago the social science history prize committee awarded the year's Sharlin book prize to a comparable work, Jose Moya's densely packed, analytical, theoretically informed description of immigration flows from Spain to Argentina (*Cousins and Strangers,*[13] which called into question several widely accepted generalizations about the social characteristics and motivations of immigrants.

The *APSR* has for years considered such pioneering descriptive works "unscientific," but this impoverished notion departs significantly from the "hard" sciences. Pick up any issue of *Science* magazine, and you will find pathbreaking (and often hypothesis-generating or hypothesis-questioning) descriptions of (to mention a few recent examples) changes in biological diversity in rain forests, observable personality differences among horses, or annual changes in carbon dioxide emissions. Without such descriptions, science is impossible. Yet our political science journals disparage "mere" description, equate science only with highly technical methods, and appear to value statistical analysis of existing data sets far above the work of scholars who painstakingly collect new data and report on the patterns they find in simple percentages, tables, and graphs.

Science relies much more on easily interpretable data displays than do our political science journals. I doubt many Perestroikans object to the methods that tell us, for example, how much our chances of having a stroke are increased if we both smoke and take birth control pills. The conclusions of few articles in the *APSR* are so straightforward, however. The usual means of data presentation is a table of numbers carried to the third or fourth decimal place and accompanied by one, two, or three asterisks. All too seldom does the author translate the inscrutable numbers into intelligible prose such as "For every thousand-dollar increase in district median income, the member of Congress's sponsorship of tax cut bills can be expected to increase by twenty-five percent."

More often than not, the tables of four-digit numbers, with or without asterisks, are followed by sweeping conclusions such as "Neither occupation nor education matter, as shown by the coefficients in model one," even

Table 12.3 Democratic Vote, 1992 General Election, in Panola County Black and White Precincts

	Percentage Voting for Candidates			Number of Votes		
Precinct	Leonard Morris	Bill Clinton	Michael Espy	State Legislature	President	Congress
Black precincts						
West Como	87.5	86.9	87.5	519	869	678
West Sardis	—	78.1	83.6	300	270	292
Crenshaw	—	66.2	84.9	—	420	449
Pleasant Grove	55.9	58.4	73.5	273	257	268
South Sardis	63.0	66.5	74.2	781	692	740
Curtis	73.0	72.1	87.9	397	359	141
Belmont-Hebron	72.9	76.0	83.2	332	300	310
Cortland	74.2	61.8	—	392	600	—
East Crowder	59.8	67.7	84.1	251	226	239
West Batesville B	80.5	76.5	82.9	809	705	725
Pleasant Mount	58.9	63.7	70.3	316	270	317
Median%	72.9	72.1	83.2			
% range	55.9–87.5	58.4–86.9	70.3–87.9			

White precincts						
East Como	35.9	37.9	58.5	365	351	342
East Sardis	—	34.6	—	—	436	—
Tocowa	43.3	33.4	—	420	362	—
North Asa	40.8	39.1	—	125	115	—
Batesville 3	35.8	25.9	—	159	320	—
West Batesville IV	42.6	39.0	—	242	228	—
Median%	40.8	53.8				
% range	35.8–43.0	25.9–39.1				
Total county vote	62.1	53.8	79.4	7,089	11,399	4,731

Sources: Wirt, "*We Ain't What We Was*," Table 4.4, p. 80. Wirt referred to mid-November 1992 issues of the *Panolian* for overlapping jurisdictions, and confirmed the data by consulting registrar records.

Note: Some voting tallies are not included due to jurisdictional lines; they are indicated by a dash. Candidates were not on the ballot in those jurisdictions. [Morris and Espy are Black.]

Table 12.4 Summary of Trade Area Development and Change in Major Party Strength, 1888–1896

Trade Area Economic Development	Vote Cast For Major Party Candidates in 1888 (%)			Vote Cast For Major Party Candidates in 1896 (%)			Change 1888–1896 (%)	
	Republican	Democratic	Total Vote Cast	Republican	Democratic	Total Vote Cast	Rep.	Dem.
5 (highest)	49.5	48.0	3,153,946	59.4	37.3	3,645,807	+9.9	–10.0
4 (high)	52.2	44.8	1,157,197	56.8	41.3	1,603,414	+4.6	–3.0
3 (middle high)	53.7	42.5	1,075,733	53.7	43.7	1,267,027	0.0	+1.0
2 (middle low)	51.4	43.9	1,825,149	53.3	44.7	2,228,294	+1.9	+0.0
1 (low)	47.9	46.7	1,908,744	48.7	49.9	2,289,874	+0.8	+3.0
0 (lowest)	37.7	60.2	2,242,864	36.1	62.1	2,474,679	–1.6	+1.0

Source: Bensel, *The Political Economy of American Industrialization*, Table 4.8, p. 261.

Table 12.5 Summary of Collective Interests Associated with Institutional Changes in Congress, 1919–1932

Case	Primary Interest	Common Carrier for Other Interests?	Compromised by Other Interests?	Coalition Shaping Change	Main Effects of Change
Senate committee consolidation, 1920	Senate capacity	Majority party (reputation)		Universalistic	Made committee system more orderly
Senate farm bloc	Policy (sectoral)			Cross-party sectoral	Hurt GOP program; started bloc activism
House rules changes, 1924	Policy (progressives)	Minority party; individual power bases	Mangled discharge rule (majority party interests)	Cross-party ideological	Boosted individual member prerogatives
Discharge rule repeal, 1925	Majority party (effectiveness)	Policy (conservatives)		Majority party	Made discharge rule ineffective
Longworth's revival of speakership	Majority party (effectiveness)	Democratic leaders' power		Party based, but with an element of bipartisan cooperation	Increased Speaker's power; established bipartisan leadership alliance
Punishment of presidential election defectors, 1925	Majority party			Partisan	Strengthened party discipline in House
House rules reforms, 1931	Individual power bases	Policy (progressives, issue-specific blocs); majority party (reputation)		Cross-party reformist (antileadership)	Attacked committee chair power; helped "special interests" force floor votes

Source: Schickler, *Disjointed Pluralism*, Table 3.1, p. 87.

Table 12.6   Vetoes of Public Bills, 1945–1992

	Total Vetoes			Vetoes in Chains		
	No.	Col.%	Row%	No.	Col.%	Row%
Total	434	100	100	176	100	41
Divided government	310	71	100	139	77	45
Unified government	124	29	100	37	21	30
Appropriations	34	8	100	28	16	82
Authorizations	400	92	100	148	84	37
[Landmark bills] Group A	34	8	100	22	12	65
[Important bills] Group B	29	7	100	19	11	66
[Ordinary bills] Group C	126	29	100	79	45	63
[Minor bills] Group D	245	56	100	56	31	23
Truman	86	20	100	19	11	22
Eisenhower	79	18	100	30	17	38
Kennedy	9	2	100	1	0	11
Johnson	15	3	100	5	3	33
Nixon	41	9	100	23	13	56
Ford	59	14	100	27	15	46
Carter	29	7	100	15	9	52
Reagan	71	17	100	34	19	48
Bush	45	10	100	22	13	49

Source: Cameron, *Veto Bargaining,* Table 2.3, p. 47.
Note: Column percentages are by category, e.g., percent unified + percent divided = 100%.

Table 12.7   Support for Decreased Immigration, 1980–1996

	Percentage Supporting Decrease		
Demographic Group	1980	1986	1996
Education			
Less than high school	79	56	74
College	44	41	49
Income level			
Less than $15,000	76	58	65
More than $50,000	42	44	54

Sources: Tichenor, *Dividing Lines,* Table 9.5, p. 276. Tichenor cited the Roper Center, University of Connecticut, 1980 Poll, and CBS News / *New York Times* monthly polls, June 1986 and September 1996.

though the conclusion is derived from only one set of data points and the selection of variables for the often misnamed and unspecified "models" frequently seems arbitrary. Another set of observations at another time, a different set of independent variables, or a different statistic tweaked in a different way might well yield a different conclusion (that is, a different set of coefficients, with or without asterisks); but interpretations of such tables are seldom modest. Perestroikans may suspect that the purpose of such tables is more to impress and mystify than to explain or encourage debate. I recently overheard two graduate students at an APSA meeting talking about an article one hoped to send off to a journal. "But Prof. X says I need to tech it up some more," said the author.

"Teching it up" is indeed what we have been doing, and articles have become less and less intelligible. Even the highly trained are often at a loss to explain or defend the statistical method employed in an article, but if only highly trained statisticians are chosen to review such articles, they may not be scrutinized by readers in a position to critique the assumptions, operationalizations, facts, or case selections. It is not uncommon to find articles in our leading journals that are statistically sophisticated and substantively quite naïve.

One solution would be to urge reviewers to closely examine substantive issues and require that simpler statistical presentations—categorical means, graphs, histograms, maps, and so on—at least accompany the "fancy" stats. It would also be reasonable to require that there be an explanation *in words* of what the numbers in the tables mean. This would challenge authors to demonstrate that they truly understand what they have done (laying to rest *one* suspicion), and it would force confrontations between claims made on the basis of four-digit numbers with asterisks, and the evidence in the more starkly visible direction of simple means, vote divisions, or graphs.

The complaint may be made that such simple statistics are too crude, or do not "control" for other relationships. One response to that complaint is to treat our "cases" with the respect due individuals, states, or countries. Rather than grinding them up statistically, we can "control" by grouping cases on the relevant variables and then reporting the simple percentages within groups. For example, Robert Carp and C. K. Rowland, in their study of patterns of judicial liberalism in presidential appointments, rather than statistically controlling for the effect of type of court case or judge's party affiliation, present the cross-tabulation in Table 12.8 using simple percentages—perfectly intelligible counting.

The more common *APSR* tables of four-digit numbers with asterisks give a false sense of precision, because the coefficients depend on the particular cases examined and differ from the coefficients that *other* statistics, subject to *other* manipulations, would find. The assumption that the asterisks—symbols of statistical significance in random samples—have some intrinsic meaning when the cases examined constitute not a sample but the entire population of counties, states, countries, or senators remains (to me at least) an odd metaphysical notion.

Table 12.8 Liberal Decisions for Three Categories of Cases by Same-Party and Opposite-Party Appointees of President Truman through President Ford

| | Criminal Justice | | | | Civil Rights and Civil Liberties | | | | Labor and Economic Regulation | | | |
| | Dem. | | Rep. | | Dem. | | Rep. | | Dem. | | Rep. | |
Appointing President	%	n	%	n	%	n	%	n	%	n	%	n
Harry Truman	22	930	32	79	44	629	42	33	62	780	63	57
Dwight Eisenhower	25	24	19	1,830	46	37	39	1,031	55	31	61	1,320
John Kennedy	25	1,881	29	189	41	991	50	123	65	994	60	161
Lyndon Johnson	36	2,207	30	121	61	1,961	51	80	67	1,168	64	119
Richard Nixon	35	95	25	1,100	44	116	38	1,219	38	76	48	839
Gerald Ford	57	7	29	42	55	11	39	67	56	9	54	54

Source: Carp and Rowland, *Policymaking and Politics in the Federal District Courts*, Appendix C, p. 179.
Note: For presidents prior to Truman the *n*'s were too small (fewer than 50 cases in each category) to use meaningfully. [Numbers in % columns are percent voting liberal.]

Table 12.9   Voting Behavior on Amendment to FY96 Bill to Prohibit Funds
for Tobacco Program, by Level of District Characteristics

District Level[a]	Farm Employment			Rural Population		
	Number Voting			Number Voting		
	Yea	Nay	% Yea	Yea	Nay	% Yea
All members						
Low	94	36	72.9	95	41	69.9
Middle	62	90	40.8	70	74	48.6
High	43	97	30.7	34	108	23.9
Agriculture Committee						
Low	—	—	—	1	0	100.0
Middle	2	9	18.2	2	13	13.3
High	6	30	16.7	5	26	16.1
Appropriations Subcommittee						
Low	—	—	—	—	—	—
Middle	1	3	25.0	2	5	28.6
High	2	5	28.6	1	3	25.0
Noncommittee members[b]						
Low	94	36	72.3	94	41	69.6
Middle	59	78	43.1	66	56	54.1
High	35	62	36.1	28	79	26.2

Source: Hurwitz, Moiles, and Rhode, "Distributive and Partisan Issues in Agricultural
Policy in the 104th House," Table 4, p. 918.
[a] Division into approximately equal thirds is based upon the values obtained for the farm
employment and rural population variables.
[b] Representatives who are not members of either the Agriculture Committee or the agriculture appropriations subcommittee.

It might be argued that space constraints in journal articles preclude putting more simple descriptive counts in tables, and encourage condensation in
one big table with four-digit coefficients. But even the *APSR* has sometimes
published articles like that of Mark Hurwitz, Roger Moiles, and David Rhode
("Distributive and Partisan Issues in Agricultural Policy in the 104th House").[14]
In this article nearly all of what we want to know appears in straightforward
tables like Table 12.9. These authors felt compelled to present a table of multivariate logit coefficients at the end of the article, but a political science undergraduate could easily follow the argument up to that point and know what she
needed to know about voting patterns on farm bills.

My plea, then, is not that we give up counting in favor of some "qualitative"
method, or that we simply adopt a quota for "qualitative" articles in journals,

including them alongside the inscrutable "techy" articles. Many propositions that interest us cannot be tested and cannot yield legitimate generalizations without systematic counting. But we can count sensibly and produce straightforward, easily intelligible tables and figures. Students can be trained to do that, and can get over the number phobias many government majors (and graduate students) have, if we let them know that they don't have to devote two years to training in upper-level statistics (at the expense of substantive courses and original data collecting) in order to do "quantitative" analysis and systematic hypothesis testing. Above all, we should not communicate to our students that science is served by ever-more-impenetrable tables.

Notes

1. V. O. Key Jr., *Southern Politics* (New York: Random House Vintage Books, 1949).

2. Michael Paul Rogin, *The Intellectuals and McCarthy* (Cambridge, MA: MIT Press, 1967).

3. Doug McAdam, *Political Process and the Development of Black Insurgency, 1930–1970* (Chicago: University of Chicago Press, 1982).

4. John Gerring, *Party Ideologies in America 1828–1996* (Cambridge, MA: Cambridge University Press, 1998).

5. Frederick M. Wirt, *"We Ain't What We Was": Civil Rights in the New South* (Durham, NC: Duke University Press, 1997).

6. Stephen Skowronek, *The Politics Presidents Make* (Cambridge, MA: Harvard University Press, 1993).

7. Richard Franklin Bensel, *The Political Economy of American Industrialization, 1877–1900* (Cambridge, MA: Cambridge University Press, 2000).

8. Eric Schickler, *Disjointed Pluralism: Institutional Innovation and the Development of the U.S. Congress* (Princeton, NJ: Princeton University Press, 2001).

9. Sarah Binder, *Minority Rights, Majority Rule* (Cambridge, MA: Cambridge University Press, 1997).

10. Charles M. Cameron, *Veto Bargaining* (Cambridge, MA: Cambridge University Press, 2000).

11. Daniel J. Tichenor, *Dividing Lines* (Princeton, NJ: Princeton University Press, 2002).

12. Jacob Hacker, *The Divided Welfare State* (Cambridge, MA: Cambridge University Press, 2002).

13. Jose C. Moya, *Cousins and Strangers: Spanish Immigrants in Buenos Aires, 1850–1930* (Berkeley: University of California Press, 1998).

14. Mark S. Hurwitz, Roger J. Moiles, and David W. Rhode, "Distributive and Partisan Issues in Agricultural Policy in the 104th House," *American Political Science Review* 95 (December 2001): 911–22.

CHAPTER 13

Lost in Translation

The Challenges of State-Generated Data
in Developing Countries

Kamal Sadiq

Bad Statistics may well be worse than no statistics, since they rigidify
the deep channels of our false flows of thought—based on a
consensus erected on the basis of random insights.

—Polly Hill (1984)

The state plays a crucial role in generating the statistics we use from developing countries. However, this involves uncritically accepting a certain amount
of neutrality on the part of the state with respect to its ideologies, domestic
prejudices, interests, and claims of efficacy for the collection of its data. In this
context, we need to heed the Perestroika network's call for making political science more relevant and grounded by examining concretely what this collection and use of data entails. In this chapter, therefore, I begin by entering the
methodological debate surrounding the challenges of using statistics from
developing countries.

My arguments will be developed around the relationship between state and
data. In particular, I am assuming that the state is the best, and sometimes the
only, source of data on many political phenomena.[1] Presently I am interested
in the problem with relying on state-supplied data in developing countries,
which is separate from the empirical question of whether other sources of data
exist. Clearly, making factual claims based on data and statistics supplied by
developing states is one way of analyzing political and social realities. It also
raises several issues that I will examine in this chapter. I hope that an analysis
of these difficulties will serve as the groundwork for either the creation of new
methods or the selection and revival of some of the elements of older methods.
Doing so will allow us to avoid these difficulties while still obtaining the data
necessary to increase our understanding of the politics of developing states. To
this end, the chapter begins by examining two questions.

First, how does one study phenomena that mobilize the state's interest in
suppressing information or lying about it? The visibility and legibility of many
political phenomena are dependent on the political character of the state,
whether authoritarian, monarchical, or totalitarian. Alternatively, they may

depend on the ideology of the regime. For example, many developing states, though democratic, may have an intrinsic interest in suppressing information about their ethnic minorities. Particular data-gathering departments may exaggerate numbers or minimize them to affect budget allocations—and not only in developing states. These factors compromise the reliability and availability of data in developing countries. They inhibit questions about such states and also highlight the weaknesses of methodological tools that depend on such data. I shall demonstrate this with some examples from my cross-regional research on migration and from debates on poverty.

Second, how does one study phenomena that bypass the state? States are not able, with the resources currently available, to monitor and control phenomena that circumvent them. Therefore, data on terrorist networks, the illegal or "black" economy (e.g., India's bazaar economy), illegal trade, illegal international financial transactions (e.g., *hawala*), and illegal migration flows are all a reflection of states' inability to control and monitor key processes within and across their boundaries. A related issue is the absence or inaccuracy of data, resulting from cultural practices that lead to, for instance, an underestimation of the contributions of groups in traditional societies. I shall elaborate on this issue later using examples, such as women's groups, to illustrate problems in data generation as well as questions surrounding the reliability of the data gathered on such issues.

The availability and reliability of data, as well as the possibilities for cross-regional research, are much better when doing research within developed states. The unavailability and unreliability of data make cross-regional research between cases within developing countries difficult. As political scientists, are we to ignore all such phenomena, where the state either lies or hides, or where the state is unable to "see," that is, the state is unable to generate data? We may have to become creative and develop methods to examine issues that do not always arise from or for the state. I shall illustrate my argument with examples from my cross-regional research on South and Southeast Asia.

Data Manipulation and Suppression

States count, monitor, and make legible many aspects of society and politics in an effort to maintain control and order. The development of almost all statistics becomes possible only with the acknowledgement, if not the encouragement of states. Hannah Arendt has argued with regard to stateless people that "the lack of any reliable statistics on the subject" is the result of leaders' wanting to ignore the problem (Arendt 1968, 279). Therefore, there are bound to be more statistics on those issues over which the state has tighter control and which it would like to publicly acknowledge. Recent ethnic conflicts and violence, increasing assertions based on gender, and issues related to race and minority rights demonstrate to us the linkages between institutions of the state and availability of data. States have an intrinsic interest in suppressing and discouraging the collection of data that challenge their assertions in the polity or that break the consensus on issues, for instance, the percentage of Hindus in Bangladesh, the percentage of Christians in Pakistan, the magnitude of poverty in India, the number of illegal Filipinos and Indonesians in Sabah, Malaysia, and so on.[2] Therefore, states obfuscate and efface certain data. Let me illustrate with an example from my fieldwork on the issue of illegal immigrants from Indonesia and the Philippines in Malaysia.

In my research I have shown how the state uses illegal immigrants from neighboring countries to "Malayize" or homogenize Malaysia.[3] The authorities at the center collaborate with their regional partners in Sabah to use census practices to incorporate an illegal immigrant population from the Philippines and Indonesia. The motive for such practices is to use illegal immigrants as voters to ensure political control by a Malay or Muslim party such as the UMNO (the United Malays National Organization).[4] At the individual level, illegal immigrants use the census by giving self-reports that deny their illegal immigrant status and, more important, use documents to prove their citizenship and acquire the rights of citizens, such as political suffrage. In my research I have analyzed the politics of estimation and classification of the illegal population. I emphasize the use of fuzzy categories by the census to create ambiguity around illegal immigration, thus facilitating immigrant incorporation—an outcome that sections of the federal and state governments appear to favor although the law disfavors it. This is an outcome that scholars using census data from Malaysia will be unaware of, particularly if they are involved in large n studies of ethnic groups or immigrants that may preclude spending too much time checking the veracity of censuses and other government reports. Usually data from the United Nations Development Program, the United Nations Children's Fund, and other United Nations agencies are dependent on the data supplied by national governments and merely replicate this misinformation. The same goes for data from regional organizations such as the Association of Southeast Asian Nations, the Asian Development Bank, and so on.

Local Malay authorities are constantly being accused of encouraging illegal immigration of Muslims from the Southern Philippines and Indonesia to Sabah, a region of Malaysia. The census is a project of the central government, but it is conducted with the cooperation of regional governments in Sabah. Census categories can be introduced and withdrawn according to the political goals of the dominant political party in Sabah. Parties dominated by West Malaysian Muslims such as the UMNO use census categories to incorporate individuals who have been engaged in illegal immigration from the Philippines to Sabah. The political calculation to provide citizenship through census manipulation was part of a long-term goal to Malayize Sabah and ensure the political hegemony of Malay-Muslim–based parties such as the UMNO. Such census manipulation also provides incentives for self-reporting by illegal immigrants to fit into Malay-Muslim categories such as "Pribumi" or "Bumiputera," terms conveying local origin.

In the 1970s the Malaysian government estimated that the population of Filipino refugees was 70,000, while the United Nations Commissioner for

Refugees estimated that their numbers were closer to 100,000 and the local community leaders in Sabah claimed that the figure was in excess of 130,000.[5] The official Malaysian *Population and Housing Census 1991* gave a figure of only 57,197 (Department of Statistics, Malaysia, 1995). There are allegations that these differences were part of a tactic to create ambiguity about this issue through unreliable and multiple figures. Controversy surrounds the changing categories used to classify and "incorporate" this "alien" population. Federal authorities, in collaboration with their regional partners, the United Sabah National Organization, and later their regional branch, the UMNO, created census categories that would deny or minimize illegal immigration. The term *Pribumi,*[6] or "sons of the soil," which was introduced in the Malaysian *Population and Housing Census* of 1980, functioned to downplay the distinction between natives and immigrants because it was not a discrete category and included indigenous as well as immigrant groups. The term *Pribumi* was introduced by a Sabah state government directive on October 7, 1982 (Regis 1989, 15–16).[7] It has the effect of collapsing all the indigenous groups classified under various headings in censuses before 1980 and grouping them along with recent immigrants, thereby creating a large undifferentiated Malay stock (see Table 13.1).

"Pribumi" was a political category as much as an all-inclusive nomenclature in the census. Many groups, including immigrants from the Philippines and Indonesia who had been included in the category "Others" in the 1970 census, were included in the generic "Pribumi" or "sons of the soil" category in 1980. Ignoring descent and ethnic boundaries between groups for classification purposes facilitated the inclusion of illegal immigrants and their children, who would qualify for citizenship and "sons of the soil" status if their parents were classified as "Pribumi." The "Pribumi" category included Malay-Muslim groups such as Malays, Bajaus, Suluks, Indonesians, and natives of the Philippines (mainly Muslim Southern Filipinos).[8] A neutral, nonpoliticized use of these categories would involve using the categories "Malay," "Bajau," and "Suluk" for only those natives who had been present in Sabah from before its independence. However, these categories were also used to absorb newly "minted" natives who had illegally arrived from the Southern Philippines. These Filipino Suluks and Filipino Bajaus were being accommodated in the generic categories of "Suluk," "Bajau," and so on.

Because the magnitude of illegal immigration was huge, illegal immigrants were spread into various Pribumi categories such as "Native of Philippines," "Suluk," and "Bajau." The category "Malay" could accommodate an illegal immigrant from either the Philippines or Indonesia. The reason several subcategories were being used to absorb illegal immigrants was that a conspicuous jump in the numbers associated with any single category could be spotted or traced and therefore become a domestic political issue for regional anti-immigrant parties such as the PBS (Parti Bersatu Sabah). At the same time, the larger overarching cover of Pribumi sent the political message of native dominance. As a result of this innovative "cooking" of the census books, Pribumi

Table 13.1   Census Categories for Muslim Filipino Immigrants in Sabah

1970 Census	1980 Census	1990 Census
Malay (listed for the first time) →	Malay	Malay
Bajau	Bajau Indonesian	Other Bumiputera: Indonesian
Other indigenous: Suluk born in Sabah and the Philippines →	Other indigenous Suluk Native of Philippines	Bajau Suluk
Others: Includes native of Philippines ↗	Others	Others: Filipino, Indonesian
		Non-Malaysian (New immigrant) **citizens** 25.1%

The 1980 Census column shows a brace grouping the rows labeled **Pribumi 82.9%**. The 1990 Census column shows a brace grouping the rows labeled **Malaysian citizens 74.9%**.

Sources: Department of Statistics, Malaysia 1983; Department of Statistics, Malaysia 1995; Regis 1989.

accounted for as much as 82.9 percent of the Sabah population in the 1980 census. The term *Pribumi,* much like the term *Bumiputera,* was a code for Muslims (Table 13.1). The term was dropped on April 24, 1985, after the opposition regional party, the PBS, came to power and made illegal immigration a major issue. By forcing the national census to back down, the PBS was seeking to protect the regional interests of its members, who were mainly non-Malay, non-Muslim local natives such as the Kadazandusuns and Muruts.

The reconfigured census of 1991 continued the incorporation but showed some of the immigrants separately. In the *Population and Housing Census 1991,* these immigrants were placed in the category "Non-Malaysian Citizens" (Department of Statistics, Malaysia, 1995). From the total population of Sabah of 1,734,685 in 1991, the non-Malaysian citizens numbered 425,175, which, after adjusting for underenumeration, was about 25.1 percent of the population (Table 13.1). This large percentage of noncitizens in Sabah's population excluded illegal immigrants who had self-reported as belonging in "Malay," "Bajau," "Suluk," or some other Bumiputera category in the census. According to the explanatory notes and definitions of the 1991 census, citizenship "refers to the *self-identification* of an individual regarding his citizenship and was not based on any official document" (Department of Statistics, Malaysia, 1991, xxxi, emphasis mine). Clearly, there was incentive to self-report as a member of a "sons of the soil" or Bumiputera group. The "Non-Malaysian Citizens" category in the 1991 census also excluded illegal immigrants who over the decade had acquired Malaysian citizenship, either by naturalization or by fraudulent means.

Within the "Malaysian Citizens" category the following was the breakdown: (1) "Others" numbered 32,210; (2) "Other Bumiputeras" numbered 255,555, or 14.7 percent; (3) "Bajaus" numbered 203,457, or 11.7 percent; (4) "Indonesians" numbered 139,403, or 8 percent; and finally (5) Malays numbered 106,740, or 6.15 percent (Department of Statistics, Malaysia, 1991, 18–20). Why were Indonesians listed as Malaysian citizens in the 1991 census? Although some may have regularized their status from illegal through marriage with a local, others might have benefited from the many "regularization" exercises that Malaysia conducts, which have the effect of legalizing and normalizing illegal immigrants. This regularization paves the way for Filipinos and Indonesians alike to be eligible for naturalization as citizens. Indonesians, a majority of whom are illegal Muslim immigrants, were included in the "Other Bumiputera" and "Others" subcategories of "Malaysian Citizens" and constituted as much as 8 percent of "Malaysian Citizens." Excluding the large Indonesian category, many of the subheadings within "Malaysian Citizens" were meant to incorporate the large influx of illegal Filipinos into Sabah, Malaysia. "Bajau," "Malay," and "Suluk" were all ethnic categories that would neatly incorporate the group of recent illegal immigrants from the Philippines. Indonesians were accommodated in the category "Indonesians," where they were carefully combined with people from other ethnic categories such as "Bugi" that overlap both Malaysians and Indonesians. Within the "Bumiputera" category, many subheadings included immigrant groups, formerly illegal, who were now "legal" citizens, having spent decades in Sabah. It is clear that census terms such as *Pribumi, Bumiputera, Bajau, Indonesian, Other Bumiputera,* and *Malay* were code words for Muslims. This practice of the census was in effect *conferring citizenship on various illegal immigrant groups.*

It is curious that 192,800 people (6.5 percent) in Sabah were categorized as Malays according to the *Monthly Statistical Bulletin Sabah* of October 1999 (Government of Sabah 1999, 9), although there were no records of large-scale migration of Malays from West Malaysia to Sabah after the initial migration of civil servants in the early years of independent Malaysia. This category included personnel of the armed forces who were stationed in Sabah, but the number of Malays was too high to be accounted for by mere transfer of officers to Sabah. As Patricia Regis points out in her study, "The term 'Malay' is being increasingly used as a generic term to describe traditionally Muslim groups who speak Malay." She further states, "It is also likely that *a number of Indonesians may have claimed to be Malays in order to be indigenized.* In fact, in the census classification system for Peninsular Malaysia they are classified as Malays" (Regis 1989, 417, emphasis mine). The same practice holds true for Muslim Filipinos.

Shifting fuzzy categories in census reports suggest a state political strategy to absorb. The tension between Malay-Muslim–sympathetic sections of Sabah and the non-Muslim Malay-based "sons of the soil" parties such as the PBS can explain the changing categories adopted to classify immigrants. Malay-based parties such as the UMNO wanted to capture the illegal vote, while the PBS wanted to neutralize their impact. However, there is incentive for mass self-(mis)reporting by Filipino illegal immigrants, as Patricia Regis pointed out; it has been done by Indonesians claiming to be Malays. While my fieldwork data, consisting of newspaper reports and observations of local conversations, suggest that capturing and classifying illegal immigrants as citizens was a matter of political calculation, it is clear that there was incentive for illegal immigrants from the Philippines (and Indonesia) to self-report as citizens. The census in Malaysia was hiding some realities, while revealing others.

These government practices present several problems for scholars researching immigration to or the ethnic composition of Sabah and Malaysia as part of a larger universe of cases. Most researchers studying Malaysia take government figures on immigration and immigrant ethnic groups at face value. Sometimes they may substantiate their national data using figures on immigration given by the International Labor Organization or regional Asian organizations. But these organizations usually take their estimates and census classifications from the Malaysian government and may back those estimates with figures given by journalists from leading magazines such as the *Far Eastern Economic Review* or *Asiaweek*. Very rarely would a researcher question the ethnic breakdown and classifications used in the official census. But as I have shown, sections of the Malaysian state have an interest in suppressing information about the incorporation of fellow Muslim illegal immigrants into Malaysia.

This is not a new phenomenon. All the following states are suspected to have misreported the magnitude of sections of their populations: Bangladesh with regard to its Hindu population, China with regard to its Tibetan population, and India with regard to its tribal population. Hania Zlotnick, from the population division of the United Nations, has pointed out how in the 1980s "the political sensitivity of worker migration in the oil-rich countries of the Middle East and North Africa . . . led to a virtual information blackout" (Zlotnick 1987, ix). Every state, democratic or authoritarian, suppresses information about certain groups or phenomena. Rogers Smith's research (1997) examining the politics by which elite groups foster a common identity and membership supportive of their governance shows us that distorting state statistics to project the preferred image of the "people" as an empirical reality is an example of this sort of politics.[9]

For many political scientists doing large *n* work and spending just a few months or no time at all in each country they select, there is a tendency to uncritically accept census and other economic data provided by the government agencies. Running regressions on immigration data based on the case I have discussed will not only give false results, but also overlook the fudging involved in the breakdown of ethnic groups that is so important for many scholars studying ethnic conflict. Also missed will be state complicity in the phenomenon being studied. That is precisely why some scholars caution us about using national data. National aggregates can be spurious, washing out regional or local circumstances and politics that may determine local inputs (Rudolph and Rudolph 1987, 347–48).

Let me elaborate with a second example. Governments in India have been known to generate data on poverty with an eye to parliamentary elections.[10] Any data showing that poverty had increased became a reflection of a government's bad performance. Therefore, successive governments have succeeded in changing the definition of poverty or found other means of fiddling with such data so that more people are shown moving above the poverty line. A recent paper on poverty by two Indian economists, J. Mehta and S. Venkatraman, shares similar concerns: "The word 'statistics' originally meant 'for the purposes of state.' The state could use statistics to ascertain the objective reality, but it could use it to camouflage the real state of affairs. We, the people of India, must demand that government uses [sic] statistics only to ascertain objective reality. If the majority in this country are poor, the government has first to admit it" (Mehta and Venkatraman 2000). Because statistics are known to us as facts, why are they are so easily manipulated? Why is there conflict over poverty statistics in India? Facts cannot be cooked—or can they?

The recent debate on whether poverty in India decreased or increased during the 1990s is an example of such an interpretation. According to the Indian government, poverty declined from 56.9 percent in 1973–74 to 37.2 percent in 1993–94 in rural India, and from 49 to 32.4 percent in urban areas (Mehta and Venkatraman 2000). However, this claim, accepted by the World Bank, was based on a National Sample Survey covering, among other things, consumer expenditures. The "poverty line" was defined as the aggregate per capita monthly expenditure of a group whose per capita, per diem caloric intake conformed to certain nutritional standards and norms. According to Mehta and Venkatraman, these caloric standards were 2435 kcal per capita per diem for rural areas and 2095 kcal for urban areas. When they adhered to these caloric norms, based on consumer expenditure figures, they found that 75 percent of the rural population and 54.4 percent of the urban population was below the poverty line. However, if one lowers these caloric standards, the figures on poverty correspond to the official government figures. Because changing the caloric norms in effect enables the government to show a larger percentage of people above the poverty line, does this mean that the official economic planners in India are manipulating the poverty figures?

A recent special investigative report in a leading Indian newsmagazine points to other strategies through which approximately fifty million poor people may have been "pushed" above the poverty line in India as a result of official state surveys that had "predetermined" poverty estimates as targets to be achieved (Sinha 2004).[11] In short, there was a recommended limit on the number of poor people a state could have, and state surveys were to achieve those targets. The point is that "cooking the books," which we have associated with Enron, WorldCom, Arthur Andersen, and other firms manipulating financial data, has been practiced by states for a long time.

Changing caloric norms in poverty data or changing ethnic group classifications in the census are illustrations of attempts by states to manipulate, and sometimes fudge, statistics. For scholars prone to doing large n work on poverty, immigration, or ethnic conflict, the results could be "hiding" more than they are revealing. In the sweep of generalizations that many of us seek, we could be "seeing" as the state wants us to see (to paraphrase Scott). For this purpose, the state often has politicians, bureaucrats, and military personnel acting as "gatekeepers," as Margaret Peil has pointed out (Peil 1983, 73).[12] Controlling research and data output on politically sensitive topics, the kind of topics that interest political scientists, is a feature of both democratic and authoritarian regimes. The state has much to hide and lie about, and a critical political science will have to take a microscopic look at political processes to be aware of any statistical manipulation of reality.[13] This is the value that careful case studies based on extensive field work provide.

State Hypermetropia

States in developing countries are not able to monitor and control many phenomena, which bypass them due to their limited resources. In effect, these states suffer from what is called "hypermetropia"—technically, the condition of farsightedness of the eyes.[14] Thus by "state hypermetropia" I mean the inability of the state to monitor and capture close details of its own polity and society. Accordingly, lack of reliable data on underground or "black" economies, landlessness, illegal money transactions, the role of women, and illegal migration flows is a reflection of the state's inability to monitor or control everything. As scholars, are we to ignore all such phenomenon that the state is unable to "see"—that is, about which the state is unable to obtain data? Legibility of people is important for the state. However, what is the validity of data in circumstances in which the state is unable to count, estimate, and monitor?[15] Are we satisfied with what we see, or are we going to go deeper into the issue by being creative? As Lloyd and Susanne Rudolph suggested in 1958, "there is a need for more political anthropology if social science as a whole is to grapple successfully with the problems raised by the study of underdeveloped areas"(Rudolph and Rudolph 1958, 244). The call to do more contextualized research, ethnographic data collection, and fieldwork is as relevant today.

Let me elaborate with an example from India: illegal immigration to Assam, a regional state in India, from a neighboring country, Bangladesh. Here I focus on two issues: (1) the difficulty of collecting information on a mobile population, many of whose members are illegal but have succeeded in manufacturing documentary citizenship, and (2) the politicized interpretation of the inadequate figures—the interest of the Bharatiya Janata Party (BJP) in magnifying the number of Muslims,[16] the Assamese Hindu panic about being overwhelmed by Bengalis in general and by Bangladeshi Hindus and Muslims in particular, the

Bangladeshi obfuscation, the probable confusion of illegal immigrants and Muslims, and so on. Here counting is exacerbated by motivational interpretations.

Illegal immigration produces a wide range of estimates and figures related to the magnitude of the immigrant population in Assam, India, as it has in other states such as Malaysia and even the United States.[17] It is an issue of national political importance in India, and yet, because of the nature of the phenomenon, the state is unable to collect reliable data or settle on some standard estimate of the numbers who immigrate. In Assam, the effects of illegal immigration have been dramatic. From 1891 until India achieved independence in 1947, the state's population grew at a rate of around 20 percent each decade. The rate shot up to 35 percent between 1951 and 1971, and touched 53 percent between 1971 and 1991, according to the census (Directorate of Census Operations, Assam, 1997, 118). The federal government fears that the unabated inflow of Bangladeshis may well end up altering the demographic character of this border state.

Not satisfied with the state census figures, I searched for a confidential document that I had heard existed. When I found the document, a confidential report sent by the governor of Assam, Lieutenant General Sinha, to the president of India, K. R. Narayanan, I learned that Sinha had this to say about the Bangladeshi immigration to Assam: "This silent and invidious demographic invasion of Assam may result in the loss of the geostrategic vital districts of Lower Assam. The influx of these illegal migrants is turning these districts into a Muslim majority region. It will then only be a matter of time when a demand for their merger with Bangladesh may be made" (Governor of Assam 1998, 18).[18] The report submitted to President Narayanan also points out the "perceptible changes" in the state's demography and how those might spur "the long cherished design of greater Bangladesh" by Islamic fundamentalists. The report, which makes startling revelations about the infiltration of Bangladeshis into Indian territory, also deals with the likely political and strategic fallout of the situation. Sinha, a retired lieutenant general of the Indian Army, noted that if the influx was not checked, "they [Bangladeshis] may swamp the Assamese people and may sever the North East land mass from the rest of India." Sinha, who had been given his new assignment by the BJP government, substantiated his statement by citing the following statistics: "Bangladesh census records indicate a reduction of 3.9 million Hindus between 1971 and 1981 and another 3.6 million between 1981 and 1989. These 7.5 million Hindus *have obviously come into India*. Perhaps most of them have come into States other than Assam" (Governor of Assam 1998, 18, emphasis mine).

Clearly guesswork as to the direction and magnitude of illegal immigration into India is at work in official circles. Moreover, the speculation that "most of them [Bangladeshi Hindus] have come into States other then Assam" means that there is a focus on Muslim Bangladeshis in Assam. A belief that a large part of the Bangladeshi immigration into Assam could be by Hindus would undermine the bogey of the "Bangladeshi Muslim" threat in Assam. Therefore, even in speculation, these estimates might be further biased. With regard to the

influx of Muslims from across the border, the report says: "In 1970, the population of East Pakistan was 7.5 crores but in 1974 it had come down to 7.14. On
the basis of 3.1 percent annual population growth rate of that period, the
population in 1974 should have been 7.7 crores. The shortfall of 6 million
people can be explained only by large scale migration" (Governor of Assam
1998, 18).[19]

Substantiating the theory of the "demographic change" of the state, the
report points out that the "Muslim population in Assam has risen from 24.68
percent in 1951 to 28.42 percent in 1991. As per the 1991 census, four districts
(Dhubri, Goalpara, Barpeta and Hailakandi) have become Muslim majority
areas. Two more districts (Nowgaon and Karimganj) should have become so by
1998 and one district (Morgaon) is fast approaching this position" (Governor
of Assam 1998, 18). According to sources in the Ministry of Home, the five
"worst-affected" border districts are Dhubri, Barpeta, Karimganj, Mangaldoi
and Cachar, "which will soon have a Muslim majority" (*Pioneer,* New Delhi,
2001). An examination of the Indian census reveals that the Hindu population
in Assam declined from 72.51 percent in the 1971 census to 67.13 percent in
1991 and that it is expected to decline even further in the coming decades
(Directorate of Census Operations, Assam, 1999, 10–16). Between 1951 and
1991 there was a 155.64 percent increase in the Hindu population in Assam. In
contrast, the Muslim population rose 219.30 percent during that forty-year
period. Between 1971 and 1991 the Muslim population growth rate was an
alarming 77.42 percent, while the Hindus registered a more modest growth rate
of 41.89 percent (Directorate of Census Operations, Assam, 1999, 10–16).

This is what the Indian census tells us about Assam. Confounding immigration scholars is the conflation of Muslims and illegal immigrants rampant
in many estimates. These figures ignore the significant indigenous Assamese
Muslim population, the large pre-independence Bengali-speaking Muslim
population, and the internal migration of Muslims (both from Bengal and
from other north Indian states). Obviously the conflation of Muslims and illegal immigrants is largely a reflection of unreliable data on this issue and the
local politics of religion in India. Hindu nationalist parties such as the BJP view
Bangladeshis as Muslims, thus ignoring Bangladeshi Hindu immigrants or
legitimizing them as representing a refugee flow that deserves a sympathetic
response from the state.

One speculative estimate that has received attention came from Indrajit
Gupta, who, during his tenure as the home minister of India, surprised everyone by casually telling the Parliament on May 6, 1997, that the government
estimated the number of illegal immigrants at nearly ten million (*India Today,*
New Delhi, 1998). Recently the deputy prime minister of India estimated the
number of illegal Bangladeshi immigrants at fifteen million, with the greatest
concentration in West Bengal and Assam (*Times of India,* New Delhi, 2003).[20]
A former senior bureaucrat in the Government of India, B. Raman, says that
"while no accurate estimate of the influx is available, many reports put the
influx from Bangladesh alone at over 20 million" (Raman 2003).[21] Others

question these estimates. For example, Muchkund Dubey, a former foreign secretary of India, has recently argued that "the figure of 15 million . . . is highly exaggerated and almost impossible to verify" (Dubey 2003). The estimate of twenty million illegal Bangladeshis may have been arrived at by including those involved in the exodus of Bangladeshis, both Hindu and Muslim, to India during and immediately after the 1971 war of liberation in which Bangladesh became an independent state (Sengupta 2003). Therefore, even though there is data manipulation, it is the inability to monitor and count the number of illegal immigrants that makes the data unreliable.

These problems of estimation are compounded by the fact that many illegal Bangladeshis have over the years been added to Indian electoral rolls; acquired state-recognized documents such as the ration card, licenses, and so on; and become active "Indians." This has led to the creation of "conventional numbers," which are "round figures that become reified in journalistic and other popular uses" (Larson and Sullivan 1987, 1475). A similar situation holds with respect to the number of Dominicans in United States during the 1980s; use of a "conventional number" of five hundred thousand became popular (Larson and Sullivan 1987, 1475). In many estimates of illegal immigration, repetition of the same figure leads to credibility, and convergence among citations becomes a sign of reliability (Larson and Sullivan 1987, 1488). Such overestimation, according to scholars, occurs "because of the difficulty of estimation, the tendency to repeat unsubstantiated estimates, and the incorrect interpretation of missing values" (Larson and Sullivan 1987, 1474). Meanwhile, the Indian government, journalists, policy makers, and scholars continue to speculate on the magnitude of illegal immigration from Bangladesh to India, which has so changed the "demographic landscape" of the North Eastern border states.

The sampling errors and non–sampling errors are at the heart of estimation problems involved in conducting surveys. For example, Delhi police launched a drive to evict illegal immigrants from Bangladesh from that city only to discover that many have documents issued to them by the Assam government and claim to be Indian citizens (*Assam Tribune,* Guwahati, 2003). For the purpose of the census, it is important to consider whether the census enumerator should ignore the residency or citizenship claims (and proof) presented by the illegal immigrants, as the police did, or categorize them as internal migrants to Delhi from Assam. Perhaps they are genuine internal migrants, much like Abdul Sobhan Khan, the subject of a story in a regional newspaper, who resided in the Goalpara district of Assam and had various state-authorized documents to back that claim (*Assam Tribune,* Guwahati, 2003). However, many censuses, such as the Malaysian and Indian censuses, adopt self-reporting as a means of identifying the citizenship or place of residence of an individual. In such circumstances, can the census enumerator, based on his intuition (or prejudice), be allowed to judge the truth of these claims in hundreds of thousands of cases? The census coverage of illegal immigrants involves making such judgments and guesses, which, in effect, creates large sampling errors.

Surveys conducted as part of the census can also miss members of immi-grant families who have moved, are leaving, or are possibly returning. Illegal immigration can have a temporary component that such censuses miss. Such temporary migration is common between Assam and neighboring regions of Bangladesh with established immigrant networks. Also missed will be return-ing illegal immigrants who may have gone back to Bangladesh for a short while. Given the lack of monitoring at the border and the preexisting net-works, illegal immigrants should not find it difficult to return to their "home-land" for personal reasons—marriage of relatives, reunion with old parents or kinsmen, payment of old debts, sale of personal property, and so on. The cen-sus or state-sponsored surveys (for intelligence or policy purposes) also miss important but basic information needed for the study of immigration patterns —the "residential" status of illegal immigrants.[22] Nonresponse is a major fea-ture of immigration surveys and official censuses. The fear of being detected by government agencies and deported causes illegal immigrant respondents to be less forthcoming. Those who have entered with fraudulent documents or are out of status are likely to go missing. Moreover, illegal immigrants lie about their status and pretend to be "citizens"; thus we cannot know which part of Bangladesh they are from, even if we guess they are from Bangladesh.

Contrary to the Indian government's claims, Bangladesh has steadfastly denied that its citizens cross over to India. Officially, the Bangladeshi govern-ment does not recognize illegal emigration to India. This presents severe prob-lems for those researchers who are hoping to arrive at numbers of emigrating Bangladeshis based on the study of a Bangladeshi census that shows a sharp decline in the Bangladeshi Hindu population. Census data with regard to minority Hindus in Bangladesh are very unreliable. There are no official state agencies responsible for monitoring and collecting data on labor emigration to India.[23] Because the Indian state has unreliable data—some based on confi-dential intelligence estimates—it will be difficult for any researcher to get at the "true" facts from Indian sources. And because of the Bangladeshi govern-ment's official stand of denial, the Bangladeshi census will not throw any light on this emigration. How, then, does one study a phenomenon that bypasses one state, is unrecognized by another, and yet is a major bilateral foreign policy issue between the two?

Let me point to another problem that researchers studying illegal or legal immigrants or citizens in poor developing countries encounter: most house-hold or population surveys in developing countries (such as South Asia or Africa) are conducted by investigators interviewing the "head" of each house-hold. In rural areas of India, which are still home to approximately 70 percent of the population, the joint family system is prevalent. Western survey systems are accustomed to targeting "individuals" as the unit of society. Surveys based on heads of households present a problem because surveyors of immigrants will have difficulty assessing and categorizing the information gathered from the head of a large extended family of illegal immigrants that comprises a household in India (Hill 1984). For instance, was the household "head" guessing correctly when he estimated the household income contribution of son and daughter-in-law number one? Was he aware that daughter-in-law number two may have secretly sold her jewelry or pilfered from the granary? How does one assess the household income of an extended family of 106 members, like the one Polly Hill discovered in Kano city of Hausaland district, which consisted of twenty-two married men and their dependents (Hill 1984, 498–99)? Though critics may argue that individuals, and not entire extended families, illegally migrate, this is not true. The contiguous borders of India and Bangladesh, along with the lack of state monitoring capacity and the complicity of sections within the state, which encourage such illegal immigration, and the historical immigrant networks contribute to the immigration of entire families over time. Those who are left behind have incentives to join the rest of the extended family across the border. Entire villages and large numbers of landless households have immigrated to Northeast India from Bangladesh. We cannot dismiss the problems arising from interviewing the "heads" of households as "mere" sampling errors. They have more to do with the social assumptions built into sampling conventions that conceive of the world as constituted by individuals.

Surveying the family of an illegal immigrant in a rural area of a developing country also requires gender sensitivity. Many women work as laborers in fields and yet are missing from the categories "Cultivator" and "Agricultural Laborer" because men householders are ashamed to admit that the women in their families work the land. The role of women is vastly underestimated in many developing countries, where there is a taboo against women's working outside. Recent studies by demographers in India have revealed that "women who did so much work in looking after cattle, milking cows and buffaloes and assisting in marketing the products of animal husbandry were more often than not recorded as merely housewives" (Bose 2004, 2). Lloyd and Susanne Rudolph have argued that the egalitarian assumptions of the random sample, that all opinions have equal weight and importance, is frequently challenged at the ground level in developing countries. When confronted by an interviewer, the response of village women was, "Why ask me? I am only an ignorant woman! Ask my husband" (Rudolph and Rudolph 1958, 238). The knowledge that a suspicious husband, father, or brother is watching from afar or waiting outside can warp any answer provided by a female respondent. To expect a "self-respecting" male head of an immigrant household to acknowledge that his daughter, daughter-in-law, wife, or other women in the family do menial jobs is to not understand the cultural norms of South Asia. Illegal immigrant women are selling cigarettes and fruits as street vendors and working as household help, agricultural laborers, prostitutes, restaurant help, waitresses, and so on. And yet the purdah-clad or scarf-wearing or *pallu*-covered immigrant women in parts of Asia and Africa are not given equal weight with men.[24] Therefore, state agencies or individual scholars find it difficult to arrive at figures on illegal immigrants' agricultural or household income, to distinguish between immigrant cultivators and laborers, and so on, based on a random sample. Obviously any such effort by an individual surveyor of immigrant populations will find women underrepresented or misrepresented. It is apparent that in such circumstances both interviewees (e.g., heads of illegal immigrant households) and surveyors are guessing, and that often involves wishful thinking. With the increasing feminization of illegal immigration in developing countries, surveyors and scholars will have to confront the "invisible" female component of the data on illegal immigration.

The contribution and role of illegal immigrant women in developing countries is an example of a category that bypasses the state and poses challenges to scholars' sample design and data collection techniques. We are then left with estimates from surveys based on the wild guesses of rural household heads being surveyed; or the paranoid guesses of a bureaucrat in the Home Ministry in his "confidential" report; or the equally unreliable guesses of intelligence, police, and state officials; or the "guesstimates" of journalists in newspapers or newsmagazines.[25] One can collate all these estimates on a chart and arrive at a nice median figure, which may be as reliable as hearsay. Therefore, in the conditions of "state hypermetropia" that exist in many developing countries, one is left with a very narrow range of issues with reliable data. The others raise a "validity" problem.

Conclusion

The validity problem poses the following question: how representative are the data we use of the problems we seek to analyze? More important for scholars of illegal immigration between developing countries is this question: are the data and their operationalization true reflections of the problem we are studying? Very often the sophistication of the statistical techniques and the parsimonious character of the statistical output hide the quality of the data being used. In studying politics and society in developing countries, it is important to be careful about what we mean by "data" and how we acquire, use, and operationalize these data. This is a widespread problem in social sciences when scholars study the developing world, where conditions are not amenable to the collection of data. Therefore, the *politics of data collection* is as important as the operationalization of the data and its subsequent use to build larger data sets that can then be used for broad comparisons—the large *n* analyses. Although some of these data problems have been noted as difficulties associated with weak statistical coverage under conditions of weak immigration control in developing countries (Zlotnick 1987, ix), others highlight the varying and sometimes ambiguous definitions used in surveys as the sources of such statistical errors. For example, Manuel Garcia Griego has explained the discrepancy between the low numbers of emigrants in Mexican sources based on state-supervised export of labor and the higher numbers of Mexican agricultural workers admitted by the United States resulting from "the procedures used to operationalize the definitions established by law, though vague definitions are also often at fault" (Griego 1987, 1246). However, I am highlighting problems with data collection and statistical coverage that go beyond questions of definitional ambiguity and lack of statistical control. Even with tighter control, better definitions, and better operationalization, we will have to confront the challenges that gender, definitional pressures by civil society, and state manipulation throw at our methods of data generation.

Therefore, I argue that greater emphasis on the quality of data and the validity of the operationalizations rather than on the "sophistication" of the analytic techniques is crucial in the study of many political phenomena in developing countries. To make this emphasis possible we need a new breed of "qualitative" and "interpretive" methodologists who will assess the reliability of statistics being used and their "validity" for the phenomena being studied. Until then, we should assume that many of our sociopolitical data sets are fraught with manipulations and "cooking," some at the individual and group levels and some at the state level.

Notes

Parts of this chapter have appeared in my doctoral dissertation (Sadiq 2003, Chapter 3) and appear in an article (Sadiq 2005), where I have used the case of census and data manipulation to show how the state is complicit in preferring illegal immigrants over citizens in Malaysia.

I thank Thomas Donahue, Ryan Harvey, Richard Ned Lebow, Susanne Hoeber Rudolph, and Lloyd I. Rudolph for their comments on this chapter.

1. A close examination of many statistics put out by international organizations, regional organizations, nongovernmental organizations, firms, and so on, will confirm that many are replicating statistics supplied by individual states.

2. West Malaysia is over one thousand miles from Sabah, a regional state in East Malaysia, and is separated from it by the South China Sea. It takes about two and a half hours by airplane to reach Sabah from West Malaysia.

3. Sections used here have appeared in Sadiq (2003) and Sadiq (2005).

4. UMNO is the powerful Malay Muslim party that controls the ruling coalition, Barisian Nasional, in Malaysia. It has a branch in Sabah that now rules the state along with other coalition partners.

5. This information comes from a report done by Bilson Kurus, Ramlan Goddos, and Richard T. Koh for the state think tank, the Institute for Development Studies, that was later published in *Borneo Review* (Kurus, Goddos, and Koh 1998, 161).

6. *Pribumi* means "native" and has the same meaning as the term *Bumiputera* (both words have roots in Sanskrit).

7. Directive CMDC 503/60. While the nomenclature "Pribumi" was adopted by the center in the 1980 census, the directive to adopt it at the regional, Sabah, level was introduced in 1982.

8. The "Malay world," according to some conceptions, extends from Singapore to the Southern Philippines. Claims to being part of the larger "Malay world" are based on language (variations of Bahasa Melayu), sultan (Malay kingship), and religion (Islam). See Shamsul 1999, 18, and Shamsul 1996, 15–33.

9. Private communication via e-mail from Rogers Smith, March 3, 2003. See also Smith 1997.

10. This parallels the current debate on unemployment in the United States between the George W. Bush administration and its critics, with the two sides marshaling "data" and making opposite claims.

11. This was a special investigation of fudged figures by the leading Indian news magazine *Outlook*.

12. See the section on "Gatekeepers," 73–77.

13. The tendency of the state to suppress and lie through data leads to a "validity" problem. What if there are data and they are not false or manipulated? The state institutions are interested in supplying data for the sake of transparency and to start a debate within the polity. In such a situation, the state may suffer from a validity problem because it is not able to convince members of the polity of its sincerity in the generation of data. Nobody, least of all regional minorities and other "natives," will believe the Malaysian government's figures on illegal immigrants and the ethnic composition of Sabah's population as shown in the census, or other such socioeconomic reports. Similarly, if the Indian government has real, unfudged data on poverty and there has been a general improvement of the poor, the government will find it difficult to convince many of its claims regarding poverty alleviation. This is a validity problem. What does a government do when it has issues that it wants to hide or suppress from public view and at the same time wants to appear transparent on related or other issues?

14. The term has been used by extension to describe the "farsightedness" of the state in monitoring details within and across its boundaries.

15. See Dorothy Solinger's excellent analysis of the flawed data on the "unemployed" in China (Solinger, 2001).

16. BJP is the Hindu nationalist party that was most recently in power in India with its coalition partners.

17. The estimates of illegal immigrants in the United States, especially from Mexico, keep going up. Every census produces a new model of estimation that is subsequently seen as not adequately capturing the illegal population. Illegal immigration, by its very nature, is hard to calculate.

18. I am citing a personal copy of this confidential report.

19. A crore is equal to ten million. So, for example, 7.5 crores is equal to 75 million.

20. Deputy Prime Minister L. K. Advani was inaugurating a conference of chief secretaries and directors generals of police on January 7, 2003, in Delhi when he gave this estimate and linked it to national security concerns. Quoted in *Times of India*, New Delhi 2003 and in Raman 2003.

21. B. Raman is a retired "additional secretary" with the Cabinet Secretariat of the Government of India.

22. For an excellent discussion of de facto versus de jure definitions of residence, see Skeldon 1987.

23. Only data regarding official labor recruitment that go through official state-recognized labor agencies is collected. This kind of labor export is sent, for example, to labor-importing states of the Middle East, states in Southeast Asia such as Singapore and Malaysia, and so on. Data on labor emigration and remittances is easily available in such cases.

24. The *pallu* is one end of the sari, the cloth worn by women in South Asia. The *pallu* is used to cover the head, and in many rural areas of India women cover their heads in the presence of men.

25. Presented with such a situation, most scholars, as has happened frequently, shy away from a topic with a lack of hard data.

References

Arendt, Hannah. 1968. *The Origins of Totalitarianism.* San Diego: Harvest Books.

Assam Tribune, Guwahati. 2003. "Most Migrants in Delhi Have Assam Papers." February 6. http://www.assamtribune.com.

Bose, Ashish. 2004. "Towards Gender-Sensitive Population Census." *Economic and Political Weekly* (Bombay), April 24, 2. www.epw.org.in.

Department of Statistics, Malaysia. 1983. *Population and Housing Census 1980,* Vol. 1. January.

Department of Statistics, Malaysia. 1995. *Population and Housing Census 1991, State Population Report: Sabah.* March.

Directorate of Census Operations, Assam. 1997. *Census of India 1991: Series 4, Assam,* Part II-A, General Population Tables. Delhi: Controller of Publications.

Directorate of Census Operations, Assam. 1999. *Census of India 1991: Series 4, Assam,* Part IV-B (2), Religion (Table C-9). New Delhi: Government of India.

Dubey, Muchkund. 2003. "Dealing with Bangladesh-II." *The Hindu,* February 6. http://www.hinduonnet.com/thehindu/2003/02/06/stories/2003020600041000.htm.

Government of Sabah. 1999. *Monthly Statistical Bulletin Sabah,* October.

Governor of Assam. 1998. *Report on Illegal Migration into Assam Submitted to the President of India by the Governor of Assam,* 18.

Griego, Manuel G. 1987. "International Migration Statistics in Mexico." *International Migration Review* 21 (4):1246.

Hill, Polly. 1984. "The Poor Quality of Official Socio-Economic Statistics Relating to the Rural Tropical World: With Special Reference to South India." *Modern Asian Studies* 18 (3): 493.

India Today, New Delhi, 1998. "Illegal Immigrants: Political Pawns." August 10. http://www.indiatoday.com.

Kurus, B., R. Goddos, and R. Koh. 1998. "Migrant Labor Flows in the East Asian Region: Prospects and Challenges." *Borneo Review* 9 (2): 156–86.

Larson, Eric, and Teresa Sullivan. 1987. "'Conventional Numbers' in Immigration Research: The Case of the Missing Dominicans." *International Migration Review* 21 (4): 1475.

Mehta, J., and S. Venkatraman. 2000. "Poverty Statistics: Bermicide's Feast." *Economic and Political Weekly* (Bombay), July 1.

Peil, Margaret. 1983. "Situational Variables." In *Social Research in Developing Countries: Surveys and Censuses in the Third World,* ed. Martin Bulmer and Donald Warwick. Chichester, England: John Wiley and Sons Ltd.

Pioneer, New Delhi. 2001. "Infiltrators May Soon Be 'the Majority' in Assam." January 15. http://www.dailypioneer.com/archives/secon22.asp?cat=\story5&d=fpage&ti=jan1501.

Raman, B. 2003. "'There Are No Bangladeshis in India!'" *Outlook,* February 4. http://www.outlookindia.com.

Regis, Patricia. 1989. "Demography." Appendix 1 in *Sabah 25 Years Later: 1963–1988,* ed. Jeffrey Kitingan and Maximus Ongkili. Sabah: Institute for Development Studies.

Rudolph, Lloyd, and Susanne Rudolph. 1958. "Surveys in India: Field Experience in Madras State." *Public Opinion Quarterly* 22 (3): 244.

Rudolph, Lloyd, and Susanne Rudolph. 1987. *In Pursuit of Lakshmi: The Political Economy of the Indian State.* Chicago: University of Chicago Press.

Sadiq, Kamal. 2003. "Redefining Citizenship: Illegal Immigrants as Voters in India and Malaysia." PhD Dissertation, Department of Political Science, University of Chicago.

Sadiq, Kamal. 2005. "When States Prefer Non-Citizens over Citizens: Conflict over Illegal Immigration into Malaysia." *International Studies Quarterly* 49 (1): 101–22.

Scott, James C. 1998. *Seeing Like a State: How Certain Schemes to Improve the Human Condition Have Failed.* New Haven, CT: Yale University Press.

Sengupta, Ramananda. 2003. "The Kid Gloves Need to Be Taken Off." *Rediff.com,* February 4. http://www.rediff.com/news/2003/feb/04ram.htm.

Shamsul, A. B. 1996. "The Construction and Transformation of a Social Identity: Malayness and Bumiputeraness Re- examined." *Journal of African and Asian Studies* (Tokyo), v. 15.

Shamsul, A. B. 1999. "Identity Contestation in Malaysia: A Comparative Commentary on 'Malayness' and 'Chineseness.'" *Akademika* (Malaysia) 55 (July).

Sinha, Rajesh. 2004. "The Poverty of Statistics: Did the Previous Regime Consciously 'Edit Out' Five Crore Indians Eligible for BPL Benefits?" *Outlook* (New Delhi), June 14. http://www.outlookindia.com/full.asp?fodname=20040614&fname=BPL+%28F%29&sid=1.

Skeldon, Ronald. 1987. "Migration and the Population Census in Asia and the Pacific: Issues, Questions and Debate." *International Migration Review* 21 (4): 1074–1100.

Smith, Rogers. 1997. *Civic Ideals: Conflicting Visions of Citizenship in U.S. History.* New Haven, CT: Yale University Press.

Solinger, Dorothy. 2001. "Why We Cannot Count the "Unemployed." *China Quarterly* 167 (September): 671–88.

Times of India, New Delhi. 2003. "Advani Asks States to Deport Illegal Visitors. January 8. http://timesofindia.indiatimes.com.

Zlotnik, Hania. 1987. "Introduction: Measuring International Migration: Theory and Practice." *International Migration Review* 21 (4): ix.

CHAPTER 14

In the House of "Science," There Are Many Rooms

Perestroika and the "Science Studies" Turn

Dvora Yanow

An op-ed essay in the *New York Times* concerning the "Central Park jogger" case raised the question of the character of evidence and truth, given that subsequent DNA analysis exonerated the five young men who had been convicted and imprisoned after confessing to the crime (Kassin 2002). Underlying the methods debates raised in much of the Perestroikan discussions is a generally unspoken set of assumptions and presuppositions concerning similar questions: How do we (political scientists) understand the character of social and political realities? What do we accept, and what should be accepted, as evidence of statements about that reality? And what kinds of truth claims can we make based on our answers to these questions?

The questions, and the debates surrounding them, suggest that political science as a discipline has at last followed other social sciences in taking the reflective turn characteristic of "science studies." By "discipline" I mean to convey a collective of academics who share a set of professional practices (research, publishing, teaching, career trajectories and hurdles) and, if not a single unifying set of research questions, a sensibility about what in the wide world of human action merits attention and analysis—an inclination to focus on questions of power and organization, and of powerlessness and disorganization, in their several manifestations, state and otherwise. Such reflection brings to the fore what are otherwise, in other circumstances, the "common"-sense, taken-for-granted, tacitly known "rules" for practicing this particular profession, at this time, in this place. This is the sort of analysis conducted in the field known as "science studies," whose cases to date have included studies of laboratory science (e.g., Latour 1987), biology (e.g., Keller 1983), and theoretical and experimental physics (Traweek 1992). In focusing attention not only on methods but also on a wide range of disciplinary practices,[1] Perestroika has moved political science under the science studies lens.

What this lens highlights is that science itself is a practice—and a rhetorical one at that—and furthermore, that there is not a single way of doing science or of being scientific. Thomas Kuhn's revolutionary study (1962)—revolutionary in being among the first to take such a reflective turn, analyzing the physical sciences using a history of ideas approach and attending to their professional practice dimensions—still assumed a single model for doing science. Kuhn posited that the path from revolutionary science to normal science (and onward) characterized all sciences; that paradigmatic unity was a characteristic of normal, "mature" science; and that the social sciences were (seemingly perpetually) pre-paradigmatic. The rhetorical argument was won right there: absent a paradigm, the social sciences fall short; who, after all, wants to be, or to appear to be, "immature"? And so political science, like other social sciences, has fought to be perceived as a science and as one possessing a paradigm.

The Perestroikan discourse implicitly challenges this formulation in its call for methodological pluralism (and for the enactment of pluralism throughout the other areas of political science practice). On the one hand, it is a call to recognize that political science does have a paradigm—both a weltanschauung and a community of scientists who have adopted it[2]—in the form of methodological positivism. Its paradigmatic standing is what gives it its strength within political science: paradigms are by definition hegemonic. On the other hand, Perestroika's call is not for an "anything goes" pluralism, but rather for the recognition that there is more than one way of doing science *while still remaining "scientific."* Implicit in this argument is a challenge to the Kuhnian path: perhaps political science (or parts of it), like other social sciences (or parts of them), is sufficiently different from physics and chemistry that it will follow a different path as it finds other, better ways to serve certain research questions than regression, path, rational choice, and other such analyses. The Perestroikan call, then, despite attempts to portray it as such, has not been for a wholesale replacement of "quantitative" methods by "qualitative" ones, but rather for an expansion of the domain of methods legitimated in the practices of contemporary political science to include others that are equally scientific, albeit in different particular ways. In hindsight, if this reflective turn continues, Perestroika may be seen as the launching of an SSPS—an association for the Social-scientific Studies of Political Science.

This chapter reflects on the "qual-quant" divide that has developed within American political science. I suggest that that taxonomy masks underlying philosophical differences, and that the masking and the unreflective character of our practices have led to silences about fundamental matters and a narrowing of the discipline and its concerns. Making some of these silences "speak"— notably, in the creation in 2003 of a "Qualitative Methods" section of the APSA—has enabled increased attention to the character of the methods subsumed under that category. I return in the end to the science studies question by reflecting on our knowledge practices, considering that the dominance of methodological positivism may be explained, among other things, by systems of knowing-learning and the status of one view of "science." If this is the case, those of us practicing political science in all its forms might better proceed about our claims with an increased measure of passionate humility.

Unmarked Category Language, Unspoken Presuppositions: Making Silences Speak

As with any paradigm, the "normal" case typically goes unmarked and, on the whole, unremarked until challenged. Position descriptions advertise for "methodologists" when what departments are searching for is candidates who use advanced statistical and other quantitative tools. One ad, for example, chosen at random from a 1999–2000 issue of the APSA's *Personnel Newsletter*, invites applications "in the field of research methodology." Although this most general field statement might be taken to designate a broad search across the full spectrum of methods, the ad delimits the meaning immediately: "We are looking for someone with strong *statistical* skills as they apply to empirical data . . . to teach *quantitative methods* at the graduate level, beginning with *first semester statistics* through *advanced statistical methods commonly used* in political science" (emphases added). With similarly generic labeling, the sole APSA section until 2003 that explicitly concerned itself with methods took the name "Political Methodology." Its sessions, however, commonly feature papers on selection bias, logistic regression, statistical applications, econometric models, computational models, stochastic models, modeling strategic action, logit and probit analyses, time series data, causal inferences, and game theory (a list compiled from two recent conference programs), only rarely reflecting the concerns of nonquantitative methods. Likewise, the section's journal, *Political Analysis*—yet another generic appellation—in its inaugural issue cast a wide net in defining its domain as "concern . . . with *the entire range* of interests and problems centering upon how political inquiry can be conducted" and saying that "any manuscript dealing with *this broad set of interests* is appropriate for submission." Yet this breadth is constricted when these interests are itemized as "measurement, estimation and specification and theory development" (*Political Analysis* 8 [Winter 2000], opposite page 1; emphases added). Textbook authors and publishers, too, typically use such general titles as *Research Methods in Political Science* but limit themselves to treating experimental or survey research design, the scientific method, and regression and other modes of statistical analysis.[3] In other words, the unmarked, norming language proclaims breadth, but its enactment reflects a narrower set of concerns. The use of similar language in various areas of disciplinary practice repeats and reinforces the same message: the research methods used in political science are quantitative, statistical, and modeling methods, period.

When shared knowledge is presumed, all manner of other options are disappeared from the room. Could we imagine, for instance, a position description inviting applications in the field of research methodology that read, "We are looking for someone with strong observational skills as they apply to empirical data . . . to teach qualitative methods at the graduate level, beginning with first semester interviewing through advanced participant observation methods commonly used in political science"? Our disciplinary house may have rooms for different subfields and areas, but the discipline's language in so many arenas of practice presents "political methodology" as having only a single orientation for analyzing the subjects that are found in those rooms. Consequently, the existence of other analytic methods, let alone the need for them, is silenced—just as political scientists instructing others in and reviewing work using these methods have been silenced. If Perestroika has done nothing else,[4] it has enabled those silences to speak.

What Is "Science"?

The challenge to the hegemonic language that equates methods with numbers-based analysis gives voice to the question of what "science" is or what it means to do "scientific" political analysis. What it means in contemporary "Western" contexts to "be scientific" or to "do science"—whether natural, physical, or social science—has been developing since the days of Copernicus, Galileo, and Newton; its philosophical elaboration took place through the nineteenth century and into the twentieth as "natural philosophy" turned into "natural science" and "social philosophy" into "social science."[5] Although it is widely believed and taught that good science proceeds according to the steps enumerated in common descriptions of "the scientific method," there are all manner of sciences, including several in both natural and physical science (not to mention social science), that proceed otherwise. Requiring political science to be scientific in one way is, then, a narrow understanding of what it means to be scientific and to do science.

From a macro perspective, what seems to characterize all sciences is a systematicity of process and an attitude of testability. This makes sense in light of the development of contemporary understandings of "science" in the seventeenth and eighteenth centuries against the backdrop of the authority- and faith-based reigns of monarchs and the church. This view of science as the systematic application of human reason in the development of universal laws, always subject to testing, extends control (or the promise of control) over the erratic, unpredictable, non-reason-based, whimsical decision making of queens and popes. As word-based, non-quantitative methods hold both of these characteristics (sytematicity and testability), they constitute scientific practices in a broader understanding of what science is.[6]

Such matters are commonly the domain of a course in the philosophy of science or social science (or a course in the history or scope of the discipline). One of the questions raised in Perestroikan discussions has concerned what has become of such courses. Many veteran discussants remember having read such subjects in their doctoral programs and bemoan their apparent disappearance.[7] One possible explanation is that the (perceived) need for advanced training in methods of statistical analysis has driven them out. Here then is yet another impact of the hegemonizing reach of the "methods = statistics" equation: it has eliminated language studies, as first computer programming (e.g., FORTRAN) and then regression analysis et al. have been accorded the status of languages. Moreover, not making explicit the grounding of this equation in particular philosophical presuppositions, let alone reflecting on and questioning it, has also driven out more philosophical-theoretical explorations of the character of social (and political) realities and their knowability. What constitutes acceptable evidence, then, is assumed rather than explored. Dissertation (and other) research becomes method-driven. I recall that in the late 1970s students at MIT were advised to locate a database that could be analyzed for dissertation research.[8] When a discussion of other sorts of methods that might be more appropriate to other sorts of research questions is eclipsed, doctoral students are deprived of an entire range of possible research topics and modes of analyzing data. So is the discipline as a whole, as generational processes unfold and students graduate into the pro-fessorial ranks and train new generations of students. It is this narrowness that has been reflected in the pages of the national association's lead journal,[9] in the Political Methodology Section's conference panels, and elsewhere.

The Qual-Quant Divide: Methods versus Methodology

The two broad schools of methodological thought commonly labeled quanti-tative and qualitative differ on what they recognize as evidence and on how to treat it. But underlying these differences are more fundamental issues. The qual-quant distinction is erroneous and misleading: "quantitative" researchers do make interpretations; "qualitative" researchers do count. The terms have become a proxy for deeper divides concerning the character of social reality and how it might be known. To rehearse these briefly (and somewhat superfi-cially), what is commonly called "quantitative" research rests on objectivist-realist ontological and epistemological presuppositions; these follow from the developments of scientific thought associated with the three nineteenth-century schools of positivist philosophy and the early twentieth-century logical positivism and attendant work in analytic philosophy. "Qualitative" research in the manner of "Chicago School" field studies (which entail partic-ipant observation, ethnographies, and "single n" case studies) rests on con-structionist ontological presuppositions and interpretivist epistemological presuppositions. These are in keeping with twentieth-century neo-Kantian, continental philosophies (hermeneutics, phenomenology, and some critical theory) and with American developments in ethnomethodology, symbolic interactionism, and pragmatism.

These concerns, and the debates, are not exclusive to political science. The philosophical discussions were conducted throughout the nineteenth and twentieth centuries, as represented in the writings of such thinkers as Max Weber, Johan Gustav Droysen, Edmund Husserl, Alfred Schutz, George Herbert Mead, William James, Hans Georg Gadamer, Paul Ricoeur, Jacques Derrida, Harrold Garfinkel, Jürgen Habermas, and Charles Taylor. The history of ideas antedates them, drawing on Immanuel Kant's notions of the role of a priori knowledge as the grounding for the critique of critical positivism (empirio-criticism) and its requirements for sense-based data, and major works have appeared in other social sciences arguing for the interpretive turn and its associated rhetorical, narrative, and linguistic ideas (e.g., Geertz 1973 in anthropology; Rabinow and Sullivan 1979 and 1987 in sociology, human development, organizational studies, etc.; and McCloskey 1985 in economics).[10]

The two sets of presuppositions differ, among other things, on whether "objectivity," commonly understood, is warranted or even possible. To draw once again on a legal context, Dahlia Lithwick (2002) comments on Justice Clarence Thomas's words concerning the meaning of burning crosses in a case involving first amendment protections. She engages the question of what role personal experience should play in "the disinterested, lucid distance" of legal judgment. On the one hand, it is deemed completely inappropriate—the position that would be articulated by methodological positivism in contemplating the role of personal experience in research. On the other hand, a close understanding of the case may not be possible *without* drawing on personal experience —the position that would be held by a constructivist-interpretivist–informed science contemplating the question of objectivity.[11] It used to be argued, especially in the context of policy analysis, that the solution to the problem was for the researcher to make her biases as explicit as possible—and then go about the research. But as Mary Hawkesworth (1988, esp. Chap. 3) has amply shown, that presupposes an objectivist take on biases—that they can be isolated, separated from the self, boxed up as it were, and set aside.

Not only do field researchers not claim to be able to step outside of themselves; these days many of them go further and argue that research processes *require* the researcher to draw on himself—on his own understandings, experiences, sense making—for provisional sense making of the situation under study, with the provisionality expressing the attitude of testability required of science.[12] Thoreau, noting that "in most books, the *I*, or first person, is omitted," asked his readers' indulgence as he followed a different course of action: "We commonly do not remember that it is, after all, always the first person that is speaking. . . . I, on my side, require of every writer, first or last, a simple and sincere account of his own life, and not merely what he has heard of other men's lives; some such account as he would send to his kindred from a distant land; for if he has lived sincerely, it must have been in a distant land to me" (1939/1854, 14). His sense is echoed in the words of the Cree hunter who, under oath in a Canadian court to testify about the fate of his hunting lands in a case concerning a hydroelectric plant, is reported to have said, "I'm not sure I can tell the truth. . . . I can only tell what I know" (Clifford and Marcus 1986, 8).

Historically, the term "qualitative methodology" encompassed the various methods used in field-based research, particularly site-based, "in-depth" ("open-ended" or "conversational") interviewing, typically within the context of ethnographic or participant-observer research. These are the methods associated with the "Chicago School" studies of organizational, social, political, and other problems and with later ones done in that vein.[13] These studies focused on the *Lebenswelt* ("life-world") of phenomenological inquiry or the artifactual expression of meaning characteristic of hermeneutic analysis, studying texts and "text analogues" (in the phrase of Charles Taylor [1971]). Studies in this mode came to be designated "qualitative" with the development of survey research and the field of statistics and with subsequent growth in the ability of computers to analyze large amounts of numerical data (e.g., those produced by surveys and content counts). The logic of the language of "quantitative" called "qualitative" into being: if statistics is quantitative analysis, then nonstatistical methods that retain their word-based, narrative form— conversational interviewing, observing (with whatever degree of participation), and studying documents—must be "qualitative" analysis. Case studies also came to be designated "small *n*" research, in contradistinction to "large *n*" surveys.

What this means is that rather than talking about quantitative and qualitative methods, we should be talking about positivist and constructivist-interpretivist methods. Because the common category structure focuses on numeracy or its presumed absence, the ontological and epistemological underpinnings of methods choices are silenced. The political science discipline, on the whole, engages methods as tools and techniques split off from any discussion of the methodological issues that underlie them—and the latter become silenced.

One of the outcomes of this absent discussion is a universalizing assumption concerning the criteria for the trustworthiness of research. "Validity" (internal, construct, external, etc.) and "reliability" are grounded in positivist ontological and epistemological presuppositions. "Qualitative" research has been called to task for not measuring up to these criteria. Increasingly qualitative researchers have been urged to do a better job in getting their small *n* studies to meet the reliability and validity criteria for large *n*, quantitative studies.[14] Yet because the traditional forms of qualitative methods take off from presuppositions different from those underlying these two criteria, they will constantly come up short when evaluated against them. The unarticulated, universalizing assumptions of positivist-informed evaluative criteria deflect attention from the ways in which reliability and validity are grounded in positivist presuppositions about reality and knowing and from the possibility that there might be other ways of assessing research trustworthiness (e.g., see Erlandson et al. 1986, esp. p. 186, for one approach).

This silencing of philosophical presuppositions and the separation of methods from methodology enables an argument that otherwise would not make sense. Some have called for the use of multiple methods (also called "triangulation") in a single research project. Understanding that ontological and epistemological presuppositions and attendant methods are intertwined renders such a move, in which multiple methods cross epistemological-ontological divides, inconceivable. Methods do not exist in a void: they are intimately bound up with a fundamental orientation toward the reality status of what those methods allow us to study and the knowability that we presume about that world. Can a researcher firmly situated within a realist ontological position conduct research informed by a phenomenological (constructivist) ontol-ogy at the same time (and vice versa)? Certainly one can imagine issues on which both survey and participant observation research might shed interest-ing light. But by the time the research question has been brought down to the level of specificity necessary for operationalization, the researcher has, implic-itly if not explicitly, taken a stance regarding whether the topic of study can be known "objectively." I cannot imagine research that could accommodate such contradictory positions.

I hold that research should be question-driven rather than methods-driven: we should be starting from what we want to know, which will lead us to the appropriate methods for gaining that knowledge, rather than letting what we know how to do drive our choice of research questions. The very framing of a researchable question presupposes a position toward the ontological and epis-temological status of the social and political world that we are studying.[15] This is not to say that we cannot educate students and practicing researchers about more than one methodology or train them in more than one method, or that textbooks cannot cover quantitative, qualitative, and interpretive method-ologies and methods. But operationalizing a research question enacts an epis-temological-ontological stance, whether or not the researcher is consciously aware of it and reflective on it.

Contesting "Qualitative" Methods:
Numbers, Words, and Philosophical Presuppositions

The increasing use of "qualitative methodology," in several social sciences, to refer *not* to research focused on meaning or "lived experience," but to research informed by methodological positivism, and the term's orientation toward positivist criteria, present another challenge to the "qual-quant" taxonomy. Traditional forms of meaning-focused qualitative research increasingly find themselves without a home among neo-"qualitative" researchers: the "quali-tative" terrain has itself become contested. This is especially clear when modes of accessing ("collecting") data are identified separately from modes of analyz-ing those data.[16] All qualitative researchers use some combination of observing (definitionally including participating; see Gans 1976), interviewing, or reading topic-relevant documents in accessing data for their studies. What researchers do with these data, though, is often quite different.

Whereas neo-qualitative researchers might include among their methods such forms of analysis as Q-sort, process tracing, path dependence, fuzzy set, necessary condition, contingency, and macro-causal analyses, old-style quali-tative researchers would list such forms of analysis as category, content,[17] conversational, deconstruction, discourse, dramaturgical,[18] ethnographic semantics, ethnomethodology, ethno-science, frame-reflective, genealogical, grounded theory, metaphor, myth, narrative (including oral histories and story-telling), participant-observation, (participatory) action, semiotics, space, and value-critical analysis, among others.[19] The difference appears to concern a comfort with words: researchers using the former, under pressure to appear as "scientific" as those using quantitative methods (but under a narrow apprehension of what it means to be scientific, as I have argued earlier), increasingly seek to turn word data into numbers or models for the sake of analysis; those using the latter retain their data in word form and invoke word-based modes of analysis. What the latter share is an orientation to meaning—not only *what* events mean, as Steinberger notes (in this volume), but *how* they mean (Yanow 1996), interpreting phenomenologically and/or hermeneutically across divides of language, culture, and/or time (see Yanow and Schwartz-Shea, forthcoming).

Today, within the APSA and other social sciences more broadly, much of the contestation about what "science" means focuses on the tension between what ever-more-complex computer technologies and older word-based approaches enable. Methods in the "qualitative" category and their underlying methodologies find themselves increasingly caught betwixt and between, as the category encompasses varieties of methods that are not in agreement about the character of evidence and the "knowability" of truth. More and more, we have a tripartite division of empirical research methods among positivist-informed quantitative research, positivist-informed or -leaning qualitative research, and constructivist-interpretive qualitative research. Because the discipline has, on the whole, dealt in its public deliberations (i.e., in journals, at conferences, and in textbooks) with methods rather than with methodology, these differences—indeed, the very questions and explorations that might have led to identifying the existence of such differences—have been silenced.

But it is not just the differences that have been silenced: one might argue, as well, that the mere existence of constructivist-interpretive methods and their presuppositions have been almost entirely disappeared—from education, from methods textbooks,[20] and from journal pages as well. To take but one example of the latter, in defining the "interpretive/conceptual" category of articles in the *American Political Science Review*—the category into which constructivist-interpretive research would seemingly naturally fall—the most recent past editor described them as "textual analyses using no quantitative data or formal analysis" (Finifter 1996). This might define political theory writings (although one has to infer what is meant by the qualifiers "quantitative" and "formal": I could imagine theorists reading and analyzing numerical texts or arguing that their analyses are quite formal, logically speaking; the qualifiers make sense only with quantitative research as the unmarked case). This treatment betrays a singular misunderstanding of the character of constructivist-interpretive empirical research, which includes analyses of numerical texts as well as acts, physical artifacts, and spoken language—Taylor's text analogues—with the analysis performed in accordance with the rules of formal logic. It also represents a sad commentary on the state of methodological knowledge within the national association, no doubt reflecting broader curricular issues.

If "qualitative" is coming to mean "methodologically positivist small n studies," and it is only such work that will find space in the pages of flagship and first-tier journals, constructivist-interpretive–informed qualitative research, which looks quite different, will continue to be rejected because it does not, and cannot, fit that image and definition. Positivist-qualitative reviewers are not any more likely than positivist-quantitative reviewers to accept constructivist-interpretive-qualitative articles, out of simple ignorance of the operative standards of those modes of analysis (leaving aside questions of methodological prejudice). Such gatekeeping, too, is part of paradigm practices.

Interpretive Research as Science

Constructivist-interpretive methods—I will at times shorten that to "interpretive" for the sake of brevity and in keeping with their designation in other fields—are not impressionistic. There is as much systematicity in them as in multivariate statistics (and as much of an attitude of testability). But it is a different sort of systematicity. These methods are not "rigorous," if that means stepwise and unyielding: when conducting a conversational interview in the field, the researcher must respond to what the respondent has just said; when observing as a participant in a field setting, this is all the more the case. The steps of this sort of research cannot be pre-specified in the way that those of statistical analysis can be "lined out."[21]

Also, because interpretive researchers insist on the importance of context in shaping local meaning—the meaning that the researcher is attempting to access—research proposals often cannot delimit the parameters of the project in the same way as proposals for a survey research project, for instance. Moreover, this sort of research proceeds much more in a circular, recursive mode than in the linear fashion suggested by the scientific method. It is, in this way, more hermeneutic—and more self-consciously so—than quantitative methods.[22] It enacts its own philosophical grounds (as does positivist-informed research, although it is less self-evident there, perhaps because of its unmarked "normalcy").

None of these characteristics, however, means that the research is not rigorous, as that term is taken, in its context of logic, to mean consisting of precise and exacting argumentation. Interpretive research adheres to a rigor of logic (what Mark Bevir [2003] referred to as a philosophical rigor) in its design procedures (choosing observational sites, for example), in its analytic procedures (which differ by method), and in the way it is written up.

Those of us doing constructivist-interpretive research are partially at fault for its misperception as nonrigorous and unscientific. We have not hitherto done a good job of making its presuppositions and its processes explicit, of articulating how it is that we do what we do. In part, this is due to the character of what it is that we are studying. Making explicit how sense making actually is done is difficult in all fields because, ironically, it is difficult to observe with only the senses. The data are not directly observable: we can see the outcomes of human acts and infer that sense has been made (or not) and inquire what that sense is, but it is most difficult to observe and describe sense making as it unfolds—precisely because, as phenomenologists argue, sense making entails the use of more than sense data, and because it is done reflectively, after the fact. This is one of the strengths of interpretive methods: they do not require all data to be directly observable—they acknowledge the ontological status of tacit knowledge (see, e.g., Polanyi 1966)—and they are, therefore, appropriate for studying subjects in which tacit knowledge figures, such as policy myths (see, e.g., Yanow 1996, esp. Chap. 7).[23] It is also ironic, then, that these methods themselves rest on tacit knowledge—a fact that, I think, researchers using these methods know tacitly, but largely do not address.

Another possible explanation of the failure to articulate the "how-tos" of this research lies in the fact that the methods are largely learned by a kind of apprenticeship (most clearly seen in anthropology and perhaps in area studies) that consists of reading others' studies, questioning one's advisor and other experienced researchers, and learning by doing. Within cultural anthropology there has been, on the whole, no need to explicate the methods, as there has been a community for whom the methodological attitude, the disciplinary history, and the literature constitute common sense, commonly shared (or so, at least, it appears to an outsider). In political science (and other fields), there is no "common" from which to make joint sense. Or the common has shifted, because once upon a time (prior to the late 1970s) such studies were not only legitimated, but mainstream.

Somehow along the way we have lost the intellectual history and attendant writings that inform these matters. They have been replaced by the shared common sense—the paradigm—of quantitative analysis and behaviorism (which is what Perestroikans have been contesting). Doctoral students from political science, public policy, organizational studies, information technology, and other departments attending a seminar two years ago at one of the major U.S. universities expressed ignorance of over one hundred years of writings in continental philosophy and other areas that would have enabled them to make the case for the field research methods they wanted to use in their dissertation research. The even more perplexing problem, however, is that they seemed incapable of exploring on their own this vast array of published writings and finding their own path among them. Is this, too, an artifact of the ideational hegemony that Perestroikans have been discussing?

Because the scientific method is so step-wise and precise, because quantitative methods lend themselves to a step-by-step delineation much more readily than do interpretive ones, because on the other hand field studies entail so much procedural flexibility and ambiguity, and because of the lack of explicit "recipe-writing" for interpretive methods, the battle to claim the one type of study as science and dismiss the other has been won and lost, on rhetorical grounds, before the research results are even in: the "rigor" of positivist-quantitative methods is enacted in the very narrative format of textbooks and in journal articles' methods sections. Interpretive researchers need to do a far better job of making our tacit how-to knowledge as explicit as possible and to reclaim the philosophical and empirical antecedents of our methods in our scholarship and in our teaching.

Concluding Thoughts: Science Studies and Questions of Knowledge

In encouraging reflection on scientific practices, science studies turns an analytic eye toward knowledge claims and disciplinary practices. In the tension between academic political science in its methodologically positivist vein and matters of political studies and practices, we may be seeing differences between two systems of knowledge. On the one hand lies "scientific" analysis in the form of technical-rational expertise. On the other is "local knowledge," the very mundane yet expert understanding of and practical reasoning about local conditions derived from lived experience that is developed in interaction among people with the programs, operations, or physical artifacts that are specific to a local context. Greenwood and Levin term the two "scholarly knowledge" and "everyday knowledge" (1998, 109).

These two systems of knowing-learning include different types of knowers and their occupational and gender characteristics, along with concomitant forms of scientific practices for producing knowledge and reasoning about it (Yanow 2004). Much as quantitative analyses enact technical-rational values and modes of thinking, interpretive methods enact the humanistic values and modes of thinking associated with local knowledge. Rooted in context and human meaning, local knowledge is the more democratic mode of knowing, much as interpretive methods are a more democratic mode of analysis.[24] Interpretive research methods may have been shunted aside because of the kind of knowledge they represent and the standing of that knowledge in society: positivist-quantitative methods representing university-based intellectual knowing have been elevated over interpretive methods that are grounded in practice-based everyday knowing (think of "hands-on" fieldwork); technical expertise associated with "brains" and with work that is (perceived as) "mental" has been elevated over local knowledge associated with "brawn" and work that is "manual";[25] and "hard" quantitative analysis that is closer to physics has been elevated over "soft" qualitative and interpretive analyses that are closer to the humanities.

Because of the political status and power that in our society adhere to "science" in its technical-rational mode, I am not prepared to yield the domain of science solely to research that is methodologically positivist. There is nothing in interpretive ways of knowing that would make them illegitimate occupants of one (or more) of the rooms in the house of Science, understood in a broader sense. Philosopher Alfred North Whitehead's "fallacy of misplaced concreteness" appears to have made no inroads into political science thinking:[26] the mathematicization of political science research has continued, unabated, until this point. But a many-roomed political science house needs, I warrant, a touch of passionate humility about its undertakings. In contradistinction to positivism's promise of universal truths, this calls for passion for the logic of one's position married to a sense of humility in the face of the narrower range of what science can claim, along with the possibility that one might be wrong (Yanow 1997). Unchecked, that passion can itself result in a kind of ideational imperialism leading to the sort of hegemonizing that Perestroika has been decrying.

It is ironic that a political science practiced in a democracy should privilege an analytic mode that celebrates a technical expertise available to the few over a local knowledge available to the many. Moreover, there is something ironic in a society that argues for demographic diversity and cultural pluralism, yet (still) searches for grand unifying theories in its social sciences. A science studies perspective calls for a practice of political science that questions knowledge claims and their sources—knowledge for whom? knowledge of what? known how?—and thinks, publicly and openly, about what those claims entail. What could be more "mature" than that?

Notes

Parts of the argument presented here have appeared in "'Qual'-'Quant' and the Methods Project," *Clio,* the newsletter of the Politics and History Section of the American Political Science Association (May 2002), and in "Interpretive Empirical Political Science: What Makes This Not a Subfield of Qualitative Methods," *Qualitative Methods Newsletter* (Fall 2003).

1. These practices range from the courses taught to undergraduate and graduate students to the textbooks used in these courses, from the advising of doctoral students on appropriate—and defendable—dissertation research to committee judgments on those defenses, from position descriptions and hiring practices to promotion and tenure decisions, from journal review and editorial practices to foundation and fellowship evaluations of research proposals. And of course those students carry the values embedded in these practices forward as the next generation of discipline-boundary monitors and gatekeepers.

2. Kuhn was criticized for lack of clarity in his use of "paradigm" to mean both a way of seeing the scientific domain in question and the community of scientists sharing that way of seeing. This duality of meaning is, however, quite in keeping with understandings of the hermeneutic circle as both a way of interpreting and the interpretive community sharing that set of interpretive rules.

3. See Schwartz-Shea and Yanow (2002), the source of these examples, for an extended, nonquantitative content analysis of fourteen methods textbooks marketed to political scientists.

4. And I do not think this is the case.

5. This is not to say that there was no science elsewhere or prior to the sixteenth century in Europe, just that contemporary debates on the philosophy of (social) science trace their concerns within this Renaissance European history. See, for example, Teresi (2002) for a discussion of the wealth of earlier forms of science developed in other parts of the world.

6. See the essays in Yanow and Schwartz-Shea (forthcoming) for extended argument and illustration of this.

7. See Schwartz-Shea (2003 and this volume), for an analysis of contemporary course offerings across political science doctoral programs.

8. In fairness, I should note that I am not referring to the Department of Political Science. Malcolm Feeley (personal communication, 2004) notes that today database research may be being driven by excessive zeal in institutional review boards' interpretations of protocols for protection of human subjects; see also Katz (2004).

9. See Pion-Berlin and Cleary (this volume). The current editor of the *American Political Science Review* (*APSR*), Lee Sigelman, has communicated his intent to change this.

10. A vast number of sources present these ideas and make these analytic arguments. See, e.g., Abbagnano (1967), Beam and Simpson (1984), Berger and Luckmann (1966), Bernstein (1976, 1983), Burrell and Morgan (1979), Dallmayr and McCarthy (1977), DeHaven-Smith (1988), Hawkesworth (1988), Jennings (1983), Passmore (1967), Polkinghorne (1983), Ricoeur (1971), Rorty (1979), Schutz (1967, 1973), and Taylor (1971).

11. "The truth," she writes, as far as justice is concerned, "likely lies somewhere between the two extremes." This debate is ongoing in interpretive social science.

12. See Krieger (1991), for example. This has also brought about increasing attention to writing itself as a method (e.g., see Clifford and Marcus 1986; Geertz 1988; Richardson 1994). I note that there is a difference between drawing on oneself and projecting oneself or one's ideas, values, etc., onto the people one studies: there is testability in the former, but bad management practices, interpersonal relations, and research methods in the latter.

13. I have in mind Blau's *The Dynamics of Bureaucracy* (1963), Kaufman's *The Forest Ranger* (1960), Lipsky's *Street-Level Bureaucracy* (1979), Selznick's *TVA and the Grass Roots* (1966), and Whyte's *Street-Corner Society* (1981/1943).

14. To increase the "robustness" of data and thereby improve small n studies under the requirements of positivist science King, Keohane, and Verba (1994) have called on small n researchers to increase the number of observations. It is a fallacy, however, that small n studies entail a small number of observations, as anyone who has conducted field studies of communities or organizations or polities knows. Each such study entails sustained observation (with whatever degree of participation) over time and/or extended conversational interviews and/or the reading and analysis of a multiplicity of agency, policy, or other documents, and each of these activities comprises multiple "observations" or data points. The meaning of "observation" differs, in other words, across research communities.

15. That said, it is also clear that scholars' personalities lead them to certain philosophical stances and methods skills; research is not entirely as "bloodless" a process as this sentence would suggest. Bill Connolly (forthcoming) notes that William James was of the view that character "inflects" such pathways.

16. Interpretive researchers typically do not "collect" their data. The data—the events studied, including settings, participants, and "props" (Murphy 1980)—stay in the "field" as researchers access them and afterward. As in the case of other common methods terms, this one appears to have been imported into the social sciences from non–social scientific practices (in this case, from those used in

collecting archaeological shards, butterflies, etc.). What researchers bring home or to their desks to analyze are their notes on (and possibly photographs or audio or video tapes of) their observations and conversations and readings (and perhaps copies of documents); the people, objects, and original documents remain in their places of origin. Perhaps this, too, enacts field researchers' disinclination to objectify or commodify their subjects. Interpretive research typically entails, then, fieldwork, deskwork, and textwork (Yanow 2000).

17. Word-based content, not the quantitative sort developed by Harrold Lasswell and Ithiel de Sola Pool.

18. Building on the work of Kenneth Burke and Erving Goffman.

19. On the analysis of symbols and myths and for other topics and further references, see Kaufman (this volume), Feldman (1995), Yanow (2000), and Yanow and Schwartz-Shea (forthcoming).

20. Babbie's is a notable, albeit limited, exception to this statement; see, e.g., his 1998 text.

21. Donald Schon (1985), drawing on Herbert Simon's work, gives a more formal definition of rigor as "well-formed problems of instrumental choice to whose solution research-based theory and technique are applicable" (15). Field research questions are no more "well-formed" than the professional practice that was his concern: the researcher cannot proceed by a simple application of techniques; she must engage in conversation with the situation, including with its participants, which means that the research "problem" is much more co-constructed, in partnership, a point made by Ruth Behar (1993), among others. See Lynch (this volume) on the rhetorical uses of "rigor."

22. I am referring here to the hermeneutic circle described, e.g., by Edmund Husserl and, more so, in Hans Georg Gadamer's extension, as the way in which learning develops. See also note 2.

23. One might argue, in fact, that the requirement that everything be made explicit is a particularly American orientation. I maintain that this explains some of our singular foreign policy failures, e.g., in the Middle East, where much is communicated without spelling it out. This orientation toward the explicit may also explain, in part, the domination of quantitative methods, as well as the challenges to the tacit dimension.

24. See note 21, on the co-construction of the research problem and, e.g., Dryzek (1990), the essays in Fischer and Forester (1993), and Schneider and Ingram (1993) in the context of policy analysis.

25. These two different modes of knowing are associated with intellectual ability on the one hand and with physical ability on the other, exemplified etymologically in the differences between "I know," from Middle English *knowen* or Dutch *Ik ken, kennen,* and "I can," from Old English *can* or *con, cunnan* or Dutch *Ik kan, kunnen.* See also *canny,* "having or showing knowledge and skill in applying it; fully competent," and *ken,* "perception; understanding" (from Middle English *kennen* and Old English *cennan,* "to make known." *American Heritage Dictionary of the English Language,* ed. William Morris, 1975, pp. 197, 717). Ralph Hummel (2001) explicates these differences at length, drawing on Georg Wilhelm Friedrich Hegel.

26. Whitehead argued that we attribute more concrete reality to mathematical variables, which are, after all, abstractions, than we do to human experience, which constitutes the "hard data" that social science observes. However, we treat

human behavior as abstract, in his view misplacing concreteness onto mathematical expressions.

References

Abbagnano, Nicola (1967). Positivism. *Encyclopedia of Philosophy,* Vol. 6. New York: Macmillan.

Babbie, Earl (1998). *The Practice of Social Research,* 8th ed. Belmont, CA: Wadsworth.

Beam, George, and Dick Simpson (1984). *Political Action.* Chicago: Swallow Press.

Behar, Ruth (1993). *Translated Woman.* Boston: Beacon Press.

Berger, Peter L., and Thomas Luckmann (1966). *The Social Construction of Reality.* New York: Anchor Books.

Bernstein, Richard J. (1976). *The Restructuring of Social and Political Theory.* Philadelphia: University of Pennsylvania Press.

Bernstein, Richard J. (1983). *Beyond Objectivism and Relativism.* Philadelphia: University of Pennsylvania Press.

Bevir, Mark (2003). Comments made during a discussion at the roundtable "Constructivist and Interpretive Methods," American Political Science Association Annual Meeting, Philadelphia, PA (August 28–31).

Blau, Peter. 1963. *The Dynamics of Bureaucracy.* Chicago: University of Chicago Press.

Burrell, Gibson, and Gareth Morgan (1979). *Sociological Paradigms and Organisational Analysis.* Portsmouth, NH: Heinemann.

Clifford, James, and George E. Marcus, eds. (1986). *Writing Culture.* Berkeley: University of California Press.

Connolly, William E. (forthcoming). *Pluralism.* Durham, NC: Duke University Press. Chap. 3.

Dallmayr, Fred R., and Thomas A. McCarthy, eds. (1977). *Understanding and Social Inquiry.* Notre Dame, IN: University of Notre Dame Press.

DeHaven-Smith, Lance (1988). *Philosophical Critiques of Policy Analysis.* Gainesville: University of Florida Press.

Dryzek, John (1990). *Discursive Democracy: Politics, Policy, and Political Science.* New York: Cambridge University Press.

Erlandson, David A., Edward L. Harris, Barbara L. Skipper, and Steve D. Allen (1993). *Doing Naturalistic Inquiry.* Newbury Park, CA: Sage.

Feldman, Martha S. (1995). *Some Interpretive Techniques for Analyzing Qualitative Data.* Beverly Hills, CA: Sage.

Finifter, Ada (1996). "Report of the Editor of the *APSR,* 1996–97." *PS: Political Science & Politics* 29, 760.

Fischer, Frank, and John Forester, eds. (1993). *The Argumentative Turn in Policy Analysis and Planning.* Durham, NC: Duke University Press.

Gans, Herbert (1976). "Personal Journal: B. On the Methods Used in This Study." In M. Patricia Golden, ed., *The Research Experience.* Itasca, IL: F. E. Peacock. Pages 49–59.

Geertz, Clifford (1973). *The Interpretation of Cultures.* New York: Basic Books.

Geertz, Clifford (1988). *Works and Lives.* Stanford, CA: Stanford University Press.

Greenwood, Davydd J., and Morten Levin (1998). *Introduction to Action Research.* Thousand Oaks, CA: Sage.

Hawkesworth, M. E. (1988). *Theoretical Issues in Policy Analysis*. Albany, NY: SUNY Press.

Hummel, Ralph (2001). "Kant's Contributions to Organizational Knowledge: Do Workers Know Something Managers Don't?" Paper presented to the Annual Conference of the Public Administration Theory Network, Leiden, the Netherlands (June 21–23).

Jennings, Bruce (1983). "Interpretive Social Science and Policy Analysis." In Daniel Callahan and Bruce Jennings, eds., *Ethics, the Social Sciences, and Policy Analysis*. New York: Plenum. Chap. 1.

Kassin, Saul (2002). "False Confessions and the Jogger Case." *New York Times*, November 1, A31.

Katz, Jack. 2004. "Subterranean Fieldworkers' Blues: Scratching toward a Common Law of Social Research Ethics." Paper presented to the Center for the Study of Law and Society, Boalt Hall School of Law, University of California, Berkeley. February 17.

Kaufman, Herbert (1960). *The Forest Ranger*. Baltimore: Johns Hopkins University Press.

Keller, Evelyn Fo(1983). *A Feeling for the Organism: The Life and Work of Barbara McClintock*. New York: W. H. Freeman.

King, Gary, Robert O. Keohane, and Sidney Verba (1994). *Designing Social Inquiry: Scientific Inference in Qualitative Research*. Princeton, NJ: Princeton University Press.

Krieger, Susan (1991). *Social Science and the Self*. New Brunswick, NJ: Rutgers University Press.

Kuhn, Thomas S. (1962). *The Structure of Scientific Revolutions*. Chicago: University of Chicago Press.

Latour, Bruno (1987). *Science in Action: How to Follow Scientists and Engineers through Society*. Cambridge, MA: Harvard University Press.

Lipsky, Michael (1979). *Street-Level Bureaucracy*. New York: Russell Sage Foundation.

Lithwick, Dahlia (2002). "Personal Trust and Legal Fictions. *New York Times*, December 17, A35.

McCloskey, Donald (1985). *The Rhetoric of Economics*. Madison: University of Wisconsin Press.

Murphy, Jerome T. (1980). *Getting the Facts*. Santa Monica, CA: Goodyear.

Passmore, John (1967). "Logical Positivism." *Encyclopedia of Philosophy*, Vol. 5. New York: Macmillan.

Polanyi, Michael (1966). *The Tacit Dimension*. New York: Doubleday.

Polkinghorne, Donald (1983). *Methodology for the Human Sciences*. Albany: SUNY Press.

Rabinow, Paul, and William M. Sullivan, eds. (1979, 1987). *Interpretive Social Science*, 1st and 2nd eds. Berkeley: University of California Press.

Richardson, Laurel (1994). "Writing: A Method of Inquiry." In Norman K. Denzin and Yvonna S. Lincoln, eds., *Handbook of Qualitative Research*. Thousand Oaks, CA: Sage. Pages 516–29.

Ricoeur, Paul (1971). "The Model of the Text: Meaningful Action Considered as Text." *Social Research* 38, 529–62.

Rorty, Richard (1979). *Philosophy and the Mirror of Nature*. Princeton, NJ: Princeton University Press.

Schneider, Helen, and Anne Ingram (1993). "Social Construction of Target Populations." *American Political Science Review* 87, 334–47.

Schon, Donald (1985). *The Design Studio.* London: RIBA Publications.

Schutz, Alfred (1967). *The Phenomenology of the Social World.* Chicago: Northwestern
   University Press.

Schutz, Alfred (1973). "Concept and Theory Formation in the Social Sciences." In
   Schutz, *Collected Papers,* Vol. 1, ed. Maurice Natanson. The Hague: Martinus
   Nijhoff. Pages 48–66.

Schwartz-Shea, Peregrine (2003). "Is This the Curriculum We Want? Doctoral
   Requirements and Offerings in Methods and Methodology." *PS: Political Science
   and Politics* 36, 379–86.

Schwartz-Shea, Peregrine, and Dvora Yanow (2002). "'Reading' 'Methods' 'Texts':
   How Research Methods Texts Construct Political Science." *Political Research
   Quarterly* 55, 457–86.

Selznick, Philip (1966). *TVA and the Grass Roots.* New York: Harper Torchbooks.

Taylor, Charles (1971). "Interpretation and the Sciences of Man." *Review of Meta-
   physics* 25, 3–51.

Teresi, Dick (2002). *Lost Discoveries.* New York: Simon & Schuster.

Thoreau, Henry David (1939/1854). *Walden, or Life in the Woods.* New York: Heritage Press.

Traweek, Sharon (1992). *Beamtimes and Lifetimes: The World of High Energy Physicists.*
   Cambridge, MA: Harvard University Press.

Whyte, William Foote (1981/1943). *Street Corner Society,* 3rd ed. Chicago: University
   of Chicago Press.

Yanow, Dvora (1996). *How Does a Policy Mean? Interpreting Policy and Organizational
   Actions.* Washington, DC: Georgetown University Press.

Yanow, Dvora (1997). "Passionate Humility in Interpretive Policy and Administrative Analysis." *Administrative Theory and Praxis* 19, 171–77.

Yanow, Dvora (2000). *Conducting Interpretive Policy Analysis.* Newbury Park, CA: Sage.

Yanow, Dvora (2004). "Translating Local Knowledge at Organizational Periph-
   eries." *British Journal of Management* 15 (March): S15–S25.

Yanow, Dvora, and Peregrine Schwartz-Shea, eds. (forthcoming). *Interpretation and
   Method: Empirical Research Methods and the "Interpretive Turn."* Armonk, NY: M. E.
   Sharpe.

CHAPTER 15

Will the Real Perestroikniks Please Stand Up?

Race and Methodological Reform in the Study of Politics

Dorian T. Warren

I was motivated to write this chapter by several observations about the relationship between the Perestroika movement and the study of race and ethnicity within the political science discipline. First I argue that many scholars of color, students of race and ethnic politics, and feminist scholars and students of gender politics have long proffered similar critiques of method- and theory-driven over problem-driven research to those motivating Perestroika adherents. These scholars have also illustrated the limitations of mainstream methodologies and theoretical approaches for understanding racialized and gendered politics.[1] However, few of these scholars have been a significant part of this most recent disciplinary insurgency. This is related to a second observation, which is that there is a tension within the subfield of race and ethnic politics around how much to challenge the quantitative methodological tools, a tension that has produced some of the more noted scholarship on race and politics legitimacy in the discipline, which has been unparalleled at any other time. This passive acceptance of the methodological hegemony of survey-based behavioralism in American politics and within this subfield, combined with the lack of engagement with the Perestroika movement, has significant implications for the training of graduate students and for the range of research questions asked.

I explore these observations and their implications through a brief overview and contextualization of scholarship on race and ethnic politics within the discipline. Next I turn to the implications of method-driven over problem-driven research in the race and ethnic politics subfield and in American politics more broadly, exploring how this impacts graduate student training. Through a discussion of my own dissertation research on the incorporation and representation of marginalized groups of workers within contemporary U.S. labor politics, I argue that a problem-driven and methodologically pluralist approach best facilitated my research. I explain why this approach is most promising for taking up cutting-edge questions of "intersectionality" and how complex processes of ascriptive inequalities of race, gender, class, and sexuality all impact politics. Finally I offer a concrete example based on the experience of

Yale graduate students that highlights some of the ways in which younger scholars can help change the state of this subfield and of the discipline for the better.

As Charles Lindblom (1998), Rogers Smith (1998, 2002), and Ira Katznelson and Helen Milner (2002) point out in several essays, the discipline of American political science has historically endeavored to serve two functions that are often in tension with each other: to legitimize and refine the project of liberal capitalist democracy, and to become more "scientific." This scientism, uncritically based on the model of the natural sciences, has driven the American politics field to become fixated on quantitative methods and on method-drivenness more generally. This impacts and is a detriment to the subfield of race, ethnicity, and politics and to those who study the processes and politics of other inequalities ascriptively based on class, gender, and sexuality. In fact, much of the literature in race and politics, especially the most mainstream work on public opinion, adheres to this narrow behavioralist and methodologically individualist approach.

The study of race and ethnicity in political science and in the social sciences more broadly has made significant inroads and contributions over the last two decades. However, these inroads have come at a price. The field has come a long way since Ralph Bunche's observation in 1941: "In respect to my own field . . . there isn't a very cordial reception for papers dealing with the Negro" (Bunche, quoted in Holden 1995). For most of the hundred-year history of American political science, work on race and politics was neither accepted in nor accessible to the field. For example, in their longitudinal analysis of articles on race in the two oldest journals of the discipline,[2] Walton Miller, and McCormick (1995) and Walton and McCormick (1997) find that of the 6157 articles published through 1990, in the 105-year history of *Political Science Quarterly* and in the 85-year history of the *American Political Science Review* (*APSR*), both published only twenty-seven articles addressing the experiences of African Americans, accounting for no more than 2 percent of all articles published. Recent overviews of the latest literature in the subfield have all argued that the impact of race and the processes of racialization in American politics are still very much neglected and need to be made more central, while highlighting the vast expansion and many contributions of the field (Dawson and Cohen 2002; Dawson and Wilson 1991; McClain and Garcia 1993; Smith 2004; Tate 2000). In particular, the research on public opinion and race has received the greatest amount of attention and is closest to the mainstream of the profession (Dawson and Cohen 2002). This work has been professionalized as the most dominant form of scholarship on race and politics in the discipline.

Yet the reason for and one of the costs of this professionalization of scholarship on race and ethnic politics has been the mainstreaming and freezing in place of a *particular kind* of scholarship on race: that of the "race relations" school. The main features of this scholarship within the social sciences, with its origins ranging from the Chicago School of sociology to Gunnar Myrdal's

(1944) classic work, include a commitment to behavioralism and methodological individualism in the form of "measuring" individuals' (mostly whites') attitudes through survey research, along with an ideological position that the "American dilemma" or the "Negro problem" is a mere blemish on our otherwise democratic and egalitarian society, as opposed to a defining, constitutive, and fundamental part of our social structure (Reed 1999; Smith 1997; Tate 2001; Walton, Miller, and McCormick 1995; Walton and McCormick (1997). This specific tradition within the field of race and politics is intimately related to the dominant methodological and ideological underpinnings of the larger discipline. As Dawson and Cohen (2002) argued in their recent assessment on the state of the subfield, "Part of the reason for our unequal levels of information regarding racial politics in the United States is political science's excessive reliance on the discipline of economics as a source of methodological and theoretical inspiration as well as our constant emphasis on the individual level of analysis. This dependence has led to the emergence of dominant methodological approaches in political science, rooted in the use of economic modeling and the individual as the unit of analysis" (488).

Moreover, as Dawson and Cohen and others point out (Reed 1999; Smith 2004), when political scientists have taken up the study of racial politics within this dominant and hegemonic framework, they have uncritically accepted and reified racial categories as given, obscuring the underlying *processes* of the political construction of racialized groups. Thus the current methodological battles within the discipline of political science should be central concerns to students of race and politics, as should the study of other ascriptive processes based on gender, sexuality, and class, and these specific subject matters should also be of central concern to those engaged in the Perestroika insurgency. Unfortunately, as the Perestroika case shows, for the most part those studying race and politics and those studying ascriptive processes are two separate and distinct communities of scholars.

The Silencing Effect?

Since the initial e-mail from an anonymous "Mr. Perestroika" appeared in October of 2000, the loose coalition of faculty and graduate students constituting this disciplinary insurgency at the dawn of the discipline's centennial come from many varied and often conflicting theoretical, methodological, and political perspectives. At times it seems as if supporters and participants agree only on resisting some abstract domination within the discipline. However, Perestroika sympathizers do broadly agree on one thing: they explicitly agree that there is within political science an epistemological and methodological hegemony of positivism, behavioralism, rational choice, game theory, and method-driven and quantitatively focused research. The remedy for this should be a principled commitment to methodological pluralism and diversity—specifically in the publication of articles in the major journals, in faculty hiring and tenure decision making, and in the demonstration of an overall respect for alternative and nondominant methodological and theoretical approaches. There is much less agreement when it comes to the specific subject matters and subfields of the politics of marginalized and ascriptively defined groups and their historic antagonistic relationship with mainstream and hegemonic methods.

One of the eleven points of the original Perestroika "call to arms" specifically addresses the role of race, gender, and sexuality in terms of the leadership of the discipline:

> 8. Why are the overwhelming majority of Presidents of APSA or editorial board members of APSR WHITE and MALE? Where are the African-Americans, Hispanics, Women, Gays, Asians—in short, where is the diversity of [the] United States and the world that APSA "pretends" to study—is somebody afraid that APSA will slip out of their hands??? (emphasis in original)

Despite this specific attention to the racial and gender composition of the APSA leadership, combined with the focus on the dominance of mainstream methods in the discipline, race and ethnic politics scholars were mostly quiet in the beginning stages of Perestroika. This is significant in that the direction of Perestroika might have been broader and its impact more effective had many more of these scholars become engaged during this early window of opportunity.

The silencing of scholars of race and politics, particularly senior and prominent ones, has come from two main sources, both with implications for younger junior scholars and graduate students. In the first case, participants within Perestroika—with a few notable exceptions, including the author or authors of the original manifesto from "Mr. Perestroika"—have either ignored or repeatedly discounted attempts to place the study of the politics of marginal groups on the reform agenda. For instance, in a posting to the e-mail list serve on September 4, 2001, I attempted to express my concern with the lack of participation from political scientists in the Race, Ethnicity, and Politics Section of the APSA and in the sociologists' Gay, Lesbian, and Transgendered Caucus in the Perestroika-organized events. As I wrote: "I didn't see that many folks from these two sub-communities of the APSA wearing our red buttons, and they are probably the MOST sympathetic (descriptively and substantively) to the main concerns of this 'movement'" (Warren 2001, emphasis in original). My message was met with silence, which in effect seemed to silence others who might have wanted to discuss the issues I had raised. But another more explicit dismissal came in the form of responses to a posting to the list serve made by a senior woman of color, Andrea Simpson. In her original posting, explicitly solicited by "Mr. Perestroika," she raised several concerns:

> As a person who has lived my life as a member of an out-group, and now makes the study of how exclusionary practices are created and maintained my life's work, I find it impossible to devise a logit or probit equation that will explain the probability of being oppressed. . . . I do want to join this

discussion, because you are right in thinking that "methodological inclusivity" will have an impact on minority scholars and their position within the discipline. If the discipline can take at least that step, then the journey to respect for questions of power and privilege will be that much shorter. (Simpson 2001a)

In a subsequent posting she continued: "I hope it is clear that I am not only concerned about giving scholars who use qualitative methods a seat at the table, but also giving a seat to those of us who care about race, gender, and class" (Simpson 2001b).

Simpson's interventions were met with hostile and dismissive responses from several Perestroika adherents who argued that the concerns she had stated have no place in this insurgency. These responses had a larger effect of silencing others for a while, particularly untenured junior scholars and graduate students who support Simpson's views and agenda. In her last posting on the list serve about the role of race, gender, and class and their relationship to Perestroika, she explicitly argued, "The point is that the study of race, class and gender is not valued in this discipline. . . . This is why scholars of color are sometimes silent on these issues. Others want to establish their perspective as the 'right' one, and condescend to tell us what we already know" (Simpson 2001c). It would be a long while before these concerns would resurface in Perestroika discussions, and their reemergence was due primarily to controversy around contested APSA elections and their impact on the race and gender composition of the association's leadership.

A second source of the silencing comes from what I perceive to be a tension between two developments. The first is an official and formal acceptance of the subfield of race and politics within the broader discipline—in the guise of an organized section, more publications in the mainstream journals, and more presence of scholars in the field in leadership positions in departments and the *APSR*. This is in tension with a second and more recent development: attempts to "rock the boat" and threaten, by means of methodological and theoretical challenges to the mainstream, this newfound legitimacy at the very moment it seems most promising and more secure than ever before.

Although this tension might present a complicated political dilemma for many students of race and politics, it unveils deeper and more fundamental questions about the long-term goals and aims of scholarship in these fields. Should we as practitioners seek *only* assimilation into the dominant norms and methods of inquiry of the discipline, which have rarely if ever been hospitable and open to our subject matter and purpose, or should we seek a broader and potentially more beneficial strategy of transforming hegemonic disciplinary norms and research paradigms?[3] Unfortunately, based on my own observations and the responses of several scholars to my public support of many of the goals of Perestroika, I am quite doubtful that the strategy of transformation is being considered. For instance, three junior scholars in the field of racial politics independently questioned the "wisdom" of my agreeing to be on a Perestroika panel at one of the major conferences in the discipline. "You must not want to get a job, much less tenure!" exclaimed one, while another softly chided me for my participation because, after all, this "is not our fight." I attribute these anecdotal yet serious concerns to the tension I described earlier.

As a result of the silencing of scholars and the tension within the subfield, there are at least three losers by my count. First, Perestroika participants and supporters are losing their best allies for fundamental reform of the discipline. Second, race and politics scholars are losing a significant and momentary political opportunity to permanently alter the study of American politics by acknowledging the centrality of race and to transform the broader discipline to serve the best interests (methodological, theoretical, and normative) of the subfield. Finally, and most important, graduate students are losing the chance to achieve a broader, more open and inclusive substantive and methodological training, which constricts the range of questions we learn to ask and the research designs we construct, both of which will ultimately impact us through-out our careers. This methodological straightjacket in the broader discipline and in the field of American politics, along with its influence on the subfield of race and politics, impedes relevant and important research on the most pressing political problems facing us today.

My primary argument is that the fixation on method- and theory-drivenness in American politics and its subsequent effect in the field of race and politics field will lead to a dangerous limitation of the range of questions asked, especially by insecure, unsure, and naïve graduate students, who for several reasons, including "market forces" and a lack of knowledge of the history of the discipline and its trends, are especially vulnerable to succumbing to this fixation. I would never have arrived at my dissertation topic or questions without the sheer luck of having advisors and graduate student colleagues who pushed me to identify a problem and a substantive question. The fixation on quantitative methods would have forced me to ask a much narrower question, which I would have probably had to abandon anyway because there are no neatly collected data available to answer it. For example, instead of asking a question such as "Why and under what conditions has there been change and variation in labor unions' politics around race, ethnicity, gender, and sexuality," I might have ended up with a question such as "What are labor unions' members' attitudes around issues of race, ethnicity, and gender, and how have they changed?"[4] The former question, a much broader one, starts from a wider conception of "politics" motivated by a larger political problem that can and does encompass the latter question's focus on members' attitudes. I could have asked the much narrower question about union members' attitudes, downloading the American National Election Study data set from the Inter-university Consortium for Political and Social Research at the University of Michigan, and run some regressions. I might have told a convincing and important story about change in union members' attitudes over time. In fact, I know I would have finished my dissertation much sooner had I chosen that strategy.[5] However, although this approach, driven not by the larger question or problem per se but by methodology and available data, would have given me an interesting and valid story to tell, it could not have told us much about the central political problem I posed at the outset: what explains the variation in unions' politics around race, ethnicity, gender, and sexuality? That approach has allowed me to study unions as political organizations and as sites of collective action and not just to study acontextual individual union members' political attitudes and behavior.

Let me be clear: I am not suggesting that I should not have written a dissertation on change in union members' attitudes around race. Rather, I think it inherently better to arrive at a research project or dissertation having started out with a broad problem and ending up with a smaller and researchable chunk of that larger question, as opposed to never asking a broader question at all.[6] Thus my argument is that the *processes* through which graduate students learn how to ask questions and formulate and design research projects are flawed, primarily through their fixation on quantitative methods and method-drivenness in the broader discipline and, as Peregrine Schwartz-Shea has shown, especially in the graduate curriculum (2001 and this volume). This curricular and disciplinary focus, according to Greg Kasza (this volume), sends the following messages to graduate students:

1. The heart of political science is its methodology, not its subject matter.
2. Statistics is the one methodology that all political scientists must learn; by implication, other methods are inferior.
3. The most suitable topics for political research are those susceptible to statistical inquiry.
4. Manipulating numerical data sets is more important than reading books, doing field work, or any other way of educating oneself about politics.

Allow me to provide another quick anecdote about method-drivenness in the political science discipline. I remember attending a conference organized by my department titled Democracy and Distribution during my second year of graduate school. The underlying political problem and question that invited thinkers and that scholars were asked to examine was "Why don't democracies redistribute downward?" The two-day conference featured panel after panel of high-tech, methodologically sophisticated models and approaches, along with vigorously argued causal explanations. Then, on the final panel on Sunday morning, Robert Dahl was asked to comment on what we had learned during the previous two days, to which he responded: "All of the papers and presentations were very interesting, and well done, but I wonder why, in seeking to answer the question 'Why don't the poor soak the rich,' no one bothered to ask the poor" (taken from personal conference notes). Dahl's simple yet profound observation illustrates how methodological hegemony can impede more methodologically open and pluralist approaches to the study and illumination of real world political problems. That is, in limiting their answers to the research question of the conference to just those provided by the available data that are amenable to quantitative analyses, the participants neglected a most likely source of answers.

Political Problems and Methodological Pluralism

I turn now to a brief explanation of how a problem-driven and methodologically pluralist approach to research has assisted me in my own dissertation work. For "problem-driven" I rely on Shapiro's definition (in this volume): "This is understood to require specification of the problem under study in ways that are not mere artifacts of the theories and methods that are deployed to study it." In my dissertation I use a multiple-method approach. I start with the assumption that the best approach to researching a question or problem depends on what the question is. Thus I use several methods and approaches to research aspects of my broader question. This strategy of "triangulation" gives me evidence from multiple sources, eliminates some of the flaws inherent in any one method, allows me to leverage several strategies of causal inference, and enables me to tell a more convincing and compelling causal story about my political problem. I actually moved to Chicago from New Haven to do "fieldwork," a term that many Americanists think applies only to comparative research.[7]

Part of my dissertation project consisted of constructing and implementing my own survey of labor unions in an attempt to capture unions' politics and not those of individual union members. One of the consequences of the fixation on quantitative methods for me in this process was that even though I had taken my required courses in "methods"—statistics, public opinion, and even survey research—I was not adequately trained in how to construct *organizational* surveys; I really knew only how to analyze already collected individual-level aggregate data. In addition, and just as important, the qualitative fieldwork itself proved to be crucial in the construction and implementation of the survey instrument and in the development of testable hypotheses. That is, if I had never gone into the field, the questions I had originally constructed for the survey would have been misguided and produced extremely unreliable and invalid responses. The discovery of several crucial "causal process observations" during my fieldwork directly contributed to my better collection of the survey data (for those observations, see Brady, Collier, and Seawright 2003). Thus the many methods I have used, all of which have served a specific purpose in helping me to answer parts of the larger question, have been complementary and even necessary to each other.

Furthermore, as I grappled with the question of how some labor unions change to incorporate previously excluded groups of workers based on race, ethnicity, gender, or sexuality, the need for more expansive, interdisciplinary, and innovative theoretical and methodological approaches became not only attractive, but necessary. In fact, to help us get at the more crucial political problems, questions, and puzzles that lay ahead of us in our field, specifically questions about how intersectionality impacts political processes, policies, and behavior, I argue that some methods are more suitable than others. For instance, attention to the many conceptual and methodological contributions of historical institutionalists seems in order. Specifically, the focus on the historical, temporal, and contextual dimensions of causation, the emphasis on the dynamic processes of social change and politics, and especially the prominence given to the study of the interaction effects of distinct causal sequences and processes all seem to be particularly useful to those studying the intersection of ascriptively defined processes and politics (Mahoney and Rueschemeyer 2003; Pierson and Skocpol 2002). In order to bring these and other methods from outside of our formal discipline to bear on the political problems impacting the politics of marginalized groups, the central goals and promises of Perestroika need to be taken seriously and will require much more engagement by scholars in our discipline—particularly those in positions of power, who have the ability to push for changes from the departmental to the associational level.

From Whence Will Change Come?

Lest we hold our breaths awaiting change from on high, let me conclude by offering a concrete example of what graduate students can do to chip away at the anti-intellectual and obscurantist fixation on method-drivenness in the discipline. Over the past several years, several faculty members in my graduate department have been in the vanguard of calling for problem-driven research over method- and theory-driven research in the discipline. Furthermore, several faculty members have been extremely involved in various ways with the Perestroika insurgency. Thus, even though this counterhegemonic approach to research and teaching in political science was part of the public face of political science at Yale, within the department students felt frustrated that these public positions were not being implemented or institutionalized at home. We could not take courses in anything other than quantitative methods (otherwise conflated with and known as data analysis or empirical methods), the only required course graduate students must take. Further, when we wanted to learn about other approaches and tools of research, we were told to go to the sociology or anthropology department to take classes in those subjects, which served further to marginalize these other approaches within the field of political science at Yale. What was the result of this? First, some students left, feeling as if political science was not the right place for them, even if their initial research interests and questions did fit. Second, the burden was on those of us who were seeking out the multitude of ways to approach the study of politics to gain the necessary tools and knowledge on our own. Finally, those who do political theory, and who use nonquantitative methods or more than one methodological approach, were left feeling as though our work "isn't really political science," and unsure about what "risks" to take in pursuing other kinds of research strategies.

Thus a few of us in the department, after complaining and griping for a while, began to organize to demand changes in our department. We called a meeting among graduate students and drafted a letter for all to sign with the following requests:

1. That courses in at least two of the following be offered each year: comparative methodologies, comparative-historical case studies in political science, genealogy of political science of history of the discipline, and philosophy of the social sciences or ontology of the discipline.
2. That a faculty seminar series be instituted in which faculty members could present different approaches to the same problem.
3. That a student study group be established to supplement the first two items.

Along with this, we distributed syllabi from other kinds of methods courses and a few on the history of the discipline. Almost all first- and second-year students signed the letter (there were forty-seven signatures, including those of several faculty members), an amazing response that went beyond our initial expectations. We then met with our department chair and presented the letter to him. He agreed that if we could get a faculty member or members to teach a qualitative methods course, he would do what was necessary to get it on the schedule and make it happen. He also agreed to fund the faculty seminar series and any other kinds of conferences or symposia we wished to organize. We secured a senior and junior faculty member to teach a course the first year, and two junior faculty members to teach a course the following year, even though many of us were not able to take either one.

Although I hope that this small yet concrete example of change in my department might serve as an inspiration for other graduate students, there is still much work that remains to be done, from reforming the APSA to fundamentally changing the ways in which departments and journals operate. Unless all of us act, regardless of the stage or status of our careers, the future of the discipline and its relevance in illuminating political problems in the world are in jeopardy.

Notes

Thanks to Cathy Cohen, Kristen Renwick Monroe, Kamal Sadiq, Dara Strolovitch, and Dvora Yanow for their comments on previous drafts of this chapter. All shortcomings are the sole responsibility of the author.

1. See Patricia Hill Collins, *Black Feminist Thought: Knowledge, Consciousness, and the Politics of Empowerment* (New York: Routledge, 2000); Sandra Harding, ed., *Feminism and Methodology: Social Science Issues* (Bloomington: Indiana University Press,

1987); Shulamit Reinharz, *Feminist Methods in Social Research* (New York: Oxford University Press, 1992).

2. The *Political Science Quarterly* was founded in 1885, the *American Political Science Review* in 1906.

3. Given that I think socialization into the dominant norms and methods of inquiry in the discipline is inevitable to some degree and especially for younger scholars, envisioning and advancing alternative strategies and approaches is necessary for making progress in the field.

4. Of course existing data would not have provided me with much data on the question of attitudes toward sexuality, and it is doubtful that I would have formulated the second research question: "what are the processes by which 'single-identity' organizations change to incorporate 'multiple-identity' issues and groups?"

5. There is the issue of securing adequate funding to support the additional time it takes to pursue labor-intensive research strategies. In fact, it took much effort to raise the money necessary to support myself during fieldwork and to fund my original survey. The intellectual and even career benefit for me is that I now have experience in writing and garnering research grants and fellowships.

6. I also endorse the notion, brought to my attention by Dvora Yanow, that there should be a role for one's own personal interests and talents in choosing research questions and approaches.

7. Although, with the recent emergence of "field experiments" as a popular method, I suspect that this view among some of my colleagues in American politics might change.

References

Brady, Henry E., David Collier, and Jason Seawright. 2003. *Rethinking Social Inquiry: Diverse Tools, Shared Standards.* New York: Rowman & Littlefield.

Dawson, Michael C., and Cathy Cohen. 2002. "Problems in the Study of the Politics of Race." In Ira Katznelson and Helen V. Milner, eds., *Political Science: The State of the Discipline.* New York: W. W. Norton.

Dawson, Michael C., and Ernest J. Wilson III. 1991. "Paradigms and Paradoxes: Political Science and African American Politics." In William Crotty, ed. *The Theory and Practice of Political Science.* Evanston, IL: Northwestern University Press.

Holden, Matthew, Jr., ed. 1995. *National Political Science Review: The Changing Racial Regime,* Vol. 5. New Brunswick, NJ: Transaction Publishers.

Katznelson, Ira, and Helen V. Milner. 2002. "American Political Science: The Discipline's State and the State of the Discipline." In Ira Katznelson and Helen V. Milner, eds., *Political Science: The State of the Discipline.* New York: W. W. Norton.

Lindblom, Charles E. 1998. "Political Science in the 1940s and 1950s." In Thomas Bender and Carl E. Schorske, eds., *American Academic Culture in Transformation: Fifty Years, Four Disciplines.* Princeton, NJ: Princeton University Press.

Mahoney, James, and Dietrich Rueschemeyer. 2003. *Comparative-Historical Analysis in the Social Sciences.* Cambridge: Cambridge University Press.

McClain, Paula D., and John D. Garcia. 1993. "Expanding Disciplinary Boundaries: Black, Latino, and Racial Minority Groups in Political Science." In Ada W. Finifter, ed., *Political Science: The State of the Discipline II.* Washington, DC: American Political Science Association.

Myrdal, Gunnar. 1944. *An American Dilemma: The Negro Problem and Modern Democracy*. New York: Harper & Bros.

Pierson, Paul, and Theda Skocpol. 2002. "Historical Institutionalism in Contemporary Political Science." In Ira Katznelson and Helen V. Milner, eds., *Political Science: The State of the Discipline*. New York: W. W. Norton.

Reed, Adolph. 1999. "The Jug and Its Content: A Perspective on Black American Political Development." *Stirrings in the Jug: Black Politics in the Post-Segregation Era*. Minneapolis: University of Minnesota Press.

Schwartz-Shea, Peregrine. 2001. "Curricular Visions: Doctoral Program Requirements, Offerings, and the Meanings of 'Political Science.'" Paper delivered at the 2001 Annual Meeting of the American Political Science Association, San Francisco, CA, August 30–September 2.

Shapiro, Ian. 2002. "Problems, Methods, and Theories in the Study of Politics, or: What's Wrong with Political Science and What to Do about It." *Political Theory* 30 (August): 596–619. Reprinted in this volume.

Simpson, Andrea. 2001a. "Andrea Simpson Speaks on Minorities/Race." Posting #775 to perestroika_glasnost2@yahoo.com., perestroika_glasnost_warmhome @groups.yahoo.com. November 12.

——. 2001b. "Andrea Simpson—On Being Relevant." Posting #774 to perestroika _glasnost2@yahoo.com, perestroika_glasnost_warmhome@groups.yahoo.com. November 12.

——. 2001c. "Andrea Simpson on Paul Gronke—On Being Relevant." Posting #784 to perestroika_glasnost2@yahoo.com, perestroika_glasnost_warmhome @groups.yahoo.com. November 13.

Smith, Rogers M. 1997. *Civic Ideals*. New Haven, CT: Yale University Press.

——. 1998. "Still Blowing in the Wind: The American Quest for a Democratic, Scientific Political Science." In Thomas Bender and Carl E. Schorske, eds., *American Academic Culture in Transformation: Fifty Years, Four Disciplines*. Princeton, NJ: Princeton University Press.

——. 2002. "Putting the Substance Back in Political Science." *Chronicle of Higher Education*, April 5.

——. 2004. "The Puzzling Place of Race In American Political Science." *Political Science & Politics* 37:1 (January).

Tate, Katherine. 2001. "Politics of Race Relations (United States)." In Neil J. Smelser and Paul B. Baltes, eds., *International Encyclopedia of the Social and Behavioral Sciences*. New York: Elsevier Science.

Walton, Hanes, Jr., and Joseph P. McCormick II. 1997. "The Study of African American Politics as Social Danger: Clues from Disciplinary Journals." In Georgia Persons, ed., *National Political Science Review*, Vol. 6. New Brunswick, NJ: Transaction Publishers.

Walton, Hanes, Jr., Cheryl M. Miller, and Joseph P. McCormick, II. 1995. "Race and Political Science: The Dual Traditions of Race Relations Politics and African American Politics." In John Dyrzek, James Farr, and Stephen Leonard, eds., *Political Science and Its History: Research Programs and Political Traditions*. Cambridge, MA: Cambridge University Press.

Warren, Dorian T. 2001. "A Yale Student Speaks." Posting #571 to perestroika _glasnost2@yahoo.com.Perestroika_glasnost_warmhome@groups.yahoo.com. September 4.

CHAPTER 16

Let a Hundred Flowers Bloom, Let a Hundred Schools of Thought Contend

Arguments for Pluralism and against Monopoly in Political Science

Lloyd I. Rudolph

Economics over the years has become more and more abstract and divorced from events in the real world. Economists, by and large, do not study the workings of the actual economic system. They theorize about it. As Ely Devons, an English economist, once said at a meeting, "If economists wished to study the horse, they wouldn't go and look at horses. They'd sit in their studies and say to themselves, 'What would I do if were a horse?'"

—Ronald Coase, *The Task of the Society*

Neither Mikhail Gorbachev's "perestroika" movement nor Mao Tse-tung's "Let a hundred flowers bloom" campaign achieved its objective in the near term. But over time they may have helped to make some good things happen. It is in that spirit that I offer a few thoughts about the case for pluralism and the case against monopoly in the theory and practice of political science.

I start making the case for pluralism and against monopoly by invoking the grand themes of a recent book by Stephen Toulmin, *Return to Reason*.[1] Toulmin argues that because rationality as found in the world is contextual and thus plural, it is at best illusory and at worst damaging to thought, knowledge, and explanation to invoke it as a universal, objective standard. The capacity of reason to help us know and act better has been damaged, he says, by a serious imbalance in our pursuit of knowledge. Reliance on rationality, understood and practiced as a mathematical form of reasoning modeled on scientific method and the quest for absolute certainties, has lowered the value of reasonableness, that is, humane judgments based on personal experience and practice. A lot of scholarship in economics and those who emulate such scholarship in other social sciences, Toulmin finds, value expert knowledge and theoretical constructs above the testimony of diverse communities and the practical experience of individuals. Toulmin argues for the need to confront the challenges of an uncertain and unpredictable world not by applying abstract theories, but by returning to a humane form of reason that accepts variability, complexity, and contingency.

Deirdre McCloskey finds that the kind of economics practiced in Ronald Coase's Nobel Prize–winning article, "The Nature of the Firm" (1937), accords with Toulmin's humane form of reason, including casuistic reasoning about and from cases.[2] McCloskey tells us that "Coasean economics is Anti-Modernist, 'Gothic,' postmodernist in its rhetoric."[3] Coase's economics is anti-modern because it doesn't draw on "the rhetoric of axiomatization, the French claim since Descartes that we know what we mean only if we know what axioms we have started with . . . and was brought to perfection as the main method of economics by Paul Samuelson. Assume a maximizing individual self-aware of his constraints and tastes, and proceed. You will then know what you mean."[4] It is "Gothic" because it doesn't engage in a search "for a grail of a unified field theory, an awakening from Descartes' Dream."[5] Coase's economics is postmodern, McCloskey argues, because it is casuistic rather than universalist. Coase uses "a case by case approach" that embodies common sense and common morality, common law rather than jurisprudential [law]," and he looks for "the stories and metaphors and facts and logics that fit the case in hand."[6]

The Perestroika movement within the APSA has been directed in large measure against the monopoly view of knowledge that practitioners of rational choice scholarship often adopt. They tend to identify with a view of scientific knowledge that claims to be based on and to produce objective, universal truths and to use categories and "facts" that are divorced from time, place, and circumstances. Here I want to argue for a pluralist view of knowing and knowledge. It starts with denying "science" a monopoly on the asking and answering of questions by recognizing the variety of ways that questions can be framed and answered and the several forms of knowledge and kinds of truth associated with multiple modes of inquiry. These include subjective,[7] moral, practical,[8] tacit,[9] and local[10] knowledge and imaginative, partial, contingent, and spiritual truth.

In a 1957 BBC talk, Isaiah Berlin spoke about how to think about rationality in the context of political science. He argued that the idea that political science rests on laws and experiments like those of physics "was the notion, concealed or open, of both Hobbes and Spinoza . . . a notion that grew more powerful in the eighteenth and nineteenth centuries, when the natural sciences acquired enormous prestige, and attempts were made to maintain that anything not capable of being reduced to a natural science could not properly be called knowledge at all." Berlin denied the claim that anything worthy of being called knowledge had to be reduced to a version of natural science. Quite the contrary: "The arts of life—not least of politics . . . possess their own special methods and techniques, their own criteria of success and failure. . . . To be rational in any sphere, to apply good judgment in it, is to apply those methods which have turned out to work best in it."[11]

One form of knowledge dismissed when the social sciences stress their claims that they are science is subjective knowledge. But need we accept the monopoly claims of objective knowledge? M. N. Srinivas died in Bangalore on November 30, 1999. He was India's leading anthropologist, and a scholar of world renown. Passages from two of his last articles offer warrants for the use of subjective knowledge in social science theorizing.[12] These passages make clear that by the late 1990s Srinivas had gone beyond explanation based on social structure and social function to an appreciation of the importance of subjective knowledge and human agency in the making and shaping of culture. As he wrote:

> Every life mirrors to some extent the culture and the changes it undergoes. The life of every individual can be regarded as a "case study," and who is better qualified than the individual himself to study?

> The value of biographical literature, including autobiography, biography, memoirs and diaries as sources for cultural and economic history, is well known. Historians regard them as essential to their work, and anthropologists working in societies with literate tradition, have also used them even when their main source of information was fieldwork. While this is as it should be, it is surprising that anthropologists have yet to look at their own lives as sources of information about their culture, especially as they are undergoing radical change. Anthropology started as the study of "the other," an exotic other, but now there are dozens of anthropologists engaged in the study of their own cultures. The culmination of the movement from the study of other to studying of one's own culture is surely the study of one's own life? The latter can be looked at as a field, with the anthropologist being both the observer and the observed, ending for once the duality which inheres in all traditional fieldwork.[13]

Srinivas was not alone in challenging the monopoly of objective truth. James Clifford's introduction to Writing Culture: The Poetics and Politics of Ethnography, illustrates the "higher realism" by telling us a story about a Cree hunter. When put under oath in a Canadian court to tell the truth, the whole truth, and nothing but the truth about his way of life in connection with a case about his people's hunting lands, he said, "I'm not sure I can tell the truth ... I can tell what I know."[14]

The Cree's response suggests that subjectivity has its own rules. The following story from the diary of Amar Singh,[15] a subjective account that I have been interpreting, indicates the kind of truth, that is, the "rigorous partiality" of self-knowledge, that we can find in a "self as other" ethnography. Amar Singh was a North Indian nobleman who in 1899 had just completed the first full year of his forty-four-year diary. He responded to a rebuke from his respected teacher, the bard (charan) Ram Nathji. In a note penciled in at the end of the 1899 volume, Ram Nathji chastised Amar Singh for writing so much about "butchery" (hunting boars and tigers, or "pig sticking") when his native Jodhpur was experiencing the worst famine in a century, a normatively worthier topic. "I ought surely to have written about the famine," responded Amar Singh, "but you must bear in mind that no opportunities were given me to study or watch it and consequently I could not write anything . . . fearing that I might put in something quite out of place. What I have written is of which I am an eye witness or have heard from very reliable sources."[16] Amar Singh, like the Cree, seemed clear about telling what he knew—things he could study and watch—and not telling about those he couldn't. His subjective knowledge was true because it was partial and contextual.

An essay Amar Singh wrote in his diary while serving in World War I, "The Importance of Keeping Records," written from the western front on October 15, 1915, shows how the absence of subjective knowledge supplied by first-person narratives can compromise voice and representation. Amar Singh was concerned that, in the absence of "eye witness" accounts, the story of Indian soldiers' contribution to the Allies' victory might be lost from view. The war had begun in early August 1914. By late September, the Indian expeditionary force had landed at Marseilles and had arrived at the northern front, where it helped to prevent the execution of the German army's Schliefen plan to encircle Paris by invading Belgium and then penetrating to the Marne.[17] Amar Singh feared that the Indian soldiers' story would fall victim to India's colonial relationship to Britain. He wrote: "To my mind it is a thing of the greatest importance to keep up a nation's records. In this we are backward. . . . Both [the Maharajas] of Jodhpur and Bikaner who have brought their own troops to fight in this world wide conflict ought to have brought their own *charans,* who are our hereditary recorders. . . . What we want is a man of learning and imagination who could and would write from personal experience. . . . The English historians will simply treat . . . the war in a very general way. . . . What we can expect is a mere mention." The absence of an "eye witness" account by a colonial subject did indeed result in reduction of the Indian troops' contribution to the Allied war effort to a "mere mention" in Imperial history.

What are the prospects for intersubjective communication and comparative generalization in the context of cultural pluralism?[18] Clifford Geertz and Richard Shweder invoke forms of life with their own ways of thinking and knowing. Geertz has taught us that cultural differences matter and that they erect barriers to communication, understanding, and explanation. At the same time, he finds space for commensurability sufficient to compare, generalize, and sometimes to explain. It is possible, he argues, for "people inhabiting different worlds to have a genuine, and reciprocal, impact upon one another."[19] They can, he holds, construct a public vocabulary that allows them to talk to each other. The scholar can transcend incommensurability too because, seeing beyond the cultural uniqueness that distinct forms of life entail, she can make cross-cultural comparisons. Command of the languages involved is usually a condition not only for mutual comprehension, but also for bridging differences.

In *Thinking through Culture: Expeditions in Cultural Psychology* Richard Shweder, like Clifford Geertz, makes a case for a pluralism of "multiple objective worlds" that are able, under certain circumstances, to converse with each other.[20] The case for pluralism finds support too from a view of culture that recognizes that it can be made as well as enacted; culture in the making as well as in the doing.[21] To view culture as constituted as well as given suggests that it is wise to avoid dichotomies such as culture versus psychology or structure versus agency as determinants of reality or truth. All four terms are involved in mutual determining processes and interactions. Shweder puts it this way: "Psyche refers to the intentional person. Culture refers to the intentional world. Intentional persons and intentional worlds are interdependent things that get dialectically constituted and reconstituted through the intentional activities and practices that are their products, yet make them up."[22]

Let me conclude by invoking one who to some readers might seem an unlikely theorist of pluralism in the social sciences. I cite Mohandas Gandhi for what he taught about relative, contextual, and partial truths and the standing of subjective knowledge. A *karma yogi,* one who believes in disciplined engagement with the world, he sought "truth in action," most notably in the theory and practice of *satyagraha.*[23] By "truth in action" he meant that there was a truth in each action, a contextual truth that had to be found afresh each time.

In the introduction to his "autobiography," Gandhi tells us that "it is not my purpose to attempt a real autobiography. I simply want to tell the story of my numerous experiments with truth, and as my life consists of nothing but those experiments, it is true that the story will take the shape of an autobiography. . . . Far be it from me," he continues, "to claim any degree of perfection for these experiments. I claim for them nothing more than does a scientist who, though he conducts his experiments with the utmost accuracy, forethought and minuteness, never claims any finality about his conclusions, but keeps an open mind regarding them. . . . I am far from claiming any finality or infallibility about my conclusions . . . [even though] for the time being . . . they appear to be absolutely correct. . . . If they were not, I should base no action on them. . . . So long as my acts satisfy my reason and my heart, I must firmly adhere to my original conclusions."

While Gandhi recognized the existence of "Absolute Truth," he also believed that mortals can at best gain "faint glimpses" of it. "As long as I have not realized this Absolute Truth," he continues, "so long must I hold by the relative truth as I have conceived it. That relative truth must, meanwhile, be my beacon, my shield and buckler." For Gandhi, practitioner of truth in action, knowledge was subjective and truth contextual and partial.[24]

Notes

This chapter is based on a paper prepared for Panel 7-1, "Perestroika: Undisciplined, Unpunished," at the APSA annual meeting on August 31, 2001, in San Francisco, California.

1. Stephen Toulmin, *Return to Reason* (Cambridge, MA: Harvard University Press, 2001).

2. McCloskey takes the view that "Albert Jonsen and Stephen Toulmin [in *The Abuse of Casuistry: A History of Moral Reasoning* (Berkeley, CA: University of California

Press, 1988)] have rescued the word 'casuistic' from the contempt into which it had fallen. . . . They take it as a thoroughly modern approach to ethics, in the context of the revival of the Aristotelian studies of the particular virtues." Deirdre McCloskey, "The Lawyerly Rhetoric of Coase's 'The Nature of the Firm,'" in *Measurement and Meaning: The Essential Deirdre McCloskey,* ed. Thomas Ziliak (Northampton, MA: Edward Elgar, 2001), 293.

3. McCloskey, "Lawyerly Rhetoric," 292.

4. Ibid., 281.

5. McCloskey draws on John Ruskin's critique of Renaissance architecture to come up with her concept of Gothic. As McCloskey tells it, Ruskin noted "that the search for a crystalline Ideal has been an incubus on classical and Renaissance, and now we may say modernist, architecture." The Renaissance's main mistake, Ruskin wrote, "was the unwholesome demand for perfection at any cost." According to McCloskey, "Ruskin's argument fits positivism in economics . . . which seeks an all-embracing, testable, Theory apart from the practical skills of the statesman, the craftsman, or the economic scientist." McCloskey, "Lawyerly Rhetoric," 292.

6. Ibid., 293.

7. Michael Polanyi, *Personal Knowledge: Towards a Post-Critical Philosophy* (Chicago: University of Chicago Press, 1962).

8. James C. Scott, *Seeing Like a State: How Certain Schemes to Improve the Human Condition Have Failed* (New Haven, CT: Yale University Press, 1998). To convey the idea of practical and often local knowledge and skill, Scott prefers the ancient Greek term *metis* to more familiar but less apropos phrases and terms such as "'indigenous technical knowledge,' 'folk wisdom,' 'practical skills,' techne, and so on" (313). He acknowledges his debt to anarchist writers (Piotr Kropotkin, Mikhail Bakunin, Pierre Joseph Proudhon), "who consistently emphasize the role of mutuality as opposed to imperative, hierarchical coordination in the creation of social order" (7). As I suggest later, Gandhi's "truth in action," often via the mutuality of truth associated with a successful *satyagraha* campaign, resembles what Scott seems to be getting at here.

9. See Michael Polanyi, *The Tacit Dimension* (Gloucester, MA: Peter Smith, 1983).

10. On *metis,* see Scott, *Seeing Like a State,* 316–19, where he stresses the localness and particularity of practical knowledge.

11. Isaiah Berlin, *The Sense of Reality,* ed. Henry Hardy (New York: Farrar, Straus, Giroux, 1996), 40–41, 50–51.

12. See my "The Self Constructing Culture: The Ethnography of the Amar Singh Diary," *Economic and Political Weekly* 35, no. 40 (2000).

13. M. N. Srinivas, "Indian Anthropologists and the Study of Indian Culture," *Economic and Political Weekly,* March 16, 1996: 657, and "Social Anthropology and Literary Sensibility," *Economic and Political Weekly,* September 26, 1998: 2528. See also his introduction to *Indian Society through Personal Writing* (New Delhi: Oxford University Press, 1998), where he observes: "It is my plea that the movement from studying one's own culture or a niche in it, to studying oneself as an ethnographic field, is a natural one. In the west, anthropology started as a study of 'the other,' generally a weaker, inferior and exploited 'other,' but in India it has largely been a study of the self or the self in-the-other. And this should extend to include one's own life. 'Sociology of the Self' should be a rich field given the diversities and unities which the members of Indian civilization, are heir to" (xi).

Andre Beteille's appreciation of Srinivas as a structural functionalist, which he was throughout most of his professional life, can be found in his "M. N. Srinivas (November 16, 1916–November 30, 1999)," *Economic and Political Weekly,* January 8–14, 2000: 18–22.

14. James Clifford, *Writing Culture: The Poetics and Politics of Ethnography* (Berkeley: University of California Press, 1986), 8.

15. See Susanne Hoeber Rudolph and Lloyd I. Rudolph with Mohan Singh Kanota, *Reversing the Gaze: Amar Singh's Diary, a Colonial Subject's Narrative of Imperial India* (New Delhi: Oxford University Press, 2000, and Boulder, CO: Westview Press, January, 2002).

16. Comments written in the margin of Amar Singh's diary for 1899, the diary's first year. The full text of the young Amar Singh's response to Ram Nathji's comments at the end of the 1899 bound diary are given below. Ram Nathji was the only person allowed to read the diary. He did so for the first three years, penciling comments in the margins and writing a summary comment at the end.

> My dear Master Sahib,
> I am indeed very grateful for the trouble you have taken to read the whole of my diary and [to] have written remarks on it. I feel very much honoured by it. You know this perfectly, that you are the only man who has yet been at liberty to do what you like with these pages which, though quite rot and a record of butchery [accounts of hunting expeditions] as you say, can yet put me to great inconvenience if known to bad characters. I ought surely to have written about the famine but you must bear in mind that no opportunities were given me to study or watch it. . . . What I have written is [that] of which I am an eye witness or [what I] have heard from very reliable sources.

17. German strategy was based on the plan prepared by Alfred von Schliefen. It provided for the concentration of the German main forces on the French front, the passage through Belgium, and a huge wheeling movement to encircle Paris.

18. I have been helped in my effort to answer this question by the fine essays in *The Fate of Culture: Geertz and Beyond,* ed. Sherry Ortner (Berkeley: University of California Press, 1999).

19. Clifford Geertz, *Local Knowledge: Further Essays in Interpretive Anthropology* (New York: Basic Books, 1983), 161.

20. Richard Shweder, *Thinking Through Culture: Expeditions in Cultural Psychology* (Cambridge, MA: Harvard University Press, 1991).

21. See "Introduction," particularly Section 2 ("Liminality: Making a Self between Two Cultures") and Section 6 ("Reversing the Gaze: The Diarist as Reflexive 'Native' Ethnographer") in Rudolph and Rudolph, *Reversing the Gaze,* 16–22, 39–43.

22. Shweder, *Thinking Through Culture,* 101.

23. Best translated "truth force," though that poorly captures the sense of the word.

24. Mohandas K. Gandhi, *An Autobiography: The Story of My Experiments with Truth,* trans. Mahadev Desai (Boston: Beacon Press, 1957, 1993), xxvi–xxviii.

PART 3

Governance

Methodology is intimately linked to APSA governance because APSA officers, especially the president, set policies that influence what is accepted as
"good scientific" work. Beyond this, Perestroika has been concerned that
there is an APSA establishment that has become entrenched and too unwilling to admit groups with new ideas. A main focus of the political activities
of Perestroika—as opposed to its intellectual activities, if we may use that
distinction—has thus been on the way in which the APSA is governed.

For the most part, the Perestroika group has advocated revising the selection
process for the APSA's officers to introduce more democracy, either through
expanding and electing the Nominating Committee or through requiring competitive elections for all offices. Perestroikans also have criticized the existing
electoral mechanisms both for privileging those nominated by the official
Nominating Committee and for using simple electoral mechanisms that keep
minorities disadvantaged. Perestroikans argue that the current process by which
the APSA Council and officers are chosen provides an advantage to established
scholars who work in well-worn intellectual grooves, and makes it difficult for
scholars who do less conventional work to gain access to the APSA power structure. In doing so, Perestroikans thus address a central conundrum of democratic
theory: democratic organizations depend on some notions of equality for
legitimacy, equality the democratic organization—be it a state or a body such
as the APSA—then promotes. But if there are inequalities in the body served by
the organization, people will participate unequally. Therefore, there are no
assurances that the organization will respond adequately to the needs of those
who are unequally represented and who do not participate equally as a result
of this inequality. Furthermore, Perestroika has argued, the institutions themselves need to be democratic and egalitarian institutionally; the institutions
themselves are relevant, not just the outcomes that are produced.

The initial Perestroika movement favored openly contested democratic elections; support for the drive for contested elections is unclear at the moment,
with many Perestroikans wanting more open democracy but also fearful that

the APSA cannot find a system that protects minority rights as fully as does the current system. My sense is that Perestroikans are now particularly concerned about the effects of elections on minority representation in the APSA for two reasons: (1) a disproportionate number of political scientists who do qualitative research are women or members of other minorities, from ethnic groups such as Latinos and African Americans to members of the Gay, Lesbian, Bi-Sexual and Transgendered Caucus, and (2) Perestroika's ideological roots in egalitarianism mean the movement would like to see the profession become more reflective of all groups in our society, from conservative to liberal political elements. The relationship between minority group politics and methodological issues is the subject of several chapters in the following section.

The question of governance itself is the focus of five chapters. The topic has been much discussed in APSA circles, and is slowly filtering into discussions focused on regional associations as well. At the national level, the APSA Council authorized Gary C. Jacobson to head a committee to look into such matters in 2002. This process, culminating in the issuance of what is commonly known as the Jacobson Report, is the subject of Jacobson's chapter on the selection process for APSA officers.

Gary C. Jacobson's chapter describes the work of the APSA Elections Review Committee. Jacobson notes that the committee recommend against mandating competition for several reasons: (1) The APSA's constitution already provides for contested elections if any *ten* of its more than thirteen thousand members want to nominate alternatives to the official slate; (2) unless elections are thoroughly rigged, mandatory competition is likely to decrease political diversity among the APSA's officers; (3) there is no authentic endogenous basis for competition at present, and making it mandatory actually may create factions and encourage factional strife within the organization; and finally (4) mandatory competition for APSA offices would discourage or waste participation by distinguished members. Overall, Jacobson argues, the current system has succeeded in providing the APSA with distinguished, responsive, and broadly representative leadership. Mandatory competition is unnecessary and would be potentially damaging to the association.

Marsha Pripstein Posusney disagrees. She was intimately involved in the debate over governance while she was on the APSA Council, and her chapter explains why she finds the existing APSA provisions for democracy inadequate. In particular, Pripstein Posusney addresses the diversity argument against competitive elections raised by the Jacobson committee and finds no merit in the claim that elections would necessarily harm diversity. Her chapter outlines several tentative ideas for alternative electoral procedures that could bring greater democracy to APSA while not threatening the gains made in representational diversity over the last few years. Pripstein Posusney's chapter reminds us that part of Perestroika's initial concern was the entrenched establishment, and that Perestroika's desire for democratic elections reflects a desire to be more, not less, inclusive.

Kristen Renwick Monroe describes the public meeting at which many of these governance issues were discussed. Her chapter presents the wide variety of opinions on this complex issue and argues that there are two problems that should be addressed in any attempt to reform. First, Monroe argues that the current system has been responsive to demands for the inclusion of previously disadvantaged groups in the APSA that have been made by women and minority caucuses. The institutional mechanisms themselves, however, privilege the in-group nominees, that is, the ones chosen by the official APSA Nominating Committee. Candidates proposed via petition are seen as challengers and run for office at a disadvantage. Furthermore, in institutional terms, the system is too dependent on the vagaries of chance in terms of good appointments to the Nominating Committee. Monroe finds it surprising, given political scientists' claims that they care about institution building, that this point has gotten lost in the debate. Second, she argues that any reforms must introduce more democratic inputs into the selection process at some point, but also must construct institutional mechanisms to protect minority rights. As currently constructed, the system responds well to demands from organized political groups clamoring for increased access, as has been the case with women and many ethnically defined minority groups. The groups that have been systematically disadvantaged, however, are those at large, nonresearch teaching universities or small colleges. These groups need the protection and nurturance an institutionalized concern for democracy and equality could provide.

Joanna Vecchiarelli Scott writes from the vantage point of a self-described implicated observer. Both by accident and by design, Scott was located at the busy intersection of multiple sites of dissent in the rhetorical war being waged for the discipline of political science in America. Situated between the Nominating Committee, on which she served during the two crucial years (2000–2002) when Perestroika was launched, the Women's Caucus for Political Science, the Perestroika movement, and her own disciplinary identity as a political theorist from a regional state university, Scott is struck by the gaps between intention and effect on all sides of this controversy. Her chapter notes the arguments of Roland Barthes about the authenticity of the reader and the text and Edmund Burke's views about the nature of representation. Postmodernists and anti-modernists alike set the tone for Scott's exploration of whether, despite the intentions of authors or the opinions of the electorate, what Scott refers to as "the virtual republic of Perestroika" should be read as a binding mandate requiring reform of APSA governance, a deconstructive Fifth Column operating inside the organization, or a mostly online "loyal opposition" whose primary impact will be limited to proposals for procedural reform. Her answers raise further questions: How can students of politics defer to the dictates of a permanent elite on research and publication, however benevolently intended? Where do we find the organized Latino, African American, Asian, and feminist groups in all of this, and how will an APSA reformed by Perestroika include them? Scott's chapter forces us to ask: Does Perestroika itself claim not to represent the opinions of the APSA membership as a whole but rather to speak selectively for particular groups that have been silenced by the APSA's hegemonic discourse? And what broader lessons on representation and governance can we draw from the Perestroika list's critical assault on the APSA establishment?

Lloyd I. Rudolph's chapter comes from a panel on how to escape the quota frame when dealing with minority representation in contested APSA elections.[1] A staunch supporter of contested elections, Rudolph sets his analysis in the context of classic work in political theory to make a strong case for member sovereignty. Rudolph begins by asking: How should we view representation in the APSA? This question then raises another: Who or what should be represented? His answer is that the APSA is a membership association of persons who choose to identify themselves as political scientists, and that the one person, one vote convention, used since the time of John Locke, should be followed. However, Rudolph does see importance in Locke's one caveat concerning majority rule, that the "majority should be able to conclude the rest;" that is, that "the rest" should feel that the majority has taken their interests or identity into account. On the other hand, Rudolph argues that the APSA also represents constituencies of diverse kinds, not all of which correspond. He concludes that the APSA should represent all individuals and constituencies. His chapter, especially taken in conjunction with Pripstein Posusney's, provides a new viewpoint on the traditional divides over the issue of elections.

Martha Ackelsberg's chapter might be read as an assessment of Perestroika insofar as it highlights the contributions Perestroika has made to political science. I include her chapter in this section, however, because Ackelsberg links her assessment of Perestroika to the question of competitive elections. She believes that Perestroika's focus has been too limited. Although Perestroika has made some progress in achieving each of its three major goals—instituting competitive elections in the APSA, increasing the methodological openness of journals, and challenging the methodological narrowness of many departments —Ackelsberg challenges political scientists concerned with such issues to think more about "ultimate ends": What are our broad goals? And what is the best way to achieve them? Specifically, Ackelsberg questions whether competitive elections can really achieve the broader goals for which Perestroika has been struggling. As a strategy for transforming both the discipline and the APSA, competitive elections may in fact yield results inconsistent with some of Perestroika's more specific goals. Ackelsberg's chapter raises important, broader questions about Perestroika's aims and focus, and is intended as a response to many questions and issues raised by other authors in this section.

Note

1. This panel was part of the meetings of the Midwest Political Science Association on April 18, 2004.

CHAPTER 17

The Case against Mandatory Competition for APSA Offices

Gary C. Jacobson

As part of its effort to make the discipline of political science friendlier to its intellectual and normative concerns, the Perestroika group has advocated revising the selection process for the American Political Science Association's officers to require competitive elections for all offices. In response, APSA President Robert Jervis (2000–2001) appointed an Elections Review Committee to review the issue and to report its findings and recommendations to the APSA Council. The report was submitted in April 2002.[1] I chaired the committee, which unanimously recommended that competition for APSA offices *not* be made mandatory. The report and recommendations were meant not to be definitive or final but to serve as a starting point for wider discussion of the selection process by the APSA Council and members. This chapter is also intended as a contribution to that discussion. I draw heavily, often verbatim, from the committee's report, but responsibility for its content is of course mine alone.[2]

The APSA currently elects a president-elect (who automatically becomes president the following year), three vice presidents, a secretary, a treasurer, and a sixteen-member Council. The president and vice presidents serve for one year, the secretary and treasurer for three years, and Council members for two years, with half elected annually. The procedure for filling these offices is specified by Article V of the APSA constitution and may be found at the association's Web site.[3] It provides for a six-member Nominating Committee (each incoming APSA president appoints three members to two-year terms) charged with proposing a slate of nominees, one for each office, that reflects the diversity of the APSA membership. If no additional candidates are proposed, the slate is elected by voice vote at the annual business meeting (held at the association's annual meeting, traditionally on Labor Day weekend). A minimum of ten members may propose additional candidates for any or all offices, in which case the whole membership is eligible to vote in an election via mail ballot after the business meeting.

To evaluate this process and possible alternatives, the Elections Review Committee gathered several kinds of information. We canvassed the entire membership via e-mail for ideas, opinions, insights, and experiences with leadership selection processes. The committee also compiled information on the diversity of the leadership chosen under the current system and on how other professional academic organizations select their officers. No one in the profession will be surprised to learn that their colleagues took a wide variety of positions on the desirability of and rationale for current or alternative electoral systems. Their responses did, however, share a common thematic focus on issues of democracy, representation, participation, accountability, and leadership quality.

Democracy

People who advocated moving to some form of obligatory competition generally shared Perestroika's view that the current system is undemocratic and therefore illegitimate. When it comes to governing, most political scientists, including those on the Elections Review Committee, have a strong bias in favor of democracy and its formal practices. The argument here is straightforward. Legitimate authority derives from consent, and elections are necessary to ensure that consent has really been given. If we believe that democracy is the only legitimate form of government for nations, parties, labor unions, and many other political entities, how can it be otherwise for our own professional organization? The current system, accordingly, falls short, reminding its more vehement critics variously of the papal selection process, elections in the former Soviet Union or one-party Middle Eastern states, and government under the raj in India.[4]

Why, then, did the Elections Committee not recommend mandatory competition for APSA offices? We had several reasons. First and most important, the APSA's constitution already provides for contested elections, via mail ballot sent to all members, for any or all of its offices if any *ten* of its more than thirteen thousand members want to nominate alternatives to the slate of candidates proposed by the Nominating Committee. Perestroika or any other group within the association that is unhappy with the official nominees and believes that other members share its unhappiness has easy recourse to the ballot box. The advent of e-mail and the Internet has made coordinating such challenges inexpensive in terms of money and time.

The minimal barrier to electoral entry provides a check on Nominating Committees, encouraging them to compose slates of candidates who are broadly acceptable to the membership. If even a few APSA members think any of the committee's choices are objectionable, they are free to propose alternatives. Moreover, if Perestroikans believe, on principle, that APSA elections should allow the full membership to choose from two or more candidates for every office, they can make sure that it happens without any change in the rules. Some participants in the Town Meeting on Governance at the APSA's 2002 annual meeting in Boston promised to do just that if the constitution is not changed to make competition obligatory. A tentative step in this direction occurred when Peregrine Schwartz-Shea, a Perestroikan represented in this volume, was nominated by petition to the 2003–04 Council.[5] If and when such candidacies arise, no defender of the status quo has any reason to object; this is exactly the sort of electoral challenge the rules are designed to permit.

Seen in this light, comparisons to leadership selection processes in dictatorships, colonial systems, or the Vatican are particularly inapt. From their memos to the Elections Review Committee, it appeared that many members were unaware or had forgotten that the APSA's constitution already provides for contested elections. Presumably those who care about the issue now know about this option and can act accordingly.

Why have so few elections been contested? Critics, Perestroikans among them, argue that the current system rigs the race, forcing those who want competition to adopt the role of insurgents, which automatically puts them at a disadvantage. This is no doubt true—as long as the only purpose for mounting a challenge is to make sure that every election is contested. If a challenge is based on substantive disagreement over association policy or direction, APSA members are, I think, perfectly capable of voting for the side they prefer regardless of who did the nominating.

The opportunity for an electoral challenge serves as a constraint on the APSA leadership, but other, more important, constraints operate on a continuing basis with or without contested elections because of the association's very nature. The APSA is not a polity or a labor union. It does not exercise coercive authority, and it does not run a closed shop. It is a voluntary professional organization that attracts and retains its members by delivering services that they value. One need not be a member to attend annual meetings or publish in its journals; anyone with access to an academic library can read its publications. Exit is always an option; a variety of other regional or field-based associations can and do compete with the APSA for membership and participation. Indeed, some leading political scientists choose not to be members, and none appears to have suffered professionally for that choice.

Because members can always withdraw their support (and have the opportunity to do so annually at membership renewal time), the association's leaders and staff have every incentive to be inclusive and responsive, as they have proven to be. The swift nomination of prominent Perestroikans to the Council and the presidency is only the most recent instance in which the association has invited dissenting voices to join the governing process. It would be perverse, I think, to read this as Machiavellian cooptation by a manipulative elite rather than as a good faith effort to be inclusive and responsive to any group of APSA members with a well-articulated grievance.

Inclusiveness and Diversity

The desire to maintain an inclusive leadership is the second main reason the Elections Review Committee advised against mandating competitive slates. The current system has, at least in recent years, succeeded in producing a diverse, broadly representative set of leaders. Data from 1996–2002 indicate that the Nominating Committees have successfully reached out to formerly underrepresented groups; women, African Americans, and Latinas or Latinos are actually overrepresented among APSA officers. The distribution of offices by major subfield is reasonably proportional, with modest overrepresentation of American politics and political theory, and equally modest underrepresentation of comparative politics and international relations. Regionally, the Northeast and the West Coast are overrepresented compared to other regions, primarily because officers are drawn disproportionately from top-ranked research universities, which are relatively more common in these regions.[6]

In recent years, care been taken not only to make each year's nominees as representative of the association's various components as possible, but also to be sure that offices are distributed over time in a way that reflects its intellectual and demographic diversity. The testimony of colleagues who have served on the Nominating Committee has left no doubt that this is a complex and challenging task whose difficulty is easily underestimated until one tries to perform it conscientiously. It is hard to imagine a wide-open election system of the sort proposed by some APSA members that could reliably reproduce the diversity of our past and current Councils. Balanced tickets are the product of smoke-filled rooms, not open primaries.

The only kind of mandatory competitive electoral process that would ensure a leadership as diverse as we now have would be one in which pairs of competing candidates were carefully matched by category, in effect twinning the current slates. To its credit, the ad hoc committee of Perestroikans who took on the task of designing a system of mandatory competition recognized this reality. Its proposal would enjoin the Nominating Committee to attend to the same diversity criteria as they do now, but with twice as many nominees as positions to be filled. It would also reserve three of the proposed fifteen Council seats for "demographic minorities" and three others for "institutional minorities." The candidates for the reserved seats would be twinned, while candidates for the remaining seats would not.[7]

Some immediate reactions to this proposal underline the dilemmas raised by opening up the selection process while trying to maintain or increase inclusiveness and diversity. The idea of minority set-asides was not well received by minority political scientists, demographic or institutional, who spoke out at the Town Meeting in Boston. It was also unclear how other diversity criteria that the ad hoc committee deemed desirable (gender, subfield, sexual orientation, region) and others that might apply (intellectual approach, professional career path) would be met if the other nominees were not also twinned. The difficulty is that the number of dimensions in which diversity can be measured is large, and any formal specification inevitably privileges some dimensions and slights others. The option proposed by some APSA members of adopting a system of proportional representation or some form of consociationalism runs into similar difficulties because it would require sorting members into a relatively small number of exclusive categories, any set of which would be arbitrary and artificial.

Of course some APSA members believe that the election process should be completely unconstrained, with no limits on who may be nominated and no attempt to ensure diversity: open up the system, the argument goes, and let the chips fall where they may. The problem here is that the chips are likely to fall in a way that produces unbalanced, unrepresentative leadership and permanently alienated factions. The dilemma is that leadership diversity can be guaranteed only under a system of mandatory competition by severely constraining choices, while "democratization" is supposed to open up choices. The less constraint, the greater the danger that an unrepresentative leadership will be chosen. The more constraint, the more the system will be open to the same criticisms as the current system. At best, mandatory competition might succeed in duplicating the current level of representative diversity; it is very unlikely to increase it.

The severity of this dilemma was acknowledged by Susanne Rudolph, also represented in this volume, who as APSA president for 2003–04 appointed a second Elections Review Committee, chaired by Kirstie McClure,[8] whose central charge was "to consider how contested elections could be made consistent with the interests of minorities, while avoiding the problems associated with set asides or quotas."[9] The committee's final report is due at the 2004 Annual Meeting in September.

The Basis for Competition

Mandatory competition would also do nothing to enhance accountability. Elections enforce individual accountability only when reelection is a possibility, and no one has, to my knowledge, advocated multiple terms for APSA officers. Elections enforce collective accountability only with the equivalent of political parties, which the APSA (fortunately, in my view) does not have. This points to a third reason for not adopting mandatory competition for APSA offices: there is no authentic endogenous basis for it. The association's members diverge in numerous dimensions, but existing cleavages tend to be crosscutting rather than mutually reinforcing. Differences in intellectual style cut across differences in area of specialization. These divisions in turn cut across differences in region or type of institution. This is healthy for the association. Were its membership to coalesce into a small number of coherent, contending factions, it would be open to the kind of debilitating conflicts that have beset some other academic and professional associations. The current selection process would not prevent such developments—any faction is free to nominate and campaign for its own slate of officers—but it is unwise to introduce artificial conflicts that might, over time, generate the real thing. If the real thing does arise—if, for example, the Perestroika group wants to elect officers sympathetic to its agenda and goals and believes that the official slate will not do—dissenters can nominate an alternative slate. Rather than being ginned up for competition's sake, competition will then reflect substantive policy differences that are important to at least some members.

The danger of provoking factional conflict over offices should not be taken lightly, because such conflict has, on occasion, damaged other scholarly organizations. APSA members with experience in other professional and academic associations have expressed a wide range of views on their leadership selection processes. By some accounts, mandatory competition works satisfactorily, with members appreciating the opportunity to exercise choice. Others accounts, however, report low voting turnout, intense factional conflict, widespread withdrawal from participation in association activities, humiliated and alienated losers, and cynicism about the quality of the winners. Low participation sometimes allows narrow, highly mobilized factions to prevail, reducing the diversity of representation. Although the APSA might be able to avoid such problems, there is a real risk that it will not. Factional competition is guaranteed to produce unhappy losers in a context in which exit is a ready option and breaking up is not all that hard to do. It would be harmful to political scientists individually and collectively if the APSA's election processes were to inspire losing factions to redirect their energies into other, more narrowly conceived, professional societies.

Leadership

There is a reasonably strong consensus that the APSA should be led by its most accomplished members. To be sure, a few members have advocated election reform as a way to turn what they see as an elitist organization into one with an egalitarian and populist culture. But even strong supporters of obligatory competitive elections usually expected the officers thereby chosen to be leading scholars and teachers. Scholarship and teaching are not egalitarian enterprises, and the APSA is not a populist organization. It is a professional association of scholars, teachers, and practitioners that ought to be led, and represented to the outside world, by its most prominent and successful members. Thus a fourth reason to reject mandatory competition for APSA offices is that it would discourage or waste participation by some of our most distinguished colleagues.

Several past presidents have reported that they would have declined to take part in contrived contests against esteemed colleagues, particularly when no real differences of principle or policy distinguished them. Mandatory competition would involve the public rejection of half or more of those who did agree to compete in what, absent concrete policy differences, are likely to be seen as pure popularity contests, discouraging at least some from further involvement in the association's governance. This would make the composition of diverse slates even more difficult, because some categories do not, as yet, enjoy deep reserves of qualified scholars.

It is noteworthy that few APSA members who have contacted the committee have expressed dissatisfaction with the actual slates of officers the present system has produced. The APSA has enjoyed distinguished, yet intellectually and demographically diverse, leadership under the current system. There is a greater prospect for erosion than for enhancement of this tradition of excellence if distinguished members are compelled to compete with one another for the honor of leading the association.

The Nomination Process

The Elections Review Committee did recommend some changes in the nomination process. Under the current system, Nominating Committee members are chosen by APSA presidents with the consent of the Council. We considered several alternatives that would relieve the presidents of this particular burden and create a more transparent and open process, including proposals similar to that made by Perestroika's ad hoc committee. The ad hoc committee would have a nine-member Nominating Committee elected by the full APSA membership by the Hare single transferable vote method from a list of forty candidates, two each made by the president, past president, and president-elect, the other thirty-four by the thirty-four organized sections. While some members of the Elections Review Committee were intrigued by the idea of using organized sections in this manner, we ultimately concluded that the sections were not a good basis for representation. They are not meant to be representative; they are self-initiated groups, quite variable in size (currently the range is from 172 to 1617 members, with a mean of 572 and a standard deviation of 254) and scope, with fluctuating and overlapping memberships. Their own internal decision-making processes vary widely in transparency and participation. Making them part of the nomination process would institutionalize groupings that ought to be allowed to arise, expand, contract, or disappear as the interests of APSA members evolve.

The Elections Review Committee could discover no alternative divisions on which to base representation on a Nominating Committee that would not require an arbitrary and artificial categorization of APSA members. We did find, however, that the APSA Council has been consistently and broadly representative of its membership. Council members are also knowledgeable about APSA governance and its various challenges. A Nominating Committee composed of a subset of present or former Council members could thus provide the breadth of representation and the knowledge of association business essential for a Nominating Committee.

Thus we proposed having Nominating Committee members chosen from the Council (excluding ex-officio members) by lot, three per year. We also considered the possibility of having the Nominating Committee chosen partially by lot from Council and partially by presidential appointment, and some committee members preferred this option. We also recommended expanding the terms of service to three years and thus the size of the committee to nine members. A larger committee, while possibly more cumbersome, would provide wider representation. The three-year term would deepen the institutional memory, which colleagues who have served on the committee told us would be beneficial. The committee would be chaired by a member who has already served on it for at least one year.

The Elections Review Committee also recommended that the process of recommending candidates to the Nominating Committee be formalized so that all APSA members have a clear idea of how and when to propose candidates. As it is now, recommendations arrive in a variety of forms, from simple letters with no documentation to elaborate files with considerable documentation. Drawing on the advice of current and former Nominating Committee members, we recommended that a clear, widely publicized set of procedures be established for receiving and processing candidate recommendations.

Conclusion

The current election system has succeeded in providing the APSA with distinguished and broadly representative leadership. It has proven responsive to emerging groups and their concerns. It has not fostered artificial conflict, but does provide for competitive elections if even a few members want to propose alternatives to the Nominating Committee's choices. Although no system is ever perfect, and some tinkering with the nominating process may be desirable, the current practice of having a single slate of nominees selected by a Nominating Committee, but open to alternative candidates or slates by petition, is better for the APSA than any of the alternatives that have been proposed. Perestroikans and others who believe, for symbolic or substantive reasons, that elections for APSA offices should always offer a choice among candidates can make it happen without any change in the association's constitution. I will be surprised, in light of the deeply held views expressed on the issue, if they do not.

Notes

1. "Report of the APSA Elections Review Committee on APSA Election Procedures," available at http://www.apsanet.org/news/elections/apsareport.cfm, May 21, 2004.

2. The other committee members were Randall Calvert, Washington University; Valerie Martinez-Ebers, Texas Christian University; Lynn Mather, Dartmouth College; Robert Price, University of California–Berkeley; and Susan Welch, Pennsylvania State University.

3. http://www.apsanet.org/about/governance/constitution.cfm, May 21, 2004.

4. All of these comparisons were made by political scientists in criticizing current selection practices.

5. She won fewer votes than all of the Nominating Committee's candidates and so was not elected.

6. "Report of the APSA Elections Committee," Appendix B, at http://www
.apsanet.org/news/elections/appendixb.cfm, May 21, 2004.

7. Five Council members would be elected each year to three-year terms; see
Mike Desch, Kristen Monroe, Marsha Pripstein Posusney, and Lloyd Rudolph, "Ad
Hoc Committee Proposal for Amending the APSA Constitution to Provide Con-
tested Elections," prepared for distribution at the Town Meeting on Governance,
APSA annual meeting, Boston, August 30, 2002.

8. Of the University of California–Los Angeles; other members include Jane S.
Anderson, University of Cincinnati; Richard L. Engstrom, University of New
Orleans; Robert A. Holmes, Clark Atlanta University; Gregory Kasza, Indiana Uni-
versity–Bloomington; Richard S. Katz, Johns Hopkins University; Kristen Renwick
Monroe, University of California–Irvine; and Michael C. Munger, Duke University.

9. http://www.apsanet.org/about/governance/electionreview.cfm, May 21, 2004.

CHAPTER 18

Democracy versus Diversity—
A False Dichotomy

A Critique of the Jacobson Committee Report

Marsha Pripstein Posusney

The *New York Times* of March 2, 2003, carried a story about Hu Dezhai, a Shanghai teacher who wanted to seek election to China's legislature. China's legislative elections operate under the system known in the former Soviet Union as *nomenklatura,* in which the ruling party chooses the candidates for office and the voters' only choice is whether to endorse them or not. The Chinese constitution, however, stipulates that anyone wishing to seek office need find only *ten* supporters to sign a petition to place the person's name on the ballot. Mr. Dezhai canvassed his acquaintances to collect signatures.

The APSA, the largest political science association in the world's most influential democracy, chooses its leadership in a manner not unlike the *nomenklatura* system. The Nominating Committee produces a slate of officers, selecting just one candidate for each available slot. Barring a petition challenge, the entire slate is ratified at the annual business meeting; in other words, only those in attendance actually vote, and voters' only option is to accept or reject the entire slate. Moreover, the Nominating Committee itself is chosen by the sitting leadership. It consists of six members, each serving a two-year term, with half of the committee changing every year. The three incoming members are appointed by the president-elect, subject to the approval of the Council. Thus the incumbent leadership handpicks those who will, in turn, choose their successors.

Most political analysts consider the Chinese system, and other past and present examples of *nomenklatura,* lacking in contestation, an essential component of procedural democracy. Yet in rejecting the call for competitive elections in the APSA, the Jacobson committee report's primary argument is that the association is already democratic. "First and most important," Jacobson writes in this volume, "the APSA's constitution already provides for contested elections . . . if any *ten* [emphasis his] of its more than thirteen thousand members want to nominate alternatives to the slate of candidates proposed by the Nominating Committee." Thus he maintains that comparisons between the APSA and authoritarian countries are "particularly inapt."

To be sure, the APSA has followed its constitution in the case of petition challenges to the official slate. The Chinese government, in contrast, kept Mr. Dezhai's name off the ballot in spite of the 110 signatures he collected.[1] But because of the advantages *nomenklatura* elections confer on the designated nominees, on the one hand, and the obstacles they impose on dissidents, on the other, these elections fall short of genuine contestation even when petition challenges are honored, and even in the absence of the repression that has characterized the authoritarian countries that championed this system.

There may be good and compelling reasons why individuals dissatisfied with the official APSA slate in practice wish to refrain from challenging it in the prescribed manner. One of these—diversity concerns—is a central reason that moved the Jacobson committee to recommend against mandatory contestation. Perestroikans concerned with protecting the rights of diverse groups within the APSA, however, have concluded instead that it is better to seek alternatives to the present system, and that diversity and democratic elections are not incompatible.

In this chapter I seek first to explain why I find the existing APSA provisions for contested elections inadequate. I then critique the diversity argument against competitive elections raised by the Jacobson committee. In the third section I explore tentative ideas for alternative electoral procedures that can bring greater democracy to the APSA while not threatening the gains we have made in representational diversity, thus showing that this juxtaposition is a false and unnecessary one.

The ideas contained herein are my own, although they were influenced by the ongoing discussions of this topic in APSA meetings and on the Perestroika list serve, as well as in Governing Council[2] meetings themselves, over the past couple of years.[3] I should also note that, although I think it is fair to say that the Perestroika movement has advocated more openness and transparency in APSA functioning in general, Perestroika itself is a discussion forum rather than an organized interest group. Thus there is no uniform position among its participants about whether to contest elections via the existing mechanisms or about what the best alternative to these elections would be.[4] Because of this, my purpose here is not to defend any particular Perestroika perspective,[5] but rather to further discussion and debate in the hope of eventually arriving at one or more alternative approaches to elections that the APSA would be prepared to seriously consider.

Flaws in the Petition System

The Jacobson committee itself summarized the negative feedback they received on the APSA's democratic mechanisms as follows: "Nominations by petition are not a realistic option; some years ago, the Caucus for a New Political Science proposed alternative candidates several times but failed to elect any of its nominees.[6] The current mechanism is obscure, imposing high transaction costs on anyone wanting to organize opposition, and pits insurgents against the establishment, which biases the outcome in favor of the official slate" (3). A rejoinder—endorsed by the committee—maintained that "the Caucus failed, not because its candidates were nominated by petition, but because they did not have sufficient support within the Association. . . . Lack of competition in recent years suggests that no one is interested or believes that a compelling case could be made to the membership to elect someone other the regular nominees."[7] I fail to see how these conclusions are supportable. They do not consider either the coordination problems or the career concerns associated with potential insurgent candidacies.

The challenges of an insurgent candidacy should not be minimized. The official slate has always been published in *PS: Political Science and Politics,* along with biographical data on the nominees. There is also a reception at the annual convention where interested members can meet the official candidates. In contrast, unofficial nominees, in the Caucus's days, faced the burden of publicizing their candidacies and their credentials on their own. I wasn't an APSA member at the time, but I am deeply skeptical that the Caucus was able to reach the membership as extensively as was the association itself.

Most of these challenges would still be faced by dissident candidates today. The Jacobson committee report suggests that "the advent of e-mail has made coordinating such challenges inexpensive and relatively easy." But even a list serve as large as Perestroika's reaches only a relatively small proportion of the APSA's total membership, and large lists, although they bring greater publicity, make systematic discussion and *decision making* more difficult. It is still unlikely, therefore, that a petition challenge could be organized in sufficient time to have the candidates' biographies publicized in *PS* along with the official slate. Today this material is publicized on the APSA Web page as well, which requires significantly less lead time, so that can help bring name recognition to insurgent nominees even if they miss the *PS* deadline. But we have no data on what percentage of the membership uses the Web page, as opposed to *PS,* to obtain candidate information.

In addition, as the committee report itself notes, there are sensitivities associated with competing for office, especially for the presidency, which is seen primarily as an honorific. Thus people may refrain from running not because they lack grievances, but because they do not wish to offend the official candidates—out of politeness, friendship, or sheer pragmatism. Academia as a profession in many ways carries the vestiges of feudalism, and although the situation of dissidents in the APSA hardly compares to the risks of repression faced by Mr. Dezhai and his counterparts elsewhere (all of whose courage is inspirational), we would be naïve to believe that challenging very prominent and powerful members of the profession could not have potentially adverse consequences for an individual's career trajectory. There is a good reason why "Mr. Perestroika" has chosen to remain anonymous.

The Current Rules and the Diversity Dilemma

A second major argument that the committee advances against mandatory competition is that it would be impossible to achieve diversity of representation along gender, racial or ethnic, geographic, and institutional lines through elections without resorting to mechanisms that could cause severe factionalism in the organization. I am not persuaded, however, that the committee considered a full range of alternatives before reaching that conclusion. Moreover, the existing provisions for democracy that Jacobson would have dissidents resort to take no account of this need. It is well known in our discipline that the electoral rules a country or organization uses have a profound effect on the outcome of the vote. With one exception, the APSA's current rules for elections triggered by petition challenges appear to be the worst choice for both fairness and diversity purposes.

If all of the APSA's leadership were to be chosen competitively under the existing rules, there would be two types of elections: "single-winner" and "multi-winner." The single-winner positions are president, secretary, and treasurer, for each of which there is only one official nominee. The elections for vice presidents and the at-large Council members are multi-winner competitions because three vice presidents and eight Council members are chosen each year.

For the vice presidents and the Council members, the existing rules call for block voting: when alternative candidates are nominated, "members shall be entitled to vote for a number equal to the number of offices in the set, and the nominees ranking highest in the poll, in a number equal to the number of offices, shall be declared elected" (APSA constitution, Article 5.1). In this type of election minorities are at a disadvantage; indeed, in county and municipal elections in the United States, at-large rules have been used historically as a way to limit representation of African Americans and other ethnic minorities.[8] Within the APSA, candidates from small or undergraduate-only institutions would also be at risk, because the likely winners would be those nominees who enjoy the advantages of affiliation with prestigious universities. Scholars from schools with large teaching loads tend to have less name recognition because they are often unable to publish as frequently as those at "Research One" institutions,[9] and are also likely to have fewer departmental colleagues and be less well networked outside of their home institution.

One way to surmount this problem would be to allow challengers to put forward a rival *slate*—which could be matched demographically to the official slate, and might even include some of its members. However, no provisions for elections by slate exist in the constitution. The Jacobson committee did consider slates as one means of ensuring diversity with *mandatory* competition, but rejected the option as conducive to factionalism. Yet if the "democracy provisions" in the constitution are being invoked, it suggests that the association is fraught with dissent anyway, so in this case the factionalism argument would be moot.

For the single-winner positions, challengers could preserve the diversity of the Nominating Committee's slate simply by proposing candidates with the same demographic profiles as the official nominees. But that assumes that only one additional nominee per position would be submitted, and there is no way anyone could control for the number of other challengers that might come forward. Moreover, in the case of more than two challengers for secretary or treasurer, the current rules call for the winner to be decided by a simple plurality rule, denying voters the right to express second choices and risking the possibility that the winner would lack majority support.[10] Only in the case of the presidency does the constitution prescribe a different system—the alternative vote—which allows voters to rank the candidates and specifies that there must be a majority winner.[11]

Thus, given the existing rules, the desire to preserve diversity is another reason that even those committed to democracy may prefer to refrain from launching an electoral challenge until the rules are changed. Indeed, this issue was discussed extensively on the Perestroika list serve prior to the 2002 petition nomination of Peregrine Schwartz-Shea; I argued on the list at the time, and still believe, that in order to protect diversity on the Governing Council any insurgent challenges should have been directed toward one of the single-winner offices.[12] However, the desire to preserve diversity cannot be taken as an indication that the membership feels no need for a greater role in the leadership selection process.

Indeed, even if we were to conclude that mandatory *regular* competition is a poor choice for the APSA, there is a need to reconsider these existing provisions for the *occasional* elections that dissident challenges might trigger. The Jacobson committee's failure to recommend this, while at the same time both claiming support for diversity and encouraging democracy proponents to use the existing mechanisms to trigger elections, is therefore quite contradictory. Worse, it sends a message that there is an inherent contradiction between democracy and diversity. At a time when numerous countries with ethnically diverse populations are emerging from authoritarian rule and struggling to find ways to achieve fair representation, this is a sad statement for the American Political Science Association to be making.

Pathways to Democracy with Diversity

The discussions that have taken place over the past few years have generated a number of proposals for expanding membership participation in APSA leadership selection while seeking to preserve diversity. The ideas in this section are the ones with which I am sympathetic, but I do not mean to preclude other possibilities.

The minimalist way for the APSA to democratize would be to allow the Nominating Committee itself to be elected while maintaining the existing provision that the committee will then nominate only one candidate for each officer and at-large Council position. Proponents of an elected Nominating

Committee have also argued that its size should be expanded, from the current six to at least eight or ten members. Expanding the size of the committee would increase the possibility that it would have diverse representation. It would also mean that the committee itself would bring to the table a wider knowledge of the APSA membership.

Aside from giving APSA members a greater say in the leadership selection process, one advantage of electing the Nominating Committee would be that it could be seen as an indication of what kind of results competitive elections for officers would produce. If Nominating Committee elections proceeded smoothly and diversity were indeed maintained, the organization could then move with confidence to competitive elections of some or all officers. In the interim, however—or if the APSA as an organization decided to persist in not regularizing competition for leadership elections—there could still be petition challenges to the Nominating Committee's slate, so the dilemmas addressed in the previous sections would still obtain. Therefore, election of the Nominating Committee only would need to be paired with changing the rules for petition challenges.

I believe that for the Nominating Committee itself, and for petition challenges to the multi-winner APSA offices, the rules should specify single transferable vote (STV) elections, a case for which is made in Lloyd Rudolph's contribution to this part of the book.[13] For the single-winner offices, the alternative vote method currently in effect only when there are more than two presidential candidates should be extended to election of the secretary and treasurer as well.[14]

As Rudolph notes, STV would allow APSA voters to give voice to, and rank, a multiplicity of concerns, be they related to demography, geography, methodology, institution type, subfield, or other issues. It could not, however, guarantee the achievement of diverse representation across all of the dimensions of concern to the APSA. I therefore think it is worth considering the idea of appointing some proportion—but not all—of the candidates for offices. There are numerous possibilities here, but for diversity purposes the most relevant would be appointing some, but not all, of the at-large Council members. If we were to elect, say, only half of the people to fill the available at-large Council seats in a given year from a pool of nominees, the remaining seats could be filled after the election, either by the Nominating Committee or by the seated Governing Council itself, based on an evaluation of any serious gaps or imbalances that resulted from the poll.

Some have objected to this approach, seeing it as a form of set-aside for minorities (implicitly, for racial and ethnic minorities), and arguing that the individuals who would be appointed under such circumstances would be viewed with less respect by the membership. However, we cannot know, in advance of competitive elections of some type, which of the APSA's various constituencies might fare poorly in competition, and it would not necessarily be the same groups each year. My own belief is that the group that would be likely to suffer the most, even under STV elections, would in fact be almost a majority of the membership—those who teach at small or non-PhD-granting institutions. Besides having less name recognition, such scholars are not cohesively organized; unlike racial and ethnic minorities, women, and sexual preference groups, professors at teaching-intensive schools presently have no status group within the APSA.[15]

Moreover, it is not clear why a "partial-appointment" approach would confer any less legitimacy on those so seated than the current "full-appointment" system does. At any given point, there are hundreds of APSA members who are qualified and able to serve as at-large Council members (a reality that has led some to seriously suggest that APSA should resort to the Athenian form of democracy and choose the at-large Council members by lot). To think that eight can and should be chosen on the basis of scholarly achievements alone, in a discipline with multiple subfields and a membership dispersed across the country in institutions of different types, is ludicrous, and this is not how things presently work. Diversity, across these as well as the various demographic dimensions already named here, has figured prominently in the Nominating Committee's deliberations, and rightfully so. We cannot know what kinds of outcomes would ensue if mandatory competition is initiated, but having mechanisms in place to protect that diversity seems a wise course to me. As the Jacobson committee report notes, the APSA is primarily a service organization, and it cannot effectively deliver services to its membership if important constituencies, whether their basis is ascriptive, professional, or of another sort, do not have a voice in leadership.

Conclusions

For better or worse, the U.S. government is currently engaged in a project to bring democracy to one of the most authoritarian regions in the world. The APSA, for its part, is currently engaged in a project to increase the public presence of political science by showing how our academic research can shed light on pressing policy issues in society. But on the critical issue of establishing democratic procedures for leadership selection in other countries, the APSA is poorly placed to comment, because we ourselves choose our leadership in a manner reminiscent of methods used by some of the most repressive authoritarian regimes. Worse still, we are the only large academic professional association to do so.

The need for diversity on the APSA Governing Council has been raised by opponents of competitive elections as a key reason for maintaining the present *nomenklatura* system. But as I have attempted to show here, there are a variety of options available to the APSA that would give the membership a greater voice in leadership selection while preserving the gains we have made in diverse representation. My list here is not exhaustive, and there may be better ideas that I have overlooked. Minimally, however, the suggestions here should demonstrate that democracy and diversity *can* be reconciled.

Minimally, too, those committed to diversity ought to be arguing for a change to the current rules for petition challenges, especially for the vice presidents and at-large Council seats. To use diversity as a club against contestation while supporting electoral rules that have historically been shown to minimize minority representation is utterly hypocritical, yet this is exactly what the Jacobson committee report does. And for the time being, unfortunately, the Council has ruled out approving any reforms to the existing system, making petition challenges under the existing rules the only avenue available for those seeking to democratize the APSA. For those of us who favor democracy and diversity, this is a difficult dilemma, and one that is sure to generate ongoing discussion on the Perestroika list serve and elsewhere. But the last people to criticize any future petition challengers on diversity grounds should be those who have resisted making any changes to the rules for such challenges.

Notes

I am grateful to Kristen Monroe for helpful comments on an earlier draft of this chapter.

1. Denzhai was reduced to running a write-in campaign, but because the Chinese system does not allow for write-ins, this meant asking his supporters to deliberately invalidate their ballots—a symbolic protest campaign. The latter is a tactic frequently used by voters in systems that hold "authoritarian elections." In the context of the methodological issues being debated elsewhere in this volume, it is worth noting here that rational choice arguments can help to explain some of the behaviors of opposition *parties* in such systems. However, they are particularly ill-suited to account for this and other types of symbolic protests by ordinary citizens under repressive conditions. See Marsha Pripstein Posusney, "Multi-Party Elections in the Arab World: Institutional Engineering and Oppositional Strategies," *Studies in Comparative International Development* 36, no. 4 (Winter 2002): 34–62, and "Irrational Workers: The Moral Economy of Labor Protest in Egypt," *World Politics* 46, no. 1 (October 1993): 83–120.

2. In this chapter I will use "Governing Council" to refer to the APSA's leadership body, which consists of six "elected" officers and sixteen at-large "elected" members, as well as several individuals appointed to special positions (journal editors, annual conference chairs). I will use "at-large Council members" to refer to the at-large seats.

3. As part of the official slate, which was uncontested that year, I was elected as an at-large Council member in September 2002.

4. It follows that, although my Perestroika affiliation is well known and I seek to advance Perestroika's core concerns as a at-large Council member, I did not view myself as an official Perestroika "representative" to the Governing Council. Nor have Perestroikans serving in the APSA's leadership necessarily voted the same way on issues pertaining to elections, or on other matters.

5. I was involved, along with Lloyd Rudolph, Kristen Monroe, and Mike Desch, with the "ad hoc committee" whose report is referred to in the Jacobson chapter. This ad hoc committee was a group of people who communicated by e-mail, and

never actually met face to face. As I indicated at the 2002 Boston Town Meeting, and as I believe is evident from a close reading of that document (especially the footnotes), the committee was in fact not united behind the proposal that was given primary attention in that report. From his chapter here, however, it appears that Jacobson neither heard my remarks in Boston nor fully read the document.

6. Based on the committee's report, this would have been in the late 1970s.

7. "Report of the APSA Elections Review Committee on APSA Election Proce-dures," available at http://www.apsanet.org/news/elections/apsareport.cfm, May 21, 2004.

8. See Douglas Amy, *Real Choices, New Voices: The Case for Proportional Represen-tation in the U.S.* (New York: Columbia University Press, 1993), 117–21, and Richard Engstrom and Michael D. McDonald, "The Effects of At-Large versus District Elec-tions on Racial Representation in U.S. Municipalities," in Bernard Grofman and Arendt Lijphart, eds., *Electoral Laws and their Consequences* (New York: Agathon, 1986), 203–25.

9. There is, nevertheless, a large number of scholars at teaching-intensive schools with admirable publication records, whose achievements are all the more impressive in light of the limited research support available to them. But their work may be overlooked simply because of the lack of prestige associated with their insti-tutions of employment. Indeed, it is too often assumed that professors at such schools either are not interested in, or have less intellectual capability for, con-ducting and publishing quality research. This elitist attitude is unfortunately reflected in Appendix B of the Jacobson committee report, which states that "dis-tinguished scholars tend to cluster in top-rated, research-oriented departments," and suggests that only by expanding the definition of "scholarly distinction" to include teaching and mentoring achievements can the historic underrepresentation in the APSA's leadership of scholars from nonelite institutions be corrected.

10. For an in-depth critique of plurality voting in U.S. governmental elections, see Amy, *Real Choices, New Voices.* See also the various documents at the Web site of the Center for Voting and Democracy (CVD), www.fairvote.org.

11. In the alternative vote method—also known as "majority preference vot-ing" or the "instant run off," voters assign a rank to the candidates, and the count-ing begins by apportioning one vote to the first-ranked candidate on each ballot. If no one obtains a majority after these "first-place votes" are counted, the candidate with the least support is dropped, and those voters who had ranked this candi-date first have their votes reassigned to their second choices. If there is still no majority winner, this process will be repeated; it continues until one candidate obtains a majority. Readers unfamiliar with this and other alternatives to plurality voting rules can find concise explanations and evaluations of them in the Institute for Democracy and Electoral Assistance, *The International IDEA Handbook of Elec-toral System Design* (Sweden: IDEA, 1997); see also the CVD Web site.

12. The results, I believe, bear out this position. Had Schwartz-Shea, a white woman from a PhD-granting institution, garnered more votes, she would have dis-placed an African American woman from a teaching-intensive school.

13. Like the alternative vote, STV elections use a preference ballot on which vot-ers rank the candidates, and the counting method begins by assigning first-place votes to each candidate. Since multiple winners are being selected, however, the threshold for any individual to win is less than a majority; it varies inversely with

the number of vacancies, so the greater the number of seats to be filled, the lower the proportion of total votes needed for election. In this manner a constituency representing, say, 10 percent of the APSA membership if its members voted cohesively, would be ensured representation as long as there were at least nine vacancies to be filled. STV differs from the alternative vote in that, after candidates who cross the threshold with first-place votes are elected, any *surplus* votes they have won are transferred to their supporters' second choices. Then, if an insufficient number of candidates cross the threshold in this manner, the lowest-ranked candidate is dropped and those votes are transferred. These iterations of "top-down" and "bottom-up" vote transfers continue until all the vacant seats have been filled.

14. Critics of the alternative vote point out that it is nonmonotonic and especially conducive to strategic voting. However, strategic voting can be a problem with any electoral system. (See Gary Cox, *Making Votes Count: Strategic Coordination in the World's Electoral Systems* [Cambridge: Cambridge University Press, 1997].) Moreover, regardless of which electoral method is used, unless someone were to conduct and publish pre-election polls of voter preferences—which seems unlikely in the APSA's case— the information needed for APSA members to vote strategically would not be available.

15. This problem may be rectified in the near future, however. To their credit, APSA presidents Theda Skocpol and Susanne Rudolph have, respectively, established and continued a task force on the Council to address the concerns of political scientists at such institutions. A status group could emerge from the work of this task force.

CHAPTER 19

Governance

Minutes from a Public Meeting

Kristen Renwick Monroe

The Jacobson committee report was not the last word on the issue of governance. Indeed the issue remains unresolved as this volume goes to press.

Because the issue of governance was one about which a significant number of members felt strongly, the APSA Council felt it imperative to provide members every opportunity to discuss and deliberate on the issue. The Council and the program chairs, W. Phillip Shively and Kathryn Sikkint, thus took the opportunity of the annual meetings in Boston (September 2002) to sponsor a town hall meeting on APSA governance. I was asked to chair the meeting because Shively and Sikkint wanted an APSA official to head it and I was then APSA vice president. I also was a fairly representative APSA member in that I shared the confusion and concern felt by many APSA members on this issue. In institutional terms, the system seems too dependent on the vagaries of chance in terms of good appointments to the Nominating Committee. Like many other APSA members, I am troubled by the fact that the most important political science association in what is arguably the most important democracy in the world has such a closed system for choosing nominees. I am troubled by the institutionalized system in which a current president chooses three people who then—in conjunction with three chosen by his[1] predecessor—choose the next president. Given the power and influence of the APSA president, the potential for self-replication of an in-group is striking. I also know that although there are formal mechanisms for challenging the officially chosen slate, they are rarely used and those who follow this route are viewed as challengers and upstarts, not as equally legitimate contenders for office. As someone concerned with the institutions and with the political culture they foster, this concerns me.

At the same time, I realize how fair and open the APSA Nominating Committees have frequently been in practice, and I know that the recent Nominating Committees have worked hard to hear complaints, to consider them fairly, and to make the reforms necessary to bring more groups into the system. My sense is that my own difficulties in finding a happy solution to these problems are shared by a wide number of APSA members.

I served on the APSA Elections Review Committee, whose report has not yet been submitted to the Council and hence is not considered here.[2] But the gist of the committee's report was to portray a wide array of options for elections used by other professional associations. Along with a few other committee members, I supported the possibility that the Nominating Committee be expanded and elected, using some type of single transferable vote, but the committee itself did not make any formal recommendations.

I note my own position at the outset so the reader will know my views on the issue of governance as it was discussed in the summer of 2002. In the rest of the chapter, however, I try to put aside whatever opinions I may have on this issue and to summarize the issues raised at the Town Meeting held on Saturday, August 31, 2002, and attended by approximately one hundred people. The discussion was wide-ranging, and I have summarized comments in brief, not via direct quotes, in order to avoid identifying any one speaker. I adopted this form because more than one person occasionally raised the same point, because my notes from the discussion are incomplete and sketchy, because I do not want to misquote anyone, and because I do not wish to quote participants by name without their approval. The following is adapted from remarks placed on the APSA Web site, with an invitation to correct or expand the basic ideas.

Background

As I understand it, much of the impetus for the current discussion of APSA voting procedures and APSA governance originated in the concerns of the Women's Caucus for Political Science (WCPS) that there had been too few women presidents and officers of the APSA. In April 2001, the WCPS asked the APSA Council to pass a resolution encouraging Nominating Committees to avoid choosing as president a person of the same gender for more than two years in a row. This nonbinding resolution was passed by the Council in April 2001. At the same time, Robert Jervis (then president of the APSA) appointed a committee to look into the question of elections. This committee was chaired by Gary Jacobson, and the report it issued to the Council in April 2002 is hereafter referred to as the Jacobson Report (see Jacobson's chapter in this volume). This report was posted on the APSA Web site, as were several responses and comments on this issue.

Comments at the APSA Town Hall on Governance, August 30, 2002

Comments are noted in the order in which they were presented.

1. We should keep the present system for four reasons: (1) There are cheap alternatives to changing the current system, i.e., any ten members of the APSA can call for an election, and contested elections then have to occur; (2) although the system may look less democratic than would be a system of contested elections, in reality the Nominating Committees do a good job of

reflecting the various constituencies of the APSA; (3) competitive elections might encourage and strengthen divisions that are now fluid and artificial and could threaten the gains made by minorities over the last few years; and (4) the presidents and vice presidents are top scholars and distinguished leaders of the profession. A survey of past presidents suggested they would not like competing over what is primarily an honor, not a substantive post from which to pursue a specific issue or policy.

2. We need to increase the legitimacy of the process by introducing democratic elections at some point. We recommend longer terms of the Council members so Council members will have a chance to understand the political issues. The Council should be expanded to consist of fifteen to sixteen seats, with five members elected each year. We should elect the Nominating Committee, because having past presidents choose the people who name their successors replicates existing power structures. We should select officers by means of transparent democratic procedures that will protect minority representation. Voting should be done by all members, not just those who attend the annual meeting.

3. We need to create institutional mechanisms to ensure representation and democracy, and not have to rely on the benevolence of oligarchs.

4. We need more data on how other organizations choose their officers and need to know what the costs to us would be if we instituted these changes.

5. Setting aside seats for certain minorities is a bad idea because most of us have many identities with crosscutting cleavages. How do we decide which identities are the relevant ones?

6. The organized sections are not democratically elected, so we should not use them to choose the members of the Nominating Committee.

7. If we go to elections, we should use approval voting, in which one can vote for as many candidates as one approves of and the candidate with the most votes wins. This is better than using single transferable votes. We could use approval voting for the president and cumulative voting for the Council.

8. The existing system does a good job of increasing minority inclusion. We don't want to lose that.

9. The issue of mandatory elections is not the only important issue of governance. We should become more inclusive but avoid becoming a labeled society with set-aside seats for certain groups. The current structure of the APSA forces the association to listen to groups that might organize.

10. We shouldn't alter the process that has increased the representation of minorities. If we go to competitive elections, we need on-site balloting, not annual elections.

11. A three-year term on the Council is taxing for parents and for teachers at schools that already are in session and therefore will lead to a bias in representation in terms of the kinds of people who can serve on the Council.

12. A set-aside seat for X group implies that there is only this seat for them. What do we mean by representation? We should think about the different interests that the APSA represents. Having on-site elections is a bad idea because it leaves out lots of people who lack financial resources to come to the conven-

tion. We should separate the principle of competitive elections from the discussion of the form of elections.

13. Most members of the APSA feel deeply alienated from the oligarchic association. We have set-asides and tokenism right now.

14. If the APSA does not institute systematic elections within a year, we will have them via the initiative procedures, because some of us will insist on them and will follow the existing constitutional provisions to ensure that we have contested elections.

15. Democracy is an important symbolic issue. We need to have competitive elections. We can figure out how to protect minority representation and still have democratic elections. For labeling to create or freeze categories of caste labels is not something that has to happen.

16. Competitive elections do not ensure democracy.

17. The system IS broken. We need research on how to best fix it. One way is to do a sample survey of membership, ask who's alienated and why. Also, have we thought about partial elections? If we do go to elections, we need to use electronic voting, not on-site voting.

18. We need to get in touch with the concerns of the membership.

19. We can look to our own research by asking what happens when we move to a fuller democracy. There is a fear that minorities will lose their rights or gains if we go to contested elections.

20. We should have competitive elections but not of the kind advocated so far. We should put all these issues up on a Web site so all members can enter the debate.

21. Competitive elections are not a magic bullet.

22. One of the main problems of the APSA is the underrepresentation of faculty at non-degree-granting institutions. How can we get better access to these people? Can we work with regional and state organization to draw these people into the political science community as represented by the APSA? Should we contact the past officers of these organizations to see if they will engage in dialogue with us on this issue?

23. How do we build more continuity into the APSA leadership? Several ways present themselves for our consideration: (1) lengthen the terms of office on the Council, (2) publicize the fact that the Council meetings are open to the general membership, and (3) have more working groups to mull over issues that the Council believes the membership cares about.

24. Can we establish closer ties between the Council and other APSA committees? Members?

25. We should ask other associations, including regional and state political science associations, how they establish better ties to non-graduate-degree-granting institutions.

26. There is a legitimation crisis within the APSA. The issue of governance is tied to the issue of elections. The Nominating Committee has made a concerted effort to bring in people too often ignored by the association. Mass elections will favor the big names. The quandary is how to reconcile these two.

27. Can majoritarianism and minority representation be made compatible? How? What is the best method?

28. Under the present APSA constitution, ten members can file a nomination that requires a mail ballot. Fifty members can file a petition and ask for a mail referendum on how the elections are held. Although according to the constitution the Council has to first consider this proposal and have the opportunity to make a recommendation, once the petition is filed, a referendum must occur.

29. We should have an elected Nominating Committee that then chooses the Council and officers. This introduces democratic elections but maintains the institution's ability to retain the kinds of representation of diverse constituencies that we want reflected in APSA governance.

And the Debate Goes On

In the summers of both 2003 and 2004, Gregory Kasza sponsored a petition nominating additional members to the APSA Council. This move was in keeping with the APSA constitution and necessitated an election because there were then more candidates than seats available on the Council. In 2003, when there was one additional candidate running, voter turn-out for the election was 4348, or 30.1 percent of all eligible APSA voters; in 2004, when two additional Council candidates ran, turn-out was 3636, or 25 percent of all eligible APSA voters (these figures come from the APSA Web site, which also notes that the figures for other similar member associations, such as the Modern Language Association, the American Anthropological Association, and the American Sociological Association, indicate that election turn-out in regularly scheduled elections usually ranges from 11 percent to 25 percent). In 2003, the one Perestroika nominee lost. In 2004, one of the two Perestroika candidates won and the other lost. Many interpretations of these results have been offered, and the jury remains out on elections.

My own sense is that people vote for candidates with high name recognition and that there is systematic underrepresentation of academics from small colleges and nonresearch universities. My personal preference would be to find a compromise that interjects some institutionalized democratic elections into the regular process of choosing APSA officers and Council members, possibly by electing the Nominating Committee. But this possibility was not recommended by the Task Force on Elections, and the issue of elections remains unresolved as this volume goes to press.

Notes

1. The pronoun was distinctly male for most of this time.
2. The report has now been received, and is available on the APSA Web site: www.apsanet.org/content_4579.cfm.

CHAPTER 20

Ironic Representation

Joanna Vecchiarelli Scott

Randolph Bourne observed, in the *New Republic* on March 11, 1916, that "the object of an education is to know a revolution when you see one." Updating Bourne's remark, I will explore the ironies inherent in what the readers of the text of political science in America "see" in the confrontation between the APSA and its reversed mirror image, Perestroika. Is Perestroika a revolutionary specter haunting the APSA? Perestroika's spokespersons are convinced that it is. "Mr. Perestroika," in a combative tone meant to dispel any questions about the movement's agenda, made it clear in an e-mail message on September 25, 2003, that "those hoping to completely institutionalize us, 'tame' us, co-opt us, save the APSA or the Midwest Political Science Association from our harsh glare, etc.—have not understood our reform or the determination with which we launched this initiative."

The mood a year earlier at the 2002 Boston national meeting of the APSA had been similarly alienated and militant. Just prior to the meeting, an open forum on governance posted on the APSA Web site provoked a number of responses, including an extended critique of existing practices from a Perestroika founding father, Greg Kasza (2002). He wrote, "I want to ask: who appointed this group of people to represent my views on elections anyway? But that is the problem in a nutshell, is it not?" Kristen R. Monroe, a founding mother, presided at a "Town Meeting" in Boston on August 30, 2002, and published a summary of the comments (see the previous chapter) on the APSA Web site under the heading "How Should the APSA Elect Its Officers and Council?" (APSA 2002). One participant believed that "most members of the APSA feel deeply alienated from the oligarchic association." Another remarked that the APSA was in the midst of a "legitimation crisis." While "the nominating committee has made a concerted effort to bring in people too often ignored by the Association," some sort of election reform was still needed. And someone else opined, "The issue of governance is tied to the issue of elections." But there was still the danger that democracy might "favor the big names."

An occasional note of paranoia has enlivened Perestroika postings as well, sliding from revolutionary zeal to petulant persecutory prose. An anonymous "autarkheia" posted a letter on March 18, 2003, in response to one of mine in which I had raised the issue of Perestroika's disadvantage vis-à-vis other organized APSA sections when it came to lobbying for representation in the governance structure. Autarkheia felt "rebuff[ed]" by those "who sit comfortable and confident in tenured offices" while the "hegemons have resort to a battery of dirty tricks . . . to block, marginalize, undercut, traduce, hamper, embarrass, baffle, downsize and fire those among us who do not have tenure. What price peace?"

Meanwhile, the APSA Council, whose pace of change is normally glacial, was moved to immediate action by the its own internal Strategic Planning Committee and by the Perestroika upsurge. Its response was to appoint a committee to study the governance structures and processes of the association. The issues were "fundamental," Gary Jacobson, the chair of the committee, wrote in the report posted on the APSA Web site (Jacobson 2002). Nothing less than the meaning of democracy was at stake. After all, we are political scientists and, more than any other of our sister academic associations, spend our careers debating the scope and limits of democracy. Yet at the same time the APSA is a collection of scholars whose primary identification is with their institutions and the practice of the discipline, not with the APSA as such. Those who don't like the fact that the president, the Nominating Committee, and those present at the business meeting, in effect, elect the leadership of political science in America can simply leave. As the Jacobson committee put it, "Is the APSA the kind of organization that, to be consistent with the values of the discipline it represents, must be democratic?" The alternative, ironically couched in the logic of rational choice that the Perestroika movement vehemently rejects, would be to think of the APSA not as a "polity" but instead as a "voluntary professional organization" from which members can simply exit at minimum cost.

Coming to no definitive conclusion on that theoretical point, the Jacobson committee did agree that that the costs of a change from self-selected voters turning up at the annual business meeting to "mandatory competition" would be too high. A general election, termed "Populist" democracy, might run counter both to the gains of minorities and women and to the quality of the leadership. The emphasis being placed on both diversity and merit as values best preserved by the current electoral system was no doubt not lost on the report's readers. That the "APSA should be led by its most accomplished members," the committee concluded, was a matter of "broad if not universal agreement." The current system has produced both a "distinguished and broadly representative leadership."

However, Perestroika's reformist revolution and the APSA's status quo stance may not be as different as they appear on the surface. At first glance, the official defense of open, rotating elite governance is as clear in the APSA document as is Perestroika's determination to storm the battlements with its postings, using the APSA's own rhetoric against it. If the APSA is so open to diverse interests, methodologies, and candidates, so the argument goes, let them prove it. Yet upon closer inspection, what can the reader see of the topography of Perestroika's own democratization? To whom does Mr. Perestroika give voice when calls for nominees and manifestos on the state of the discipline appear on the list? From the identity of "Mr. P." to its decision-making processes, Perestroika's online presence is much more opaque. This is particularly ironic because, even though Perestroika is a movement that eschews institutional entrapment, its members spend a great deal of online and conference time in detailed deconstruction of the institutional policies and practices of political science in academic departments and in the governance structures of the APSA.

Indeed, if nothing else, Perestroika has certainly acted on the APSA's official policy promoting the "encouragement" of the practice of political science (APSA Constitution, Preamble) by provoking a long-overdue debate on the future of the study of politics in America. Perestroika takes direct aim at the hegemonic methodological biases that shape the way departments of political science teach the discipline to their graduate students; hire and promote new colleagues; control access to the *American Political Science Review,* the *American Journal of Political Science,* and the *Journal of Politics;* and, until recently, maintain a lock on the governing structures of the APSA. Mr. P is still an anonymous online personage and comes close to, but always steps back from, naming Perestroika as an organized pressure group or explicitly stating that when the self-identified leadership cadre take action they do so as representatives of the collective membership. Mr. P. is unelected and unaccountable to anyone other then the Yahoo list serve manager. Although electoral democracy has been one of the twin poles of Perestroikan ideology—the other being the dethroning of rational choice and "large n" empiricism as the defining disciplinary paradigms—the list serve has never claimed that its authenticity as a forum, or as a "movement," depends on its being the authoritative voice for an identifiable majority of list serve members, let alone a silenced majority of APSA qualitative researchers. Nonetheless, Mr. P's assault on the APSA establishment is conducted in the classically inclusive language of institutional representation and governance. In other words, various discourses of representation, equally abstract, are being marshaled by both Perestroika and the APSA establishment, even while both organizations are operating beneath the surface through networks of influence and power.

Postmodern Perestroika

For me as a political theorist, the question of Perestroika's positioning in the debate on the future of American political science invokes a conflict between solidarity and critical thinking. Decoding the fraught terrain between the APSA and Perestroika turns up an unexpected blend of both Roland Barthes's and Gilles Deleuze's late-twentieth-century refusal to privilege "authors" and Edmund Burke's classic eighteenth-century defense before the electors at Bristol of an elected representative's right to virtually represent the best interests, if not the immediate preferences, of the citizens. Undeniably, what appears by any measure to be a radical pluralization of the APSA establishment, including its publications and elected representatives, has emerged in Burkean fashion from the sequestered deliberations of the APSA Nominating Committee, presidents, and Council, in the absence of "contested" elections. For the first time in its history, the APSA will have had three women presidents in a row: Theda Skocpol, Suzanne Huber Rudolph, and Margaret Levy. A study by Kirstie McClure, commissioned by the 2003 APSA Council, found that the pluralization trend is decades in the making, and has resulted in the overrepresentation of women and minorities when compared to membership demographics, although non-PhD-granting institutions continue to be less visibly represented. The facts speak to the emergence over time of a consensus, compounded of politics and ethics in equal parts, cutting across officially and unofficially organized groups, and resulting in a major sea change in leadership if not in the nomination and electoral process itself.

Nonetheless, some outspoken Perestroika list members are explicit in their relegation of the goal of diversity to secondary status behind the demand for contested elections, whatever their outcome. As Ron Libby wrote on March 31, 2003, "What is the purpose of having competitive, democratic elections for APSA offices? Is it to give the appearance of representative leadership or is it to fundamentally reform the association?" Libby claims indifference to disciplinary affirmative action and sees a fundamental opposition between representation of plural identity groups and "INTELLECTUAL diversity." In the most recent contested election generated by a Perestroika challenge, that of October 2004, three candidates were fielded. One of them, Harvey Mansfield Jr. of Harvard University, defeated a Nomination Committee candidate for the first time. The results, not unexpectedly, verified the patterns of previous contested elections. Candidates from Big Ten, Ivy League, and other major research universities had pulled the most votes. Some observers viewed the Perestroika nomination of Mansfield as "cynical," because it was done with the voting patterns of 2003 in mind rather than the goals of the Perestroika movement. Others thought it a brilliant piece of insider game playing to use the institutional conservatism of APSA members against their own official nominees.

John Dryzek takes a different approach. In his chapter of this volume he wishes a friendly "Pox on Perestroika," pointing out that Perestroika's advocacy of intellectual pluralism is "uncritical." Hurling taglines as epithets across a disciplinary no-man's land does not solve the problem of what Perestroika as a collectivity advocates for. Then there's "Mr. Pravda," a list member as anonymous as Mr. P, who accuses the Perestroika list of bad faith. The revolutionaries, he claims, are outsiders only in their rhetoric, when in fact they are established political scientists who are just seeking their fifteen minutes of Andy Warholian fame by getting themselves more space in the APSA's flagship journals. Others lament that the list lacks a common strategic denominator and indulges in a form of wishful thinking that never specifies "what is to be done" to make political science as a discipline and as an organization more directly reflective of political reality.

Perhaps the answer lies in the postmodern aura of Perestroika. Rather than an organized assault on the APSA establishment, it seems more like one of Deleuze's (1987) rhizomes spreading across the surface of cultural discourse by means of offshoots that appear disconnected but are really linked by a common taproot (24–25). Roland Barthes's (1977) resistance to ascribed, fixed meaning also seems germane (142–43). The Perestroika list's discourse is multicultural, conducted in the languages of both protection of group rights and plebiscitary democracy, balancing the seemingly opposed strategic goals of institutional change and chat room consciousness raising. Even more ironically, the visible (online) and vocal (at conferences) leadership of Perestroika persists in describing itself as "individuals" in virtual motion, as well as a collective movement with an institutional agenda. The September 25, 2003, e-mail message continued by saying, "This is not meant to replace APSA or recreate it, it is meant to be the critical conversation outside its corridors that ignites multiple initiatives by individual scholars. So, prepare for more initiatives, as ever increasing number of individuals start questioning the status-quo. But remember to have your morning coffee here."

Perhaps joining the list is no more incendiary than reading the *Village Voice,* or perhaps *The Onion,* as one downs an espresso and begins another frustrating day as an underground qualitative researcher. Yet the coffee house protest movement is also above ground, organizing panels at national and regional meetings and, in September 2003 and 2004, running alternative candidates for the APSA Council in order to activate the association's by-laws, which mandate a general mail ballot when the Nominating Committee's list of nominees is appropriately challenged. In this respect, the list is more the equivalent of Tom Hayden's "The Port Huron Statement" or V. I. Lenin's "What Is to Be Done" or Malcolm X's "Ballots or Bullets" in its focus on multiple levels of insurgency. A founding and very visible member of Perestroika, David Pion-Berlin, remarked on the illusive nature of the Perestroika landscape just after a Perestroika list member, Peregrine Schwartz-Shea of the University of Utah, emerged in 2003 as the one challenger to the APSA's nominated slate. On October 6, 2003, he noted how "interesting" it is that so many Perestroika list members "still refer to Perestroika as a movement, and not just a discussion group." More confusing still, "those who want to open it up to a dozen different topics (also) refer to it as a movement." Still others want it to have no strategic purpose but simply to be an unstructured forum for "the airing of views."

At the same time, there has also been dismay among Mr. P's readership occasioned by the free-floating conspiracy theories, petulant bitterness, factual errors, and, again ironically, the nonrepresentative nature of most of the list's e-mail leadership—comparativists, qualitative methodologists, normative theorists, and disgruntled doctoral students from PhD-granting institutions, particularly the Ivy League. Perestroika's parallel virtual universe only infrequently engages the concerns of the "traditional" organized sections of the APSA representing gender, ethnic, and regional interests. The latter reflect the Jacobson Report's concerns that the effect of mandated contested elections for the Nominating Committee and the Council will have the effect of rolling back their hard-won gains.

What is the "reader" to do? In addition to the seven hundred list serve members, Mr. P., and the circle of advisers named publicly online in 2003, there are external readers whose angle of vision is crucial to Perestroika's future: the APSA leadership cadre, roughly thirty people, and beyond them the fourteen thousand paid-up members of the association. Everyone reads what the authors of the "text" of the Perestroikan movement write. The founding mothers and fathers of Perestroika read their own and others' postings for the purpose of making policy decisions that appear to commit the entire movement to action. Then too, APSA Council leaders include a number of Perestroika list members, myself included. We also "read" Perestroika and act according to our best understanding of what is appropriate for the discipline as a whole. Perestroika seems like the reincarnation of the Caucus for a New Political Science, this time focused not on opposition to the discipline's acquiescence to the war in Vietnam but on the theory and practice of the discipline and its governance bodies. Yet functionally, there is little difference between APSA and Perestroika "readers" who act on their sense of the "text." Both would agree with Burke that "your representative owes you not his industry only, but his judgment," which "he betrays, instead of serving you, if he sacrifices it to your opinion."

The Perestroikan Candidate

In 2003 the multiple ironies of the Perestroika-APSA standoff began to cascade as a Perestroikan leader, Gregory Kasza, announced on the list shortly before the APSA national meeting in Philadelphia that he had privately convinced Peregrine Schwartz-Shea to run as a challenge candidate for the APSA Council in 2004, forcing a general ballot of the membership. This proved to be a case study in the tactics and strategy of Perestroika, and would be repeated a year later with some variations. Schwartz-Shea was to run not as a candidate endorsed by the Perestroika movement or as part of a Perestroika slate for other offices, but as a single individual nominated by other individuals, who happened to be Perestroikans. Two others of us were also Perestroika list members but had been selected "officially" by the APSA Nominating Committee: in 2004 the challenger list was expanded, but again targeted only the Council.

Online list members and observers struggled to articulate the status of a candidate who was, and yet was not, at the vanguard of the Perestroika movement. Right from the beginning the question of whom the challenger in fact "represented" was a problem because the list had debated online whether alternative candidates should be run but had never come to a consensus publicly. Without a formal organizational structure, with no elected leaders and no procedures for arriving at policy decisions, the list has, in effect, no way of speaking with one institutional voice. Yet it can act with the implicit endorsement of the membership as long as the leaders who act in its name are known publicly to be Perestroikans and speak in the language of Perestroika: methodological pluralism; institutional, intellectual, gender, racial, and ethnic diversity; and open electoral processes.

Perestroikan opponents of challenging the APSA slate argued that targeting the president and vice presidents or the Council without first having a plan in hand to reform the electoral process in such as way as to protect the gains of women and minorities was a self-defeating prospect. One-to-one challenges of single-member offices would look like personal vendettas, and the decision to force the Council slate onto the ballot would invite an aggregate majority to vote down the challenger. Again the hegemons would win. What political scientists all knew to be the case in their own research on elections in democracies seemed suddenly germane to the internal politics of the discipline. Mass electoral democracy and storming the hierarchies of privilege within the APSA might not be compatible activities.

Nonetheless, Peregrine Schwartz-Shea ran as a de facto Perestroika challenger, a white woman from a PhD institution. She became, in effect, cannon fodder to make a point about contested elections but not necessarily to win the day. Another martyr and yet another would stand in front of the guns of the establishment year after year until constitutional change could be achieved. This stated goal (Kasza, Town Meeting) took the identity crisis of Perestroika to another level of ambiguity. This was not a coffee klatch, a chat room, or even an intellectual forum but a "movement" crossing boundaries from the outside to the inside of the APSA, in fact but not in name.

Even if the candidate represented no greater "diversity" than the APSA official slate, the point was the challenge, and not the outcome. Gregory Kasza made the case for alternative nominations in clearly institutional terms, invoking the Perestroika list collectively by using pronouns such as "we" and "our." Kasza extrapolated from what he took to be majority opinion among Perestroikans in favor of "competitive elections at APSA" to a strategy of using the current APSA by-laws to force a mail ballot. A completely alternative slate, which he noted might very well lose in an open contest, seemed to Kasza neither strategically sound nor representative of list serve opinion. But, he argued, a test case of one or two candidates for Council might meet both requirements. The list members who opposed the rush to wholesale competitive elections as a first tactic would, he implied, accept using the existing rules to effect a limited outcome. "Our purpose should be to institutionalize competitive elections, not to commandeer the association." The effect of Schwartz-Shea defeat was never discussed.

More than a year before the election, on March 10, 2002, Suzanne Rudolph spoke online as a Perestroikan and as the newly elected APSA president (but not "elected" in a general poll of the membership) to say that the timing of contested elections was less important to her than the strategic goal of a "transparent, accountable process" that would eventually produce "democratic nomination(s) and competitive elections" but also would guarantee diversity in the leadership. Rudolph was gently pushing the postmodern *Village Voice* identity of Perestroika down to submerged taproot status, invoking instead her vision of Perestroika as a movement, forcing a quickening of the pace of constitutional change. This despite the fact that Rudolph's name had emerged from the inner politics of the caucuses and the APSA Nominating Committee. Later, before the general election of 2003, she sent an e-mail message to the APSA electorate on October 21 reminding them to vote by October 29 and framing the narrative of the first APSA general election in over thirty years largely in Perestroikan terms. She wrote that recourse to the membership had been "triggered by a petition process from individual APSA members to establish a contested slate." She then drew a causal connection between the challenge and structural reform. After this election she would create a forum to think of "alternative ways to institute democratic processes for APSA leadership selection" that also take into account "multi-cultural representation."

Nonetheless, by October 30 the APSA members learned of election results in which, with a response rate of 30.1 percent, the entire APSA Nominating Committee slate had been elected. The Perestroika "reform" candidate came closest to beating not the "hegemons," but an African American woman doing community-based public administration at a small regional public university. Ironically, majority rule in practice turned out to mean endorsement of the APSA status quo, in its commitment both to racial and gender diversity and to the dominance of gatekeeper institutions like the University of Michigan, Texas A&M, Duke University, and Brown University. Consternation and explanations abounded on all sides. President Rudolph responded by creating a committee on electoral reform to study ways in which, if contested elections were to become the norm, they might be conducted in ways that would preserve the "diversity" in the association rather than undermine the hard work of the minority and women's caucuses. By September 2004, Kristie McClure's committee had completed a much-debated report which, among other notable achievements, had collected data demonstrating that non-PhD institutions are themselves approaching 50 percent of the APSA membership but remain significantly underrepresented in APSA governing bodies. The remedies proposed, however, remain suggestions that so far lack majority support.

Let the Reader Beware

Both the logic of the reform movement and explicit debates among the members amply demonstrate that the Perestroika list has no formal structure by design, not by inadvertence. Calls for institutionalizing the list along the lines of an "organized section" of the APSA have been rejected by the predominant voices on the list. As of January 2005, Perestroika listers continue to argue that democratic, open discussion is facilitated precisely by the absence of institutional hurdles and rules of engagement, as well as by the tolerance of anonymous postings. From a tactical perspective, the challenge to the establishment is intensified in proportion to its elusiveness.

During the 2003 APSA meeting in Philadelphia the newly nominated president of the APSA, Margaret Levi, remarked to Council members that she had been denied membership in Perestroika. Gary King, a newly nominated vice president, had had the same experience some months earlier, as had others whose "hegemonic" affiliations made them suspect. To add a bit of wartime theatrics, a set of "playing cards" with their faces and those of others similarly targeted had been circulated among some insider Perestroikans. Presumably the intent was to invoke the U.S. Army's search-and-destroy list of enemy Iraqis. An uproar ensued, disclaimers flew, and Mr. P publicly (but still anonymously) took both responsibility and the bold step of proposing the appointment of a council of wise counselors to assist in filtering members and postings. Apologies were made for the unintended appearance of blacklisting and the previously excluded were welcomed to the list. No guarantees were given that the filtering process would not continue, but there were assurances that it would not be arbitrarily undertaken by a single individual.

From the perspective of the governance question, however, the most interesting outcome of the accountability controversy was that the list of people "nominated" by Mr. P for the advisory role almost exactly duplicated the list of the founding Perestroikan leadership, whose postings appeared regularly and who chaired and organized Perestroika panels at the APSA meetings. There was no open call for candidates, and no mechanism for voting. At the same time Mr. P had made the accountability issue a public matter for the first time. And, also for the first time, academics with public faces, names, and voices had been assigned advisory roles to the still invisible

In an ironic mirroring effect, Perestroika's process of leadership self-nomination and "election" in the absence of dissent oddly shadows the rotation of elites in the APSA governance processes that Perestroika has mercilessly critiqued. There are echoes here of the APSA's Jacobsen Report which concluded: "In sum the current selection system has provided the Association with distinguished and broadly representative leadership. It does not foster artificial conflict, but does provide for competitive elections if even a few members want to offer alternatives to the official nominees." The APSA and Perestroika are in many ways parallel camps in the conflict over the fate of political science in America. It is an odd battle, with combatant "readers" boundary crossing at will and reporting back on the enemy's fortifications. Leadership cadres of Perestroika are intermingled with those of the APSA. The demand for democracy hurled at the APSA bounces back upon Perestroika, but the former's track record since 1903 is by far the more problematic, and hence vulnerable to critique. Yet, as Michael Bernhard remarked online on April 4, 2003, Perestroika itself is not of one mind on the issue of whether "democratic competition and representativeness are necessarily at odds with each other." The two positions could be reconciled, he believed, by implementing the Perestroika leadership's proposal (2002) for use of the Hare single transferable vote, or some variety of proportional representation. This would constitute the core of Susanne Rudolph's proposal for electoral reform as president of the APSA.

Marsha Pripstein Posusney, a Council member and a founding mother of the Perestroika movement, is a boundary-crossing observer and from the beginning resisted Greg Kasza's initiative to mount a challenge to Council nominees On March 31, 2003, she posted a message saying that unless the APSA constitution was first amended to protect diversity across a broad range of measures, forcing a general vote on Council nominees would result in unintended consequences, because "there are two Perestroikans among the eight council nominees, and a third is a participant in the new 'elections and diversity' listserve." Pripstein Posusney pointed out that though the Jacobsen Report sidestepped the "representation" issue by saying that diversity is best served by the status quo, the Perestroikan Council challenge "risks displacing some minority nominees" and producing "winners . . . with the greatest name recognition . . . from prestigious universities." And in fact the election outcome confirmed her concerns.

Everyone who joins the list—or, more accurately, who is permitted to join —has become part of a reform movement that has no official institutional identity other than its evocative name and a self-identified leader, Mr. P. When Mr. P speaks, he directs his speech acts only to the faithful and does not call for specific action. The founding fathers and mothers, constituted as a self-selected leadership cadre, do engage in actions as members of the APSA, and simultaneously as Perestroikans. Such acts are de jure the acts of individuals, however coordinated, and do not express any formal mandate from the membership. Discussions, not votes, precede them. Occasionally a Perestroikan "reader" raises an equivalent concern about both democracy and representativeness inside Perestroika itself. Or, as Pripstein Posusney said, "Perestroika . . . has already been accused by some of only being concerned with the career trajectories of graduate students and junior faculty at top schools." The issue for her is not so much internal Perestroika governance but rather the danger of rushing into contested elections without providing guarantees of diverse representation in APSA governance.

When the terms "democratic competetiveness" and "representativeness" are turned back on the Perestroika list (as in Michael Bernhard's posting of April 4, 2003), postmodern ironic ambiguity proliferates. The governance norms of Perestroika seem to come closer to Lenin's democratic centralism than to the open democracy that Perestroika advocates for the APSA. On the one hand, Mr. P's September 25, 2003, posting on "transparency" declares in favor of the silenced and disenfranchised. Perestroika, rather than being a forum for those who want to find ways to penetrate the existing methodological establishment, is dedicated to forcing the profession to accommodate different visions of political science. The goal is "bringing back those who have been excluded from the discipline's associational life . . . the vast majority of qualitative scholars . . . [who] sat on the sidelines during the 1980s and the 1990s, disarmed by the trope of science while department after department, journal after journal, and association after association were taken over." On the other hand, Mr. P sees no contradiction in declaring that the way to avoid the problem of blacklisting and other filtering errors is to "accept Rogers Smith's suggestion to create an 'umpire'-like advisory group," a sentiment endorsed that same day by other prominent Perestroikans. Leaving no doubt about the selection process, Mr. P presents a list of ten "very active" members "who have spent large amounts of time in not just the discussions here but also other concrete perestroika related activities." One wonders what would have happened if list serve members had expressed dissenting opinions on the idea of the "umpires," or proposed alternative nominees' serving as such. The incoming APSA president, Susanne Rudolph, expressed an opinion that the umpires should be a "light presence, not a highly rationalized organization" (cited in an e-mail message posted by Mr. P. on September 25, 2003). Her suggestion reflects a countercultural resistance among Perestroikans to the restrictions that institution-building imposes on revolutionary movements. Leadership yes, electoral democracy no, at least while Perestroika is a movement of "individuals" in motion.

Rhizomes and Readers

Both as an online coffee house forum and as a de facto organized movement for reforming the discipline of political science in America Perestroika has been very public, efficient in targeting leading "hegemons" and effective in forcing issues of democracy and representativeness to the surface of APSA consciousness. Judging by the ratcheting up of debate on the future of the discipline in the corridors of APSA conferences, and the creation of a new journal, *Perspectives in Political Science,* Mr. P's list has made remarkable progress.

The core irony remains, however. As a list serve, Perestroika is an undemocratic aggregate of readers and texts presided over by a self-designated leadership, though its central mission is the democratization of the APSA. Most list serves display such characteristics, with unseen moderators and filters. There is no such thing as free and open discussion on Yahoo nowadays. However, Mr. P's list is no ordinary list serve, nor is it a one-person blog. It began in 2000 as a spontaneous eruption of discontent within the discipline of political science against the capture of departments, journals, and conferences by rational choice modelers and empiricists, largely American in their research focus. The battle cry was "representativeness"; the argument was that the portrait of the discipline presented by the "hegemons" was false. Forcing a wedge in the rotation of status quo–oriented elites in leadership positions at the APSA through electoral reform emerged from the outset as a tactical priority. Yet the process of becoming a de facto organized pressure group while retaining the free-form appearance of an online list serve has raised the questions of what exactly Perestroika's text message is and how its readers inside and outside the movement should act on it.

Deleuze argues that his favored form of rhizomatic writing "has no begin-ning or end: it is always in the middle between things, interbeing, *intermezzo*. His description is an apt metaphor for Perestroika. Unlike vertical, structural entities (like trees), rhizomes are less interested in self-definitions ("to be") than in the conjunction "and . . . and . . . and" (Deleuze and Guattari 1987, 25). Its deliberate ambiguity is both its strength and its weakness. Hegemony of the modelers and the data crunchers is undoubtedly a bad thing. Indeed the two have little in common except an opposition to the "soft" science of area and cultural studies, political theory, and any form of political science practiced in the academic hinterlands beyond their control. Perestroikans also have little in common except their contrapuntal advocacy of "qualitative methods" and research questions that range beyond the standard fare of American politics. What will come after the "and . . . " remains a question mark.

Edmund Burke (1774) may be summoned up at this point to expound further on his right to read the text of the electors' mandate in a way that conformed to his "reason" and his "conscience," whether they agreed or not. Might not Mr. P and his umpires, together with the APSA "elected" and, as of this year, actually elected bodies, be understood similarly? Aren't, in Burke's words, "*authoritative* instructions, *mandates* issued, which the member is bound blindly and implicitly to obey, to vote, and to argue for, though contrary to the clearest conviction of his judgment and conscience . . . a fundamental mistake"? Particularly because APSA constitutional arrangements allow for the member-ship to challenge its leaders, the absence of challenges until 2003 would lead the gentle reader to assume that the electors are satisfied with the status quo. And even after the 2003 challenge, the results simply reinforce that opinion.

As Roland Barthes reminds us (1977, 147) from the other side of modernity, "the death of the author" is an accomplished fact because the text is perpetu-ally rewritten by its readers, who infuse it with their plurality. The Perestroika list serve "in the multiplicity of writing" presents its readers and leaders with texts that are to be "disentangled," not definitively "deciphered." One can fol-low the path of arguments as they lead here and there, yet there is no central singular or visible meaning. The APSA would seem to be a rather differently structured phenomenon, even if its leaders as "readers" exercise the same priv-ileges espoused by Burke, Barthes, and Deleuze. There is nothing ambiguous about the APSA's de jure structure. Under the "Governance" link on its Web site it publishes all of its Council minutes, the constitution, and its by-laws. To this extent it is a thoroughly modern, rather than postmodern, institution. Nonetheless, for both the APSA and Perestroika, leaders and policies "emerge," much as did nineteenth-century British Tory prime ministers, from its inner networks and negotiations rarely exposed to public scrutiny. Periodic ratifica-tion of nominees and policies is all that is required of those who turn up at the business meetings.

Mr. P's list has no such carapace of rules and regulations; it has only the online conversation and its self-selected umpires, who periodically transform the coffee-house conversation into a movement targeted at the transformation of the APSA. In Barthean terms, this model frees readers, who in this case are the list serve's leaders, to transform the texts of their constituents' opinions. This translation can be called an "anti-theological activity, an activity that is truly revolutionary," because to "refuse to fix meaning" makes it possible to re-create what Perestroika, and even the APSA, appear to be and perhaps actually are. In the end, perhaps Perestroika is best understood as a political rhizome whose nature demands that the APSA's borders be not only transparent but also completely permeable to different readers and texts. The Perestroika list, made up as it is of APSA members, is perfectly positioned to move back and forth through the membrane of the APSA's meetings, journals, and elections. This definition would exclude for the present an institutionalized structure, including elected candidates and slates for APSA elections, but might not in the future if the membership of the list wants to clearly police its own borders. The costs of this reversion to border patrolling would be high, particularly in the closure of conversations across trenches and, in the end, the failure of the revolution. But then there is always the coffee house.

References

APSA. 2000. "How Should APSA Elect Its Officers and Council? A Town Meeting Discussion." Report on Elections: APSA Plenary Session, moderated by Kristen R. Monroe. August 30. http://www.apsanet.org/news/elections/electionsforum .cfm.

———. Ad Hoc Committee Draft: A Conversation about Election Provisions for the APSA Constitution. Mike Desch et al. August 21, 2002. Link superseded by http://www.apsanet.org/imgtest/Final doc for web.pdf, as of 2004.

Barthes, Roland. 1977. "The Death of the Author." In *Image, Music, Text,* trans. Stephen Heath. New York: Hill and Wang. 142–48.

Bourne, Randolph. 1964 [1916]. "The Price of Radicalism." In *Randolph S. Bourne: War and the Intellectuals: Collected Essays 1915–1919,* ed. Carl Resek. Indianapolis: Hacket Publishing Co.

Burke, Edmund. 2000 [1774]. "Speech at the Conclusion of the Poll." In *Empire, Liberty and Reform: Speeches and Letters,* ed. David Bromwich. New Haven, CT: Yale University Press. 48–57.

Deleuze, Gilles, and Felix Guattari. 1987. "Introduction." In *A Thousand Plateaus: Capitalism and Schizophrenia,* trans. and foreword by Brian Massumi. Minneapolis: University of Minnesota Press. 3–25.

Jacobson, Gary et al. 2002. Report of the APSA Elections Review Committee on APSA Election Procedures. April. http://www.apsanet.org/news/elections/ electionsforum.cfm.

Kasza, Gregory. 2002. Posting in Elections Forum. August 21. http://www.apsanet .org/news/elections/electionsforum.cfm. Link superseded by http://www .apsanet.org/imgtest/Final doc for web.pdf, as of 2004.

CHAPTER 21

Introducing Democracy in the APSA

The Case for Member Sovereignty and
Constituency Representation

Lloyd I. Rudolph

For the past several years, members of the APSA have been debating the question of whether the APSA should institutionalize democratic authority by providing for regular elections. The reports of two committees set up to consider the question, one appointed by President Robert Jervis in 2001 and headed by Gary Jacobson, the other appointed by President Susanne Hoeber Rudolph in 2003 and headed by Kirstie McClure, were "received" but not acted upon by the APSA Council. This chapter addresses some of the issues in this continuing debate.

I start with the question "How should we think about representation in the APSA?" This question raises another: "Who or what should be represented in the APSA?" I start to answer these questions by observing that the APSA is a membership association of persons who choose to identify themselves as political scientists. From this I conclude that a prime objective of representation should be the representation of the members. In our democratic era,[1] that translates into one person, one vote. The convention since Locke's time about representative government under conditions of equal citizenship and equal voting has been majority rule. Locke did introduce one caveat concerning majority rule, that the "majority should be able to conclude the rest," that is, "the rest" should feel that the majority had taken their interests or identity into account. James Madison, in *Federalist* 10, expressed a deeper reservation about majority rule when he spoke of remedies to check majority tyranny. On the other hand, the APSA is populated not only by members but also by theorists, international relations scholars, comparativists, or Americanists who identify themselves as a constituency or as persons from PhD-granting institutions or "teaching-intensive" institutions. From this I conclude that another objective of the APSA should be the representation of constituencies.

I take Locke's caveat and Madison's reservation about majority rule as an opportunity to investigate how the APSA might find ways and means for the majority to be able to "conclude the rest" and to provide remedies against the possibility of majority tyranny. Doing so raises questions in my mind—and I hope in my readers' minds—about minority rights and about the other identities, interests, and purposes that APSA members hold to be relevant to their membership in the APSA. The problem is how to combine member sovereignty with constituency representation.

The U.S. Constitution manages to do this.[2] The self-conscious, organized, and active "minority" when the Constitution was being drafted was the "small states" led by New Jersey. The Constitution begins with the words "We, the people," which established popular sovereignty in an era in which monarchical sovereignty was the norm. Popular sovereignty implied democracy based on equal citizenship and majority rule. But, as has already been noted, Madison (and other founders) were concerned, inter alia, about majority tyranny. And a constitutional draft could not be agreed upon, much less subsequently ratified by the required nine of thirteen states, unless the interests and concerns of small states for representation and rights were satisfied. The response was to provide for the possibility of majority rule via elections to the House of Representatives and to provide for minority rights and representation by treating large and small states alike in the Senate, in which each state has two votes. The small state constituency was recognized and accommodated by a suitable institutional arrangement that, until amended in 1916, provided for indirect election of senators by state legislatures. Nobody called that a system of set-asides, reservations, or affirmative action. Rather, they used the language of adequate representation, recognizing that majoritarianism could be inimical to fair representation.

The reason I have gone through this exercise of examining how the U.S. founders combined member sovereignty with constituency representation is to help us imagine how this possibility might be provided for in the APSA. Presently visible constituencies that might make plausible claims to representation include teachers from non-PhD-granting institutions, political scientists not affiliated with academic institutions, members of the thirty-nine organized sections of the APSA, and members of the four major subfields.[3]

In addition to such "functional constituencies," de facto arrangements and current practice reveal the existence of demographic constituencies based on things such as race, ethnicity, gender, and sexual preference. Current formal and informal arrangements provide for status groups and caucuses that make it possible for such demographic minorities to be heard.

None of the functional and demographic constituencies are constitutionally represented, although new language about diversity in the by-laws signals their significance to the APSA. There are a variety of ways that the APSA can provide for member sovereignty and constituency representation. I would like to consider a few here.

Member representation presumably means consulting members' opinions about who will represent them. At the moment we work under a system of virtual or proxy representation. Nominators select our representatives by imagining whom we would elect if we voted, and if we voted to maximize representation of diversity. Instead of this system of virtual or proxy representation, we should have a system that would require that members be consulted by means of elections that let them choose.

The challenge of elections is to balance member sovereignty with constituency representation. Having an elected Nominating Committee is one way to establish member sovereignty. Inducting the single transferable vote (STV) is a plausible way to promote (but not guarantee) constituency representation. Without going into technical detail about how the results are accomplished, it can be said that the STV obviates the possibility of majority tyranny by eliminating majority rule and makes possible constituency or minority representation by privileging first and second preference votes.

That brings me back to how the Nominating Committee might be elected by the whole membership in a way that represents a wide range of constituencies. Let us say we want to elect via STV and on an annual basis a nine-member Nominating Committee. Each of the thirty-nine organized sections could be asked to choose one person every other year, for example, twenty per year, for a slate of candidates. Those twenty could be joined by ten candidates chosen by the Council and five each chosen by the president-elect and the president, for a total of forty. The current sixteen-member Council could be elected, too. At present, eight Council members are chosen by the Nominating Committee to serve a two-year term. An elected Nominating Committee, keeping in mind the kind of concerns to represent diversity that the current Nominating Committee is enjoined to respect, could slate sixteen candidates, of whom the APSA members would be asked to vote for eight, or it could slate a larger number, say twenty-four, with eight to be elected via STV.

An elected Nominating Committee could choose two or three persons to stand for election as president-elect. If two, the election would be by majority, if three, by plurality. Another option consistent with member sovereignty would be to have an elected Nominating Committee choose the president-elect.

You may have noticed that I have been speaking of functional and demographic constituencies rather than of minorities. I do so in order to conceptualize the membership in terms of members as citizens on the one hand and members with other identities and interests on the other. Isn't it reasonable to think of ourselves simultaneously as an APSA member and as an international relations member of the APSA? I think of myself as a U.S. citizen and as a citizen of the State of Vermont and as a freeman of the town of Barnard, Vermont. I vote and pay taxes in all three contexts.

I go to such lengths to point out the multiple-constituency nature of our lives in order to make a case against the language of affirmative action, reservations, and set-asides. Such language assumes the possibility of discrimination against disadvantaged minorities and the need to provide for equality of opportunity in initial conditions or outcomes. The downside of affirmative action, reservations or set-asides, is stigmatization, the accusation that one is where one is because of what one is, not because of what one has accomplished. If we think of the APSA as composed of a variety of constituencies to be represented, like the constituency of small states that sought representation in the writing of the U.S. Constitution, we can provide for both pluralism and universalism in our understanding and our practice of APSA direct and indirect elections.

Some object to elections because their outcomes are uncertain. Elections run the risk of resulting in outcomes that some or even many will find unsatisfactory or undesirable. I want to remind members of the APSA that not having elections in order to avoid uncertainty and to hold on to certainty means living with the status quo. Certainty in this context means keeping things as they are. Now some might welcome keeping things as they are. "The APSA isn't broken," they might say, "so let's not fix it." But without elections at some level the APSA won't have member sovereignty, and without member sovereignty authority in the APSA will lack legitimacy. Like Voltaire, we will be satisfied with enlightened despotism.

Elections at some level also will address another lacuna in the APSA, the lack of an adequate public sphere. You may have noticed that the election-by-petition for members of the Council was the occasion for lively and constructive discussion not only of matters relating to the possibility of elections but also of other important substantive matters. It was as if sleeping members, a membership coasting on tacit consent at best, woke up to find that there were and are pressing issues affecting the lives and interests of political scientists. How will the APSA respond, for example, to the shrinking number of tenure-track jobs, the growing reliance on temporary employees, and demands by graduate teaching assistants that they be given the right to unionize and bargain?[4] What about the effort to install political supervision over area centers and the monitoring of faculty political affiliations? Then there is the continuing question of the quality and inclusiveness of APSA journals. Elections will enlarge and enliven an APSA public sphere. We should be talking to each other more than we do under the current status quo. Doing so will provide not only the legitimacy but also the transparency and accountability that are, to my view, lacking under the current status quo.

Notes

This chapter was originally prepared as a paper for a panel organized and chaired by Peregrine Schwartz-Shea titled "Escaping the Quota Frame: Conversations on Minority Representation in Contested APSA Elections" at the Midwest Political Science Association Annual Meeting on April 18, 2004, in Chicago, Illinois.

1. Some have argued, e.g., the Jacobson committee in their report, that APSA members view the APSA as a service organization. They join and pay dues to buy services. By this reading the identity of political scientists as scholars, teachers, intellectuals, and professionals does not require them to think and act collectively about the values and interest that accompany these components of their identity.

2. I am excluding for the moment the idea and practice of individual rights, the kind of institutional arrangements that were provided after the fact by amendments to the U.S. Constitution providing for a "bill of rights."

3. All members are asked to declare a major subfield, of which the principal ones are theory, international relations, comparative political science, and American political science.

4. See Karen W. Arenson, "Pushing for Union, Columbia Grad Students Are Set to Strike," *New York Times,* April 17, 2004.

CHAPTER 22

Confessions of a Confused Democrat

Some Thoughts on Representation and
Governance in the APSA

Martha Ackelsberg

Although I've been on the Perestroika list serve almost since the beginning, and have been in general agreement with most of the stated goals of the movement, I have some serious questions about the direction of Perestroika's activities and, in particular, its focus on competitive elections in the APSA. Nevertheless, Perestroika's commitment to methodological and other forms of pluralism has meant that participants in its discussions are prepared to listen to, and engage with, many alternative perspectives. I offer this chapter as part of that continuing conversation.

Before I embark on the critical dimensions of my argument, however, I want to acknowledge the significant impacts Perestroika has had on the discipline of political science, and on the governance of the APSA, in the four years of its existence.

First, Perestroika has been a clear voice raising the issue of methodological pluralism in the profession. That voice is increasingly loud at meetings of the APSA and its regional subgroups, and has gotten good press beyond the walls of the convention centers. It has been very important to those who are studying politics outside the major centers of the discipline to know that there are others with similar perspectives. (At the same time, it bears mentioning that it is probably *easier* to practice a less "methodologically correct" political science if one is not on the faculty of one of the major institutions. In some ways, that is an unexpected "perk" of teaching in a less elite context.) And, I am sure, the existence of Perestroika—and the debates it has stimulated—has helped overcome the isolation and alienation of many graduate students.

Second, Perestroika's voice and activism have directed (more) attention to questions of methodological openness in the major journals of the profession. Perestroika has not, of course, been solely responsible for this—changes in the *American Political Science Review* (*APSR*) were underway even before Perestroika was formed—but it has certainly helped to push the process along. And we *have* made progress, both in terms of the appointment of the new editor of the *APSR* and in the launching of *Perspectives on Politics*. *Perspectives* is already adding an important different "voice" to the discipline; and although the

APSR may be changing more slowly than many of us would like, it *is* changing. More work remains to be done; but we have made an important start. And changes in the national association, and in its journals, are also sparking parallel moves in the regional associations.

Third, of course, Perestroika has had a significant role in forwarding the choice of Susanne Rudolph as president of the APSA. Again, the fact of the nomination cannot be attributed solely to any one group: the Women's Caucus for Political Science had begun a process of challenging the APSA's Nominations Committee to give serious consideration to women candidates a number of years earlier and, together with a variety of caucuses and status committees of the association, had offered names and exerted pressure to effect the change. Nevertheless, the organization exhibited, and the agitation coordinated, on the part of Perestroika surely had an important impact as well.

Despite these significant achievements, however, I believe Perestroika's focus has in fact been too limited. As I understand them, there have been three major elements of that focus: instituting competitive elections in the APSA, increasing the methodological openness of journals, and challenging the methodological narrowness of many departments. These are important, each in its own way. And as I've suggested, Perestroika has made some significant contributions to changing the discipline in these respects. I think it is also important, however, to think more about "ultimate ends": What are our broader goals? And what is the best way to achieve them?

More specifically, I want to raise some questions about competitive elections, and the (implied or assumed) connection between competitive elections and the other sorts of changes for which Perestroika has been struggling. To the extent that competitive elections have been proposed as a strategy for transforming both the discipline of political science and the APSA, I am concerned that the strategy may yield results inconsistent with some of Perestroika's more specific goals. I will end by raising some broader questions about Perestroika's aims and focus.

Some Problems with Competitive Elections as a Strategy

It is my sense that many Perestroikans who argue in favor of competitive elections for the APSA have assumed that such elections will necessarily be more democratic than the system we have now; and that the institution of competitive elections will somehow be the key to achieving all further desired changes in the association. Like many I know in the Women's Caucus; in the Lesbian, Gay, Bisexual, and Transgendered Caucus; in the Latino Caucus; in the Asian Pacific American Caucus; and on the various status committees, I have real questions about this assumption. It is important to ask: What is the evidence for this claim? What definitions of "democracy" are being used? Which groups are likely to be advantaged by competitive elections, and which may lose ground?

Additionally, I think there is an assumption that changing the *structures* (specifically the electoral structures) of the APSA will change the *politics* of the

discipline. Here I have my doubts. We've had a lot more impact on the institutions of this organization in the last ten years—*without* formal democracy—
than any institutionally based analysis would lead us to think possible. And,
given that *many* in this discipline—and in this organization—are more conservative in a whole variety of dimensions than are most of the members of
Perestroika, I am not convinced that more formal "democracy" is what we
need, or want.

Before I go any further, however, I must acknowledge the anomalous nature
of my position and my argument. I have long been a partisan of participatory
democracy: much of my research is focused on participatory democratic social
movements; I teach courses in democratic theory; I am, in general, an advocate for greater democracy in virtually every political context in which I find
myself. Yet, in the context of the APSA, I am very wary of (at best) and probably opposed to (at most times) a change to contested elections, at least under
any electoral framework of which I am aware.

It is true, of course, that the initial enthusiasm for competitive elections
among Perestroika's membership has been moderated somewhat over the
years—not the least in response to concerns raised by members of the various
caucuses and status committees mentioned earlier. Thus, for example, when as
president of the APSA Susanne Rudolph appointed a committee to explore (for
a second time) the possibility of instituting competitive elections in the APSA,
she charged the committee "to consider how contested elections could be
made consistent with the interests of minorities, while avoiding the problems
associated with set asides or quotas."[1] The rest of this chapter is devoted to an
exploration of the questions evoked for me by this charge.

Let me turn, first, to a discussion of what I take to be the advantages and the
disadvantages of the present system. On paper, the existing system seems
closed and very limited: presidents of the APSA appoint members to the Nominating Committee, the committee selects a slate, and, absent a challenge,
those nominated are declared elected. This system does not *sound* particularly
democratic—or representative. And for many years it wasn't; rather, the leadership simply reproduced itself, yielding a set of officers and committee members who were largely white, heterosexual, and male and from elite research
institutions.

Over the years—particularly during the Vietnam War—there have been a
number of challenges to the Nominating Committee's slate, at least some of
which led to the proposal of alternative slates, and resolution via mail ballots
(in accord with the association's by-laws). Most of the would-be challenges
were not very successful, at least not in the short run; the alternative slates
were not elected. Indeed, the one successful challenge of which I am aware—
undertaken in 1973—was mounted by members of the Caucus for a New
Political Science, and its success was probably due in no small part to a well-
coordinated (and -financed) campaign that would probably cost in the range
of $10,000 to $15,000 to mount today. And this alternative slate was com-

posed of political scientists who were all well published and well known within the profession, even if they were known as "mavericks."[2]

Although, technically speaking, it could still be the case that the nomination process produces clones of the existing leadership, in recent years that has not proven to be the case. The potential reasons are many: the change might be attributed to the long-term effects of earlier challenges, to pressures from below, or to an increasing awareness of the changing demographics of the profession. In any case, over the past five to ten years Nominating Committees have become somewhat more broadly based, and they have looked increasingly broadly within the organization for nominees.

This process has been helped immeasurably, in the past five years or so, by the concerted efforts of a number of groups—most especially by the Women's Caucus for Political Science, in coalition with a variety of caucuses and status committees. These groups worked together to put more, and different, names before the Nominations Committee, and before the president of the APSA, to encourage both the committee and the president to name a broader range of people both to the Nominations Committee and to other posts (a process that resulted in the nominations of Theda Skocpol and Susanne Rudolph, in particular).

In short, things have begun to change. Both the Council and the officers of the APSA are much more broadly representative than they have been before. Perestroika has surely been *part* of this process; however, it did not initiate it, nor—to my mind—did it *lead* it.

In the midst of the pressure—largely from Perestroika—to institute competitive elections in the APSA, virtually *all* the caucuses and status committees have expressed serious concern about, if not outright opposition to, such a change. Why should this be the case? Because there are many groups of people who are present in the association in *relatively* small numbers, but who have been working hard—and with increasing success—to change the institutions and practices of the organization. The leadership of the APSA looks *very* different now than it did ten years ago. It is much more diverse, not only in terms of its representation of racial-ethnic minorities and of women, but also in terms of its representation of those from nonelite, non-research-focused universities, (occasionally) those concerned with issues affecting or research about sexual minorities, and those who are proponents of less mainstream methodologies.

That is not to say that the structures—or the outcomes—of the nominations process are perfect. But it is to point out that if we were to shift to competitive elections, these groups would very likely *lose* ground to those who come from elite, research-focused institutions and who use more traditional research methodologies.

Why, then, the push for contested elections in the first place? Is this simply an ideological preference resulting from the belief that we are a political science association, one that professes as among its goals the education of our citizenry for democracy, and therefore we ourselves ought to be governed by democratic procedures? Or is there some assumption (or hope) that contested elections will lead to different and, ideally, better results than the existing system produces? My own sense, from reading postings to the Perestroika list serve and talking with members, is that the latter is the case: those who argue for competitive elections expect that competitive elections will generate a "better" slate of candidates, one more conducive to the methodological and political diversity that are among Perestroika's most cherished goals. I would ask, however, "Better by whose definition, and better for whom?"

As I mentioned earlier, I think this perspective is based on an assumption that changing the structures (specifically the electoral structures) of the APSA will change the *politics* of the discipline. But such is not necessarily the case. In the past ten years—and without any formal change in the structures of the association—those of us who have been pressing for a more representative leadership have had considerable success: women, scholars of color, those who identify as gay, lesbian, or bisexual, and those who teach at small liberal arts colleges have made their way into the leadership of the APSA, and into a variety of committee appointments, in numbers considerably beyond what any institutional analysis might have led us to expect. Here, in fact, I think of an analogy related to women's winning the right to vote: as many scholars have pointed out, women may have had as much, if not more, impact on state and federal social policy in the years *before* achieving the right to vote than they had in the decade or two *after* doing so.[3] Let me be clear: I do not mean to argue that women would have been better off without the right to vote, but I do mean to suggest that attaining that right was not the simple route to equality that many of its proponents expected it to be.

Further, I strongly suspect that most members of the APSA—and most practitioners of political science—are more conservative in a whole variety of dimensions than are most members of Perestroika. Therefore, a move to more formal democracy in the form of competitive elections will not necessarily accord the proponents of Perestroikan views more power than they already have. Indeed, I think it likely that those committed to changing the association to make it more broadly representative have, in fact, had considerably more power under the existing system of nominations than they or we would ever have under a more formally "democratic" system.

Another and equally compelling question is "Who or what are to be defined as 'minorities' in a reconstructed system?" Of course there are electoral systems that can be configured to ensure the representation of minorities—the Hare system of single transferable ballots, for example, or various systems for weighted voting. But what interests or minorities would we be attempting to represent or protect? Are we talking about racial-ethnic minorities as defined by the U.S. Census Bureau? Do we mean to include in the category of minorities those who identify as gay, lesbian, bisexual, or transgendered? What about women, who are surely not a minority of the U.S. population but are a minority of APSA membership? What about those who are not faculty members at the most prestigious, PhD-granting, universities? What of those who teach in small liberal arts colleges? Or in religiously-affiliated institutions? How about those who are at the margins of the profession in terms of the methodologies they use? Or those who teach in institutions located away from the major centers?[4] We might want to represent or protect any or all of these groups; but to devise an electoral system that would protect all (or even many) of them would appear to be virtually impossible. Yet the existing system of nominations does a remarkably good job of ensuring some measure of representation for those in many, if not all, of these categories—not the least because it can recognize that people may "fit" more than one of them at the same time. I certainly do not mean to argue that the only kind of representation for which the APSA should strive is that defined by various ascriptive characteristics. What I do mean to suggest is that "the interests of minorities" are neither self-evident nor simple to protect.

Beyond the question of defining which minority interests we are talking about, and how to take them into account, is the problematic framing of the issue in terms of avoiding "set-asides and quotas." Both of these terms have been badly treated in the press and in public policy discussions in recent years, reflecting what appears to be a generalized backlash in the United States against programs promoting greater equality and social welfare. The claim, of course, is that set-asides and quotas are both ways of guaranteeing seats—a "place at the table"—to those who would not otherwise garner them by their own "merits." In response, advocates of affirmative action have pointed out that for generations members of the dominant group were given all—or virtually all—the seats, despite *not* having won them in a full and fair contest.[5] To insist now on a "full and fair contest" leaves intact the previous decades (if not centuries) of unfairness. In short, the counterargument goes, some affirmative action is necessary to ensure *meaningful* equality of opportunity.[6]

This line of argument holds for the APSA as well. It is important to mention, however, that I do not think that recent Nominating Committees have used either "set-asides" or "quotas," whatever it might mean to do so. In that respect, I fear that the charge given to the recent APSA Elections Committee raises red flags unnecessarily. Rather, my sense is that Nominating Committees have responded to nominations, suggestions, lobbying, and an overall changing climate within the association (and the country) by producing slates that have been broadly representative (though not in any rigid, formulaic, way) of at least *some* of the diversity of the association. Those slates have not been perfect; many individuals and groups have taken issue with the particular combination of persons present in the leadership at any given time. Nevertheless, the process has probably produced slates that have actually included more women, more members of racial-ethnic minority groups, more people from nonelite institutions, and more of those doing somewhat "nonmainstream" research than would have been achieved *either* by contested elections *or* by some rigid formula of quotas or set-asides. And I believe that the resulting slates have in fact been better (both for those of us committed to the broader reformist goals of Perestroika and for the healthy growth and future of the

APSA) than any slate that would likely be achieved through competitive elections. Indeed, given the demographics of the association's membership, were we to introduce competitive elections I fear we would be more than likely to come up with officers and Council members who would be overwhelmingly white, male, heterosexual professors at elite institutions who are doing the sort of mainstream research that a majority of people in the profession (though not, presumably, in Perestroika) would recognize as "legitimate."

In short, I fear that, in the guise of trying to come up with a system that will protect the gains we have made in creating governing bodies that are somewhat representative of the range of people and views in the APSA, we will end up with procedures that really *do* look like either quotas or set-asides, and will, in fact, produce leadership that will be less representative, and have less legitimacy, than the governing bodies we have achieved through hard-fought battles over the past five years.

Broadening the Focus

Now let me return, albeit briefly, to my earlier claim that, despite its revolutionary self-image, Perestroika has, if anything, set its sights too low. Perestroika discussions have tended to focus largely on the practice of political science in a few of the most prestigious departments. I'm all for changing them where possible. But it is important to remember that *most* people who engage in political science in the United States are *not* members of (or even trained by) these departments. And that is *especially* true for women and members of various minority groups. Methodological openness is a real issue; but what about representation of a much more traditional sort—for example, what proportion of full professors in the major university departments are women?[7] What proportion are people of color? Does anyone in Perestroika care? Without falling into a rigid and unthinking essentialism, I suggest that these questions may be connected to what types of political science are being practiced.

Finally, let me introduce a related issue: there has been so much focus on elections, journals, and methodology that relatively little attention has been paid to the relation of political science to the most pressing *political* issues of the day. Most of the people with whom I speak and exchange work don't follow the Perestroika list serve very closely; for them, much of what is discussed there does not seem relevant. Why are we not talking more about issues such as imperialism, growing income inequality (both in the United States and between the North and the South), devastation of the environment, the increasing prevalence of violence, the use of fears of terrorism to curtail civil liberties? People in Perestroika have much to say about these issues. Why have political scientists had so *little* to say in public forums, the news media, and the like? What can we do to increase the numbers of those who are engaging in research about the things that matter most to the world—and working to get their findings out to those who could benefit from them? Addressing these questions—rather than instituting competitive elections in our professional association—would result in a much more significant *political* impact, with potentially revolutionary consequences for the society and the polity in which we live.

Notes

This chapter developed out of comments I delivered at the Perestroika reception that was part of the 2003 Annual Meeting of the American Political Science Association, Philadelphia, PA, August 29, and at the roundtable "Escaping the 'Quota' Frame" at the Western Political Science Association, March 11, 2004. I am grateful to Kristen Monroe for encouraging me to speak at the former and to develop my comments in written form, and to Peregrine Schwartz-Shea for organizing the latter event and asking me to participate in it.

1. The first exploration, of course, was that undertaken by the so-called Jacobson committee, which reported in 2003, and did not recommend a change to competitive elections (see Gary Jacobson's chapter of this volume); the second committee, chaired by Kirstie McClure, reported in 2004. The explanation for the appointment of the committee—and its charge—is available at www.apsanet.org/about/governance/electionsreview.cfm. Its report is available at www.apsanet.org/about/governance/electionreview.pdf.

2. I am grateful to Ken Sherrill for posting this information to the Perestroika list serve. Ken was campaign manager for the challengers in that election.

3. See, for example, Suzanne Lebsock, "Women and American Politics, 1880–1920," 35–62, and Nancy Cott, "Across the Great Divide: Women in Politics before and after 1920," 153–76, both in Louise A. Tilly and Patricia Gurin, eds., *Women, Politics, and Change* (New York: Russell Sage Foundation, 1990); Seth Koven and Sonya Michel, eds., *Mothers of a New World: Maternalist Politics and the Origins of Welfare States* (New York: Routledge, 1993); Kathryn Kish Sklar, *Florence Kelley and the Nation's Work* (New Haven, CT: Yale University Press, 1995); Vivien Hart, *Bound by Our Constitution: Women, Workers, and the Minimum Wage* (Princeton, NJ: Princeton University Press, 1994); and Linda Gordon, ed., *Women, the State, and Welfare* (Madison: University of Wisconsin Press, 1990).

4. My sense of the complexities of this question was much enriched by Paul Gronke's contribution to the roundtable on which we both participated, "Escaping the Quota Frame," at the March 2004 meetings of the Western Political Science Association in Portland, OR.

5. See, for example, Philip Green, *Equality and Democracy* (New York: New Press, 1998); Lani Guinier, *The Tyranny of the Majority: Fundamental Fairness in Representative Democracy* (New York: Free Press, 1994), and "Lift Every Voice," 273–312, in her *Lift Every Voice: Turning a Civil Rights Setback into a New Vision of Social Justice* (New York: Simon and Schuster, 1998); and Anne Philips, *Engendering Democracy* (Cambridge, MA: Polity Press, 1991), and *The Politics of Presence* (Oxford: Oxford University Press, 1995).

6. See the extended example in Green, *Equality and Democracy*, 120–24.

7. Recent work by Janet Boles suggests that women constitute approximately 23 percent of regular, full-time faculty members in the top twenty-five political science departments, ranging from a low of about 14 percent to a high of 32 percent. Data are available from Janet Boles; I am grateful to Bahram Rajaee for alerting me

to the existence of the data. See also Robin Wilson, "Women in Higher Education: Where the Elite Teach, It's Still a Man's World," *Chronicle of Higher Education,* December 3, 2004, available at chronicle.com/free/v51/i15/15a00801.htm. On the "stalled" advancement of women in political science, in particular, see "Report of the NSF Workshop on Women's Advancement in Political Science," March 4–5, 2004 (available from the APSA National Office).

PART 4

The Journals

Because much of what political scientists do is publish, the avenues for publication—and any possible methodological bias evidenced by the major journals in the field—were a crucial battleground for Perestroika. As this volume goes to press, critical changes have been made, with two of the most important political science journals, the *American Political Science Review* and *Perspectives on Politics,* shifting their focus and expanding the type of work they publish as scientifically legitimate. Less change has occurred at the regional level, with many of these journals still heavily oriented in favor of works that are rational choice, behavioral, quantitative, or formal modeling in nature. Reaching out to these journals, and convincing them of the value of methodological pluralism, remains a major goal of Perestroika. Because this process remains ongoing, the following chapters detailing the process by which change occurred at the level of the national association thus take on particular interest.

No one is better able to speak to this issue than Sven Steinmo, who took the extraordinary step of "running" for the APSA Council with the stated goal of changing the *American Political Science Review (APSR)*. His chapter details the recent history of the efforts to broaden the intellectual and methodological perspectives of that journal. It explores the reasons behind these reform efforts and then offers a personal account of the author's foray into the politics of the APSA. The central implications of Steinmo's chapter are (1) that the focus of the *APSR* had become so narrow that it had very few defenders (hence "the emperor had no clothes") and (2) that the APSA itself was an organization remarkably open to change and adaptation. The chapter concludes on a somewhat hopeful note about the future of both the *APSR* and the association.

The chapter by David Pion-Berlin and Dan Cleary also addresses the methodological bias of the *APSR*. As the flagship journal of political science, the *Review* is supposed to display the best scholarship that the discipline has to offer, regardless of methodological orientation. However, Perestroikans have argued that practitioners of nonmathematical research have been systematically excluded from the pages of the *Review*. Pion-Berlin and Cleary address this claim through a content analysis of all articles published in the *Review* between 1991 and 2000. Their analysis demonstrates the near absence of qualitative research in the *APSR* and, by contrast, the hegemonic position occupied by statistical studies. The authors believe this imbalance, which they find was persistent and varied little from one editor to the next, can be attributed to a systematic editorial bias practiced by the *APSR*. They hypothesize that the journal has repeatedly stacked the deck against qualitative work through the selection of reviewers and the adoption of criteria that have placed an excessive emphasis on technical proficiency. Though many qualitative specialists have undoubtedly chosen not to submit their work to the *Review,* that decision itself was a product of historical bias that discouraged submissions from qualitatively oriented scholars and led them to pursue alternative outlets for their work. Pion-Berlin and Cleary argue that although editorial changes finally may be underway, such changes must be institutionalized if they are to survive transitions from one editor to the next.

These changes are the subject of the chapter by Lee Sigelman, the new editor of the *APSR,* and one who has done much to respond to Perestroika's concerns and build better bridges for communications. According to Sigelman, with the possible exceptions of death and taxes, nothing has seemed as inevitable as widespread dissatisfaction with the premier research journal in political science, the *APSR*. His chapter outlines his agenda as the editor who assumed office at the peak of such dissatisfaction, much of which was focalized by the Perestroika movement. Sigelman presents a brief "progress" report on how this agenda had played out in practice a year and a half into his term as editor. Sigelman's chapter stands as a valuable model for other journal editors who wish to broaden the nature of their base.

Jennifer Hochschild's chapter builds on Sigelman's by dealing with the birth of the APSA's new journal, *Perspectives on Politics* (*POP*), which she herself edits. This chapter describes the many forces that came together over a few years—in a brief window of opportunity in which problem, policy, and political streams came together—to create the new journal, which is comparable to but different in character from the *APSR*. A combination of disaffected members of the APSA, entrepreneurial presidents and staff members of the association, committees that did their homework, pressure from Perestroika in its early days, and the discovery of a way to break through budget constraints led to the invention of *Perspectives*. Whether the journal can satisfy all of its constituency's demands and hopes remains to be seen, but the journal's initial issues, under Hochschild's editorial guidance, which is widely judged to be sensitive and energetic, are encouraging.

Perestroikans concerned with the receptivity of the political science journals to creative, innovative, and nontraditional approaches to political science have fared less well in producing change in the regional journals. Perestroika's demands that "science"—more broadly conceptualized—continue to move forward, not remain stuck in paradigms that are outdated or limited, and encourage new thinking and new ideas have often engendered harsh responses from sitting editors and members of editorial boards, as if even raising the issue is somehow to express disloyalty. One of the places where the emotional level of discussion has been most intense has been in the Midwest Political Science Association (MPSA), a major regional association with a journal, the *American Journal of Political Science* (*AJPS*), that aspires to be the top journal in political science. Yet unlike the recent editors of the *APSR* and *POP,* who have made consistent efforts to reach out to disaffected groups, the editors of the *AJPS* are widely perceived as having remained steadfastly committed to a view of science that most Perestroikans find limited, narrow, and out of date in its attachment to numbers for the sake of numbers.

Many Perestroikans have tried to engage the MPSA in dialogue about this issue. This attempt is illustrated in Gregory J. Kasza's chapter. In this quantitative piece Kasza takes seriously the issues raised both by Perestroika and by the defenders of the *AJPS,* constructing a systematic evaluation of the type of research published in the MPSA's journal to determine whether the journal, in fact, tends to publish more statistical and quantitative articles than other types of material. Kasza finds that the publication does indeed privilege the statistical and quantitative, and that this bias has increased since 1960. Of course, as he notes, conclusions about the cause of this bias are speculative. But the data do suggest to Kasza that the *AJPS* editors—and members and officers of the Midwest Association—who genuinely care about broadening the base of intellectual activity in that association need to be more proactive in welcoming diverse forms of research, perhaps by sponsoring special issues or commissioning a more diverse kind of manuscript submission, as Hochschild has done so effectively at *POP.*

In the final chapter of this section, the editors of the *AJPS,* Kim Quaile Hill and Jan E. Leighley, counter Kasza's critique. First they delineate four major research goals that might be pursued in a scholarly article: description, conceptualization, hypothesis testing to create general theory, and applied research concerned with understanding particular phenomena. With that in mind, they then note that as *any* scientific discipline matures, there is a shift toward the latter kinds of productions. Practitioners in established sciences, particularly those working on the intellectual frontier, are more concerned with hypothesis testing and applied research than with descriptive or conceptual efforts, and these goals tend to call for more analytical, mathematical methods. Hill and Leighley see the *AJPS* as a general publication journal dedicated to presenting the best work on the intellectual frontier in political science; thus, they argue, it is only natural that the *AJPS* should receive and accept a higher proportion of articles that involve quantitative methods. Finally, they say that as editors they are required to deal with some eight hundred submissions a year, a volume of material that precludes anything overtly Machiavellian in their decision-making process.

CHAPTER 23

The Emperor Had No Clothes

The Politics of Taking Back the APSR

Sven Steinmo

Teaching to the Test

Few political scientists would advocate introducing a national standardized test to measure faculty performance or potential job candidates in political science. Such a test would threaten both our academic freedoms and the quality of our graduate education, because it would create incentives to "teach to the test." I believe that much of the frustration and anger expressed through the Perestroika movement was in part evoked by the fact that the *American Political Science Review* (*APSR*) has become something analogous to a standardized test in many political science departments across the country. I further believe that the increasing methodological and intellectual narrowness of this journal did in fact undermine the quality of our graduate training as well as intellectual freedom within our profession.

The complaints against the *APSR* are well known. The facts of the journal's methodological or quantitative bias are documented in the chapter of this volume by David Pion-Berlin and Dan Cleary. But so what? There are lots of specialized journals in political science. Why should it bother me or anyone else that the *APSR* is so narrow or specialized? Why not just be content to publish elsewhere? There are, after all, plenty of outlets for good work. The answer, of course, is obvious: the *APSR* is *the* journal.

How many times have you heard "We have to train our graduate students so that they can publish in the *APSR*" or the corollary, "We need to hire someone who can teach our graduate students to publish in the *APSR*"? These are arguments for "teaching to the test." We have all heard advocates of this position argue that we should interview or hire candidate *X* over candidate *Y simply* because candidate *X* is more competent in the particular methodologies favored by the *APSR*. Indeed an even more pernicious argument (yet one all too common) is that we *should not* interview or hire candidate *Y* or *Z* because he or she cannot teach the kinds of methodologies that must be used to publish in the *APSR*—*no matter how important the candidate's work or how profound his or her ideas.*

Of course Professor Robert Jervis is correct when he admonishes his colleagues not to fall into this kind of trap (see Jervis chapter in this volume). But unfortunately the implication that political science departments should simply pay less attention to publication in the *APSR* and instead look to the intrinsic merit of our colleagues' work is not likely to be achieved in many departments in this country. Why? In most departments, publication in the *APSR* counts for more than publication in any other journal because we have no objective standards of merit in social science. Thus when making a case for tenure or promotion before deans and committees who are not political scientists, we are often drawn to easy markers. The *APSR* is such a marker. Similarly, when political science departments struggle for scarce resources within their universities, the simplest and most powerful indicator of departmental merit is often the number of publications in the national association's officially sanctioned journal. No private journal or regional journal has this power.

Because the *APSR* had become the equivalent of a national standardized test *and published only some types of political science,* scholars who chose to pursue other types of political science were competitively disadvantaged compared to those who "wrote to the test." Rational actors understood this. Thus, when faced with choices about graduate training, we all confronted powerful incentives to add more and more sophisticated methodological training to our programs.

Given limited resources and pressures to graduate our PhDs more quickly, the decision to teach more methodology came with costs: program after program in the United States cut back on language requirements, theory requirements, and field survey requirements, and—and in my view most frightening— many departments began rolling back or eliminating comprehensive field exams. In short, methodological sophistication has come at the cost of intellectual and substantive depth and breadth. Is this because political scientists agree that "breadth" requirements are bad—that political scientists do not need broad training? Hardly. Rather, even advocates of breadth and depth want our students to do well in the job market. We know that as job candidates our students will face the same questions and issues that we fight over in our own departments. One way or the other, they too will be confronted with the question "Can you teach to the test?" In short, as the technical requirements for publication in the *APSR* have increased, the breadth requirements in our PhD programs have decreased. In my view, we have impoverished our programs— not to mention our students and our discipline.

If the *APSR* was neutral to methodological, theoretical, and epistemological orientations and did indeed publish the best work across the many subfields of political science, many like myself would have much less to worry about. But this clearly has not been the case.

From Apathy to Anger

Perhaps there was little new or unique in these complaints about the *APSR* and its effects on our profession (see Samuel Beer's chapter in this volume). Very clearly, many people have long resented the narrowness of the *APSR* and the impact of that narrowness on our profession as a whole. According to an official APSA study conducted in 1998, nearly half of all political scientists had serious complaints about the *APSR*.[1] Certainly the Perestroika movement that erupted in October 2000 was at least in part motivated by similar frustrations with this journal. The obvious question was "Why had nothing been done about it?" And, beyond that, "Why, have so many political scientists continued to subsidize a journal that is not relevant to their research or teaching, and may even undermine their profession?"

By the late 1990s I personally had grown very frustrated and angry with this state of affairs. By then I had several friends and colleagues who had dropped out of their professional association as a specific protest against the *APSR,* and several others who had told me that they simply threw the journal away when it arrived in their mailboxes. The final straw for me came while participating on a search committee in 1997. I was particularly attracted to a specific candidate who studied American political development (APD). The candidate had just finished his PhD, had extraordinarily positive letters of recommendations from some of the top Americanists in the world, and already had a book manuscript accepted by Princeton University Press. I argued that we should interview this candidate, but was outvoted by my colleagues on the committee. Their argument for rejecting this candidate out of hand was quite simple: "He will never publish in the *APSR*." One colleague went on to argue, "It may be OK for you comparativists to not publish in the *APSR*. But for Americanists it is essential." When I asked how my colleague knew this young candidate would "never" publish in the *APSR,* he responded, "The *APSR* doesn't publish that kind of work." Of course I knew he was right. The point was not lost on me. The rejection of this candidate had nothing to do with his intellectual or scholarly merit; it was simply that his qualitative work in APD was "not the kind of work" that is publishable in the APSA's professional journal. In short, the *APSR*'s methodological bias eliminated this candidate—and many others—from the pool of acceptable candidates in American politics at the University of Colorado. I was despondent and furious.[2]

At this point I decided to try to figure out how and why we as an association had gotten ourselves into this situation. If so many people were upset with the editorial policies of the *APSR,* and if the *APSR* is as influential and important as I believe it is, why doesn't it change? Why, I asked many colleagues and friends, don't we do something about this?

The virtually universal response was "Any effort at reform would be wasted effort." This argument held that the *APSR* had long been the domain of highly specialized, very quantitative types of political scientists—and there was simply nothing that could be done about it. History seemed to prove this fact. When pressed, however, no one who made this argument seemed to know where the journal's policies were made, how editorial decisions were made, or how they could be changed. It was simply assumed that nothing could be done. At best there was enormous apathy, at worst a sense of conspiracy. The common attitude seemed to be *"They* don't publish 'our' kind of work. And *they* never will. . . . You are simply wasting your time to try to change this long-standing fact." When I asked who "they" were, the only substantive answer I could get was "The editor" or "The editorial board." I went on to ask who chose the editorial board and discovered that the editor chooses the board.[3] The next obvious question, of course, was "Who chooses the editor?"

Taking Back the *APSR*

In December 1998 I sent an e-mail message to a small number of colleagues requesting that they nominate me for a position on the Executive Council of the APSA. When one colleague, Mark Blyth, asked, "Why in the hell would you want me to do that?" I told him, "To take back the *APSR.*" He told me that if I would write up a short campaign platform, he'd send it around and attempt to generate some more support. I wrote the following:

December 16, 1998

"Take Back the *APSR*" is about getting a journal that is more representative of the actual reading/publishing interests in the profession. There is massive dissatisfaction with the journal today (according to a study done by the APSA this summer). It is a no brainer as to why. So, I say, Take It Back. Give it to the members rather than to a particular methodological/theoretical group. The issue is that the *APSR* is run as a closed shop. If I understand correctly, and I think I do, under current rules the *APSR* board is self-selecting. I would love to be on the board, but there is no point of access under current rules as I understand them. So, ever the institutionalist, I say, get on the APSA Council and propose changing the rules. It seems to me incredible that an association of political scientists would allow their main journal to be governed by such undemocratic processes—especially when there is such dissatisfaction with the way it is run today.

I have two specific alternative proposals for the *APSR:* First, open the board to a democratic process. Let all members select the board. This, I believe, would force the *APSR* to be more representative in its editorial policies. Alternatively, allow APSA members to opt out of getting the *APSR* (and opt out of subsidizing it). Instead each member could choose to receive an alternative journal (which could be worked out by contract with a host of journals). This latter alterative would "let a thousand flowers bloom," and reduce the subsidy we all give to a particular type of political science.

Let me be perfectly clear. I am not suggesting that we make it "easier" to publish in the *APSR*. Instead, I am saying that we should have an *APSR* that satisfies THE READERSHIP better than the current one does. I know many, many, political scientists who do not read the journal (which they must buy nonetheless) and many who resent subsidizing a journal they get no use from. On that note, by the way, the "Book Review" section could easily be put together with *PS,* which is useful to a lot more members of the association.

I really don't know if the voting for Council makes a difference. But in the *PS* this month (page 884) there is a ballot.

So, use it. We'll see what happens.

Sven Steinmo

Blyth sent this "platform" around to those on his e-mail list that he usually reserves for jokes (perhaps he thought I really was just joking). But he added:

Personally, I think this is a wonderful idea. We all know about collective action problems, so let's not even go there. Please take the time to find the requisite form in this month's *PS* and nominate Sven Steinmo, University of Colorado, Boulder, to the APSA Council. Things will only get better if we try. Please feel free to forward this to anyone you might think would be sympathetic.

Sincerely, Mark

The response was really quite astounding. Though this e-mail/platform never had anything like the visibility of the Perestroika letter sent around approximately two years later, it did have an impact. I was told that I received more than seventy individual nominations to the APSA Executive Council and that this was a record for the association. Much to my surprise, I was nominated by the Nominating Committee that spring and began my term in the fall of 1999.

The Emperor Had No Clothes

My firm expectation was that when I finally did get into the "corridors of power" I would be ignored or discounted. Like many eventual Perestroikans, I simply assumed that the association was effectively run by a cabal of elites who managed the profession (and their journal) to suit their own needs and intellectual preferences. I assumed that if anything was to be done, it would require a systematic and sustained effort against the well-organized and coherent opposition of intransigent elites. I fully assumed I would fail.

What I actually found, however, was quite different. The APSA Executive Council was not populated by any coherent group. In fact, it was quickly obvious that the Council was instead made up of people with a very diverse set of interests from across the profession. I soon learned that the Nominating Committee goes to great pains to include representatives from all over the profession. I was genuinely surprised. My colleagues sitting around the Council table in fact were very diverse (much more so than a typical political science department) in terms of age, race, gender, sexual orientation, and so on, as well as size and status of school, region of the country, and substantive or theoretical orientation.

I soon came to the opinion that a key problem in the association—and a key problem for the governance of the *APSR*—was precisely that there was so much diversity on the so-called Executive Council that it was difficult for this committee to do much beyond approve the suggestions presented to them by the APSA president, his or her subcommittees, and the association's staff. The real work and power, I discovered, were to be found not on the Council, but instead on the ad hoc or working committees, as well as on the APSA staff. Visions of smoke-filled rooms and episodes of *Yes, Minister* came immediately to mind. The APSA Council looked remarkably like a classic Parliament (a.k.a. a rubber stamp).

But even rubber stamp parliaments are not powerless. They can, at a minimum, withhold their stamp. Perhaps more important, they can be mechanisms for bringing policy ideas or voter discontent to the executive.[4] Because I had been nominated to the Council with a specific agenda, I decided to poll other members of the Council to see how they felt about the *APSR*. Somewhat to my surprise, I found that the general discontent with the *APSR* was widely shared by those on the Executive Council. By my count, at least, a majority of Council members supported the idea of making the *APSR* a broader and more intellectually pluralistic journal. Indeed a large percentage of the APSA Executive Council members admitted to me quite frankly that they too did not read, were not interested in, and were quite frustrated with the *APSR*. Even the incoming APSA president, Bob Keohane, admitted to a small group of us at a breakfast meeting in 1999 that he was very sympathetic to our complaints and that a central reason that he had helped start the journal *International Organization* had been his frustrations with the *APSR*.

Probably because of my activism on this issue, President Keohane asked me to serve on the Strategic Planning Committee, which was charged to examine a host of broad policy issues and practices of the association. We were specifically mandated to examine APSA publications.[5] Of course I assumed that it would be on this committee that the *APSR* reform initiative would be killed. Committees are, after all, the deathbeds of many good ideas. Several of the committee members, moreover, were quantitatively oriented political scientists who had published a number or articles in the *APSR*. Much to my surprise, however, even on this committee, and even among several of the members who had published in the *APSR,* there was little support for a narrow, methodologically driven professional journal. It is probably fair to say that some members of this committee were initially unaware of the deep frustrations of many APSA members with the journal, but it would be equally fair to say that they were remarkably open to the concerns that I along with several other members on the committee raised. No one attempted to defend an editorial policy that de facto excluded some types of political science on the basis of methodology, theory, epistemology, or orientation. To be sure, some committee members initially doubted that such a bias existed (or believed that, if it did exist, it was the fault of those who did not send their work to the *APSR* for review).

It was precisely at this time (winter of 2000) that the Perestroika storm erupted. What began as a single e-mail message soon blossomed into a major movement. Articulated by many of the profession's most highly acclaimed scholars, the enormous frustration within the profession was impossible to ignore. Though certainly the efforts to reform the *APSR* were already well in motion by the time Perestroika took off, there can be no denying that this movement added a huge momentum, legitimacy, and urgency to our reform efforts.

In the end, the Strategic Planning Committee concluded as follows: "There are problems with the *APSR*. . . . The problems are sufficiently worrisome as to suggest corrective actions be taken at this time, so that the *APSR* can be the true flagship journal for our discipline that it aspires to be." Noting that member disaffection with the journal was a serious problem for the association, the committee specifically argued, "The central source of this dissatisfaction is rooted in the widespread perception that the work published in the *APSR* represents the best cutting-edge scholarship of some fields of the discipline and of some theoretical and methodological approaches, but not of others. To the extent these perceptions are valid, the *APSR* can not be considered the discipline's flagship journal."[6] No one would defend an intellectually narrow journal. The emperor had no clothes.

Reforming the *APSR*

The Strategic Planning Committee made few specific policy suggestions, in part because we felt that these substantive policy decisions should be made by the Council and in part because the Council was concurrently in the process of selecting a new editor for the journal. This was a delicate and difficult process in its own right, and we were loath to complicate this process with a set of very specific mandates. The committee concluded that it would be better to present the issues strongly to the Council and allow them to integrate consideration of these issues into the process of selecting of the next *APSR* editor. Clearly our report and the growing pressure from the Perestroika movement placed substantial pressure on the selection committee to find a new editor who would be open and responsive to the demands for greater intellectual, theoretical, and methodological diversity.

In my opinion, the selection committee recommended an ideal candidate to change the *APSR:* Lee Sigelman. Professor Sigelman is a broad-minded, intellectually open, and remarkably tolerant scholar. Equally important, he took the concerns of those in the Perestroika movement and the *APSR* reform movement very seriously indeed. He addressed these concerns very specifically in his comments to the Council in 2001. I believe that he is now making, and will continue to make, significant progress toward improving and broadening the *APSR*.[7]

I did not believe, however, that simply choosing a new editor was enough. The problems and concerns many had expressed vis-à-vis the *APSR* had not been the product simply of narrow editorial policies. Moreover, no matter how sincere the current editor was (and I believed he was quite sincere), he would be in his position for only a few years. Structural changes were also necessary.

In 2001 the APSA Council made three additional and extraordinarily important policy decisions, each intended to bring about greater intellectual diversity in the publications of the APSA. First, the *APSR* editorial board must now be specifically approved by the APSA Council. The editor is specifically charged to demonstrate the intellectual and methodological diversity of the editorial board he or she proposes. Second, the Council initiated a new journal, *Perspectives on Politics (POP)*, with the intention that it publish broad review essays and surveys of the discipline.[8] Finally, the Council also has moved to delink APSA membership from *APSR* subscription.[9] The logic here is that if the *APSR* (or, for that matter, *POP*) is subjected to market pressures it (or they) will be forced to be more responsive to its (or their) readership.

Taken together, these reforms imply a sea change for the *APSR*. As things now stand, the editor is specifically mandated to broaden the intellectual and methodological diversity of the articles published in the *APSR*. Second, the editorial board will henceforth be selected by a fundamentally more open and democratic process than in the past. Finally, APSA members will have the option of not receiving the *APSR* if it does not serve them.

The Politics of Political Science: Lessons Learned

The most obvious lesson that I have drawn from my own personal experience is that the APSA can be a remarkably responsive organization. This organization, in my experience, is *not* run by a cabal of elites—either from the East Coast elite universities or from the Midwest public schools. Instead, a critical problem for the association and for its members is apathy.

I can also say with conviction that the *APSR* does not currently exercise a methodological bias in its editorial policies. But the journal can publish only work that is sent in for review. The journal's long history still hangs over it, and many scholars apparently do not send in their work to the *Review* for fear that it will not be treated fairly. If constructivists, interpretivists, case study analysts, and so on wish to see much more of "their" type of work published in the *APSR,* they must (we must) send it in for review. The *APSR should* be a highly competitive journal. It *should* be difficult to publish in this journal—but this fact should not dissuade nonquantitative scholars from taking a shot at it.[10]

Finally, we must continue to apply political pressure to the APSA and its journals to value intellectual diversity—both in the association's publications and at its annual meetings. The Perestroika movement in particular has had a powerful impact in the last couple of years. But there should be no doubt that the battle for intellectual diversity is far from over. To be sure, those with a much narrower vision of what should constitute political "science" have been set on their heels, but they are not likely to recede into the night. If the struggle for intellectual diversity is to be won, it must be sustained politically for years and years to come.

I began this chapter suggesting that the *APSR* had become something analogous to a national standardized test in political science and that this test was clearly biased in favor of a very narrow version of political science. I believe the *APSR* is now a more open and diverse professional journal than it was just a few years ago. It is less "standardized." Only time will tell, however, if the changes discussed here will have similar consequences for the profession as a whole. I certainly hope so.

Notes

1. In 1998 the APSA conducted a random survey of past and present membership. The key findings of this survey were that for the most part members were largely satisfied with or ignorant of the majority of the association's endeavors—with one glaring exception. This survey revealed enormous frustration with and anger toward the *APSR*. Nearly half of respondents expressed negative attitudes—and often very negative attitudes—toward the *APSR*. No other function, program, or publication of the APSA evoked anything like the outpouring of ill will that was expressed toward the *APSR*.

2. We went on to hire a young candidate who had published in the *APSR*. Nothing in my comments here or elsewhere should be interpreted to suggest that I believe that publishing in the *APSR* was a mark of poor scholarship. I was (and continue to be) an enthusiastic supporter of the candidates we eventually did hire. My point here is that the methodological bias in the publishing output of the *APSR* eliminated a number of candidates from consideration—irrespective of these candidates' intellectual or scholarly merit. I am quite confident that my department is in no way unique in this regard.

3. It is significant that at that time the editor was given complete freedom to choose any editorial board he or she preferred. Surprisingly, the editor did not even have to submit his or her board nominations for approval to the APSA Executive Council.

4. Reforming the APSA governance itself has not been a major priority on my agenda. But it has become clear to me that one of the problems for the APSA in terms of democratic governance is that Council members are appointed for two-year terms. Given the enormous number of complicated issues that the Council votes on at each meeting, it is very unusual for Council members to take strong stands on issues. Few members come to the Council with a specific policy agenda. More often than not, new members are overwhelmed by each meeting's agenda during their first year and are loath to introduce new issues or complications during their second year when they are unable to follow these issues through. Moreover, given the very tight agenda facing the Council at each of its biannual meetings, there is very little opportunity to bring new issues to the table—especially when these issues (such as changing the *APSR*) require a great deal of consideration and are likely to evoke considerable controversy . . . and when it is already 4 p.m. and Council members want to get out of the room.

5. For a discussion of the origins of the Strategic Planning Committee and its early deliberations, see Catherine Rudder, "Executive Director's Report, 2000," http://209.235.241.4/PS/septoo/rudder.cfm. For the full report of the Strategic Planning Committee, see APSA Strategic Planning Committee, "Planning Our Future," http://209.235.241.4/new/planning/finalreport.cfm.

6. APSA Strategic Planning Committee, "Planning Our Future," 18.

7. Professor Sigelman has initiated a series of reforms and changes in editorial policy, including taking great care to construct a broadly diverse editorial board and creating an executive committee that is specifically charged to review his editorial policies and decisions. For a list of his editorial policies, see "Letter from the Editor" in the March 2002 issue of the *APSR.*

8. Perhaps I should note that I was not in favor of this new journal initially. My skepticism grew out of the fear that the creation of such a journal could take the pressure off the *APSR* to be broader and more intellectually diverse. Although it would not necessarily be the case that there would be a division of labor between the *APSR* and *POP* along methodological or epistemological lines (and I see nothing in the policies of the current editors of these two journals that should lead in this direction), I believe we must vigorously guard against this development in the future.

9. The Council subsequently decided to table this decision. According to the minutes of the fall 2003 Council meeting, "The rationale for the [journal choice] recommendation was the newness of Perspectives on Politics, and the recent changes made to the APSR. Susanne Rudolph noted the original discussion regarding journal choice was not about money or discounts, but was a critique of the APSR prior to Lee Sigelman's editorship. Since then, under the leadership of Lee Sigelman, many changes have been made to the format and review structure of the journal. The benefits of such changes have not yet been realized, so it would be unwise to implement journal choice at this time." This policy is to be reviewed at future Council meetings.

10. The *APSR*'s Executive Board conducted a two-day in-house examination of *APSR* editorial policies in March 2003. The members of the committee created for this purpose paid particular attention to the issue of bias in the selection of reviewers or the interpretation of reviews. Given the enormous volume of manuscripts the *APSR* deals with, we were in fact quite impressed with Mr. Sigelman's efforts to be impartial and objective as well as his efforts to overcome the legacies he had inherited. We found no evidence of any kind of systematic methodological or epistemological bias on the part of the editor or the reviewers (somewhat surprisingly, the toughest reviewers are those who share the author's epistemology). The fact remains, however, that the APSR is simply a difficult journal to get into. That is as it should be.

CHAPTER 24

Methodological Bias in the *APSR*

David Pion-Berlin and Dan Cleary

Introduction

The *American Political Science Review* (*APSR*) has long been considered the flagship journal in political science. It is the official journal of the APSA. Countless rankings place the *Review* at the top of the heap, whether based on reputation, quality, or impact. Not surprisingly, an individual's stature in the discipline is invariably and immeasurably enhanced through publishing in the *APSR*. It is the same for departments themselves; they can move up in the rankings by hiring professors who publish in the *Review*. The *APSR*'s standing and importance in political science seem unassailable.

For this reason, it is especially imperative that this journal's practices be held up to the closest scrutiny. The *Review* is a general-interest journal whose mission is to publish the best political science regardless of field, subfield, topic, or approach. Past editors have said so explicitly. For instance, Ada Finifter said: "The *Review* is open to articles in any field or on any subject about which political scientists do research."[1] Finifter boasted that the *Review* deals with all the important political issues of our time, everything from conflict in Bosnia to democratization in Mexico to minority representation in the U.S. Congress.[2] Although typically the *Review* receives more submissions in American politics than in the other fields, topical quotas are never imposed at any point in the process. And yet editors proudly point out that acceptance rates are remarkably similar across all fields. This suggests to them that all reviewers, regardless of their area of expertise, consistently apply similar standards of evaluation when assessing a manuscript's merits.[3] It may be tough to get an article into the *Review* (with acceptance rates hovering around 10 percent historically), but at least everyone is treated fairly, or so the editors would want us to believe.

Obviously the *Review* has an enormous stake in maintaining impartiality. Any intentional bias in favor of or against a particular type of scholarship would call into question not only the journal's commitment to fairness, but its ability to faithfully display the best research that the discipline *as a whole* has to offer. For many years Perestroikans and others have had their doubts as to whether the journal has behaved in an unbiased fashion, at least with regard to methodological questions. It seemed as if articles by those doing non-mathematical, empirical work were seldom seen in the pages of the *Review,* perhaps because the journal had not given those scholars a fair shake. That is a serious charge, because if proved true it would expose a significant disjuncture between what so many political scientists actually do and what is found in the flagship journal. In 1991 Richard Betts suggested, in the absence of a statistical survey to the contrary, that "quantitative research, game theory, and formal modeling comprise the nearly exclusive content of the journal apart from articles in political philosophy."[4] He said that the concentration on these subjects and methods seemed highly disproportionate to the orientations of political scientists in general. If he were proven correct, it would make those in the field wonder whether the *APSR* was fulfilling its mission or whether it was behaving more like a specialized journal with appeal to a much smaller fraction of APSA members.

Of course there has never been any proof of methodological bias in the *APSR,* and former editors would deny up and down that the *Review* has practiced discrimination against any one type of research. In fact, until very recently editors had never even catalogued the submission and publication of manuscripts according to method. So a fundamental piece of data eluded us that would allow us to answer the question "Just how frequently does top-caliber, qualitative research appear in the *Review?*" The analysis that follows is devoted to answering that question, and others. We were interested in knowing whether statistical studies occupied a hegemonic position in the journal; how mathematical modelers and normative theorists fared; whether acceptance of qualitative research varied much over time, and if so, whether that was a function of the editor in charge; and finally, whether researchers using certain kinds of methodologies had better success than others in getting repeat articles published.

Following the presentation of the data, we will launch into an interpretation of the trends. If in fact qualitative research has not had a good showing in the *APSR,* it may have been for any number of reasons. Perhaps practitioners of nonmathematical research do not submit their best work to the *APSR,* or their best work is simply not good enough to pass muster with the *Review*'s gatekeepers. If the former, there may have been solid reasons for abstention, and those may have had something to do with the editorial practices of the *APSR* themselves. We will reflect on what those practices are and have been, and conclude with some observations about the *Review*'s future under new stewardship.

A Content Analysis of *APSR* Articles by Method

It seemed to us quite fitting to undertake a quantitative analysis of *APSR* publication practices over time in order to ascertain whether nonquantitative work has been underrepresented in the *APSR,* and if so to what degree. What follows are the results of a content analysis conducted on all articles appearing in the *APSR* between 1991 and 2000. We included in our analysis full-length articles as well as research notes. Let us first define the methodological categories. One can, we suppose, quibble with these classifications, but they seemed sensible to us. The qualitative analysis articles described those empirical studies that relied on verbal explanations based on an array of evidence drawn from archives, interviews, newspapers, and so on. When numbers were reported, they were used for illustrative and not statistical purposes. Admittedly, there is considerable variation within the qualitative category. It is employed here as a catch-all for numerous approaches, including single (including critical) case studies; structured, comparative case studies; legal case study analysis; comparative historical analysis; path-dependent approaches; process tracing; constructivist and interpretive empirical research; and so on. The use of one catch-all category will drive home the point about systematic exclusion that we will discuss later.

Articles defined as statistical were ones that used probabilistic means of analysis, including correlation analysis, ordinary least squares regression, probit and logit regressions, pooled time series, chi-square analysis, and so on. Articles that employed mathematical or formal modeling were written by strategic game theorists who used analyses of simple one-shot 2-by-2 games, repeated games, or extended (treelike) game. This category included a smaller number of articles by scholars who used economic kinds of models such as production functions. Finally, theory pieces were those *nonempirical* studies that reflected on the writings of a classic or contemporary political theorist; that took on an important theoretical tradition such as rational choice, Marxism, or postmodernism; or that analyzed a concept such as the state, democracy, interests, collective action, and so on. These can also be labeled conceptual or thought pieces.

We perused every article published in the *APSR* during this period to look for evidence of methodological preference. Our overall findings appear in Table 24.1. Although this was a time-consuming task, it was also a relatively clear-cut one. It did not require us to make countless judgment calls, because the authors were quite explicit about their research designs and methods. Occasionally a piece stood at the border between one approach or another. For example, some legalistic articles had a qualitative flavor, but were tossed into the theory camp if they lacked an empirical investigation of actual judicial decisions. Also, there were articles that deployed more than one methodology; those are reflected in Table 24.2.

As Table 24.1 demonstrates, over the course of a decade 53 percent of all articles accepted for publication in the *APSR* were statistical in nature, 21 percent were mathematical modeling pieces, 25 percent were theory pieces, and 1 percent were qualitative. A total of *only five wholly qualitative pieces appeared* in the *APSR* during this ten-year period, despite the rich diversity of approaches included within this method category. Table 24.1 also reveals the hegemony of statistical approaches relative to political science inquiry within the journal.

Table 24.1   *APSR* Articles According to Method, 1991–2000

Year	Number of Articles	Statistical (%)	Math Modeling (%)	Theory (%)	Qualitative (%)
1991	48	30 (62.5)	11 (22.9)	7 (14.6)	0 (0.0)
1992	50	27 (54.0)	7 (14.0)	15 (30.0)	1 (2.0)
1993	49	20 (40.8)	15 (30.6)	13 (26.5)	1 (2.0)
1994	47	22 (46.8)	12 (25.5)	13 (27.7)	0 (0.0)
1995	44	20 (45.4)	12 (27.3)	11 (25.0)	1 (2.2)
1996	37	16 (43.2)	6 (16.2)	14 (37.8)	1 (2.7)
1997	39	21 (53.8)	3 (7.6.0)	14 (35.6)	1 (2.5)
1998	42	27 (64.3)	8 (19.0)	7 (16.7)	0 (0.0)
1999	35	22 (62.9)	7 (20.0)	6 (17.1)	0 (0.0)
2000	34	20 (58.8)	7 (20.6)	7 (20.6)	0 (0.0)
Total[a]	425	225 (53)	88 (21)	107 (25)	5 (1)

Source: Authors' calculations.

[a] These figures have been rounded off to the nearest integer.

Pieces using the statistical approach accounted for more than half of all pub-lished articles, and in some years (1991, 1998, and 1999) they represented almost two-thirds of the collection. In no year did they account for less than 40 percent. Statistical articles turned up more than twice as often as those using mathematical modeling or theory, but there was no clear trend upward or downward over time.

Articles by game theorists seemed to have had their strongest showing in the mid-1990s and have tapered off since. That took us a bit by surprise, because it seems as if the preference for modeling of this sort has persistently grown in the profession over time. That theory has such a respectable niche in the *APSR*, accounting for one quarter of all published pieces, may be news to some who had imagined that the journal was a showcase for only quantitative research. It would be more accurate to call it a showcase for quantitative *empirical* work. For decades *nonempirical* thought pieces have been featured regularly in the *Review*. Some Perestroika colleagues believe it's not all good news for theory, however, contending that theorists who have taken on more contemporary and less arcane issues are often subjected to hostile reviews by empirical political sci-entists and have a lower probability of getting published.[5] In the absence of a more refined content analysis—one that could distinguish between classical and contemporary themes—we can't settle this issue one way or the other.

Of course it is column six of Table 24.1 that reveals the most disturbing data. Here is the clearest evidence to date that the *APSR* has failed to publish the best work by qualitative political scientists. Over the span of a decade, qualitative scholars have been, with only five exceptions, nowhere to be found on the pages of the *APSR*.

It could be argued that Table 24.1 overstates the case for the exclusion of qualitative empirical work because it does not consider the many articles that may have combined methods. There might have been more qualitative work than meets the eye, because it may have been subsumed within other categories. Table 24.2 shows what we found when we looked for evidence of mixed methods within each article. Included is a category for articles using experimental designs, defined as those that analyzed feedback from human subjects in laboratorylike conditions. All experimentalists used either statistical or mathematical models to interpret their results. Thus their approach was collapsed into the statistical or mathematical modeling categories in Table 24.1, but is broken out here.

Interestingly enough, very few *APSR* authors are methodological pluralists. For example, only 9.7 percent of statisticians bothered to combine statistical approaches with game theory, case studies, or experiments. Likewise, only 13.6 percent of game theory modelers chose to combine game theory with qualitative, statistical, or experimental approaches. Statistical pieces that included case study analyses equaled only 4.4 percent of all the quantitative articles, and modelers who used case studies amounted to just 5.6 percent of the cohort represented in the *APSR*. As low as these figures are, they give the *Review* the benefit of the doubt, perhaps too much benefit. We say that because the statisticians who used some qualitative, case study material in the ten articles shown in column four did so sparingly and only to illustratively buttress their results. Most often, case study analysis amounted to no more than a page or two of text. Thus most of the pieces that "mixed" these categories were overwhelmingly statistical and only slightly qualitative. The same was largely true for the pieces by game theorists who occasionally resorted to case study analysis.

Table 24.3 shows what we found when we took a look at the choice of methods in pieces published under different *APSR* editors. The articles we looked at spanned the terms of three editors: Samuel Patterson (1991), G. Bingham Powell (1992–95), and Ada W. Finifter (1996–2000). Admittedly the sample sizes in terms of number of issues and number of articles under each editor are not nearly proportional because we have not represented Patterson and Finifter's full terms in office (as their terms of office overlapped years before and after our1991–2000 study period) . Nonetheless, was there any discernible difference in the methodological distribution of articles from one steward to the next? As shown, statistical design articles had their strongest showing under Patterson and theory articles their worst, with qualitative articles not registering at all. Under Powell there was more of a balance between methods, but just barely. Game theory articles had their weakest showing under Finifter. But these differences were slight. A Cramer's V test (results shown in Table 24.3) demonstrates a weak and insignificant association between editors and the distribution of articles that they published across methods. It mattered little who was at the helm. The most important finding was that qualitative approaches fared very poorly *regardless* of who was editor.

Table 24.2   APSR Articles, Single and Mixed Methods, 1991–2000

Year	Number of Articles	Statistical	Statistical + Qualitative	Math Modeling	Math Modeling + Qualitative	Math Modeling + Statistical	Qualitative	Experimental Design + Statistical	Experimental Design + Math Modeling	Theory
1991	48	29	1	10	1	0	0	0	0	7
1992	50	25	2	5	0	1	1	0	1	15
1993	49	18	2	11	1	2	1	0	1	13
1994	47	18	2	10	2	0	0	2	0	13
1995	44	19	0	11	1	0	1	1	0	11
1996	37	15	1	6	0	0	1	0	0	14
1997	39	19	0	3	0	0	1	2	0	14
1998	42	26	1	7	0	0	0	0	1	7
1999	35	19	1	7	0	0	0	2	0	6
2000	34	19	0	6	0	1	0	1	0	7
Total	425	207	10	76	5	4	5	8	3	107
Percentage of total		49	2	18	1	1	1	2	1	25

Source: Authors' count of articles.

Table 24.3   Methodological Distribution of *APSR* Articles by Editor, 1991–2000

Editor	Statistical (%)	Math Modeling (%)	Theory (%)	Qualitative (%)	Number of Articles
Patterson	62.5	22.9	14.6	0.0	48
Powell	46.8	24.2	27.4	1.6	190
Finifter	56.7	16.6	25.7	1.0	187
Total					425

Source: Authors' calculations.
Note: Cramer's V value = 0.102 (range is from 0 to 1). Significant = 0.185.

Our final numerical analysis was designed to allow us to see whether some scholars had an easier time repeating publication in the *APSR* than others. Was there some methodological pattern to their success or failure? We grouped authors in two categories: those who published twice in the journal and those who published more than twice (three, four, or five times). We wanted to see how many authors could publish two or more times as a percentage of all authors within their methodological category. The data are shown in Table 24.4. Eyeballing the percentage data, one can see that statisticians had a slight edge in terms of publishing twice, and modelers had the edge in publishing more than twice. Theorists were in third place, and qualitative practitioners had no repeat successes of any kind.

Another way of looking at these data is to sort them by dominant methods for each tier of repeat success. For example, we counted the number of authors as a percentage of all authors who published three times and who preferred statistical approaches, and so forth. The results are shown in Table 24.5. As shown, statisticians and modelers dominated at each level. Combined they

Table 24.4   Repeat Publication Success in the *APSR* by Method, 1991–2000

	Statistical	Math Modeling	Theory	Qualitative
Number of authors[a]	338	103	99	5
Two times	52	13	8	0
Percentage[b]	15	13	8	0
Three, four, or five times	16	8	4	0
Percentage	5	8	4	0

Source: Authors' count of articles.
[a] Number of authors exceeds the total number of articles in the journal because of co-authorship.
[b] These percentages have been rounded off to the nearest integer.

Table 24.5   Dominant Methods by Tier of Repeat *APSR* Publication Success, 1991–2000

	Three Articles		Four Articles		Five Articles	
	No.	%	No.	%	No.	%
Statistical	18	55	4	57	2	67
Modeling	10	30	2	29	1	33
Theory	5	15	1	14	0	0
Qualitative	0	0	0	0	0	0
Total	33	100	7	100	3	100

Source: Authors' count of articles.
Note: Percentages have been rounded off to the nearest integer.

accounted for 85 percent of all who published articles three or four times and 100 percent of those who published five times. Theorists trailed well behind, and qualitative specialists did not register.

Data Interpretation: Does It Show the Presence of Bias?

How should we interpret the data presented? Why have so very few qualitative studies been published in the *APSR?* On the face of it, it seems unfathomable that, given the sheer volume of high-caliber, qualitative empirical research out there, so little of it would show up in the *Review.* Former *APSR* editor Ada Finifter, in her APSA Web-based response to the Perestroika revolt, shifted the blame to the rest of us for having chosen not to submit our manuscripts to the journal. She wrote: "Any lack of representation of particular subfields or methods results overwhelmingly, if not entirely from self-selection by authors of where to submit their articles."[6] She sarcastically quipped that "an automatic veto is imposed on all non-submitted manuscripts."[7]

Of course it is tempting to just chalk up all of these trends to submission rates, especially if one assumes that the review process is impartial. No submission, no acceptance; end of story. There are two issues here. The first is this: is lack of submission principally to blame for the near absence of qualitative work? The second is this: if abstention has occurred, to what can it be attributed?

Self-selection is undoubtedly a contributing factor to the huge imbalance reported. There are historical reasons that scholars of a certain type have opted not to submit their best work to the *APSR,* reasons having to do with the editorial practices of the journal itself. Those reasons will be treated later. But self-selection is clearly not the sole reason, according to Finifter's own data on submission and acceptance rates. Beginning in 1996–97, the editor broke out analytical categories to facilitate comparisons according to method. Her categories are not equivalent to those used in this study, but there is some overlap.

Articles were divided into five areas: quantitative, formal, formal and quantitative, interpretive/conceptual, and small n. The interpretive/conceptual category, which dominates the normative theory field, seems to refer to nonempirical thought pieces and textual analyses, although that was not made clear. Although the small n category was not explicitly defined, there is little doubt that by default it was intended to refer to qualitative, empirical studies of one case or a handful of cases.[8]

According to the official data, 2 percent or forty-one of the 2042 manuscripts submitted to the *APSR* between August 1995 and August 2000 were of the small n variety. Of those *none* was published by the *Review!*[9] Clearly this was not a problem of self-selection, because forty-one manuscripts had been sent in. If the review process had been unbiased, in light of the overall acceptance rate for the *APSR* at the time of 10.1 percent, we would have expected about four of those manuscripts to be accepted.[10] Our own analysis presented in Table 24.1 found a total of three qualitative studies published by the *APSR* from 1995 through 2000. Naturally the discrepancy can be attributed to differences in the time frames reviewed and to method categorization. But it is sadly ironic that the editor's own analysis delivers an even gloomier assessment of the gross methodological imbalances present in the journal than does ours.

How could the results be so skewed if the review process is, as every former *APSR* editor agrees, rigorous, evenhanded, and objective and if readers are chosen with great care? Potential reviewers are culled from a huge online database of more than sixteen thousand political scientists, and final decisions are made only after extensive consultation with relevant members of the editorial board, who apparently suggest "balanced packages" of reviewers for each manuscript.[11] The editor then selects reviewers "who are writing in similar areas as the manuscript under review," "who have the expertise to review the manuscript," and, as far as can be judged, "can be expected to provide a fair and impartial review that neither favors nor disadvantages the author."[12] The result of this process is supposed to be the selection of appropriate readers who are knowledgeable about the subject material and who apply consistent criteria for assessment. Finifter has said that "reviewers in all fields use similar or comparable standards of evaluation."[13] What, then, is the problem?

One insight can be gleaned from the editor's analysis of the *APSR* data. Finifter's figures revealed a modest imbalance between the proportion of articles submitted and published according to analytical methods. Whereas quantitative pieces were somewhat overrepresented (48 percent of those submitted, 55 percent of those published) nonquantitative articles—which lumped together small n and interpretive/conceptual articles—were somewhat underrepresented (32 percent of those submitted, 25 percent of those published).[14] Note that this grouping disguises the much more serious imbalance afflicting the small n (qualitative) studies compared to all others. Be that as it may, the editor attributed the disproportion she found to two factors: (1) all manuscripts that are completely unsuitable for the *APSR* because they are either advocacy or descriptive pieces happen to belong to the nonquantitative category, and

(2) there is a greater chance that reviewers will question authors' conclusions and interpretations in articles that do not present quantitative data.[15]

The first explanation makes us question what the editor and her reviewers had in mind when they designated pieces "descriptive." Is the term a euphemistic reference to more historical, small *n* studies? At the very least, we must wonder whether some percentage—however small—of the truly analytical qualitative pieces were summarily dropped from consideration because they were deemed too "descriptive." Indeed, in commenting on the disproportionately lower acceptance rates for comparative politics pieces between 1995 and 2000, Finifter said, "The only obvious reason . . . is that reviewers sometimes feel that detailed case studies of single countries that are included in this category are better suited to more specialized comparative politics or area studies journals than to *APSR*."[16] The language is troubling: why are such articles not suited to the *Review?*

The second explanation raises a suspicion that there is an imbalance in the review processes deriving from methodological bias. If a qualitative piece poses an interesting puzzle, has a strong theoretical argument, demonstrates a command of the facts, and applies an appropriate method, why should more questions be raised about its findings? Why shouldn't scholarly peers be able to agree that small *n* studies can clear the bar as easily as can large *n* studies?

There are two plausible hypotheses that could answer this question. The first is that a much more disparate group of peers is repeatedly chosen to review case study research. They may not work in the same subfield, share epistemological beliefs, or deploy similar methodologies, and they can't agree on the merits of a study. Their widely differing assessments leave the editor with sufficient doubts and little choice but to reject the manuscript. Editors are naturally cautious: if they are to make mistakes, they routinely prefer to commit the "type 1 error," where a worthy manuscript is rejected, than a "type 2 error," where a poor manuscript is accepted. Lack of reviewer consensus causes them to lean toward rejection. But this does raise questions. Given the long-term pattern of near-total absence of qualitative work from the pages of the *Review,* why haven't *APSR* editors made more conscientious efforts to assemble like-minded teams of small *n* reviewers? Could they not have dug a little deeper into their vast data troves to find experts who were "on the same page," as it were, much as they repeatedly did when it came to finding reviewers for statistical and formal modeling studies?

The answers to those questions may reside in the second hypothesis. It could be that the review teams *were* homogenous, and that, as past editors have alleged, their standards for quality measurement were more than similar or comparable across fields and subfields; they were identical, the product of long-standing *APSR* norms that subtly or explicitly influenced how most readers approached their materials. And those norms privileged technical methods over nontechnical methods. According to this hypothesis, reviewers were very much reading off the same page; they shared a single-minded attention to and admiration for technique. They took comfort in the precision that comes with the presentation and manipulation of numbers. For them, a Pearson's R, an r^2, beta terms, and T-tests of significance render more reassuring demonstrations of association or causation than do nonnumerical alternatives. They found it easier to concur with those authors whose conclusions were based on hard (authoritative?) data, and therefore recommended publication of such authors' work with fewer questions asked. Conversely, they were distinctly uncomfortable at having to wade through the less precise but by no means less persuasive forms of evidence found within verbal arguments and interpretations, historical research, and structured comparisons. Accordingly they raised more objections.

These reviewers may very well have been subfield experts, and yet may have demonstrated a methodological hostility and intolerance that raises serious doubts about their credibility as reviewers. Should one or more readers be resolute in their belief that a small n study does not and *cannot* pass methodological muster, it matters little whether those readers call themselves Latin Americanists, Asianists, culturalists, peasant specialists, or what have you. In this scenario, the application of similar if not uniform standards to all manuscripts is completely inappropriate, because it stacks the deck against those who do nontechnical, nonmathematical work.

Conversely, uniformity has its distinct advantages for others. Let's return to Tables 24.4 and 24.5 for a moment. Anyone who has repeatedly published in the *APSR* in the span of a decade must be doing something right. On the face of it, these are impressive achievements, even extraordinary. Yet they raise serious questions about bias in the other direction. If over a ten-year period an author has managed to publish, say, four or five times in the *APSR*, as ten political scientists have, that means that the author has successfully landed an article in the *Review* every two to two and a half years. How could that have been possible if everyone faced the prospects of a 10 percent acceptance rate? Has it been a matter of sheer brilliance on the part of these political scientists, has it been luck, or some of both? Or do they face different odds because of the nature of their work and the research communities that assess their scholarship?

Those top ten authors were, as stated previously, either statisticians or modelers, with one exception (a theorist). Of those who published three times within the decade, 85 percent were statisticians or modelers. It is our contention that these mathematicians had an easier time repeating because they operated within tighter-knit communities of methodologically like-minded scholars. Moreover, they could depend on the *APSR* editors to tap those communities repeatedly for empathetic reviewers. Scholars outside of these cohorts were never solicited for reviews because they were "nonspecialists" who could not possibly understand the material, or so the excuse went. The more sophisticated the math, the more imperative it became that *all* those asked to review any given article have the requisite methodological skills. Theoretical and substantive knowledge may also have been relevant, but would have taken second place to technical proficiencies. Here the second hypothesis seems relevant. The obsession with mastery of technique shared by a more homogenous collection of readers may have created a positive bias in favor of the best mathematical political science.

Absent confessions by the editors, we will never know which of the two hypotheses is valid. But if it is the second, the whole notion that the application of consistent criteria—in anything but the most general sense of that term—will somehow impart greater fairness to the review process is wrong. Political science is a hugely diverse discipline. The range of problems, subjects, areas, and countries that are covered, and the range of approaches used, is simply staggering. When it comes to doing high-quality research in our discipline, there are many ways to skin the proverbial cat. Indeed there must be, because the vast range of interesting problems political scientists write about do not invite uniform methodological solutions. Those journals like the *APSR* whose mission is to publish the best research across all fields and subfields of the discipline need to be especially sensitive to that fact. This requires not only the adoption of less narrow and rigid standards of evaluation, but an appreciation of the idea that quality comes in different packages depending on the topic studied and methodological preference. Ada Finifter admitted as much, saying that measures of "quality" could vary by subfield, requiring "*differentially* rigorous evaluations" (emphasis ours).[17] That observation, by her own admission, was never translated into a reformed editorial practice.

Judgments of merit have to respect the diversity of methodological traditions present across subfields by assessing each tradition on its own grounds. For example, small *n* structured comparisons put a premium on case selection and conceptual equivalence across cases to achieve some measure of scientific control. Single case studies stack the deck against themselves by testing hypotheses that are "least likely" to hold within a given country. Process-tracing and path-dependent analyses emphasize timing, sequences, and chains of causality. There are perfectly reasonable ways of sizing these studies up *on their own terms* without having to inappropriately import criteria devised for statisticians or formal modelers.

The Journal versus the Discipline

Then what about those who never bothered to submit their work in the first place? Were they simply not interested in publishing in the *Review?* That would seem absurd. No one would want to avoid earning the enormous status and respect that come with publishing in the flagship journal. Moreover, why would political scientists not want their research to benefit from exposure to the much wider audience of a general-interest journal? It seems equally unlikely that small *n* scholars were simply discouraged by the official rates of acceptance. Many who have not published in the *Review* have turned to other journals with comparably low rates. Year in and year out, purely qualitative

316 DAVID PION-BERLIN AND DAN CLEARY

studies turn up in field-specific journals such as *World Politics, Comparative Politics, International Organization,* and the *International Studies Quarterly.* Acceptance rates for these journals have ranged from 10 percent to 13 percent.[18]

Let us turn the tables on the *APSR* editors for a moment. Let us assume that refusal to submit is a function of a historical editorial bias going back decades and probably of the kinds we have described earlier. If self-selection still plays a role today, it is only because of discriminatory practices of the past that so discouraged qualitative specialists that they simply gave up trying to get articles published in the *APSR.* Collectively, these scholars surmised that their real probability of acceptance was far lower than the average rate of 10 percent. This calculation was especially salient for junior scholars. Given the pressures of the tenure clock, it was more rational for them to submit elsewhere, where the odds were better, than to spend an enormous amount of time on an *APSR* piece that had a slim chance to no chance of acceptance. After a while, the systematic bias caused abstention to take on a life of its own, as word got about the subfields that the *Review* was, for all intents and purposes, "off limits" to a certain group of political scientists. So abstention was the most rational response that qualitative social scientists could have adopted to a journal whose "gates" seemed practically closed to them.

Of course if that group of scholars had constituted a small minority of the profession, their omission from the flagship journal, while objectionable, would not have ruffled so many feathers. But one of the most damaging features of the *Review*'s exclusion is that it flies in the face of the demographics of political science. It is a profession populated by vast numbers of qualitative specialists—a profile that developed decades ago. Even during the heyday of behavioralism, many of the early self-proclaimed "revolutionaries" were an eclectic lot. Though they extolled the scientific virtues of survey research, they were also critical of its ahistorical character and warned of its descent into triviality.[19] At the same time, they were remarkably tolerant of nonquantitative empirical research because they had practiced it themselves.[20] Among those who counted themselves behavioralists during the early 1960s were scholars like David Truman, Robert Dahl, and David Easton, who had achieved acclaim through their landmark qualitative studies and would all become presidents of the APSA. If many of the early revolutionaries were methodologically broader minded, you wouldn't know it from reading the *APSR* during the 1960s. The brand of behavioralism featured in the *Review* was one that had conflated systematic, rigorous methods with quantitative techniques. Beginning in 1962 or thereabouts, statistical studies came to dominate the pages of the *Review,* issue after issue.[21]

By the end of that decade, however, serious challenges to behavioral orthodoxy were being mounted. Behavioralists were taken to task for their scientific arrogance, for being oblivious to the huge political changes swirling about them, for preaching value-free science at a time when values seemed important, and for acting as apologists for the U.S. political system. In 1969 APSA President David Easton declared that the behavioralist era had ended and a postbehavioral era had begun.[22] Apparently news of the revolution's demise never reached those in the editorial offices of the *Review,* who were too busy keeping the fires burning.

Postbehavioralism never amounted to a new revolution, but rather was a lingering testimony to the way in which political scientists had dispersed from the once hegemonic center. The discipline was described as being adrift, fragmented, divided, or situated at separate tables.[23] David Easton would later say, "There are now so many approaches to political research that political science seems to have lost its purpose."[24] Obviously, these descriptions reflected displeasure among some and a nostalgia for the "good old days" when a common sense of mission had unified the profession. But they were also realistic appraisals of a discipline whose demographics, by the 1970s, defied any narrow categorization. Political science was increasingly populated by a huge collection of area studies and international relations specialists whose range of substantive interests and analytical or methodological approaches knew no bounds. Droves of scholars were heading to the Third World to do fieldwork in particular countries, and returning to write up their findings in the form of critical and comparative case study analyses. By the 1980s and into the 1990s, even Americanists were fanning out, bringing us important new insights using historical and institutional modes of inquiry.[25] These methods blossomed alongside others, and yet, once again, one would not have found so much as a clue about that trend in reading the *APSR* during those times. While the discipline was experiencing a methodological diaspora of sorts, the *Review* was busy guarding the mathematical home front. The schism between what political scientists were doing and what the *Review* was publishing had widened further.

That schism should have deeply troubled generations of *APSR* editors. How could their journal uphold its virtuous claim that it represented the very best that the discipline as a whole had to offer if it systematically turned its back on important subpopulations within political science? If editors were wearing methodological blinders, as they contend, if they indeed valued good theoretically informed scholarship regardless of the methodological tools deployed, one would think that somewhere along the line they would have issued a distress call: why are the numbers so appallingly low for qualitative work, and what can be done about that? If succeeding editors had adopted a strategy of recruiting top-flight qualitative manuscripts to correct for the enormous historical disadvantages these methods had suffered at the hands of previous editors, some trend line of improvement would be visible in the data presented in Tables 24.1–24.5, given how much superb qualitative research there has been. But no such trend is visible, and clearly no corrective measures were taken to produce a more balanced product.

Final Thoughts on the Future

This study should remove most doubts about whether there have been methodological imbalances on display in the pages of the *APSR* over long periods of time. Our hypotheses that editorial bias was the culprit are well founded. The production and reproduction of bias began decades ago, and certainly continued throughout the 1990s. What are the chances that these trends will persist into the future? Or is change visible on the horizon?

John Kingdon has suggested that political agendas are altered when there is a fortuitous confluence of problems, policies, and politics. There must be an accumulation of unattended grievances of sufficient magnitude to cause widespread concern; policy advocates must be ready with the right prescriptions; and leaders must sense that the time is right to opportunistically seize upon those prescriptions. These elements develop independent of one another but sometimes converge so that "solutions become joined to problems, and both of them are joined to favorable political forces."[26] Are we at such a junction in our discipline, a junction where real change can occur within the APSR and perhaps within other political science journals?

Methodological bias has accumulated for decades, and the patience of those who have been discriminated against has worn thin. "Mr. Perestroika" emerged in October of 2000, and his manifesto for change struck a resonant chord with many of the disenfranchised within political science. Shortly thereafter, a new editor was appointed to the APSR. These developments had the makings of a useful convergence. On the Perestroika list serve, ideas (including those expressed by us) were circulated widely about what should be done to reform the APSR and the institutions associated with it. We argued that because the disenfranchised have been discouraged by historical editorial practices, they could not be expected to submit articles to the APSR unless there were clear signs that the journal was prepared to change its policies first.[27]

In response to our plea and the pleas of other Perestroikans that the new APSR editor, Lee Sigelman, make the first move, Sigelman delivered a message to the Perestroika list detailing a new vision for the journal and a series of concrete proposals he would implement upon assuming editorial responsibilities (his message was revised and later published in the March 2002 issue of the APSR). Sigelman admitted that he had come on board amid "widespread expressions of discontent among political scientists, discontent directed . . . at the APSR itself." He acknowledged that complaints about the APSR had taken on a "special resonance" with the emergence of the Perestroika movement. He stated that the Review has not reflected nearly as well as it should have the "rich, theoretical, methodological, and substantive variety" our discipline has to offer.[28] To remedy that situation he appointed a new editorial board that he believes reflects the discipline's diversity, and charged that board with the mission of encouraging a much wider array of submissions. Other proposals include expanding the pool of reviewers, allowing authors to recommend readers, sending reviews to the other readers to make the process more transparent to all, lifting the requirement that all accepted manuscripts receive three positive recommendations, and making page limits more flexible to allow for longer qualitative pieces.[29]

Since that time there have been marked changes in the *APSR*'s methodological profile. From September 2002 to February 2004, a total of seventy articles appeared in the *Review*. By our count, ten of those, equal to 14 percent of the total, have been purely qualitative in orientation. These articles have used illustrative data or case study, interpretive, historical, or constructivist analyses. This showing represents a substantial increase over the historical trends. It also substantiates the hunch that with real changes in editorial and review practices, it is relatively easy for a top-flight journal to find and publish high-caliber qualitative work. Of course plenty of room for improvement remains, because the great majority of empirical pieces are still mathematical in orientation. But we are pleased that the Perestroika movement has had a positive impact on our flagship journal. The *APSR* is beginning to look more like the discipline it is supposed to represent.

Unfortunately, we cannot yet say the same for the journals of two of the key regional political science associations: the *American Journal of Political Science* (*AJPS*) and the *Journal of Politics* (*JOP*). The *AJPS* is the official journal of the Midwest Political Science Association, and the *JOP* is the official journal of the Southern Political Science Association. Past and present editors of these journals have not practiced what they preach. They insist that their publications are, and always have been, open to all kinds of political science without regard to methodological preference. They point us to their official Web sites, which state that their journals seek "manuscripts that make outstanding contributions to scholarly knowledge about notable theoretical concerns, puzzles, or controversies in any subfield of political science" (*AJPS*), or that they "strive to maintain a balanced representation of all areas within political science" (*JOP*). But Gregory Kasza (see his chapter of this book) and Ron Libby have surveyed articles from the *AJPS* and the *JOP*, respectively, over the course of decades and have found extreme methodological biases against articles by researchers who use qualitative methods that persist to this day.[30]

In response to a request for new editorial guidelines that would directly encourage submissions of nonmathematical scholarship and that would broaden the pool of potential manuscript reviewers, the *JOP* editor stated that the journal exhibits no bias and that nothing more needs to be done.[31] The editors of the *AJPS* announced the selection of an editorial board that they claim signals "a new openness" given the diverse fields of scholarship represented by its members. But a careful look at the methods these board members employ and the publication outlets they choose for their own work raises questions about how much the *AJPS* is likely to be renovated. Based on methodological self-descriptions and journal choices, forty of the forty-four board members resort to purely or mainly statistical and formal modeling methods, two are nonempirical theorists, and two are predominantly qualitative scholars. The board members are also extremely narrow in their choice of publication outlets. Despite the fact that the *AJPS* professes to be representative of all political science fields, only very rarely have any of its board members published in the four leading journals of comparative politics and international relations.[32]

To insist that the *AJPS* and the *JOP* really are methodologically impartial—even in the face of overwhelming evidence to the contrary—is a lot like insisting that Fox News is "fair and balanced." The skeptical viewing public doubts the latter message, and the discerning journal reader is unmoved by false claims of these journals' "openness." The *AJPS* and *JOP* editors must make real, not cosmetic, reforms if their journals are ever to—for the first time in literally decades—become venues for the rich diversity of approaches that is political science.

As for the *APSR,* positive editorial changes may indicate that we are at a kind of critical juncture in the evolution of the flagship journal and its relation to the discipline. If this juncture is indeed critical, the journal should establish a new and lasting trajectory of editorial practices. Because editors come and go, there must be some mechanism for ensuring that today's innovations will become tomorrow's standards. The current editor may very well pass the baton on to someone who is equally committed to making the journal more representative, but he may not. Policies must be institutionalized if they are to last more than a fleeting moment in the *APSR*'s long history. As a hedge against future reversals, it may be advisable for the *APSR* editorial board and the APSA Council itself to go on the record as endorsing the current practices as official journalistic policy that is not subject to change by executive fiat. Should the journal revert to its former practices, the APSA members should be free to redirect their dues to the purchase of some other political science journal. In the final analysis, it will fall upon those "outside the tent" to serve as watchdogs over those who are inside. It is the dissenters from methodological hegemony whose interests are at stake, and it is they who will have to continue to insist that the discipline's flagship journal publish the best that we all have to offer.

Notes

The authors thank Martin Johnson for statistical guidance offered in the preparation of this chapter.

1. Ada W. Finifter, "The 1997–98 Sail on the Flagship *APSR,*" *PS: Political Science and Politics* 31 (December 1998): 897.

2. Ada W. Finifter, *"APSR* Editor Responds," *The American Political Science Association Online,* February 28, 2001, http://www.apsanet.org/new/planning/APSReditor.cfm.

3. Finifter, *PS: Political Science and Politics* 31 (December 1998): 900–901.

4. Richard K. Betts, "APSA Publications Committee Discussion of *APSR,*" memo to APSA Publications Committee, March 15, 1991, 4.

5. Bonnie Honig, communication on the Perestroika list serve, November 7, 2000, perestroika_glasnost_warmhome-owner@egroups.com.

6. Finifter, *"APSR* Editor Responds."

7. Ibid.

8. We prefer our categorization to that of the former *APSR* editor, though there is obvious overlap. Most troubling is her interpretive/conceptual category, which

seems to be completely nonempirical but is not explicitly defined that way. Finifter refers to articles in this category as "textual analyses using no quantitative data or formal analysis." See Ada Finifter, "Report of the Editor of the *APSR*, 1996–97," *PS: Political Science and Politics* 29 (December 1996): 760. But it would seem as if these are thought pieces even though some are lumped within the American, comparative, and international relations fields. By suggesting that these are the nonquantitative studies Finifter gives the impression that far more qualitative empirical work has been published than is the case.

9. Ada Finifter, "*American Political Science Review* Editor's Report for 1999–2000," *PS: Political Science and Politics* 33 (December 2000): 925.

10. Ibid., 922.

11. Ada Finifter, "Report of the Editor of the *American Political Science Review, 1995–96*," *PS: Political Science and Politics* 29 (December 1996): 762.

12. Ibid., 762.

13. Ibid., 761.

14. Finifter, "*APSR* Editor's Report for 1999–2000," 925.

15. Ibid., 922.

16. Ibid.

17. Finifter, "Report of the Editor, 1995–96," 761.

18. Fenton Marton and Robert Goehlert, eds. *Getting Published in Political Science Journals: A Guide for Authors, Editors, and Librarians,* 5th ed. (Washington, DC: American Political Science Association, 2001), 20, 45, 53, 149.

19. Robert Dahl, "The Behavioral Approach in Political Science: Epitaph for a Monument to a Successful Protest," *American Political Science Review* 55 (December 1961): 763–72.

20. James Farr, "Remembering the Revolution: Behavioralism in American Political Science," in James Farr, John S. Dryzek, and Stephen T. Leonard, eds., *Political Science in History: Research Programs and Political Traditions* (Cambridge: Cambridge University Press, 1995), 198–224.

21. It is ironic that if the aforementioned icons of political science had tried to get published in the *APSR* by submitting in article form the kind of research that had won them acclaim, they probably would have been turned down—and perhaps they were.

22. David Easton, "The New Revolution in Political Science," *American Political Science Review* 60: 1051–61.

23. Heinz Eulau, "Drift of a Discipline," *American Behavioral Scientist* 21 (1977): 3–10; Gabriel Almond, "Separate Tables: Schools and Sects in Political Science," *PS: Political Science and Politics* 21 (Autumn 1988): 828–42.

24. David Easton, "Political Science in the United States: Past and Present," in James Farr and Raymond Seidelman, eds. *Discipline and History: Political Science in the United States* (Ann Arbor: University of Michigan Press, 1993), 299–300. He added that we are in an era of a more "relaxed understanding of science," in which nonmathematical but certainly scientific, rigorous, and sophisticated modes of analysis occupy vast portions of the discipline (305).

25. Stephen Skowronek, *Building a New American State: The Expansion of National Administrative Capacities, 1877–1920* (Cambridge: Cambridge University Press, 1982). See also various issues of the journal *Studies in American Political Development.*

26. John Kingdon, *Agendas, Alternatives, and Public Policies* (Boston: Little, Brown, 1984), 21.

27. Lee Sigelman, e-mail message to the Perestroika list serve, May 10, 2001, perestroika_glastnost_warmhome@yahoogroups.com.

28. Lee Sigelman, "Notes from the New Editor," *American Political Science Review* 96 (March 2002): ix.

29. Ibid., x.

30. Ron Libby, "Methodological Bias in the *Journal of Politics,* 1993–2002," unpublished report released on the Perestroika list serve in May 2003 and available from the author.

31. William Jacoby, editor of the *Journal of Politics,* e-mail message to the David Pion-Berlin, October 1, 2002.

32. Results based on a June 2003 unpublished study by David Pion-Berlin of *AJPS* board members. Pion-Berlin examined board members' Web pages and vitas, and also found their journal articles through online Current Content searches. The four leading journals in comparative politics and international relations are *Comparative Politics, World Politics, International Organization,* and *International Studies Quarterly.*

CHAPTER 25

The *APSR* in the Perestroika Era

Lee Sigelman

Many of those with whom I talk about the *American Political Science Review* (*APSR*) assume that I must feel cursed to have become editor during a period of widespread discontent with intellectual currents in the discipline, the governing institutions of the profession (ranging from individual departments through the APSA), and, perhaps most pointedly, the *APSR* itself. This discontent took on a special resonance during the Perestroika era, but it is well to bear in mind that, in the words of Robert Salisbury (2001, 767), "complaints about *APSR* . . . have been perennial features of life among political scientists."

Rather than considering myself cursed by the timing of my editorship, I see myself as blessed by the unique opportunity it has presented to respond constructively to the challenges that our discipline faces and to make common cause with many in the Perestroika movement. In my "Notes from the (New) Editor" in the March 2002 issue of the *APSR,* I addressed some of these challenges and discussed the role I hoped the *APSR* would play in coming years (Sigelman 2002). Here I draw on those notes and go on to present an interim "progress report" a year and a half into my term as editor.

Some Perspectives on the Mission of the *APSR*

I begin with the proposition that political science is hardly a "discipline" at all in the sense of being a distinct branch of learning. Instead, it is a crazy quilt of borrowings from history, philosophy, law, sociology, psychology, economics, public administration, policy studies, area studies, international studies, civics, and a variety of other sources. Any real coherence in political science exists, if at all, only at the broadest conceptual level, in the form of our widely shared interest in power, the "authoritative allocation of values for society," "who gets what, when, how," and the like.

This overriding intellectual diversity endows political science with vibrancy, energy, and openness to new and often challenging perspectives. Even so, I sense that in many ways we have become less of a discipline over the years. When I entered the profession some three decades ago, virtually everyone seemed to be reading and discussing certain contemporary canonical works (those of Robert Dahl, David Easton, Gabriel Almond and Sidney Verba, Anthony Downs, Theodore Lowi, and Peter Bachrach and Morton Baratz, among others). I am hard pressed to think of many equivalents today. These days it is harder than ever to find a center of intellectual gravity in our discipline. More and more we are a confederation of narrowly defined and loosely connected, or even disconnected, specializations. Our heightened specialization is further fragmenting our already disjointed discipline, to the extent that most of us have little knowledge, understanding, or appreciation of what our colleagues in other subfields are doing.

For many years, the most widely expressed criticisms of the *APSR* in particular were "It doesn't publish the kind of work that interests me," "It's biased against my kind of work," "I have no idea what most of those articles are even about," and "I don't even open it when it arrives." Defenders countered that the *APSR* was doing a good job of publishing the best papers that were submitted to it, and that the problem, if there was one, was that those who felt aggrieved rarely submitted their work to the *APSR,* thereby creating a vicious circle. A second line of defense was that there is nothing unique to political science about the fact that those in one subfield neither understand nor appreciate what those in other subfields are doing. This, it was said, is an inevitable byproduct of specialization and other aspects of disciplinary "progress," not specifically an *APSR* problem.

Over the years, and especially in the years immediately before I became editor, the contents of the *APSR* were more diverse than many critics acknowledged. Still, I found it impossible not to agree that the rich theoretical, methodological, and substantive variety of our discipline was not being reflected nearly as well as it should have been in the pages of our premier research journal. At the same time, I also found it impossible not to agree that the problem of the vicious circle was real. That did not mean, though, that it had to be accepted as inevitable. Moreover, even though the increasing divergence of theoretical perspectives and analytical techniques and the proliferation of specialized vocabularies were, to some extent, signs of advancement and pluralism, they were undeniably impeding broader communication. Some of those with whom I talked were more concerned about this than others were, but no one thought that, as a discipline, we were doing as much as we should to make our ideas accessible to one another, let alone to others.

My goal as the incoming editor, then, was to try to make the *APSR* into an important vehicle for overcoming this isolation, for building and sustaining a sense of intellectual community among political scientists. I wanted the *APSR* to be the showcase for the best research from the wide array of theoretical orientations, substantive foci, and methodological approaches that comprise our discipline. I looked forward to a time when opening up the *APSR* when it arrived would give political scientists a sense of invigoration about all the interesting work their colleagues were doing. I wanted the *APSR* to move as far and as quickly as possible in that direction, by publishing a broad representation of the very best work being done throughout political science and by enhancing the likelihood that this work would actually be read.

The obvious question was how to go about trying to translate that mission into reality.

Steps Taken

The first task, and in many ways the main task, was conversational. Immediately upon being named the incoming editor (a year before assuming the editorship itself), I began talking with people, the great majority of whom I had never met, to let them know what I had in mind and to solicit their advice about goals, priorities, procedures, pitfalls, resources, people, or virtually anything else. Some of these conversations were face-to-face, others electronically mediated; some were one-on-one, others in group settings. Among other things, I contacted every one of the APSA's organized sections and status groups to solicit suggestions, spoke at dozens of gatherings of various sorts, made extensive use of e-mail to broaden the circle further, and posted to the Perestroika discussion list. The outpouring of advice I received in these venues proved immensely valuable, and the responses I received when I tried to articulate the mission described earlier were gratifying. Many Perestroikans, in a willing suspension of disbelief, volunteered their advice and assistance, and these offers were gratefully accepted. On the Perestroika discussion list, I came to be referred to as "the well-intentioned new editor of the *APSR*"—a description I chose to interpret as a compliment even though I recognized that it was often intended as a polite put-down of what was seen as a quixotic effort.

An early priority was to assemble a slate of *APSR* editorial board nominees for approval by the APSA Executive Council. The editorial board must be composed of productive scholars to whom the editor can confidently turn for wise counsel, and I was especially determined that the board should reflect the diversity of the discipline. I consulted widely and received scores of suggestions. The ultimate result was a board of forty-four members, all brand-new to service on the editorial board. This is an exceptionally accomplished and diverse group with whom I am honored to be associated, and both individually and collectively they have more than borne out my initial confidence in their wisdom, energy, and commitment. By their very presence on the board, these forty-four members symbolize a genuine desire to receive a wider array of submissions than have come to the *APSR* in the past and a determination to conduct a fair, thorough, and timely review process.

Six editorial board members (four drawn from the major subfields of the discipline and two at large) agreed to serve as an executive committee. In designating an executive committee, my intent was twofold. First, this would be a group of manageable size to which I could turn for advice or other forms of assistance on matters involving procedures, policies, and the like. Second, and perhaps more important, although I expected to receive a great deal of feedback from authors, reviewers, readers, and others, I considered it appropriate for the operation of the editorial office and my own performance to be subject to periodic review. The executive committee is performing that review function. At this writing, the first scheduled review is still a few months off, but at that time the executive committee will assess the fairness, competence, and timeliness of the review process and of my decisions, and will offer any recommendations that follow from its assessment.

After sifting through numerous ideas for procedural reforms—many of which emanated from all the conversations mentioned earlier—we put in place several modifications of the review process intended to open it up and make it more transparent. We tried in several ways to expand the already large pool from which reviewers were drawn. For example, we began inviting those who submit a paper to suggest the names of appropriate reviewers of their paper. We also began sending copies of all the reviews of a paper to all the reviewers, along with a copy of my decision letter (all rendered anonymous, of course). The rationale underlying these changes was that increasing the transparency of the review process would boost authors' and reviewers' confidence in the process and their sense of involvement in it. Note that this rationale involved an element of risk, for making the process more transparent had the potential to undermine confidence if people didn't like what they were seeing; I am reminded of the old saw about the dangers of watching sausage being made. So far, though, the results of this greater transparency have been extremely positive.

In my conversations in various forums during the year before I assumed the editorship, an oft-voiced criticism was that work published in the *APSR* tended not to be intellectually exciting or venturesome; descriptions such as "narrow," "conventional," "mainstream," and "boring" were common. In response, I ventured the opinion that getting a paper accepted by the *APSR* might often be something like the process involved in winning the Olympic gold medal in figure skating. That is, what seemed to matter was that one not make a major mistake, so the best strategy was to play it safe by not trying anything risky. That problem was that a paper that received two genuinely enthusiastic reviews and one decidedly negative one could well be more interesting and important than a competent paper that had nothing seriously "wrong" with it. Thus I promised to try to diversify the *APSR*'s portfolio by investing in some "speculative" or "growth" stocks along with the normal "blue chips," that is, to be open to work that was new, different, and perhaps too controversial or too far outside the mainstream to receive unanimously positive reviews.

Another aspect of the "narrow" and "boring" charge stemmed from the manner in which authors were presenting their research rather than from the nature of the research per se. Responding to that problem, I challenged authors to communicate to a broader audience than they were probably used to addressing:

> It is the obligation of authors to make their research accessible to prospective readers, not by "dumbing it down" but by effectively conveying what they are trying to find out and why this quest is so worthwhile. . . . The real

key lies in careful editing and rewriting designed to open lines of communication rather than to close them. It is not reasonable to expect researchers who use complex formal or statistical models to conduct tutorials on their methods as a part of reporting their work; or to hold those whose research focuses on a certain nation or a certain political thinker responsible for introducing the rest of us to the most basic aspects of their subject matter before turning to the specific issues of concern; or, more generally, to require researchers to eschew all but plain, simple English. Moreover, it is naive to expect that . . . those who are untrained in formal or statistical modeling will suddenly become avid and knowledgeable consumers of the technical portions of a statistical or formal presentation, or that those who had previously shown little or no interest in a certain region or thinker will suddenly yearn to master the subtlest nuances thereof. But it is neither unreasonable nor naive to insist at the very least that as political scientists we can and should clearly communicate to a broad range of other political scientists what we are trying to do and why it matters. (Sigelman 2001, 2002)

In deciding whether a paper should be published in the *APSR,* I have made it a habit to ask whether the authors did everything they legitimately could to broaden its accessibility and appeal. Generally I have concluded that they didn't, so I have prodded them to spell out very clearly at the outset what their basic research question is and why it is so interesting and important that readers who might otherwise ignore their analysis should instead invest their time in it. To do that, I have encouraged authors to reach out to a diverse audience of potential readers who cannot be assumed to have specialized knowledge of their subject matter, and then to come back at the end of the paper to the questions that motivated the analysis in the first place. I have been disheartened that such prodding on my part was necessary, but I have been gratified by the response of the authors and by the consequent improvements in their papers.

Other pertinent changes have included applying our forty-five-page limit on manuscripts flexibly in order to make publication in the *APSR* a more realistic prospect for those who do qualitative, "thick-descriptive," or case study–based research; making more sparing use of "revise and resubmit" invitations, which are now confined to situations in which I am confident that if the authors implement a relatively narrow and specific set of revisions, the revised paper would indeed warrant publication in the *APSR;* using my "Notes from the Editor" in each issue to provide sneak previews of articles in order to tempt readers to look at work to which they might not otherwise pay attention; and yes, putting striking colors and attractive images on the cover. (As a student of symbolic politics, I was especially pleased to have a peace symbol adorn the first such cover.)

Some Early Returns

The first sign of progress that I hoped and expected to see after becoming editor was a greater volume of submissions. Having more promising papers to consider would itself be a good thing, but I also hoped that an enhanced flow of manuscripts would bring us more papers from parts of the discipline that had been underrepresented in the *APSR*'s pages. My expectation that we would begin to receive more submissions was based on the efforts that I, the members of the editorial board, and many others were taking to make it known far and wide that we were eager to receive more papers than the *APSR* had gotten in the past, that we were working to ensure that the review process would run as it should, and that we aspired to publish the best article-length work across the full range of our substantively, theoretically, and methodologically diverse discipline.

This expectation was fulfilled beyond my most optimistic expectations. From September 2001 through August 2002, my first year as editor, the *APSR* received 56 percent more submissions than it had the year before. This surge in submissions wasn't a one-year wonder: at this writing, midway through year two, submissions are up *another* 15 percent or so.

A major goal, of course, was to achieve greater diversity in the manuscripts we received. In this regard, it would have been unrealistic to expect wholesale changes in the short run. Suspicions and habits built up over the course of many years could hardly be overcome simply by the brave words and good intentions of a new editor and editorial board, and even a sudden surge of submissions from a previously underrepresented subfield could be offset by the continuing or enhanced flow of submissions from another field. That achieving this goal was going to be a longer-term project came through clearly at the end of our first year, when we classified the papers we had received. Categorized in terms of analytic approach (quantitative, formal, interpretive/conceptual, or "small n"), these papers closely resembled those that had been submitted in the recent past. However, some early signs of change could be gleaned from the substantive distribution of submitted papers—and in particular from the declining dominance of submissions about American politics. (This does not mean that the number of American politics–focused submissions declined. Because the total number of submitted manuscripts increased sharply, the absolute number of American politics papers increased even while their proportion of the total was dropping.)

We also made a concerted effort to speed up the review process, and in spite of the start-up status of our office, the disruptions we experienced because of the September 11 attacks and the anthrax scare, and the unprecedentedly large number of submissions we received, this effort met with success. We generally managed to get submitted manuscripts out for review within a day of receiving them; our reviewers typically met or bettered the target dates we assigned; and we kept the process running expeditiously at the decision stage, too. As a consequence, our median turn-around time was just thirty-nine workdays from the day a paper arrived through the day I signed the decision letter.

A key question is whether certain types of papers fared better than others. The answer is that so far, rejection rates have varied very little across papers representing different approaches to and subfields of political science. Rejection has been no less likely for papers representing the approaches and the subfields that are often assumed to enjoy "most favored" status at the *APSR* (formal and quantitative papers and those focused on American politics) than it has been for other papers. Indeed, if anything, the "batting average" of papers from supposedly favored approaches and fields has been lower than that of other papers, though it would be unwise to make much of these minor differences. The only difference that really stood out was that, relative to the papers we received during the year, those that were accepted for publication substantially *over*-represented interpretive/conceptual submissions and *under*-represented quantitative and formal ones.

Conclusion

Now in its ninety-seventh year, the *APSR* is very much a work in progress. During the short period in which I have been editor, I think considerable progress has been made in some important respects (but then I would, wouldn't I?). In some other respects, progress has proven frustratingly, but not surprisingly, slow, but I hope and trust that the progress that has been made will carry over into those areas as well.

References

Salisbury, Robert. 2001. "Current Criticism of APSA Is Nothing New." *PS: Political Science and Politics* 34 (December): 767.

Sigelman, Lee. 2001. "Foreword." In *Style Manual for Political Science,* rev. ed., 5–8. Washington, DC: APSA Committee on Publications.

Sigelman, Lee. 2002. "Notes from the (New) Editor." *American Political Science Review* 96 (March): viii–xvi.

CHAPTER 26

Inventing *Perspectives on Politics*

Jennifer Hochschild

The invention of *Perspectives on Politics* provides a small but tidy example of John Kingdon's classic model of the politics of change in *Agendas, Alternatives, and Public Policies:* problem, policy, and political streams came together in a brief window of opportunity, helped along by some savvy policy entrepreneurs and political brokers. As a result, an organizationally dense institution broke with its usual practice of incremental change and moved in a new direction. We do not yet know if a second classic model, Frank Baumgartner and Bryan Jones's theory of punctuated equilibria, will obtain in this case. If it does, the journal has begun a process that is developing a momentum, institution, constituency, and equilibrium of its own that will change the discipline of political science.[1]

Origins of *Perspectives*

In the three years after 1998, a vague dissatisfaction about the APSA that had been bubbling among its members under the surface for a while came sharply into view. An array of actors understood the problem in different terms and initially proposed different solutions to it. However, one policy proposal that had seemed infeasible—that a new APSA journal be created—suddenly became a realistic option, and it was soon discovered to respond to many of the particular forms of the general dissatisfaction. None of this was automatic; matching the problem and the policy solution required a string of actors both in official positions of responsibility in the association and in unofficial positions of considerable influence. But it happened, and the APSA has a new journal, *Perspectives on Politics*. It remains to be seen whether the journal will in fact resolve the dissatisfaction, in all of its disparate and even contradictory versions, or whether the cycle must eventually begin again. But in the meantime, the old equilibrium has been broken, and a new one is being formed and consolidated.

The APSA office first officially noted frustration in analyzing the results of a survey of members and former members that was conducted in July 1998.

Although response rates were very low, so the validity of the results could be (and was) questioned, the survey revealed important concerns. Over two-fifths of the current members who responded, and half of the former members who responded, expressed displeasure with the *American Political Science Review* (*APSR*); it headed the list of APSA activities and endeavors with which respondents were unhappy.[2] In the open-ended section of the survey, respondents criticized the *APSR* for being "too narrow, too specialized and methodological, and too removed from politics," in the words of the report of the results.[3] People wrote that it "'covers one small corner of the discipline,'" that it is "'virtually useless for my teaching preparations and research specializations,'" and that it is not "'reflective of the range of research methods and approaches in the discipline.'" (Others were more positive about the *APSR*, noting its increasing methodological and substantive diversity and praising the book review section.)

The report on the survey raised questions for the association to address. With regard to "each . . . publication: . . . could it operate more effectively, could it encompass a broader array of intellectual interests that fall under the purview of political science? . . . We should also ask what is missing that ought appropriately to be offered by APSA. . . . In particular, we might ask ourselves whether . . . the Association . . . is too narrow in its intellectual orientations." The report concluded that "one function of a scholarly society is to set and sustain intellectual standards—a task of particular relevance to the leading journal of the profession."

Despite these suggestions, not much happened with regard to the APSA publications portfolio during 1998 and early 1999. The issue came up several times during the presidencies of Kent Jennings (September 1997 through August 1998) and Matthew Holden (September 1998 through August 1999), and the Administrative Committee and other groups discussed several models for a new journal.[4] But the association was facing budgetary problems and the prospect of a much larger crisis if membership (and thus revenue from dues) declined and costs continued to rise, so no one thought it feasible to consider the expensive undertaking of starting a new journal.

But suddenly the latent dissatisfactions surfaced more urgently. Sven Steinmo of the University of Colorado at Boulder had started a small e-mail campaign in 1998, calling on political scientists to "take back the *APSR*"; he was elected to the APSA Council in 1999 on that platform. On the Council he found, to his surprise, "enormous diversity [and] lots of sympathy for my idea," including that of the new president, Robert Keohane.[5] In September 1999, Keohane appointed a Strategic Planning Committee (SPC), to be chaired by Paul Beck of Ohio State University. The committee was guided by a "Draft Design for a Strategic Planning Process," which had been written earlier by the APSA's executive director at that time, Cathy Rudder. Rudder justified a strategic planning process in terms of the dissatisfaction and lack of knowledge revealed by the 1998 survey, the worrisome budget trajectory, and large changes in society. As she wrote: "Longer-term trends of generational change, the changing environment in higher education, the possibilities offered by the Internet, and globalization of political science . . . present challenges but also offer exciting opportunities for our future."[6] Keohane explained his support similarly: "This proposal was motivated in part by dissatisfaction with APSA's publications, as well as by a general view that any organization needs, periodically, to examine itself in a long-term perspective."[7]

The SPC was asked, among other things, "to make recommendations on the most pressing issues and critical choices that must be made, including those pertaining to . . . publications." It worked throughout the year, frequently publicizing its developing arguments and seeking responses from APSA members. As *PS* reported, "There has been a remarkable level of member participation in strategic planning in focus group . . . , Hyde Park sessions . . . , in print and email submissions to the relevant committees, in email discussion groups, and even the public press."[8] Its report to the Council in August 2000, "Planning Our Future," did not recommend creation of a new journal.[9] The SPC did, however, find "problems with the *APSR* that . . . are sufficiently worrisome as to suggest corrective actions be taken at this time." These included lack of theoretical and methodological breadth, research that is "so highly specialized that it is inaccessible and unappealing to the general disciplinary readership," and the fact that it is "falling behind" technologically, especially with regard to electronic publishing.

The SPC made several recommendations to address these problems, mainly urging "more space for the publication of papers" through electronic publication of articles, as well as giving readers access to peripherals such as data and archives. It also urged the association to "provide a venue for high quality peer-reviewed essays that function to integrate cutting edge research for a broad readership." It considered starting a separate journal to include book reviews, review essays, and integrative articles, but rejected the idea on the grounds of expense and its preference for moving toward electronic publication.

Nevertheless, at least some members of the SPC "liked the idea" of a new journal that was about to be proposed by the Publications Committee. Paul Beck said later when he presented the SPC report to the APSA Council, "I voiced support for the idea of a new journal," he said, "feeling that I was fairly representing what the SPC's sentiments would be in this new situation."[10] As a participant now recalls the situation, "The impetus [for a new journal] came from the SPC and they were responding to the widespread feeling that the discipline was suffering from the effects of over-specialization" (private communication with author, August 12, 2002).

Inventing *Perspectives*

While the SPC was considering whether an electronic *APSR* would solve the problems now recognized by most of the people involved, the Publications Committee was moving in a different direction. Chaired by Bert Rockman of Ohio State University, it proposed at the same August 2000 Council meeting that the APSA start a new journal. After much discussion of the focus, feasibility, and timing of this endeavor, the Council unanimously approved a motion reading:

> The APSA will publish expanded book reviews and more integrative essays no later than January 2003 in a form—electronic and/or print, in an existing or new publication—to be decided. An ad hoc Publications Implementation Committee, appointed by the President and approved by the Council will be established to recommend to the Council plans to carry out this resolution. The committee will report to the Council at its next meeting, April 21, 2001, and will have a completed plan in place for Council approval in time for its August 29, 2001 meeting.

The minutes recording this motion gloss it immediately with this: "By 'integrative essays' the Council has in mind both essays that review the literature in an area and articles that are less specialized than our normal research and span larger parts of the discipline. The latter might also involve the application of political science to questions of public policy."[11]

The minutes of the Council meeting at which this action took place are informative (and thoroughly daunting to a new editor!) about the array of views on what the new journal should, and should not, do. Setting aside financial and technological questions, members wanted a new journal to give sufficient attention to policy concerns, debated whether the association's journals should be set in competition with one another by giving APSA members an option on subscriptions, sought to ensure that the new journal would expand the number of book reviews and review essays offered, encouraged broad integrative essays, looked for ways to expand readership beyond APSA members (or even political scientists), searched for ways to make the new journal attractive to teachers and practitioners, queried the effects of the new journal on *PS*, and raised the specter of unintended consequences for the *APSR*. The whole issue was then passed to the Publications Implementation Committee (PIC), to be chaired by Helen Milner of Columbia University.

By this point, the problem, policy, and political streams were converging, with the assistance of some entrepreneurs and brokers. The general problem—disaffection from the APSA and dissatisfaction with the *APSR*—was widely recognized. Few people, at least among the vocal actors who have left a record, disagreed that the problem was real and legitimate and both needed and deserved a serious response. The 1998 survey and Steinmo's unofficial e-mail campaign had brought the problem to the surface, but they were catalysts more than causes; something else would probably have generated the same activity had they not existed.

Possibilities within the policy stream were also converging on some sort of new journal as a critical element of the solution to the problem. As one central figure wrote, "The big debate in 2000 was not whether to have such a journal—there was almost unanimity on this—but whether it should be all-electronic."[12] Some uncertainty persisted; views on the record about what was needed ranged from "a movement . . . to disestablish the *APSR* journal from the Association"[13] to adding pages to the *APSR*. But the Council's resolution did demonstrate a big step toward consolidating a policy response.

The political stream that made this response possible included several elements: pressure from increasingly restive (and dues-paying!) members, intimations of a way to finance publication of a new print journal without unduly straining the APSA budget, willingness to consider using additional funds from the endowment or the Trust and Development Fund if needed, a shared perception of the need to take and to be seen taking decisive action, genuine excitement about the intellectual possibilities of a new journal, and skillful leadership by committee chairs, association staff, and a string of presidents.

The political stream received a big surge from the emergence soon after the 2000 Council meeting of the Perestroika movement. An anonymous "Mr. Perestroika" sent a "manifesto" to a small number of political scientists, and it spread rapidly through the profession. The *New York Times* wrote about "these Internet guerillas who have been fomenting revolt. . . . Their target? The leaders of their professional organization . . . and its journal."[14] Rogers Smith, then of Yale University, wrote an "Open Letter" that had collected over 225 signatories (including myself) by the time it was published in *PS* in December 2000. It urged various changes in the *APSR* to make it more responsive to an array of methods or epistemological frameworks and more attentive to "the great, substantive political questions that actually intrigue many APSA members, as well as broader intellectual audiences." It also called for "pursuing the suggestions both for an electronic *APSR* and a separate 'book reviews' journal" but pointed out that "we, the undersigned, do not represent . . . any consensus on just what should be done."[15] Sven Steinmo published a commentary in December 2000 pointing to the same problems but noting that "while there is a great deal of agreement about the problem, there is little agreement about what to do about this problem." He suggested several solutions, adding that he was "not enthusiastic" about "a separate book review journal" for fear that it "might simply be seen as 'second tier,' . . . [and] could allow the *APSR* to become even narrower." He continued, however, that "in defense of the proposal, taking the book reviews out of the *APSR* could allow for more space and thereby longer, and more different, articles."[16]

By the fall of 2000, there was a new, energetic, and voluble list serve for people interested in the concerns motivating Perestroika. Rogers Smith wrote in September 2000 (on a different list serve) about the difficulty of "get[ting] non-quantitative empirical work . . . published in some top political science journals" and the fact that "some departments value publications in those places almost to the exclusion of all else."[17] A few months later, a participant on the Perestroika-Glasnost list serve reported that she had accepted a nomination as vice president of the APSA and would "keep pushing for more democratization and change in both the major journals and in the national association."[18] Within a single week in February 2001, a range of suggestions for APSA journals were proffered and debated on the Perestroika list serve. They included the following:

- "a two-journal format, one stressing work advancing formal/ quantitative technical rigor, one stressing work of substantive interest to a wide audience";
- "choice of journals. . . . If APSA members are permitted to vote with their subscriptions, the results will change the universe of journals very dramatically";
- "subject . . . the *APSR* . . . to a quota system during a given length of time . . . after which we would hope that it had 'learned' non-discriminatory practices";
- "put the book reviews in *PS*";
- "breakup by creating multiple *APSR* flavors . . . into an *APSR A, B, C, D*, etc. [which would create a] more thematically-focused and reader-responsive mix of journals";
- "split it in half by subfield: *APSR-A* for American, Theory, and Methods . . .; and *APSR-B* for IR [international relations] and Comparative";
- "each quarterly issue could have two parts, one devoted to general political science as is the case now but with more diversity and openness, the other to one of the four sub-fields"; and
- "more pluralism in the selection of the editor [of the *APSR*] and the editorial board."[19]

And there were others. Although some endorsed the idea of a new journal, several Perestroikans expressed skepticism. Joe Carens of the University of Toronto summarized these concerns: "I worry about the idea of a second journal devoted to overview and public relevance articles. . . . It may be more interesting to read. . . . But will articles in it matter professionally in the way *APSR* articles do? If an article appears in the *APSR*, it is harder . . . to treat it as second class. That's why I'm for keeping a single journal and changing it."[20]

While all of this was transpiring, the PIC (now operating under APSA President Robert Jervis) developed plans to implement the Council resolution of August 2000. Its members decided that the association's financial situation permitted them to recommend a new stand-alone, printed journal of the same magnitude as the *APSR*. "The big breakthrough was that Cathy Rudder learned from consultants that she was using on another project that we could increase the price we charged to libraries if we added an additional (& valued) journal in the package. Before then we didn't see how we'd be able to finance it & thought we'd have to make do with adding issues or pages to the *Review*, at least at the start."[21] Substantively, the PIC agreed that the journal "would include integrative essays, state of the discipline type essays, book reviews, reviews of literature in other disciplines with relevance to political science, conceptual and methodological essays, as well as a policy forum for debates on current policy issues among other new materials."[22] The journal might also provide "forums for debate [and] articles similar to those found in *Science* magazine." Articles would be solicited but subsequently reviewed, after extensive consultation between authors and the journal's editor(s). The journal would also encourage proposals, the most likely of which would follow the same process of editing and review as articles.

The PIC added other missions for the new journal to pursue beyond those already canvassed in the August 2000 Council meeting. It "might increase the visibility of the profession externally and possibly attract new members," as well as enable political scientists to "connect with and contribute to public policy debates. . . . The committee stressed that it should publish a very wide range of scholarship" while "remain[ing] distinct from the *APSR*" (whose new editor, Lee Sigelman of George Washington University, was simultaneously extending the range and accessibility of *APSR* articles).[23]

The PIC formalized those views into recommendations, which the Council debated and accepted in principle in April 2001.[24] Sixteen members agreed, and two dissented. Soon after that, President Jervis appointed a committee, chaired by M. Kent Jennings of the University of California–Santa Barbara, to search for an editor or editorial team. The committee put out a call for applications and nominations,[25] and recommended candidates to the president of the association (by then Robert Putnam) in January 2002. I was appointed editor in March 2002 with Council approval, and the Council further approved five associate editors in June 2002.

The Context of *Perspectives*

Any confluence of problem, policy, and political streams occurs within a context, and it helps greatly if forces in that context are all tending in the same direction. That was the case with *Perspectives*. Most generally, several key actors pointed out that comparable professional associations offer their members an array of journals that serve slightly different purposes. As the PIC noted, "All . . . other social science associations . . . publish more than two journals. Although History . . . publishes only two main journals, Economics offers its members choice among zero to three journals out of the three it publishes. At the other extreme, Sociology offers its members choice of 2 among about 8 journals that it manages."[26] Political scientists with ties to other disciplines, especially but not only economics, found that those disciplines were greatly strengthened internally by having several flagship journals with distinct profiles. In addition, political scientists pointed out that they are much more likely to use ideas and literatures from other disciplines when those disciplines offer integrative literature reviews and articles written to be accessible to people outside particular subfields; presumably influence could move in the opposite direction if we, too, published articles of interest to and accessible to people outside political science.

More particularly, several disciplines are seeking to balance journals focused on technical reports of individual research with journals or magazines reaching out to a wider audience. Economists pioneered this effort many years ago with the *Journal of Economic Literature* and the *Journal of Economic Perspectives;*

those journals clearly were (and remain) models for *Perspectives on Politics.*[27] The American Sociological Association more recently began *Contexts,* which seeks to "get . . . the meat and potatoes research out to the public," in the words of its founding editor, Claude Fischer.[28] Faculty at Yale Law School have started a nonprofit journal, *Legal Affairs,* which calls itself (on its home page) "the magazine at the intersection of law and life."[29] Neither the people who created *Perspectives* nor the original editorial team aimed at a predominantly non-academic audience, but political science is clearly joining a trend of seeking to make scholarly research more accessible and influential beyond the academy.

Another contextual factor connects more directly with Perestroika. The *Guardian* of London put it this way: "No one expected an argument about the use of mathematical modeling and 'rational choice theory' in politics and economics research journals to blow up into an academic uprising which has spread from France to the rest of continental Europe, Britain, and north America." It described the emergence in France in June 2000 of the "post-autistic economics" movement, which rejects the dominance of neoclassical economics in favor of "a plurality of approaches adapted to the complexity of the object studied." And it said that after moving to Spain and Great Britain, "in the United States the movement ignited in political science."[30] The *Guardian* has many specific facts wrong in this article, but the overall point is important: there is a broad impulse, across continents as well as disciplines, to move at least some research in the social sciences away from the focus on "science" and more toward a focus on "social," variously defined in particular contexts.

But a dichotomy between would-be scientists and would-be humanists or policy actors is too simple, even misleading intellectually as well as politically. Helen Milner, chair of the PIC, points out:

> There was a general sense that . . . journals that reviewed and assessed the progress of the field in less technical terms, brought high-level theory to bear on policy questions, and evaluated the results of a large number of empirical papers on a single topic were much needed in political science. . . . Indeed, the research areas most in need of such journals are often the most technical ones, where 'normal science' leads to very specialized research. Progress requires the periodic review of small, cumulative findings. I think that many non-Perestroika scholars (and everyone on the PIC) would be very disappointed if the new journal did not serve their needs as well.[31]

More pointedly, "No one in authority believed the *Review* . . . should be 'hard science' and the new journal 'soft.'"[32]

Perestroika and *Perspectives*

So the various problem streams merged into one policy solution, and political entrepreneurs and brokers enabled that solution to break through the old equilibrium and jolt us into a new one. Journalists have made a direct causal link between the emergence of Perestroika and this breakthrough. In the words of one writer for the *Chronicle of Higher Education:* "Since the association received the letter of complaint in November [2000], it has announced that it will start a new journal."[33]

That simple causal story is mistaken; the crucial decision to support publication of "expanded book reviews and more integrative essays" was taken in August 2000, and the PIC was well into its work of implementing that mandate before Perestroika emerged. But a more complex and subtle causal story is persuasive. For instance, "Criticisms of our situation in [1998 and] 1999 . . . were crucial in moving the process forward; so in a sense some of the energy that fueled the Perestroika movement surely was part of the whole process." Or "The complaints in the open letter I drafted and on the e-list . . . probably added some sense of urgency to get the new journal." Or "Perestroika's timing was superb in that the movement publicized a range of views (especially on APSA's publications) that had already become widely (indeed, almost universally) shared among political scientists or at least within the APSA 'establishment.'"[34] Many streams merged to force open this window of opportunity, to mix metaphors in a way that no editor should permit.

Some Perestroikans (like some other political scientists) remain uncertain about how much the new journal can open up the discipline of political science to new (or very old) epistemologies, methods, and questions, and can bring together the scattered and even antagonistic components of our fragmented discipline. There remains concern also that the *APSR* will remain the flagship journal, and that *Perspectives* will occupy an honorable second place. Those of us working on *Perspectives* are all too aware of the grounds for skepticism; we can only strive to overcome them while recognizing that the journal's constituencies and purposes are multiple, probably overambitious, and certainly contradictory. There is plenty of room for a first-class *APSR* focused on reports of a wide array of particular empirical and philosophical endeavors, and for a first-class *Perspectives on Politics* focused on broad, integrative essays that cut across subfields or disciplinary boundaries and that bring politics and policies back into the center of political science. The proof is in the pudding, and settled convictions about the impact of *Perspectives* will necessarily be a long time in coming.

However, I cannot resist pointing out that the new journal is publishing excellent articles on the applicability of just war theory to the new war on terrorism, the role of neuroscience in understanding political leadership, the role of power in equilibrium-seeking models of rational choice, the creation of democratic space through popular protest, and more. It publishes articles by untenured assistant professors and occupants of named chairs, by scholars in small liberal arts colleges and large universities, by people seeking better syllabi and people seeking new research paradigms, by charter members of Perestroika and opponents of it, by political scientists and the rest of the world. The associate editors and I have solicited articles and symposia, commissioned essays by public officials and journalists, and responded to an unending stream of unsolicited manuscripts and proposals. Articles from *Perspectives* are now being cited in more recent scholarly articles, taught in classes, and discussed in seminars. The new journal seems to be working; how well it will fulfill its many purposes over the long run, of course, is not for the first set of editors to determine.

Whether *Perspectives* succeeds or fails depends in the end on whether political scientists and others continue to generate excellent and exciting proposals, papers, and responses to solicitations. As Steven Walt of Harvard University put it in the *Chronicle* article on Perestroika, "You can't fight something with nothing. You can't plead for tolerance without having something good to put forward." The editors await your best manuscripts!

Notes

1. John Kingdon, Agendas, Alternatives, and Public Policies (Glenview, IL: Scott, Foresman, 1984); Frank Baumgartner and Bryan Jones, Agendas and Instability in American Politics (Chicago: University of Chicago Press, 1993).

2. That may be because it was one of the few APSA activities and endeavors about which many respondents had an opinion; the survey showed that a lot of people were simply unaware of most APSA services, activities, and publications.

3. "How Are We Doing? Assessments of APSA Programs by Members and Former Members" (no author or date).

4. The most explicit proposal that I know of at that point was for a journal modeled after *Science,* in which cutting-edge research would be presented to a broad readership in ways that showed its importance while making it accessible to nonspecialists.

5. Sven Steinmo, conversation with the author, January 21, 2003.

6. Cathy Rudder, "Draft Design for a Strategic Planning Process," www .apsanet.org/PS/septoo/rudder.cfm.

7. Robert Keohane, e-mail to the author, August 12, 2002.

8. Robert Hauck, "Editor's Note," *PS,* December 2000, 735.

9. APSA Strategic Planning Committee, "Planning Our Future," www.apsanet .org/new/planning/finalreport.cfm.

10. Paul Beck, e-mail to the author, August 13, 2002.

11. "Draft Minutes, APSA Council Meeting [of August 30, 2000]," *PS,* December 2000, 973.

12. E-mail to the author, August 12, 2002, from a writer who wishes to remain anonymous.

13. E-mail to author, August 17, 2002, from a writer who wishes to remain anonymous.

14. Emily Eakin, "Think Tank: Political Scientists Leading a Revolt, Not Studying One," *New York Times,* November 4, 2000, B11.

15. "An Open Letter to the APSA Leadership and Members," *PS,* December 2000, 735–37.

16. Sven Steinmo, "Perestroika/Glasnost and 'Taking Back the *APSR,*'" www.apsanet.org/new/planning/steinmo.cfm. Debates over the *APSR* itself are not relevant to this chapter. To pursue that issue, see Ada Finifter, "*APSR* Editor Responds," www.apsanet.org/new/planning/apsreditor.cfm; letters by Robert

Jervis and Gregory Kasza in *PS,* December 2000, 737–41; Lee Sigelman, "Notes from the (New) Editor," *American Political Science Review* 96 (March 2002): viii–xvi.

17. Rogers Smith, e-mail message headed "Law and Society and Law and Courts Post," to Law and Courts Discussion List lawcourts-l@usc.edu, September 27, 2000.

18. Rita May Kelly, e-mail message headed "David Pion-Berlin on Theda's Selection," to perestroika_glasnost_warmhome@yahoogroups.com, February 3, 2001.

19. In order, Rogers Smith, Anne Norton, Margaret Keck (two bulleted suggestions), Timothy Luke, and Stuart Kaufman, all February 5, 2001; Lloyd Rudolph, February 6, 2001; David Mason, February 7, 2001.

20. Joe Carens, e-mail message headed "Joseph Carens Again, . . . Supports Lloyd Rudolph Reform Agenda from Lloyd Rudolph," to perestroika_glasnost _warmhome@yahoogroups.com February 7, 2001.

21. E-mail to the author, August 14, 2002, from a writer who wishes to remain anonymous.

22. APSA Publications Implementation Committee, "Discussion and Resolution of the Publications Implementation Committee," www.apsanet.org/new/ planning/picrecommendations.cfm.

23. Ibid.

24. "Final Minutes, APSA Council Meeting . . . , April 21, 2001," in *PS,* December 2001, 924. Members of the Publications Committee concurred with the PIC, but worried that a journal of the requisite quality could not appear as early as winter 2003. The Publications Committee recommended that the journal begin no later than winter 2005.

25. www.apsanet.org/new/planning/newjournal.cfm.

26. APSA Publications Implementation Committee, "Discussion and Resolution of the Publications Implementation Committee," www.apsanet.org/new/planning/ picrecommendations.cfm.

27. The PIC said that the new journal "would combine the features of the *Journal of Economic Literature* with those of the *Journal of Economic Perspectives*" (minutes of the Publications Committee, February 16, 2001). It also proposed that the new journal be called the *Journal of Political Science Literature,* which was the name under which the Council approved the PIC's recommendations in April 2001. Luckily, wiser heads intervened at some point and changed the name to *Perspectives on Politics.*

28. Claude Fischer, conversation with the author, May 23, 2002, www.sfgate .com/cgi-bin/article.cgi?file=/chronicle/archive/2002/07/30/DD197569.DTL. More formally, "*Contexts* brings the best of sociological research to the general public in a concise, accessible, and engaging way. *Contexts* tells teachers, journalists, civil servants, and policymakers about important developments in social research" (Claude Fischer, "From the Editor," *Contexts* 1 [Spring 2002]: iii).

29. www.legalaffairs.org. More formally, "Law and lawyers matter deeply in the United States and around the world, and that literate, probing, wonderful writing about the law is found too rarely in even the best general newspapers and magazines. Our goal is to present this kind of writing regularly and to stir a challenging, vibrant conversation about the law—broadly defined to include everything from the increasingly political nature of state courts . . . to the role of adoption in settling disputes in Micronesia." Lincoln Caplan, "Legal Affairs," *Legal Affairs,* May–June 2002, http://www.legalaffairs.org/aboutus/aboutus_fromeditor.html.

30. Kurt Jacobsen, "Education: Higher: Unreal, Man: Political Scientists Have Turned Guerillas in an Attempt to Shake Off the Stranglehold of the Dogmatic, Unworldly Theory That Dominates Their Discipline," *Guardian,* April 3, 2001, 12.

31. Helen Milner, e-mail to the author, August 18, 2002.

32. E-mail to the author, August 14, 2002.

33. D. W. Miller, "Storming the Palace in Political Science," *Chronicle of Higher Education,* September 21, 2001, 16.

34. E-mail to the author, August 11, 2002; Rogers Smith, e-mail to the author, August 15, 2002; e-mail to the author, August 12, 2002. The authors of the first and third e-mail messages quoted here wish to remain anonymous.

CHAPTER 27

Methodological Bias in the
American Journal of Political Science

Gregory J. Kasza

Emulating David Pion-Berlin's study of the *American Political Science Review* (*APSR*), I have classified articles in the *American Journal of Political Science* (*AJPS*) by research method using these categories:

Statistics: articles that analyze empirical, numerical data sets using statistical techniques such as regression or correlation.

Mathematical or formal modeling: articles that use deductive reasoning to develop formal models.

Philosophy or theory: articles on philosophers such as Plato and articles that explore questions such as "What is political culture?" without examining specific empirical cases.

Qualitative empirical research: articles that explore empirical subjects without using statistical techniques.

Excluding brief research notes and authors' responses to comments, I reviewed all articles in pairs of years to trace the evolution of the journal's editorial policy (see Table 27.1). Two difficulties arose in categorizing the articles. First, many articles of the last twenty years fall between the statistics and modeling categories. Conceptually, modeling and statistics appear distinct, but in practice they are usually coupled. The typical article discusses a model and then applies it to a statistical data set. There is no clear divide between formal and statistical models, because even statistical models generally include "assuming that" or "what if" propositions. After reading the abstracts and conclusions of the articles and paging through them, I placed them in the one or the other category based on whether the author put more emphasis on the modeling or the empirical issues, but in some cases the decision was arbitrary.

The symbiosis of modeling and statistics is significant. Though modelers and statisticians share the goal of forging a hard science of politics, many scholars have questioned whether they are guilty of the same sins. In particular, many who share Perestroika's critique of rational choice would absolve statistics of similar failings. This is muddled thinking. Judging from the *AJPS*,

Table 27.1   A Classification of Articles in the *AJPS* by Research Method, Selected Years, 1960–2001

	Statistics (%)	Modeling (%)	Philosophy (%)	Qualitative Empirical (%)
2000–2001	71.7	18.6	7.1	2.6
1995–96	89.1	3.0	1.0	6.9
1990–91	63.7	29.7	2.2	4.4
1985–86	65.1	27.7	3.6	3.6
1980–81	65.4	17.3	4.9	12.3
1975–76	76.5	8.6	3.7	11.1
1970–71	62.3	3.3	8.2	26.2
1965–66	29.3	2.4	7.3	61.0
1960–61	9.4	0.0	15.6	75.0

Source: Author's calculations.

modeling exercises without statistics are rare, and statistical exercises without modeling are untypical.

The common fusion of modeling and statistics excludes consideration of nonquantifiable, empirical information. Articles that begin by evaluating a mathematical model, modify that model to improve it, and then apply the amended version to a numerical data set never transcend the sphere of numbers. Methodological pluralists who use statistics selectively along with qualitative data, in the manner of Robert Putnam or Peter Katzenstein, must understand that this is not the modus operandi of most numbers crunchers. One must return to the 1960s to find much methodologically pluralistic work of this type in the *AJPS*. If a valid research design should include the many types of information relevant to a topic, be they numerical or not, most articles in the *AJPS* fail the test. Thus the notion that one can censure deductive theory for the ills of hard science while absolving statistics of blame is mistaken. The reason that modelers and statisticians form such a cozy partnership in political science is that they are largely one and the same group of people.

A second difficulty of categorization concerned qualitative empirical articles. Many articles in this category, though not using statistical procedures such as regression, still involved mainly or exclusively the analysis of numerical data (see Table 27.2). The big shift to hard science in the *AJPS* occurred in the late 1960s. In the editions I covered from 1970 to 2001, thirty-two of the fifty-two articles that I classified as "qualitative empirical" were mainly nonstatistical analyses of numerical data. Thus many readers may conclude that my findings exaggerate the amount of qualitative research in the *AJPS*. Remove the countable aspects of phenomena such as elections, surveys, and executive appointments, and there has been little left to read in this journal since 1970.

Table 27.2   Qualitative Empirical Articles in the *AJPS* That Use Mainly Numerical Data, Selected Years, 1960–2001

	Qualitative Empirical Articles	*Qualitative Empirical Articles Using Mainly Numerical Data*
2000–2001	3	0
1995–96	7	5
1990–91	4	3
1985–86	3	3
1980–81	10	5
1975–76	9	5
1970–71	16	11
1965–66	25	9
1960–61	24	5

Source: Author's calculations.

There is no way to verify an author's motives, but it appears to me that many contributors to the *AJPS* chose their subject matter because it was open to quantitative analysis, not because of its substantive importance. The numerical minutiae of American politics get more attention from the journal than big issues in that or any other subfield. For instance, there are more pieces on the composition of U.S. congressional committees than on social welfare, environmental pollution, or war. This fascination with legislative committees defies comprehension if not for its amenability to statistical research. Few articles ask if these committees produce good government or how they might produce better government. In most respects, good government is not countable.

When I circulated the results of my review to the journal's editors and to the president of the Midwest Political Science Association, I invited them to respond on the Perestroika list serve, which they did. Quoting from the masthead of the journal, which proclaims that the *AJPS* is "a general review journal open to all members of the profession and to all areas of the discipline of political science," they averred that the journal has never favored any particular type of research or methodology. They pointed to the paucity of submissions from qualitative researchers as the main reason that their work is underrepresented in the journal's pages. Assuming that these sentiments are sincere, why do qualitative researchers not submit more work to a prestigious journal like the *AJPS?* The answer is that even in the absence of conscious editorial discrimination, there is an editorial bias at work here that drives qualitative scholars away.

The editors of the *AJPS* are hard-scientific scholars. Presumably they do hard science because they consider it the best form of research, and inevitably most of their contacts are people who do similar work. They read the research of other scholars who do hard science, join them on conference panels, contribute to their collective volumes, and so forth. There is nothing wrong with this until one pretends that it does not influence the way they edit a journal.

Qualitative research cannot get a fair hearing from editors who believe that it is inferior and who call upon like-minded scholars to referee it. These editors must judge qualitative research inferior, or they would be doing it themselves. They must select mainly like-minded referees, because most of their close associates think as they do. The reason that qualitative researchers (myself included) do not send work to journals like the *AJPS* or the *Journal of Politics* is that most of their referees judge our work by standards we do not accept. My experience with generic political science journals is that their referees tend to be PhDs in research design who apply inappropriate standards of method to my work and say nothing about its substance. Most are not even in the same field of study.

Hard-scientific scholars do not receive such prejudicial treatment. Not once since I joined the professoriate in 1983 has a journal editor sent me a piece of quantitative research or deductive theory to referee. Not once has an editor sent me an article on American politics. Evidently the editorial elite do not believe that I am qualified to judge such work. And they are right. But why, then, do these editors imagine that somebody who has been doing regression analysis for the last twenty years is qualified to judge qualitative scholarship? Does it not show contempt for qualitative research to suppose that a hard scientist is fit to pass judgment on the qualitative scholar's years of archival study and field work? This is the bias that hard-scientific editors bring to the evaluation of qualitative research.

The only lasting remedy for journals like the *AJPS* is a radical restructuring at the top. Why must such journals have only one editor? Recognizing the deep divisions that exist in the discipline and the limits of any one person's competence, why not appoint separate editors for deductive theory, quantitative analysis, qualitative empirical research, political philosophy, and "other stuff," and let the contributors decide who should adjudicate their work? If the *AJPS* adopted such a collective editorship, it would receive a flood of qualitative manuscripts. As it is, after sitting at the roulette wheel for forty years and seeing the little ball stop repeatedly on "statistics" and "formal modeling," only a dummy would bet on a different outcome.

The record of the *AJPS* is regrettable. This is not a journal designed to serve a small sect of scholars practicing a particular approach to political study. It is the publication of the Midwest Political Science Association, whose thousands of members support it with their dues. As such, it should represent the many types of excellent research that political scientists do, not restrict itself to such a narrow range of scholarship. Yet nowhere is the dictatorship of hard science more prominent than in the *AJPS*.

CHAPTER 28

Science, Political Science, and the *American Journal of Political Science*

Kim Quaile Hill and Jan E. Leighley

As the editors of the *American Journal of Political Science* (*AJPS*), we welcome the opportunity to engage in dialogue about the concerns of the Perestroika movement and to respond to characterizations from that movement of the editorial policies of and articles in the *AJPS*. In this chapter we respond to criticisms found in Gregory Kasza's chapter assessing the articles published over the last twenty years in the *AJPS*. We also address other concerns posed by Kasza in an earlier statement of Perestroikan principles (Kasza 2001). We begin by summarizing the key concerns expressed in those two writings, and then we discuss each concern in turn.

The Concerns of the Perestroikans

Kasza's chapter addresses the character of the scientific articles published in the *AJPS,* so most of our remarks will focus on these articles as well. Two additional points regarding the focus of our essay should be noted. First, we recognize that in his earlier work Kasza (2001) also lamented what he characterizes as a decline in the role of political philosophy in our discipline. Yet the *AJPS* publishes, by Kasza's own accounting, as much political philosophy at present as it has in any period except the very first biennium for which he provides data. Second, we are equally concerned here, as is Kasza, with research on substantive political topics. Thus we join Kasza in not discussing research on methodological matters per se, even though the *AJPS* does publish a notable amount of such research.

In his chapter Kasza makes three key assumptions about scientific research and the *AJPS*. (1) He assumes that there exists a meaningful distinction between "hard" science that principally employs quantitative data to address its research questions and "qualitative" research that does not (although he characterizes the methods of the latter kind of scholarship only as "without statistical techniques"). In earlier work Kasza argued that what he calls hard science restricts methodological pluralism. He calls for more diversity in research methods; yet that call appears to be motivated largely by what he perceives as the declining status of area experts in our discipline. Indeed he styles area experts as "the richest source of political theory" for the study of substantive politics (Kasza 2001, 597). (2) Kasza also assumes that quantitative research rarely addresses topics that are substantively or otherwise important. In particular, he concludes that such research ignores how the goal of "good government" might be advanced. In his 2001 work, Kasza made this same argument, suggesting that hard science ignores contemporary problems of applied or topical importance. (3) Kasza further assumes that what is published in the *AJPS* represents "the journal's editorial policy" and the biased preferences of the editors.

Kasza's empirical work presents a count of types of articles published in the journal over time.[1] Based on his assumptions, stated earlier, and reflecting on the articles, which he has counted by category and time period, Kasza concludes that too little qualitative research is published in the *AJPS*, that too much hard science is published there, and that qualitative research scholars thus are discouraged from submitting their work to the *AJPS*.

Types of Scientific Research and Their Place in the Evolution of Scientific Knowledge

We disagree, first, with the labels Kasza employs in his initial assumption about the distinctions that characterize different kinds of scientific research. In particular, we find the term "hard science" meaningless. We know of no well-established characterization of approaches to scientific research, but two distinctions appear useful for that purpose. The first distinction takes account of the *goal* of a particular research project and the written report on it that might be appropriate for journal publication. The second distinction takes account of the *method,* meant in a very general sense, by which the goal of the research might be pursued. We distinguish four common research goals, and briefly note the different methods that might be appropriate for each one. We describe those four goals individually, but we recognize that at times one scholarly article might pursue more than one of them simultaneously.

Some scientific research offers literal *description* of actual political events, processes, or institutions. Such work could be meant to stand alone in providing original observational evidence about the character of a given phenomenon, for example, on which later work with other goals might be based. Alternatively, it might be intended as part of a typological exercise—work little appreciated or pursued in political science at present but work that has been quite valuable in other sciences. Descriptive work might rely on casual observation conveyed entirely in prose, or it might rely on rigorous qualitative analysis or systematic quantitative evidence. In the former two cases it would be fairly labeled qualitative, while in the latter case both systematic data and relevant, summarizing statistical procedures might be employed.[2]

Another goal for scientific work that might produce a paper suitable for journal publication would be *conceptualization*. Here one moves in one respect or another from the particular to the abstract. One might seek to create general concepts that apply to many particular cases. One might attempt to elucidate how several general concepts relate to each other and thus combine to form a broad explanation for particular phenomena—what we usually think of as general theory.

We can readily imagine research that seeks to advance conceptualization that employs entirely qualitative evidence, as Kasza uses that term. That is, it could be based, for example, on the inductive assessment of nonquantitative evidence from a small-sample case study. But conceptual work might also rely on intensive statistical assessment of quantitative data from multiple cases intended to measure and distinguish particular concepts. Conceptualization and theory construction are also common goals of so-called formal theory in our discipline. Such deductive theory construction might be entirely non-quantitative in Kasza's terminology. That is, it might eschew empirical evidence of any kind for logic and pure mathematics.

A third research goal would be *hypothesis testing to create general theory.* Such research offers empirical tests of propositions about relations among abstract concepts. Methods can vary here, too. Qualitative methods as described by Kasza are employed by some scholars to pursue this goal (cf. King, Keohane, and Verba 2001). Other scholars, of course, employ quantitative evidence on multiple cases that is assessed by one or another statistical method. Regardless of which method is used to evaluate the evidence for particular hypotheses, the hypotheses themselves might arise from any of a host of sources—from conventional wisdom, prior qualitative research, deductive theory, or prior work of various kinds employing statistical data.

As a final research goal we distinguish *applied research concerned with understanding particular political phenomena,* and usually their causes or consequences. While such work has literally applied objectives, it also characteristically adopts some "theoretical" expectations about the phenomena under study. For example, evaluations of the consequences of specific government programs routinely adopt expectations about the causal processes intended for a program that are either stated in program law or are imposed by the scholar carrying out the analysis. Expectations imposed by the authors of such research may arise out of normative preferences or general theory that has been developed by research pursuing the third goal discussed earlier.

Program evaluations represent only one category of applied research. Yet all of the types of such research that we can envision also begin with some assumptions, or "theory," as a foundation and proceed to conclusions about the degree to which valued political or social goals are achieved. As is the case with the third goal of research we distinguished earlier, applied scholarship may employ any of various kinds of methods. Indeed, taking the subject of program evaluation as an example again, there are rich research literatures that address both qualitative and quantitative evaluation approaches (e.g., Mohr 1995; Patton 2002). One can find similar methodological variation for all kinds of applied research.

Now recall Kasza's conclusions about articles currently published in the *AJPS*—that the preponderance of them employ quantitative data analyzed by statistical methods, that too few of them employ qualitative methods, and that this imbalance is unfortunate. The preceding explanation of different kinds of scientific scholarship, together with some common observations from the history of science, leads to far different conclusions about the publication patterns Kasza observes with his counting of articles.

Three circumstances are commonly observed in the historical development of every science. First, all of the four separate scholarly goals outlined earlier remain important regardless of whether a science is relatively young or relatively advanced. Second, as a discipline matures, an increasing proportion of the scholarship on the intellectual frontier of knowledge pursues either the third or the fourth objective we have outlined as at least one of its goals. Yet such research usually relies in part, too, on the second goal of conceptualization. Thus description per se becomes a less common research goal. And conceptualization becomes closely integrated with efforts to test theory empirically, whether for its general or for its particular implications. Third, as a scientific discipline matures, systematic empirical evidence analyzed with advanced statistical or mathematical methods begins to displace relatively qualitative methods. Roles remain for all kinds of methods, even in highly advanced sciences. But in general, work at the frontier more commonly relies on tools that allow the use of increasingly precise measurement of concepts, samples of cases intended to offer broad generalizability, and modes of analysis that can allow scholars to extract and evaluate the information in precise measures taken across multiple cases.

These trends in scientific goals and methods are accompanied by compatible changes in scientific publishing, especially in journals. The most noted developments here are specialization and stratification. Most scholarly disciplines, whether scientific or not, begin with a small number of journals that publish all kinds of research (although the research in young disciplines is not highly differentiated in terms of the goals and methods described earlier). As disciplines mature, their journals multiply. Some of them seek particular niches based on subject matter, the goals of the scholarship, or even the methods characteristically employed in the scholarship. Thus there exist today political science journals with highly specialized subject-matter concerns. There are also journals that seek to publish only work pursuing particular goals, such as applied scholarship or scholarship that addresses topical policy concerns from normative or "good governance" perspectives. There are also journals that publish only work using one methodological approach.

Stratification among journals also arises in maturing disciplines. Some journals, like the ones that would fit into the particular categories listed earlier, become mediums of communication among specialists instead of the discipline at large. Other journals are recognized as general ones whose goal is to publish scholarship that is both path-breaking in its particular field and potentially of interest to all members of the discipline. In political science, the

American Political Science Review, the *Journal of Politics,* and the *American Journal of Political Science* have been long recognized as general journals.

Another way of describing the goals of general journals is to say that they seek to publish the best scholarship on the intellectual frontier of the discipline. Recall, then, the character of the work that appears on that frontier as a discipline matures. It is more likely to be of the type that Kasza calls "hard science" and that we have described as seeking to test the implications of theory with especially systematic data and methods. But it is not exclusively of this type. Thus it is no surprise to us—indeed, it is to be expected—that the *AJPS* publishes more of the latter kind of scholarship today than it did twenty years ago. The journal would be failing at its mission if it did otherwise.

Our earlier argument suggests, of course, that the *AJPS* is not unique in terms of how the scholarship published there has evolved. The trends that Kasza documents for the *AJPS* are evident as well in the histories of the *American Political Science Review* and the *Journal of Politics.* Considering the social sciences more broadly, these trends are equally apparent in the histories of the *American Economic Review* and the *American Sociological Review.* Were we to go far enough back in time, we could chronicle similar evolution in the scholarship of chemistry, physics, or any of the physical sciences. The universality of such changes is testimony to the accuracy of our characterization of how sciences evolve.

Of course the ambition of general journals, whether the *New England Journal of Medicine* or the *AJPS,* to publish only path-breaking research is never perfectly realized. Editors, reviewers, and authors do not always agree on what constitutes path-breaking research. So there will be times when a potentially path-breaking manuscript is rejected in the review process or when a modest intellectual advance survives to publication. Indeed, as Cole (1983) vividly indicates, discriminating what is especially valuable in research on the intellectual frontier is not an entirely rational process *in any science.* Thus the *AJPS* publishes today both path-breaking research and research that will have little or no influence on the future course of scholarship.

Does the Scientifically Advanced Research Published in the *AJPS* Address Unimportant Topics?

In response to Kasza's concerns that quantitative research rarely addresses substantively important topics, we provide here a list of representative research questions taken from articles that were published in the *AJPS* in 2004.

- What factors affect citizens' willingness to trade civil liberties for security in the post-9/11 world?
- How does Americans' trust in other countries influence their foreign policy attitudes, their perceptions of foreign nations, and their willingness to take military action against Iraq?
- What are the effects of the duration and timing of civil wars on economic growth in both the war-torn nation and nearby nations?

- Do South African "truth commissions" lead to truth, tolerance, and reconciliation?
- What are the effects of oil wealth on regime survival, political protests, and civil war?
- Does the need to run for election to office influence the impartiality of judges, and how does this experience affect judges' sentencing practices?
- How do potential candidates' decisions about whether to run for office lead to the underrepresentation of women in elected offices?
- What are the roles of race and racial environment in the implementation of sanctions for recipients of aid through the Temporary Assistance for Needy Families program?
- How does partisanship affect welfare retrenchment in advanced industrial societies?
- What is the relationship between democracy and human rights violations?
- What is the role of foreign direct investment by multinational enterprises in creating worker insecurity?
- What is the effect of campaign advertising on democratic participation in and knowledge about presidential campaigns?

We leave it to the reader to determine whether such papers address meaningful issues, despite their reliance on quantitative analytical procedures.

Do the Articles Published in the *AJPS* Reflect the Preferences of the Editors as to What Should Be Published?

In general terms, we hope the journal does indeed reflect our preferences as to its contents. But one must understand what those preferences are. From the beginning of our editorship we have proclaimed the following simple editorial policy: *the AJPS seeks manuscripts that make outstanding contributions to scholarly knowledge about notable theoretical concerns, puzzles, or controversies in any subfield of political science.* We have stated that policy widely since we became the *AJPS* editors—in all our written announcements about the journal, in response to all individual queries, and in at least one public forum on journal publishing at every annual meeting of the Midwest Political Science Association and of the American Political Science Association.

Despite our pledge to review papers in any subfield of political science, we receive more in some fields than others. And we are captive to what is submitted to the journal for review for publication. What is submitted, however, is shaped in part by long-standing custom and practice. Journals acquire reputations and stature that influence how members of the scholarly community perceive them and what work these scholars decide to send the journals for review. We interpret the evolution of the publishing trends that Kasza documents for the *AJPS* as having arisen in good part because the discipline at large came to recognize the status of the *AJPS* as a general journal and responded accordingly.

To some extent, we are also captive to the peer review process. Even scholars who share values about the substantive and theoretical importance of particular research questions, as well as preferences as to optimal methodological approaches for addressing those questions, often disagree about the contribution of a particular manuscript. Thus the individual preference of every scholar involved in the determination of a peer review decision, whether as a reviewer or as an editor, is to a notable degree subsumed to the collective judgment that arises out of that process.

Finally, although we personally like some manuscripts more than others, we make no efforts to engineer the fate of those we ourselves admire. Doing so would violate the trust the discipline invests in journal editors. Frankly, the practical demands of shepherding about eight hundred manuscripts a year through the review process leave us no time for such machinations. Our most critical editorial responsibility, and the task on which we spend the vast bulk of our time, is managing that large number of submissions to provide serious reviews in as timely a manner as possible. Beyond that, we seek to make decisions about the fate of manuscripts in a fair and reasoned manner. In the end, our influence over the content of the journal is far less than that of our authors and reviewers. The time demands associated with managing the editorial affairs of the journal, along with the nature of the scholarship that is submitted and the collective character of the peer review process, explain why that is the case.

Notes

1. We would have done this counting of papers by category differently, but we will accept it as providing a reasonably representative portrait of how some categories of scholarship published in the journal have changed over the last forty years.

2. Our discussion here of descriptive research and of how it relates to other research goals is heavily influenced by our recognition of political science as a preparadigmatic science in Kuhn's (1996) conception. Yet Kuhn (1996, 25–28) offers a useful discussion of the importance of such research in a paradigmatic science.

References

Cole, Stephen. 1983. "The Hierarchy of the Sciences?" *American Journal of Sociology* 89 (July): 111–39.

Kasza, Gregory. 2001. "Perestroika: For an Ecumenical Science of Politics." *PS: Political Science and Politics* 34 (September): 597–99.

King, Gary, Robert O. Keohane, and Sidney Verba. 1994. *Designing Social Inquiry.* Princeton, NJ: Princeton University Press.

Kuhn, Thomas. 1996. *The Structure of Scientific Revolutions.* Chicago: University of Chicago Press.

Mohr, Lawrence B. 1995. *Impact Analysis for Program Evaluation.* Thousand Oaks, CA: Sage.

Patton, Michael Quinn. 2002. *Qualitative Research and Evaluation Methods.* Thousand Oaks, CA: Sage.

PART 5

Graduate Education

A major concern of Perestroika has been graduate education and how it replicates the existing ideological paradigm by imposing a narrow view of science on students. In this regard, Perestroika was in tune with currents already circulating in the discipline; the 2002–03 APSA president, Theda Skocpol, made this one of her central concerns, convening a task force that included several prominent Perestroikans.

The Task Force on Graduate Education issued its preliminary report, written by Christopher Achen and Rogers M. Smith, in 2004. The final report is included here, and, at the request of the Task Force members and of former president Skocpol, I wish to make it clear that this was an initiative of the APSA president and Council, not a "Perestroika" initiative, and was developed by a diverse and inclusive committee. While Perestroika supported the initiative, the move to establish the Task Force was not spurred by any one section of the discipline, and the recommendations speak to all members of the association. I am grateful to the APSA for allowing us to reproduce the report in this volume.

Peregrine Schwartz-Shea, now perhaps best known as the Perestroikan who ran for the APSA Executive Council in the 2003 elections, actually first became active in Perestroika because of her interest in graduate education. She focuses her chapter on the doctoral requirements and offerings in methods and methodology. What is the state of doctoral training in methodology? Do students have the opportunity, and do they receive the encouragement, to understand the breadth of possible approaches for studying politics? Or does their training produce a narrow and exclusionary view of what constitutes legitimate social-scientific knowledge? In her chapter Schwartz-Shea addresses these questions via a survey of the doctoral curricular requirements and offerings of fifty-seven programs, covering an estimated 61 percent of the graduate student population and 90 percent of the top fifty programs according to the National Research Council rankings. Her focus is the broad area of "methods": language, quantitative-statistical methods, qualitative methods, and philosophy of science. Specifically, Schwartz-Shea examines how requirements and offerings fit together at the program level in order to assign each program to one of three ideal types: (1) those that, via the curriculum, equate "methods" and "empirical research" with quantitative-statistical training; (2) those in which the meaning of "methods" is open to both quantitative and qualitative understandings of research; and (3) those in which the curricular message is split between these two possible conceptualizations as a function of field. The distribution of programs across these ideal types provides the parameters for a thought experiment that demonstrates the ways in which student talents and phobias are nourished, corrected, or neglected. Schwartz-Shea concludes by arguing that the benefits of department specialization cannot excuse doctoral curricula that produce method-driven researchers.

Leslie E. Anderson has similar concerns with the current state of graduate education. Her chapter describes a course she teaches each fall in the Department of Political Science at the University of Florida. The course is required of all incoming doctoral students in their first semester and helps fulfill the basic requirements for a doctorate in political science across all subfields in the department. The course presents the various methods of collecting data, both qualitatively and quantitatively, as tools in a toolbox. The students are charged with learning how to use all the different tools in the toolbox and with understanding which kinds of research are most appropriate for each method. They must learn as well the strengths and limitations of each method or tool so that they will understand that, whatever method they use, some aspect of the process of research discovery will be enhanced but other elements of discovery limited. The students learn the various methodologies through a combination of doing actual research in groups and individually, reading about the methods, and hearing from other faculty and graduate students during classroom visits. The methods introduced in the course Anderson teaches include participant observation, survey research, in-depth interviews of various kinds, focus groups, archival research, and use of electronic databases and statistical analysis packages, particularly SPSS (Statistical Package for the Social Sciences). Anderson concludes that students often respond to this pluralist presentation of methods by choosing to use both qualitative and quantitative methods in their own research and by becoming open-minded about and respectful of different kinds of data collection and analysis. Her chapter, taken in conjunction with the reading list in the appendix, provides concrete illustration of how courses in graduate methods might be modified to allow for a more pluralistic approach to political science.

Gregory J. Kasza focuses on a closely related issue, one that is the basis of a central claim by Perestroikans and one that strikes at the heart of our professional existence: the concern that an overemphasis on quantitative methods is reflected in a systematic bias present in the training and hiring of new political scientists. Kasza argues that the use of mathematics in political science lies at the heart of the current debate over methods. Research using statistics or formal mathematical models dominates our association journals, he claims, and the study of these hard-scientific methods has become the core of graduate education. Kasza's chapter challenges the hegemony of statistical research by arguing that there are aspects of every political phenomenon that resist quantification. It then makes an effective case that the exclusion of uncountable information from statistical research compromises the objectivity, precision, and generality that are its selling points. Kasza concludes is that a genuine methodological pluralism should replace the current fascination with quantitative analysis.

Hayward R. Alker continues on Kasza's themes, drawing on the particularly rich methodological diversity of Alker's teaching and scholarship to derive seven principles of methodological pluralism. Using his experience in teaching theory, philosophy of inquiry, modeling, data analysis, and methodology courses as part of a unified yet pluralistic PhD curriculum, Alker suggests and illustrates four components of what he calls pedagogical pluralism. First, Alker argues that we should reflexively teach a discipline's multiple research practices as emulatable and criticizable objects of sociohistorical inquiry, including their epistemological or methodological aspects. Second, we must sociologically historicize and internationally contextualize the development of a discipline's core theories and methodologies. Third, we need to recognize and teach a plurality of knowledge interests such as the Habermas-Radnitzky distinction among positive, practical-hermeneutic, critical-emancipatory, and cosmological knowledge interests. In doing so, we should give equal attention to the variety and richness of nomothetic and ideographic historical research. All of this will expose students to a variety of research paradigms, agendas, programs, and discourses. Finally, Alker argues that we should consider reconceptualizing political science and the social sciences more generally, and think of them as disciplines bridging the humanities and the natural sciences.

CHAPTER 29

2004 Report to the Council

APSA Task Force on Graduate Education

[Following is a reprint of the final report presented by the APSA Task Force on Graduate Education to the APSA Council. The reprint is unchanged except for minor format changes.]

I. Introduction

In spring 2002, APSA President-Elect Theda Skocpol appointed this Task Force on Graduate Education, representing a variety of institutions, political science subfields, scholarly backgrounds and methodological viewpoints. She asked its members to report on ways to strengthen graduate education in political science. The Task Force quickly concluded that no single structure of graduate training could be appropriate for the wide range of institutions offering graduate instruction in political science, and that departments must decide for themselves what programs best suited their capacities and interests.

We also found, however, that we agreed on certain basic principles that all graduate programs could and should seek to embody, even if in widely differing forms. The principles are not so broad as to be meaningless or trivial, so they are also not uncontroversial. Still, we believe that most political scientists will on reflection come to endorse them. We also found that we could readily identify a number of steps that departments and the APSA can undertake, and often need to undertake, to fulfill these principles in ways that fit their circumstances. This report describes the principles and their rationales and then reviews a series of options for their pursuit by individual departments and institutions and the APSA.

The APSA Task Force on Graduate Education included Christopher H. Achen (Princeton University), Cristina Beltran (Haverford College), Cathy J. Cohen (University of Chicago), David Collier (University of California–Berkeley), Edie Goldenberg (University of Michigan), Robert Keohane (Duke University), Kristen Monroe (University of California–Irvine), Rogers M. Smith (University of Pennsylvania), and Michael Wallerstein (Northwestern University).

II. Principles for Graduate Education in Political Science

Half a century ago, an APSA committee attempted to set goals for political science and proposed changes in departmental structures to achieve those goals (Dimock et al., 1951). Among their recommendations were proposals for improved graduate training, including better advising systems, deeper training for teaching, more inter-institutional cooperation, more information for prospective graduate students, and a more unified perspective on the study of politics. In our own deliberations fifty years later, we found ourselves returning to these perennial issues in the education of graduate students. While the specifics have changed, the underlying challenges have not.

Like our predecessors, the Graduate Task Force believes that, despite the diversity of substantive interests and approaches visible in contemporary political science, there are some beliefs and commitments that genuinely serve to unite our discipline. Although these commitments often have to be pursued in varying fashion because of the distinctive resources, student needs, and intellectual strengths and interests of different departments, we believe they can serve as common guides that can assist departments in structuring effective graduate programs in a wide variety of contexts.

1. Perhaps most foundational is the belief that politics is often if not always of fundamental importance to human life—so that *exploration of how far politics can help explain human experiences and help resolve human difficulties is one of the primary tasks of intellectual life.* This belief in the importance of politics is what motivates most students to enter political science. Graduate education should equip them to pursue the questions this conviction raises, not divert them from substantive political interests.

2. Of equal importance is the belief that *political scientists must seek to analyze politics in the most intellectually honest and rigorous ways they can.* We may differ on how to pursue this goal—but not on its centrality to our work.

3. Most if not all political scientists also affirm that *the complex subject matter of politics must be studied using many methods* if we are to obtain the greatly varying sorts of data, form the wide range of powerful descriptive and explanatory concepts, and engage in the many sorts of inferential testing that we need to achieve rigorous analyses.

4. *Studies of ethical norms and normative commitments, including those in our own work, are central to the study of politics.* Their rigorous analysis, clarification, and evaluation belong not only in the subfield of political theory, but in many other parts of the discipline as well.

5. We also affirm that *the discipline today must address a diverse range of long-neglected subjects, including the political experiences of traditionally marginal groups,* using all appropriate methods. Doing so

requires attracting to the discipline and aiding the development of scholars with backgrounds and perspectives more varied than those that have long characterized our field.

6.   We believe that *it is essential for political scientists to be able to communicate clearly to each other and to broader publics why and how the aspects of politics they study are helping us to achieve improved understandings of substantively important features of human life.* Not all aspects of all political science research can be accessibly expressed and shown to be significant to wide audiences, but our core concerns and claims can and must be.

7.   Finally, we share the view that *a serious graduate education includes a broadly informed perspective on the discipline.* In contemporary academic life, research excellence is prized and rewarded. Research requires specialization and a focus on the new. Thus "cutting edge" methods and theories have a natural appeal to young scholars in any methodological tradition, and they may be tempted to put most of their energy there. However, excessively narrow training can lead to myopic perspectives and unduly parochial research.

Members of the Graduate Task Force are concerned that, for historical reasons, graduate training in many departments is now almost bifurcated. Some students stress credentials in quantitative analyses and formal modeling at the expense of other sorts of methodological, historical, and substantive preparation, with the risk that their seemingly sophisticated analyses repeat the intellectual blunders and blindnesses of fifty or more years ago, which have long been recognized and overcome in other parts of the profession. Other students acquire qualitative and historical research skills to deal with the American presidency or the legal process, for example, but then find themselves without the tools to interpret sensibly public opinion polls about the president, or to evaluate the quantitative evidence in legal debates over capital punishment. Students of political theory are too often intellectually separated from the other graduate students, with resulting losses to both sides.

Intellectual and methodological narrowness harm the profession as a whole, and they can limit the rigor and substance of the research each of us does individually. Equally importantly, they can stifle the skills needed for effective pedagogy, especially in undergraduate teaching but also in graduate mentoring, and for accessible writing aimed at broader publics. Teaching, public service, and research all require a breadth of training in intellectual traditions and open-mindedness about methodological tools.

Imperative as all these commitments are, achieving these goals is hard. We recognize that efforts to pursue them will challenge any graduate program and that few if any graduate departments can hope to do equal justice to them all. Disparate goals require trade-offs. What may seem like minimally sufficient training in particular methods such as statistical analysis, formal modeling, philosophical reasoning, ethnographic analysis, in-depth interviewing, modes of textual interpretation, foreign language training, and more can be so extensive as to leave little time to learn other methods—much less the sorts of rich contextual knowledge of various arenas of politics that insightful concept formation usually requires. Broadening the composition of graduate student populations and faculties is also a major challenge, and departments must then go on to address the special problems minority scholars face. Amidst competing pressures, goals of promoting diversity in the topics and membership of the political science profession can lose out to a range of other concerns.

The Task Force believes, however, that departments can respond to these sometimes conflicting imperatives in many appropriate ways, while still successfully conveying the shared core professional commitments delineated above. There is, in fact, no other intellectually respectable choice. Meeting those commitments will require changes in many graduate programs. We now turn to those issues.

III. The Structure of Programs and the Allocation of Resources

The values that we have enunciated will only have a positive impact on graduate education if they are implemented in an integrated and reinforcing way. Crucially, scarce resources need to be allocated in ways that maximize the opportunities of able graduate students to gain the training that they need in a demanding intellectual and professional environment. Departments of political science will need to request sufficient resources from university administrations, but in a time of financial stringency we can only do so credibly if we are using those resources wisely.

With these considerations in mind, we put forward the following suggestions:

1. Program Breadth   A common structural problem—resulting from successful innovation in our field—faces all Ph.D. programs in political science. Through the scholarship of ever-growing numbers of political scientists, no longer concentrated in the U.S. but working throughout the world, all subfields contain increasing amounts of knowledge, acquired through a broader range of methods. For example, technical competence in mathematics and statistics has become essential for political scientists in many areas of the discipline—and required levels of technical competence are becoming more demanding. Yet political science remains a largely problem-driven discipline, and neither the number nor variety of political problems is declining. Indeed, the types of subjects and activities that seem important for understanding politics continue to grow, and those subjects continue to innovate and to extend their activities around the globe. The results of this double process of innovation—by political scientists and those we study—are increasing tensions in graduate programs between both substance and technique, and breadth and depth.

No Ph.D. program should turn out broadly but superficially educated dilettantes. Yet there is a real danger that excessive specialization could drive out imaginative reconceptualizations of politics, generated by explorations of relationships between subfields, and between political science and other disciplines. In the long history of the profession dating to the Greeks, we have learned a great deal from such reconceptualizations. Much would be lost if a new generation of political scientists found themselves so narrowly focused on particular sub-fields, using specific methods, that they could not learn from one another, or from scholars in other disciplines, using different methods.

We recommend that each program ensure that first and second year graduate students are exposed to a variety of approaches to political science— qualitative and quantitative, descriptive, interpretive, and explanatory—and to multiple substantive issues, viewpoints, and subfields of the discipline. Each student should also get deep training in at least one significant research area. This combination of breadth and depth is the necessary core of any good graduate education in political science. We believe that a well structured and balanced program of coursework in the first two years will go far toward ameliorating the excessive narrowness and seeming aridity of graduate work about which students have long complained (see the survey in Bennett et al., 1969).

As noted above, a major consequence of the increasing specialization and diversity in political science is that few if any graduate programs can offer state-of-the-art training in all methods and in all substantive areas. Coverage of the field is uneven in even the very large departments. Mid-size departments have no choice but to specialize to some degree.

Some amount of specialization is also highly desirable. Scholars working with a particular methodology or in a particular area of substantive research benefit from working in close proximity to others with similar intellectual interests. From the point of view of graduate training, it is preferable for departments to offer in-depth training in a few things rather than superficial training in many things.

Thus some departments may well choose to specialize in particular approaches to political science. Large departments may be able to do so while offering a balanced exposure to a variety of quantitative and non-quantitative methods, and to substantive as well as methodological training. But other departments may have to rely more heavily on individual student advising and mentoring, guided by explicit concern to see that each student is made aware of the whole range of topics and methods in political science appropriate to the student's interests.

Departments may also choose to work with other programs in their university that provide in-depth training in statistical, ethnographic, linguistic, interpretive or other skills the departments cannot offer themselves. They may establish partnerships with geographically proximate but substantively or methodological disparate departments at other universities. They can support the participation of their students in special training programs open to graduate students from across the country, as discussed below.

A few departments have recently begun to restructure their program to feature the study of various sorts of substantive political problems, such as the design and operation of institutions and issues of conflict and violence, rather than traditional subfields such as comparative politics, American politics, and international relations. This approach may help to communicate that political science is about substantive political issues and that a variety of methods are appropriate for their study. Other departments may choose to proceed differently.

Whatever their curricular choices, all departments retain a fundamental duty to familiarize their students, at least in general terms, with other approaches. All should advertise their own specializations clearly when students are applying for graduate school. And all should help their students to work elsewhere, or even transfer, if those students are not thriving within the program as established. Finally, all departments should seek to achieve appropriate demographic diversity of their faculty and student populations and to insure that members of groups recently added to the ranks of the profession are suitably supported.

2. Specialized Training   Some students will want to go beyond this core program, to get deeper training in more than one subfield of political science or in some branch of another discipline, such as economics or law. Preparation of that kind is increasingly common and necessary in political science. We urge departments and universities to take note that their students may need to undertake extra training and that doing so will lengthen time to degree. Additional financial support should be available for students requiring an extra year's training, or more, to accomplish this purpose. Without that extra funding, students will rush to finish before the money runs out.

3. Fellowship Packages   To make recommendations (1) and (2) workable for students, universities should reconsider fellowship packages that are too rich in the first year or two, relative to funding available in the fourth, fifth, and sixth years. The Committee particularly recommends providing more support for students to complete dissertations, without having to teach, when they are within a year of doing so. It makes more sense to us for students to teach in their second to fourth years, while they are completing course work and devising plans for their dissertations, than to have them continue teaching when they could be concentrating their efforts on finishing dissertations already in progress.

4. Diversity Strategies   The APSA's Minority Identification Program; its support for the Ralph Bunche Summer Institute, now held at Duke University; its Minority Fellowships and endowments within the Centennial Center; its pre-APSA Annual Conference workshops for scholars of color; the Road Show outreach effort of the APSA Committee on the Status of Latinos y Latinas in the Profession, among other efforts, have all helped to recruit and prepare more students of color interested in political science and to assist them in their careers. However, much remains to be done by all of us to achieve a profession more representative of America's, and ultimately the world's, population.

Many universities also have programs for faculty mentoring of minority undergraduates interested in pursuing Ph.D.s. Departments should participate in these and similar efforts, such as recruitment letters targeted to traditionally black colleges and to programs in racial and ethnic studies, and gender studies, in order to expand the pool of qualified applicants from diverse backgrounds. Many departments also use an affirmative action advocate on their graduate admissions committee or some other institutionalized system to assure that minority applicants receive careful, comprehensive consideration going beyond standardized test scores. But it is vital for such admissions efforts to be followed by departmental and university programs to provide minority students with intellectual and social support; by a broadly shared faculty willingness to mentor students who may come from less familiar educational and social backgrounds; by a curriculum that does not treat issues of race, ethnicity, gender and sexual orientation as marginal political science concerns; and by student and faculty reward systems that recognize outstanding work done by scholars with diverse backgrounds and interests. As part of this general process, the APSA has established a mentoring program for women and minorities which can be accessed via the APSA website. Although it currently focuses on the special issues of gender and minority status among graduate students and faculty, this program could be extended to the undergraduate level.

5. International Students   Foreign students have become a substantial presence in many graduate program. All of them, but especially those from non-English speaking countries, face special challenges. Not only must they live and work in a less familiar language and culture, but their substantive interests may vary from those of American students. The job market at home may function quite differently from the American model, making it hard for them to prepare for it here. Moreover, during their graduate training, undergraduate teaching may be difficult for them, thereby eliminating a major source of funding. Travel costs, visa regulations, and fellowship restrictions may also add to their burdens.

Most universities with graduate programs now make special provision for improving the English language skills of foreign students. We urge that these programs be continued, supplemented by special university offices responsible for enhancing the social and intellectual experience of foreign students. At the department level, we encourage faculty to be alert to the special needs of international students, and to structure programs to meet the coursework, advising, and funding needs.

6. Professional Ethics   The basic principles of professional ethics are clear. All of us should practice intellectual honesty in our scholarship and teaching. We should treat all students and colleagues respectfully, according them appropriate recognition for their work and avoiding all forms of harassment and intimidation. We should conscientiously fulfill our responsibilities as teachers and institutional citizens, even as we seek to pursue our research agendas, contribute to our communities, and care for and enjoy our families. But especially for those entering the profession, it is often less clear just what their obligations and prerogatives are in a whole host of particular situations. Some departments have established workshops on professional ethics and/or adopted formal guidelines. In one form or another, all departments must strive to convey concrete standards of professional ethics to their graduate students, most of all by following them.

7. **Teaching and Research Experience** Good graduate programs include opportunities for students to serve both as teaching assistants/graduate student instructors (TA/GSI), and as research assistants (RA). Indeed, we consider the roles of TA/GSI and RA both to be essential elements of a graduate education. Serving as a TA/GSI under a fine, experienced undergraduate teacher is an excellent way to learn how to teach, especially when combined with departmental seminars and monitoring practices focused on teaching. Likewise, being an RA provides essential insights into how to do research.

We encourage departments to set up formal mechanisms to help graduate students become better instructors. Faculty advice and constructive suggestions are often very valuable. Departments should consider having faculty members visit the class meetings of their TA/GSI at least once in each course taught.

Departments also need to consider what special training may be necessary to help graduate students from other countries be effective in today's U.S. classroom. More generally, all graduate students must learn to address constructively the impact of many kinds of diversity on classroom environments and teacher/student relationships. If their university has not already begun such training, departments should do so themselves.

But diminishing returns set in for both teaching assistantships and research assistantships when pursued merely as a way of receiving financial support year after year. Departments should provide sufficient support for graduate students that they do not have to work as TA/GSI's or RA's in ways that are detrimental to their intellectual and professional development. Working in one of these roles should not be allowed to inhibit students from gaining the broad and deep knowledge necessary to be first-rate political scientists, or from making rapid progress toward completion of their dissertations, once they are fully engaged in their research and writing.

8. **Structured Evaluations and Advising** Departments need to have systematic procedures in place to keep track of students' progress and to assess whether that progress is satisfactory. An average time to degree that is overly long ought to stimulate departmental discussion about the appropriateness of requirements and the adequacy of advising. On the other hand, because some students need deep training in more than one area, our Task Force does not recommend rigid criteria for time to degree. Rather, departments should remain flexible in allowing graduate students to pursue individualized programs that

reasonably suit their intellectual needs and interests. Departments should engage university administrators in conversation about the meaning of averages in calculating time to degree.

Departments must be willing to drop students from their programs who are not making satisfactory progress despite appropriate support. Doing so could free up resources for more successful students, to give them additional years of support for in-depth study as mentioned under heading (2).

Evaluation procedures need to be clearly explained to graduate students, and the evaluators need to be well informed and fair. Thus departments need to pay attention to advising and mentoring of all graduate students, while taking into account the fact that students vary in their independence, and that stubbornness or even recalcitrance may suggest originality rather than bad character. Each student should have access for advice to more than one faculty member. Patterns of having one or two faculty members advising all minority students should be resisted.

Some departments have instituted a mandatory review of each graduate student at the end of the first year, attended by more than one faculty member of the student's choice, and another such review at the end of the second year. Registration for the following year is blocked until the meeting is completed, thus ensuring that students make the appointments and faculty keep them. These half-hour meetings provide an opportunity for students to discuss their concerns and receive pertinent advice at critical points of their student careers. Excessive narrowness or lack of focus can be visible from the transcript, as are academic difficulties of other sorts. Students also have the opportunity, if they wish, to talk about their financial concerns, illnesses in their families, and other matters that might otherwise go undetected.

Thus we recommend that departments set up both procedures for regular graduate student evaluations and also formal mechanisms by which regular faculty advice to individual graduate students is not just recommended in laissez-faire fashion, but is instead a reality for each student.

Finally, departments should recognize that burdens of advising fall unevenly on faculty members for a variety of reasons. They should endeavor to ensure that—particularly with respect to untenured faculty—unequal advising and supervising burdens do not hinder the intellectual development and professional advancement of any category of faculty. Departments should be especially sensitive to the additional burdens often placed on faculty of color, as well as on women faculty.

9. Graduate Student Associations   Associations of graduate students can play a very important role in the education of graduate students, by sponsoring seminars and practice job talks, assisting in faculty hiring and graduate student recruitment, providing advice to junior graduate students, representing student interests to the faculty, and sustaining a minimal degree of social life. Such associations should be encouraged, since the intellectual community they help create will make possible all the goals we have discussed in this report.

10. **Informing Prospective Graduate Students**   Many prospective students choose among graduate programs with knowledge of little more than the geographical location of the university, the ranking of the department, and the terms of their financial aid package. Relatively few have a clear idea of the type of training they want or need.

If departments described themselves clearly in their application materials and websites, students applying to graduate programs would make fewer mistakes. And if applicants had a good source of centralized information about the types of training available and the departments where such training is offered, the matching of students to graduate programs would work better than it sometimes does at present. APSA can play an important role in that effort.

The Task Force recommends that the APSA publicize how undergraduates can use its Graduate Student Website to link to departments offering Ph.D. programs and that the website add links to Master's programs. The website could give a list of things that students might like to think about as they consider graduate education. These could include a list of the categories of information provided on individual departmental web sites, along with brief instructions on how to locate those sites. Such a list might therefore include items like the following:

Graduate Program URL
Contact Information
Graduate Degrees Awarded
Ph.D. Program Objectives
Ph.D. Program's Distinctive Attributes, e.g., Joint Degrees
Financial Aid
Diversity Programs
Requirements for the Ph.D.—Skills, Coursework
Recent Student Papers and Presentations
Professional Preparation—Research, Teaching, Other Professional
    Development Activities
Other Academic Roles, Preparation for Careers Outside the Academy
Placement Outcomes, Average %
 Placed and Types of Placement, Placement Procedures
Average/Maximum Time to Degree
Graduate Student Organizations

The APSA might revise its "Graduate Programs: Questions to Ask" program so that the APSA's website, staff representatives, and member departments all advise undergraduates exploring graduate programs to consider the following topics, which departments should also be prepared to address:

Methodological focus, placement experience.
Actual availability of faculty of different specialties in specific departments; average time to degree.

Funding.

The nature and quality of faculty involvement with students, as evidenced by which faculty members have chaired dissertations, published joint articles, etc.

The existence of divisive departmental cleavages on disciplinary issues, such as views toward "science", behavioralism, quantitative/ qualitative methods, formal modeling, rational choice or other political science perspectives.

The climate for women and other minorities in a department, its university, and its community.

Resources for students with spouses, children or significant others.

How the department assesses student progress.

Departments should especially make potential applicants aware of the APSA initiative providing website information on "Graduate Programs: Questions to be Asked" regarding professional preparation and training. Ph.D. departments are being invited to indicate that they are prepared to answer the questions; departments that agree are to be listed as "Rostered" departments. The APSA could revise its "Earning a Ph.D." brochure to include a section on "Applying to Graduate Programs: Questions to be Asked" that could be a companion to the "Rostering" Questions. All of this material needs to be more readily accessible from the general APSA website, including links to pertinent activities of the APSA Task Force on Mentoring and the APSA Committee on Education and Professional Development.

11. Informing Enrolled Graduate Students and Connecting Them to the Profession   No matter how hard the profession tries, some student vagueness about their future graduate educations is inevitable. That fact is neither surprising nor blameworthy. In many subfields, the undergraduate curriculum does not acquaint students with the methods commonly applied by active researchers. Hence choices of graduate programs made in good faith during the undergraduate years may result in unhappy surprises during graduate school. Inevitably, minds change during a graduate education, alternate paths open up, and students may find themselves intellectually marooned in a program ill suited to their interests or abilities. What can be done to help a graduate student who develops a strong interest in the politics of the Middle East in a department without a Middle East specialist, or someone who becomes fascinated with game-theoretic models of international conflict in a department where such work is absent among the faculty?

One answer is collaboration among departments. In the field of statistical methods, collaborative training is well established. Since 1962, the Summer Program in Quantitative Methods administered by the Inter-University Consortium for Political and Social Research, or ICPSR, at the University of Michigan has offered summer courses in both introductory statistics and a variety of advanced topics. Both faculty and students from around the country come to

Ann Arbor to participate in courses and workshops that last from two days to four weeks. Over time, the course offerings have expanded to include courses in mathematics and formal theory. No department of political science can offer courses in the full array of statistical techniques that political scientists have found useful. Many students, even students from departments that offer strong quantitative training, receive important benefits from being able to supplement the courses offered in their home departments with the variety of basic and specialized courses offered in the ICPSR summer program.

The ICPSR summer program is the most well known, but it is not the only inter-departmental training program. Students with an interest in survey research methods can find a variety of specialized courses in the Summer Institute in Survey Research Techniques, offered by the Survey Research Center at the University of Michigan. Within the past two years, two new inter-departmental training programs have been established. The National Science Foundation [NSF] funded the establishment of an annual four-week Summer Institute in Empirical Implications of Theoretical Models, or EITM, for four years. The purpose of EITM is to provide graduate students with specialized training in both the content of formal models and the appropriate quantitative methods for testing formal models.

In addition, the discipline now has an annual training institute for training in qualitative methods. The Consortium for Qualitative Research Methods, or CQRM (web address http://www.asu.edu/clas/polisci/cqrm) offers an intensive two weeks of instruction in the philosophy of science and qualitative methods in social science at Arizona State University once a year. Like the EITM, the CQRM has successfully recruited top scholars to teach state-of-the-art research techniques in their respective areas. We urge the NSF and other funders to support this sort of qualitative as well as quantitative research training in the social sciences.

Subject to space limitations, all of these programs are available to graduate students in any Ph.D. program for a fee. One obvious thing that departments can do to improve their graduate programs is to provide funding for students to attend one of the training institutes in quantitative or qualitative training. (Since NSF funds EITM, students do not need funding from their home department to attend. All that students need is encouragement to apply.)

As valuable as such training programs are, a one-week or four-week course is no substitute for working closely with a faculty member on a research project or dissertation over an extended period of time. One program that might be expanded or emulated is the Traveling Scholar Program of the Committee on Institutional Cooperation or CIC. The CIC is a forum for institutional cooperation among the eleven members of the Big Ten Athletic Conference, plus the University of Chicago. The Traveling Scholar Program is an agreement among the CIC universities that allows a graduate student to study for up to a year at another CIC university. A student who wishes to spend a year at another CIC university must obtain the approval of both departments. Students remain registered in their home department. The host school provides the student with access to libraries and other university facilities. The home department provides the student with financial assistance. Credits earned are automatically transferred to the home department.

The Traveling Scholar Program enables a student who acquired an interest in Middle Eastern politics or game-theoretic applications in international relations to spend a year in a CIC school with a strong program in Middle East studies or game theory. Negotiating an exchange program among 12 schools is clearly better for both the students and the universities than a series of bilateral exchanges. From the university administration's point of view, participating in such an exchange allows the university to expand what can be offered to its students relatively cheaply. Departments may worry that participating in such an exchange reduces the pressure on the administration to allow the department to hire enough faculty to cover the discipline, but complete coverage of the discipline is no longer feasible. Expanding the Traveling Scholar Program to include a large number of graduate departments seems like a practical way to increase opportunities for graduate students to acquire deep training in more areas of research and more methodological approaches than any single graduate program can offer. Expansion will, however, require top -level administrative support. The APSA as well as member departments should contact provosts or presidents belonging to the AAU [Association of American Universities], the Ivy League, the PAC-10 [Pacific-10 Conference], and similar university associations to encourage them to institute or expand Traveling Scholar programs. And because the APSA and political science more generally are becoming ever more internationalized, efforts to incorporate departments outside the United States in similar cooperative arrangements should also be pursued.

A final way in which the faculty of departments collaborates in training graduate students is in organizing graduate student conferences. The Society for Comparative Research, for example, holds an annual graduate student conference that is open to graduate students in sociology and political science who are doing comparative research, with faculty participating as discussants. Graduate students also attend the summer meeting of the Political Methodology Section of the APSA, where a part of the meeting is dedicated to graduate student posters. Faculty circulate around the poster room, learning about each student's work and giving informal, one-on-one advice and suggestions. These annual conferences present a good opportunity for graduate students to present their dissertation research to a broad audience and to meet other students from around the country who are working on similar topics.

Students can only avail themselves of these opportunities if they are aware of them. APSA is a crucial source of knowledge about research and training opportunities for political science graduate students. Thus departments should participate in APSA's programs of importance to graduate students, including its announcements of specialized training programs open to graduate students across the country. APSA can also sponsor training and mentoring sessions as part of the annual APSA meetings, as it has done in the past, to aid students whose departments cannot provide some forms of preparation.

IV. Preparing for Professional Careers

Though graduate training occurs primarily in large research universities, a great many attractive jobs are available in small public and private colleges, public comprehensive universities, and community colleges. Many political science Ph.D.s find exciting employment outside academia as well. Though here, too, departmental responses can legitimately vary, all graduate programs should seek to prepare their students for the greatest range of job opportunities they can.

The APSA currently participates in an interdisciplinary Preparing Future Faculty (PFF) program, described on the Association website, that is exploring new ways that departments can provide appropriate preparation for today's academic job market. That program's principles rightly stress preparing students not only for research but also for teaching and service within academic communities. They call for departments to create formal mentoring systems for teaching and professional development, which can include workshops or elective courses on teaching and course development, along with individual faculty mentoring of teaching assistants. Such systems should include discussion of the varying demands of different institutional settings, such as the emphasis on interdisciplinary teaching in many small colleges and in interdisciplinary programs with hiring powers; the varying emphases on teaching, research and service as grounds for promotion that junior faculty encounter in different settings; issues of professional ethics; and the differing challenges presented by the diverse class, educational, gender, racial, ethnic, and religious backgrounds of students at various types of institutions. Professional development programs should also include fostering student awareness of emerging uses of new technologies in both teaching and service work.

Beyond these PFF recommendations, we believe that departments should assist graduate students in preparing job talks and application materials for a variety of types of institutions. They should also work with institutional career planning and placement centers whenever possible to develop workshops and advisory systems that can help students seeking non-academic careers. Departments with small graduate programs also might work with larger ones to initiate workshops and short courses offered to graduate students at the APSA's annual meeting, as has occurred in the past. Topics can include learning to teach, preparation for the job market, concerns of minority scholars, and much more. The APSA annual meeting can also be an occasion for graduate studies directors to meet to discuss common concerns, including minority scholar identification, recruiting, and mentoring. Similar sessions can be undertaken as part of regional meetings.

Though departments must decide for themselves whether and how their curriculum should be structured to assist students not seeking academic jobs, it is also desirable to encourage broader faculty acceptance that business, government, and nonprofit careers can be appropriate goals for Ph.D. students.

V. The Need to Study Ourselves:
Career Paths in Graduate School and Beyond

In our deliberations, the Committee often found ourselves asking questions about the career paths of political scientists. How does dissertation support affect initial job placement? Do faculty at liberal arts colleges often move to research universities? How do the experiences of racial, religious, and economic minority, LGBT [lesbian, gay, bisexual, and transsexual], and female assistant professors differ from those of males from traditionally privileged backgrounds? How do they differ from each other? Unfortunately, though speculation about each of these questions abounds, none of the answers is reliably known.

The Association is in an excellent position to study its own members and learn the answers to these and many other questions that arise in the course of APSA business. We believe that studying ourselves in this way would pay for itself. Put the other way, making Association recommendations and policy in a state of self-ignorance is an expensive way to proceed.

Thus the Committee recommends that the American PoliticalScience Association begin a panel study of the careers of political scientists. Designing such a study is a job for specialists, and we make no pretense of doing so here. However, we recommend that scholars at all stages be included in the sample, from graduate school on. An initial survey of demographic and career information, supplemented by occasional attitudinal studies, would pay immediate dividends. Then as the years passed and longitudinal data became available, the profession could stop guessing about how we live and which policy changes work effectively.

We recognize that a survey of this kind will cost APSA some money. We also recognize that special efforts will have to be made to keep information confidential and to prevent the identification of individual scholars from the data in the surveys. But these are familiar problems from surveys of other small populations, and they have well tested and effective solutions well known to survey professionals. Thus, while there are many details to be worked out and approved by the Association in consultation with those administering the survey, we believe that the project is feasible, ethical, and eminently worthwhile. We urge the Association to consider it.

VI. Conclusion

The challenges of providing adequate graduate education in political science today are more daunting than ever before, but they are not insurmountable. Political scientists share some vital commitments. We believe that politics matters. We seek to identify and illuminate truly important political topics. And we try to do so as rigorously and honestly as we can, while recognizing that many kinds of knowledge, methods, and perspectives are necessary for the discipline as whole to study politics well. If, whatever their distinctive strengths and specializations, all graduate programs seek to make students aware of all of the different types of training and assistance available, in their department and beyond; if they support students materially and intellectually in the pursuit of all forms of training most pertinent to the students' own interests; and if throughout their graduate training activities departments and graduate student mentors seek to communicate these shared commitments, then much can be accomplished.

No department can now do the job alone. Yet through individual and collaborative efforts guided by our shared professional commitments, the discipline of political science as a whole can provide an appropriately broad, accessible array of graduate training. Only this combination of dedication, cooperation, and mutual respect will suffice to educate the next generation of political scientists fully, responsibly, and effectively.

> Respectfully submitted,
> *Cristina Beltran, Haverford College*
> *Cathy J. Cohen, University of Chicago*
> *David Collier, University of California-Berkeley*
> *Edie Goldenberg, University of Michigan*
> *Robert Keohane, Duke University*
> *Kristen Monroe, University of California-Irvine*
> *Michael Wallerstein, Northwestern University*
> *Christopher H. Achen, Princeton University, and*
> *Rogers M. Smith, University of Pennsylvania, Co-Chairs*
> March 23, 2004

References

Bennett, Douglas, Morris Blackman, Frederick Eisele, James Paul, and Kenneth Sharpe. 1969. Obstacles to Graduate Education in Political Science. *PS* 2, 4: 622–641.

Dimock, Marshall E., Harold M. Dorr, Claude E. Hawley, E. Allen Helms, Andrew E. Nuquist, Ruth G. Weintraub, and Howard White. 1951. *Goals for Political Science.* New York: William Sloane Associates.

CHAPTER 30

The Graduate Student Experience

"Hegemony" or Balance in Methodological Training?

Peregrine Schwartz-Shea

Graduate education is, and is meant to be, a transformative experience. Student potentialities are developed, honed, and shaped via a process of professional socialization and attention to substantive content. Students acquire substantive expertise, but they also learn (implicitly if not explicitly) disciplinary and field norms about how to conduct research, norms about the proper purposes of research, and, most important, norms about what counts as legitimate social-scientific knowledge.

Because the social sciences are located at the intersection between the sciences and the humanities, there is considerable variation in disciplinary understandings about what counts as legitimate social-scientific knowledge. Some of the more interdisciplinary fields, such as communication and educational studies, enact broad definitions of knowledge such that researchers use interpretive techniques adapted from the humanities as well as more traditional quantitative-statistical methodologies. Other disciplines, such as economics and psychology, enact more exclusive definitions of knowledge that emphasize quantitative-statistical approaches as the most legitimate form of research.[1]

In this chapter I document the variation of political science norms about research and knowledge using the lens of doctoral program curricular requirements and offerings from fifty-seven departments. What is particularly useful about requirements and offerings is that they reflect the collective decisions of faculty "on the ground"; that is, curricular requirements and offerings provide the structural parameters within which, on a daily basis, individual faculty work with and train those who will ultimately replace them in the discipline. This evidence base provides the means for inquiring about variations in the graduate experience by program type, specifically about the extent to which students acquire inclusive or exclusive understandings of what counts as legitimate knowledge. Whereas other disciplinary indicators may challenge Perestroikan claims of methodological hegemony (for example, the breadth and variety of organized sections in the APSA), doctoral education provides some of the clearest evidence in support of the Perestroikan claim that political science enacts exclusionary definitions of legitimate knowledge.

In what follows, I first describe the evidence base, discuss coding issues, and assess limitations of a curricular approach to understanding variation in graduate education. Then I describe the development of the typology of programs, present the distribution of programs across the typology, and then use these findings to conduct a thought experiment about graduate experiences as a function of student potentialities and program placement. In the final section, I address the difficult issue of department specialization: are departments obligated to legitimize the full spectrum of approaches to knowledge?

Data Set and Methodology

Fifty-seven doctoral programs were selected based on the criteria of graduate program size and three sets of rankings,[2] the 2001 *U.S. News & World Report* (*U.S. News*) ranking,[3] the National Research Council (NRC) ranking (as published in *PS*, 1996), and the ranking system of Ballard and Mitchell (1998) published in *PS*. The sample includes 43 percent of the 132 doctoral programs identified in the 1998–2000 *APSA Graduate Program and Faculty Guide* (351–52) and 90 percent of the top fifty NRC programs. It also includes approximately 61 percent of the graduate student population as estimated using the program size numbers from the *Guide*.[4] Small program size was the reason the five top fifty NRC programs were *not* included in the data set, whereas the distinct ranking system of Ballard and Mitchell accounts for the selection of particular programs ranked lower or not ranked in the NRC and *U.S. News* systems. For the list of doctoral programs included and their associated codes, see the appendix to this chapter.

For each program, two primary sources were used: (1) department program descriptions and course listings from university bulletins available through the database College Source, and (2) department Web sites. If program information was incomplete or there were inconsistencies between these two sources, e-mail communication with staff and faculty was used for clarification. In a few cases, graduate program guides were obtained by mail. These sources were used to create an extensive record for each program: 121 variables as well as a template-based description including idiosyncratic descriptors and synthetic judgments, for example, the likely implications of particular concatenations of requirements. Initial coding was conducted by a research assistant,[5] and then I checked and corrected it after completion of the template-based description. Completing and verifying the data for each program required approximately two hours from the research assistant and four hours on my part.

For each department, three sets of questions guided the investigation:

1.   Are there any program-wide requirements? Or, are requirements decided by each field?
2.   What are the curricular definitions of "methods" and "methodology?" That is, are "methods" courses exclusively quantitative or are courses in qualitative methodology offered or required as well?

3.   To what extent are philosophy of social science and the scope and/or history of the discipline offered or required at the doctoral level?[6]

Aggregate percentages for the fifty-seven programs have been reported elsewhere (Schwartz-Shea, 2003) indicating disciplinary coverage of and requirements in language, philosophy of science, scope or history of the discipline, quantitative methods, qualitative methods, and game theory.[7] Here I rely on the template-based description to classify each program into one of three categories, based on what the curriculum communicates to graduate students about the legitimacy of various methodological approaches to knowledge and knowledge-making. Before explication of the typology, however, some additional issues require clarification—the coding and limitations of a curricular approach.

For the most part, the coding was straightforward, but two areas need discussion. First, the meaning of "qualitative methods" must be carefully defined, because the term is used in a variety of ways in the discipline. To capture this diversity, "qualitative methods" should be understood as an umbrella term encompassing positivist and interpretive epistemological perspectives of the access to "words" (for example, interviewing, selection and construction of cases) and analysis of them (for example, content analysis or semiotics). Courses in qualitative methods cover topics such as field research, in-depth interviewing, textual analysis, case studies, ethnography, historical research, and assorted interpretive techniques (from metaphor analysis to deconstruction). Courses in "quantitative methods" cover standard statistical topics (descriptive statistics and measures of associations) and forms of multivariate analysis as well as experimental methods, survey research, and econometrics. Though use of the "quantitative-qualitative" terminology is useful for the purposes of curriculum assessment, it has been criticized on several grounds.[8] I agree with much of this criticism and admit that the construction of these crude categories of courses contributes to the reification of the misleading "quantitative-qualitative" distinction. Nevertheless, for the purposes of curriculum review, these categories are appropriate to the task of describing existing courses.

There is another complication that is relevant to counting the number of qualitative courses offered in a program. Whereas quantitative course titles are rarely field-identified, qualitative courses often have field-identified titles such as "Case Study Methods for Comparative Politics" or "Textual Analysis in Political Theory." Course titles matter because a field-identified course title narrows the range of clientele, whereas a general title invites students of any field to consider the method as applicable. Thus, for the calculation of statistics reported later, a field-identified qualitative methods course title received half credit (0.5) whereas an "unmodified" qualitative methods course title received full credit (1.0).

A second coding issue involves the extent of program coverage of particular topics, such as qualitative methods or philosophy of science. Such content may be covered in a "stand-alone" course focusing on the particular topic or in a "catch-all" course that covers a smattering of topics. Catch-all required introductory courses are common, attempting to cover some combination of philosophy of science, scope of the discipline, history of the discipline, design, and methods. The coverage of stand-alone courses can be inferred from course titles and catalog descriptions. Identifying and inferring the content of catchall courses is tricky because they have a variety of titles (from "Scope and Methods" to "The Nature of Political Science" to "Design and Methods") that may or may not match the content of the catalog descriptions. In a few such cases I was able to obtain syllabi. Though syllabi are a better indicator of instructor intent, catalog descriptions formalize the general outlines of course content and thus may guide future course instructors.

Inferences as to precisely what is covered are less reliable for catch-all than stand-alone courses, though for any particular content, for example, philosophy of science, coverage will obviously be greater in stand-alone than in catchall courses. For the purposes of counting whether particular content was required, I chose a generous decision rule, that is, mere mention of the relevant content in the course description meant the program received credit for covering the topic. Thus the depth of coverage of the specific content is overestimated in the areas of philosophy of science and qualitative methods. In addition, the data on program requirements are generally more reliable than those on course offerings, because new courses are often taught under temporary specialty catalog numbers before achieving individual catalog titles and numbers, and courses in the catalog may not have been taught in years.[9]

Though it is useful to think about variations in the graduate student experience in terms of curricular requirements and offerings, several caveats should be kept in mind. First, the data set is cross-sectional, so longitudinal inferences are not warranted. Second, the research questions focus on programwide rather than field requirements and on variation in method and methodology rather than on variation in theoretical approaches. These decisions were a function of resource limitations but also of the judgment that methodological and epistemological training interact with theoretical training in critical ways. Thus theoretical diversity may be supported *or* undercut by curricular requirements and offerings in methods and philosophy of science.

Third, a major premise of the study is that course requirements and offerings reflect substantive judgments about the value of particular content in the doctoral curriculum. But for a variety of reasons (from problems of collective action to institutional constraints), the graduate curriculum does not perfectly reflect what members of the discipline most value. Geological metaphors are useful for understanding the connection (or lack thereof) between curricular structures and disciplinary values: courses and requirements are laid down like sedimentary layers, at times reflecting the interests of long-departed faculty; the earthquakes and volcanoes of full-blown curricular revisions are comparatively rare but can be dramatic in their consequences. Though "the faculty" is collectively responsible, individual members exercise different levels of influence as a function of the structure they encounter upon entering the department, their tenure status, field power within the department, expertise, and happenstance. This caveat about individual responsibility aside, curricular offerings, and particularly doctoral requirements, are a faculty's collective, formal enactment of its vision for graduate education, and students must operate within the given curricular structure or invest time in getting around it.

A fourth issue concerns the relative importance of curriculum in doctoral education; a study of curriculum cannot capture the significant roles of graduate advising and mentoring, much less the informal interaction and socialization that occurs over a multiyear process. But while mentoring and socialization are critical processes, they still take place within a curricular structure that can support or subvert them. Finally, it might be objected that it would be preferable to ask students directly about their understandings of what constitutes legitimate social-scientific knowledge. Existing surveys of doctoral education (The 2000 National Doctoral Program Survey 2001; Golde and Dore 2001), however, focus on issues such as overall student satisfaction, time to degree, and career preparation with no questions specific to methodology and epistemology.[10]

The Typology

As political theorists and interpretive researchers emphasize (Stone 1988; Yanow 2002), category creation is never a neutral, value-free endeavor. Researchers decide what and how to count with a purpose in mind. The impetus for the research presented in this chapter grew out of my years of participant observation in the discipline as someone hired to teach quantitative methods who then began reading the interdisciplinary literature on feminist epistemology and methodology. As a result of the latter exploration I began to compare our discipline to others. Specifically, not only was there an apparent lack of courses in qualitative methods, but the very definition of a "methodologist," in APSA personnel advertisements but also in common usage, was someone specializing in the measurement of variables and analysis of large n data sets using regression, analysis of variance, and other statistical techniques. Analysis of selected research methods texts marketed to the discipline provided systematic evidence of this narrow understanding of methodology; that is, the texts communicated in subtle and not-so-subtle ways the superiority of quantitative-statistical approaches to research (Schwartz-Shea and Yanow 2002). In sum, diverse disciplinary indicators appeared to equate legitimate social-scientific knowledge with quantitative-statistical approaches (even, at times, erroneously equating "empirical" exclusively with "quantitative" research). This study seeks to assess the extent to which this is also the case in doctoral education.

Aggregate statistics reported elsewhere (Schwartz-Shea 2003) document the strong position of quantitative-statistical methods, the comparatively weaker position of philosophy of science and scope of the discipline, and the marginalized position of language and qualitative methods based on the same fifty-seven programs examined here. Though informative, such aggregate statistics cannot reveal how program requirements and offerings fit together to present students in a particular program with a set of options, or what those options communicate to them about what constitutes legitimate social-scientific knowledge. Analysis at the department level is required to get a sense of these issues. Even in its purest form, that is, abstracted from institutional and market pressures, graduate program design involves complex judgments involving a variety of interrelated issues: breadth-depth tradeoffs, time to completion of degree, the extent of programwide versus field-based requirements, and so on (Schwartz-Shea 2002). Departments have found myriad ways of meeting this challenge, producing complex combinations of required courses, required competencies, and structured choices. To make sense of this complexity requires some classificatory scheme. The three categories used here, each of which represents an "ideal type" of program, were developed inductively based on immersion in the "thick descriptions" available in the template database, that is, curricular requirements and offerings, but also, where available, field descriptions and department self-representations. After the three ideal types were developed, individual programs were assessed against the types and classified in one of the categories.

The ideal types and coding complications are described in detail later, but briefly, ideal type 1 enacts exclusionary definitions of legitimate knowledge, narrowing the meaning of method and methodology to quantitative-statistical approaches. Ideal type 3 enacts inclusive definitions, offering and legitimizing both quantitative and qualitative training. Ideal type 2 is "split," encouraging or requiring a sorting by substantive field such that some students receive quantitative-statistical training whereas others receive linguistic training. Though the development of these ideal types has a critical purpose, it is essential to note that the assignment of a particular program based on this single criterion should not be read as an indictment or an endorsement of the substantive training available in the program as a whole. Doctoral education is a complex phenomenon, and the disciplinary variation described here is a function of historical antecedents, collective decisions and nondecisions, the evolution of organizational practices, and substantive debates over the nature of legitimate social-scientific knowledge.[11]

The Ideal Types

Table 30.1 presents the curricular components that define each ideal type of program in terms of required language competency, a quantitative methods requirement, a philosophy of science requirement, the offering of a qualitative methods course, and the number of quantitative courses "on the books," that is, listed in the university catalog. Each program was assessed against

Table 30.1   **Primary Characteristics of the Ideal Types**

Curricular Characteristics	Category 1	Category 2	Category 3
Language competency required?	No	In some fields	Yes
Quantitative-statistical course required?	Yes	In some fields	Yes
Philosophy of science course required?	No	An option only	Yes
Qualitative course offering?	No; possibly a field-identified course	Possibly a field-identified course	Yes
Number of quantitative-statistical course offerings	High (four to six)	Medium (two to four)	Low (one to two)

Source: Author's own design.

these primary indicators, but, where available, I considered program and field representations—some of which will be presented later to give flesh to the bare bones of the ideal types.

Other secondary indicators that aided me in program classification included the existence and role of three fields: methodology, formal theory, and political theory. In the case of methodology, 45 percent of programs offer such a field, and the way in which that field was represented could be directly examined. In the case of formal theory, I counted the number of course offerings and noted whether an examination field in formal theory was offered, which is the case for 16 percent of the programs. Though the presence or absence of a formal theory field or courses was not a determining factor in classification of programs, it is relevant. In this I concur with Kasza's (2001) judgment that the behavioral revolution and its associated quantitative perspective of method laid the groundwork for the acceptance and growth of the game-theoretic approach. This approach has, in turn, reinforced the quantitative perspective of method as evidenced in this study by field titles such as "Formal Theory and Quantitative Methods," "Formal and Quantitative Analysis," and "Formal Models and Methodology" offered by 14 percent of the programs studied.[12]

In the case of political theory, is it a strong field in the sense of having a minimal number of faculty? Or is it combined with other fields such as formal theory or methodology? Whereas programs' coverage of American politics, comparative politics, and international relations is greater than 96 percent at the aggregate level, only 72 percent offer a political theory field, 7 percent offer a field combining political theory and methodology, and 5 percent offer a field combining political and formal theory. In addition, the position of political theory in a department can be a bellwether for views on the meaning of "science." Specifically, is theory marginalized by the tendency to reify the distinction between political theory and "the empirical fields"? The division of labor reflected in "fields" is appropriate when it recognizes a distinct purpose of political theory, that is, reflecting on questions of political values to which empirical evidence cannot provide answers. The institutional division of labor is detrimental, however, when it replicates the facts-values dichotomy, obscuring the similarities of those doing normative and empirical research: both make arguments, both use evidence, and both are ineluctably political. Reification is problematic because it communicates to "nontheory" (or "empirical field") students the particularity (or peculiarity or irrelevance, depending on student inclinations) of the political theory field, a division of labor in which "philosophers" worry over "values" (using primarily "words") whereas "scientists" theorize and test "reality" using quantitative-statistical tools.

Because the categories are ideal types, individual programs do not always perfectly fit their assigned type. There are three possible coding complications. First, because each judgment was a synthetic one based on the myriad bits of available evidence for any program (for example, field descriptions, requirement "opt-out" opportunities, definitions and field titles, and so on), there are cases where a single feature "runs against the grain" of the program as a whole, but that single element is not sufficient to change the overall coding judgment. For example, a category 1 program (47) requires one unspecified political theory course "unless completed as an undergraduate." Second, because field descriptions and program representations were not uniformly available and because representations do not always match curricular deeds, I adopted the decision rule that curricular patterns were the primary determinative of program classification in one of the three categories. In short, curricular criteria trumped program representations. Finally, as will be detailed later, there are some coding complications peculiar to each category type.

Program and Field Representations and Coding Complications

The archetypal program for category 1 is Rochester, and the clarity of its vision was the work of a notable entrepreneur, William Riker. As the Rochester Web site itself observes: "The program began in the 1960s, and the Department is regularly ranked in the top handful of political science departments in the country, a development characterized by Berkeley's Nelson Polsby as 'one of the great success stories of department-building in the annals of political science and perhaps of American higher education' (*PS* Fall 1984)." In terms of the program's vision for doctoral education, the Web page states:

> The structure of training in the Ph.D. program is based on two convictions. One is that political science has a unique subject matter that requires specialization. . . . Our other conviction is that, in the next generation, all the social sciences, including political science, will become increasingly formal in theory and will rely increasingly on quantitative evidence. Foreseeing

this future, we have designed a program to help students successfully participate in it. While many of our graduate students write dissertations and
pursue careers that apply traditional methods, they have been trained to
be able to read and evaluate *all* the literature in their fields, no matter how
technical. (Emphasis added.)[13]

I have identified Rochester explicitly because its example is so well known and
because the match between the Web site language and the program requirements and offerings is consistent. There is no language requirement, and the
course requirements are (1) PSC 480, Scope of Political Science ("a philosophical analysis of the logic of theory construction in political science"); (2) PSC
403, Mathematical Modeling; (3) PSC 404, Introduction to Statistical Methods;
(4) PSC 405, Multivariate Statistical Methods; and (5) one political philosophy
seminar, usually PSC 581, Classic Paradigms of Political Inquiry ("an examination of the leading models of political order, both Cartesian and pre-Cartesian")
or 582, Political Economy II. Additional course offerings include four more
courses in the quantitative-statistical category as well as one in the philosophy
of science and a field-identified course in qualitative methods (Comparative
Political Analysis). Most revealing, the template entry shows that of the eight-
een courses listed in the catalog *under* political theory, half are game-theoretic.
    Even in this archetypal program, however, there is not a perfect match with
the ideal type. In particular, there is a stand-alone course in philosophy of science on the books as well as coverage in the required scope course, an optional
political philosophy seminar in the requirements, and a field-identified qualitative methods offering. Phrases from the catalog course descriptions for PSC
480 and 581 were added earlier to give some sense of what is covered in each
course. To fully understand this program, one would need to inspect syllabi for
these two courses in order to see the extent to which "the philosophical analysis" of 480 and the "leading models" of the optional 581 are inclusive or exclusive of ideas that would challenge Riker's vision. Nevertheless, the bulk of the
evidence is consistent with ideal type 1, particularly the required modeling
and statistical sequence (PSC 403, 404, and 405), which communicates to students the centrality of these approaches for all fields offered in the program.
    The assumed centrality of quantitative approaches can be communicated
without requiring any courses. If—due to recruitment—practically all faculty
think that the only legitimate or the "best" social-scientific research is quantitative research, a lack of formal requirements does not necessarily translate
into diverse offerings, much less support for methodological diversity. At a
more subtle level, inspection of the catalog for program 47 reveals that courses
are arrayed by field, but four courses in statistics and five courses in modeling
and game theory are listed in the "general" category. Other theoretical approaches are listed within field categories, implying that statistics and modeling are relevant to all fields in ways that other theoretical and methodological
approaches are not. Finally, it is often the case in program materials for cate-

gory 1 programs that "method" is identified with "quantitative" research, as in the following course description and field statement.

> POLS 7030. *Methodology* in Political Science. 3 hours.
> The use of *quantitative* methods in political science research. Topics range from descriptive statistics through regression analysis. (Program 16, emphases added.)

> *Methodology*
> Since we believe that a strong background in *research methods* will be essential for political scientists in the 1990s, we provide a rigorous training in the application of *statistical methods and formal models* to political analysis. Coursework in analytic methods includes introductory training in mathematical methods and statistics as well as more advanced modeling, econometric, measurement and time series analysis. (Program 35, emphases added.)

In summary, the defining characteristic of category 1 programs is that these programs define "method" and "empirical research" as quantitative research in their course requirements and offerings, thereby legitimizing an exclusive understanding of what constitutes social-scientific knowledge. A key caveat is that many category 1 programs (as is evident in the Rochester case) require catch-all introductory courses in which there may be some exposure to philosophy of science or to research design (which may admit the existence of qualitative modes of data access such as interviewing or field research). For category 1 programs, however, this exposure in catch-all courses receives little or no reinforcement in other requirements or offerings. Thus I had comparatively little difficulty in categorizing programs that fit category 1; as when using any ideal type, there were a few difficult decisions (two out of thirty assignments) for which an argument might be made for a different categorization.[14]

For programs in category 3, the defining characteristic is a breadth of methodological offerings and requirements across the quantitative-qualitative spectrum. A program constituting this ideal type would require language competency, a quantitative methods course, and a course in philosophy of science. There would still be several quantitative courses on the books but fewer than in category 1, because faculty resources would be devoted to a qualitative methods course, above and beyond any field-identified qualitative methods courses. In terms of secondary characteristics, political theory would not be a marginalized field, *nor* would game theory courses be absent from the curriculum.

What makes program classification a bit trickier in category 3 than in category 1 is that the program materials will sometimes retain what might be called a category 1 residual—that is, there is still a tendency to equate "empirical" work with formal and quantitative work. For example, consider the following statements from two different category 3 programs:

> In *quantitative* methods, where a carefully structured program is particularly valuable, the department has developed an optional sequence preparing students for *empirical* research. (Program 7, emphases added.)

> Recently the Dean authorized an exciting new venture, the creation of a Center for *Basic* Research in Social Science which will boost research and teaching using *quantitative* methodologies across many disciplines. (Program 17, emphases added.)

That said, for programs in category 3, there is a curricular affirmation of qualitative methodologies so that students who choose to pursue qualitative research are given the message that this is both possible and acceptable (or normal rather than deviant). For this ideal type, there were a few difficult decisions (one out of twelve assignments) for which an argument might be made for a different categorization.[15]

There are no statements for programs in this category as succinct as the Rochester statement, perhaps because the programs wish to decouple methodological approaches from substantive-theoretical concerns or, more carefully, to emphasize the preeminence of substantive concerns over the desire to apply a tool or even a theory. This is advisable because of scholars' tendency to "fall in love" with their tools (Gigerenzer and Murray 1987) and also with their chosen theory (Rule 1997), forgetting the broader purposes of social science research. Thus here are two program statements (to give some flavor of the category 3 programs):

> This breadth of scholarship is valued at [program 7]. So, too, is an emphasis on the profound questions of political life, from the sources of war and the meaning of justice to the development of representative democracy. It is this commitment to understanding fundamental issues that distinguishes [program 7] and its graduate program.

> Our objective is to be a place where most faculty and graduate students are fluent in theory. . . . [Program 23 is] designed for graduate students who seek broad training, who are inspired by large questions about politics and who aspire to develop considerable strength in more than one field.

One shouldn't make too much of such broad statements, but it could be argued that they represent a subtle critique of disciplinary practices that value precision at the cost of being mundane or trivial. As Shapiro (2002) expresses this point: "Part of the disaffection with 1960s behaviorism . . . [was that it seemed to many] to be both utterly devoid of theoretical ambition as well as detached from consequential questions of politics, frankly boring" (613).

Note, also, that neither of the program descriptions just presented uses the word "qualitative." The use of that word is indicative, however, in part because of its absence in category 1 programs. Consider the following statement, from a category 3 program that more directly discusses issues of method and methodology:

> The Department emphasizes the importance of acquiring expertise in social science research methods. As professional social scientists, graduates of the program should be familiar with methods of generating, analyzing, and interpreting *both quantitative and qualitative* data. Students should know how to *formulate hypotheses,* operationalize concepts, construct measures, and test hypotheses with appropriate data. *At a minimum, students should master basic statistics* and, where appropriate for their interests, a more advanced knowledge of statistics and mathematical models of politics. Students should *also* develop, according to their interests, knowledge of various methods of data collection, such as survey methods, psychological testing, content analysis, documentary research, case analysis, and participation observation, *and the appropriate methods for analyzing these data.* (Program 27, emphases added.)

Some of this statement reflects the category 1 residual described earlier. For example, basic statistics should be mastered, whereas data collection is an "also." In addition, the third statement about hypothesis testing procedures assumes a positivist perspective of research. Nevertheless, the final statement recognizes qualitative as well as quantitative data access and, what is particularly rare, implicitly acknowledges the existence of methods of qualitative data analysis (which could be either positivist or interpretive).

Developing the characteristics of ideal type 2 proved most challenging. The coding complication is differentiating a split program from a program in category 3 in which the discussion of method may be blurred by category 1 residuals. The decision rule is still curricular. Many of the Web statements from category 2 programs would seem to communicate the sorts of sentiments that would indicate category 3 placement. And many of the programs offered a course in qualitative methods or had healthy political theory fields (that is, both indicators of a category 3 program).[16] When it came to program *requirements,* however, these category 2 programs either defined "empirical" in quantitative terms or allowed or encouraged those in "empirical fields" to do so. In short, these programs replicated in their methodological requirements the descriptive-prescriptive or facts-values disciplinary reification discussed earlier. For this ideal type, there were a few difficult decisions (two out of fifteen assignments) for which an argument might be made for a different categorization.[17]

As an example of a split program, consider selected field descriptions from a single program (program 49):

American Political Institutions and Processes focuses on the variety of political institutions, ideas, groups and practices that comprise and surround American government. Examples include . . . . As the examples imply, the American field shares interests (and faculty) with related fields such as . . . . Our large and diverse faculty teaches a wide array of courses that represent the theoretical and methodological breadth of research in American politics. . . . Faculty and students draw upon numerous analytic techniques and methods, including formal theory, political economy, historical and documentary research, and quantitative and qualitative analysis. . . . Students are strongly advised to become fully competent in the quantitative and/or qualitative methods relevant to their research specialties. They should also equip themselves to be "intelligent consumers" of other prominent methods and approaches.

The field of *comparative politics* is devoted to the explication of the similarities and differences in the practice of politics and the characteristics of political institutions across temporal and geographical space. It seeks to develop the most general statements possible about political life, applying them to the understanding of particular political phenomena in specific times and places. We are a large and diverse group of scholars who employ a wide range of methods (quantitative and qualitative) and theoretical perspectives to the study of almost every area of the globe. This permits students a broad range of choices in their subjects of study and methods of analysis. No single approach or theoretical perspective can pretend to hegemony in comparative politics today.

Methodology is centrally about statistical theory and methods. Political theory adapts and develops ideas from statistics to the empirical study of politics, in much the same ways as do econometrics in Economics or psychometrics in Psychology. . . . Courses in Methodology are designed to be useful to students wishing to conduct rigorous analysis of empirical questions in American Politics, Comparative Politics, International Relations, Political Behavior, Formal Theory, Public Law, or Public Policy; to understand and be able to criticize articles in these fields in the leading political science journals; to contribute to the leading political science journals themselves; to be able to stand up to methodological criticisms of others; or to make original contributions to political methodology itself.

Political Behavior as the term is most commonly used in political science, means the politics of ordinary citizens. . . . But how do people come to think, feel, act as they do? This is the domain of political behavior. . . . Students writing dissertations in the field, however, are strongly encouraged to make Methodology one of their other fields, or at least to take two or more methodology courses. It is virtually impossible to do cutting edge research in Political Behavior without well-honed quantitative skills.

To summarize, the first two field descriptions, for "American Political Institutions and Processes" and "comparative politics," emphasize breadth and diversity of approach and include the term "qualitative." The statement for the comparative politics field ends by observing, "No single approach or theoretical perspective can pretend to hegemony in comparative politics today." The field descriptions for "Methodology" and "Political Behavior" provide striking contrasts. The broad category of methodology is narrowed to statistics, which, in turn, is associated with "empirical" research, "rigorous analysis," and publication in the "leading" journals. The statement for political behavior begins with a focus on the meaning of politics for ordinary citizens ("But how do people come to think, feel, act as they do?") and ends by concluding that it is "virtually impossible" to address these broad issues except with "well-honed quantitative skills."

The split revealed in the field language is then replicated in the program requirements, which encourage student sorting: (1) proficiency in one language *or* two research methods courses beyond the required courses; (2) after two required courses, choice one of the following: Studies in Political Theory and Philosophy *or* Introduction to Formal Political Science. This case, however, also illustrates the difficulties involved in coding, because the program's two required courses may expose graduate students to alternative perspectives. The two required courses are Statistical Analysis in Political Science I and Problems in the Study of Politics, the latter described as "normative orientations in research, theory formation and empirical assessment, various conceptions of explanation and historical development of the social sciences." The impact of the second required course would depend greatly on how this course description is explicated in the syllabus. Are alternative "conceptions of explanation" taken seriously or simply dismissed?

There *are* examples of similar splits within category 1 programs in which a particular field language resists the dominant curricular definitions (for example, the American politics field description for program 38). But these programs are still coded in category 1 because there is no significant curricular impact that would match the field's rhetorical resistance (though it may be the faculty responsible for such resistance who are offering the few qualitative methods courses offered by programs in this category). Likewise, there are claims of methodological diversity on the Web sites of some category 1 programs (programs 2, 5, 22, and 47). But these claims are often contradicted by other Web site language, and, most important, they are not substantiated in the curricular requirements or offerings.

To summarize, classification of each program was a synthetic judgment based on all available evidence, but it was always a judgment in which curricular criteria trumped program representations. Though resources constraints made a reliability check infeasible, the approach was systematic and questionable classifications have been identified. Most important, the overall findings reported in the next section would not be likely to change dramatically if three or four programs were shuffled to neighboring categories.

Findings

Table 30.2 presents the percentage and number of programs classified into categories based on the three ideal types, descriptive statistics for the various curricular elements, the NRC rankings, and the codes of the programs studied.

After the programs were assigned to the categories, descriptive statistics were calculated using the variables data. Three of the five curricular characteristics used to define the ideal types are cleanly supported by the descriptive statistics. First, language requirements follow a clear pattern across the three types: only 7 percent of category 1 programs require language competency in contrast to 42 percent of category 3 programs, and category 2 has the most programs (6) with a choice between language and statistics. Second, the percentages of programs with a quantitative-statistical course requirement demonstrate the clear emphasis on quantitative methods in category 1 programs: 83 percent have a quantitative requirement compared to approximately half of the programs in categories 2 and 3. It was also possible to calculate the *number* of required quantitative-statistical courses: on average, category 1 programs require one and a half such courses compared to approximately one for programs in categories 2 and 3. Third, the average number of qualitative offerings follow a clear pattern, with the fewest in category 1 programs (less than half a course) and the most in category 3 programs (close to a course and a half).[18] *Examination of the distribution of 25 qualitative courses that are not field-identified provides additional support for this characteristic: programs in category 3 offer 64 percent of these courses compared to 20 percent for programs in category 2 and 16 percent for programs in category 1.*

Two of the five curricular characteristics require more explanation. The statistics for the philosophy of science requirement are anomalous. Fifty-three percent of category 1 programs receive credit for requiring some philosophy of science, usually in a required, catch-all scope course. This percentage increases for category 2 programs, but unexpectedly decreases for category 3 programs. This may be explained by the fewer, on average, required courses in these category 3 programs (about one course) in comparison to those in category 1 (two and one half courses). Further examination of the data on stand-alone philosophy of science course offerings supports this explanation: 83 percent (10/12) of category 3 programs offer a stand-alone course compared to 73 percent (11/15) of category 2 programs and only 40 percent (12/30) of category 1 programs. In terms of the number of quantitative course offerings (as contrasted with required courses), I had reasoned that category 3 programs would offer fewer quantitative-statistical courses in order to make room for increased offerings in qualitative methods. Though category 3 programs do offer more qualitative courses, they offer, on average, as many quantitative courses as programs in categories 1 and 2.

Table 30.2 documents notable variation in disciplinary views on the legitimacy of different approaches to knowledge and knowledge-making. The 53 percent of programs in category 1 communicate through their curriculum that

Table 30.2 Distribution of Fifty-Seven Programs across the Ideal Types, with Descriptive Statistics

Category Number and Title	1 Empirical = Quantitative	2 Split	3 Empirical = Quantitative and Qualitative
Percentage and number in ideal type	53% (30)	26% (15)	21% (12)
Language competency required	7% (2/30)[a]	13% (2/15)[b]	42% (5/12)[c]
Quantitative course required	83% (25/30)	47% (7/15)	50% (6/12)
Average number of quantitative courses required[d]	1.60 (0.99)	0.80 (0.71)	0.71 (0.62)
Philosophy of science coverage required	53% (16/30)	60% (9/15)	25% (3/12)
Scope course required	53% (16/30)	47% (7/15)	25% (3/12)
Average number of required courses[d]	2.43 (1.74)	1.27 (1.16)	1.25 (1.74)
Average number of offerings[d]			
Qualitative	0.37 (0.39)	0.63 (0.67)	1.46 (0.62)
Quantitative	3.67 (1.39)	2.93 (1.33)	3.67 (1.50)
Game theory	2.07 (1.17)	1.13 (1.30)	1.83 (1.40)
Of the 25 qualitative courses,[e] percentage offered, by category	16% (4/25)	20% (5/25)	64% (16/25)
NRC rankings	2, 3.5, 5, 8, 9, 11, 17, 18, 20, 22, 24, 25, 27, 30, 32, 33, 34, 35, 38, 41, 44.5, 47.5, 53, 54, 56, 63, 84; 3 unranked programs	7, 14, 14, 19, 27, 27, 29, 38, 44.5, 47.5, 50, 54, 57, 63, 66.5	1, 3.5, 6, 10, 12, 13, 16, 21, 23, 36, 42, 67
Program codes	2, 3, 4, 5, 8, 14,16, 19, 20, 21, 22, 24, 25, 28, 31, 32, 35, 36, 37, 38, 40, 43, 47, 48, 53, 56, 57, 58, 60, 62	11, 12, 15, 18, 26, 33, 34, 39, 42, 44, 45, 46, 49, 51, 59	7, 9, 10, 13, 17, 23, 27, 29, 30, 41, 54, 55

Source: Author's own design and count.

[a] Excludes one program with a choice between language and statistics.

[b] Excludes six programs with a choice between language and statistics.

[c] Excludes two programs with a choice between language and statistics.

[d] Standard deviation in parentheses.

[e] This number includes only those qualitative courses with unmodified titles.

empirical research is quantitative research. Does such a message merit the charge of "hegemony"? That is difficult to know on the basis of curriculum alone, but certainly the association between empirical research, quantitative research, and "sophistication and rigor" that appears in some of the program representations does legitimate quantitative research and delegitimate other forms, both positivist qualitative and interpretive.[19] In contrast, the 21 percent of programs in category 3 communicate through their curriculum that empirical research is both quantitative and qualitative. Qualitative courses are part of their curricula, but so are quantitative-statistical courses and, unexpectedly, so are game theory courses. On average, category 3 programs offer almost the same number of game-theoretic courses (about two) as programs in category 1. Clearly these programs deserve the moniker of "balanced."

Later I explore the implications of these findings for graduate education using a thought experiment. But before beginning, it is essential to note that there is no clear association between the NRC rankings and the ideal types. Top twenty programs, for example, are prevalent in each type. If the Ballard and Mitchell (1998) ranking approach were used, this conclusion might well change, because that ranking approach emphasizes (though not exclusively) what Luke (1999) calls "journal science"—research employing quantification and modeling. The NRC is the broader ranking system because a reputational system can take into account the different publishing habits by field and the role that faculty books and other activities play in developing program reputation.

A Thought Experiment

A natural follow-up to this research would be in-depth interviews with doctoral students in programs across the distribution of ideal types. Short of that, however, the following thought experiment is offered as a way of analyzing not only the end result (that is, views about what constitutes legitimate knowledge), but also the way in which different student potentialities are encouraged or thwarted by the curricular structures of programs of the three ideal types. Even if pertinent interview evidence were available, a thought experiment would still be useful because part of the issue is this: how would graduate student X, with a particular set of talents, be different if she had attended *this* program rather than *that* program? The findings from Table 30.2 provide structural parameters for conducting such an inquiry.

The thought experiment could be conducted in a variety of ways. One approach would be to posit a student with a particular substantive interest—say, development politics in sub-Saharan Africa or language politics in the United States—in order to ask whether the methodological training he or she would receive would be appropriate to that interest. It would be important to conduct such a thought experiment because fields and issues of methodology combine in significant ways. Most notably, case study methods may be more relevant than quantitative-statistical methods for the comparative politics field, where reliable statistics are not always available. Though this approach to the thought experiment would certainly be pertinent, my purpose is different in that I want to consider the ways in which graduate education does (or does not) encourage particular talents or predilections that students bring to a program. Moreover, students' substantive interests typically evolve during the years of graduate education, often as a function of their environment. Put another way, it is important to emphasize that doctoral students are, and at some level must be, focused on survival—acquiring mentors, passing comprehensive examinations, constituting a committee, and choosing dissertation topics that are both feasible and marketable. In this process, they learn what approaches are valued by faculty in their program (that is, what it means to do legitimate social-scientific research in a particular field); students may assume such values are universal in the discipline and the social sciences, particularly if they do not take a stand-alone course in philosophy of science.

Consider the possible doctoral experiences of two stereotypical entering U.S. graduate students, one numbers-phobic and the other word-phobic, who intend their major fields to be political theory and American politics, respectively.[20] Put in the affirmative, the numbers-phobic student lacks a talent for mathematics but has considerable facility with language, not only in terms of foreign language but also in terms of writing and other forms of word-based analysis. In contrast, the word-phobic student is drawn to and enjoys mathematics, finding the ambiguity of words frustrating.

If the two entering students have these phobias, talents, and field interests, it may be essential to their success that these students' undergraduate advisors —the ones writing the letters for admission to graduate school—steer them toward programs appropriate to their interests and proclivities. If the matching mechanisms are working,[21] the stereotypical word-phobic American politics student would be steered into category 1 programs (or perhaps category 2 programs), where she would have few reasons, or opportunities, to learn anything at the methodological level about word-based approaches to the discipline. She would emerge from five to six years of doctoral training heavily invested in quantitative and possibly formal modeling approaches and thereby convinced of their necessity for addressing political problems (at least for the period of time necessary to obtain tenure). If, in contrast, this student went into a category 3 program, her training would be predictably less "rigorous," where *rigorous* is a code word for quantitative-formal approaches to politics. Instead, the emphasis would be on the substantive theoretical questions, and the possible means to answer them would be, simply put, broader—neither elevating quantitative methods nor ruling out qualitative ones; she might even be exposed to interpretive epistemological and methodological orientations as relevant to research in "empirical" fields. In short, she would emerge after five or six years as a markedly different sort of scholar—one driven by a problem-driven approach to the study of politics rather than a method-driven approach (Shapiro 2002).

Because of the special position of political theory within the discipline, the stereotypical numbers-phobic doctoral student faces a different set of possible outcomes. First, there are simply fewer programs from which to choose and, more important, fewer possibilities for future employment. Second, there are strong political theory programs in category 1 (for example, program 2),[22] so he might end up in such a setting. Because many nontheory and even some theory faculty in these programs are unlikely to challenge a normative or empirical field reification, the student may be "left alone" to do "what it is that theorists do." He might even be allowed to opt out of the statistical requirements applied to those in empirical fields (in programs 4 and 38, for example). But in a category 1 program he would find himself "at odds" with his fellow graduate students, whose sensibilities about the nature of valuable work in the profession were being developed in particular directions. He would have some clue as to these sensibilities (if not allowed to opt out of quantitative requirements) and would acquire some as a function of his minor fields, but few of his peers would understand his research orientation given category 1 requirements and the likelihood that few of his peers would choose political theory as a minor field. Depending on the particular category 1 program, he might develop relationships with faculty and students outside of political theory in fields such as public law, public administration, or women and politics. The curricular requirements he would be expected to meet would be quite similar if he ended up in a category 2 program, but because of the split among faculty by field, there would be more relevant course offerings in fields outside of political theory, and possibly more faculty and peers appreciative of the role of "word analysis" in the discipline. Whether his experience in a category 3 program would be markedly different would depend on the extent to which the program had worked to build bridges between political theory and empirical fields (Jennings 1988). Certainly his peers in American politics, comparative politics, and international relations would be more open to him, or, put in negative terms, his peers would *not* have been given the curricular message that political theory has a very particular and narrow role to play in the discipline. In summary, for the political theory student in contrast to the American politics student, the issues raised in this study appear to have less bearing on his graduate training per se (that is, he might flourish in a program of any of the ideal types by developing close working relationships with political theory faculty). But the issues are highly relevant to the nature of the discipline he would inhabit upon obtaining employment.

Now imagine a different sort of student, a numbers-phobic American politics student. If the matching system was not working or for other reasons he ended up at a category 1 program, what would his options be? Perhaps he would gravitate to another major field, say comparative politics or public law, or drop out of graduate school, or attempt to switch programs. Or, out of a desire to succeed, he might simply convince himself that a "word" approach to understanding American politics is clearly not "rigorous" or "scientific"; he would learn the quantitative-statistical tools and apply them as his faculty committee members advised in order to get publications in order to get a job in order to get tenure. Yet if that same student went to a category 3 program, the question would be What are your substantive interests? And only then, What combination of methods should you learn to pursue answers to your substantive questions? In programs of this ideal type, substantive rigor is not defined in terms of particular methodologies or even particular theoretical approaches; it is defined by a careful justification of the significance of the research question and by choice of appropriate means of addressing that question.

Discussion

This set-up of the thought experiment is obviously artificial because talents in the domains of words and numbers need not be so asymmetric. But assuming its usefulness for the sake of argument, there are two possible responses to these student potentialities. One response is that any systematic phobia should be addressed so that student weaknesses may be mitigated so that the students can become more balanced scholars. Indeed, a common rationale for requiring quantitative courses is this compensation or balancing argument; that is, it is assumed that students drawn to the undergraduate major are numbers-phobic. A required quantitative course or competency *can* be effective in lessening phobia. But there can be an unintended narrowing consequence, because too often quantitative courses are perceived as "*the* methods courses." Moreover, to the extent that those with a word phobia go undiagnosed, they may take refuge in the false notion that quantitative skills are particularly difficult to develop and yet particularly valuable.[23] Whereas it is typical for political theory students (who are assumed, consistent with the stereotype just stated, to be numbers-phobic) to be forced to take a quantitative-statistical course, it is much rarer for American politics students (who are assumed, consistent with the stereotype just stated, to be word-phobic) to be required to take a political theory course. Aggregate statistics show that 66 percent of the studied programs require a quantitative methods course for students in all fields, whereas a political theory requirement for students in all fields is much more rare at 18 percent (Schwartz-Shea 2003).[24]

A second response is that even if it is agreed that phobias should be addressed, it is also clear that particular talents should be nurtured, or at least not thwarted. The needs of those with numerical talents are clearly met for any field, particularly in category 1 programs, but if a student is particularly talented linguistically, these talents may be appreciated and nourished only in particular fields, such as comparative politics and political theory, or in the 21 percent of programs in category 3.[25] Of course at practically any university throughout the country, such courses are available in departments of sociology, anthropology, communication, education, social work, philosophy, or English. But at a time when graduate students are "taking on" their professional identities as political scientists, seeking out these courses would seem to require faculty encouragement and, in some cases, a mentor's defense of such courses to graduate advisors or other members of the student's supervisory committee. In contrast, the student who takes her third course in quantitative methods is not likely to be called upon to defend that choice, but will likely be seen as "acquiring the requisite technical skills" for her professional career.

The word-talented student interested in American politics has a special problem because, judging from many field descriptions, the American politics field is overidentified with quantitative methods. For example, in one of the programs with the greatest breadth of methodological offerings, the field advice for those who major in American politics is this: "[You should learn the] quantitative methodologies that professionals in this field use to conduct their research. For most students, this will involve taking Multivariate Political Analysis" (program 27). Contrast this with the statement from the comparative politics field in the same program: "Students should be familiar with cross-national comparative statistical analyses of large numbers of countries, with comparative studies of small numbers of countries, and with the uses and limitations of survey research and cross-sectional studies, as well as those of case-study and historical analyses." Given the breadth of research questions, the ability to use the U.S. states or counties as units of analysis, and the significance of historical and case study research to the American field, this statement should apply to its students as well. This is a clear case of the methodological tail wagging the substantive dog.

In their defense, American politics field faculty would emphasize their commitment to the student.[26] "If you choose this field," they might say, "you must know these methods"; the unstated part of the sentence is "to survive." This view, however, defines American politics publishing primarily in terms of journals. Examination of the field in terms of both journals and books reveals greater opportunities to do empirical work that is primarily qualitative even in traditionally quantitative areas such as electoral studies (Hart 2000; Mayhew 2002; Menefee-Libey 2000). Thus students in the American field *also* deserve to be trained in both quantitative and qualitative methodologies so that they will be aware of the range of possible methods they should consider for their substantive research questions. It is ironic that American politics students who wish to acquire a broader perspective of method must usually take a methods course identified with comparative politics—as if case study methodology is not ubiquitous across all fields. Most broadly, those students with word talent deserve the same nurturing as those with numbers talent.

What of category 2 programs and the sorting by field that their program structures require or encourage? A sorting approach to curricular requirements is appealing because it is one way to recognize some of the particular needs of fields. Moreover, it could be argued that methodological issues are best covered at the field level rather than in a more abstract cross-field approach. Yet these advantages need to be assessed against the disadvantages. Most prominently, if sorting is interpreted to mean giving up entirely on programwide requirements, that begs the question of what makes political science a discipline rather than a collection of fields, and it can contribute to the reification of the political theory–empirical fields division of labor. Additionally, program structures that encourage entering students to specialize from the very beginning of the program—whether through sorting or a lack of programwide requirements—contribute to problems of disciplinary communication because these students are never exposed to, much less learn to appreciate the value of, what researchers in other specialties do.

More important to the purposes under consideration here, it is clear that while a sorting approach would—at least in programs of ideal type 3 (and to a lesser extent in those of type 2)—allow students to build on their strengths, it is not clear that they would voluntarily take those courses that would mitigate their weaknesses. Thus, returning to our hypothetical stereotypical students, it would be the numbers-phobic political theory student who would most likely take the qualitative methods and philosophy of science courses, shunning an optional quantitative methods course. Similarly, the word-phobic American politics student would most likely take the quantitative methods offerings and shun the qualitative methods and philosophy of science courses. One can imagine a case in which both students, though they had a similar interest, say poverty policy, would by the end of their doctoral program find it difficult to communicate across the epistemological-methodological divides their respective training had encouraged.

What curricular structure would produce awareness and balance for *both* of our hypothetical stereotypical students? If the logic of the thought experiment is sound, programwide requirements should be seriously considered. There are a variety of ways to skin the curricular cat, including required courses, required competencies, and structured choices from both inside and outside the department (for example, one required course from of a list of qualitative methods courses offered in political science, sociology, anthropology, communications, and so on).[27] For simplicity's sake, however, and also consistent with the logic laid out in the thought experiment, consider three programwide requirements: a stand-alone philosophy of science course covering the gamut of epistemologies from positivism to phenomenology, a course in qualitative methods, and a course in quantitative methods. Only after fulfilling these programwide requirements would students sort themselves and specialize as a function of field interests.

Whether three required courses, and particularly these three required courses, would be politically feasible would vary greatly among programs, because at the aggregate level there is considerable variation in curricular structure: 30 percent of the programs studied have no programwide required courses, 33 percent require one to two courses, and 37 percent require between three and six courses (Schwartz-Shea 2003). In terms of ideal types, category 1 programs require almost three courses on average compared to only one for category 2 and 3 programs and, as Table 30.2 shows, these are typically quantitative courses for all the ideal types. Thus in some cases reform would mean challenging existing quantitative requirements in order to make space for courses in philosophy of science and qualitative methods. This would involve challenging taken-for-granted assumptions about the particular value and centrality of quantitative methods and making the case for the usefulness of qualitative methods and the centrality of philosophy of science training.[28]

In other cases, reform would first necessitate building cross-field coalitions to promote the idea of programwide requirements. One possible objection is that requiring three courses might mean that students would begin publishing later in their programs. The early specialization encouraged by field-based requirements *may* enable professional success, that is, publishing before degree completion, obtaining tenure-track employment, and working efficiently toward tenure. But is sacrificing the initial breadth in training (represented by these three required courses) detrimental to disciplinary communication and to the quality of scholarship? It might be argued that the discipline would be better served in the long run by encouraging doctoral students to acquire the breadth that will assist them in pursuing interdisciplinary problem-based research not only with the natural sciences but also with the humanities (Wallerstein 1999). This line of argument leads to a related debate on whether the academic incentive system rewards mere quantity in publishing and thus discourages the incubation of ideas that would improve the quality of published research.

Is Department Specialization Best?

One purpose of the thought experiment is to emphasize the ways in which doctoral education is a transformative endeavor. As the proverb says, "As the twig is bent, so grows the tree." Tenure can free faculty to some extent, but the years from entering a doctoral program to achieving tenure usually span more than a decade, and it may be difficult—or there may be few organizational and disciplinary rewards for taking the time—to retool or to think in new or unaccustomed ways. Clearly, however, doctoral education and research require the depth produced by specialization; any single research project requires epistemological-methodological-theoretical coherence. A discipline of dilettantes is not desirable. Yet to make an informed choice to acquire specialized methodological training, students require an awareness of the range of possibilities. Because of the imperfections in the system that matches students to programs as well as the undesirability of method-driven research, departments should legitimize and cultivate awareness of the full range of methodological possibilities.

A likely response to this argument is that the discipline as a whole is better off when there is no single model of graduate education. Program structure is up to faculty, and there are significant economies of scale that come from hiring a number of like-minded faculty. As Jervis asked rhetorically in his 2001 WPSA presentation, Who would question that the discipline is better off with a Rochester in its midst? Isn't this the very definition of diversity—programs with competing visions? In response to this objection, it is important to distinguish between theoretical and methodological diversity. There is, at the very least, a modicum of theoretical diversity in the discipline, and Jervis may be correct when he says that that everyone feels like an embattled minority (see his chapter in this volume). But as my research documents, for over half of the programs studied, methodological diversity and balance is lacking, and this privileges particular theoretical approaches. Thus, while program structure and theoretical emphasis is indeed up to faculty, an appeal to "diversity" and "competition" at the disciplinary level should *not* mean agreeing that some programs should continue to promulgate the error of equating empirical research with quantitative-statistical research. A quantitative methodological hegemony is not defensible in any single program because it trains students to do method-drive research.

And even for those departments that choose to specialize in a particular theoretical approach, a useful rule of thumb might be this: the greater a department's uniformity, the greater its ethical obligation to expose its doctoral students to the full range of methodological-epistemological positions and debates. If this rule of thumb is followed, such a department's students will be better equipped to communicate effectively with their "research others" in the many disciplinary tasks that require cooperation across these methodological-epistemological divides, for example, student supervisory committees, hiring and tenure processes, and peer review. Graduate education should be a transformative experience, but it should not foreclose intellectual openness and curiosity.

Appendix: The Fifty-Seven Programs Analyzed

School Name	Code	School Name	Code
University of California–Berkeley	2	University of Houston	19
University of California–Los Angeles	3	University of Illinois–Urbana-Champaign	20
University of California–Santa Barbara	4	Indiana University–Bloomington	21
University of California–San Diego	5	University of Iowa	22
		Johns Hopkins University	23
University of Chicago	7	University of Kansas	24
Claremont Graduate Schools	8	University of Kentucky	25
Columbia University	9	University of Maryland–College Park	26
University of Connecticut	10	Massachusetts Institute of Technology	27
Cornell University	11	Michigan State University	28
Duke University	12	University of Michigan–Ann Arbor	29
Emory University	13		
George Washington University	14	University of Minnesota	30
Georgetown University	15	University of New Mexico	31
University of Georgia	16	New York University	32
Harvard University	17	CUNY Graduate Center	33
University of Hawaii	18		

School Name	Code	School Name	Code
SUNY–Albany	34	University of Southern	
SUNY–Stony Brook	35	Carolina–Columbia	46
University of North Carolina–		Stanford University	47
Chapel Hill	36	University of Texas A&M	48
University of North Texas	37	University of Texas–Austin	49
Northwestern University	38	University of Virginia	51
University of Notre Dame	39	Washington University	53
Ohio State University–		University of Washington	54
Columbus	40	University of Wisconsin–	
University of Pennsylvania	41	Madison	55
Princeton University	42	Yale University	56
University of Rochester	43	University of Arizona	57
Rutgers University–		University of California–Irvine	58
New Brunswick	44	University of Colorado–Boulder	59
University of Southern		Florida State University	60
California	45	Rice University	62

Notes

Portions of this chapter were presented at the 2001 Annual Meeting of the American Political Science Association, San Francisco Hilton and Towers, August 30–September 2. Support provided by the Faculty Fellow Program and the Tanner Humanities Center at the University of Utah. The support is much appreciated. Thanks also to those who provided feedback on earlier drafts, particularly Matthew Burbank but also John Francis and Dvora Yanow.

1. Sometimes the status of entire disciplines is institutionally ambiguous. On some campuses history is located in a college of the humanities, whereas in others it is housed in a social science college. Similarly, psychology is usually located in the social sciences, but it can also be found in schools of natural science. Thanks to Dvora Yanow for this insight.

2. Debates over the validity of program rankings are intense, with some defending reputational systems, others championing "objective" publication-based ones (e.g., Ballard and Mitchell 1998), and still others questioning the whole enterprise. For additional discussion, see Schwartz-Shea (2001a, 11). Whatever one's views on rankings, this selection of programs covers a substantial portion of disciplinary programs and the doctoral student population.

3. According to the Web site active during the period of data collection (http://www.usnews.com/edu/beyond/gradrank/gbpolisci.htm), the 2001 *U.S. News* Graduate Rankings for Political Science were based on data from 1998.

4. In the *Guide,* the figure for "Number of Students Now in Ph.D. Program" was not available for five of the fifty-seven programs studied. These numbers were obtained during the June 2000–August 2001 time frame for data collection of this project. To calculate the percentage I used the denominator given in the *Guide* under "Totals Adjusted for Missing Data," 7,765.

5. Thanks to doctoral student Hasan Kosebalaban for his careful work.

6. Throughout the remainder of the chapter I use the term "philosophy of science" as equivalent to "philosophy of social science."

7. "Formal theory" seems to have replaced "game theory," "rational choice theory," and "public choice theory" to a substantial degree in course titles. The other phrase synonymous with formal theory is "positive political theory."

8. Authors as diverse as King, Keohane, and Verba (1994, 5) and Flyvbjerg (2001, 196) decry the distinction as spurious, though on quite distinct grounds. For further discussion, see Schwartz-Shea and Yanow (2002, 480–82).

9. The appearance of new courses is particularly significant when it comes to qualitative methods; that is, my descriptive study has a moving target due to the Perestroika movement (which began in October 2000) within the discipline. For example, in response to the Perestroika e-mail discussions, graduate students at Yale University requested changes in the methods offerings of their program. However, given the substantive complexity and collective action problems involved in changing departmental requirements, it seems likely that the disciplinary portrait painted here is still quite accurate.

10. Golde and Dore (2001) do have five questions on the "effectiveness of program structures" (Table W-16, revised February 2002), but these are very broad. For example, 70.4 percent of doctoral students across eleven disciplines (not including political science) agreed that "coursework has given a broad foundation of knowledge in the field."

11. Other than criticizing the narrow disciplinary understanding of "method" and "empirical research," I do not engage these debates here. But see Schwartz-Shea (2001b).

12. For more detail on field coverage and field combinations of methods, political theory, and formal theory, see Schwartz-Shea (2001a), Tables 4 and 5 and pp. 29–30.

13. To ask the question whether Rochester graduates would be able to fully comprehend a semiotic reading of a public policy document is to render the Rochester vision partial.

14. Programs 25 and 56. For program 56 I have "extracurricular" knowledge about changes that would indicate placement in category 2 instead of category 1 (see note 7), but I chose to use only the formal curricular information.

15. Program 13.

16. "Healthy" political theory fields exist in category 1 programs as well, of course. The issue is the relationship to the "empirical fields," a complex topic in the discussion of which both sides share responsibility for the way in which the division of labor is understood.

17. Programs 15 and 39.

18. Recall that for the calculation of this statistic, a field-identified qualitative methods course title received 0.5, whereas an unmodified qualitative methods course title received a 1.0. The range of number of offerings in a program varied from zero to 2. In contrast, the range for quantitative methods offerings is 1 to 6, nearly all with unmodified titles.

19. For a published example of this attitude, see Dowding (2001, particularly 95–97), who implies that analysis that is not "formal" cannot be rigorous.

20. The more extreme contrast would be between students choosing the fields of political theory and formal theory, and the reader can substitute that possibility. I chose American politics because of its near-universal offering by the programs in my sample, whereas far fewer programs offer formal theory as a field.

21. This presumption is open to question. Are those writing the letters able to keep up with trends in doctoral education by program? Moreover, family and funding factors are often critical in such decisions as well. Potential graduate students can now use the Web to acquaint themselves with doctoral programs—though whether they can "read between the lines" or see through departmental representations the way I have here is debatable. As important, when mistakes are made, exit by graduate students from one program and entrance to another is both costly and risky.

22. The *U.S. News* ranking of the top five political theory programs as reported in *PS*, June 1996, 148.

23. For a response to the argument that quantitative-statistical methods are particularly difficult and particularly valuable, see Schwartz-Shea (2003).

24. Programs that require "one course in political theory" (not specified) are 13, 27, 33, and 47. Programs that require a specified course are 19, 26, and 43. Three programs require two courses or an examination: 12, 15, and 17. Program 43 is a less convincing case given the two courses listed. It would depend on the syllabi. There are five programs that require some coverage of qualitative methods (8, 10, 11, 54, 60), so adding the ten programs with a political theory requirement to the five programs requiring qualitative methods means that coverage of "word approaches" is required in 26 percent (15/57) of programs. I don't mean to simplistically equate what goes on in a political theory with what is covered in a qualitative methods course. Rather, both are in the "nonquantitative" category.

25. At the aggregate level, 56 percent of programs offer no qualitative methods course, not even a field-identified one (Schwartz-Shea 2003).

26. Another quotation illustrates this problem as well as the error of equating "empirical" with "quantitative" research: "The [program 48] Political Science faculty includes specialists *in all aspects of American politics.* The predominant orientation of the American politics faculty is to address major substantive questions from both theoretical and empirical perspectives. As a consequence, students selecting American politics as a major field will need to *develop statistical and computer skills characteristic of the mainstream of empirical research in the field*" (program 48, emphases added). The point is to recognize and question the self-fulfilling nature of this perspective.

27. Extracurricular approaches such as guest lectures might be effective, though much would depend on the strength of department norms of attendance.

28. See note 23. I have argued for a required philosophy of social science course elsewhere (Schwartz-Shea 2002).

References

Ballard, Michael J., and Neil J. Mitchell. 1998. "The Good, the Better, and the Best in Political Science." *PS: Political Science and Politics,* December, 826–28.

Dowding, Keith. 2001. "There Must Be an End to the Confusion: Policy Networks, Intellectual Fatigue, and the Need for Political Science Methods Courses in British Universities." *Political Studies* 49: 89–105.

Flyvbjerg, Bent. 2001. *Making Social Science Matter: Why Social Inquiry Fails and How It Can Succeed Again.* Cambridge: Cambridge University.

Gigerenzer, Gerd, and David J. Murray. 1987. *Cognition as Intuitive Statistics*. Hillsdale, NJ: Lawrence Erlbaum Associates.

Golde, Chris M., and Timothy M. Dore. 2001. "At Cross Purposes: What the Experiences of Doctoral Students Reveal about Doctoral Education." A report prepared for The Pew Charitable Trusts, Philadelphia, PA. www.phd-survey.org.

Hart, Roderick P. 2000. *Campaign Talk: Why Elections Are Good for Us*. Princeton, NJ: Princeton University Press.

Jennings, Bruce. 1988. "Political Theory and Policy Analysis: Bridging the Gap." In Edward Bryan Portis and Michael B. Levy, eds., *Handbook of Political Theory and Policy Science*. Westport, CT: Greenwood Press.

Jervis, Robert. 2001. "A Community of Scholars or a Scholarly Community? Controversies in Disciplines and Public Life." APSA Presidential Address, presented at the Annual Meeting of the Western Political Science Association, Las Vegas, NV, March 15.

Kasza, Gregory J. 2001. "For an Ecumenical Science of Politics." May 15 posting to the Perestroika list serve.

King, Gary, Robert O. Keohane, and Sidney Verba. 1994. *Designing Social Inquiry: Scientific Inference in Qualitative Research*. Princeton, NJ: Princeton University Press.

Mayhew, David R. 2002. *Electoral Realignment: A Critique of an American Genre*. New Haven, CT: Yale University Press.

Menefee-Libey, David. 2000. *The Triumph of Campaign-Centered Politics*. New York: Chatham House.

Luke, Timothy W. 1999. "The Discipline as Disciplinary Normalization: Networks of Research." *New Political Science* 21 (3): 345–63.

The 2000 National Doctoral Program Survey. 2001. "Survey Results." http://survey.nagps.org/compare.php?category=0&type=165. October 17.

National Research Council. 1996. "Appendix Table P-36: Relative Rankings for Research-Doctorate Programs in Political Science." *PS: Political Science and Politics,* June, 146–48.

Rule, James B. 1997. *Theory and Progress in Social Science*. Cambridge: Cambridge University Press.

Schwartz-Shea, Peregrine. 2001a. "Curricular Visions: Doctoral Program Requirements, Offerings, and the Meanings of 'Political Science.'" Paper presented at the Annual Meeting of the American Political Science Association, San Francisco, September.

Schwartz-Shea, Peregrine. 2001b. "Knowledge Metaphors: Epistemology, Disciplinarity, and Progress." Paper presented at the 2001 Annual Meeting of the Western Political Science Association, Las Vegas, NV, March.

Schwartz-Shea, Peregrine. 2002. "Issues in Curricular Design." *Clio: Newsletter of Politics and History, An Organized Section of the American Political Science Association* 12 (2).

Schwartz-Shea, Peregrine. 2003. "Is This the Curriculum We Want? Doctoral Requirements and Offerings in Methods and Methodology." *PS: Political Science and Politics* 36 (3): 379–86.

Schwartz-Shea, Peregrine, and Dvora Yanow. 2002. "'Reading' 'Methods' 'Texts': How Research Methods Texts Construct Political Science." *Political Research Quarterly* 55 (2): 457–86.

Shapiro, Ian. 2002. "Problems, Methods, and Theories in the Study of Politics, Or: What's Wrong with Political Science and What to Do about It." *Political Theory* 30 (4): 596–619.

Stone, Debra A. 1988. *Policy Paradoxes and Political Reason.* Glenview, IL: Scott, Foresman.

Wallerstein, Immanuel. 1999. "The Structures of Knowledge, Or How Many Ways May We Know?" In Wallerstein, *The End of the World as We Know It: Social Science for the Twenty-First Century.* Minneapolis: University of Minnesota, 185–91.

Yanow, Dvora. 2002. *Constructing "Race" and "Ethnicity" in America: Category-Making in Public Policy and Administration.* Armonk, NY: M. E. Sharpe.

CHAPTER 31

Graduate Education
in a Pluralist Context

The Metaphor of a Toolbox

Leslie E. Anderson

This chapter provides a perspective of the conduct of graduate education within a pluralist intellectual and methodological context. At the University of Florida I offer a course on research design required of all doctoral students in their first semester. The syllabus is included in edited form as an appendix to the present chapter. My course, entitled The Conduct of Inquiry, has two principal goals: (1) to excite students about doing scholarly research and encourage them to find an intellectual puzzle that fascinates them and (2) to create an atmosphere in which students feel free to choose their own data collection methods as best suit their intellectual puzzle, defining that puzzle first and only then choosing the method of data collection.[1] In the Department of Political Science at the University of Florida, this course is offered as a companion to another course providing a pluralist view of the scope and epistemologies of political science.[2] Other courses offered in the department but later in the graduate curriculum include courses on many levels of quantitative data analysis, survey research, and qualitative methods. The department offers a "methods" major and minor and frequently sends students to the Michigan summer program in research methods. Yet in the first semester my task is to help students connect with their intellectual excitement about a question and to introduce them to a multitude of ways of collecting data.

I begin the course with a metaphor. I ask the students to imagine that they have been given a new toolbox as a birthday gift. Inside are many different tools, some of which they may recognize or even have used before, but others of which they have never seen previously. Over the duration of this course they will learn to use all the tools in the toolbox, finishing the course comfortable with all of them and feeling that they know how to use them all. I suggest that some tools in the toolbox will be more appropriate for some projects, while others will be better for other tasks. Yet every tool in the toolbox has its use, and their task will be to learn how to use all of them. In the course of their own research, they will probably use only some of those tools, particularly in the first project, which is the dissertation. But a career is long, and one never knows what tools one will need in some subsequent project. Therefore they must learn the uses of all the tools in the toolbox and be able to use all of them should the need arise.

Getting into the Field

The first month of the course is spent doing research. My goal is to get the students doing research first and only then reading about how to do it. I know, and they quickly learn, that they will make mistakes in this first research task. But those mistakes matter far less than the intellectual excitement generated by actually getting into the field and by collecting data and trying to understand a new phenomenon. Because neither funding nor publication rides on this first research experience, it matters less how perfectly they do it and more that they become excited by doing it. Thus the first few weeks are spent reading examples of three different kinds of research while also doing the research itself (see syllabus).

After the first class meeting students are given three reading assignments. These are Gary King, Robert Keohane, and Sidney Verba's *Designing Social Inquiry,* particularly the discussion of survey research, Alan Wolfe's *One Nation after All,* an example of in-depth interviewing, and Clifford Geertz's "Deep Play: Notes on the Balinese Cockfight," an example of participant observation. In the second class I divide the students into three groups: a survey research group, an in-depth interview group, and a participant observation group. The first two groups are then instructed to move off into separate groups and decide what research project they would like to conduct for the next three weeks.

Unlike the other two groups, the participant observation group is instructed to spend several weeks observing the University of Florida football mania known as "gator mania" or "gatorism." Their task is to attend football games, observe and participate in the communitywide picnic known as "tailgating"; circulate in university bars, fraternity houses, and sorority houses; wander around campus; go to parties; talk with "gators"; and generally partake of the football culture that dominates the Gainesville campus every fall semester. The gatorism team is also required to get away from Gainesville, visiting the small communities outside Gainesville, going to bars and watering holes outside town, and observing gatorism from outside the campus. The gatorism team is permitted to wear school colors, wear opposition colors, or wear clothing that supports no particular team. They are allowed but not required to attend away games. But in the case of away games, they are required to observe the gatorism phenomenon on the Florida campus even when there is an "away" game.

Observing gatorism, of course, is a huge task and one that would take more than a few weeks if a researcher worked alone. But the students are working in a group of six to nine people. They coordinate their efforts and are able to "cover" multiple aspects of gatorism at the same time. They then meet regularly to exchange notes, compare interpretations, and plan further strategy. The gatorism team works nearly all day every Saturday for the first month of the semester. Their task is to learn what gatorism tells us about the University of Florida, about north Florida, about the state of Florida generally, and about U.S. society broadly. This task is made even more interesting by the fact that, inevitably, the gatorism team always includes several students who are not from the United States and many who are not from Florida. Their interpretations, juxtaposed against those of Florida natives, make for a fascinating tension and a contrast of perspectives.

While the gatorism team has its task clearly delineated for it, the other two teams are free to choose their own research subjects. In the first working class meeting, I circulate among the three groups, sitting with them for a period of time and offering suggestions or advice. Over the five years that I have offered this course, the survey research team has generally decided to survey University of Florida undergraduates, generally about political attitudes. Every other year is an election year, and the survey research group usually chooses, in the election years, to ask undergraduates about their political opinions. Once the survey research team has chosen its subject and its respondent pool, they are required to write a survey instrument and bring it to class for class perusal and inspection. Inevitably the class has questions about and criticisms of the wording of the instrument, and the survey research group is then forced to rethink or reword some of their questions. Later in the semester all of the class will be involved in collecting survey research data and using the survey instrument, so it is essential that the entire class understand the survey research team's project, feel comfortable with the instrument, and feel able to administer it. By the time the survey research group has written and then revised the instrument with class input, the entire class feels that they are involved in the survey research project and that they have an interest in the survey results.

The third research team, the in-depth interview team, has generally had the greatest latitude in choosing a research subject. Over the several years that this seminar has been offered, in-depth interview teams have chosen to interview Florida undergraduates, Florida faculty members, and low-income members of the Gainesville community. Each choice includes a series of research lessons that I try to bring to the attention of the entire class. If the in-depth team chooses to interview undergraduates, I remind them that they are choosing to research a respondent pool for whom they (probably) have some (or a lot) of disdain. I suggest that they try to be aware of this and that they take steps to conceal this attitude so as to allow the research to proceed unaffected by it. I also suggest that there will be times in their research when they do not particularly like their interview subjects, but that they can still interview them and learn from them.

If the in-depth interview team chooses to interview faculty, what I call "elite" interviews, they will in all likelihood be interviewing a group who are very busy (especially at the outset of a semester), who may have little interest in or time for the research subject, and who may even view graduate students with some disdain. Again, such a choice brings with it other learning experiences. The students have to learn to deal with having their requests for interviews rejected, with working with an interviewee who has very little time, and with interviewing a subject who is highly educated and very intelligent. All of these constitute challenges that accompany this type of research and this type of subject. But they are lessons that may be needed for the students' own research at some future date.

Finally, if the in-depth interview team chooses to interview low-income Gainesville residents, that choice opens up yet a third set of challenges. Again we discuss these in class. I call these "non-elite" interviews and suggest that there might be times in the students' own future research where they might want to interview "nonelites." The nonelite interview places the students in a situation where their subjects view them with awe, may want to impress them or make a good impression on them, and may even be a little afraid of them or intimidated by the interview circumstance. I suggest that the students need to be aware of these dynamics and do what they can to lessen their impact on the interview itself, while still proceeding with the interview and learning as much from it as they can. Nonelite interviews among low-income Gainesville residents also raise other challenges that on-campus interviews do not. For example, students need to be concerned about issues of safety. "Do not endanger yourselves!" is a charge that I leave them with. "You can conduct this research without placing yourselves in danger, so please be certain that you do so." Over the course of initiating this research, the students figure out ways to conduct it without running undue risks. They then report these back to the class as a whole. For example, they work in pairs and enter dangerous neighborhoods only in twos or threes and only during the daytime. They also interview the poor away from their homes, perhaps inviting them for coffee or a hamburger and conducting the interview in a restaurant near campus.

The research projects chosen, particularly by the survey research group and the in-depth interview group, tend to present different kinds of problems and challenges, so no two groups and no two classes have exactly the same experience. Throughout the first weeks of the class, however, we discuss the research projects underway and deal with any problems that present themselves. I suggest to the students that part of being a successful researcher is taking each problem and challenge as it presents itself and then figuring out how to deal with it at the time and in the moment. The point is to stay focused on their own research question. Giving the student teams latitude to choose their own research topic invariably gives them the motivation to be sufficiently resourceful to overcome whatever problems the field presents. This, of course, is what the researcher has to do in the real world. These students begin to do it the first month of graduate school.

At the University of Florida, all research involving human subjects requires approval from the Florida Institutional Review Board (IRB). This is true even in cases like these, where the research is being conducted without funding and where no publication of the results is intended. In my class, both the in-depth interview team and the survey research team must receive approval for their studies from the IRB. This university research requirement constitutes something of a bureaucratic headache for these teams, particularly because they are required to complete their research in one month's time. I discuss with the class the reasons for IRB oversight and suggest that they charge one team member with working closely with the IRB. That person should be an individual of exceptional patience. Once the students learn that they are required to obtain IRB approval for their research, they always manage to get approval in time to conduct and finish their research. The experience then prepares them for what lies ahead when they turn to doing predissertation summer research or research for the dissertation itself.

Opposition and Learning: Teaching the Tool

As these three teams develop their projects and conduct their research, there is invariably a range of reactions to the research process. Some students like the methodology they are assigned to use; others dislike it or distrust its results. I respond to these concerns by asking them to jot down some notes on their response to the tool and why they like it or dislike it. I ask them to bring such thoughts to the class when they present the results of their research project. I suggest as well that some researchers are particularly good at one method of data collection, while others find some data collection methods unusually difficult or distasteful. I suggest to the class that their own personal tastes should be a part of the picture when they choose a research methodology, and therefore it is important to be attentive to which methods they like and dislike and why.

Among highly intellectual, professionally oriented, serious doctoral students, there is inevitably some negative reaction to an assignment that asks them to observe and participate in gator mania on several football Saturdays of their first month in graduate school. Some students respond with disbelief and horror. Others characterize gatorism as "distasteful," "offensive," "infantile," "juvenile," and generally what they came to graduate school to avoid rather than to embrace. As a scholar myself, I am sympathetic to such reactions, especially when the practice makes it impossible to accomplish any serious work anywhere on campus during football Saturdays. Additionally, students from developing nations or students who have lived extensively in poor countries are often horrified by the expenditure of large amounts of money on gator clothing, toys, flags, and even football tickets. All of these reactions become part of the participant observation exercise.

However, I use this negative response as a teaching tool for these students. I suggest that there may well be other instances in which they will not like the subject they are studying. In fact, there is nothing inherent in research that requires that one always like one's subjects or one's subject matter. What if, for example, they were doing research on the Aryan Nations or the Skinheads or perhaps on Islamic fundamentalists? In such cases they might find their research subjects distasteful or offensive but, perhaps precisely for that reason, realize that participant observation was the least obvious and least intrusive tool with which to begin their research. I also suggest to the students that researchers often begin a research project with a preconceived attitude about the subject but find that that attitude was wrong, partially wrong, or simply incomplete.

When I suggest to the gatorism students that they are studying the use of the tool (participant observation) more than the subject itself (gatorism), they become less resistant to the assignment. Additionally, inevitably they find that their preconceived images of gatorism were incomplete and that there is more to it than they imagined. Normally students also find that there is something positive to the football mania, normally more than they had guessed. Finally, I suggest to them that if they find the phenomenon primarily a negative one, possibly the information it gives about the university, the town, and even national society is primarily negative. In the end, there is nothing inherently wrong about arriving at that conclusion so long as an effort has been made to view the phenomenon as dispassionately as possible. In the end, we cannot ask more of ourselves as researchers than that.

When the student research teams present their research results, they are charged with teaching the tool they have used, as well as with reporting on their findings. They bring to their presentations the assumption that other classmates have not used this particular tool and it is their responsibility to present the tool as thoroughly and objectively as possible so that others can decide whether they want to use it in their own research. As in the case of the gatorism team, usually some members of each of the other two teams have decided that this particular data collection tool would not be their first choice. Others have become very enthusiastic about the tool. Both groups share their opinions with the class as a whole, along with their reasons for those opinions.

Usually some students on the survey research team have very much liked doing surveys, while others have found that they always wanted to ask more questions and more open-ended questions. For those who wanted to pursue the research subject in greater depth, I suggest that in their own research designs survey research might be supplemented with in-depth interviews. Additionally, this team has usually begun to discover some of the mistakes they have made by the time they get around to presenting their work to the class. They may realize that they have not done a random sample, have introduced bias in their sample selection, or have made various mistakes with the instrument itself. I think looking at their results and at the mistakes they have made is a better way of teaching them the importance of using the correct survey methods than is an approach that discusses the methods extensively before putting the students in the field. Having done the work already and seen the problems, they are motivated to learn to do survey research correctly and to take the time to learn correct sampling techniques, the need for a pilot study to perfect the instrument, and the need to avoid bias in the interview process itself. I then tell the students that our department offers an advanced doctoral seminar in survey research where they can learn the exactitudes of this method. If they are really interested in this method or think they will use it in their own research, they might think about taking that seminar.

Among the survey research team, there is usually one or more students who know just a little about quantitative analysis. They undertake to present their results with modest levels of analysis, using frequencies, perhaps bivariate cross-tabs, and some discussion of significance levels. I encourage these modest forays into quantitative analysis because they arouse students' curiosity about quantitative analysis. There are always students who perceive that they are primarily oriented toward qualitative analysis. I suggest to them that using quantitative analysis is like training a powerful microscope on one's data and discovering patterns therein that are not visible to the naked eye. However, such patterns can normally be distinguished only when one has a relatively large amount of quantitative data. As the class discusses the quantitative data and vote choice results, usually some members of the class begin suggesting further analysis beyond what the team itself has done: "Well, did you try running this opinion divided by gender?" is a question often raised. Or "What about the subgroups of Protestants: Baptists, Presbyterians, Methodists? Do you think there would have been vote choice differences there?" When these kinds of questions emerge, and particularly when they come from someone who has previously been skeptical or hostile toward quantitative data analysis, I am pleased to see that even these skeptics have begun to grasp some of the attractions of large n research. In the face of such growing curiosity about the possibilities of quantitative analysis, I remind the students that all of them will be doing survey research over the next several weeks as part of their class assignment. They will all receive a copy of the "class data set" before the end of the semester, so if they wish to pursue some of the questions or interests that have arisen they will soon be free to do that on their own with the full data set at their disposal. I also remind them that later in the semester there will be an introductory class on SPSS (Statistical Package for the Social Sciences) analysis, so if they want to learn how to do frequencies and cross-tabs they can learn those techniques then. I tell them, too, that beyond this course the department also offers classes on quantitative analysis at beginning, intermediate, and advanced levels. If they want to learn these techniques, there were be plenty of opportunities to do so.

The in-depth interview team is also charged with teaching their tool. Across the years, the teams have chosen to accomplish that task in different ways. One year, as part of their presentation, the team staged a mock interview with an unresponsive interviewee:

Interviewer: So what do you think about U.S. foreign policy?
Interviewee: Yeah
Interviewer: So, yeah? What do you think?
Interviewee: I dunno.
Interviewer: Do you have an opinion?
Interviewee: [Silence.]

When the team staged this mock interview, they used it to teach their classmates about the problems with this method of data collection. "You will inevitably come across interviewees who either cannot or will not be responsive," they suggest. "What do you do?" Some students on this team have found that they were pretty good at building rapport, pulling out answers, and getting an interviewee to engage. Others have found this unattractive and felt subjects should not be pressured to respond. The team members then recount their experiences with the interviews, times when they felt they were successful and why. One year the in-depth interview team chose to include some elite interviews and interviewed faculty members at the University of Florida. One student reported that she had been shocked and hurt when a faculty member had refused an interview and said he did not have time. The student was disbelieving, thinking, "Of course the faculty should support my doing my research!" When this subject came up, I talked about the need to be relatively thick-skinned. Potential respondents may well be unwilling to participate in the study, and after all, no one has any obligation to help us with our research or participate in our studies. Additionally, when doing elite interviews, we are dealing with important, powerful people who face enormous demands on their time and energy. In such circumstances the rejection rate is certain to be higher, but the key is not to take such rejection personally. The student should just move on and find someone who will participate in the study.

Similarly, when this group has chosen to interview nonelites, the poor, or very low-income respondents, they have encountered a different series of problems and challenges. They usually do not have friends or contacts among this socioeconomic class, and they need someone (an employer, a minister) to help them make such contacts. They discuss their efforts to find a gatekeeper, someone who would help them gain access to respondents. They talk about finding a safe place to meet the respondents and gain their confidence. They talk about building rapport with someone who feels intimidated, inadequate, and inferior and who is poor, uneducated, and often a member of an ethnic minority. On this team, too, there are usually some students who are better at this technique than others, and the team talks about who is good at this technique, why, and what the others learned from that individual.

In 2001, one week before the Twin Towers were struck in New York, the in-depth interview team had decided to interview foreign students about their opinions of U.S. foreign policy. When the terrorist attacks took place, their chosen research subject suddenly became much more complicated and sensitive. Again I suggested to the class that one does not control one's research environment in the social sciences and that huge catastrophic events like this do sometimes happen right when we are trying to get our research done or precisely during the one year for which we have funding to conduct research. The question becomes how to work with the changed circumstances and how to get the research done as well as possible in the new environment.

In 2001 the class found their entire research environment touched by the acts of terrorism, and this particularly affected the in-depth interview team because of the subject they had chosen to study. To their surprise, most foreign students were eager to express solidarity with the United States and reluctant to opine that perhaps U.S. foreign policy could have contributed to the terrorist attacks. Many were anxious to distance themselves from the terrorists. At the same time, the foreign students were not very surprised that the attacks had happened, and the student surveyors were able to uncover such attitudes in their interviews. Finally, the in-depth interview team tried deliberately to seek out Islamic students on campus for interviews and found the door almost totally closed in their faces. The student group Islam on Campus absolutely refused to be a gatekeeper or to help the students contact Islamic students for interviews. When the students did, inadvertently, stumble across one Islamic Turkish student who agreed to be interviewed, they found that the interviewee clearly did not want to talk about the terrorist attacks at all. The team members who interviewed him characterized the subject of terrorism as "a huge elephant in the room that everyone knows is there but everyone pretends not to see." All of this became a useful teaching opportunity. The students learned that sometimes doors will absolutely be closed in their faces, and their task will be to conduct the research some other way. Other times they will sense that interviewees consider some subjects totally off limits. As interviewers, their task is to figure that out and respect those boundaries.

The in-depth interview team often has concerns that are the mirror image of the concerns expressed by the survey research team. The in-depth interview team has information with extensive depth and color but only a small number of respondents. Some of them feel their results are inadequate because they cannot present quantitative patterns. I suggest that there are methods and computer programs for turning qualitative information into quantitative data, but that by the same token their data have a richness that is instructive. One year the in-depth team decided to study attitudes about social and economic inequality and to contrast such attitudes among elites (whom they defined as university professors) and among the poor (Gainesville's low-income residents). In reporting on the results, one team member declared that he thought this method worked only for elite interviews because the professors knew a lot, were well read, and could provide full answers to the questions. He didn't think the method worked for uneducated respondents. But a classmate from another team then pointed out that he had become most animated when he talked about the low-income responses to questions about inequality. "Clearly you learned a lot from these people, even if you don't think you did and even if they are uneducated," she reminded him. "I think the method works for the uneducated also and you just proved that it does."

Finally, the gatorism team reports on its observations. Generally students have positive as well as negative views of what they have seen and end up concluding that the practice of gatorism reflects both negative and positive aspects of university life and of society more generally. Students recognize that football Saturdays provide an opportunity for community camaraderie, playfulness, and togetherness. Only in such circumstances can strangers embrace each other or have lengthy friendly conversations. Foreign students, particularly those who watch soccer in Europe or Latin America, remark that gatorism provides a surprisingly safe sports event. Children and entire families can attend a game without the threat of violence among the fans. The participant observation team also recognizes that the university and the town both profit substantially from gator mania.

At the same time, the team recognizes that football Saturdays constitute a time when university academics are totally subordinated to football, and that tells them something about the University of Florida and about the balance of power between athletics and academics at the university. They describe ways that football epitomizes relations of power in the state of Florida and at the university. Gatorism also reflects a kind of glorification of violence, with strong overtones of sexism, racism, and classism, wherein women and the low-income classes are secondary citizens or are excluded entirely and the only place an African American can feel comfortable in the stadium is on the playing field.

In the end, the team's evaluation of gatorism is more negative than positive. Indeed, it would be surprising if a team of professionally oriented doctoral students did not arrive at such a conclusion. Yet I remind them that politics can be quite ugly, and if they have come to study politics they will not be able to avoid that aspect of it entirely. Empathy is hard to teach and perhaps even harder to learn. Yet empathy does not mean sympathy, and if they can arrive at an empathetic understanding of gatorism and of the people who embrace it, they have taken a step toward becoming astute observers of politics, whether or not they like what they see.

The class considers these multiple perceptions of gatorism, and we discuss how one would continue the study of football mania using other research methods. Frequently students have recognized that precise survey questionnaires can now be constructed using questions that previously were only incompletely formulated. Others suggest that the true or unusual nature of Florida gatorism would be uncovered fully only by studying football mania at other university campuses, particularly universities with nationally ranked football teams but higher academic rankings than the University of Florida has. Finally, students suggest that the role of athletics in campus culture is understudied in our society but could be the subject of an entire sociopolitical project that could use multiple research methods. Students agree that using the participant observation research tool is an important way to begin research on a topic they know little about or might not, at least initially, know how to study.

Moving beyond the Team Research Projects: The Class Data Set

Beyond working on the team research projects I have described, students in the class are also required to contribute to the class data set. An extension of the survey research team project, this class project extends through most of the semester, or through election day if it is an election year. As described earlier, the subject of the research is determined by the survey research team, and they initiate the research and report their initial findings with their team research project. They then distribute questionnaires to the rest of the students and ask them to perform between fifteen and twenty-five additional surveys. When the results of all these surveys are combined, the class data set usually has an *n* of between 400 and 500.

The second semester of their first year, most students in the course will move together into a beginning course on quantitative data analysis. The professor for that course knows that the first-year class is collecting a class data set and bringing it with them to her course. She then assigns homework using that class data set. She also uses the exercise to show what mistakes have been made in collecting the data in the data set and how those can be corrected. For the students, this provides continuity from one class to the next and from one term to the next. Additionally, the students have a vested interest in the class data set: they were involved in constructing the questionnaire themselves, and they helped collect the data. This prior involvement makes them more motivated to learn the exercises they need learn to analyze these data and others than they would be if they were using only "canned" data.

The Other Tools in the Toolbox

Apart from collecting the data for the class data set, the students in my class spend the rest of the semester learning about other ways of analyzing and collecting data. These include archival research, content analysis, focus groups, additional in-depth interviews, electronic data collection, and the statistical program of SPSS. Throughout the middle five weeks of the course students read about these methods of collecting data and also hear from researchers who are using the various methods. When it is relevant, I draw on my own research to talk about examples of several of the different kinds of data collection methods.[3] Additionally, the class entertains visits from faculty members or advanced graduate students who use the particular data collection method under study. Over the course of the semester, the students hear about how departmental members have used or are using content analysis, focus groups, and in-depth interviews. One class is spent in the library with one of the research librarians, who summarizes for the students what kinds of data are available over the Web and through the electronic library resources. In all cases, efforts are made to talk with the students about real, ongoing research rather than discussing data collection in an abstract way. Additionally, I try to combine examples of research projects from comparative politics, American politics, and international relations, because these are the main fields that the students themselves represent.

An Introduction to SPSS

One of the most important classes in this course is the one on which the students are introduced to SPSS during a three-hour working session. On that day the students move from our regular classroom to the computer center, where one classroom provides a separate computer work station for each student. From there they can access SPSS on the university server. I ask a faculty member or graduate student to run this particular class session. The classroom allows the instructor to work on a computer at the front of the classroom while the instructor's own computer screen is projected onto a large overhead screen in front of the class. This set-up means that all the students can see their own personal screens and also see the instructor's screen at the same time. With an advanced graduate student, I circulate among the students in the class, looking over their shoulders and trying to help them keep up with the instructor and the main screen.

At the beginning of the class the students are provided with a handout and a set of data to input. The students begin by learning to open a spreadsheet in SPSS and inputting data. From there they move on to a larger data set and learn first frequencies and then basic bivariate cross-tabulations. By the end of this class session, the students have learned to access SPSS and input data and have begun the first steps of statistical analysis. They have done so in a setting that does not allow students to fall behind or to slip through the cracks. The instructor for that session, the advanced graduate student, and I are able to provide enough attention to the students so that all of them learn the lesson for that particular class session. The following semester, when they enter their first course on statistical analysis, they will build on the lessons they have learned about SPSS in this first semester.

Also during this class students are introduced to the treasure trove of secondary data available for analysis through the Interuniversity Consortium for Political and Social Research, of which the University of Florida is a member. Students are also encouraged to begin thinking abut attending the Interuniversity Consortium for Political and Social Research (ICPSR) Summer Program at the University of Michigan during the course of their graduate careers. We tell them as well where they can find a summary of the ICPSR databases and how they can access those data.

The Final Research Project

For their final research project, the students are required to write the research design and methods section of a dissertation proposal. I instruct them not to write about the theoretical background of the design and not to cover any literature review. Instead, the bulk of their attention is directed toward telling us what they plan to do for their research, specifically how they intend to collect data, and how much the entire project will cost.

I tell the students that they are applying for a grant of $15,000 and that they should plan a budget and data collection design that will cost approximately that amount. The last three weeks of the semester, students present their research designs to the class as a whole. In their presentations they must tell what kind of data collection methods they will use and why, how they will go about collecting the data, what obstacles they expect to encounter, and how they intend to overcome any such problems. Students give a minimalist summary of their research question and puzzle, but in their presentations they do not give an extensive overview of the literature or the theoretical context. Instead they focus on how they will collect data.

These projects tend to be quite elaborate. Students put a great deal of effort into researching how they will do the projects they would ideally like to do with $15,000 in funding. Often they search the Web, quite frequently in other languages, to learn the costs of travel, subsistence, and research in other nations where they hope to conduct research. They also search university Web sites to learn what it will cost them to hire assistance in the form of translators or research assistants. Students who plan to do research inside the United States similarly calculate the costs of living and research in the various locations they intend to visit. Over the years, students have created very varied research designs that have moved from content analyses of political speeches to research on AIDS in Africa to mail and in-depth interviews of legislators in developing democracies. Generally speaking, most students come forward with a project that entails more than one method of collecting data. Their projects combine survey research and in-depth interviews or archival research and content analysis. By the end of the course, as is its intent, they feel comfortable with most of the tools in the toolbox and with most of the various methods of collecting data. Additionally, they have come to understand that each data collection method has both advantages and limitations. They often choose to combine data collection methods so that they can get a fuller picture of their research by allowing the various methods to enhance or compensate for each other.

By presenting their research plans to the class as a whole, the students also benefit from having multiple heads focusing on their own research designs. When there are potential problems with a design or when there might be a better resource to use or a better way of doing a given task, having the entire class think about it together invariably improves the research design. The final projects handed in at the end of the semester in hard-copy format are always better as a result of the class presentations.

Mission Accomplished

For doctoral students in many political science programs, courses on "methodology" and "research design" often tend to be unhappy experiences. Students enter these courses because they are required, but often exit them drained of their intellectual excitement and passion for research. This "death of passion" has two causes. First, research design and methodology courses often focus on design and methods exclusively, without linking them to intellectual questions, as my course does. As a result, students end up thinking about methods and design separate from intellectual puzzles. Second, many design and methods courses deliberately stress and encourage the use of some data collection methods and some kinds of data analysis, presenting them as *inherently superior* to other methods of data collection and analysis. For the most part, the preference is for quantitative methods of data collection and analysis. Because quantitative methods are presented as superior, students receive the message that they had better choose a question that will allow them to produce data that can be analyzed quantitatively. If by some unfortunate chance they happen to be interested in an intellectual question that does not lend itself to quantitative data collection and analysis, they are out of luck and may also be drained of intellectual curiosity. Additionally, those who are qualitatively inclined may end up resentful of quantitative methods, blind to their advantages, and hostile to using them.

My course avoids these various pitfalls. Focusing first on an intellectual puzzle and only then on design and methods gives the students a prioritization that preserves their passion and curiosity. Telling them that the choice of methods is theirs and that all methods have assets and limits allows them to avoid thinking that some methods of data collection and analysis are superior. Those who are qualitatively inclined become more open to learning quantitative techniques but do not feel forced to do so. In fact, they are more open precisely because they are not forced toward quantitative methods. And those who are quantitatively inclined do not feel or act fundamentally superior to other students and realize that their preferred techniques also have limits.

One additional benefit comes from the design of this course and the way that it is conducted: by listening to each other present their individual research designs and realizing how widely varied are the different interests represented, the students develop a camaraderie that will last throughout the first year of their doctoral program and into the second year. By the end of the class, it is clear that the students see themselves as beginning scholars engaged in a long-term task. That task starts with the need to learn the substantive material in their area of interest and continues with the need to design and conduct an original study that will become the focus of their dissertation. The students acquire a sense of purpose and a long-term perspective that extends beyond the class itself, beyond their first semester, and beyond their first year in the doctoral program. They have an idea where they are going and seem excited about getting on with the task.

Finally, by talking together throughout the term about different kinds of research, the students develop a mutual respect for each other that is rare and valuable. This respect translates into respect for each other's chosen methods of data collection and analysis. The students understand that each and every individual will come up with a separate and unique research puzzle and that true scholarship requires that they do so. They understand as well that the pursuit of solutions to that puzzle will necessitate data collection methods that are appropriate to that research question and to the context in which the research will be carried out. They understand that each data collection method has both assets and limitations. There is no sense in which they emerge from the course thinking that some kinds of research, some kinds of data, or some methods of data analysis are superior. Instead they are focused on intellectual questions and on allowing the data collection method to emerge in response to those questions rather than the other way around. Their mutual respect and their generalized openness to multiple methods of collecting and analyzing data produces the pluralist perspective of research that our department is seeking to create. These young scholars then become a joy to train.

Appendix: Conduct of Inquiry, Professor Leslie Anderson

This course is about research methodology. As such it does not have a specific substantive focus, nor will you be asked to become knowledgeable about a substantive matter. Rather I seek to introduce you to a variety of research methods, both qualitative and quantitative. As graduate students and scholars you will eventually be asked to design and complete a research project of your own. By the end of the course my hope is that you will feel sufficiently comfortable with all of these methods that you would be willing to attempt any one of them or any combination of them if the question you ask requires it. The goal will be to permit you to ask any question you dream of—and then to have in your hands the tools you will need to answer it.

Consider the following metaphor. You are the recipient of a brand-new toolbox. Inside are some tools you have seen before and others you have never laid eyes on. In this course we will examine each tool separately, putting it to use ourselves, reading the work of others who have used it, or listening to the research stories of still others who use these tools. By the end of the class you will feel comfortable with the entire toolbox and every implement in it. You will be able to carry it around wherever your research takes you, and you will always be able to use all those tools to answer your questions. This is the purpose of this course.

Coursework

There is nothing more deadly than spending a semester reading what others have to say about "methodology." Therefore you will spend a considerable amount of time for this course in the field actually doing different kinds of research. Your readings will be a supplement to what you are doing in the field.

In Part I you will read briefly an introduction to three different kinds of research: participant observation, interviews, and survey research. After you do that reading I will divide the class into three teams. Each team will spend a few weeks conducting research in that genre and then report the results of that research to the class.

In Part II we will move carefully through a series of research methodologies, reading and hearing about each. During this part of the course we will have class visits from other political science professors and one research librarian, all of whom use different methods in their research. They will tell us what they do and why they have chosen these specific methods. During Part II you will also be introduced to Lexis-Nexis, a source of electronic information and data.

In the last part of the course you will design a research project on a question that interests you in the field of your own substantive interests. You will have several weeks to prepare that design, and you will present it to your classmates during class in the final weeks of the semester. When you present it to your classmates, the class and I may raise questions about some of your design or make corrective suggestions. You will then have a chance to revise your design before turning it in to me on the due date. You are expected to take these criticisms seriously and to change your research design according to the criticisms and questions.

Reading List

Books
1. Gary King, Robert Keohane, Sidney Verba, *Designing Social Inquiry*
2. H. Russell Bernard, *Research Methods in Anthropology: Qualitative and Quantitative Approaches*
3. Robert Putnam, *Bowling Alone*
4. Alan Wolfe, *One Nation after All*
5. Robert Putnam, *Making Democracy Work*
6. Theodore Rosengarten, *All God's Dangers: The Life of Nate Shaw*
7. Charles Tilly, *Popular Contention in Great Britain 1758–1834*
8. Catherine Fosl, *Subversive Southerner: Anne Braden and the Struggle for Racial Justice in the Cold War South*

Articles
1. Clifford Geertz, "Deep Play: Notes on the Balinese Cockfight"
2. Katherine Bischoping and Howard Schuman, "Pens and Polls in Nicaragua: An Analysis of the 1990 Pre-election Surveys"
3. Leslie Anderson, "Neutrality and Bias in the 1990 Nicaraguan Preelection Polls: A Comment on Bischoping and Schuman

Course Outline

Date	Topic	Readings
Part I		
August 24	Getting started	Geertz, "Balinese Cockfight" Putnam, *Bowling Alone* Wolfe, *One Nation after All* (read any four chapters and be prepared to report your opinion of each) King, *Designing Social Inquiry*, pp. 12–33

Date	Topic	Readings
August 31	Dividing into teams	
September 7	Discussion of fieldwork, any problems or snags	
	Survey team presents questionnaire for class feedback	
September 14	No class; do fieldwork	
September 21	Interview team presents results	

Part II

Date	Topic	Readings
September 28	Archival work	Bernard, pp. 336–39 Putnam, *Making Democracy Work,* Chap. 5 Fosl, *Subversive Southerner* (please make sure you spend time with Fosl's epilogue, notes, and bibliography)
	Professor Beth Rosenson visits class to talk about archival research for her new book	
	Survey team presents results	
October 5	Participant observation team reports on gatormania	Bernard, Chap. 13
October 12	Content analysis	Bernard, Chap. 9 Tilly, entire book (beginning with Appendix 1)
October 19	Nonelite interviews	Bernard, Chaps. 10, 11 Rosengarten, *All God's Dangers*
October 26	Survey of Lexis-Nexis and other online data sources	
November 2	Elite interviews/focus groups	Bernard, Chaps. 8, 10 Putnam, *Making Democracy Work,* Appendix A and Chaps. 2–4
November 9	Survey research: public opinion data, ICPSR data sets, Michigan summer program	
November 16, 23, 30	Class presentations	
December 7	Research design projects due	

Notes

I am indebted to Lawrence Dodd, Dennis Galvan, and Michael Martinez, who read an earlier version of this chapter and offered helpful comments. Interaction with Kristen Renwick Monroe and the other contributors to this volume has been inspiring and heartwarming, and I am grateful for the opportunity to work with them.

1. The syllabus for this course is included as an appendix to this chapter.

2. My course, The Conduct of Inquiry, and the companion course, Scope and Epistemologies, are taught in tandem during the first semester to incoming doctoral students. Scope and Epistemologies is taught by Lawrence Dodd; the syllabus is available at http://www.clas.ufl.edu/users/ldodd.

3. An example of work that draws on fieldwork and extensive nonelite interviews with peasants in rural villages is Leslie E. Anderson, *The Political Ecology of the Modern Peasant: Calculation and Community* (Baltimore: Johns Hopkins University Press, 1994). An example of multimethod work that draws on survey research and analysis, content analysis, fieldwork, and in-depth interviews is Leslie E. Anderson and Lawrence C. Dodd, *Learning Democracy: Citizen Engagement and Electoral Choice in Nicaragua, 1990–2001* (Chicago: University of Chicago Press, 2005).

References

Anderson, Leslie. "Neutrality and Bias in the 1990 Nicaraguan Preelection Polls: A Comment on Bischoping and Schuman." *American Journal of Political Science,* Vol. 38, 1994, 486–94.

Bernard, H. Russell. *Research Methods in Anthropology: Qualitative and Quantitative Approaches,* 3rd ed. Walnut Creek, CA: AltaMira Press, 2002.

Bischoping, Katherine, and Howard Schuman. "Pens and Polls in Nicaragua: An Analysis of the 1990 Pre-election Surveys." *American Journal of Political Science,* Vol. 36, 1992, 331–50.

Fosl, Catherine. *Subversive Southerner: Anne Braden and the Struggle for Racial Justice in the Cold War South.* New York: Macmillan, 2003.

Geertz, Clifford. "Deep Play: Notes on the Balinese Cockfight." *Daedalus,* Winter 1972, 1–37; rpt. in Clifford Geertz, ed., *Myth, Symbol and Culture* (New York: W. W. Norton), 138.

King, Gary, Robert Keohane, and Sidney Verba. *Designing Social Inquiry: Scientific Inference in Qualitative Research.* Princeton, NJ: Princeton University Press, 1994.

Putnam, Robert. *Bowling Alone.* Paperback edition. New York: Simon & Schuster, 2001.

Putnam, Robert, with Robert Leonardi and Raffaella Y. Nanetti. *Making Democracy Work: Civic Traditions in Modern Italy.* Princeton, NJ: Princeton University Press, 1993.

Rosengarten, Theodore. *All God's Dangers: The Life of Nate Shaw.* New York: Knopf, 1974.

Tilly, Charles. *Popular Contention in Great Britain 1858–1834.* Cambridge, MA: Harvard University Press, 1995.

Wolfe, Alan. *One Nation after All: What Middle-Class Americans Really Think About: God, Country, Family, Racism, Welfare, Immigration, Homosexuality, Work, the Right, the Left, and Each Other.* New York: Viking, 1998.

CHAPTER 32

Quantitative Methods

Reflections on the Files of Recent Job Applicants

Gregory J. Kasza

An empty technicism prevails in much of political science. The triumph of methodology over substance is evident from the labeling of academic schools. Before the mid-1980s, substantive political ideas identified most schools: we were elite theorists, pluralists, modernization theorists, dependency theorists, neo-statists, and so forth. Now methods identify the major schools: we are game theorists, quantifiers, or qualitative researchers. What are the political ideas of today's schools? As schools, they do not have any. The few groups organized around substantive ideas, such as postmodernists and feminist thinkers, seem marginalized by that very fact. Fewer political scientists today dream of forging a new theory of class conflict than of concocting a new form of regression analysis or a new puzzle like the prisoners' dilemma. Once upon a time, the debates that stirred the discipline involved different views of politics; now they involve methodology and imaginary games.[1]

Many in the Perestroika movement that seeks to reform political science blame this situation on the formalistic, unempirical character of rational choice theory, but quantitative methods may be more at fault than deductive theory for the technicism that plagues the discipline. Judging from today's graduate education, statistical methodology is the core of political science. I have sat on search committees in comparative politics for five of the past seven years. Training in quantitative methods is the only shared trait of junior job candidates. In a study of fifty-seven top doctoral programs, Peregrine Schwartz-Shea discovered that 66 percent of them required courses in quantitative methods, as opposed to just 16 percent with a foreign language requirement.[2] But whether due to requirements or to the influence of advisors, all students study statistics. David Pion-Berlin and Dan Cleary found that between 1991 and 2000 the *American Political Science Review* published 225 articles using statistical methodology and 88 articles of mathematical modeling, but only 5 pieces of empirical qualitative research (see their chapter in this volume). In a parallel survey of the *American Journal of Political Science,* I discovered that in the years 1985–1986, 1990–1991, 1995–1996, and 2000–2001 the journal published 283 articles of statistics and 74 of mathematical modeling, including many articles that straddled the two categories. These accounted for over 90 percent of the articles published in each two-year period. By contrast, the journal published only 14 articles of political philosophy and 17 of qualitative empirical research (see my earlier chapter in this volume).

Perestroikans advocate methodological pluralism, that is, we believe that scholars should develop diverse methodological skills and apply them as the subject matter and research materials dictate. The political science establishment sometimes pays lip service to this principle, but its practice belies such rhetoric. The dominance of quantitative methods is such that no one can rethink the nature of political inquiry today without making an issue of this.

What is statistical or quantitative methodology? It is not the mere reporting of numbers. No scholar analyzing an election would omit the numerical results to say that one party got "a lot more" votes than another. Courses in statistics are not about putting numbers in columns. Quantitative methodology comprises mathematical calculations that measure causal or correlative relationships between sets of numbers and the empirical phenomena they purport to represent. There is no statistical methodology without the use of measurements such as regression coefficients and significance tests. I do not doubt the utility of statistics as a partial aid in interpreting data that naturally take numerical form. The question I raise in this chapter is whether quantitative methodology and the hard-scientific ambitions underlying it deserve to dominate the graduate curriculum and our leading journals as they do today. I will ignore the use of mathematical notation in nonempirical research, where it is often an affectation rather than a method.

What explains the ascendancy of statistics? Its attractions are objectivity, precision, and generality. Quantification seems more objective than other methods because mathematics, and not the deficient human mind, produces the theoretical result. The essence of quantitative methods is the scholar's abdication of judgment in favor of a judgment rendered by mathematical calculations. Indeed, if statistical methodology did not surpass the unassisted human mind in its analysis of numbers, what purpose would it serve?

Precision seems an obvious benefit of quantitative research. Probability statements are the stuff of political theory, and words cannot match numbers for a precise expression of probability. Generality is our virtue of virtues. Scientific theory embodies general truths. To arrive at general truths, the mainstream view is that research should include as many cases of the phenomenon under study as possible. Quantitative research can accommodate many cases, so it appears more scientific than the alternatives. Studies of just one or a few cases are said to suffer from a "small n problem" because they cannot produce general conclusions. Even scholars who defend qualitative, small n projects often do so apologetically, averring that their utility lies in areas where the quantitative study of many cases is unfeasible.[3]

All professions seek to differentiate themselves from amateurish ruminations about their subject matter. This is easy to do in technical fields such as engineering, but difficult in regard to politics, about which most people hold passionate opinions. Quantitative methodology produces precise yet general truths about politics that are apparently free of passion and opinion and well beyond the grasp of amateurs. Evidently statistics is the standard by which today's political science defends its credentials as a profession: thus the centrality of quantitative methods in graduate education and in our top journals.

This professional ideology has many flaws. Some relate to the difficult and often subjective decisions involved in gathering data and choosing appropriate statistical instruments. But those problems arise largely within the quantitative school, and this chapter will not challenge quantitative methodology mainly on points internal to it. Rather, I wish to explore the methodological implications of a simple statement about the nature of politics: *there are aspects of every political subject that resist meaningful quantification.* Some aspects of politics resist quantification by their very nature. History, culture, leadership, and power have features that numbers cannot capture. Information from certain types of research materials may also resist quantification, regardless of their topic. Laws, speeches, interviews, and diaries are materials that often defy mathematical translation.

If one concedes the existence of nonquantifiable elements in political life, the case for making statistics the core of the discipline collapses, for this admission leaves the quantifier with only three options: to exclude the uncountable, to quantify the uncountable in an illegitimate way, or to abandon a purely quantitative methodology for a methodologically pluralistic approach in which *qualitative judgments must predominate.* All three options strip quantitative research of the objectivity, precision, and meaningful generality that are its selling points.

Objectivity and Precision

Many quantifiers exclude uncountable data from their work. This strategy undermines both objectivity and precision. Every important political subject has its nonquantifiable aspects. Even regarding elections, a subject suited to statistical analysis, nonquantifiable elements such as the charisma of candidates and electoral fraud demand attention. The only objective way to approach an empirical question is to examine relevant research materials and facts whether they are countable or not. To exclude the uncountable a priori is a subjective distortion of political reality because the exclusion springs from a methodological bias, not from a judgment that something was unimportant to politics. Instead of adopting a method that suits the facts, the exclusion of uncountables distorts the facts to suit the method. It is just as capricious to exclude the uncountable as it would be to exclude the countable aspects of politics from research.

One example of excluding the uncountable is "content analysis," which is poorly named because it removes the content of written materials from research. "Content analysis" involves counting the times that words or topics appear in speeches, laws, or other documents instead of reading them. A language is not its dictionary; grammar turns words into meaningful expression. But for the resolute quantifier, textual exegesis involves qualitative judgments and is therefore objectionable. The scholar thus counts the number of times that the word *state* or the subject *local government* appears in a text rather than analyzing what is written about it.[4] To avoid the modest subjectivity of interpreting a text, quantifiers render themselves illiterate.

Careerwise it matters not, for "content analysis" governs the profession. Faculty judge their junior colleagues at tenure time by counting, not reading, the articles they have published in association journals that carry mainly quantitative research. And the profession judges our departments by counting the number of such articles that we publish and how many times they are referenced in yet more unread articles. (Somehow when rating the research output of departments, our mathematical wizardry does not extend to counting scholarly books or articles in area studies journals, both of which contain predominantly qualitative research.) And the circle is complete. The saddest comment one can make about political science today is that if we evaluated each other's work by reading it rather than counting it, this would cause a revolution in the way we conduct our business.

To exclude the uncountable also undermines precision. Quantitative methodology always produces a result that is precise *in form*. But its precision *in relation to the phenomenon it seeks to explain* depends on the precision of the descriptive data that enter the equation, not on the formalistic precision of the statistical measurements that result. If the input data do not contain precise indicators of the political subject, the precise form of the outcome is misleading. All scholarship abstracts from the infinite details of the real world. Regardless of approach or method, every scholar must choose to highlight certain facts over others. But the standard for making this choice should be our reading of politics, not methodological convenience. Quantifiers who exclude the uncountable have removed much of politics from the picture even before the process of abstracting relevant facts begins. At any given level of abstraction, then, they cannot offer as precise an account of their subject as can a methodological pluralist.

To avoid excluding the uncountable, the quantifier may instead force uncountables into numerical form. This invariably trivializes or distorts these elements, damaging both objectivity and precision. One measures "corporatism" by counting the labor federations in a country, or obstacles to economic growth by counting the number of interest groups. Studies that use proxy measures to force-quantify uncountables typically leave us understanding less about their topics than we might learn by reading the newspaper. A profession should offer a rich, nuanced account of its subject matter, but the quantification of the world offers a stripped, distorted view.

To summarize thus far: All important political phenomena have uncountable aspects. Every purely quantitative study must either exclude those aspects arbitrarily or quantify them in a trivial way. In the process, statistical procedures that are objective and precise *as procedures* produce studies that are subjective and imprecise in relation to politics.

Generality: The Large *n* Problem

Large *n* studies, which maximize the number of cases under investigation, underlie the quantifier's claim to superior generality, but the uncountable aspects of politics pose a special problem for large *n* research. It is easy to gather statistical data on many countries from bodies such as the Organization for Economic Cooperation and Development, Freedom House, and various polling organizations. There is no similar shortcut for studying the uncountable aspects of politics. Because the task of mastering the uncountables in many political settings is formidable, large *n* studies are those most prone to exclude them. When they do, generality comes at the price of scholars' not knowing what they are talking about. The large *n* problem is this: *the more cases scholars include in a study, the less likely they are to grasp the full range of information pertinent to understanding those cases.*

How large an "*n*" is too large? If scholars are unable to master the uncountable as well as the countable aspects of politics in the cases they are studying, their "*n*" is too large, be it 2 or 20. If the investigators do command the varied sources of information about their subject, even a study of twenty cases might avoid the large *n* problem. But how many scholars doing quantitative studies of even seven or eight countries demonstrate qualitative knowledge of their cases?

Some quantifiers believe that they can generalize from statistical data and leave the nonquantifiable aspects of a topic for others to address. We might label this the *Time on the Cross* syndrome after the famous study of American slavery that limited itself entirely to numerical data.[5] But if there are uncountable aspects of every political problem, the analysis of quantitative data can never be an autonomous endeavor. The only sound way to evaluate any one or two aspects of a political subject is within their broader context. The notion that one can scrutinize the numerical aspects apart from the rest and rely upon statistics alone to weigh their significance is mistaken. Statistical measurements cannot gauge the impact of variables that do not fit into mathematical equations. Only a methodological pluralist can evaluate the countable and uncountable aspects of politics together. The paradoxical conclusion is that only qualitative researchers are able to do valid statistical analysis.

An illustration: the official number of child abuse cases in Japan increased over 1000 percent in the 1990s. There were no changes in the law or in reporting procedures to explain the increase. Imagine how a large *n*, quantitative study of child abuse in thirty countries might analyze this phenomenon. Japan's economy stagnated in the 1990s. Divorce rates rose. Crunch the numbers on unemployment and divorces, and the Japanese data would support a theory linking these causes to child abuse. In fact, the rise in reported child abuse reflected mainly a growing awareness and redefinition of the problem in public discourse. Citizens' groups and the mass media focused attention on child abuse by means of surveys, hotlines, and news stories. Anthropologist Roger Goodman concluded: "It is doubtful whether there is more child abuse in Japan at the start of the 2000s than there was at the start of the 1990s. The figures . . . simply demonstrate a dramatic change in people's awareness of what constitutes abusive behavior and a greater preparedness to pass on concerns . . . to the state authorities."[6]

Only a methodological pluralist examining all aspects of the topic could produce the correct analysis. Given the ubiquity of uncountable factors in politics, quantitative methods offer no escape from judgment, even as pertains to the quantitative dimensions of a study. Only someone with a firm qualitative grasp of a subject can discern the real meaning of that regression coefficient. In this sense, quantitative methods do not produce more objective results than do qualitative methods. We must evaluate statistical measurements as we would any other piece of information. Does statistics itself leave us any choice? There are no firm statistical rules for assessing the substantive meaning of a measurement such as a regression coefficient. There is no way to argue on purely statistical grounds that it must reach a given threshold to matter, or pass another threshold to constitute a sufficient causal link. Such determinations require a background of qualitative research and entail judgments that are neither more nor less objective than those involved in evaluating any other type of information.

The reason for preferring small n studies is not, then, as Arend Lijphart has suggested, because large n studies are unfeasible. In most cases, it is because small n studies alone permit scholars to master the many facets of their subject, that is, to know what they are talking about.

Unsurprisingly, small n studies have provided most of the seminal ideas that have advanced comparative politics over the last fifty years. Consider a short list of areas in which achievements have resulted from small n studies with minimal or no assistance from quantitative methods:

Late development—Alexander Gerschenkron (Russia)
Consociational democracy—Arend Lijphart (the Netherlands)
Modern pluralism—Robert Dahl (New Haven, Connecticut)
The moral economy of the peasant—James Scott (Vietnam, Malaysia)
Neostatism—Alfred Stepan (Peru); neo-Marxists (adapting Gramsci's
    essays on Italy)
The developmental state—A.J. Gregor (Italy); Chalmers Johnson (Japan)
Social capital—Robert Putnam (Italy)
Authoritarian regimes—Juan Linz (Spain)
Modern corporatism—Philippe Schmitter (Brazil, Switzerland)[7]

A few large n, quantitative studies, such as Ronald Inglehart's work on postmaterialism, have made major original contributions. But even most large n

studies that have produced pathbreaking findings, such as Samuel Huntington's *Political Order in Changing Societies,* Juan Linz and Alfred Stepan's *Breakdown of Democratic Regimes,* or Giovanni Sartori's *Parties and Party Systems,* have been nonquantitative efforts. As a rule, the best large *n* research comes from scholars who read and write books, not from people who gather and interpret numerical data sets. The authors of these qualitative large *n* studies often know their cases intimately. Their large *n* represents an accumulation of in-depth, small *n* studies, and their work is thus free of the large *n* problem that afflicts so many quantitative projects.

The normal pattern of field development in comparative politics has been for a scholar studying one or a few cases to produce a great theoretical insight, which other scholars then refine and modify in projects of similar scope. The field has not developed mainly by applying ever more sophisticated methods of quantitative measurement. Valid general truths about politics do not emerge from research that systematically excludes or distorts nonquantifiable information.[8]

Those whose love affair with statistics springs from "economics envy" might consider the parallel analysis of Tony Lawson, whose critical work on econometrics has inspired the post-autistic economics movement for the reform of economics (www.paecon.net):

> In their . . . programmatic stances, mainstream economists refer to many substantive items which their official ways of proceeding cannot accommodate without severe strains. Such items even include the basic economic categories of choice, institutions, markets, money, social relationships, uncertainty, and change. . . . Econometricians . . . are in effect committed to a *particular* formulation of the post-Humean scientific ideal. . . . According to this thesis, for every (measurable) economic event or state of affairs y there exists a set of conditions or events, etc., $x_1, x_2 \ldots x_n$ say, such that y and $x_1, x_2 \ldots x_n$ are regularly conjoined under some (set of) "well-behaved" probabilistic formulation(s). . . . The feature of modern economics which is remarkable here is the minimal concern that is shown either for tailoring methods to insights available regarding the nature of the social world, or for explicitly determining the sorts of conditions under which chosen methods would be appropriate. This is despite a dearth of successes according to criteria which the discipline sets itself. Rather, methods and procedures are formulated according to the nature or degree of their technical sophistication, or their conformity with *a priori* conceptions of proper practice, or some such. . . . The most telling point against this econometrics project is the *ex posteriori* result that significant invariant event regularities, whether of a probabilistic kind or otherwise, have yet to be uncovered in economics, despite the resources continually allocated to their pursuit.[9]

Notwithstanding the signs that qualitative, small *n* research produces the most fertile theoretical insights into politics, the pursuit of generality continues to foster quantitative, large *n* projects. Generality has become such a Holy Grail for political scientists that it deserves a radical rethinking. Are general truths always superior to particular truths? This is not a live question for most scholars, regardless of their methodological colors. Most have settled the issue in favor of the general, for two reasons. First, general truths are the stuff of science, and even most critics of quantitative methods embrace the scientific project. Second, there is an unspoken assumption that every key aspect of politics has a valid general explanation. If we haven't found it yet, we just haven't looked hard enough. This is the Great Social Science Prejudice, to assume that everything important that happens makes general theoretical sense. Woe to the job applicant porting a dissertation that explains a particular political phenomenon without couching it in the form of general truth. The faculty immediately judges this person less intelligent than those who come bearing generalities. Write a biography for a dissertation, and you may as well skip your job search and start waiting tables at once.

The notion that general truths are always a greater achievement than particular truths is nonsense spread by people whose commitment to an abstract conception of science outweighs their desire to understand politics. It cannot be argued on the basis of what is important to politics itself. Which matters more for understanding the politics of the twentieth century: The program of the Communist Party of the Soviet Union, or the programs of Communist movements in general? The impact of Stalin's leadership, or the general traits of effective leaders? The reasons that Soviet Communism collapsed, or general features of the breakdown of nondemocratic regimes? And if what is most significant in politics is not necessarily amenable to general theory, how should we react to this finding? Should we ignore what is politically significant to flatter our theoretical and methodological pretensions, or put politics first, and science second?

The reason that the study of politics matters is not because it is open to the formulation of general laws. It is because politics decides bread-and-butter and life-and-death issues that affect all of humanity every day. Stalin caused the deaths of over twenty million people. No one should feel bound to offer a scientific excuse for studying his life.

Suppose we do discover a great general truth about some empirical political subject. How useful or general can it be in a changing world? Will the same theory of revolutions or wars work in eras of different weapons technology? Will the same theory of class conflict work in eras of different industrial structures and labor markets? Politics is a moving target. All empirical political knowledge is historically grounded because politics is a historical phenomenon, and this limits the general validity of any explanation. Lasting general truths require a lasting reality to which they might apply, and in political science we do not have such a reality to work with.[10] Only the normative aspects of politics are open to enduring general theory, something we ought to remember when pondering the place of classical political philosophy in the curriculum.

To be sure, even if one's goal is to explain a single case, general patterns based on comparative research can be enlightening. I play the devil's advocate on this point, however, because the emphasis on generality has exceeded rational bounds. Many scholars now accept or reject explanations based solely on their generality. They would discard a superior explanation of case *x* for an inferior one only because the latter applies to more cases. There is no surer sign of the triumph of scientism and methodology over truth in the study of politics.

Many key aspects of politics do not have valid, generalizable explanations. That is why political scientists whose main concern is to understand politics must read and occasionally write narrative history: to grasp the impact of the particular, the accidental, the unpredictable exercise of free will in political affairs. To leave particular explanations to the historian is not an option. Only by charting the realm of the particular can a political scientist know the proper reach of general theory. Only a competent historian can become a competent political scientist.

Statistics in Graduate Education

This, of course, is not what we are teaching the next generation of scholars. Instead we offer them a curriculum whose only universal requirement is quantitative methodology. What does this convey to our students?

- The heart of political science is its methodology, not its subject matter.
- Statistics is the one methodology that all political scientists must learn; by implication, other methods are inferior.
- The most suitable topics for political research are those susceptible of statistical inquiry.
- Manipulating numerical data sets is more important than reading books, doing fieldwork, or any other way of educating oneself about politics.

The effects of this education are clear in the many applicant files I have read. Today's dissertation writers, even those who obviously favor other methods, feel obligated to incorporate some quantitative element in their research. They may be working on political systems about which quantitative data are notoriously unreliable. No matter; they will find some way to include statistics in their studies. Even when the quantitative element is a small part of their work, it is usually the part they highlight in their job talks. This may not put their research in the best light, but they believe it is necessary to get a job. Sadly, at many research universities they are probably right. This is not methodological pluralism; it is methodological dictatorship. Why is it imperative that a dissertation on Ghanaian nongovernmental organizations, Argentine political development, French bureaucracy, or the U.S. Congress use quantitative methods at all?

What should we teach our students about the use of statistics in political science?

- Given the presence of uncountables in the political world, there is no such thing as a valid research design limited to numerical data and quantitative methods.
- Given the need to interpret statistical measurements in light of nonquantifiable variables, the notion that quantitative methods offer superior objectivity, precision, or reliable generality is largely an illusion. In political science, there is no escape from judgment and its attendant insecurities.
- Quantitative methods may enhance the study of data that come naturally in numerical form, but we must reexamine all modes of statistical measurement in light of the ubiquity of uncountables in politics. Methods textbooks typically note the problems with statistics and then proceed to give instruction without solving those problems or directing us to substantive studies that illustrate their solution.[11] Students today must not take such instruction at face value. Because statistics is the methodological dogma of our time, it demands severe scrutiny.
- The study of politics will never become a hard science with the precision, objectivity, or generality of the physical sciences. It is not the lack of more refined methods, but the nature of the social world, that makes it so. If you require the exactitude of the engineer, study engineering. Political science is not for you.

Above all, today's graduate students must grasp that methodology is not the foremost factor in producing good research. Given the current overemphasis on statistics, I endorse the view of most Perestroikans that we must expand education in qualitative methods. But the roots of the quantification problem lie in the notion that we can reduce good research to a set of methodological skills, and qualitative researchers must not perpetuate that falsehood. Our libraries are full of brilliant studies that are methodological travesties. Think of Alexis de Tocqueville tramping around the United States without a sample or a questionnaire. And there are scads of methodologically sound works that teach nothing very interesting about politics. How can this be?

All methodology, be it training in statistical measurement, conducting interviews, or doing textual exegesis, is mere mechanics. Methods are techniques to facilitate the gathering and processing of different types of information. In this, they can be useful. They cannot tell us what issues our research should address, what information is relevant to understanding them, what is true or false in the information we gather, or what conclusions to draw from it. Yet good scholarship depends on the answers to just these questions.[12]

At least three elements should take priority over methodology in graduate education:

Political philosophy. Training should begin with a full exploration of the normative, ontological, and epistemological bases of politics and political knowledge.

Empirical foundations. Students should master the politics of three or four countries, examining political life in its historical, economic, and cultural context. Someone who aspires to theorize about bureaucracy or party systems or political culture ought first to study several real-world examples of these things.

Analytical reasoning. This involves the study of concept formation and different approaches to political research. An "approach" is a way to divide politics into parts for analysis. The parts might be classes, elites and masses, groups, processes of change, individuals, values, regimes, and so forth. The choice of approach is a critical step in any research project, because it largely fixes the type of argument or explanation that will result. This choice should never be based on methodological criteria. Indeed a common abuse of quantitative methodology is that it masquerades as an approach, with the method dictating that one should dissect politics into whatever parts are countable.

"Skills," including methodology and languages, would come fourth, with a correction of the current imbalance between statistics and foreign language study, and a healthy dose of qualitative methods.

Perhaps the greatest appeal of the hard-scientific methodologies that predominate today is that they seem to offer graduate students a pat formula for success: "master this skill, apply it conscientiously, and you, too, can join the club." The educational plan outlined here offers no such formula, but it will lead more students to good scholarship than the methods-based education we are offering at present. The truth is that there is no pat formula, methodological or otherwise, for producing good scholarship. It may be an unsettling truth, but perhaps the truth would be a good place to start as we seek to fashion a more persuasive defense of what we do as a profession.

In conclusion, I will restate that this entire argument regarding quantitative methods follows from an assertion about the nature of politics, namely, that there are uncountable aspects of every significant political subject. I stress this point because the case against making statistics the core of political science depends upon it. If the key aspects of most political phenomena can be meaningfully expressed in numbers, quantitative methods should form the heart of political science. If they cannot be, statistics should play a secondary role in our work. It would be gratifying if those who dispute this analysis would address this substantive question about the nature of political life in their rebuttals. Ultimately, the consideration of methods should always focus on their relationship to the real world of politics.

Notes

My thanks to the following people for their comments on drafts of this chapter: Michael Desch, Tom Dumm, John Harbeson, Patrick Thaddeus Jackson, Gary King, Ralf Juan Leiteritz, John Mearsheimer, David Pion-Berlin, Sanford Schram, Peregrine Schwartz-Shea, Rogers Smith, and Ernie Zirakzadeh.

1. In this chapter I will refer to "politics" and "political reality" with the casual abandon of a naïve empiricist, as I think befits the subject matter and most readers. Ontological questions deserve extended treatment, but that would distract from my purpose here.

2. Peregrine Schwartz-Shea, "Is This the Curriculum We Want? Doctoral Requirements and Offerings in Methods and Methodology," *PS: Political Science and Politics,* vol. 36, no. 3 (July 2003): 380.

3. For instance, Arend Lijphart, "Comparative Politics and the Comparative Method," *American Political Science Review,* vol. 65 (1971): 682–93. For a systematic review of methods texts that confirms this apologetic approach to qualitative research, see Peregrine Schwartz-Shea and Dvora Yanow, "'Reading' 'Methods' 'Texts': How Research Methods Texts Construct Political Science," *Political Research Quarterly,* vol. 55, no. 2 (June 2002): 457–86.

4. One recent job applicant wrote in his research statement that he had spent two to three months in each of several countries to count the number of times that issues of local government were mentioned in parliamentary deliberations.

5. Robert William Fogel and Stanley L. Engerman, *Time on the Cross: The Economics of American Negro Slavery* (Boston: Little, Brown, 1974).

6. Roger Goodman, "Child Abuse in Japan: 'Discovery' and the Development of Policy," in Goodman, ed., *Family and Social Policy in Japan: Anthropological Approaches* (Cambridge: Cambridge University Press, 2002), 149.

7. A common question at job interviews is "What scholars have most influenced your intellectual development?" Surprisingly, applicants bearing high-tech, quantitative dissertations often name the scholars I have listed here or others doing qualitative, small *n* research. I haven't put these job candidates on the spot by asking them why they were not doing the type of research they seemed to admire so much in their elders, but I would certainly like to know.

8. Am I mistaken? Have I overlooked a large number of purely quantitative, large *n* studies in comparative politics that (1) do not unfairly exclude uncountables, (2) do not quantify uncountables in a specious manner, and (3) constitute original, theoretical contributions to knowledge that are comparable in importance to those listed earlier? If so, I beseech the reader to send me their titles with a brief explanation of their significance, so that I can be instructed. This is not a rhetorical request. When challenged by the movement for a "post-autistic economics" (an unfortunate slogan for a worthy enterprise—see www.paecon.net), Europe's neo-classical economists responded publicly and forthrightly to criticism. Unfortunately, the Perestroika movement has elicited little response from mainstream scholars in political science. This leaves reformers to assume the worst, namely, that mainstream scholars are unable to defend their practices, or that they are so secure atop

the discipline that they feel no need to respond. An abiding stimulus for the Perestroika protest is the sense that political science has taken the wrong path without a full public debate of the relevant issues. In the long run, such a debate can have no losers. I am grateful to quantitative scholars like Gary King and Paul Gronke who have participated in the Perestroika debates. I am chagrined that they are so few.

9. Tony Lawson, *Economics and Reality* (London: Routledge, 1997), xii, 8, 70, 76.

10. "Economics, then, in a more obvious way than natural science perhaps, is necessarily historical-geographical. In addition, if by virtue of their dependency upon human agency, social structures must be continually reproduced, it follows that economics is concerned with inherently dynamic matters. . . . Clearly, if society is intrinsically dynamic, social science must be alert, and its methods tailored, to this condition." Lawson, *Economics and Reality*, 34.

11. For example, textbooks mention the difficulties of finding proxy variables for factors that are not naturally countable, and warn against "omitted variable bias," noting that the omission of a key independent variable from a regression equation can bias the measurement of the variables that are included. For instance, see Paul D. Allison, *Multiple Regression: A Primer* (Thousand Oaks, CA: Pine Forge Press, 1999); Gary King, Robert O. Keohane, and Sidney Verba, *Designing Social Inquiry: Scientific Inference in Qualitative Research* (Princeton, NJ: Princeton University Press, 1994). But if there are important, uncountable features of every political problem that resist reasonable quantification, how can a regression analysis take into account all key independent variables? These books never state the obvious conclusion that follows from their reasoning, namely, that statistics is of limited use in political science.

12. For a sophisticated demonstration that rule-based analysis embodies a simplistic, nonexpert level of intellectual mastery, see Bent Flyvbjerg, *Making Social Science Matter: Why Social Inquiry Fails and How It Can Succeed Again* (Cambridge: Cambridge University Press, 2001).

CHAPTER 33

On Curricular Perestroika

Seven Principles of Methodological Pluralism

Hayward R. Alker

Curriculum reform is a sensitive subject, especially at the doctoral level of university training, where professional disciplinary identities are shaped, renewed, and redefined. Core—that is, required—courses teach the disciplinary identities, interests, truths, modes of inquiry, and other competencies certified by successful performance on disciplinewide or subdiscipline-specific "screening," "qualifying," or "comprehensive" exams. Restructuring such core courses, the broader curricula they help center, or the examinations directed toward certifying such competencies can easily raise issues about professional identities, the disciplinary centrality of certain kinds of work, and privileged research and teaching directions, issues about which faculty members and professionally oriented graduate students care passionately.

With its concern for restructuring and renewing the disciplinary institutions of American political science, from its beginnings in the fall of 2000 the Perestroika movement has raised curricular issues about the definition, teaching, and development of political science. These concerns caught my attention and evoked my support.[1] Shortly after I joined the Perestroika list serve, I circulated on it a version of my syllabus for the spring 2001 semester of a broadly shaped, required methodology course, IR513, in the School of International Relations PhD program at the University of Southern California (USC). The course, which I have regularly taught at USC since 1995, is entitled Social Scientific and Historical Research Methods: Introduction to Research Design, and the syllabus is included in edited form as an appendix to the present chapter. The syllabus was subsequently recirculated by "Mr. Perestroika" with the comment "Excellent," and it became the basis for some further discussion on the list serve and for my participation on Perestroika panels at the APSA in August 2001 and 2002 and at the Western Political Science Association meeting in March 2002.[2]

The present chapter provides a more extended version of my views on the design and teaching of such "philosophies of, methodologies of, or conduct of inquiry" courses as ways of helping to integrate PhD curricula in political science and international relations within a pluralistic philosophical-methodological-ontological framework. It has grown out of my current teaching in the School of International Relations at USC, as well as my earlier teaching of a required course entitled Philosophies of Social Science in the political science PhD program at MIT and, even earlier, my graduate student education in the "scope and method" of political science, international relations, and public policy analysis at Yale under the separate and distinctive tutelages of Robert Dahl, Karl Deutsch, Robert Lane, Harold Lasswell, and Charles Lindblom.

The reader will better understand the syllabus for IR513, the design and teaching of which has been so central to my thinking on these issues, if he or she knows the following. At USC we have required international relations PhD students to take an international relations theory course plus three out of four slightly more specialized domain overview courses. Additionally, they must take an overview research methodology course (which has been IR513) and a social-scientifically oriented multivariate data analysis course. Later on in their graduate careers, students must take a more specialized and advanced methodological course pointed toward the preparation of a doctoral dissertation. A few years ago, we removed the requirement of a second semester of advanced international relations theory.[3]

Because each specific philosophy, methodology, or conduct of inquiry course has its own special features, developed in a context of other curricular options, complements, and requirements,[4] I think it wise to proceed here at the broader level of the principles and goals I have tried to embed in the different parts of our core curriculum, especially IR513. Thus I shall avoid making claims as to which specific readings should or must be included in a particular course of this sort at another institution.[5]

Because the exchange in question is methodologically oriented, resonant with previously cited Perestroika commitments to including feminist perspectives, and part of the broader curriculum associated with IR513, but not of that course per se, I shall concretely illustrate several of the points suggested here with references to a published exchange among J. Ann Tickner (1997, 1998), Robert Keohane (1998), and Marianne Marchand (1998). Methodological pluralism is fostered not only by individually conceived pluralistic courses, but also by having multiple teachers of different methodological approaches at the same university and, more broadly, teachers who are in dialogue about the options that should be covered in core curricula.

Pedagogical Principles

Perhaps the best way to start such a review of pedagogical principles is with the following reflexive commitment:

Pedagogical Principle 1   *Social-scientifically and historically oriented scholar-teachers should treat their own discipline's multiplicity of sociohistorical research practices as emulatable and criticizable objects of sociohistorical inquiry, including, but not limited to, their philosophical, epistemological, and methodological aspects.*

By way of exposition, I should note that I have not only interpreted IR513's commitment to "historical and social-scientific" subject matters in terms of serious attention to the distinctive methodological literatures of the different disciplines involved, including historians' own historiographic literatures.[6] I have also treated reflexively the subject matter of the course itself, taking a sociohistorical look at research practices, including their justificatory elements. Thus research practices and designs are described not merely in terms in the philosophies of inquiry used to justify actual or potential practices, such as Popper-Lakatosian critical rationalism,[7] but in terms of the criticizable and commendable motivations of actual individual pieces or lines of research. Rather than assume that some nice-sounding philosophical doctrine guides (and therefore is heard as justifying) particular research practices, one needs to discover concretely what the guiding motives, principles, or institutional interests were and discuss the appropriateness and validity of these standards, and others perhaps more relevant.[8] What should one emulate, and what criticize, in which circumstances? Surely these are appropriate questions to seek to answer from the perspective of a critically oriented historian or social scientist of research practices.

Reflectively, the student needs to think of others' or of one's own research as joining, and taking sides in, or somehow transcending ongoing controversies about how a discipline should conduct itself. Seeing specific research activities as part of larger, but particular, sociohistorical groupings of research practices is parallel to taking Thomas Kuhn's description in Imre Lakatos and Alan Musgrave (1970) of his classic study of scientific revolutions (Kuhn 1970, originally 1962) as primarily a historically based exploration of the "psychology" of science, an exploration of the dynamics of multifaceted "disciplinary matrices" centered in paradigmatic or exemplary "ways of seeing" rather than the typical "philosophy" of (natural) science text with historical examples.

Let me give a somewhat more sustained example of what I have in mind. Hayward Alker and Roger Hurwitz (1980, 2001) and Alker (1996, 303–31) follow Rom Harré and Paul Secord's (1972) paradigmatically revolutionary advocacy of a "new psychology" in recommending an ethnomethodological or dramaturgical approach to studying how people actually play iterated prisoner's dilemma games, contrasting it with rational choice, game learning, and social psychological conflict resolution research paradigm complexes. Their illustration of Harré and Secord's distinction between "old psychology" and "new psychology," described as research paradigm complexes (RPCs), both suggests what Kuhn's (new) psychology of science might look like and exemplifies my synthetic conception of "research paradigm complexes,"[9] a merger of Kuhn's, Lakatos's and Jürgen Habermas's contribution to the debate about how best to characterize progress in the natural, human, or social sciences.

One could think of the "new psychology" of Table 33.1 as an interpretively or hermeneutically oriented revolution in psychological paradigms associated with perspectives that were partly incommensurable and partly overlapping with the experimentally oriented "old psychology" of David Hume, Wilhelm

Wundt, B. F. Skinner, and Robert Zajonc. The richness of this contrast—defined more comprehensively than specific research programs—argues for trying to save Kuhnian notions of scholarly paradigms and Habermas's concern with multiple (positive, hermeneutic or interpretive, and emancipatory) knowledge interests in our vocabulary for assessing contributions to knowledge.[10]

As any casual reader of sociological studies of science is aware, social-scientific disciplines play social roles vis-à-vis individuals in their environing societies and vis-à-vis their individual members. Some of these roles enable collective capacities, while others limit them. Unless we include the relationships between a set of research practices and the environing society—as Habermasian critical theory requires—the broader, historically situated appraisal of such relationships in terms of social betterment or detriment are not possible. For example, the emancipatory interest of "new psychology" in the discovery or improvement of collective human capacities is broader than the primary Enlightenment-inspired goal of "old psychology," knowledge enhancement.[11] Michel Foucault would say that disciplines help discipline their members in many ways: limiting their approved ways of doing things is associated with spending more effort and developing greater competences in approved ways of proceeding.

A number of related principles are closely associated with the taking of a sociohistorical perspective.

Pedagogical Principles 2 and 3   *As a way of enhancing student methodological possibilities and discernment, sociologically historicize and internationally contextualize the development of a discipline's core theories and methodologies. An appreciation of a discipline's internationally recognized classics suggests the appropriateness of considerable methodological tolerance concerning shareable standards of knowledge enhancement.*

Teachers of required discipline-training courses are faced with some hard choices about what to include and exclude. Associated with these are potential sins of commission and omission: their students' prospects for getting and keeping good academic jobs are diminished when they are not adept at theory-method mixes that personnel search committees or research proposal reviewers consider the sine qua non of disciplinary literacy or competence, while their ineptitude vis-à-vis alternative approaches damages these students' ability as future teachers to encourage their own students and impress evaluating superiors when substantive interests appropriately point in such alternative directions. In a situation in which both perestroika and glasnost—restructuring and opening toward greater pluralism—are called for, the resulting choice dilemmas are only heightened.

One of the hard choices concerns the wide practice of requiring the statistics of general linear modeling of all political science PhDs.[12] As the pressure to become more competent in calculus-based statistical skills increases, what usually gets excluded are those historical and recent traditions of empirical

Table 33.1 Old and New Psychology Research Paradigm Complexes (RPCs)

RPC Framework	Old Psychology	New Psychology
Core beliefs (conceptual or metaphysical pretheories and their negative heuristics)	Mechanistic model of humans; Humean causation wherein the mode of connection of cause and effect is not part of empirical science; radical behaviorism; positivism; verificationist theory of meaning; operationalist definitions	Shift from a physiological theory of movements to the study of meaningful social actions; Hampshire's anthropomorphic model of man; the dramaturgical standpoint; an "open souls doctrine"; the standards of negotiating accounts, not obtaining absolute truth
Originating exemplars and positive research heuristics	Wundt's physiological psychology; laboratory research defined in terms of the additive manipulation of independent variables; behavior under the control of environmental variables	Austin's theory of speech acts; Chomsky's "generative grammars" possibly extended into social life; Miller, Galanter, and Pribram on plans and the structure of behavior; reliance on conceptual systems embedded in "ordinary languages" to generate self-monitoring "accounts" of rules, plans guiding meaningful behavior
Symbolic relationships, including testable theories	Skinnerian theories of environmental conditioning and intervening variables; relying on statistical models of S-(O)-R relationships	Systems theory, especially Macfarlance's treatment of homeostasis; the ascription of "powers" via the formula: If C_1 v C_2 v ... C_n, then B in virtue of N, where the Cs refer to conditions, Bs to behaviors, and N to natural powers and liabilities; a typology of role-rule models and episodes

A literature evidencing theory "successes" and new puzzles	The literature (including research programs) on animal learning experiments as trait psychology; Zajonc's social psychology	Chomsky's discoveries of transformational rules of human grammars; Chomsky and Levi-Strauss on deep structures of meaning; Berne, Garfinkel, and Goffman on games people play
A relevant scholarly community	Adherents of radical behaviorism; typical psychological experimentalists	A mixture of linguistic philosophers, psychologists and sociologists focused on meaning and people's agency
External research situation	Emulation of natural science according to the false philosophy of logical positivism and its near relatives	The later Wittgenstein's writings on psychology and "language games"; the search for generative models of natural and social powers by mature sciences (in Kuhn's sense)

Source: Alker and Hurwitz (2001), based on Harré and Secord (1972), especially Chapters 1 and 2.

inquiry grounded in nonprobabilistic treatments of uncertainty, argumentation, intentionality, and linguistically mediated probative reasoning. Nonetheless, I have found it valuable to take examples of political and international relations analysis from earlier periods of political-historical research; a historical (and international) perspective helps one better see the "fads" or "biases" in contemporary (American) methodological advocacy. Let me mention only two such related historical vantage points, starting with Paul Lazarsfeld's own historical review of the field of statistics, and going back to Thucydides' Sophistic and Aristotle's post-Sophistic conceptions of scholarly political-historical inquiry.

As argued, illustrated, and documented in Lazarsfeld 1961 and in Alker 1984 and 1996, Chapters 1, 2, and 12, statistics originated in what might now be ideal-typically described as a quantitative, Gallilean mode and as a less quantitative, partly qualitative, Aristotelean mode of inquiry. Seen as a twenty-five-hundred-year-old, often-productive controversy about knowledge growth, the literature on the explanation-understanding controversy surely deserves extended treatment in courses on the conduct of social-scientific inquiry. Indeed this contrast is regularly cited by Tickner in the Tickner-Keohane-Marchand exchange cited earlier, but is not given serious attention in most of the statistically or positivistically oriented methodology literature of recent political science.

Another hard choice in designing core curricula concerns the relative attention given there to the internationally recognized classics within a field. My reanalyses of Thucydides' Melian Dialogue have led me to the view that Thucydides' training by the Sophists of his day allowed him, through the careful reconstruction of reflective, practically oriented debates, to probe deeply, in an engaged but detached manner we can describe as at once dialectical, humanistic, and scientific, into the characterological and historical roots of the Athenian tragedy his *History of the Peloponnesian War* so powerfully tells. Reflection on this most ancient classic of political science and international relations has helped rationalize and justify a whole range of more or less contemporary humanistic or scientific research methodologies. Sophisticated, operationalized research alternatives to statistical inference,[13] nondeductive argumentation, interpretive inferencing via Weberian ideal types or Schank-Abelson frame- or scripts-based computational linguistics, narrative-based explanation, practical (rather than game-theoretic) rationality are just some of these unconventional possibilities spread throughout IR513 and elsewhere.

I have become a neo-classicist from simultaneously teaching both classical social and political theory and contemporary research methodologies. The exhilaration can be catching, and one's sense of methodological tolerance broadened, if one is flexible enough to recognize rational, truth-seeking minds at work, whatever the particulars of their circumstances.

Even more controversially, during the cold war I came to believe that a rich but largely neglected repertoire of methodological possibilities can be found in a close, critical reading of the classics of the Hegelian-Marxist tradition and the

Frankfurt School of Critical Theorists, including the writings of Karl-Otto Apel, Antonio Gramschi, Georg Lukacs, Herbert Marcuse, Enrique Cardoso and Ernesto Faletto, and Jürgen Habermas. But to appreciate these classics and others, one has to recognize that different ontologies and differently formulated truth standards are at work in these writings than those assumed in much contemporary American quantitative political science.[14] The history of the historical-sociopolitical sciences gives us several such rich alternatives if we don't limit ourselves to the illusion that systematic political inquiry began and largely developed in twentieth-century America, and that statistics is an adequate methodology for addressing almost all important epistemological issues!

Because it illustrates the importance of internationalizing methodological discussions in today's world, Dutch feminist Marianne Marchand's plea (1997) for such internationalization is worth discussing here. Marchand criticizes Tickner for taking too homogeneous a cross-cultural approach, focusing on the American "mainstream" in a discipline too much dominated by American scholars in her (and Tickner's) view. She wishes to celebrate more the ontological and epistemological diversity of feminist scholarship, but mentions misunderstandings in feminist exchanges with other critically oriented international relations scholars similar to those noted by Tickner.

Even though Tickner sees herself as a bridging scholar because of her Anglo-American background and her studied attention to British writers, especially Hollis and Smith and Linklater, Marchand's European concerns are serious ones. Although they are not homogeneous, overlapping American and European standards on many issues are diverging, perhaps including scientific ones as well. At least in the Gramschian tradition, power, supremacy, legitimacy, and hegemonic standards of respectable scholarly inquiry are deeply interconnected. Couldn't some of this divergence be political, and shouldn't we be critically aware of, and try to do something about, the possible distorting effects of such politics?

During the long cold war between "Communism" and "The Free World" (to use American terminology), there were several similar epistemological-ontological dimensions of that conflict as it entered the international academic arena. One of them was the conflict between philosophies of scientific inquiry, with Soviets officially preferring a dogmatic version of Leninist "dialectical-materialism," West European Marxists more flexibly clustered around dialectical, critical approaches, and most pro-Western Anglo-American social scientists preferring some form of traditionalism, operationalism, Weberian positivism, logical empiricism, or Popperian critical rationalism. Surely some of the passions surrounding the Kuhn-Lakatos controversies are linked to earlier cold war positions; also, many Americans' instant repugnance toward the dialectical-hermeneutic tradition of inquiry just as certainly has cold war overtones. Much of my own exploration of what Radnitzky calls the continental hermeneutic-dialectical tradition of metascience was designed to get at the roots of that tradition and rationally appraise their uses and misuses.

I have found, to my amazement, that these roots may best be described as the classical humanistic tradition of philosophy and history, one blending explanatory and instrumental, practical-hermeneutic, and emancipatory objectives. Hence, the following:

Pedagogical Principle 4 *Recognize and teach social-scientific and historical research methodologies defined in terms of a plurality of knowledge interests. Following Habermas, Brooke Ackerly, Roy Bhaskar, R. G. Collingwood-Toulmin, William Dunn, and Gerard Radnitzky, I organize my own teaching in terms of knowledge interests that are positive (prediction, explanation, instrumental value realization), practical-hermeneutic (oriented toward achieving collective understanding concerning appropriate actions), critical-emancipatory (removing false necessities), and cosmological (painting an actual, possible, desireable world picture).*

Methodology courses in behaviorally oriented political science departments have often been conceived as introductions to particular tools, techniques, or methods. One recalls the problem of which readings to assign on "experimentation and simulation," "content analysis," or "survey analysis" or on "archival" and "participant-observation field research." My own early years as a political scientist found me, as a specialist in "aggregate data analysis," teaching an advanced summer course in multiequation statistical and simulational modeling at the Inter-university Consortium for Political and Social Research in Ann Arbor. But what a liberation it has been to realize from my international, historical, and multidisciplinary readings and conversations that such courses were usually straightjacketed by the assumption of one overriding, rigorously scientific, knowledge interest: prediction, explanation, and instrumental control. Habermas places all of these concerns within a "positive" knowledge interest, obviously linked to the Comptean tradition of positivism, or naturalism, as it rode through nineteenth-century academe on the backs of Isaac Newton, Antoine-Laurent Lavoisier, Charles Darwin, and the other giants of natural science.

Once Habermas had helped me to distinguish hermeneutic and emancipatory knowledge interests from positive ones, I was able to connect the linguistic revolution in twentieth-century philosophy to my own work as a political scientist. Methodological issues concerning coding reliability and validity took on a much richer set of meanings when seen in practical-hermeneutic terms.[15] The acts of understanding that are quintessential to cross-national and cross-cultural diplomacy—the characteristic subject matter of traditional international relations—gained new autonomy and respect within my mind. Marxism, psychoanalysis, feminism, and humanism were legitimated in their emancipatory concerns. The Enlightenment's emancipatory goals were allowed reentry into the social sciences as I now, more broadly, understood their goals.

Although a continuum of epistemological-ontological orientations and knowledge interests could be distinguished within contemporary Western epistemologies alone,[16] historical, Western, and non-Western multicivilizational perspectives enrich this vantage point considerably. According to the first three pedagogical principals stated earlier, I think it potentially valid to question whether theoretical and epistemological-ontological positions are influenced by one's national or ideological political perspective. Doesn't presumed identification with one nation's hegemonic stature in the world tend to emphasize the development of positive, problem-solving knowledge capabilities in the training of that nation's citizens and international guests?[17] Aren't revolutionary states in the international system—whether Leninist or Islamicist—more likely to value emancipatory or cosmological knowledge interests in their publicly supported social-scientific teaching? I wonder how many recent foreign-born and -raised social-scientific graduates of secularly defined American universities would report serious epistemological or cosmological differences as a problem in returning to their homeland in search of a teaching position.

Historicizing and internationalizing a particular form of knowledge brings fruitful insights as well as new complexities; systematic exposure to the disciplinary perspectives and competencies of several disciplines is also conducive to improved professional and methodological sophistication. Hence:

Pedagogical Principle 5   *A pluralization of political-scientific research possibilities is further enhanced by systematic exposure to a multiplicity of disciplinary research paradigms, agendas, programs, and discourses, taught in a way that reveals their individual limitations as well as the actualities and possibilities of transdisciplinarity.*

This set of reflections on methodological pluralism has already repeatedly invoked the principle of multidisciplinarity. We have visited vicariously a revolutionary moment in the disciplinary history of psychology, and argued statistical training options with sociologists, for example. Gender studies within political science and international relations, but also the humanities more generally, have frequently provided us with alternative methodological orientations. The positive and negative research heuristics of different research programs can be seen more clearly this way too. Surely many American political scientists have also visited at the least the econometric shores of economics and the middle floors of its grander game-theoretical edifices. One's own disciplinary riches and limitations—and the reality of the borrowing, imitating, and shunning that connect and divide disciplines—become more clearly apparent through such multidisciplinarity.

The advantages of such recognitions can be linked with multidisciplinarity, but I think it preferable also to introduce an allied notion of transdisciplinarity. Like computer science, statistics is both a multiparadigmatic discipline (with Fisherians, Bayesians, nonparametric data analysts, and so on) and a transdiscipline; it provides conceptual or technical assistance to empirical scholars in many other disciplines. Transdisciplinarity refers to, and builds on, the kind of (usually practical or philosophical) insights that come from a recognition or deployment of truths and fashions cutting across and through particular disciplines. It is what makes the incommensurability of Kuhnian old and new paradigms only partial. It is what helps explain parallel and divergent developments in particular disciplines.

Consider the subject of rationality, one of the leitmotifs of IR513. Even better, from the vantage point of transdisciplinarity, consider the virtues of teaching a multiplicity of conceptions of human rationality in reconstructing plausible research hypotheses and possibilities, giving priority to those practically and communicatively oriented conceptions that bridge gaps between theoretical and practical forms of knowledge. Explicitly included in IR513 are classical and modern-computational practical reasoning; dialogical reasoning; formalized instrumental rationality (economics, game theory); social, legal, and political rationality (in Diesing's and Toulmin's senses); Weberian instrumental and value-oriented rationality; and Habermasian communicative rationality. Doesn't the transdisciplinary recognition of these multiple research possibilities liberate the serious scholar from local or personal compulsions to think scientifically in terms of only one such conception?

This brings me to another historical derivative of the previous pedagogical principles, one partly mentioned by Keohane (in the quotation in note 16):

Pedagogical Principle 6   *Consider history: to fully appreciate the limitations of nomothetic—law- or generalization-seeking—social science, the genuine pedagogical pluralist needs to present and teach intellectually strong cases for ideographic research, such as that made by historians for the historical study of particular actions, events, episodes, or processes. Assimilating this activity into the preliminary descriptive work of generalization-seeking social-scientific history is not sufficient.*

Walking around thinking we are little Newtons undervalues the importance of ideographic studies, of the unique particulars of individual lives. Taken from a paper, my "Cliometrics Revisited" (Alker 2002b), which begins with a wake-up call for those identifying exclusively with a naturalistic conception of social science, Table 33.2 summarizes an important late nineteenth- and early twentieth-century case for conceiving history as a nongeneralizing science of particular events, episodes, and processes.[18] This wake-up call comes from R. G. Collingwood's stunning version of this argument in his *The Idea of History* (1994, originally 1946): "The processes of events which constitute the world of nature are altogether different in kind from the processes of thought which constitute the world of history" (217). Although in the last analysis I do not believe that processes of thought arise from outside the world of nature, I am very sympathetic with Collingwood's methodologically "idealist" effort to focus on the constitutive role of the inner aspect of events, that is, the thoughts, usually expressible in human language, giving them meaning and direction rather than their outer aspects, by which Collingwood means material bodies and their movements. For him an action is "the unity of the outside and inside of an [historical] event" (213).[19]

Table 33.2 Ten Theses Derived from Collingwood's *The Idea of History*

Thesis C1. The distinction between natural processes and historical processes. "A natural process is a process of events [especially or exclusively their outsides, which may be all they have], an historical process is a process of thoughts" (216).

Thesis C2. There are many distinctive features of historical processes, such as:
C2A. The "first step towards grasping the peculiar characteristics of history" is "the recognition that the historical process creates its own vehicles," such as the creation of classical Rome or modern England (49).
C2B. "A process is historical only when it creates its own laws" (83).
C2C. "The historical process is at bottom a logical process" involving rational self-knowledge (117).
C2D. "This element of process [whereby something is always changing into something else] is the life of history" (163).
C2E. "The positive peculiarity which distinguishes thought from mere consciousness is its power of recognizing the activity of the self as a single activity persisting through the diversity of its own acts" (306).

Thesis C3. The ideality of history, as object of study. "All events that are objects of historical thought are events which are not happening because they have ceased to happen" (pp. 439 f, 412 ff).

Thesis C4. "The Copernican Revolution in the theory of historical knowledge" (240). "For the common-sense theory, historical truth consists in the historian's conforming to the statements of his authorities; Bradley has seen that the historian brings with him to the study of his authorities a criterion of his own by reference to which the authorities themselves are judged" (240; see also 236 f on the "autonomy of historical thought").

Thesis C5. The ideality of historical inquiry: "History as re-enactment of Past Experience." "Historical knowledge is the knowledge of what mind has done in the past, and at the same time it is the [critical, reconstructive] redoing of this, the perpetuation of past acts in the present. . . . Its objective is . . . an activity of thought, which can be known only in so far as the knowing mind re-enacts it and knows itself as so doing" (218; see also 209 and 306 f). For "if history is ideal, it cannot be a single, self-contained body of fact awaiting discovery, it must be a growing and changing body of thoughts, decomposed and recomposed by every new generation of historical workers" (456).

Thesis C6. Contemporary history as a science. Contemporary history is a science that seeks to discover res gestae: actions of human beings that have been done in the past; from another angle, "All history is an attempt to understand the present by reconstructing its determining conditions," its past necessities, and its future possibilities (420–22).

(continued)

Table 33.2   (Continued)

Thesis C7. The resistance to nineteenth-century positivism ["philosophy acting in the service of natural science" (126 f] played a complex, determining role in the late nineteenth-century development of scientific history, as well as in Collingwood's own account of the development of scientific history.

Thesis C8. "Our knowledge that human activity is free has been attained only through our discovery of history" (315)."The disappearance of historical naturalism . . . entails . . . that the activity by which man builds his own constantly changing historical world is a free activity" (315).

Thesis C9. Progress as created by historical thinking. "It is only through historical thinking that [progress] comes about at all. The reason for this is that progress . . . happens in only one way: by the retention in the mind, at one phase, of what was achieved at the preceding phase" (333).

Thesis C10. The situated and dialogical building of historical knowledge. Once the ideality of history and historical facts is recognized—"it was so" and "the historical evidence now to hand indicate that it was so" are treated as equivalent. In the construction of the truer, dialectically structured narratives they seek, historians must attempt to discover multiple sources related to the question they are asking, and seek to uncover the frame of mind behind them using principled but concrete practical reasoning, as well as their historical, natural–scientific, and technical knowledge. The process has many features of dialogical argumentation, interpretive analysis, and judgment—in particular the (virtual) cross-examination of witnesses and the imaginative, hypothetical, context-sensitive decomposition and reconstitution of objects and texts from the past (see especially 234–57, 268–82, 377–88, 410, 415–17, 490–96).

Source: This table first appeared in Alker 2002. These theses are derived from Collingwood 1994.

What, then, really stimulates my phenomenological or methodological imagination is the challenge presented by Collingwood's various quotations—five of them are gathered in Thesis C2 in Table 33.2—for political science and international relations scholars aspiring to be scientific. How, for example, do we theorize, operationally represent, measure, model, and deduce empirically testable implications about processes that "create their own laws" (Thesis C2B)[20] or change the identities of things or constitute relatively enduring historical individuals? Do not psychometric or econometric time-series methodologies butcher such complex realities, turning them into consumable but lifeless entities in the interests of staying "operational" or statistically identifiable? More generally, how do we operationalize and analytically manipulate the historicity of a particular society what I (citing Olafson) define as "the time-ordered self-understanding of a continuing human society" implied by Collingwood's Theses C5 and C9 about the "Ideality" and the potentially "progressive" nature of history?[21]

The productive surprises in Collingwood's historiography continue. Political science is not the only social science debating revolutionary paradigms and competing research programs. History itself may have gone through a Kuhnian revolution in its growth toward maturity, a scientific revolution that took place in Europe about one hundred years ago. And this revolution was premised not on Newtonian models of timeless, universal laws or Darwinian evolutionism, but on the study of time-bound particulars and local, changing entities and changing laws! Besides locating the basis for history's scientific awakening in the later nineteenth-century idealism of Bradley, Croce, and others, Collingwood provides another stunning argument for history's unique contribution to the discovery of humankind's emancipatory possibilities in concrete situations through the contemporary, reflexive, critical recovery of the reflected-upon past. And his treatment of the dialectical role that (Comptean) nineteenth-century positivism (or naturalism) played in stimulating or insulting historians into developing a defensible and distinctive methodological version of their calling suggests related thoughts about resurrecting and then writing about today's political science.

However, there are more things to be said about Collingwood's freedom-respecting reluctance to generalize, as is made clear in Anthony Giddens's introduction to Max Weber's *The Protestant Ethic and the Spirit of Capitalism* on the IR513 reading list. That introduction and Fritz Ringer's historically nuanced account show that Weber was in the middle of an epical battle for the soul of the sociohistorical sciences. Weber's synthetic bridging effort, his comparative sociology of economies and societies, and his comparative religious sociology of the rise of Western civilization to its unparalleled dominance at the end of the nineteenth century came from a respect for the "characteristic uniqueness" of each society or civilization. Causal explanations, if sought, must be sought in, through, and beyond the particular configurations of meaningful social actions and institutions.

Good historical sociologist that he is, Robert A. Hall organizes his educational study of scholarly discourses and practices, of *Cultures of Inquiry* (1999) along both particularizing and generalizing lines, giving them equal and separate attention. Such a balanced presentation presupposes the respect for the particular and the individual that is a hallmark of the ideographic approach to history that I have tried to celebrate here. Particularizing practices include value-oriented "situational histories," specific narrative histories, theoretically informed "configuational histories," and interpretive or explanatory historicism. Generalizing practices, again ordered in terms of the same kinds of formative discourse, include "universal histories," theory application narratives, theoretically oriented analytic generalization, and contrast-oriented explanatory or interpretive comparisons (Hall 1999, 178 and passim).

Pedagogical Principle 7   *A refreshing, exciting, but still modest sense of intellectual centrality for political science is possible if we think classically of it, and of the social sciences more generally, as intermediary, bridging disciplines between the humanities and the natural sciences.*

The Weberian example, like Hall's uses of four forms of discourse to organize his generalizing and particularizing orientations toward sociohistorical inquiry, has a high pedagogical moral, one I take to be of a transdisciplinary sort. Just as these writers seek to benefit from their difference-respecting but trans-disciplinary study of historical particulars, so we political scientists should also think refreshingly, classically, of ourselves. My own journeys through time, disciplines, and cultural-ideological-geographic spaces have taught me that the greatest classics of political inquiry have combined humanistic and scientific impulses (Alker 1996). As bridging scholars, we can link and cut across the humanities (where discourse and gender studies often can be found, as well as philosophy and history departments) and the natural sciences (which Kuhnian pycho-histories can help us to see in new lights as well). A broader set of recognized and legitimated knowledge interests allows and encourages this enhanced self-understanding. Knowledge cumulation can be more broadly defined as well.[22] Wouldn't such a more central, if still intermediary, role be grand—in the life of the mind, of the university, and of our own societies!

Appendix

Professor Hayward R. Alker   School of International Relations

Social-Scientific and Historical Research Methods: Introduction to Research Design (IR 513, Spring 2001)

Purposes: Great debates have located international relations (IR) within history and the humanities, the practical or diplomatic arts, the quasi-naturalistic sciences, and the constructivist social sciences. Familiar-to-IR-student discussions about "explanation versus understanding," "constructivist" versus "naturalistic," and "theoretical" versus "policy-oriented" are actually part of methodological discussions, which we will here selectively sample.

This course is designed reasonably historically and experientially to introduce the academically oriented graduate student of IR to the philosophically self-conscious historical and social-scientific research practices of their professional peers in history and the social sciences. These practices involve schools of thought, disciplinary or paradigmatic orientations, research programs, and knowledge interests embedded in research contexts. Linked to motivating "logics" or philosophies of inquiry are qualitative and quantitative methodologies and designs implementing such logics. Competent practitioners can also provide situation-specific justifications for and *constructive* criticisms of such research practices, informed by an understanding of the relevant discipline's history and traditions of research practice. Only such forms of competence justify the making of "rationally redeemable validity claims" (Habermas's term) that help constitute general or particular bodies of knowledge justifiably described as "truthful," situationally "adequate," "historically accurate," "mature," "cumulative," or "scientific." This course aspires to cultivate in the student a moderate yet discriminating level of competence in delineating, constructively criticizing, and rationally applying or choosing among such research practices.

Philosophies of Knowledge Growth (Epistemologies), Methodologies of Inquiry, and Research Methods: Following Lakatos, the course treats methodologies as applied epistemologies, and research methods as replicable procedures giving form and content to these methodologies in particular theoretically and historically structured research contexts. Giving priority of place to the empirical, explanatory focus of "positive" or "naturalistic" social-scientific inquiry, the first half of the course will review a variety of increasingly sophisticated modes of explanatory research practice, including Weberian historical sociocultural and socioeconomic inquiry. Weberian efforts to integrate interpretive and explanatory research logics will serve, after a brief look at constructivist approaches, to point us toward more humanistically or hermeneutically oriented historiographic literatures This means that we shall next turn historical-philosophical lenses on history itself, that is, on the nature of historical inquiry (the subject of the required texts by Ringer, Iggers, and Hall). Finally, we shall look at evaluative methodologies, paying special attention to the truth-uncovering and emancipatory potential of deliberatively oriented feminist social criticism. We shall thus explore and synthesize what Habermas would describe as the scholarly knowledge interests of offering valid, I hope causal, "explanations," "enhancing practical understandings or clarifying meanings," and facilitating "progressive, or enlightened, human development." These deeply held concerns are at the heart of much debate about international inquiry. (Together, such readings in philosophy, historical inquiry, and social science [PHISS] methodology constitute the PHISS part of the course.)

Laboratory Focus: Besides reading about and critically or constructively discussing research practices and procedures, we shall retrospectively engage in them. This means learning by doing, by actively participating in research efforts. Most of this work will be emulative attempts to understand, rehearse, reproduce, explore, and extend select pieces of exemplary research. As should become apparent by the middle of the course, the laboratory exercises are designed to help the student bridge some of the most challenging "gaps" identified in the IR literature: first, that between scientific (causal) explanation and humanly oriented shared "understanding" as the guiding purpose for socio-historical inquiry; second, that between Enlightenment-inspired theoretical or practical inquiry and skepticism about the genuineness of social-scientific knowledge enhancement or its historically progressive contributions. Topically, we shall look at experimental, historical , participatory, and statistical efforts to provide causal explanations for, "narrative intelligibility of," "practical knowledge about," "lessons drawn from," and "explanatory understanding of" various phenomena.

Additionally, starting from Van Evera's notion of a good dissertation research proposal, as modified by the remainder of course readings, the student will prepare a ten- to twelve-page research proposal building on and attempting to go beyond an article, chapter, or book assigned as required reading in IR500 or one of the four domain overview courses.

Appropriate Background Knowledge: This course is oriented toward students in or considering entering an IR PhD program. An overview treatment of IR theories, such as that in IR500, is assumed as background to define the characteristic foci of this rich interdisciplinary field of study; similarly, an undergraduate introduction to empirical research methods (ideally like that found in IR211) is also largely presupposed; those without such background are strongly advised to sit in on IR211 (as taught this term by Dr. Andrus).

Required Work, Purchases, Grading: The grading will reflect the equal importance of the PHISS reading and the lab work. Evaluation formats will differ for these two parts of the course but will include the following elements in the proportions indicated:

- Procedural summaries of two optional readings in this syllabus, to be made available to the class on or before the day the reading is listed (except the first two weeks), 15%
- Midterm take-home exam, 20%
- Lab exercises, 20%
- Student research proposal, 15%
- Closed-book final exam focused on Parts III and IV of the syllabus, 20%
- Class attendance and participation, 10%

There will be several to-be-purchased photocopied packets of required materials. Additionally, free handouts will often be given out in class, but only there, and only to students present at that time. Books by Van Evera, Weber, Ringer, Ackerly, Hall, Iggers, and Juarerro (see assignments under Course Outline for titles) are to be purchased. Alker and Hurwitz's monograph will be distributed as a gift. If you can't afford any of these, individual copies of these (and all required reading materials) will be on reserve in Leavy Library.

Students requesting academic accommodations based on disability are required to register with Disability Services and Programs (DSP) each semester. A letter of verification for approved accommodations can be obtained from DSP when adequate documentation is filed. Please be sure the letter is delivered to me (or to a TA) as early in the semester as possible. DSP is open Monday–Friday, 8:30 a.m.–5:00 p.m. The office is in Student Union 301, and their phone number is (213) 740-0776.

Course Outline
I. Introduction and Overview

January 8. Course Overview: Contemporary Social-Scientific and Historical Methodological Perspectives

Required: 1. Ngaire Woods, Introduction and Chapter 1, *"Explaining International Relations since 1945."*

2. H. R. Alker, "Introduction: Voyages of Rediscovery," pp. 1–20 in Alker, *Rediscoveries and Reformulations* (Cambridge: Cambridge University Press, 1996).

3. H. R. Alker and R. Hurwitz, "Paradigms, Paradoxes, and Scientific Progress," Chapter 2, pp. 28–42 in *Resolving Prisoner's Dilemmas* Washington, DC: APSA, 1980.

4. Georg G. Iggers, *Historiography in the Twentieth Century* (Hanover, NH: Wesleyan University Press, 1997, pp. 1–19.

5. H. Alker, "Learning from Wendt," *Review of International Studies* 26 (1) (2000), pp. 141–50.

6. John R. Hall, "Prologue," pp. 1–5 in Hall, *Cultures of Inquiry: From Epistemology to Discourse in Sociohistorical Research* (New York: Cambridge University Press, 1999.

7. H. R. Alker, Jr., "Historical Argumentation and Statistical Inference: Towards More Appropriate Logics for Historical Research," *Historical Methods* 17 (3) (Summer 1984): 164–73. See also erratum, 17 (4): 270.

8. Brooke A. Ackerly, "Silent Voices and Everyday Critics," Chapter 1, pp. 1–32 in Ackerly, *Political Theory and Feminist Social Criticism* (Princeton, NJ: Princeton University Press, 2000).

Optional: H. Alker, "The Dialectical Logic of Thucycdides' Melian Dialogue," pp. 23–63, and "Aristotelean Political Methodologies," pp. 64–103 in Alker, *Rediscoveries and Reformulations,* op. cit. in this syllabus. Here I suggest three kinds of Aristotelean political science, including a Rescher-based model of practical-dialogical knowledge cumulation.

Laboratory: Graphing Arguments, Debates, Reasoning Processes. Lab will meet during the week of January 15, but not on January 15, which is a holiday; it will be an extension of required item 7 based on a coding manual written by Karapin and Alker.

II. The Search for Scientific Explanations of Politics and International Relations

January 22. "Barefoot Positivism," with Hempelian and Processual Approaches to Qualitative Case Studies
Required: 1. Steve Van Evera, *Guide to Methods for Students of Political Science* (Ithaca, NY: Cornell University Press, 1997), pp. 7–121.

2. Carl G. Hempel, "The Function of General Laws in History," chapter 3, pp. 43–54, reprinted variously, e.g., in M. Martin and L. C. McIntyre, eds., *Readings in the Philosophy of Social Science* (Cambridge, MA: MIT Press, 1994).

3. Stephen Van Evera, Chapter 7, 193–239, in Van Evera, *Causes of War* (Ithaca, NY: Cornell University Press, 1999). This chapter is on the causes of World War I.

Optional: 1. A. L. George, "Case Studies and Theory Development," pp. 43–68 in P. G. Lauren, ed., *Diplomacy: New Approaches in History, Theory and Policy*

(New York: Free Press, 1970), and A L. George and T. J. McKeown, "Case Studies and Theories of Organizational Decision Making," in *Advances in Information Processing in Organizations* 2 (1985): 21–58.

2. G. King, R. Keohane, and S. Verba, *Designing Social Inquiry* (Princeton, NJ: Princeton University Press, 1994).

3. Van Evera, *Causes of War,* op. cit., remainder.

January 29. Statistical, Large n, *or Quasi-Experimental Approaches to Explanatory Causal Analysis*

Required: 1. H. Blalock, *Causal Inference in Nonexperimental Research* (Chapel Hill: University of N. Carolina Press, 1964), pp. 1–30 (approx.).

2. D. T. Campbell, "Reforms as Experiments," pp. 261–89 in Campbell, *Methodology and Epistemology for Social Science: Selected Papers,* ed. S. Overman (Chicago: University of Chicago Press, 1988). This article is correctly famous for its creativity, its Popperian scientific acumen, and its suggestion of evaluation standards beyond those of statistical significance.

3. H. R. Alker, "Causal Inference and Political Analysis," in J. Bernd, ed., *Mathematical Applications in Political Science,* Vol. 2 (Dallas: Southern Methodist University Press, 1966). A synthesis of biometric, econometric, and Simon-Blalock causal inference techniques linked to modern questions of political analysis.

Optional: 1. Wm. N. Dunn, "Reforms as Arguments," and D. T. Campbell, "Experiments as Arguments," *Knowledge* 3 (1982): 293–326 and 327–37, respectively. Campbell graciously concedes that experimental standards of inquiry, which are the foundation of the "hard" natural sciences and the analogical basis of his quasi-experimental approach to causal inquiry, are in fact structured argumentation practices.

2. Gary King, *Unifying Political Methodology* (New York: Cambridge University Press, 1989), especially a later chapter.

Partly Required Examples (one of which will form the basis for different versions of the following lab):

B. M. Pollins, "Global Political Order, Economic Change, and Armed Conflict: Coevolving Systems and the Use of Force," *APSR* 90 (1) (March 1996): 103–17.

N. Choucri and R. North, *Nations in Conflict: National Growth and International Violence* (San Francisco: W. H. Freeman, 1975), sections on the authors' basic simultaneous equation model.

Walter Enders and Todd Sandler, "The Effectiveness of Antiterrorism Policies: A Vector-Autoregression-Intervention Analysis," *APSR* 87 (4) (December 1993): 829–44.

N. Sambanis, "Partition as a Solution to Ethnic War: An Empirical Critique of the Theoretical Literature," *World Politics* 52 (4) (July 2000): 437–83.

Laboratory: Dynamic Graphs of Causally Oriented Explanatory Research Practices, Including Hollis, Rescher, D. T. Campbell, W. N. Dunn, etc.

February 5. Paradigms, Research Programs, and Evolutionary or Revolutionary Epistemologies.

Required: 1. Thomas Kuhn, "Postscript," pp. 174–210 in Kuhn, *The Structure of Scientific Revolutions,* 2nd ed. (Chicago: University of Chicago Press, 1970).

2. I. Lakatos, "Falsification and the Methodology of Scientific Research Programs," pp. 91–195, and S. Toulmin's chapter, pp. 39–47 in I. Lakatos and A. Musgrave, eds., *Criticism and the Growth of Knowledge* (Cambridge: Cambridge University Press, 1970).

3. John A. Vasquez et al., "Forum" on "The Realist Paradigm and Degenerative vs. Progressive Research Programs," *APSR* 91 (December 1997): 899–934.

4. J. G. March and Johan P. Olson, "The New Institutionalism: Organizational Factors in Political Life," *APSR* 79 (1984): 734–49, OR J. D. Fearon, "Rationalist Explanations for War," *International Organization* 49 (3) (1995): 379–414.

Optional: 1. D. T. Campbell, "Evolutionary Epistemology," pp. 413–63 in Paul A. Schilpp, ed., *The Philosophy of Karl Popper* (La Salle, IL: Open Court, 1994).

2. Graham Allison, "Conceptual Models and The Cuban Missile Crisis," *APSR* 63 (1969): 689–718. This uses Mertonian and March-Simon paradigm notions.

3. Paul Diesing, *How Does Social Science Work?* (Pittsburgh: University of Pittsburgh Press, 1991). A sympathetic but different account.

4. Stephen Toulmin, *Human Understanding* (Oxford: Clarendon Press, 1972). One of the earliest and best book-length treatments of evolutionary epistemology.

Laboratory: The student will be required to try to fit Fearon's game-theoretic tour de horizon or March and Olson's interdisciplinary synthesis of rational choice institutional history and historical sociology paradigms into the Alker-Hurwitz conception of a "games and decisions" research paradigm complex, and discuss the adequacy of the paradigm for this purpose. Both Kuhn's "disciplinary matrix" reformulation of his "paradigm" idea and Lakatos's "sophisticated methodological falsificationism" are at the root of the research paradigm complex notion.

February 12. Evolving Research Paradigm Complexes and Dramaturgical Politics
Required: 1. Alker and Hurwitz, *Resolving Prisoner's Dilemmas,* op. cit., 1–27, 45–123.

2. Review R. Axelrod, *The Evolution of Cooperation* (New York: Basic Books, 1984), or Axelrod's review of the evolutionary study of complex adaptive systems at the beginning of his *The Complexity of Cooperation* (Princeton, NJ: Princeton University Press, 1997).

3. Rom Harré and Paul Secord, *The Explanation of Social Behavior* (Lanham, MD: Rowman and Littlefield), 1972, especially Chapter 1 and the analytical summaries beginning subsequent chapters.

4. Review H. Alker, "Introduction" pp. 1–20, and Chapter 9 ("Beneath Tit for Tat"), pp. 303–31, in Alker, *Rediscoveries and Reformulations,* op. cit. (required in IR500).

MIDTERM TAKE-HOME EXAM DUE TUESDAY, FEBRUARY 20, 10 A.M. The student will choose a way of assessing scientific progress based on the previous readings of this course; justify its appropriateness for application to one of the substantive topics covered in IR500, a domain course, or the previous readings; and discuss the extent to which knowledge has cumulated in these terms. This exam should be completed individually, WITHOUT COLLABORATION.

February 26: Weberian Socioeconomic History
Required: 1. Max Weber, *The Protestant Ethic and the Spirit of Capitalism,* intro. by Anthony Giddens (London: Unwin Hardin, 1989). Read entire book, including introduction.
2. G. Hernes, "The Logic of the Protestant Ethic," *Rationality and Society* 1 (1) (1989): 123–62.
3. Randall Collins, "Weber's Last Theory of Capitalism," pp. 19–44 in Collins, *Weberian Sociological Theory* (Cambridge: Cambridge University Press, 1987).
4. N. G. Onuf, Chapter 6, pp. 196–227, in Onuf, *Worlds of Our Making: Rules and Rule in Social Theory and International Relations* (Columbia: University of Southern Carolina Press, 1989). In this chapter Onuf discusses Weberian political societies. Optional: Barry O'Neill, *Honor, Symbols, and War* (Ann Arbor: University of Michigan Press, 1999).

March 5. A Deeper Look at Weberian Theories of Social Interaction and Subsequent Philosophy on Intentional Action and Causation, Seen as Contextual or Processual Challenges to the Adequacy of Causal or Structural Equation Modeling
Required: Fritz Ringer, *Max Weber's Methodology: The Unification of the Cultural and Social Sciences* (Cambridge, MA: Harvard University Press, 1997), OR Alicia Juarrero, *Dynamics in Action: Intentional Behavor as a Complex System* (Cambridge, MA: MIT Press, 1999), the first 100 pages (on the philosophy of intentional action and the inadequacies of Newtonian and Humean causation). You will not be directly examined on Juarrero in this course; it is here for your enlightenment.
Optional: 1. H. Alker, "Are There Structural Models of Voluntaristic Social Action?" *Quality and Quantity* 8 (1974): 199–246. Pay particular attention to the framework of analysis for resolving collective action problems, the examples of the prisoner's dilemma and collective security operational regimes or rules, and the dialogically structured conclusions.
2. Daniel Little, *Micro-Foundations, Method, and Causation: On the Philsophy of the Social Sciences* (New Brunswick, NJ: Transaction Publishers, 1998). Chapter 10 on causal realism is particularly suggestive.

3. J. G. Bennett and H. R. Alker, "When National Security-Seeking Policies Bred Collective Insecurity: The War of the Pacific in a World Politics Simulation," in Karl W. Deutsch et al., *Problems of World Modeling* (Cambridge, MA: Ballinger, 1977). This chapter combines a Weberian approach to the dynamics of overlapping but distinct international hierarchies based on class, status, and power with Simon-March organizational process modeling and multiagent adaptive simulations.

SPRING VACATION
March 19. A Stunning Convergence: The Dynamical Hermeneutics of Complex Adaptive Systems and the Social Constructivism of Onuf, Kratochwil, Searle, Sylvan, Alker, and Wendt
Required: 1. Alicia Juarrero, *Dynamics in Action,* op. cit., remainder of book, OR N. G. Onuf, "Constructivism" (Chapter 1), "Law and Language" (Chapter 2), the part of chapter 4 subtitled "Regimes" (pp. 145–59), and "Presumption of Anarchy" (Chapter 5, pp. 163–95) in *Worlds of Our Making,* op. cit. The section of "Regimes" includes collective security and mutual insecurity maintenance through nuclear deterrence; Chapter 5 critiques the liberal presupposition of the "cooperation under anarchy" literature. This is a pioneering book on contemporary constructivism grounded in Austin-Wittgenstein-Searle speech act theory and in the writings of Weber, Habermas, Kratochwil, etc.
2. Stephen Majeski and David Sylvan, "How Foreign Policy Recommendations Are Put Together," *International Interactions* 25 (4): 301–32. An especially accessible, partially LISP-encoded version of constructivist methodology based on grounded sociology, speech act theory, and argumentation analysis. OR G. Duffy, B. Frederking, and Seth A. Tucker, "Language Games: Dialogical Analyses of INF Negotiations," *International Studies Quarterly* 42 (2) (June 1998): 271–94. This article uses Rescher-Alker dialectical logic, speech act theory, and Onuf's concept of a mutual insecurity system to explain the Gorbachev-Reagan INF breakthrough in at the end of the cold war.
3. Review from IR500 Alker, "Communicative Rationality and the Modernity Problematique" (on Weber, Keohane, and Habermas), pp. 228–37, and "The Presumption of Anarchy in World Politics" (on Ashley, Habermas, Bull, and Deutsch), pp. 362–93 in Alker, *Rediscoveries and Reformulations,* op. cit.
4. Review from IR500 Wendt's articles on causality and constitution and his "Anarchy Is What States Make of It," *International Organization* 46 (1992): 391–425, as well as Alker's "Learning from Wendt," op. cit.

Laboratory: After forming two groups, we will focus on flow-charting the research procedures in Majeski-Sylvan or Duffy-Frederking-Tucker.
Optional: 1. Norman Denzin and Yvonna Lincoln, "Preface" and "Introduction," pp. vii–34; Valerie Janesick, "The Dance of Qualitative Research Design: Metaphor, Methodolatry, and Meaning," pp. 35–56; J. C. Morse, "Designing Funded Qualitative Research," pp. 56–85; and Anselm Strauss and Juliet Corbin, "Grounded Theory Methodology: An Overview," pp. 158–183 in Denzin and

Lincoln, eds., *Strategies of Qualitative Inquiry* (Thousands Oaks, CA: Sage Publications, 1998).

2. John O'Dell, "Bounded Rationality and the World Political Economy," mimeo, matched with Douglas Walton's flow charts of simple and complex satisficing practices, pp. 106–113 in Walton, *Practical Reasoning: Goal-Driven, Knowledge-Based, Action Guiding Argumentation* (Lanham, MD: Rowman and Littlefield, 1990).

3. John R. Searle, "Rationality in Action," unpublished manuscript.

4. Mark Turner, "The Methodology of the Social Sciences," unpublished manuscript.

5. Brian Frederking, *Resolving Security Dilemmas: A Constructivist Explanation of the INF Treaty* (Brookfield, VT: Ashgate, 2000).

III. Historical Sources, Schools, and Sociohistorical Discourses in Twentieth-Century Historiography

March 26. An Overview of Twentieth-Century Historiography
Required: 1. Iggers, *Historiography in the Twentieth Century,* op. cit., pp. 23–148. Obviously Ringer's, Onuf's, and Collins's treatments of Weber were more thorough, so bear them in mind. Review Iggers's first chapter as well.

2. Gay Tuchman, "Historical Social Science: Methodologies, Methods, and Meanings," pp. 225–260 in Denzin and Lincoln, eds., *Strategies of Qualitative Inquiry,* op. cit.

3. Review from IR500 Alker's version of Olafson's "essence of history: historicity," in his *Rediscoveries and Reformulations,* op. cit., 386–93.

4. Hidemi Suganami, "Agents, Structures, Narratives," *European Journal of International Relations* 5 (3) (Sept. 1999): 365–86.

Don Steury, a professional historian, will be a guest for this class.

Optional: 1. Joyce Appleby et al., *Knowledge and Postmodernism: In Historical Perspective* (New York: Routledge, 1996), OR Appleby, Lynn Hunt, and Margaret Jacob, *Telling the Truth about History* (New York: Norton, 1984), especially the discussion of postmodernism.

2. B. Buzan and R. Little, *International Systems in World History* (Oxford: Oxford University Press, 2000), especially the methodological discussions of neo-realism, the English School, Wallerstein, and Braudel, pp. 1–110.

3. H. Spruyt, *The Sovereign State and Its Competitors* (Princeton, NJ: Princeton University Press, 1994).

4. G. Barraclough, *Main Trends in History,* expanded edition (New York: Holmes and Meier, 1991).

Laboratory: There will be an introduction to IR-relevant historical research resources by a professional librarian.

ONE-PAGE PROPOSALS CONCERNING THE STUDENT'S CHOICE OF A TOPIC FOR HIS OR HER RESEARCH PROPOSAL DUE IN PROFESSOR ALKER'S MAILBOX BY MARCH 29. (See April 23 assignment.)

April 2. Historical Discourses

Required: Hall, *Cultures of Inquiry,* op. cit., pp. 33–166, 169–228. Start by reviewing his introduction to "The Third Path." Were there more time, you could optionally read and discuss any of the numerous sociohistorical studies Hall mentions.

Optional: 1. Lynn Hunt, ed., *The New Cultural History* (Berkeley: University of California Press, 1989), and V. Bonnell and L. Hunt, eds., *Beyond the Cultural Turn* (Berkeley: University of California Press, 1999).

2. S. Toulmin, *Cosmopolis: The Hidden Agenda of Modernity* (Chicago: University of Chicago Press, 1990).

3. Consuelo Cruz, "Identity and Persuasion: How Nations Remember Their Pasts and Make Their Futures," *World Politics* 52 (3) (April 2000): 275–312.

IV. Issues of Global and Local Governance

April 9. Deliberatively Oriented Argumentation and Cosmopolitan Political Theory

Required: 1. Thomas Risse, "Let's Argue: Communicative Action in World Politics," *International Organization* 54 (1) (Winter 2000): 1–40.

2. J. Habermas, *The Inclusion of the Other: Studies in Political Theory,* ed. C. Gronin and P. De Greiff (Cambridge, MA: MIT Press, 1999), "Editors' Introduction," pp. vii–xxxii, and Part V, "What Is Meant by Deliberative Politics," pp. 239–64.

3. Ackerly, *Political Theory and Feminist Social Criticism,* op. cit., review "Silent Voices and Everyday Critics" (Chapter 1, pp. 1–32) and read "A Third World Feminist Theory of Social Criticism" (Chapter 2, pp. 33–72).

Optional: 1. Books on postmodern or postcolonial IR by Christine Sylvester, David Campbell, Michael Shapiro, James Der Derian, Marianne Marchand and Jane Pappart, or Chandra Mohanty.

2. David Held's books on globalization and cosmopolitan democracy, especially D. Held and A. McGrew, eds., *The Global Transformations Reader: An Introduction to the Globalization Debate* (Oxford: Blackwell's, 2000).

3. Paul Diesing, *Reason in Society: Five Types of Decisions and Their Social Conditions* (Westport, CT: Greenwood Press, 1976, originally 1962). A highly accessible, more general (and earlier) version of Habermas's, Risse's and March-Olson's arguments about types of rationality and social action.

4. Stephen Toulmin, *Being Reasonable,* in press. An argument for "early Modern" practical reasoning. This book was subsequently published as Stephen Toulmin, *Return to Reason* (Cambridge, MA: Harvard University Press, 2001).

April 16. An Emancipatory Methodology of Constructive, Feminist, Social Criticism

Required: 1. Ackerly, *Political Theory and Feminist Social Criticism,* op. cit., pp. 73–203.

2. Alker, "Emancipatory Empiricism," pp. 332–354 in his *Rediscoveries and Reformulations,* op. cit.

Dr. Ackerly will be a guest lecturer for the discussion of her book.

Optional: Books by Benhabib, Mouffe, Nussbaum, Sen, Butler, or Waltzer, as cited by Ackerly.

V. Conclusions

April 23. Student Research Proposals

There is no reading assignment, but reviewing the Course Overview materials assigned January 8 might be a good way to encourage stocktaking. With special reference to Chapters 3–5 in Van Evera, *Guide to Methods for Students of Political Science*, op. cit., and Morse's Tables 3.2 and 3.3 in Denzin and Lincoln, *Strategies of Qualitative Inquiry*, op. cit., each student will orally, and in writing, present a ten- to twelve-page research proposal following one or more of the research methodologies outlined (and perhaps flow-charted) in the required or optional readings of the course. The student may continue within the subject domain of his or her take-home midterm, but may also pick a new substantive focus related to material covered in IR500 or any of the four graduate domain courses. The research proposal should not be one written for another methodology course.

IN THE SCHEDULED EXAM PERIOD, THERE WILL BE A TWO-HOUR CLOSED-BOOK FINAL EXAM FOCUSING ON THE ASSIGNED READINGS FOR PARTS III AND IV OF THE COURSE AND ON THE FINAL OVERVIEW OF RESEARCH PRACTICES IN PART V OF THE COURSE.

Notes

1. See the original statements and news articles as re-presented in the present volume. In the spring and fall of 2001, as part of our own curricular discussions, I circularized my colleagues in the School of International Relations at the University of Southern California with a brief statement by "Mr. Perestroika" calling for a "more open and diverse" discipline in "gender, racial, ethnic, and methodological terms" and for overcoming the alienation of many political scientists from the APSA and the *American Political Science Review* and from associated teaching, publishing, and hiring practices. I also included Gregory Kasza's influential posting on the Perestroika list serve (Kasza 2001).

2. See Alker 2000a,b. A version of the present chapter was presented at a pedagogically oriented qualitative methods panel at the 2004 APSA Annual Meeting.

3. Previously the advanced IR theory course had been an alternative to a second specialized empirical research methods course. The recommended multivariate data analysis course was not required, but could be taken as a way of partially satisfying the empirical research methods requirements.

4. For example, in academic year 2002–03 at USC, I added some of the advanced statistical or computational papers that had been used in IR513 the year before to the end of my version of the required Multivariate [Data] Analysis course, and thus took them out of my subsequent version of IR513.

5. Indeed, USC's advanced teaching of political science and international relations has now changed. New PhD students. are admitted into a new Politics and International Relations PhD program, for which we require a year-long sequence of classical theories courses, as well as a course offering an overview of the philosophies or methodologies of inquiry (IR513 or an alternative), a multivariate data analysis course, and an advanced research methodologies course. Both John Odell and I teach advanced qualitative methods courses building on IR513; mine, called Text, Talk and Context, focuses more on "constitutive" relations as they have been defined and uncovered in legal, philosophical, sociopolitical, and computationally oriented linguistic literatures, while his, in ways parallel to the more quantitatively oriented multivariate analysis course, takes a "pragmatic positivist" approach to discovering causal explanations.

6. Citing Sandra Harding, Ann Tickner (1997, 622) also argues reflexively: "Feminist analysis insists that the inquirer be placed in the same critical plane as the subject matter."

7. Keohane (1998) uses the popular Lakatosian term "research program" to describe such activities and challenges feminists to lay out empirically oriented, multistep research agendas. He would have done better—if he didn't intend to take sides on the epistemological controversies with which Imre Lakatos and Karl Popper and Thomas Kuhn are identified—if he had added non-Lakatosian terms for describing justifiable research practices. Consider, for example, a commitment to Kuhnian "normal" (paradigm-governed) or "revolutionary science," Alker and Hurwitz's (1980) synthetic commitment to "research paradigm complexes" (including research programs, but shaped by contextual knowledge interests of the sort recognized by critical theorists), or Hall's (1999, 23–29) anti-foundationalist commitment to "cultures," "discourses," or "phrase regimens" of inquiry rather than to conventional naturalistic, discipline-constituting "epistemologies."

8. Regarding the development of such standards, Tickner (1997, 621) emphasizes what Jürgen Habermas would call an emancipatory knowledge interest: "Most feminists are committed to the emancipatory goal of achieving a more just society, which, for them, includes ending the oppression of women."

9. The main paper developing this concept (Alker 1976) was supported by a National Science Foundation grant to a pedagogical resources development project (also known as Learning about Political and Social Science (LAPSS) of the APSA. For reasons that were never clear to me, the volume in which it was to appear, edited by Donald Stokes and Sheilah K. Mann, was never published. An abbreviated version (Alker 1982), after limited distribution at the 1979 Moscow Congress of the International Political Science Association, finally appeared in a Polish journal. One can see a narrower but rather high-quality version of disciplinewide discussions of Lakatosian (and other) philosophies of inquiry in Elman and Elman 2003. It is to the credit of contributors to this new volume, such as Jack Snyder and John Vasquez, and their editors, that they bring in additional philosophical perspectives, even though the volume's initial natural science–oriented, Lakatosian framing does not encourage them to do so.

10. Although Keohane (1998, 193) is right in seeing Tickner as a "bridge-builder between scholars with broadly common purposes but very different preoccupations," his own model of science takes its canons from the natural sciences (195). He advocates a positivistic conception of science as systematic empirical inquiry

through conjectures, theory-based deductive inferences, and causal hypothesis testing (196). He doesn't respond to Tickner's advocacy of situated, hermeneutic and emancipatory, conversational methodologies derived at least in part from the humanities (Tickner 1997, 619 ff.).

11. To take Tickner seriously, without necessarily agreeing with her, one needs to look for alternative epistemologies, with alternative notions of emancipation and its relationship to the practice of social science. The quote of hers in note 8 continues: "The Kantian project of achieving this [emancipatory] goal through Enlightenment knowledge is problematic because of feminist claims that this type of knowledge is gendered" (Tickner 1997, 621). The ethnomethodological or discursive orientation of Rom Harré's philosophical-psychological writings might be helpful in this regard for those seeking an alternative scientific conception. Citing feminist (Benhabib 1986) and many other works, John R. Hall traces the relationships among value discourses, objectivity, and pluralism in research styles, including emancipation and explanatory social-scientific goals, from Kant, Hegel, Marx, and Weber through Simmel, Adorno, Habermas, Lyotard, Appleby, and Benhabib in Chapter 2 of his *Cultures of Inquiry* (1999, 33–71). Hall's text, and Brooke Ackerly's critical feminist approach to emancipation, which is more closely linked to the literature on deliberative democracy, figure significantly in IR513. It is a pity that authors such as Stephen Van Evera, Gary King, Keohane, and Sidney Verba don't reference this literature.

12. For an insightful, nuanced, but still provocative sociohistorical treatment of "general linear reality" and associated statistical practices, see Andrew Abbott, Chapter 1, "Transcending General Linear Reality," pp. 37–63, and Chapter 3 ("The Causal Devolution"), pp. 97–125 of his *Time Matters* (2001). Here is another place in which there are methodological tradeoffs between statistically oriented treatments of nominal, ordinal, and interval scale measurement and a philosophically more sophisticated treatment of phenomenological characterization. Thus Tickner (1997, 619) states: "With a preference for hermeneutic, historically based, humanistic and philosophical traditions of knowledge cumulation, rather than those based on the natural sciences, feminist theorists are often skeptical of empiricist methodologies that claim neutrality of facts." Her conversations with Keohane recall James C. Coleman's encounter with Garfinkel's ethnomethodology, based on the suspension or phenomenological bracketing of everyday attitudes, and what Chris Hart describes as ethnomethodology's suspension of "the general principle explaining social order through generalization" in his epistemologically pluralistic *Doing a Literature Review* (1998, 66). Sociology seems to be somewhat more methodologically pluralistic in this regard, because sociology graduate students almost routinely learn forms of network analysis that are not linearly represented.

13. As an alternative to the Hempelian hypothetical-deductive model of science loved by "barefoot empiricists" (Van Evera's self-description) and probabilistically enshrined in Simon-Blalock causal modelers, including me (Alker 1984, 1996), consider the dialectical logic of probative inquiry proposed in Nicholas Rescher's *Dialectics* (1977). The literature on psychological implication and interpretation using frames and scripts also belongs here, as well as many treatments of linguistic presuppositions and implicature. Gavan Duffy and his associates (1998) build directly on my earlier Rescherian analysis of Thucydides' Melian Dialogue, but

within a sophisticated Wittgensteinian approach to conversational linguistic inferencing.

14. See in particular the brilliant recovery of Marx's ontological "philosophy of internal relations" by Bertell Ollman, Habermas's multivalent treatment of validity claims within a communicative rationality, Marcuse's and Olafson's reformulations of Martin Heidigger's "historicity," and Hayden White's metahistorical treatment of nineteenth-century historians' compositional practices, as discussed in Chapters 5, 6, 8, 10, and 12 of Alker 1996.

15. Thus, in my view, for political scientists and international relations scholars, the little-known Dunn-Campbell debate on reforms as (naturalistic) experiments or as (humanistic) arguments (Campbell 1982, 1988; Dunn 1982) matches the importance of the Kuhn-Lakatos debate from the 1970s. I have highlighted this debate even further in the 2003 and 2004 versions of IR513 because Dunn builds so well on Stephen Toulmin's contributions to argumentation theory—his casuistic, or jurisprudential, account of human reasoning capabilities—and because both Dunn and Campbell evidence parallels with Toulmin's impressive earlier evolutionary account of the growth of scientific knowledge.

16. In Alker 1996 ("Introduction") and IR513, I re-present this continuum from Alker 1980 as ranging from "Dialectics/Dialectical Hermeneutics" to "The Hermeneutics of Scientific Revolutions" to "Critical Rationalism/Methodological Falsificationism" and finally to "Positivistic Logical Empiricism." With a different historical lens, Keohane (1998, 195) suggests a related positivist–post-positivist continuum, characterized in terms of "more or less nomothetic theoretical claims, and to aspirations of greater or less adherence to canons associated with natural science." He writes: "Scientific success is not the attainment of objective truth, but the attainment of wider agreement on descriptive facts and causal relationships, based on transparent and replicable methods." He further asserts that generalizers value descriptive work and recognize that some issues are not amenable to statistical analysis because of "complexity, contingency, and lack of homogeneity between the units to be compared." Although commendable, this intellectual flexibility still stops short of the recognition of the plurality of knowledge interests noted in my Pedagogical Principle 4, stated earlier.

Neither Keohane, Marchand, Tickner, nor I have given the riches of non-Western traditions of inquiry the attention they deserve; work by Fred Dallmayr, Johan Galtung, and Sandra Harding is exemplary in this regard.

17. For example, one of the many virtues of Dunn's previously cited subsumptive treatments of Donald Campbell's Popperian descriptions of threats to validity in experimental and quasi-experimental work is his development of a list of "type III errors," errors in problem formulation. One reason that few feminists in the United States or Europe are eager to do large n statistical studies is their belief that the measurement practices presupposed by such studies suffer from many type III errors, which require prior correction.

18. Compare Chris Hart's review of ethnomethodology (1998), John A. Hall (1999), and the much-cited literature by Alexander George and his political science collaborators on process tracing in individual cases. Examples are the 2001 and 2003 IR513 syllabuses (George and McKeown 1985; Bennett and George 2001). The sociologists Hart and Hall seem so much more adept, classically and philosophically

speaking, at drawing out the methodological significance of their proposals than the extremely talented political scientists mentioned here.

19. Besides such eminent historiographers, I should also mention cognitive anthropologists such as Edwin Hutchins (author of *Cognition in the Wild*, 1996), cognitive linguists such as George Lakoff and Mark Johnson (1999), and linguistic philosophers such as James Higginbotham (see Higginbotham et al. 2000) for critical alternative perspectives from the humanities and the cognitive sciences of this (ironically self-damning) claim: "Event history models have become a dominant method of analysis in the study of international relations." This quote is the first sentence in the abstract of (Box-Steffensmeier et al. 2003).

20. I once used the quote forming the basis of Thesis C2B as the central focus of an essay question on a USC "core screening exam"!

21. I review six or seven different ways of "operationalizing" historicity in Alker 1996 (386–93), but from among these I am most enthusiastic about the recursive, self-modifying, and self-running operation of the LISP computational routines suggested in Chapter 5 of that volume. At the ontological level, I find Andrew Abbott's writings (especially Abbott 2001), Juarrero's (1999) synthesis of action philosophy, historical hermeneutics and Prigogine's biological complexity theory, and work in progress by William Connolly on different kinds of temporal processes most stimulating. One could also usefully compare Alex Wendt's treatment of the ideality of international system changes with Collingwood's older notion of the ideality of history. See my "Learning from Wendt" (Alker 2000), for details and citations.

22. In the 2004 version of IR513 I concluded with an American-European discussion of dialogue and knowledge synthesis (Hellmann et al., 2003), which produces many resonances with the earlier Dunn-Campbell debate and suggests humanistic cumulation notions appropriate to the major two-part division of IR513 between (overlapping) naturalistic and historical-humanistic approaches to sociopolitical inquiry.

References

These references include all the works cited in the notes and the text, but not all those referred to in the appendix.

Abbott, A. (2001). *Time Matters.* Chicago: University of Chicago Press.

Alker, H. (1976). "Learning How to Do Analysis in Political and Social Science." MIT, mimeo.

Alker, H. (1982). "Logic, Dialectics, and Politics," pp. 65–94 in H. R. Alker, Jr., guest editor, *Dialectical Logics for the Political Sciences: Poznan Studies in the Philosophy of the Sciences and Humanities,* Vol. 7. Amsterdam: Rodopi.

Alker, H. R., Jr. (1984). "Historical Argumentation and Statistical Inference: Towards More Appropriate Logics for Historical Research." *Historical Methods* 17 (3): 164–73. See also erratum in 17 (4): 270.

Alker, H. (1996). "Introduction: Voyages of Rediscovery," pp. 1–20 in Alker, *Rediscoveries and Reformulations.* Cambridge: Cambridge University Press.

Alker, H. (2000). "Learning from Wendt." *Review of International Studies* 26 (1): 141–50.

Alker, H. (2002a). "Curricular Perestroika: Further Comments on Schwartz-Shea's 'Curricular Visions.'" Paper presented at the Annual Meeting of the Western Political Science Association.

Alker, H. (2002b). "Cliometrics Revisited: Including 'Scientific History' in the Methodological Pedagogy of Political Science." Paper presented at the Annual Meeting of the APSA.

Alker, H. R., and R. Hurwitz (1980). "Paradigms, Paradoxes, and Scientific Progress," Chapter 2, pp. 28–42 in Alker and Hurwitz, *Resolving Prisoner's Dilemmas*. Washington, DC: APSA.

Alker, H. R., and R. Hurwitz. (2001). "Reasons, Causes, Games, Lessons and Evolution in Inequitable Sequential Prisoner's Dilemmas." Paper given at the Annual Meeting of the International Studies Association, Chicago, Feb. 26.

Benhabib, S. (1986). *Critique, Norm and Utopia*. New York: Columbia University Press.

Bennett, A., and A. L. George (2001). "Case Studies and Process Tracing in History and Political Science: Similar Strokes for Different Foci," Chapter 4, pp. 137–66 in C. Elman and M. F. Elman, eds., *Bridges and Boundaries: Historians, Political Scientists, and the Study of International Relations*. Cambridge, MA: MIT Press.

Box-Steffensmeier, J. N., D. Reiter, and C. Zorn (2003). "Nonproportional Hazards and Event History Analysis in International Relations." *Journal of Conflict Resolution* 47(1): 33–53.

Campbell, D. T. (1982). "Experiments as Arguments." *Knowledge* 3: 327–37.

Campbell, D. T. (1988). *Methodology and Epistemology for Social Science: Selected Papers*, ed. S. Overman. Chicago: University of Chicago Press.

Duffy, G., B. Frederking, and Seth A. Tucker (1998). "Language Games: Dialogical Analyses of INF Negotiations." *International Studies Quarterly* 42 (2): 271–94.

Dunn, William N. (1982). "Reforms as Arguments." *Knowledge* 3: 293–326.

Elman, C., and M. F. Elman, eds. (2003). *Progress in International Relations Theory: Appraising the Field*. Cambridge, MA: MIT Press.

George, A. L., and T. J. McKeown (1985). "Case Studies and Theories of Organizational Decision Making." *Advances in Information Processing in Organizations* 2: 21–58.

Giddens, A. (1992). "Introduction," pp vii–xxvi, Max Weber, *The Protestant Ethic and the Spirit of Capitalism*. London: Routledge.

Hall, John R. (1999). *Cultures of Inquiry: From Epistemology to Discourse in Sociohistorical Research*. New York: Cambridge University Press.

Harré, R., and P. Secord (1972). *The Explanation of Social Behavior*. Lanham, MD: Rowman and Littlefield.

Hart, C. (1998). *Doing a Literature Review: Releasing the Social Science Research Imagination*. London: Sage.

Hellmann, G., F. Kratochwil, Y. Lapid, A. Morovcsik, I. B. Neumann, S. Smith, F. Harvey, and J. Cobb (2003). FORUM: Are Dialogue and Synthesis Possible in International Relations? *International Studies Review* 5 (1): 123–53.

Higginbotham, J., F. Pianesi, and A. Varzi, eds. (2000). *Speaking of Events*. New York: Oxford University Press.

Hutchins, E. (1996). *Cognition in the Wild*. Cambridge, MA: MIT Press.

Juarrareo, A. (1999). *Dynamics in Action: International Behavior as a Complex System*. Cambridge, MA: MIT Press.

Kasza, G. (2001). "Perestroika: For an Ecumenical Science of Politics." Posted August 2 on the Perestroika list serve (perestroika_glasnost_warmhome @yahoogroups.com).

Keohane, R. O. (1998). "Beyond Dichotomy: Conversations between International Relations and Feminist Theory." *International Studies Quarterly* 42: 193–98.

Kuhn, T. (1970). *The Structure of Scientific Revolutions,* 2nd ed. Chicago: University of Chicago Press.

Lakatos, I., and A. Musgrave, eds. (1970). *Criticism and the Growth of Knowledge.* Cambridge: Cambridge University Press.

Lakoff, G., and M. Johnson (1999). *Philosophy in the Flesh: The Embodied Mind and Its Challenge to Western Thought.* New York: Basic Books.

Lazarsfeld, P. F. (1961). "Notes on the History of Quantification in Sociology: Trends, Sources, and Problems," pp 147–203 in H. Woolf, ed., *Quantification: A History of Its Meaning in the Natural and Social Sciences.* Indianapolis: Bobbs Merrill.

Marchand, M. (1998). "Different Communities/Different Realities/Different Encounters: A Reply to J. Ann Tickner." *International Studies Quarterly* 42: 199–204.

Rescher, N. (1977). *Dialectics: A Controversy-Oriented Approach to the Theory of Knowledge.* Albany: SUNY Press.

Tickner, J. A. (1997). "You Just Don't Understand: Troubled Engagements between Feminists and IR Theorists." *International Studies Quarterly* 41: 611–32.

Tickner, J. A. (1998). "Continuing the Conversation. . . ." *International Studies Quarterly* 42: 205–10.

PART 6

Assessment

Readers will have to reach their own assessment of the claims made by Perestroikans. Are things as bad as the more extreme Perestroikans claim? Have Perestroikans focused on the critical problems, or are Perestroikans merely grumbling unduly? Can the political science community respond and correct these problems without major upheaval? Does it want to make such changes? The last section offers a variety of initial assessments in order to stimulate discussion and independent judgment on these important issues.

This section opens with a chapter in which Timothy W. Luke raises critical questions for those who see themselves as politically engaged political scientists desiring to institutionalize the practices of Perestroika. Luke cautions that we must constantly ask what is at stake in this move. In seeking not to reform but to transform the discipline, Luke argues that Perestroikans must ask, For whom does the movement speak? To whom does it speak? And what does it work toward? How can Perestroikans turn their fine words into good works? Responding to arguments voiced by others in this volume—John S. Dryzek and Peter J. Steinberger in particular—Luke focuses on the methodological debates and reminds readers that we must answer the difficult questions about what we do, why we do it, and what utility our deeds have beyond small conversations, individual careers, and the relatively minor literatures political scientists have been producing for decades.

Maurice J. Meilleur's chapter highlights a problem with the role methodology plays in the renewed debates over social and political inquiry that the Perestroika movement has fostered. Meilleur argues that there is ample historical and conceptual evidence that the model of science dominant in political science disengages it from political practice, and from the problems citizens face in lived political experience. Nonetheless, Meilleur argues, critics have failed to challenge this model directly, and instead have simply rejected its application to politics. This leads to detachment and insularity in their own work. Debates between these factions over methodology thus quickly become debates over professional identity. Despite the rhetoric of relevance and democratic engagement in these controversies, advances on these fronts have been negligible. Against the drawbacks to framing the debates over reform this way, Meilleur amplifies calls made by Charles Lindblom (1997) and Rogers M. Smith (1997) for a problem-driven political science and echoes themes raised in the chapters by Samuel H. Beer, Theodore J. Lowi, and Susanne Hoeber Rudolph. His chapter connects Perestroika positions to an account of the disadvantages of political science as a discipline defined by its commitment to a set of methods and to a pragmatic instrumentalist account of social inquiry that offers a way of rethinking the place of methodology in reforming political inquiry.

John S. Dryzek writes from Australia to assess the Perestroika movement in U.S. political science. His chapter addresses both political-organizational and intellectual-methodological aspects of Perestroika. If the methodological debate remains undeveloped, Dryzek argues, the movement may shift power within the profession, but otherwise will have little effect on the practice of political science. A faltering hegemony faces only an empty pluralism with which the discipline already has plenty of experience. Dryzek's chapter points to a critical disciplinary pluralism that attempts to redeem the promise of Perestroika by inquiring more closely than have Perestroikans themselves into what relevance, problem orientation, and intellectual pluralism can and ought to mean.

Rogers M. Smith's chapter also offers a broad assessment of the discipline, from one of the senior players in the Perestroika debate. Smith focuses his assessment by asking about the various means and meanings of doing "good political science." Smith notes that many political scientists implicitly or explicitly hold the view that works in political science can be ordered according to how scientific they are. Smith finds that randomized field experiments are placed at the apex, a broader range of statistical studies just below, and a large but unscientific mass of more "qualitative" studies are relegated to the bottom. His chapter makes a powerful argument that this hierarchy applies only to certain scientific tasks of inference testing and that doing good political science requires the formation of substantively significant hypotheses. These hypotheses often can be generated only through more "qualitative" methods and via more varied forms of inference testing as well. To devalue these components of political science research, Smith concludes, is to risk cultivating a field in which little of substance grows.

The volume concludes with two chapters from non-Perestroikans, chapters that attempt a balanced assessment of some of the issues raised by Perestroikans. Robert Jervis was president of the APSA during the year that the Perestroika controversy first received attention within the profession and the elite media. He sees the Perestroika movement as a fundamentally healthy force, but argues that it was often either unclear or misguided in the choice of its targets. Its real complaint was about the direction of the discipline, but it initially concentrated much of its ire on the APSA, which actually had relatively little influence. Jervis argues that Perestroika's criticisms of the *American Political Science Review* acted as a bridge between Perestroika's unhappiness with the association and that with the discipline, but even here the movement failed to focus on the essential nature of the problem, which was a combination of self-selection on the part of authors and the tendency of departments to make publication in the *APSR* essential for promotion. Jervis explains Perestroika's emphasis on the *Review* in terms of departments' heavy use of *APSR* publication as a touchstone for tenure, behavior he finds is an abdication of their professional responsibility to judge the quality of the work itself. Although this is not a fault of the APSA, the association had to take it into account when selecting a new editor for the *Review*. Behind some of these arguments Jervis finds important issues about toleration within the discipline. He argues that we need to distinguish between kinds of tolerance, and furthermore, to come to grips with principled arguments in favor of training and hiring scholars who do the kinds of research that we believe are most productive and important. Jervis also distinguishes between different motives for diversity of approach and method, and argues that it is striking that we do not think that the lack of political diversity affects our research. In closing, Jervis points out that even highly diverse departments can be quite harmonious if the members respect each other's work.

Peter J. Steinberger's chapter raises doubts about the possibility that Perestroika will reform the discipline. He argues that Perestroikans address serious and troubling questions about institutional and personal ethics, but that ultimately their case is overstated. Perestroikans have much to say about methodological issues in political science—particularly concerning the role of mathematics—much to say about the social structure of the discipline itself. They also express very strong views about a range of institutions, including professional associations, learned journals, and academic departments within colleges and universities. However, focusing on Gregory Kasza's discussion in the September 2001 issue of *PS: Political Science and Politics,* Steinberger looks at some of these claims in detail, and thereby attempts to raise some very real doubts about the Perestroika project itself. He argues that the quantitative-qualitative distinction is at best overstated—it describes a difference of degree, not kind—and that claims about the inevitable invalidity, sterility, and irrelevance of large *n* statistical studies are unpersuasive. Steinberger further argues that concerns about the establishment of a hegemonic "normal science" within the discipline are misplaced, especially in the light of Kuhn's own account of normal and revolutionary scientific endeavor. Finally, he argues that the institutional reforms endorsed by many Perestroikans are troubling insofar as they propose political solutions to what are, in principle, scholarly and scientific questions.

CHAPTER 34

Caught between Confused Critics and Careerist Co-Conspirators

Perestroika in American Political Science

Timothy W. Luke

These comments begin, but do not complete, a critique of American political science. They come from a quarter of the discipline occupied by the "Perestroika in Political Science" movement. Open hesitation marks them from the onset, because the critics and enemies of the Perestroika movement are too quick to conclude far more than is warranted from this movement's tentative remarks, sparse texts, and e-mail traffic. Whether they reduce Perestroika to just another collective action scam by self-seeking careerists (Mr. Pravda 2002) or cast a pox upon Perestroikans for being disgruntled aristocratic counter-revolutionists (Dryzek 2002), the opposition to Perestroika remains real. This chapter pushes back, and it perhaps presses forward.

An Opening?

It does not "speak for" Perestroika. It simply "speaks with" the Perestroika movement in an effort to make political science problem-based, people-centered, and politically grounded rather than technique-based, methodology-centered, and profession-grounded. The former set of engagements might make American political science useful for progressive social transformation, an idea that once animated its founders during the early 1900s, but the latter preoccupations are certain only to deepen its scholasticism, a trend that has deadened political science since the 1950s. Like the Caucus for a New Political Science in the 1960s and 1970s, the Perestroika movement of the 1990s and the 2000s seeks to realize—through many of its currents and claims—a new critical, popular, problem-oriented approach to political analysis. The caucus always was much more, and sometimes much less, than this project (Ricci 1984); and the Perestroika movement has proven to be quite similar in some respects.

After nearly four years of gathering support, the Perestroika in Political Science movement now is deeply wedged in the conflict between politics and epistemics, methodologies and materialities, allies and enemies, critics and conspirators. These comments aim to serve as a corrective both for Perestroika's critics and for its co-conspirators. Perhaps successes are coming Perestroika's way, but failures also can follow from its actions. This study will sift through some of these contradictory tendencies.

As those who see themselves as politically engaged political scientists ask how to institutionalize the practices of Perestroika in Political Science, they must rethink what is at stake in this move. In seeking to transform, and not merely reform, American political science, we must ask, For whom does this movement speak? From where does it work? What does it work toward? And to whom does it speak? If Perestroika in Political Science is to be something more than just another "small conversation" (Ricci 1984), albeit perhaps more global, intense, and well-intentioned than some conversations that have preceded it, how can its members and supporters turn fine words into good works?

Perestroika in Political Science, American political scientists' reactions to the Perestroikan critique, and indeed all of the contributors to this book are engaged in disciplinary boundary work that contests the discipline's organization of knowledge. The responses of American political science, like most other social sciences, to Perestroikan criticisms "entail a certain power-relayed refusal of reflexivity" (Messer-Davidow, Shumway, and Sylvan 1993, 10) embedded at the core of the profession since its inception. Perestroika in Political Science arises at a propitious moment inasmuch as even the most hide-bound reader of the *American Political Science Review* (*APSR*) was willing to concede by 2001 that the cold war was truly over. For decades, in Stephen Fuller's words, "not only the twentieth-century political climate but also the ontological demands of political science" had served effectively "to stereotype politics as a Bismarckian realpolitik, where the goal is always the containment, but not the resolution, of political differences" (Fuller 1993, 139).

Our discussions, then, must answer the difficult questions about what we do, why we do it, and what utility our deeds have beyond the small conversations, individual careers, and minor literatures produced by political scientists for decades. The professional correctness that has stunted the intellectual life of this discipline is powerful and pervasive. That "Mr. Perestroika," and far too many of his (or her) supporters, believe that anonymity is the ideal speech situation from which to address one's colleagues is quite telling. This discipline, like most academic schools of study, creates its own culture of professional persecution, and many must endure disciplined discourses of disciplinary coercion and correction while working in the shadows of their allegedly more methodologically rigorous colleagues. Such reflections might be, in the end, a pathetic exercise, because our discussions, at best, are a call for caution rather than a manifesto for fresh action or a prolegomena to a new philosophy. However, all too often over the past few years, the manifesto and prolegomena, as styles of address, have been misinterpreted, ignored, or dismissed out of hand in the profession, so perhaps a note of caution can be heard and heeded.

Inoculating against Mr. Pravda and the Pox?

The acerbic observations of "Mr. Pravda" (2002) about everyone currently at work in American political science are mildly amusing at a few turns, but mostly insulting at almost all the others. His parables about a Land of Pollysigh beset by an unending war between the Quantoids and the Luddites is undoubtedly a thinly disguised version of the hell as a vocation he (or she) endures somewhere in American higher education. The key strategic issue for Mr. Pravda is not a class struggle, but rather the battle for resources: "apser reserves." Everyone in the fable, and therefore everyone everywhere almost all the time, is "rational," because Quantoids and Luddites both want to control *APSR* space and "enhance" their "income stream."

Perestroikans, however, are just like the denizens of Pollysigh: "they have joined together to—further their utility! This is a coalition of people that agrees on exactly one thing: they all want their work to appear in *APSR* so they can experience the career benefits (read: income and prestige) that come from publication in the discipline's top journal" (Mr. Pravda 2002). Thus, in quite ad hominem terms, Mr. Pravda denounces these careerist co-conspirators as "bonded together in the most Downsian of alliances." In his strange nightmare of methodological miscegenation the dependencia theorist marches with the Reaganite international security jock, the Straussian philosopher crawls into bed with the postmodernist feminist, the unrepentant Marxist allies with the draft-dodging cold war international relations realist, the clueless Albanianist stands shoulder to shoulder with the National Association of Scholars paleocon. Even worse for Mr. Pravda, the dreaded mainstream in the APSA mostly turns out to be full of squishy liberals who have capitulated to the unholy alliance of oddball careerists banded together in Perestroika, causing Mr. Pravda to conclude that it is all about self-service, or "the blatantly self-interested goals of tenure, promotion, wealth, and fame" (Mr. Pravda 2002).

Here Mr. Pravda implicitly endorses Bruno Latour's (1987) visions of "science in action" by describing professional life as one of science networks at war. In Mr. Pravda's predictable little world, methodology is destiny, and subfields, paradigms, or ideologies do not, and should not, mingle. Perestroika is so upsetting because this unlikely conspiracy of allegedly crass careerists has been pulled together by the income-enhancing aura of the *APSR*. At a time when public support for state universities and stock market portfolios at private schools are near all-time lows, it is difficult to believe that someone truly holds to this raw reading of the scholarly heart and mind. But, even with this commentary, Mr. Pravda just gives us another warmed-over version of treasonous clerics' selling out their beliefs and principles for, in this case, big raises, *APSR* bylines, and the career-enhancing power of being counted among the ranks of Perestroika in Political Science.

John Dryzek's reading of Perestroika in Political Science (2002), on the other hand, is much more useful, and Dryzek makes, as usual, very constructive points about the value of a critical political science. Nevertheless, his text comes off at times as that of a cranky corporate fat cat dismissing everyone in "the environmental movement." The deeper roots of this reaction formation must be found elsewhere, but the trunk and branches of it all trace out into a general put-down of Perestroikans as a crowd of pox-worthy aristocratic counter-revolutionists.

As a well-known expert on the environmental movement, Dryzek knows better. Perestroika in Political Science, as a movement, is quite diverse, is internally divided, and lacks a single cohesive program. Yet when Dryzek fixes upon any one Perestroikan text, or voice, it is not unlike would happen if a conservative analyst of the environmental movement in the United States were to single out a single text, or voice, in Earth First, the Wilderness Society, Greenpeace, or Resources for the Future in an attempt to obtain a definitive insight into the thinking of *all* environmentalists. Many Perestroikan texts are remarks made on the fly for a list serve. Despite associations triggered by the name, Perestroika is not a vanguard party, it has no politburo, and its founder is no democratic centralist. So casting a pox upon all of Perestroika is uncomfortably like glibly condemning all environmentalists for tree-hugging.

Dryzek's own surveys of the political science profession (1986 and 1992) are respectable and well known. Nonetheless, his perspective remains quite Anglo-American, Anglo-Australian, or Australian-American; it hardly scratches the surface of non-Anglophone political science. Like Mr. Pravda, he drifts toward a more mainstream, white, male, center-left, liberal statist view of political science: nonwhite, female, hard left or hard right, conservative, populist takes on political science are pretty much ignored in Dryzek's polemic. After rubbishing Perestroikans for tooting their own horns, which remains a well-known occupational hazard in academe, he presses down quite hard upon his Habermasian horn by pointing to the merits of deliberative discursivity in reshaping environmental policy analysis (see Dryzek 1986, 1990, and 1992; Dryzek and Leonard 1988). Admittedly, some voices for, or from, Perestroika in Political Science may not ring with new methodological departures; yet do we really have one here?

All too often in American political science, methodological training is essentially a form of epistemic programming meant to stipulate one ontology, one epistemology, one axiology (see King 1998; Shepsle and Bonchek 1997; King, Keohane, and Verba 1994; and Easton 1971). Once the stipulations take hold, what is labeled uncritically "rigorous methodological training" usually bends one to craft data, models, and theories in ways that produce disciplines, disciples, and disciplinarity. And as the credo of rigor is embraced, the method acting of professional correctness takes hold. These trends are strange, given the mainstream's disbelief in timeless traditions. In fact, according to Messer-Davidow, Shumway, and Sylvan (1993, vii), "for only two centuries, knowledge has assumed a disciplinary form; for less than one, it has been produced in academic institutions by professionally trained knowers." However, there are few disciplinary formations about which it is as safe to say, as can be said of American political science, that scientific disciples are so disciplined by their disciplines.

Arguing about method, however, has proven to be a famously wasteful pursuit in American political science for decades. It distracts energies from concrete political analysis, perpetuates feeble mythologies about science and its practices, and induces behavioral expectations about consuming and producing a peculiar code of professional correctness (Luke 1999). The mainstream case for more "rigorous methodology" in American political science is, in most instances, a strange modernization narrative that implicitly casts, at any one time, many commonly used methodological practices in political science as traditional, conventional, or even backward simply because they are not as formalized, axiomatic, or data-based as those existing beyond some disciplinary boundary (Luke 1985). In turn, the "methodologically rigorous" believe that those other disciplines elsewhere—economics, psychology, physics, biology, and so on—are truly methodologically sophisticated. In response to such external pressures, one finds the discipline's methodological modernizers from within and above cajoling and coercing any and all laggards to acquire the latest cutting-edge methods from elsewhere as soon as possible.

Over the years, political science has changed under the influence of other more highly regarded disciplines. Whether influenced by physics, economics, or psychology, these proponents of "modernizing" political science from within bring with them "particular methods or techniques" as well as "an agenda, an attitude, and a language" (Messer-Davidow, Shumway, and Sylvan 1993, 6) to underpin their putative programs for making new progress. Many highly regarded political scientists, like Gary King (1998), pretend that the development of the political science discipline mostly turns upon the creation of new methods to analyze political data. Quite often, such methods are not necessarily cutting-edge, and they typically are not suitable for political applications. Ordinary citizens also find that they are not easily comprehended, and normally such methods are mathematicized. Mathematicization can create exactitude, but it also can turn literary obscurantism into numerate obfuscation (Agger 2000). With a typical colonial cringe, users of the other "anti-modern" or "pre-modern" methods then accede to the more modern, newer mathematical ones. Yet it is very unclear that methodological modernization produces new technical control, contextual understanding, or revolutionary guidance (Lowi 1992). Instead these practices mostly propagate a new type of "science talk" among the modernized, which stigmatizes and denigrates the unmodernized (Agger 1990) but produces no real scientific progress.

Reading methodological tracts, such as King's *Unifying Political Methodology* (1998), Shepsle and Bonchek's *Analyzing Politics* (1997), or King, Keohane, and Verba's *Designing Social Inquiry* (1994), one finds a tremendous ignorance of much contemporary philosophy and history of science among the so-called "state-of-the-art" methodologies for American political science. By remaining faithful to methodological precepts of Newtonian physics, Darwinian biology, or Lavoisierian chemistry, King, Keohane and Verba (1994) defend the Baconian virtues so cherished by most American political scientists. That is, as Fuller (1993, 129) asserts, they assiduously generate a knowledge that sustains the current political order while remaining fairly disconnected from the material realities of the world that accepts this order.

Here, however, the presumptions of Perestroika tie back to its members' willingness to crack open the Pandora's box of politics, especially professional-technical politics, in American political science. Actually, there is little rhyme or reason that can be tied solely to methodologies and their putatively superior predictive performance in the distribution of professional spoils. Universities, colleges, departments, and the disciplines they host are political structures and systems. Who gets what, when, where, and how in them is not usually a function just of more rigorous methodological sophistication. Rather it is an always-shifting outcome of network wars (Latour 1987), and one would expect different networks to go after each other's alliances, followers, and products in the fashion that we see here (Latour 1988). This is not unseemly: it is often the heart of the matter. Not to talk about these realities of political science in action is to ignore, once again, what political scientists do (Easton 1971). Another performative contradiction, however, arises from the mainstream inasmuch as the professed devotion of the methodologically rigorous to observing empirical behavior ignores the data about such sectarian behaviors. Thus it also overlooks the difficulties experienced by professors of political science who "fall short" for the methodology modernizers.

As Timothy Lenoir notes (1993, 77), the temptation for most scientists, and indeed for many political scientists, is to normalize their disciplines as the accumulated stable results of prior research activities that have become canonical. This unimaginative approach, however, has "the undesired consequence of conflating what goes on at the site of research with disciplinary activity." Yet it is quite clear that cutting-edge scientists "at the research front do not perceive their goal as expanding a discipline," and that "most novel research, particularly evident in contemporary science, is not confined within the scope of a single discipline but draws upon work of several disciplines. If asked, most scientists . . . would say they work on problems. Almost no one thinks of her- or himself as working on a discipline" (Lenoir 1993, 77). Many mainstream political scientists, of course, have denied these trends as they have taken up the tasks of defending "the discipline" against Perestroikans, who tend—as this volume illustrates—to be more ecumenical, less worried about boundary work, and concretely centered "on problems" in their analyses.

A problem-centered political science should be a politics-centered discipline, not one based upon analytical fads that are shared professionally among a community of experts. While political science should heed the state, it ought not to be a simple servitor of state strategies—whether are anti-Communism or homeland defense strategies. As the discipline's many analytical failures during the cold war illustrate, the political complexities of the contemporary post-9/11 world cannot be grasped by a special scientific discipline that pumps out a one-dimensional party line about whoever or whatever is being cast as the political regime's absolute enemy.

Dryzek's amusing alliterative assault on both the incumbent mainstream of *APSR* hegemonists and an insurgent sidestream of disgruntled Perestroikans is not without its merits. He somewhat dismisses some linkages as rare (political philosophy and area studies), finds commonalities few would contest (everyone supports interdisciplinary studies), and voices frustrations about programmatic uncertainty (an inadequate and empty pluralism necessarily results). He vents his own frustrations about the careerist side of the Perestroikan resistance, and clicks his tongue over "the luminaries" from big-name, top-twenty departments such as Yale, Chicago, Harvard, Penn, or Indiana, who apparently suffer from false consciousness, commit professional suicide, or dabble in elite treason by hanging out with this suspicious lot.

To assume, however, that most Perestroikans "are prominent members of some of the most highly-rated departments of political science in the United States, and authors of books with top university presses," and that they are collectively poised to take over "the remaining parts of the discipline they do not control, notably the *APSR* and the formal offices of the APSA" (Dryzek 2002, 11) verges upon delusion. Many Perestroikans are critical pluralists, they toil away in nonprestigious departments, many are younger faculty members or graduate students, and they have little interest in wresting away control of the APSR or the APSA from the mainstream. Life is too short to plot big intrigues over such Lilliputian stakes. In fact, many Perestroikans are committed to waging a much deeper campaign for cultural transformation out in the departments and in the discipline at large: reforming all journals' editorial practices, redirecting graduate education standards, rethinking departmental hiring and promotion procedures, and reshaping professional organizations to make them more open and democratic. They do this while pursuing different methodological goals (pluralism in approach, problem-driven research, political groundedness, and interdisciplinary openness) and respecting alternate disciplinary subcommunities (area studies, political philosophy, minorities, and women).

Perestroika, then, stands for more than "mere toleration and ecumenicalism" (Dryzek 2002, 17). It also has backed careful comparative-historical critique, nonethnocentric community-based understanding, and perhaps, like the Caucus for a New Political Science in its better moments before it, giving more say in society to the downtrodden, outsiders, or the people mainstream political science ignores. All of these goals have their own problems, but this broadly based set of strategies is where many Perestroikans anchor themselves.

The Discipline as Tactics for Ontic Stabilization?

Nature and Society are essentially contested concepts, and arguments about the merits of Perestroika in Political Science constitute another episode in the struggle over its constantly contested core. At the same time, for most political scientists the centrality of a pure, objective, unmediated Nature or Society in the attainment of modern scientific knowledge is an idea that is dying very hard (Dryzek 2002). From the vanguard of Newtonian physics in the seventeenth century to the rearguard of data-driven political science in the twentieth century, many schools of modern science have naïvely assumed that their methodologies provide a privileged basis for knowledge of what is "real" in Nature or Society with their rigorous methodological mapping of enduring processes "out there" in the domains of the natural, the social, and the political (Foucault, 1970; Latour 1993; Deleuze and Guattari 1994; and Husserl 1970).

Those making such unsullied observations, in turn, are believed to propound a true knowledge of some objective reality. Such knowledge often is idealized by mainstream political scientists in the mathematical proofs of physics, and its hybrid applications in everyday life are widely believed to be the foundations of modernity's technological proficiency. When all is said and done, then, humanity is believed to know how the world of Nature and Society work because of its disciplined application of instrumental scientific methods for observation, experimentation, and verification (Lyotard 1984). Rigorous political scientists typically buy this "science talk" whole hog, and they work hard to corner some of this action—even if it does not really exist (Agger 2000).

Perestroikans, on the other hand, share a disquiet about these epistemological, ontological, and technological articles of faith in modernity. Celebrants continue to praise the system of positive science, and its derivative technologies, for a demonstrated ability to raise industrial output, overcome deadly diseases, speed up methods of travel, and produce a longer, richer human lifespan. Few of them, however, discuss how these same modes of scientific knowledge and technical action also generate noxious byproducts, cause new afflictions, create frustrations from mobility, or perhaps detract from the quality of life (Luke 1989). Consequently, many movements of people—scientists and laypersons alike—have arisen to question, or to openly protest, formulas for legitimating scientific authority and technical power by referring to putatively pure rational naturalistic knowledge (Husserl 1970). Of course these resistance movements are not universally welcomed, because the cultural privilege, political power, and economic property of many are deeply entwined in these modes of scientific production (Foucault, 1979). Nonetheless, more resistance movements seem to develop and spread with each successive generation.

In its emergent days, positive science put forth foundational epistemologies for dividing facts and values, theory and observation, experiments and explanations, or truth and opinion in order to challenge religious-feudal authority, whose place, power, and property rested upon other epistemic grounds in early modern society (Lyotard 1984). Once those traditional enemies were overcome, however, science and technology increasingly shifted their legitimating discourses toward operational achievement, or technical-economic performance, and away from epistemological incorrigibility, or real knowledge of the inherent rationality of Nature or Society. Consequently, the nineteenth and twentieth centuries saw bourgeois science and industry using their technical command of the objective forms of Nature as the great "out there" to create greater wealth and knowledge for the "in here" of market economies and societies (Foucault, 1980b).

Despite its professed intellectual pluralism, however, American political science almost never examines any of the sociological sources of its continuing successes, at least not within the narrow ambit of its own little disciplinary worlds (Almond 1996). Strangely enough, American political scientists remain among the most recalcitrant disbelievers in the notion that disciplines serve as political structures interconnecting larger systems of political economy and the academic production of disciplinary knowledge. Nonetheless, as Lenoir asserts (1993, 72, his emphasis), *"Disciplines are dynamic structures for assembling, channeling, and replicating the social and technical practices essential to the functioning of the political economy and the system of power relations that actualize it."*

Seeing how disciplines discipline their producers and consumers helps us understand the social construction of political-scientific knowledge by disclosing the conventional understandings manifest in the acts and artifacts generated within the knowledge cultures of American political science. The disciplinary lore of this academic community, however, does not acknowledge its own social construction. Instead, many mainstream practitioners (for instance, King, Keohane, and Verba 1994) still purport to show that political science is a very special project of data-driven, positivist explanation intent upon discovering more general tendencies, testing deductive nomological propositions, and confirming naturalistic laws of human behavior (Almond 1990). Seeing these practices as pure epistemological necessity, most political scientists discount the possibility that less pure sociological contingencies maintain such knowledges (King 1998; Shepsle and Bonchek 1997). If it does anything, political science in the United States, like most of the social sciences, aids in the reproduction of social control for industrial democracy, suburban consumerism, or liberal capitalism by ontologically stabilizing a system of disciplinary assumptions about our collective life (Foucalt 1991).

As Pierre Bourdieu asserts (1991, 106), any effective social science "must include in its theory of the social world a theory of the theory effect which, by helping to impose a more or less authorized way of seeing the social world, helps to construct the reality of that world." The locked-up but streamlined vision of the social world entailed by the methodological armamentarium of King, Keohane, and Verba (1994) completely assumes, wittingly or unwittingly, responsibility for systemic acts of epistemic constitution whose inner logics, necessities, and structures must remain suppressed, forgotten, or hidden. Their visions of the proper scope and correct method for political science are clearly "programmes of perception" (Bourdieu 1991, 106) aimed at empowering them and all whom they can enroll in their networks. Adopting these methods, then, leads to accepting "a certain claim to symbolic authority as the socially recognized power to impose a certain vision of the social world, i.e. of the divisions of the social world. In the struggle to impose the legitimate vision, in which science itself is inevitably caught up, agents possess power in proportion to their symbolic capital, i.e. in proportion to the recognition they receive from a group" (Bourdieu 1991, 106). Despite its professed devotion to empirical observation, American political science tends to float about in the clouds of an abstract idealism when its practitioners get wound up in methodological discussions of "the discipline."

Lacking much sociological sense, then, many political scientists tend to ignore significant characteristics of their own work. As Lenoir observes (1993, 72), "Disciplines are the infrastructure of science embodied above all in university departments, professional societies, text books, and lab manuals. . . . At the same time, the discipline helps to structure scientists' relationships to particular institutional and economic contexts. Disciplines are the institutional mechanisms for regulating the market relations between consumers and producers of knowledge. They also are instruments for distributing status; by grounding expertise and skill, discipline sets boundaries and demarcates hierarchies of experts and amateurs." This neglect of their own sociological situation is then coupled with an enduring "genesis amnesia" about American political science's disciplinary origins. Thus the scope and methods of this profession are mired in "the objectivist apprehension which, grasping the product of history as an *opus operatum*, a *fait accompli*, can only invoke the mysteries of pre-established harmony or the prodigies of conscious orchestration to account for what, apprehended in pure synchrony, appears as objective meaning, whether it be the internal coherence of works or institutions such as myths, rites, or bodies of law, or the objective coordination which the concordant or conflicting practices of the members of the same group or class at once manifest and presuppose (inasmuch as they imply a community of dispositions)" (Bourdieu 1977, 79). Dazed by such disciplinarity, methodologists like King, Keohane, and Verba (1994) do treat analytical practices as an *opus operatum* in order to train others to serve, wittingly or unwittingly, as producers and reproducers of their peculiar vision of "objective methods."

Therefore, the drill of discourse in political science reveals knowledge shaping and shifting with power in many remarkably useful ways (Barnes and Bloor 1982). Virtually all of them, however, undercut the true freedoms promised by liberalism, democracy, and markets of liberal democratic capitalism. Rational choice theorists routinely illustrate the economic irrationality of voting, the coalitional strangulation of public goods provision, and the inefficiency of democratic decision making (Luke 1987). Voting behavior specialists reshape the public into psychodemographic niche markets whose buttons usually can be pushed with sufficient air time and advertising money to produce specific voting outcomes. Public opinion analysts reveal how truths and untruths can be vended effectively in the news cycle to paralyze individual initiative or mobilize collective outrage. Many normative theorists tear up foundationalist ethics, rationalizing the agonistic free play of moralizers that leaves many citizens unclear and uncertain about how to behave. The reduction of politics to psychosocial behavioral events, rational choice acts, or ungrounded discursive agonism permits the enunciative modalities of other more cohesive structures to circulate as productive power behind, below, or beyond the liberal humanist anthropology that most political scientists unconsciously accept as normal.

In this fashion, mainstream American political science promotes the smooth operation of other disciplinary practices among the general population through the "facticity" granted to its first principles: ontological, epistemological, psychological, and social (Poovey 1998). The inherent conservatism of most political scientists, and much of political science, becomes an ontological stabilizer that enables liberal capitalist democracy to assume that this is the best of all possible worlds and is certain to bring all of the best into the world (Latour 1993). Simplistic modernist assumptions about human agency, structural stability, natural predictability, defensible values, or useful knowledge underpin most political scientists' normalizing studies of who normally gets what, how, where, when, and why (Almond 1996).

Creating a Critical Political Science?

Aspirations for realizing the goals of Perestroika in Political Science reticulate many of the major institutional pressures rolling through American university life. That is, "truth," or at least new research findings, must be delimited, defined, and delivered as new knowledge by trained specialists to fellow specialists, student cohorts, and interested laymen through the existing conduits of academic disciplines and departments (Jacoby 1994). Thinking about politics is immediately parsed through the collegiate order and the departmental organization of "real political science" as another method for ignoring the traditions of political theory. As a result, political theory has been on life support in American universities since the behavioral revolution of the 1950s (Gunnell 1986).

At that moment in the cold war during the 1960s when the discipline's many analytical failures became apparent, the "mainstream" of the discipline began neglecting at best, or persecuting at worst, most political theorists merely because they studied "loosely defined concepts such as justice, liberty, freedom, equality, and so forth," and therefore they and their work were "doomed to remain in the nonscientific realm" (Ricci 1984, 145). Usually allowed to remain on university payrolls to allow for the fulfillment of core curricular requirements by undergraduates, academic political theorists have been fighting tooth and nail against simple-minded methodological parochialism for nearly six decades in the disciplinary trenches dug deeply along the methodological fronts of most departments. Yet many of the deans, provosts, and chancellors managing American universities continue to doubt the utility of social science as such, so professional scope and methods partisans in political science continue struggling to control these educational entrenchments as political science departments fight with rival units in philosophy, history, sociology, and economics over which discipline is "more scientific" than the others (Agger 1989; Jacoby 1994).

Self-certain "real" political scientists have dismissed political theorists as deluded traditionalists who are content with "endless academic gnawing on the small bones of Kant" (Catlin 1956, 815), while they, on the other hand, are scheming to become more modern, scientific, and empirical theorists who work at explaining what *is* rather than judging what *ought to be*. They do this because they believe life scientists, mathematical scientists, and physical scientists share their epistemic prejudices about critical, ethical, or normative thinking. The disciplinary prestige systems at work in so many departments always bring these reminders to political theorists from the "big names" in "the mainstream," who rarely tire of reminding everyone that "theorizing, even about politics, is not to be confused with metaphysical speculation in terms of abstractions hopelessly removed from empirical observation and control" (Lasswell and Kaplan 1952, 63).

Perestroikans are quite conversant with the trained incapacities that make conceptual confusions like these so strong in the discipline's mainstream, and they must not be ignored. The fact that such utterances rest upon other metaphysical abstractions enforced by fiat with little countervailing empirical observation and control is, of course, downplayed in the mainstream, but this incredible ignorance aggravates the overall uselessness of political science to the larger world off campus. In modern societies whose populations co-exist with huge technostructures, environmental degradation, and bioengineered organisms, the behavioralist ideologies of the cold war that still pretend to divide "what is" from "what ought to be" need to be broken apart. Whether one uses the large bones of Kant, or the small anomalies observed in the dismal results produced by so many empirical analyses, it is essential for Perestroikan political scientists to show that mainstream political science has failed for many reasons. One of them is that "the basic concepts and hypotheses of political science," despite the claims to the contrary of Lasswell and Kaplan (1952, xi) and their contemporary mainstream heirs in the schools of rational choice or empirical analysis, are still chock-full of "abstractions of political doctrine or what the state and society *ought* to be."

In fact, most mainstream political science is actively engaged in writing, and then legitimating the writing of, liberal capitalist ontographies (Luke 1987). That is, the nation-state as a type of territorial, population, production formation must serve as a standing reserve, a resource supply center, and a waste reception center while providing markets with multiple sites for the productive use of resourcified flows of energy, labor, information, and matter. Flexible abstractions such as Nature and the Nation are always already active political assets. Still, their fungibilization, liquidification, and commodification cannot occur without expert intellectual labor to prepare, produce, and then provide them for the global marketplace (Luke 1997). Perestroikans must resist the normalization projects that liberal schools of ethics and economics have sustained for many nations along with the rise of modernity (Latour 1993).

While one might agree, in part, with Mearsheimer's observations (2001) that the contemporary will unto mathematicization in American political science is much more than an instance of methodological parochialism, the collision of mathematical and verbal modelers or data drivers and text treaders over formalizations and discursivities is, in fact, another small window opening out to the ostensible origin, and the enduring entrenchment, of the modern political subject. Oddly enough, accounting for the methodological fetishism of American political science perhaps can allow us to answer Michel Foucault's questions in "What Is Enlightenment?" (1984, 29). That is, "How are we constituted as subjects of our own knowledge: How are we constituted as subjects who exercise or submit to power relations? How are we constituted as moral subjects of our own actions?" The mathematicized analysis of individual action by individual analysts in mainstream political science simultaneously helps to propound a modern notion of individuality employed by power to erase its presence and process as well as to produce individuals with modern notions by exercising power (King 1998).

The epistemic formation that permits certain points to be thought, believed, and said in mainstream American political science is actually quite old, extending at least as far back as Galileo or Hobbes (Husserl 1970). Discourses of scope and method in political science, like all discourses, are "a distribution of gaps, voids, absences, limits, divisions" (Foucault 1972, 119). These ruptures and aporias shape scientific discussion and subjective activity in ways that silence some statements, enable others to be made, and generally set the conditions of truth. The autogenerative potentialities of methodology become "in the density of discursive practices, systems that establish statements as events," as well as "an anonymous field whose configuration defines the possible position of speaking subjects" (Foucault 1972, 128, 122).

Mainstream political science largely still holds that the truth is somehow "out there" in "the world," first to be uncovered, and second to be made to speak in terms of these historically contingent patterns now deputized into processes of making citizens. "Discourse," then, according to Clifford (2001, 30–31) "is where truth happens, rather than where it is discovered, reflected or revealed. Truth happens as statements bound together by their sameness, constituting a community of truth, a domain of knowledge in which, and only in which, such statements make sense." For American political science, APSA meetings and the APSR are key venues where truth happens, and statements about their truth constitute a discursive community of truth about an APSA and APSR domain of knowledge in which statements about politics make sense only in discourses as historical, contingent, and common statements about individuals and politics in the modern(izing) world economy.

Therefore mathematicization is about ontology and ethics as much or more than about epistemics and methodology (King, Keohane, and Verba 1994). To mathematicize is also to ontologize in a particular fashion, casting the world as a reality that one can quantify, measure, and count as well as classify and categorize by such metrological interventions with some useful material effect (Porter 1996). Mainstream political science buys into, rationalizes, and reinforces these discursive maneuvers that let this "truth" happen. Yet the impulse to quantify and classify also is integrally connected to how we are constituted as subjects of our own knowledge, how we are constituted as subjects who submit to power relations, and how we are constituted as moral subjects of our own actions.

One can argue that the modern regime of bio-power formation, as it was first described by Foucault (1980a, 138–42), has not been attentive to the complex role played by Society, Nature, and the Economy in the equations of modernizing biopolitics. The controlled tactics of inserting human and non-human bodies into the machineries of industrial and agricultural production emerged as part and parcel of strategically adjusting growth in human numbers to the development of industrial capitalism. Under this regime, systems of power or knowledge brought "life and its mechanisms into the realm of explicit calculations," making the manifold disciplines of scientific knowledge and discourses of state power into a new type of productive agency that led to the "transformation of human life" (Foucault 1980a, 145) with the Industrial Revolution. Once this threshold of control had been crossed, scientific experts began to survey, study, and supervise as many interactions of human economics, politics, and technologies as possible because the collectives continually call into question all human beings' existence as living beings (Luke 1999). Upon this premise the special sciences, like mainstream American political science, were founded in the nineteenth century (Ricci 1984). Unfortunately, what has followed is perhaps not true enlightenment, but rather Mr. Pravda's war of all against all to publish in the big-name, mainstream journals.

A Closing?

Caught between confused critics and careerist co-conspirators, what might the rank-and-file Perestroikans do? First, their aspirations for restructuring, redirecting, and revitalizing political science are sound. In many ways, American political science has been distorted since its birth by the ideological agendas of the twentieth century. A discipline devoted to understanding power beyond the terms first raised by 1917 in Russia, by 1933 in Germany, by 1945 in Central Europe, by 1949 in China, or by 1954 or 1975 in the Third World might be truly useful, but it failed at this task in the struggle against anti-liberal fascism, communism, and nationalism (Luke 1989). Now it also must continue evading 2001 in Afghanistan or Iraq, along with the knotty question of homeland security, in the United States, in order to succeed. Second, a political science directed at power and authority in all its forms, not merely those of the polis as Aristotle prejudged them two millennia ago, might tell us more about how to live amid the facts of Nature and the artifacts of techno-science. Clearly the political science we have now is incapable of thinking about how public life is formed, and misformed, by systems of technoscience in today's built and unbuilt environment (Latour 1993). Third, another way of teaching, learning, and communicating is being made possible, both locally and globally, by digital discourses above and beyond those sustained by print literacy. Training new professionals, teaching new students, and testing new communicative conventions beyond those of the twentieth-century research university could occupy many political analysts for quite some time to come. And fourth, there are tremendously threatening problems that American political science could address, but thus far has not, or has not addressed well.

What are these big problems, and how might American political science address them today? That one must ask already tells a great deal (Almond 1988). Neo-liberal ideas and ideologues have spent much of the past three decades gutting public services, lowering the social wage, degrading environmental protections, and coarsening public debate. Many collective goods such as local schools, public universities, major museums, pension systems, road grids, basic infrastructure, health care, public utilities, and public transportation are running at the ragged edges of near collapse. In 2001 one out of every thirty-two Americans was in prison, on probation, or somehow otherwise in the charge of the criminal justice system. A very unequal distribution of power and wealth is crippling human development at the local, national, and global levels of the human community.

Ugly new racial, ethnonational, and religious conflicts are resurfacing at many sites after slowly simmering under ideological bubbles during the cold war years. Vast areas of the old socialist bloc are suffering under the transition to liberal democratic capitalism, but the liberal democratic capitalist countries are sweating out an economic downturn, crony capitalist scandals, political gridlock, and ecological overshoot. Against this horizon, many political scientists continue bickering in minor journals, such as *Political Research Quarterly* or *Public Choice,* over which techniques for pooling data sets are best suited to the analysis of electoral campaigns long past or over obvious trivialities, making the smallest decisions in human politics seem like fascinating collective action problems. Political science will not address pressing public problems because the scientific politics of what methodology to privilege beforehand still consumes far too many careers with indecision, misdirection, and disinformation.

Many American political scientists, as Dryzek (1986) rightly observes, lack a clear understanding of the history of their discipline, and they increasingly have no training in, or respect for, the practices of philosophy, sociology, anthropology, psychology, or geography. Some accept economics, some embrace statistics, and some dabble in mathematics, but very few are conversant in traditions outside the liberal democratic beliefs of cold war America. And this ignorance shows in the unsophisticated, uninformative, and unhelpful counsel that a heavily disciplined reading by mainstream political science (whether data-driven or formal axiomatic) can give to anyone engaged with daily political struggles.

Ultimately, few truly care about political scientists and "the findings" they offer to the larger public. A century after the discipline's founding, a PhD in political science is not a necessary credential in the nation's political life. Indeed, it actually can be a handicap in a world run by people holding JD, MBA, or MS degrees. The White House occasionally invites a political scientist or two in for a meal or a meeting, but usually that person is chosen from some good notice in a *New York Times* book review or from some passing civic fashion coincidentally related to one's lifework. A strong review by the *APSR* brings little attention, because practically no one reads it; and the APSA refuses to make political interventions, so its say-so means almost less than nothing.

Of course political scientists, or at least APSA members, sometimes join governments. Yet those who do rarely are not from the *APSR*-centered core's "A list." Instead they typically are second stringers, odd outsiders, Ivy League mandarins, or emigré intellectuals. Whether Hubert Humphrey, George McGovern, Samuel Huntington, Ralph Bunce, Zbigniew Brzezinski, or Condoleezza Rice, few self-respecting, big-time *APSR* authors would regard any of these personalities "real" political scientists. The larger pool of opinion leaders for the mass public still get their "political science" from *Harpers,* the *Atlantic,* the *New York Times* magazine, or middle-brow books from a Borders "New Non-Fiction" table. Virtually no one outside the circle of professional political scientists subscribes to the *APSR,* the *American Journal of Political Science* (*AJPS*), the *Journal of Politics* (*JoP*), *Political Review Quarterly* (*PRQ*), or *Polity,* and not many of those who do subscribe actually read them.

Beyond producing its unread publications, which are materially entangled (and hence count for something here) in the careerist struggle for tenure and promotion, the APSA stages its annual meeting every year and provides some added member services. Beyond providing generic group death and disability insurance, discounts on other unreadable scholastic publications, cheap tickets to APSA meetings, and periodically issued surveys of what many academics pretend is "cutting-edge research," the APSA does very little. It no longer aspires to guide the nation's public life, it bars members from making political pronouncements in any collective manner, and it produces a largely unscientific run of self-referential literature by and for college professors.

Because the APSA brings eight thousand to ten thousand souls en masse to some major American metropolitan locations, and because the local papers usually have slow news days in late August (or because their editors delight at sending up any crowd of bearded boffins), the contents of this or that APSA convention paper might capture a few lines of copy in the *Boston Globe,* the *San Francisco Chronicle,* or the *Washington Post.* Likewise, Dave Broder or George Will might pull a lead for a column from an APSA roundtable. Once the Labor Day weekend closes, however, this "impact" is used to wrap yesterday's coffee grounds as the association and its members return to their home campuses for another year. Regional meetings in Chicago, Atlanta, Houston, or Long Beach usually get even less notice; and despite their best efforts to emulate the *APSR,* the *AJRS,* the *JoP,* and *PRQ* garner even less attention on the national or world stage. In fact, these regional journals are increasingly callow copies of the *APSR*, leaving the definite impression that papers rejected by any of them will be "under review" until they connect at any of the other three.

Perhaps all of Perestroika's co-conspirators are careerists. Because we do not know who "Mr. (or Ms.) Perestroika" is, we will never know if good work for reform got him or her a job at Yale, Michigan, or Stanford. However, the work of Perestroika should move us to ask if working to get and keep a position at such places should be all that we worry about, work toward, and wish to occur. By and large, the vast majority of Perestroikans do not work at Chicago, Penn, or Harvard, and they do not publish books with the big-name university presses. Moreover, professing an affiliation with Perestroikan political science is not the royal road to success, despite Mr. Pravda's diatribes and John Dryzek's poxes. On the contrary, as far too many anonymous comments on the Perestroika list serve suggest, in most departments a tie to Perestroika is a major "career negative" rather than giving a real boost to one's vita.

As Easton (1971) suggests, political science is, in large part, "what political scientists do." What political scientists do, however, remains quite diverse. To produce some semblance of coherence and advancement, a parochial disciplinarity does emerge, making "the discipline," in large part, "central to the micropolitics of knowledge production" (Lenoir 1993, 75). Despite many political scientists' pretenses to finding meaningful objects, definitive subjects, and certain agendas, few of these outcomes emerge from today's university institutions, publishing practices, or academic rituals. Associating and disassociating fields, bounding and unbounding objects, centering and decentering discourses unfold through contingent historical practices that are made slightly conventional, or somewhat canonical, simply through constant use in what political scientists do (see King, Keohane, and Verba 1994; Shepsle and Bonchek 1997). As a discipline, then, American political scientists find that "stabilization of numerous, diverse local practices occurs through their position in the broader context of an *economy of practices*. Discipline is crucial for organizing and stabilizing this heterogeneity. Silent but powerfully operating, discipline is what makes disunified science work" (Lenoir 1993, 75, his emphasis).

The efforts of Perestroikans in American political science have highlighted the heterogeneity of the discipline and questioned the economy of practices used to stabilize the production of mainstream political science work. Perestroika in Political Science pushes the merits of side-streams and undercurrents, rushing down deeper courses of conceptual flow to redefine what the scientific field of political science is, has been, and should be. The tussles in the discipline directly underscore Bourdieu's sense of scientific fields, which he regards (1975, 19) as the "locus of competitive struggle, in which the specific issue at stake is the monopoly of scientific authority, defined inseparably as technical capacity and social power, or, to put it another way, the monopoly over scientific competence, in the sense of a particular agent's socially recognized capacity to speak and act legitimately (i.e., in an authorized and authoritative way) in scientific matters."

This discussion has suggested, as has Bourdieu, that there is no transcendent context of rational justification that renders some scientific hypotheses more credible than others. Thus the usual explanation as to why some forms of political science dominate in any given journal, department, or university rests on the cultural, economic, political, or social qualities of those contexts, and not on some intrinsic epistemological merit in the mainstream practices of doing political science. Consequently, in elucidating the context of knowledge production, consumption, circulation, or accumulation in American political science, one must see how fully political science still is a very flexible form of narrative social knowledge, just as much as, or even more than, it is a rigorous system for producing trustworthy technical knowledge about this economy, government, and society (Lyotard 1984). American political science can be reclaimed to better guide collective decisions about our common problems, and the work begun by "Mr. Perestroika" represents a strong start down that path.

Ironically, the same decades that have brought thousands of newly minted political scientists into the academic ranks of our professional life also have witnessed the discipline at large doing very little to check the tremendous corrosion of public life, the cracking of many civic institutions, and the corruption of once vital democratic practices. One needs only to listen to the cynical, mean-spirited qualities of someone like Mr. Pravda to understand why American political science has so little useful understanding to offer to the larger American public. And the celebratory spirit surrounding the APSA's centennial cannot negate the discipline's very serious neglect of real-world politics. For all of its advances, the "normal science" produced by adherents of political science's disciplined systems of methodologically rigorous knowledge has failed to anticipate, or even adapt to, many major political changes, ranging from the end of the welfare state to the implosion of state socialism to the maldevelopment of the Second, Third, and Fourth Worlds to the wild spread of social chaos in many countries to the terrorist attacks of the 1990s and 2000s.

At this juncture, too much is in doubt, and at stake, in the nation's civic life for the hermetic discourses of mainstream political science to remain entirely self-absorbed in a discipline that regards its epistemic realism, technocratic operationalism, and apolitical professionalism as true "advances" for human scientific work (Goodin and Klingeman 1996). While we need not accept the pox Dryzek places on Perestroika, his appeal to everyone to find a critical political science is ultimately very sound. There are other subjugated knowledges lying outside of the existing disciplinary ambit of mainstream American political science. And their insights must be seriously reconsidered if American political science is to deal effectively with the crises that now challenge the governance structure, civic order, and university system that historically have sustained it.

References

Agger, B. 1989. *Reading Science: A Literary, Political and Sociological Analysis.* Dix Hills, NY: General Hall.

Agger, B. 1990. *The Decline of Discourse: Reading, Writing and Resistance in Postmodern Capitalism.* New York: Falmer Press.

Agger, B. 2000. *Public Sociology: From Social Facts to Literary Acts.* Lanham, MD: Rowman and Littlefield.

Almond, G. 1988. "Separate Tables: Schools and Sects in Political Science." *PS* 20 (December): 828–42.

Almond, G. 1990. "The Nature of Contemporary Political Science: A Roundtable Discussion." *PS* 23 (March): 34–36.

Almond, G. 1996. "Political Science: The History of the Discipline." In *A New Handbook of Political Science,* ed. Robert Goodin and Hans-Dieter Klingemann. Oxford: Oxford University Press.

Barnes, B., and D. Bloor. 1982. "Realism, Rationalism and the Sociology of Knowledge." In *Rationality and Relativism,* ed. Martin Hollis and Steven Lukes. Cambridge, MA: MIT Press.

Bourdieu, P. 1975. "The Specificity of the Scientific Field and the Social Conditions of the Progress of Reason." *Social Science Information* 14: 19–47.

Bourdieu, P. 1977. *Outline of a Theory of Practice.* Cambridge: Cambridge University Press.

Bourdieu, P. 1991. *Language and Symbolic Power.* Cambridge, MA: Harvard University Press.

Catlin, G. E. G. 1956. "The Function of Political Science." *Western Political Quarterly* (December): 815.

Clifford, M. 2001. *Political Genealogy after Foucault: Savage Identities.* New York: Routledge.

Deleuze, G., and F. Guattari. 1994. *What Is Philosophy?* New York: Columbia University Press.

Dryzek, J. 1986. "The Progress of Political Science." *Journal of Politics* 48: 301–20.

Dryzek, J. 1990. *Discursive Democracy: Politics, Policy, and Political Science.* New York: Cambridge University Press.

Dryzek, J. 1992. "How Far Is It from Virginia and Rochester to Frankfurt? Public Choice as Critical Theory." *British Journal of Political Science* 22: 397–417.

Dryzek, J. 2002. "A Pox on Perestroika, A Hex on Hegemony: Toward a Critical Political Science." Paper presented at the APSA annual meeting.

Dryzek, J., and S. Leonard. 1988. "History and Discipline in Political Science." *American Political Science Review* 82: 145–60.

Easton, D. 1971. *The Political System: An Enquiry into the State of Political Science.* Chicago: University of Chicago Press.

Foucault, M. 1970. *The Order of Things: An Archaeology of the Human Sciences.* New York: Vintage.

Foucault, M. 1972. *The Archeology of Knowledge and the Discourse on Language.* New York: Pantheon.

Foucault, M. 1979. *Discipline and Punish: The Birth of the Prison.* New York: Vintage.

Foucault, M. 1980a. *The History of Sexuality,* Vol. 1: *An Introduction.* New York: Vintage.

Foucault, M. 1980b. *Power/Knowledge: Selected Interviews and Other Writings, 1972–1977.* New York: Vintage.

Foucault, M. 1984. "What Is Enlightenment?" *The Foucault Reader,* ed. Paul Rabinow. New York: Pantheon.

Foucault, M. 1991. *The Foucault Effect: Studies in Governmentality,* ed. G. Burchell, C. Gordon, and P. Miller. Chicago: University of Chicago Press.

Fuller, S. 1993. "Disciplinary Boundaries and the Rhetoric of the Social Sciences." In *Knowledges: Historical and Critical Studies in Disciplinarity,* ed. E. Messer-Davidow, D. R. Shumway, and D. J. Sylvan. Charlottesville: University Press of Virginia.

Goodin, R. and H. Klingemann. 1996. *A New Handbook of Political Science.* Oxford: Oxford University Press.

Gunnell, J. 1986. *Between Philosophy and Politics: The Alienation of Political Theory.* Amherst: University of Massachusetts Press.

Husserl, E. 1970. *The Crisis of European Science and Transcendental Phenomenology.* Evanston, IL: Northwestern University Press.

Jacoby, R. 1994. *Dogmatic Wisdom.* New York: Free Press.

King, G. 1998. *Unifying Political Methodology: The Likelihood Theory of Statistical Inference.* Ann Arbor: University of Michigan Press.

King, G., R. O. Keohane, and S. Verba. 1994. *Designing Social Inquiry: Scientific Inference in Qualitative Research.* Princeton, NJ: Princeton University Press.

Lasswell, H., and A. Kaplan. 1952. *Power and Society: A Framework for Political Inquiry.* London: Lowe and Brydone.

Latour, B. 1987. *Science in Action.* Cambridge, MA: Harvard University Press.

Latour, B. 1988. *The Pasteurization of France.* Cambridge, MA: Harvard University Press.

Latour, B. 1993. *We Have Never Been Modern.* London: Harvester Wheatsleaf.

Lenoir, T. 1993. "The Discipline of Nature and the Nature of Disciplines." In *Knowledges: Historical and Critical Studies in Disciplinarity,* ed. E. Messer-Davidow, D. R. Shumway, and D. J. Sylvan. Charlottesville: University Press of Virginia.

Lowi, T. 1992. "The State of Political Science: How We Become What We Study." *American Political Science Review* 86 (March): 1–7.

Luke, T. W. 1985. "Reason and Rationality in Rational Choice Theory," *Social Research* 52 (Spring): 65–98.

Luke, T. W. 1987. "Methodological Individualism: The Essential Ellipsis of Rational Choice Theory." *Philosophy of the Social Sciences* 17 (September): 341–55.

Luke, T. W. 1989. "Political Science and the Discourses of Power: Developing a Genealogy of the Political Culture Concept." *History of Political Thought* 10 (Spring): 125–49.

Luke, T. W. 1997. *Ecocritique: Contesting the Politics of Nature, Economy and Culture.* Minneapolis: University of Minnesota Press.

Luke, T. W. 1999. "The Discipline as Disciplinary Normalization: Networks of Research." *New Political Science* 21 (3): 345–63.

Lyotard, J. F. 1984. *The Postmodern Condition: A Report on Knowledge.* Minneapolis: University of Minnesota Press.

Mearsheimer, J. 2001. "Methodological Parochialism vs. Methodological Pluralism." Paper presented at the APS annual meeting. See Perestroika_Glasnost_Warmhome@hotmail.com.

Messer-Davidow, E., D. R. Shumway, and D. J. Sylvan. 1993. "Introduction: Disciplinary Ways of Knowing." In *Knowledges: Historical and Critical Studies in Disciplinarity,* ed. Messer-Davidow, Shumway, and Sylvan. Charlottesville: University Press of Virginia.

Mr. Pravda. 2002. "Some Thoughts on Perestroika and Political Science." See Perestroika_Glasnost_Warmhome@hotmail.com.

Poovey, M. 1998. *A History of the Modern Fact: Problems of Knowledge in the Sciences of Wealth and Society.* Chicago: University of Chicago Press.

Porter, T. 1996. *Trust in Numbers.* Princeton, NJ: Princeton University Press.

Ricci, D. 1984. *The Tragedy of Political Science: Politics, Scholarship, and Democracy.* New Haven, CT: Yale University Press.

Shepsle, K., and M. Bonchek. 1997. *Analyzing Politics.* New York: Norton.

CHAPTER 35

After Methodology

Toward a Profession of Political Science

Maurice J. Meilleur

I wish to highlight in this chapter a problem with the role of methodology in the debates the Perestroika movement has renewed over social inquiry and the nature of political science. My point of departure is a claim that the philosopher Peter Manicas made in his Romanell Lecture to the American Philosophical Association's Pacific Division in 1992 about the conflict between naturalism and anti-naturalism.

Naturalism, to use the definition Manicas borrowed from Ralph Barton Perry and Marvin Faber, is "the generalization of the sciences"—the idea that we can study the social and cultural world with the same methods we use to study the natural world (1992, 59). A naturalist argues that the natural sciences (especially physics) are the paradigmatic sciences; for social inquiry to be scientific, it should emulate them. Anti-naturalists, by contrast, argue that there are too many "epistemological and ontological differences" between the physical and the social worlds for such emulation to work (60). Something about human society and culture escapes the methods of physical science; they may be appropriate for studying rocks and trees and stars, but they are not appropriate for studying humans. This disagreement has taken the form of debates between positivists and neo-positivists against philosophers of hermeneutics, poststructuralism, and cultural studies, among others, over the proper way to study human culture and society.

Manicas claimed that the irony of these debates was that naturalists have a fairly dim idea of how the natural sciences actually work. They idealize a view of science that lost any influence it might have had among natural scientists long ago. Anti-naturalists, however, do exactly the same thing. "Anti-naturalisms thrive," Manicas argued, "because, beginning with the debates of the last decades of the nineteenth century, both sides of the argument have shared in assumptions about both nature and culture and about what natural science is. They still do" (1992, 61). Philosophers of both persuasions become fixated on the methodological conditions of their profession instead of on more interesting and concrete questions about the world. Because their image of science is flawed, the question of whether to apply it to society is poorly framed from the start; the more they pursue it, the more they isolate themselves both from the practices of science and from the problems that properly drive inquiry in the first place.

Manicas's claim is directly relevant to the contemporary debate in political science over the possibility and nature of a science of politics. Thanks to the work of intellectual historians and political scientists, there is little doubt either about the influence of what Richard Bernstein (1976) calls the "positivist temper" in the mainstream academic study of politics or about the connections between this temper and a number of political and intellectual consequences, among them a persistent disengagement of the discipline from political life. But critics of the positivist temper, I will argue, have in the past helped to reinforce that temper in ways that disengaged their own work from politics. The mainstream's methodological and political problems to one side, critics have argued that there is no difference between a positivist-tempered political science and wholesale philosophical positivism, that any "science" of politics must depend on a strict distinction between facts and values, that a true political science requires researchers to reduce politics to "one big principle," and thus either that a positive social science makes no sense or that it would be monstrous (see Bernstein 1976, xiv). Thus, rather than challenging the influence of positivism on models of political science, these critics simply have rejected the idea of a science of politics altogether, and with it the real political questions the mainstream tried to address. Worse yet, debates between these factions over the methodology of inquiry tend quickly to become debates over professional identity—that is, over who the "real" students of politics are.

Against these positions I want to sketch the outlines of a pragmatic instrumentalist account of social inquiry, informed largely by the work of John Dewey, that offers a way of rethinking the place of methodology in reforming political inquiry. My argument will amplify calls of Charles Lindblom, Rogers Smith, and Ian Shapiro for a problem-driven political science by connecting their positions (a) to an account of the disadvantages of defining political science in terms of its commitment to a set of methods, and (b) to Dewey's understanding of reconstructive social inquiry and the public role of the scholar, whom he sees as one who contributes to the conditions under which democratic knowledge can emerge.

It is necessary first to clarify what this positivist temper is that so dominates the mainstream academic study of politics in the United States before moving to a discussion of the unfruitful debates that surrounded it. (By "mainstream" I mean those political scientists "who conceive of their discipline as one that differs in degree and not in kind from the well-established natural sciences, and who are convinced that the greatest success is to be found in emulating, modifying, and adapting techniques that have proven successful in our scientific understanding of nature" [Bernstein 1976, xv].)

Timothy Kaufman-Osborn has usefully defined positivism as the theory of science that "(1) advances a nomological conception of knowledge, one that identifies the end of inquiry with the construction of causal explanations relating the occurrence of specific events through reference to universal laws that predict an invariant relationship between certain antecedent conditions and their necessary consequences; (2) claims that a presupposition of such knowledge is the generation of a neutral language whose content stands in some isomorphic relationship to the antecedently existent objects it describes;[1] and (3) affirms the ideal of value-free knowledge" (1991, 229).[2]

Mainstream political scientists differ over the essential features of a positive science and over exactly how one can apply them to the study of human behavior (consider, for example, the differences between empirical-quantitative and formal-rational choice approaches to political inquiry). But, as Bernstein writes, there is a "remarkable unanimity" among mainstream social scientists over "the epistemological and logical features of empirical theory" (1976, xv–xvi) that corresponds to the elements of Kaufman-Osborn's definition: causal explanation, neutral observation and description, and value-free inquiry.

One must distinguish positivism in political science from a more thoroughgoing philosophical positivism, but it is hard to miss how positivism has influenced the development of a self-consciously scientific study of politics—how mainstream political scientists, like philosophical positivists, tend to "[recognize] only two models for legitimate knowledge: the empirical or natural sciences, and the formal disciplines such as logic and mathematics." From their point of view, historical and philosophical approaches tend "to confuse fact and value, descriptive and prescriptive judgments," and thus "do not lend themselves to systematic, rigorous formulation by which they can be empirically tested." This distinction—marked historically either by a "break" between pre- and post–scientific revolution thought or by a more continuous evolution from the "latent promise" of earlier studies to their consummation in contemporary social science—marks the positivist temper's naturalistic interpretation of science, driven as it is by the "conviction that the aim of the social sciences is the same as that of the natural sciences" (Bernstein 1976, 43).

Further, there is an inherent tendency in the mainstream positivist temper toward some form of social engineering (however attenuated). "The ideal has long been cherished," Bernstein writes, "that the advancement [of social and political science] must bring progress toward ideals and social goals accepted by reasonable human beings"; as difficult as finding and using this knowledge may be, "this goal—this regulative ideal—is still advanced by social scientists" (1976, 52). Here the goal and the test of positivistic inquiry converge—the proof of sound inquiry, even if impractical or politically unfeasible or distasteful—is control.[3]

How the study of democracy fared in political science shows the consequences of this positivist temper as it developed in the twentieth century. During the first part of that century many American political scientists became familiar with European research in psychology—like that of LeBon and Freud—and with how social scientists such as Graham Wallas were applying its findings to political questions (see Wallas 1921). They witnessed the propagandizing, hysteria, and general public irrationality that accompanied wartime mobilization during the First World War. They also knew about new experimental and quantitative techniques for studying human intelligence and the pessimistic findings that studies based on them (such as the army IQ tests conducted by Robert Yerkes and Lewis Terman) were generating. Finally, incidents such as the Scopes "monkey" trial in 1922 were enough to convince many of them that most people's emotions and prejudices drive their behavior.

As Edward Purcell has shown, from the 1920s on, political scientists cited these developments to explain why Progressive reforms depending on the informed participation of citizens had largely failed. They concluded that any theory of democracy based on what Walter Lippmann called the unrealistic idea of the "sovereign and omnicompetent citizen" could only perpetuate bad government and obstruct real democratic reform (Lippmann 1925, 21). Democratic theorists instead began to develop democratic theory in "realist" and descriptive directions, trying to specify the institutions and mechanisms by which political leaders could conduct political affairs for the common good and handle public input without succumbing to popular ignorance and irrationality. To build a more democratic society while disregarding citizens' limited intellectual, emotional, and ethical capacities was wishful thinking and poor science.

This approach to democratic theory drew severe criticism in the late 1920s and the early 1930s from critics inside and outside political science who felt such a narrow focus on institutions and behavior could never defend the values of democracy against the threats that totalitarian regimes in Europe and Asia, and extremist political movements in the United States, were beginning to pose. Defenders did their best to explain that positivist-tempered, value-free inquiry was really the best protection against these threats and that their critics, coming as many did from religious or metaphysically committed positions the scientists described as "absolutist," were themselves the real threat to democratic progress (Purcell 1973, Chapters 7–8, 10).

The debate changed after the Allied victory in World War II. Scientific democratic theorists stopped trying to explain how the United States might achieve democracy and began to ask how democracy in the United States had succeeded against the odds. Though they still believed democratic theory had to be causally explanatory, neutrally descriptive, and value-free, a functioning American democracy became their premise instead of their goal. If American democracy was working, and if intelligent and skillful participation was beyond most citizens' abilities, American democracy must come from our configuration of political mechanisms and practices. One could recognize a healthy democracy by these mechanisms—regular competitive and orderly elections, representative government, the rule of law, organized interest groups, and so on. In the 1950s and the 1960s the theory of pluralism, a proceduralist and institutional view of democratic theory, was based on these arguments.[4]

Pluralism did not depend on citizens' views or abilities at all, beyond a few core agreements over procedure. More extreme examples of this kind of theory

—what Peter Bachrach called theories of "democratic elitism," such as Joseph Schumpeter's account of competing elites in *Capitalism, Socialism, and Democracy* (1942)—suggested a "democracy without citizens."[5] Even much less overtly elitist theorists began to define democratic legitimacy as stability and the absence of social conflict. In their hands democratic theory became a body of apologism for a government presumed already to be democratic.[6]

Purcell (1973) argued that by building the American political status quo into their models of democracy, scientific democratic theorists simply recast their normative commitments as empirical axioms. This was how they finally solved the problem of both claiming allegiance to democracy and pursuing and empirical science of democratic politics. That the civil rights movement of the 1950s and the free speech and anti-war movements of the 1960s caught mainstream political science flat-footed, however—as members of the Caucus for a New Political Science argued—suggests that this solution was also making their work less empirically engaged. Also, assuming the general incompetence of the individual citizen as a background condition for the scientific study of democracy allowed political scientists to neglect inquiry into the causes of this incompetence.[7] They focused instead on how institutions and the dynamics of public opinion allowed the American polity as a whole to overcome the shortcomings of American citizens.

Strong commitments to pluralism did not survive internal criticism; both conservative critics such as Samuel Huntington and more liberal critics such as Walter Dean Burnham and Theodore Lowi—not to mention some of the founders of the approach, such as Robert Dahl and Charles Lindblom—found too many holes in the theory, and too many pathologies in the American political process it was supposed to underwrite, for it to survive.[8] Although it does live on in attenuated forms in the political parties, interest groups, and political socialization literature, nothing really arose to take its place as a defining form of positivist-tempered democratic theory. In mainstream political science, democratic theory as such now resides in the introductory and concluding paragraphs of journal articles and book chapters.

Critics of this mainstream can point to the history of scientific democratic theory to show that the positivist temper in political science has disengaged researchers from the critical study of American politics. But many of these critics, such as Manicas's anti-naturalists, demonstrate a methodological dualism that obscures the model of science they share with the mainstream. They do not engage the mainstream model at the level of practice to offer an alternative working account of scientific inquiry. Instead they reject its application to politics; wanting no part of science, they argue for their own approaches to inquiry, similar to the ones Manicas associated with anti-naturalists, and that John Gunnell associated with a "dispersed" political theory: hermeneutics, phenomenology, various brands of post-structuralism, and cultural studies (Manicas 1992, 67–68; Gunnell 1993). Because these critics believe the mainstream model of science is valid on its own terms, and because they do not engage the practice of scientific inquiry, the interminable and fruitless debate between naturalism and anti-naturalism in philosophy appears in political science as the interminable and fruitless debate over whether it is possible to study politics scientifically.

Regarding this problem, too, democratic political theory is a good illustration of the drawbacks to this debate. On Gunnell's reading, by the beginning of the 1950s political theorists interested in normative and prescriptive theory felt distinctly marginalized in political science in the face of positivism and pluralism.[9] But where political scientists generally tended, as Seidelman and Harpham argue, to think of political crises as crises in the study of politics, and where mainstream political scientists thought of political crises as crises of a science of politics, those theorists opposed to any (positivist-tempered) science of politics thought of political crises as crises of the decline of political thought. Many argued in one form or another that the modern age—or, in particular, the rise in the late nineteenth and early twentieth centuries of modern science, technology, and social organization—had eclipsed political thought, and therefore politics, properly understood. Their writings, Gunnell writes, depicted "a world-historical drama in which politics appeared as reflections of the movement of political thought" (1993, 253). Democratic and other theorists in this vein set themselves squarely against behavioralism and positivism, which they thought were the chief embodiments of modernism, and reasserted the case for the history and exegesis of canonical texts. They tied their own work to the tradition they were resuscitating, arguing that political experience and historical change reflected changes in political thinking and that only the recovery of political thought could reform and rejuvenate politics.

This, wrote Gunnell, led to "the development of an intellectual, and professional, patrimony and identity for academic political theory that lifted it out of the past and present of political science" (1993, 255). By the 1960s there was a significant gap between the "traditional" and the "scientific" understandings of theory, or between what we might call the "normative" and the "empirical" or "positive" understandings of theory (261).[10] This gap grew over the 1960s as the distance between what behavioral political scientists were studying (party systems, voting, public opinion dynamics) and what was happening in American politics (the civil rights movement; the Vietnam War; student activism around issues of class, race, and gender; and so forth) finally brought political science into crisis. In 1967–68 a series of internal empirical, methodological, and normative criticisms of pluralism combined with protests against the structure of professional governance (i.e., the APSA) to produce an organized reform movement called the Caucus for a New Political Science.

The professional and methodological challenges that the Caucus posed produced plenty of heated debate and a good deal of resistance among supporters of the scientific hegemony, but only a few years later the rancor had subsided significantly (thanks largely, writes Gunnell, to the efforts of diplomats such as Sheldon Wolin and David Easton, and of some who eased off their initial hard-line positions, such as Karl Deutsch). The anti-mainstream theorists had by protesting guaranteed themselves an institutional and professional base in political science, and now no longer had directly to confront a positivist temper as a check on their work. Enough thinkers on both sides accepted the division between traditional or normative-historical theory and empirical or formal theory that a professional pluralism of a sort could emerge. Once this split was institutionalized, practitioners of a science of politics lost what Gunnell called a "distinct reflective dimension," while "the conversations of political theory floated free of their origins, and of what had been, however attenuated, their practical roots" (1993, 269). Disagreements over science lasted into the 1970s because the institutional armistice had emerged before everyone on both sides was ready to disarm, and when the factions met directly, little of the divisiveness of the earlier open conflicts had dissipated. But as the groups continued to grow apart, this debate faded.

How the anti-science political theorists translated the debate over social science in their own ranks is instructive. Divisions between different strands of political theory (such as those attracted to the work of Leo Strauss and Quentin Skinner or the various adherents of liberalism, libertarianism, or communitarianism) drew the theorists' attention further inward. Their criticisms of the mainstream, positivist-tempered science were "distinctly external," writes Gunnell, "less an internal critique of the logical and epistemological assumptions of behavioral science, which it also tended to equate with the practices of natural science, than an attack on the very idea of a science of politics and on a very broad range of positivism" (1993, 269). Their positions rested on the philosophical traditions of inquiry to which theorists had committed themselves—increasingly influenced by their institutional neighbors in philosophy and cultural studies—rather than on the ways that political and other social scientists were actually practicing (or aspiring to practice) science. Thus the anti-science faction had escaped the hegemonic control of positivism only to reinforce it simply by contrasting it with the new practices and disciplines outside the profession to which they had attached themselves.

This institutional split also freed the critics from any obligation to political experience and the specific problems of political life. As much as the Caucus had fought for reform in the name of engagement, by the 1970s critics of the mainstream devoted themselves to what Gunnell calls "a world of specialized scholarly projects" (1993, 271). Even the few attempts in theory to form a rigorous post-positivist discussion of inquiry and engagement, and to bridge the gap both between theory and practice and between the university and the world of politics, ultimately engaged not positivist scientific practices themselves, but rather the academic philosophical conversations surrounding those practices.

It is easy to see why the works of (to mention Gunnell's examples) John Rawls, Robert Nozick, Michael Walzer (to a degree), critical theorists and the later Frankfurt School, and Jürgen Habermas, regardless of their original contexts, in the hands of political democratic theorists were perhaps "about" politics but had little practical context.[11] The issues in these and other works of democratic theory upon which the anti-mainstream faction had chosen to focus—like theorists' various interpretations of liberalism, individualism, or relativism—"were detached from their practical roots and transformed into philosophical, that is, epistemological problems" (Gunnell 1993, 273). Only rarely did theorists address what a "critical academically based political theory" would look like. Ironically, from Gunnell's point of view, as unfeasible as a positivist-tempered model of science was as a way of connecting the academy to the world of politics, and as disengaged as it was from political experience, the mainstream was "in many respects more proximate to political life than the emerging conversations in political theory"—closer to politics, that is, than the faction that had broken away from it in the name of precisely that sort of engagement (273-74).

In the end, the critics, having tried to recapture democratic theory from the scientists, failed to connect the world of their own inquiry to the world of politics. Like their scientific counterparts, they could not bring themselves to critically appraise their own institutions, nor could they step into political life as citizen-participants, as such a project ultimately would require them to do. Thus Gunnell ends his account: "By the end of the 1980s, the principal conversations in political theory ceased to speak about actual politics, let alone to it. . . . Even when an aspect of political theory had a distinct practical-issue counterpart and constituency, it was difficult to resist the attachment to the tokens of academic authority and the siren of esotericism and to speak in a manner that was not opaque to all outside the academy or even those standing outside the specialized language of subdisciplines" (1996, 277).

This history suggests that unreflectively and uncritically to reject a positivist-tempered science of politics grounds professional identity in a commitment to methodology no less firm than the mainstream's. This turns deliberation between the factions over the proper choice of methods for investigating specific problems into fights over professional allegiance and disciplinary boundaries while failing also to challenge the influence of the positivist temper by offering a competing account of inquiry.

Debates over methods, inside the factions, tend to be either too self-affirming or too abstract to hold any critical edge; as they move past those boundaries and become fights over professional identity, they distract practitioners from engaging the larger problems of politics. Because both factions apparently assume without much further argument that academic political science is uniquely suited to produce the expert knowledge necessary for political practice and reform, the factions—especially the reformers—frequently invoke in their debates larger questions of political practice that their own approaches preclude their addressing. Yet, having institutionalized their divisions, their debates now validate each other's existence, so the absence of political engagement is no longer a pressing issue. Not only is it hard to get political scientists from either faction to see themselves as citizens in the same sense as non-academics; it is even harder for them to see why the disparity matters.

Given these considerations, two general issues should properly ground any conversation about the prospects for reform in political science. First, neither faction can yet get past the discussion of foundations in inquiry to address upon what exactly the knowledge they seek to generate or contribute to political life would be based. Second, both factions lack a critical account of the role of the public scholar. As much as both sides have sought and proclaimed the ideals of relevance and engagement, neither has generated an account of how to connect the academy to politics or of how scholars should comport themselves as citizens and contributors in public life.

A Deweyan pragmatic instrumentalist model of science and social inquiry addresses both these issues. Dewey's account of reconstruction and his discussion of public scholarship in a democracy together offer an altogether different way of defining political inquiry, and suggest a more fruitful conversation about reform than what we can expect from the established factions in political science.

Reconstruction   Dewey argued that disequilibrium between our habits, beliefs, and practices, on the one hand, and our environments, on the other, is what drives humans to inquire into the world. We rearrange, sort, update, and purge our habits, beliefs, and practices to maintain or restore equilibrium. Thus inquiry is reconstruction. We judge our reconstruction based on whether we can move past the problem and project new and better goals for acting and judging. "Reconstruction" can also refer to how we systematically reshape specialized areas of inquiry and bodies of knowledge, as Dewey did in *Reconstruction in Philosophy* (1920).

"Reconstruction" also implies that inquiry without intelligent change is incomplete. The world is always in flux, and our habits and beliefs will change as the world changes, even if only slightly. The question for Dewey was never if we (should) inquire, but how. Because we have developed the tools of language and reflective self-consciousness, humans can refine inquiry to permit them intelligently to control their environment, where human action can reasonably make a difference. "Science" is what Dewey called refined inquiry organized around logically self-consistent and coherent systems of generalizations about our experience (1938, Chapter 2).

Dewey's account of logic shows how reconstruction provides a sounder understanding of inquiry, scientific and otherwise, than these unfounded distinctions allow us to develop. One of the more controversial claims Dewey made was that logic is an empirical science. Logical forms are not prior to human experience and reflective consciousness. Nor are they a quality of material reality—they do not lie coiled in rocks and social groups and trees and stars waiting for us to discover them. Logical forms are properties of relationships between parts of the world that accrue to them when we inquire into those relationships (1938, 479–80). We can never finally be certain that we have distilled the proper elements of logic and inquiry from instances of practice; we have to justify our reconstruction of those elements prospectively as we use them. Thus they are both empirical and a product of human thought and experience, and they transcend the categories of "objective" and "subjective" (64–66).

The debate in political science over what scientific inquiry is reveals from Dewey's perspective a persistent misunderstanding about inquiry. The persistent idea that physics is the "true" model of science is a fine example of this confusion. Physicists deal with subject matter they can quantify and with relationships they can express in equations. There is no consciously reflexive relationship between them and their subject matter when they experiment and generalize. They have succeeded so well at transforming their observations into laws and theories, and at explaining and predicting phenomena, that others seeking the authority of science, such as political scientists, have tried to recreate those laws, theories, explanations, and predictions in their own fields. But the surest way to get the principles of inquiry wrong is to confuse those principles with particular practices (1938, 70–72). Science is any regularized form of inquiry leading to self-consistent and mutually coherent systems of generalizations about the ways that parts of the world interact. We can study any subject matter that lends itself to those systems scientifically, no matter how rudimentary or provisional our generalizations will be (Dewey 1903, 116–17; see also Dewey 1958 [1922]). The laws and theories of physics as such do not tell us what science is any more than its subject matter could.

Also, there is no ontological or metaphysical division between facts and values or between objective and subjective ways of knowing the world. These are only provisional categories we use to think about experience critically. Because inquiry engages both empirical and normative questions, the criteria of successful inquiry provide the basis of judgment and evaluation, and both ground and vindicate those criteria in empirical observation. The test of a reconstructed principle is to ask whether one could deny it without contradicting the goals of solving a problem in a way that opens up new avenues of exploration and new ends-in-view (Dewey 1938, 35).

Public Scholarship   Dewey disliked any rigid social division of intellectual labor and thought the idea of a rule of experts particularly odious. Even if we assume the most impersonal and altruistic motives for seeking such power, no study of society could ever reach a complete account of the world, or stand a chance of properly reconstructing the practices and institutions and traditions necessary to solve public problems, if it excluded the experiences and perspectives of the public (1954 [1927], Chapter 6, esp. 205). Not only would doing so omit facts and perspectives without which one could not pursue the most pressing problems of the day; it would also abandon the task of improving the level and conduct of public inquiry. It is from contributing to and participating in public dialogue that researchers discover and identify the problems that should properly drive inquiry in the first place. Social inquiry divorced from the lived experience of citizens thus fails both from a democratic standpoint and on its own terms.

This does not preclude inquiry for its own sake, and it does not mean that researchers should establish the validity of their arguments or conclusions by popular referendum. But scholars' agendas and the criteria by which they justify and vindicate their inquiry properly draw upon and find their ultimate ground in the experience of associated life. In this sense even the most specialized research in a democracy is public.

A discussion of public scholarship abstracted from the problems and resources of particular communities of inquiry risks encouraging a distinction between theory and practice that pragmatic instrumentalism denies. Specifying the conditions under which public scholars can work out their proper roles in a democracy is easier, because those conditions are also conditions under which the knowledge necessary for the emergence of a democratic public can emerge. Because the contribution of public scholars is to help produce that knowledge, it follows that the role of public scholars is to help as best they can to create and maintain the conditions under which that knowledge can emerge. Those conditions are as follows.[12]

1. Citizens' inadequate sense of themselves as a public thrives on misunderstandings, errors, half-truths, and superstitions. The first job of public scholars is to inquire into what Dewey called the "problems of men" rigorously and thoroughly, and to spread sound information as widely as possible to prevent actors from manipulating other citizens by misinforming and deceiving them.

    Very specialized inquiry might be too arcane or complex to expect a direct translation; also, scholars may need professional journals and conferences to refine their methods of inquiry or test preliminary findings. But ultimately the goal of inquiry is to inform and improve public discourse. We should address questions that will advance the flexibility and scope of human activity and purposes, and someone must connect even the most esoteric inquiry to these questions.

2. We cannot trust the public to handle the best social inquiry if citizens have no idea that inquiry is even necessary. Already by Dewey's time, political and economic actors had fostered a pervasive culture of secrecy and reticence. It is the task of scholars in a democracy to oppose this culture by serving the values of truthtelling and openness, in their own work and in their assessment of public issues, events, and decisions.

3. In their critical roles, scholars must appeal to terms and principles of argument and evidence that permit a constructive conversation about alternatives. Their inquiry must link facts, analysis, and

judgment to specific mechanisms that bring them to bear on a situation. This does not mean scholars should never criticize the status quo without a fully thought-out alternative in hand. But all criticism must point to the means by which it could make a difference.

4. It is important to extend as far as possible the bounds of the public and our sense of the consequences of our individual and common actions; this creates a background against which pursuing the first three conditions makes more democratic sense. Thus scholars should work to criticize and restrain any social, economic, or political movements to manipulate public bias and prejudice against actual or potential parts of the public, and to eradicate that bias and prejudice as far as possible in the first place. They must especially be on guard against reinforcing or extending bias and prejudice themselves, either by incorporating them into their work or by assisting others who do so. In this capacity, public scholarship serves the values of reflective social self-criticism and humility.

5. The formal and informal institutions of public life must encourage intelligent inquiry and action. Thus public scholars must promote the attitudes, tools, and practices that permit citizens to bring their own experience and knowledge to bear on public problems as far as they can. They must resist publicly and persistently uncritical or unreflective conservatism and unhealthy social, economic, political, and intellectual divisions of labor. They must also resist uncritical or unreflective projects of reform or revolution. Scholars should not presume any authority other than what they can defend based on the reconstructed standards of inquiry. To contribute intellectually to public discourse requires them voluntarily and openly to submit to the standards they invoke and defend in the course of their work, subject to public democratic control.[13]

A Deweyan pragmatic approach to political inquiry would transform political science from a discipline, based on a set of methods, into a profession, based on a set of problems. Two of the clearest statements of the advantages for political science of such an approach appeared in a pair of articles Charles Lindblom and Rogers Smith wrote for *Dædalus* in 1997.

Lindblom argued that behavioralism, by "drawing practitioners' attention to a careful choice of method of inquiry—that is, of *how* to study—[may] have drawn their attention away from a careful choice of *what* to study" (1997, 231; emphasis in original). Further, political science "has not much practiced the scientific method as conventionally described and cannot do so; yet it venerates conventional scientific method, and hence suffers from continuing self-reproach and consequent disorientation"; it is "snared, crippled to a degree, and unclear about appropriate aspirations because it does not resolve the contradictions between long-standing ideas about method on the one hand and feasible products [of research] on the other" (233–34).

Surveying discussions of the accomplishments of political and social scientists (such as Deutsch et al. 1971, Bell 1982, and Almond 1990), Lindblom (1997) found no mention of "discoveries" or "findings."[14] What political scientists have been doing is collecting and cataloging political facts; generating checklists of questions to ask about the political world; assessing the consequences of political events and decisions; designing new party, electoral, and administrative systems; and correcting mistaken ideas about politics circulating among citizens and leaders (and political scientists). And of course American political scientists have been discussing methodology. These are not meaningless or useless activities. Still, "nothing that political science ever achieved," Lindblom wrote, "was *unarguably* or *demonstrably* necessary to any major social venture. That is to say, whatever humankind achieved in the period, we cannot find an unmistakable dependence of that achievement on any contribution from political science" (1997, 241; Lindblom's emphases). His point is not that political science is worthless; rather, he concludes that any argument for its worth must rest on something other than developing policy expertise from an unworkable model of science.

This history suggested to Lindblom that political science was better thought of not as a "field of conventional scientific inquiry," but as a set of ongoing debates. And this might not be such a bad thing; "political science as a debate," he wrote, "might be political science at its best" (1997, 242–44). Practitioners suffer from a series of persistent difficulties: internal standards for research prospectuses, Lindblom argues, remain quite vague; there are no obvious logical directions to research connecting one project to the next; the patterns of flexibility and rigidity at educational and research institutions and in political contexts vary too much to permit those programs to form; and political scientists have not reflected much on the "comfortable axioms" about democratic politics they have nurtured, on their naïveté about the political world, on the people whom their work most directly benefits, or on the intellectual "impairments" they share with other scholars and with lay citizens. Relaxing the pressure on political science to be a policy science would allow political scientists to address some of these shortcomings while possibly making virtues of their institutional necessities.

Rogers Smith (1997) argues that American political science has been shaped by "two often conflicting desires: to serve American democracy and to be a true 'science'" (253).[15] He describes a cycle in which political scientists in successive generations attacked older practices and approaches they felt were insufficiently scientific and too naïve about the promise of democracy. Trying to make their discipline more scientific, they were frustrated by their inability to turn their work to the support of democracy. They spent their later years focusing more on democratic politics, but a new group of political scientists judged their work to be outdated and naïve, and the cycle began anew. Smith also notes that successive generations were increasingly comfortable with a political science that existed for its own sake, and correspondingly less hostile toward their institutions even during their later, more critical years.

The Caucus for a New Political Science was a slight variation on this pattern; the younger scholars and older dissenters of which it was comprised criticized positivist and behavioral models of science for being, as Smith puts it, "dangerously complacent, ethnocentric, and (hence) undemocratic." The Caucus and its allies had opened back up some institutional space in academic political science for what was then being called "political philosophy" and had provoked some changes in professional governance and journal editorial policies, but having done so they disengaged themselves from the pro-science faction rather than continuing with an alternative vision of social-scientific political inquiry. Thus, much as Gunnell argued, Smith sees the 1970s as a period in which normative political theory became more insular and abstract, while "much of the rest of political science . . . seemed quiescent, still working through the critical assaults of the late 1960s and looking for new directions" (1997, 262–63). None of the approaches either faction developed in this period gave American political science a way out of its science/democracy impasse or brought the factions back together.[16]

This does not surprise Smith, because he believes that political science will never discover any "grand theory or special methods that can generate a unique 'science of politics'" (1997, 253). The problem is not political scientists' motives: "Most political scientists have genuinely believed it right, good, and exciting to further true knowledge about politics by the best methods available to us, an enterprise it is natural to call a 'science of politics.' And most have also genuinely wished to aid American democracy, however deep their reservations might run about its current form." Political science is valuable because the problems of "government institutions, political movements and ideology, [and] human power relationships" are too important "to deal with piecemeal, incidentally, and with only partial mastery of relevant knowledge," as other disciplines tend to do (275). But any publicly useful results of such a study of politics will never come from a "deductive general theory of politics like neo-classical economics."

Instead, Smith claims, the "distinctive mission" of political science "must be cast in terms of its subject matter"; it should "explore in the most rigorous ways all topics that are arguably politically fundamental, with special attention to those that are predictably neglected, for both intellectual and political reasons, by governmental and private-sector analysts, politicians, and the media. That . . . is about as scientific and as serviceable to democracy as we can honestly get" (1997, 253–54). As Lindblom had argued in *Inquiry and Change* (1990), Smith writes that social scientists should pursue "the questions that lay people in society care about but lack the skills to explore." They should pay particular attention to "topics of which lay inquiry and understanding may be impaired in various ways, most of which are political." The agenda must reflect "what people are experiencing as problems in their lives . . . modified by informed identification of topics they would probably perceive as problems if not for specifiable impairing influences, especially systems of unequal power" (275–76).

Smith believes that political science is "the discipline that is and must be most centrally concerned with structures of power that can dominate people's lives and consciousness in ways that are often neither necessary nor desirable. . . . For of all the many people researching political issues . . . we academic political scientists are best equipped institutionally to challenge prevailing wisdom and explore what may prove to be truths about politics that are neglected or unpopular because they go against the grain" (1997, 276).[17] In this way Smith extends Lindblom's suggestion that political science think of itself as a set of debates; he claims political scientists are at their best "when we are intellectual gadflies, rigorously questioning and testing accepted political truths, exploring ignored possibilities, courting unpopularity by offering suggestions that markets are not likely to reward and that people in power are not likely to approve. . . . Self-consciously critical research and teaching, along with preserving and extending existing knowledge about politics, should always be the heart of our academic work" (278).[18]

Theodore Lowi, one of the leaders of the Caucus for a New Political Science, has dryly observed that by the late 1960s that movement already had been "converted into the Caucus for a New Political Science Association" (quoted in Seidelman and Harpham 1985, 199). I am concerned, as should be anyone committed to rethinking academic political inquiry, that a similar fate awaits the Perestroika movement unless committed reformers can shift the question of methodology to the level of practice in a way suggested by Dewey's understanding of reconstruction and public scholarship.

Continued political marginality and hyperprofessionalism are not the only threats about which reformers should be worried. The understandable frustration that accompanies professional marginality, combined with the perception that one is "really" engaged in larger compelling political struggles, might drive some to support institutional fixes precisely as anti-democratic as the practices that to that point had shut critics out. Even short of this outcome, if reform finally means only making room in departments and journals both for those who think that the now-dominant model of political science is possible and desirable *and* for those who think that it is impossible or undesirable, we will still be mired in the same professional morass, and we will have moved not a millimeter closer to a more "democratic" political science in any but the most superficial or narrowly institutional sense of the word.[19]

Ultimately, the point of reform must be not to make the practice of political science better—and the debates over the possibility of a science of politics, as Manicas's example suggests, are unlikely to do this anyway—but to contribute to the practices of democratic politics. To this end, Dewey's pragmatic instrumentalist approach to inquiry suggests that political science must cease trying to be a discipline defined by its methodological commitments. It must move beyond methodology, beyond what Shapiro (in this volume) calls method- and theory-driven forms of inquiry, toward a profession defined by its subject matter—the problems of political life.

Notes

1. Practically everyone who does social inquiry and plans to share his or her findings with others is a realist of one form or another. But, as Dorothy Ross argues, American social scientists at the turn of the twentieth century had a unique justification for their realism: their continued commitment to American exceptionalism. The revolutionary upheavals of modern science (especially the impact of Darwinism) and their realization in technological innovation, industrial capitalism, large-scale demographic changes (immigration and urbanization), and radical political movements challenged many Americans' beliefs in a stable world in which America was above the flaws and misunderstandings of other older nations. Social scientists could discover regular laws of society (including politics) that defined a process of regular development and change. Knowing these laws would allow one to see past surface impressions and individual experience to bring institutions, behavior, interests, and skills into harmony. The American exceptionalist ideal became something that unfolded in history as political institutions and practices evolved away from ideological or interest-based struggles for power.

2. Important institutional and political constraints helped reinforce this assumption, including the political affinities of most political scientists, the demands of university administrations, the requirements of potential sources of funds, and the political climate surrounding and infusing academia. But one overlooked source of this understanding of objectivity is a deeply-seeded social meliorism, the roots of which extend back to the first days of the American colonies. This was, among other things, a belief, based on a providential understanding of history and human action, in the motive power and moral significance of unadorned facts. From this arose among many Americans—clergy, newspaper writers and book authors, and ultimately scholars—the belief that the facts speak for themselves with compelling moral force. For more on this see Hall (1989) and Nord (1990).

3. I have drawn these accounts from Crick (1959), Ricci (1984), Seidelman and Harpham (1985), Gunnell (1986, 1993), Manicas (1987, 1998), Ross (1991), Smith (1994), and Ball (1995).

4. Or, rather, on its rebirth: David Truman's *The Governmental Process* (1951) joined Truman's own analysis to the work Arthur Bentley had done decades earlier in *The Process of Government* (1908).

5. Seidelman and Harpham (1985) used this phrase to label Harold Lasswell's "politics of prevention." See Lasswell 1960 [1930], Chapter 10. For a more recent example of elitism, see also W. Russell Neuman's discussion of the possibilities of mass democracy in *The Paradox of Mass Politics* (1986).

6. See especially Purcell (1973), Chapters 11 and 13. Pluralist democratic theory dovetailed with the "minimalist" view of public opinion emerging from research by scholars at Columbia (Lazarsfeld, Berelson, and Gaudet 1948 [1940]; Berelson, Lazarsfeld, and McPhee 1954) and later at the University of Michigan (Campbell et al. 1960; Converse 1963, 1964).

7. Exceptions to this pattern—like V. O. Key's *Public Opinion and American Democracy* (1961) and Robert Lane's *Political Ideology: Why the Common Man Believes What He Does* (1962)—while critical of the approaches of many behavioralists to the low levels of political knowledge and competence of citizens, tended to blame these problems on the misunderstanding, misbehavior, or misguidance of elites.

8. See Huntington (1975), Burnham (1970), Lowi (1979), Lindblom (1990), and Dahl (1977, 1991).

9. I bracket here Gunnell's larger and more tendentious argument that the "Weimar conversation" German émigrés brought into American political science scholarship is largely to blame for the shape of the division, if not for the division itself, between empirical and normative or historical political theory.

10. Gunnell aptly cites two volumes that appeared in 1962 that show the depth of this division: *Essays on the Behavioral Study of Politics,* edited by Austin Ranney, in which Evron Kirkpatrick claimed that the empiricists had won the "war" for a science of politics against the historical and traditional understandings of theory, and *Essays on the Scientific Study of Politics,* edited by Herbert Storing, in which the Straussians savaged the subject in their volume's title, and in which Strauss himself accused the scientists of being atheists and modern-day Neros. See Kirkpatrick (1962), Storing (1962), and Gunnell (1993), 257–59.

11. Gunnell dismisses Rawls and Nozick for being disconnected from any concern with real political experience—they are professional philosophers, he says, not engaged social critics. He does grant that Walzer, Habermas, and the critical theorists may be better grounded (at least, in the case of the Germans, in their home country). The point of Gunnell's discussion, however, is how these thinkers all fared in the hands of American theorists who did not feel obligated to connect their own thought and writing to what Gunnell calls the "concrete" conditions and problems of politics.

12. I have taken these conditions from Dewey's discussion (1954 [1927]) in Chapter 5, especially pp. 166–84.

13. James Bohman (1999) has done an excellent job of describing what sorts of mechanisms could ensure that publics would hold intellectuals to these standards.

14. A survey of the first two *State of the Discipline* volumes, edited by Finifter (1983, 1993) and the four *Political Science: Looking to the Future* volumes edited by Crotty (1991), one might argue, bears out Lindblom's observation.

15. David Ricci has also made this argument, in *The Tragedy of Political Science* (1984).

16. Smith (1997) mentions one possible exception to this pattern—the rise of historical institutionalism and "middle-level" theory—but he claims this is at best speculation and explicitly refuses to defend any specific claims about its potential (270–73).

17. Smith (1997) recognizes there are plenty of potential barriers to this critical role for academic political science, including institutional ones of the sort that have until now encouraged political scientists to pursue positivist models of science in the first place, and political ones as well: because political science is so well suited to this sort of inquiry, "it is therefore also the discipline whose agenda is most likely to be shaped and distorted by the systems of belief and power that favor the status quo (even as the status quo evolves)." He continues: "The profession's aspirations to be a science and to serve democracy are themselves evidence of those facts, even if I think those hopes defensible, for they clearly reflect dominant values in America. Hence political scientists should be concerned, more so than other scholars, to define an intellectual agenda that does not simply maintain and extend the political understandings favored by the powerful" (276).

18. Both Lindblom (1997) and Smith (1997) raise the possibility that political scientists might in their work raise doubts about one or more aspects of democratic politics. Lindblom writes: "The case against democracy is not without merit, and the argument needs to be kept open indefinitely. It is therefore not the function of political science to promote or defend democracy, though it may be your function or mine to do so, just as it may be your function or mine, in a competition of ideas, to attack it" (248). Smith argues that the truths political scientists help citizens uncover may "undermine faith in democracy," but that citizens in a democracy need to know about them. Without dwelling too long on this point, however, note that the problem-driven political science both authors describe requires the institutions of a critical democratic public sphere. The point of both arguments seems to be to encourage in the profession a John Stuart Milllike skepticism regarding received truths, but I invite the reader to investigate .

19. See John Dryzek (this volume) for more on the potential problems of disciplinary pluralism.

References

Almond, Gabriel. 1990. *A Discipline Divided.* Newbury Park, CA: Sage Publications.

Ball, Terrence. 1995. "An Ambivalent Alliance: Political Science and American Democracy." In *Political Science in History: Research Programs and Political Traditions,* ed. James Farr, John S. Dryzek, and Stephen T. Leonard. New York: Cambridge University Press.

Bell, Daniel. 1982. *The Social Sciences since the Second World War.* New Brunswick, NJ: Transaction Books.

Bentley, Arthur F. 1908. *The Process of Government: A Study of Social Pressures.* Bloomington, IN: Principia Press.

Berelson, Bernard, Paul F. Lazarsfeld, and William N. McPhee. 1954. *Voting: A Study of Opinion Formation in a Presidential Campaign.* Chicago: University of Chicago Press.

Bernstein, Richard J. 1976. *The Restructuring of Social and Political Theory.* New York: Harcourt Brace Jovanovich.

Bohman, James F. 1999. "Democracy as Inquiry, Inquiry as Democratic: Pragmatism, Social Science, and the Cognitive Division of Labor." *American Journal of Political Science* 43 (2): 590–607.

Burnham, Walter Dean. 1970. *Critical Elections and the Mainsprings of American Politics.* New York: W. W. Norton.

Campbell, Angus, Philip E. Converse, Warren E. Miller, and Donald E. Stokes. 1960. *The American Voter.* New York: Wiley.

Converse, Philip E. 1963. "Attitudes and Non-Attitudes: Continuation of a Dialogue." In *The Quantitative Analysis of Social Problems,* ed. Edward R. Tufte. Reading, MA: Addison-Wesley Publishing.

———. 1964. "The Nature of Belief Systems in Mass Publics." In *Ideology and Discontent,* ed. David E. Apter. New York: Free Press.

Crick, Bernard R. 1959. *The American Science of Politics: Its Origins and Conditions.* Berkeley: University of California Press.

Crotty, William J., ed. 1991. *Political Science: Looking to the Future.* 4 vols. Evanston, IL: Northwestern University Press.

Crozier, Michel, Samuel P. Huntington, and Joji Watanuki. 1975. *The Crisis of Democracy.* New York: Trilateral Commission / New York University Press.

Dahl, Robert A. 1977. "On Removing Certain Impediments to Democracy in the United States." *Political Science Quarterly* 92 (1): 1–20.

———. 1991. "Reflections on A Preface to Democratic Theory." *Government and Opposition* 17: 292–301.

Deutsch, Karl, S. Platt, and D. Senghaas, 1971. "Conditions Favoring Major Advances in Social Science." *Science* 171 (5 February): 450–59.

Dewey, John. 1903. "Logical Conditions of a Scientific Treatment of Morality." *Decennial Publications of the University of Chicago,* first series 3: 115–39.

———. 1920. *Reconstruction in Philosophy.* New York: H. Holt and Company.

———. 1938. *Logic: The Theory of Inquiry.* New York: H. Holt and Company.

———. 1954 [1927]. *The Public and Its Problems.* Chicago: Swallow Press.

———. 1958 [1922]. *Experience and Nature,* rev. ed. New York: Dover Publications.

Finifter, Ada W., ed. 1983. *Political Science: The State of the Discipline.* Washington, DC: American Political Science Association.

———, ed. 1993. *Political Science: The State of the Discipline II.* Washington, DC: American Political Science Association.

Gunnell, John G. 1982. "Interpretation and the History of Political Theory: Apology and Epistemology." *American Political Science Review* 76 (2): 317–27.

———. 1986. *Between Philosophy and Politics: The Alienation of Political Theory.* Amherst: University of Massachusetts Press.

———. 1993. *The Descent of Political Theory.* Chicago: University of Chicago Press.

Hall, David D. 1989. *Worlds of Wonder, Days of Judgment: Popular Religious Belief in Early New England.* New York: Knopf.

Huntington, Samuel. 1975. "The United States." In *The Crisis of Democracy,* ed. Michel Crozier, Samuel P. Huntington, and Joji Watanuki. New York: Trilateral Commission / New York University Press.

Kaufman-Osborn, Timothy. 1991. *Politics/Sense/Experience: A Pragmatic Inquiry into the Promise of Democracy.* Ithaca, NY: Cornell University Press.

Key, V. O. 1961. *Public Opinion and American Democracy.* New York: Knopf.

Kirkpatrick, Evron. 1962. "The Impact of the Behavioral Approach on Traditional Political Science." In *Essays on the Behavioral Study of Politics,* ed. Austin Ranney. Urbana, IL: University of Illinois Press.

Lane, Robert. 1962. *Political Ideology: Why the Common Man Believes What He Does.* New York: Free Press.

Lasswell, Harold. 1960 [1930]. *Psychopathology and Politics.* New York: Viking.

Lazarsfeld, Paul F., Bernard Berelson, and Hazel Gaudet. 1948 [1940]. *The People's Choice: How the Voter Makes Up His Mind in a Presidential Campaign,* 2nd ed. New York: Columbia University Press.

Lindblom, Charles E. 1990. *Inquiry and Change: The Troubled Attempt to Understand and Shape Society.* New Haven, CT: Yale University Press.

———. 1997. "Political Science in the 1940s and 1950s." *Dædalus* 126 (1): 225–52.

Lippmann, Walter. 1925. *The Phantom Public.* New York: Harcourt Brace.

Lowi, Theodore. 1979. *The End of Liberalism: The Second Republic of the United States,* 2nd ed. New York: W. W. Norton.

Manicas, Peter T. 1987. *A History and Philosophy of the Social Sciences.* New York: Basil Blackwell.

——. 1992. "Nature and Culture." *Proceedings and Addresses of the American Philosophical Association* 66 (3): 59–76.

——. 1998. "John Dewey and American Social Science." In *Reading Dewey: Interpretations for a Postmodern Generation,* ed. Larry A. Hickman. Bloomington: Indiana University Press.

Neuman, W. Russell. 1986. *The Paradox of Mass Politics.* Cambridge, MA: Harvard University Press.

Nord, David P. 1990. "Teleology and News: The Religious Roots of American Journalism, 1630–1730." *Journal of American History* 77: 9–38.

Purcell, Edward A., Jr. 1973. *The Crisis of Democratic Theory.* Lexington: University of Kentucky Press.

Ricci, David M. 1984. *The Tragedy of Political Science: Politics, Scholarship, and Democracy.* New Haven, CT: Yale University Press.

Ross, Dorothy. 1991. *The Origins of American Social Science.* New York: Cambridge University Press.

Schumpeter, Joseph. 1942. *Capitalism, Socialism, and Democracy.* New York: Harper Torchbooks.

Seidelman, Raymond, with Edward J. Harpham. 1985. *Disenchanted Realists: Political Science and the American Crisis, 1884–1984.* Albany: State University of New York Press.

Smith, Mark C. 1994. *Social Science in the Crucible: The American Debate over Objectivity and Purpose, 1918–1941.* Durham, NC: Duke University Press.

Smith, Rogers M. 1997. "Still Blowing in the Wind: The American Quest for a Democratic, Scientific Political Science." *Dædalus* 126 (1): 253–87.

Storing, Herbert J., ed. 1962. *Essays on the Scientific Study of Politics.* New York: Holt, Rinehart, and Winston.

Truman, David B, 1951. *The Governmental Process: Political Interests and Public Opinion.* New York: Knopf.

Wallas, Graham. 1921. *Human Nature in Politics.* New York: A. A. Knopf.

CHAPTER 36

A Pox on Perestroika,
a Hex on Hegemony

Toward a Critical Political Science

John S. Dryzek

Although the Perestroika reform movement that began in 2000 has shaken U.S. political science, the paucity of productive methodological argument meant that the dispute became political rather than intellectual. The discipline, like James Bond's vodka martini, has been shaken but not stirred. The movement may change the balance of power within the profession but otherwise leave the practice of political science unchanged. This chapter is intended to help move methodological debate, with "methodology" taken in its broad sense of reflection upon the conduct of inquiry (so it also covers epistemology). The existing—now faltering—hegemony (identified with rational choice theory and quantitative methods) may be indefensible, but Perestroika may portend only an empty pluralism in its place. I discuss a critical disciplinary pluralism as a way of making the best of existing political science practice— and redeeming Perestroika's promise.

Space limitations preclude full documentation of the impoverished state of the methodological debate, though a flavor can be gained by looking at a symposium of articles by disciplinary stars organized to address the issues raised in the Perestroikan critique, published in the June 2002 issue of *PS: Political Science and Politics* under the title of "Shaking Things Up? Thoughts about the Future of Political Science." One common theme that emerges from the symposium is the degree to which the contributors point to their own work as a model. Asked to reflect upon the shape of the discipline, these distinguished political scientists reflect mainly on, and implicitly advocate, their own work. Strikingly, none of the contributors, even those associated with hegemony, opposes pluralism in the discipline.

Hegemony: The Phantom Menace

In this *PS* symposium and beyond, hegemony receives no explicit defense.[1] In this section I will try to explain why, and attempt to identify the best arguments I think can be made on its behalf. The hegemonic target identified by

Perestroikans is variously described as hard science, technicism, quantification, and an attempt to impose a "normal science" discipline on political science (see, for example, Kasza 2000a), as revealed in the pages of the *American Political Science Review* (*APSR*) and similar journals (the *American Journal of Political Science, International Studies Quarterly, Journal of Politics,* and *Political Research Quarterly*). Rational choice theory is often seen as central to the hegemony in the discipline, but it is not the totality. In fact, any attempt to combine rational choice analysis with quantification immediately encounters a problem of methodological discontinuity. This is for two reasons. First, most quantitative analysis in political science does not test hypotheses derived from rational choice behavioral assumptions, being quite eclectic in these terms (indeed, often scorned by rational choice theorists for exactly this failing). Second, rational choice theorists rarely subject their predictions to quantitative tests. If they did, they might find, as have their counterparts in economics, that the R^2 that can be squeezed out of their models is small by the standards that quantitative political scientists are used to. Economists are not worried by this fact because their paradigm is unchallenged within their discipline. Small percentages of variance explained are not allowed to undermine the legitimacy of the basic neo-classical microeconomic approach, for the only empirical question has to do with the comparative weight of different variables that the paradigm identifies as important, not with their overall success in explaining variance. Turning back to political science, when rational choice theorists do put their deductions to explanatory use, the findings are often disappointing (Green and Shapiro 1994).

Given that rational choice theory and quantitative approaches are not easily reconciled, it is not surprising that no *methodological* defense of hegemony in the discipline has been launched in response to the Perestroika critique—beyond rhetoric on behalf of science, the generalizability of models, systematic empirical knowledge, testable hypotheses, and the like. One of the most thoughtful responses to date is the editorial by Ada Finifter (2000) defending the *APSR*, at least, against the critics. But Finifter's is not a methodological defense of hegemony. The substance of her argument is that what is published in the *APSR* represents the best of what is submitted, such that if Perestroikans do not like what is published, they ought to submit more of their own work (see also Jervis 2000). Finifter approaches (but does not quite reach) a methodological defense of hegemony in the journal at only two points. The first (viii) is where she argues that, in contrast to what the critics aver, the *APSR* does not ignore articles that deal with "great political issues. Rather the intent is to obtain more systematic and reliable information about them." She does not explicitly equate "systematic and reliable" with "deductive and quantitative," but goes on to point out that the critics should not infer that articles containing statistics or mathematical symbols cannot "deal with great political issues." The second (ix) is where she argues that "the article that appeals to a broad scholarly audience of political scientists may be a chimera" because the discipline is so fractured. This implicitly replies to Gregory Kasza's (2000b) conjecture that articles with a broad appeal get sent to a broad set of referees, while articles with narrow appeal get sent to a narrow set of referees. Given that consensus is more likely among the latter, Kasza avers, the *APSR* discriminates in favor of articles with narrow appeal to specialists. Kasza's conjecture is consistent with the facts of what is published in the *APSR,* but so is Finifter's second point. I see no way to resolve their difference that would not violate the confidentiality of the *APSR*'s reviewing process. However, Kasza's argument does not explain the absence of specialized articles outside the *APSR*'s standard fare of rational choice, statistics, and Straussian political theory.

The fact that hegemony in the discipline has received no methodological defense probably indicates that it is indefensible. Indeed, *any* integrative program that one might propose for the discipline in its entirety (such as the heroic one offered by David Laitin [2001]) is almost certainly doomed. The reason is precisely the discipline's existing pluralism: trying to impose a common program on that pluralism really is like trying to herd cats. And if Perestroikans get their way, the cats will become even harder to herd.

The best argument on behalf of hegemony I can think of is that at least it provides some common focus. When rational choice theorists and other "hegemons" look at the discipline they see not a republic that they rule, but rather a plethora of principalities undertaking all manner of inquiries—the "organizational chaos" of which Laitin (2001) speaks. But the chaos (or, more neutrally, plurality) is actually intellectual as well as organizational. Hegemony at least gives us a center of sorts to struggle over—even if that center is internally incoherent. In this sense the current state of the discipline is an identifiable center plus considerable pluralism. What would happen were Perestroika to be successful to the degree that it demoted that center to just one approach among the many that make up the discipline? This question is actually quite easy to answer because we have several models of political science—or, rather, of political *studies,* to use the terminology favored by Perestroikans such as Susanne Rudolph (2002) and Rogers Smith[2]—available elsewhere in the world to look at. A pluralistic model of political studies with minority interests in statistical methods and rational choice theory captures quite well the state of the discipline in the United Kingdom and Australia. It would be very hard to muster an argument to the effect that the discipline is stronger in either of these two countries. In the United Kingdom, such reform impetus as exists would look to a hegemonic U.S. model of political science (Dowding 2001).

The claim that the hegemony in the discipline at least gives us something to contest may be the best argument that can be made on its behalf, but it is not an adequate one (which perhaps explains why hegemons themselves do not make it). The argument makes sense only as a holding action against disciplinary fragmentation, with no claim that it will yield intellectual progress or a discipline with greater problem-solving capacity. Can Perestroika deliver in these terms?

The Perestroikan Alternative

What Perestroika favors is a bit harder to pin down than what it opposes, in part because of its proclaimed diversity as a movement. A search of key Perestroika documents, letters (especially to *PS: Political Science and Politics*), and published interviews with Perestroika luminaries produces the following list:

- Pluralism in approaches to the subject matter of politics.
- Problem-driven research (as opposed to method-driven research).
- Relevance to important political questions and policy issues.[3]
- Area studies.
- Political studies rather than political science.
- Political philosophy.
- Interdisciplinary inquiry.
- Reform of the APSA to make it more open and democratic.
- Reform of the editorial practices of the *APSR*.
- Reform of departmental hiring and promotion practices.

The last three of these points are organizational rather than intellectual. The first seven points have methodological aspects that merit scrutiny. One problem here is that the points as stated cover quite a diverse range of orientations, not all of them interested in one another (for example, political philosophers generally have little interest in the atheoretical bent of area studies). And at least one—interdisciplinary inquiry—could be shared by the existing hegemony; rational choice theory began as interdisciplinary inquiry involving economics and political science.

Some Perestroikans might believe, with Timothy Luke (2002, 8), that "arguing about method is a famously wasteful pursuit in American political science that distracts our attention from concrete political analysis." Luke argues that the emphasis should be on the political struggle within the discipline: "Who gets what, when, where, and how is an always shifting outcome of network wars. . . . Yet, this is not unseemly, it is often the heart of the matter" (8). As if to drive home the movement's diversity, Luke is careful to point out that he is speaking "with Perestroika" but not "for Perestroika" (1). This diversity of the movement might seem to fit comfortably with its commitment to intellectual pluralism, or what Kasza (2001) calls "ecumenical science." I will now argue that a gesture in the direction of pluralism is inadequate without sustained attention to what pluralism can and ought to mean in methodological terms. I take my bearings from Mary Parker Follett (1918, 10): "The pluralists have pointed out diversity, but no pluralist has yet answered satisfactorily the question to which we must find an answer—what is to be done with this diversity?" (quoted in Schlosberg 1999, 53). I will focus on the first three items in the list given earlier, first, because there appears to be consensus among Perestroikans[4] that they constitute the methodological core of the movement, and second, because taking them seriously points (I argue) directly to a critical political science beyond Perestroika.

Perestroika's Empty Pluralism

Perestroika's advocacy of pluralism requires explanation in light of the existing pluralism in the discipline. This pluralism may not extend to the *APSR* and its imitators, several large Midwestern departments, or the University of Rochester and its doppelgangers, but it is alive (if not necessarily well) just about everywhere else. A look through the program for the annual APSA meeting reveals a remarkable range of topics and approaches. Organized sections of the APSA and new journals in ever more specialized subfields proliferate. In Gabriel Almond's (1990) lament for the lost hegemony of what he calls "the broad cafeteria of the center," we are increasingly sitting at "separate tables" as the discipline fragments into ever finer subdivisions.

In this light, one position that cannot hold is that more disciplinary pluralism will mean more politically relevant, problem-driven research. Rogers Smith states that "the ultimate objective is to create a political science that speaks clearly and accessibly to substantive important questions about politics. The problem is that there is, for good reasons, no consensus about just what such questions and such work really amount to. So, as a practical matter, we have to seek in the first instance to create space in the discipline for a greater variety of kinds of political inquiry" (Colloquy Live 2001). But if particular pieces of political science do not already "speak clearly and accessibly to substantive important questions about politics," more pluralism will make not the slightest bit of difference. In the words of Nike, if this is what you want, "Just Do It!"

Actually some people are already doing it. The field of environmental politics is pretty much defined by its concern with some major political problems. Almost invariably, people enter this field because they are environmentalists, not because they have a particular theory or method they want to try out. None of this research is published in the *APSR* or its imitators, and much of it is not well understood by the rest of the discipline, at least if Laitin's (2001, 9–10) comment about environmental politics is anything to go by. Laitin says it provides the discipline only with an independent variable that can affect the real stuff of politics—for example, when it comes to questions such as "How have ecological issues transformed political parties?" (10) The real questions of environmental politics take exactly the opposite form: for example, "How do party systems promote or impede the resolution of ecological problems?"[5]

There is no logical connection from the degree to which the discipline is pluralistic to the degree that it produces problem-driven research. Susanne Rudolph avers, "A wish to have broader answers drives you to multiple methodologies" (quoted in Miller 2001, 2). This may well be true for particular pieces of research, but it is not true when it comes to the shape of the discipline as a whole, because multiple methodologies lead to multiple answers, not to broader ones. The only conceivable connection is probabilistic: if more kinds of research are done, then, purely by chance, there will be a greater likelihood that at least some of them will be problem-driven or speak to important political questions. But exactly the opposite result is also plausible: more pluralism means more specialization means narrower framing of questions, to the detriment of any more widespread conversation, within the discipline or beyond.

Lessons from Our History

The connection between multiple methodologies and problem-driven research has been made at least once before in the discipline's history, in the policy sciences idea first proposed by Harold Lasswell in the late 1940s (see especially Lasswell 1951).[6] Lasswell advocated inquiry that would address the great issues of the age, such as the threat of war, the emergence of a "garrison state," the undermining of democracy. Lasswell thought the policy sciences were to be "contextual, problem-oriented, multi-method," requiring the best that political science (and other social sciences) could offer. There is little in Lasswell's mantra with which a Perestroikan could disagree. The contextual aspect is stressed by Sanford Schram (2003), who, after endorsing Perestroika, declares, "My political science would find its standards of knowledge in asking whether scholarship can demonstrate its contributions to enriching political discourse in contextualized settings." (Some of Lasswell's other proclivities, such as his psychoanalysis of political pathologies and his advocacy of propaganda to save democracy from itself, would of course be more controversial.) We would do well, then, to ask what happened to the policy sciences movement, and why. The movement is still alive, in the Yale-based Society for the Policy Sciences and in the journal *Policy Sciences*. But far more prevalent is the narrower case-based work that is the staple of the Policy Studies Organization and its journals. The policy sciences approach remains a minority taste within one subfield, a far cry from Lasswell's heroic ambitions.

At the very time Lasswell wanted the discipline to take on the great issues of the age in contextual and multimethod fashion, political science began a revolution that took it in a very different direction (which, paradoxical as ever, Lasswell himself also supported). Behavioralism had a scientific and positivist self-image, also favoring quantitative methods. Policy relevance was not an immediate aim—though that would supposedly come in time as reliable scientific findings accumulated. The reasons for behavioralism's success have been well documented, if not always agreed upon (see Farr 1995). To the behavioralists themselves, it was a matter of replacing legalistic, formalistic, and impressionistic work with a systematic search for reliable knowledge based on study of the actual behavior of political actors. To their critics, it was about securing respectability within the U.S. university system (Ricci 1984), appealing to funding sources, or about depoliticization in the early cold war.

The contemporary hegemony is constituted in part by the commitment to quantification that is one legacy of the behavioral revolution. (As David Easton [2001] notes, in the 1950s behavioralists could complain that they were unfairly excluded from the *APSR*. As late as 1956, editor Harvey Mansfield Sr. was hostile to behavioralism, a situation remedied only by his replacement.) But it was not behavioralism that first prevented the discipline from speaking "clearly and accessibly to substantive important questions about politics," in Rogers Smith's words. As David Ricci (1984) and Raymond Seidelman and Edward Harpham (1985) point out, the tragedy of American political science since its very inception has been its failure as a "reform science" that would be taken seriously in the political system. The reasons for this failure are varied. Ricci believes that the U.S. university system has always demanded the trappings of science, which has proved inconsistent with any more practical emphasis on political problems or the great conversation of democratic development. Seidelman and Harpham believe it is the recalcitrance of the political system that reform scientists wanted to improve. Such discipline history should give us pause for thought. The American science of politics was founded in the late nineteenth century. Its failure to speak "clearly and accessibly to substantive important questions about politics" has been constitutive of the discipline from the beginning, not a feature that arrived with behavioralism or rational choice theory.

In this light, Lasswell's failure to reorient the discipline to make it relevant to the great questions of political life is just one of a string of failures. But closer examination of the reasons for this particular failure is quite instructive if Perestroikans want to do better. Of course explaining why something did not happen is much more challenging than explaining something that did happen. Perhaps the behavioral revolution got in the way. But the real reason may be that the intellectual demands of his approach were massive. Under behavioralism, one could learn a technique and apply it. Lasswell's policy sciences required individual policy scientists to be as superhuman as Lasswell himself, to have a detailed grasp of a wide range of social-scientific (and other) approaches.

What Is to Be Done with Diversity?

If such knowledge is beyond the capacity of one individual, the obvious alternative is to try to increase capacity by involving several or many individuals. Attempts have often been made to coordinate such efforts hierarchically and bureaucratically; this works for relatively simple problems, but not for more complex problems (as Richard Nelson [1977] pointed out long ago, this can get us to the moon, but not solve the problems of the ghetto). F. A. von Hayek (1979) argued that the market was the best device for integrating fragmentary bits of knowledge held by individuals. Karl Popper (1963) made a similar kind of argument about the capacities of liberal open societies (and against their authoritarian competitors) to make use of diffuse bits of knowledge in policy making. These models cannot be applied directly to the contemporary practice of social science. Popper's argument for the comparative rationality of liberal democracy was itself derived from his account of an ideal (natural) scientific community, with policy reforms analogous to scientific experiments. However, pluralism for Popper meant only different vantage points from which to criticize particular policy reforms, not deep intellectual pluralism of the sort we observe in political science. But Hayek and Popper were right that *some* mechanism for integration is needed. And this highlights what is currently missing from Perestroika's pluralist program.

Perestroika advocates pluralism, but does not say what is to be done with this pluralism, or assumes (with no specification of a mechanism) that pluralism will somehow lead to a more politically engaged and relevant discipline. Without such analysis, pluralism becomes relativism in which there are no critical standards with which to make good (contextual) decisions across competing approaches to the study of politics. Such relativism will not disturb the hegemons: recall that Finifter (2000) and Jervis (2000) argue that the *APSR* is already open to all parts of our fragmented discipline equally; it is simply that some people choose to make more use of it.

My conclusion to this point is that hegemony in political science is indefensible but that, as it stands, the Perestroikan advocacy of an uncritical disciplinary pluralism will not produce anything much better. The Perestroikans have not answered Mary Parker Follett's question: "What is to be done with this diversity?"

Toward a Critical Political Science

Let me start from Perestroika's stated commitment to problem-driven inquiry. Problems are aspects of the world that need explaining or remedying. Not just any problems will do; rational choice theorists are justifiably criticized for the narrowness with which they define problems, and for the consequent lack of relevance of their solutions to significant political problems.[7] A progressive and defensible discipline is one whose capacity to address significant problems increases with time. (I will address the question of how to recognize problem significance in a moment.) Given political complexity and intractability, we need all the help we can get from a variety of research traditions. Having a range of effective research traditions at our disposal is conducive to the progress of political science, conceptualized as a growing capacity to cope with contingency in the problems faced by the discipline (Dryzek 1986, 315–17, 1990, 205–8). My only quarrel with the Perestroikans here is that their pluralism with no critical standards will not produce progress so defined because it is unable to make judgements across research traditions in terms of the quality of their contributions to problem solving. This inability stifles the critique of rational choice theory's problem-solving narrowness.

Our search for critical standards can begin by looking closely at the circumstances of problem definition. It is against such problems that progress ought to be assessed, but these problems do not have a brute existence, let alone weight. As Stephen White (2000, 744) puts it: "Problems do not fall like apples from a tree into the lap of an entity called 'society.' There is always the question of how a problem is defined and who in society does the defining. What is crucial here is to understand that this normative issue now must be seen as a matter on which political scientists will always have to take a position."

In terms of who does the defining, if it is only the practitioners of a particular research tradition, the result is scholasticism. If it is only political scientists more generally, that is more defensible in the social-scientific dimension, but it would still fall short in terms of political relevance. The more defensible answer is that problems faced by the discipline get defined in a social process in which both political scientists and other political actors participate. It is against this set of (changing) problems that the progress and rationality of political science as a discipline ought to be addressed.

The conditions of this broad social process of problem definition are crucial. Such social processes can be distorted by money, power, and ideology. Defensible problem definition, and so a defensible discipline, can exist only if such distortions are recognized, criticized, and counteracted. This critical commitment is not a matter of preference; it is a matter of cognitive rationality. Elsewhere I have developed a more elaborate argument on how principles of communicative rationality can be brought to bear here (Dryzek 1990, 209–13). Communicative rationality is the degree to which communication oriented to reciprocal understanding is free from domination, deception, self-deception, manipulation, and strategizing (Habermas 1984). But whether or not one accepts this particular criterion, *some* critical normative standard is necessary.

Such a critical commitment is especially important when ideological hegemony distorts the disciplinary agenda. As Ido Oren (2002) demonstrates, American political science has been powerfully shaped by shifting enemies and friends in U.S. foreign policy. During the cold war, funding priorities for area studies were largely determined by who might need to be subverted or invaded. Research programs with a hint of class analysis were downgraded in favor of those with an ontological individualism (so, for example, in voting studies the University of Michigan's psychological approach forced out the social determinism of Paul Lazarsfeld's Columbia school in the 1950s). In the wake of September 11, 2001, it became harder to describe the malfunction of the presidential election system in the previous year as relegating the United States to the ranks of the world's more dubious democracies.

A putatively rational and progressive discipline can, then, be judged in terms of the adequacy of its plurality of research traditions in relation to problems defined in social processes that transcend the discipline's boundaries and reach into the larger polity. The circumstances of problem definition must themselves be subject to critical scrutiny. But this goes only so far: the imagery here is of a set of research traditions that periodically get judged according to changing problem sets. This begs the question of what we should do as political scientists to get our research traditions in better shape. That is, how ought we to cultivate our discipline?

A critical pluralism necessitates engagement across research traditions, not just mere tolerance of different approaches, and not just communication of findings (as advocated by Jervis [2002] and Monroe [2002]). It is only in their engagement with one another all the way down that the shortcomings, or indeed the strengths, of particular approaches can be exposed. Approaches can emerge strengthened as well as weakened by such encounters, which constitute an alternative to evaluation of an approach against some absolute standard of adequacy. Consider rational choice theory. When Donald Green and Ian Shapiro (1994) apply absolute standards of explanatory adequacy to the approach, they find it falls far short. Their critique is correct but unimportant when viewed in light of the need for engagement across traditions; Green and Shapiro offer no alternative tradition with which rational choice theory might engage.

Green and Shapiro and their critics alike miss the point. It is best not to think of rational choice theory as explanatory theory; rather, rational choice theory shows what *would* happen if political actors behaved according to its behavioral precepts of strategically rational maximization (Johnson 1991). The predictions generally involve disorder: underprovision of public goods, universal nonvoting, manipulation of legislative processes, arbitrariness and instability in collective choice, domination of policy making by well-organized minorities, rent seeking by officeholders, Pareto suboptimality in public policy, and so forth (as Brian Barry and Russell Hardin [1982] summarize, "rational man and irrational society"). The trick, then, is to figure out ways in which the behavioral proclivities that yield such dire results can be curbed by alternative forms of rationality. Such alternatives can be revealed only by a research tradition capable of recognizing both the individual motivation assumed by rational choice theorists and alternative wellsprings of human action. I believe the one best equipped is critical theory, which has a place for strategic rationality, but also develops at great length an alternative communicative rationality (Schiemann 2000). This particular means of engagement removes the positivist self-misunderstanding of rational choice theory and reveals its critical potential (Dryzek 1992). Thus strengthened, rational choice theory becomes better equipped to address at least one of the great political issues of our age: the increasing marketization and hence the individuation of social and political life (Offe 1987). The combination of rational choice and critical theory can elucidate the consequences of this individuation and investigate institutional and other means for curbing it. Mere tolerance across research traditions could not produce this outcome. Nor could simple communication of findings from one subfield to another. Nor could unremitting condemnation of the Green and Shapiro sort. Rather, critical engagement needs to go all the way down.

James Johnson's (2002) cautionary tale of the encounter of culturalist ("interpretive") and rational choice traditions shows why such engagement must be seen as critical. He argues that an unrecognized conceptual problem bedeviling cultural explanation will also undermine any combination with rational choice. The combination ought to be fruitful, because "given that symbolic forms have force, the [rational choice] models help us to conceptualize more precisely why strategic actors seek to deploy them for political advantage" (234). Unfortunately, Johnson argues, cultural analysis lacks any mechanism to explain the causal force of symbolic factors. Thus analyses such as the study of state transitions undertaken by Robert Bates, Rui de Figueiredo, and Barry Weingast (1998) "ultimately reduce symbolic action, and hence culture, to strategic considerations" (Johnson 2002, 243). What starts as engaged pluralism turns into rational choice reductionism. But this encounter has at least highlighted a deficiency in cultural explanation that its practitioners must rectify.

In a different arena, Jeffrey Berejikian (1992) shows that critical engagement need not be hobbled by conceptual problems. Drawing on macrohistorical structural (Skocpol 1979) and microeconomic (Popkin 1979) explanations of revolutionary peasant action, he begins by showing that an adequate structural account requires microfoundations in a model of individual peasant agency. But structuralism is not thereby reduced to individual rational action. Rational choice explanation itself fails because it cannot explain why peasants sometimes take the huge risks that revolutionary action demands. Berejikian then defines a "social frame" as the "perception by individuals that participation in the existing social-structural arrangement means either gains or losses" (652). Behavioral decision theory tells us that individuals will take on much greater risks if they believe the status quo involves loss from some reference point. The key task of revolutionary leadership is therefore to convince peasants of a losses frame. Thus social structure does have causal force, but it is mediated by the perceptions of it that revolutionaries can propagate. Within this frame, individual peasant decisions about whether to revolt are decisive. This intellectual engagement encompasses structure, rational agency, and ideology.

Rules of Engagement

Hazards of the kind Johnson has identified notwithstanding, without productive encounters across research traditions there is no discipline as such, only an organizational entity that is not worth contesting in intellectual terms, a mere holding tank. Let me draw some concrete implications from this seemingly innocuous starting point.

First, *engagement across traditions means that to begin with we need research traditions* with identifiable ontologies, theories, and methods. This requirement immediately causes problems for kinds of inquiry with little conceptual content; descriptive policy studies might fall into this category, as would journalistic political commentary.

Postmodernists interested in destabilization of rigid understandings might object here that they have no interest in creating a research tradition of a more disciplined kind. This seems to be a particular problem for "critical" meta-theorists in international relations (IR); see their responses to Robert Keohane's (1988) demand that the IR critics produce a research program of their own. For example, Richard Ashley and R. B. J. Walker (1990, 398) scorn "paradigmatic conceits" that block the thought necessary to cope with an international system full of paradox. But even postmodernists of this sort require something to destabilize. So if realism, liberalism, and other traditions did not exist, critical meta-theorists of IR would surely have to invent them. The implication of my first point is not that all approaches to inquiry need "hardening" into research traditions with explicit ontology, theories, and methods. Such hardening may work against engagement by making different traditions look like monoliths that can only compete, losing the subtle variations that create points for dialogue (Reus-Smit 2002). But they do need hardening to the point at which they are able to engage other research traditions.

The other holdouts against well-defined research traditions might be area specialists, but the case knowledge that area studies generates can be put to comparative use not just in testing theories (King, Keohane, and Verba 1994) but, more significantly, in generating and refining theories. The exemplary work of Theda Skocpol (1979) does not simply test a theory of revolution in a comparison of cases; it also develops that theory in the context of comparative case analysis. While violating positivist precepts about deductive theory development followed by empirical test, Skocpol demonstrates just how productive can be engagement between theory and area studies all the way down.

Second, *engagement requires mutual intelligibility across research traditions*. One of the failings of rational choice theory is the predilection of some of its practitioners for complicated mathematics. The important findings of rational choice theory can be stated in simple terms in plain language. Only the esoterica requires the ultra-formalization that makes reading the *APSR* like trying to read the phone book upside down (as one of my colleagues puts it). Words as well as mathematical symbols can become unintelligible, and one does not have to read too far into critical theory or postmodernism to find plenty of examples.

The toughest issue here is not the need for clear language (though that is surely important). Mutual intelligibility can be blocked to the degree different traditions have theoretical terms that are not easily translated and that compete as central explanatory factors. Yet examples I have already adduced show that the causal force of culture can be reconciled with rational choice theory's emphasis on calculation, and that structural explanation and ideology can be interpreted in light of behavioral decision theory when it comes to peasant revolution. Flexibility in theoretical commitments is crucial here. For example, the encounter I described earlier between rational choice theory and critical theory can be productive only to the extent that rational choice theorists are prepared to allow that their behavioral assumption is contingent. Similarly, Ashley's (1984) identification of the critical potential in realist theories of IR requires realists to let go of their assumption that states necessarily maximize relative power under anarchy, and open themselves to a world of reflection and intersubjective understanding.

Third, *engagement means applying standards beyond those internal to particular research traditions,* such that an "anything goes" pluralism cannot stand. Most straightforwardly, the standard in question is success when it comes to resolving socially determined problems (see the preceding). Particular pieces of research can be evaluated in these terms, but when it comes to cultivating the discipline, an even more consequential factor is the record of a research tradition over time as it confronts series of problems. Engagement means that we can also assess felicitous (or indeed disastrous) combinations of research traditions in light of the critical problem-solving standard. My earlier discussions of rational choice's engagements with, respectively, critical theory and cultural explanation suggest that we have enough material to begin assessing the results of these engagements. The need to assess them over time and different contexts means we should not be overly quick in discarding a tradition. It might prove amenable to resuscitation if it can find the right partner; or indeed, it might fortuitously find itself able to speak to a new set of problems that arise. The latter perhaps explains the resuscitation of political culture inquiry in the 1990s, now under the "social capital" heading. Such analysis spoke directly to American anxieties about social disintegration amid increasing prosperity.

The general point here is that it is reflective disciplinary practice that should be decisive when it comes to comparative evaluation of research traditions; standards themselves come out of contests and debates across different traditions of inquiry. Accordingly, it makes sense to speak of the problematics of engagement rather than of any eternal rules of engagement.

Conclusion

In the wake of Perestroika, the only defensible political science is pluralistic. But the discipline has to be critically pluralistic in two ways not recognized by Perestroikans. The first is in adopting a critical and ultimately democratic orientation toward the political circumstances in which problems get defined and weighted. The second is in critical engagement across traditions of inquiry, whose results can be assessed in terms of this changing problem set. Mere toleration and ecumenicalism will not do.

Notes

Previous versions of this chapter were presented at the 2002 Annual Meeting of the APSA, at the Department of Political Science at Northern Arizona University, and at the Political Science Program at Australian National University. For comments and criticism I thank James Bohman, James Farr, Robert Goodin, Todd Landman, Stephen Leonard, Tim Luke, and Sanford Schram.

1. Todd Landman (2002) claims to be "rebutting Perestroika." However, his argument is on behalf of method against an emphasis on substance. Given that Perestroika opposes only methodological hegemony, not method as such, his rebuttal

misses the target and, while compelling in its argument for method as systematic inquiry, does not attempt to defend hegemony.

2. Colloquy Live, "The Perestroika Movement in Political Science," *Chronicle of Higher Education,* September 19, 2001. Accessed online at http://chronicle.com/colloquylive/2001/09/Perestroika/, p. 4.

3. Bonnie Honig (2002) criticizes the relevance criterion, but in doing so allows that this is one matter on which all Perestroikans agree—herself excepted.

4. With the exception of Honig (see footnote 3) and Timothy Luke (2002), who disdains methodology.

5. Equally irksome is the frequent comment that the environment is just a "policy area." Political ecologists might reply that politics is just a particularly problematic subsystem of the global ecological system.

6. Prior examples might include nineteenth-century moral science and some of the efforts of Charles Merriam.

7. But see Landman (2002) for an account of the degree to which systematic comparative inquiry (both large *n* and case study) has produced findings relevant to important issues of development and democracy.

References

Almond, Gabriel. 1990. *A Discipline Divided: Schools and Sects in Political Science.* Newbury Park, CA: Sage.

Ashley, Richard K. 1984. "The Poverty of Neorealism." *International Organization* 38: 225–86.

Ashley, Richard K., and R. B. J. Walker. 1990. "Reading Dissidence / Writing the Discipline: Crisis and the Question of Sovereignty in International Studies." *International Studies Quarterly* 34: 367–416.

Barry, Brian, and Russell Hardin. 1982. *Rational Man and Irrational Society?* Beverly Hills, CA: Sage.

Bates, Robert H., Rui J. P. de Figueiredo, and Barry Weingast. 1998. "The Politics of Interpretation: Rationality, Culture, and Transition." *Politics and Society* 26: 603–42.

Berejikian, Jeffrey. 1992. "Revolutionary Collective Action and the Agent-Structure Problem." *American Political Science Review* 86: 647–57.

Colloquy Live. 2001. "The Perestroika Movement in Political Science." *Chronicle of Higher Education,* September 19. Accessed online at http://chronicle.com/colloquylive/2001/09/Perestroika/ p. 3.

Dowding, Keith. 2001. "There Must Be an End to Confusion: Policy Networks, Intellectual Fatigue, and the Need for Political Science Methods Courses in British Universities." *Political Studies* 49: 89–105.

Dryzek, John S. 1986. "The Progress of Political Science." *Journal of Politics* 48: 301–20.

Dryzek, John S. 1990. *Discursive Democracy: Politics, Policy, and Political Science.* New York: Cambridge University Press.

Dryzek, John S. 1992. "How Far Is It from Virginia and Rochester to Frankfurt? Public Choice as Critical Theory." *British Journal of Political Science* 22: 397–417.

Easton, David. 2001. "Remembering Herb." Accessed online at http://www.apsanet.org/new/simon/easton.cfm.

Farr, James. 1995. "Remembering the Revolution: Behavioralism in American Political Science." Pp. 198–224 in James Farr, John S. Dryzek, and Stephen T. Leonard, eds., *Political Science in History: Research Programs and Political Traditions.* Cambridge: Cambridge University Press.

Finifter, Ada. 2000. "Editor's Notes." *American Political Science Review* 94: viii–xiv.

Follett, Mary Parker. 1918. *The New State: Group Organization and the Solution of Popular Government.* New York: Longmans, Green and Co.

Green, Donald P., and Ian Shapiro. 1994. *Pathologies of Rational Choice Theory: A Critique of Applications in Political Science.* New Haven, CT: Yale University Press.

Habermas, Jürgen. 1984. *The Theory of Communicative Action I: Reason and the Rationalization of Society.* Boston: Beacon Press.

Hayek, Friedrich A. von. 1979. *Law, Legislation, and Liberty: The Political Order of a Free People.* Chicago: University of Chicago Press.

Honig, Bonnie. 2002. Remarks made at Perestroika reception, Annual Meeting of the American Political Science Association, Boston.

Jervis, Robert. 2000. "APSR a Reflection of Its Submissions for Better or Worse." *PS: Political Science and Politics* 33: 738–39.

Jervis, Robert. 2002. "Politics, Political Science, and Specialization." *PS: Political Science and Politics* 35: 187–89.

Johnson, James. 1991. "Rational Choice as a Reconstructive Theory." In Kristen Monroe, ed., *The Economic Approach to Politics.* New York: HarperCollins.

Johnson, James. 2002. "How Conceptual Problems Migrate: Rational Choice, Interpretation, and the Hazards of Pluralism." *Annual Review of Political Science* 5: 223–48.

Kasza, Gregory J. 2000a. "'Technicism' Supplanting Disciplinarity among Political Scientists." *PS: Political Science and Politics* 33: 737–38.

Kasza, Greogory J. 2000b. "Rethinking *APSR* Review Policy." *PS: Political Science and Politics* 33: 739–41.

Kasza, Gregory J. 2001. "Perestroika: For an Ecumenical Science of Politics." *PS: Political Science and Politics* 34: 597–99.

Keohane, Robert O. 1988. "International Institutions: Two Approaches." *International Studies Quarterly* 32: 379–96.

King, Gary, Robert O. Keohane, and Sidney Verba. 1994. *Designing Social Inquiry: Scientific Inference in Qualitative Research.* Princeton, NJ: Princeton University Press.

Laitin, David D. 2001. "The Political Science Discipline." Paper presented at the Annual Meeting of the American Political Science Association, San Francisco.

Landman, Todd. 2002. "Rebutting Perestroika: Method and Substance in Political Science." Unpublished paper, University of Essex, England.

Lasswell, Harold D. 1951. "The Policy Orientation." Pp. 3–15 in Daniel Lerner and Harold D. Lasswell, eds., *The Policy Sciences.* Stanford, CA: Stanford University Press.

Luke, Timothy J. 2002. "Caught between Confused Critics and Careerist Co-Conspirators: Perestroika in (American) Political Science." Paper presented at the Annual Meeting of the American Political Science Association, Boston.

Miller, D. W. 2001. "Storming the Palace in Political Science: Scholars Join Revolt against the Domination of Mathematical Approaches to the Discipline." *Chronicle of Higher Education,* September 21, 2001. Accessed online at http://chronicle.com/free/v48/i04/04a01601.htm.

Monroe, Kristen Renwick. 2002. "Interdisciplinary Work and a Search for Shared Scientific Standards." *PS: Political Science and Politics* 35: 203–5.

Nelson, Richard R. 1977. *The Moon and the Ghetto: An Essay on Public Policy Analysis.* New York: Norton.

Offe, Claus. 1987. "Democracy against the Welfare State." *Political Theory* 15: 501–37.

Oren, Ido. 2002. *Our Enemies and US: America's Rivalries and the Making of Political Science.* Ithaca, NY: Cornell University Press.

Popkin, Samuel. 1979. *The Rational Peasant: The Political Economy of Rural Society in Vietnam.* Berkeley: University of California Press.

Popper, Karl. 1963. *Conjectures and Refutations.* London: Routledge and Kegan Paul.

Reus-Smit, Christian. 2002. "Imagining Society: Constructivism and the English School." Unpublished paper, Department of International Relations, Research School of Pacific and Asian Studies, Australian National University, Canberra.

Ricci, David M. 1984. *The Tragedy of Political Science: Politics, Scholarship, and Democracy.* New Haven, CT: Yale University Press.

Rudolph, Susanne Hoeber. 2002. "In Defense of Diverse Forms of Knowledge." *PS: Political Science and Politics* 35: 193–95.

Schiemann, John W. 2000. "Meeting Halfway between Rochester and Frankfurt: Generative Salience, Focal Points, and Strategic Interaction." *American Journal of Political Science* 44: 1–16.

Schlosberg, David. 1999. *Environmental Justice and the New Pluralism.* Oxford: Oxford University Press.

Schram, Sanford. 2003. "Return to Politics." *Political Theory* 31: 835–51.

Seidelman, Raymond, and Edward J. Harpham. 1985. *Disenchanted Realists: Political Science and the American Crisis, 1884–1984.* Albany: State University of New York Press.

Skocpol, Theda. 1979. *States and Social Revolutions.* Cambridge: Cambridge University Press.

White, Stephen. 2000. "Taking Ontology Seriously in Political Science: A Reply to Mayhew." *PS: Political Science and Politics* 33: 743–44.

ing, and that statistical testing of precise, logical models is generally second best. And I accept that when we can credibly answer significant political questions through such methods, we should do so. I think it is understandable, indeed necessary, for these claims to be communicated in our systems of preparation for, and financing and publication of, scientific studies of politics.

Yet I still think the image of the methodological pyramid that Lijphart's article implicitly conveys is a misleading one. A profession that embodies only that message, and not more, would not produce as many scholars doing genuinely good political science research as it should. What is necessary is not the same as what is sufficient.

A more adequate conception of the challenges of doing good political science must call attention to a set of plain truths that often are not effectively communicated in the sorts of methodological admonitions I have cited so far. It must explain the reasons that our successes in inference testing have in fact been fairly limited, reasons that may well persist indefinitely. More fundamentally, it must indicate that doing political science involves many tasks that are just as important as good inference testing. Lijphart himself has since contended, for example, that sometimes we can do better political science through well-structured small n case studies than through statistical methods, because in some respects the latter are less suited to exploring the validity of the concepts used to structure them (Lijphart 1975).[4] When this and a number of other points are taken into account, we may still believe that, in regard to the tasks of scientific inference testing, political science methods are arrayed in the sort of pyramidal hierarchy his 1971 article implied. But we are likely to see that when it comes to doing what can be judged, on balance, substantively good political science, our methods fall into a more horizontal alignment, with the contributions of nonquantitative research modes playing at least as large a part as those of statistical ones.

The reasons that we cannot take inference testing as the sole gauge of quality in political science research include not only the fact that we can expect to perform randomized field experiments on only a relatively narrow range of significant political questions, as all but the refreshingly zealous Don Green and Alan Gerber concede. It is also true that, at its best, the logic of inference serves only to increase our confidence in estimating things we cannot know with certainty, and that particular statistical methods, at their best, are only imperfect techniques by which to implement the analysis of data in accordance with a strict logic of inference. Different methods have different strengths and weaknesses that make some more appropriate for analyzing certain sorts of data than others; Charles Ragin and others have recently argued that in fact standard quantitative statistical methods sometimes push us to package our data in distorting ways, so inferences based on "fuzzy set" data are actually more reliable (Ragin 2000). Though that claim may be disputed, what is undeniable is that all statistical methods of inference testing are at best imperfect quantitative approximations of logical estimations of things we do not really know.

These limitations apply, of course, to all scientific inference testing. But they matter more for political science than for many other endeavors because of two further sobering realities. The first is that, on an enormous range of political topics, we do not have very sound large *n* data sets to subject to statistical analyses. We are usually dependent on data gathered from many different sources using different, none too comparable, techniques. Those sources often are governmental or nongovernmental organizations with agendas and assumptions that overtly or subtly shape the definitions, measures, and data-gathering and -reporting methods they employ in varying ways.

Furthermore, on many important but unconventional topics we simply do not have substantial quantitative data sets at all. Perhaps our most robust and refined data sets, our quantitative "gold standards," are on American public opinion and voting behavior. But the first sets are limited in time, in the questions asked, and in the degree to which they adequately sample a diverse range of minority groups, among other shortcomings. The second are only as reliable as their use of very different systems for counting votes, along with very different levels of honesty in reporting votes, permits them to be. And there is a vast range of significant questions about American politics—including questions about internal dynamics of workplaces, families, racial, ethnic, and religious groups, and social movements; about the historical development of governmental institutions; and about the normative appeal and defensibility of American ideological traditions—that we cannot pursue very far using either data set. Some dimensions of those issues can be examined by gathering more pertinent and reliable statistical data, but far from all.

Finally but most important, it is also true that if any analysis of theories and data is to produce worthwhile results, it must be an analysis that considers hypotheses about politics that are substantively illuminating—neither trivially true nor transparently wrong. If a project is defended via the claim that the immediate question seems banal but is likely eventually to contribute to some more significant understandings, we need to be given reasons for believing, because we cannot simply do everything. We must also test all our hypotheses against data that are not only empirically reliable but also well chosen and organized to test those hypotheses, which is often not true of standard quantitative data sets. This means that "good" political science does not *only* require good inference testing (by whatever methods seem most suitable). It also requires, *at least as centrally,* good hypotheses about worthwhile questions, as well as wisely structured data.

Few of the points made so far seem genuinely disputable; but their upshot is that, if we are honest, we should recognize that although inference testing is essential to the scientific study of politics, the reality is that political science can rarely achieve tests of inference that are truly intellectually compelling. We rarely can do field experiments; statistical methods are at most a clearly inferior second best, even if we have good data; in actuality, the trustworthiness of our statistical analyses is often limited even more by the obvious limitations of the quantitative data we have available to us, and sometimes by forms of quantification that distort rather than adding precision; and in any case, on many important topics we cannot do statistical analyses at all. Even when we can employ experiments and statistical analyses, although they can often give us more confidence in our inferences about descriptions and explanations for the political world, they can do literally nothing to ensure that we are drawing inferences in regard to hypotheses that are genuinely substantively interesting.

The Indispensable Role of Contextual Knowledge

Let me add two further, more legitimately debatable, points. My last contention raises the question of how scholars come up with substantively interesting hypotheses and larger theories about politics. I think Aristotle was correct to assert that in this regard, political science is not like mathematics or many of the natural sciences. In those endeavors, young scholars relatively untainted by "thick descriptive" knowledge of the world can often come up with illuminating new hypotheses, because they can most easily imagine novel logical possibilities overlooked in conventional thinking and depictions. But in political science, the logical possibility that never before entered any human mind rarely proves to have much power in accounting for behavior shaped by such human minds. People just don't often turn out to be acting in ways that no one ever thought they were.

The challenge for us of good hypothesis formation is usually quite different. We often have so many different thoughts about the ways political actors are acting that we need fairly extensive immersion in the empirics of our subject matters to be able to make good judgments about what topics and hypotheses are worth pursuing. It is admittedly an oversimplification, but it seems generally true, that in studying politics we need to know a lot rather than a little about the political world to come up with good hypotheses and theories. In other intellectual endeavors, such as number theory or theoretical physics, it may actually help to know only some things about the world rather than a lot.

This point suggests that political scientists might well be advised to gain a great deal of contextual knowledge about contemporary and historical political phenomena in the course of their graduate training and subsequent research. And they may want to become skilled in methods of historical analysis, in-depth interviewing, detailed case studies, and ethnographic observation that can enrich their knowledge of particular topics and help them to generate valuable new descriptive and explanatory categorizations and hypotheses, out of their own observations *and* out of receptivity to the understandings of those they study. Often we literally cannot imagine the specific mechanisms that may explain the patterns we find in statistical data until we explore some instances of the phenomena in question, up close and personal and in detail. Political scientists may also want to have some real familiarity with the great historical texts of political philosophy, political sociology, and political science, for reflection on such works frequently helps to inspire new descriptive and explanatory hypotheses. And, at a minimum, this knowledge can save scholars from reinventing wheels.

This more inclusive view of the challenges and methods involved in doing good political science seems to me desirable for another controversial reason. I submit that in addressing some important political questions, inference testing is actually the fairly easy part of our job, even though all I have said about the limitations of our inference-testing capacities is correct. We cannot produce a survey research design that allows us to say with the confidence of a randomized field experiment that George W. Bush's popularity ratings benefited from his response to the September 11 attacks. We also do not need to do it. To anyone with a minimal knowledge of the history of Bush's popularity ratings, and presidential popularity ratings more general, it is silly pedantry to say that we cannot confidently infer this causal relationship from these data.[5]

Similarly, when Jeff Tulis argued that presidential speeches changed substantially in form, audience, and content from the nineteenth century to the twentieth, it did not matter that his "ns" in the different categories of speech were too small to permit statistically significant analyses. Statistical significance is not the same as substantive significance. Tulis mapped all the pertinent historical data, and the evidence plainly showed the contrasting patterns he had initially defined on the basis of only parts of that data. So even this "low-tech" statistical technique justified confidence in his descriptive inference, which he then further buttressed with broader historical research (Tulis 1987, 140). It is hard to see how any more sophisticated statistical techniques would actually have served to strengthen the overall persuasiveness of his argument.

Finally, in my own somewhat iconoclastic work on nineteenth-century American citizenship laws, it has been evident to all my critics that if one accepts that I have correctly categorized thousands of citizenship statutes and judicial decisions, the evidence overwhelmingly supports my claims for a "multiple traditions" descriptive and explanatory account of U.S. citizenship instead of claims for a "Hartzian liberal hegemony." Critics have thus focused on arguing either that my categorization scheme is intrinsically misguided, or that the data are not being properly categorized under it. Knowing they would and should so argue, I devoted much of my text to defending my categorizations, not to statistical inference testing of the data set of citizenship laws and rulings I had generated (Smith 1997).[6] By doing so I may appear to have "ducked" the scientific challenge to test my claims statistically; but to me doing this represented a choice to focus on the genuinely questionable part of the analysis. Those questionable judgments might have been submerged if the text had featured what would have been overwhelmingly supportive quantitative presentations and analyses of the data thus decisively categorized. To surface the categorizing judgments and to make and defend them convincingly, I needed more historical and textual interpretive methods of analysis and exposition.

Implications for Doing Better Political Science

The conclusions I draw are, first and foremost, that in its training, financing, and publication systems the political science profession must not only feature and reward sophisticated efforts at scientific inference testing or logically precise formal modeling. We should also feature and reward, at least as prominently, methods and scholarship that help us to formulate and advance substantively interesting questions and hypotheses about politics. Work that rigorously states and tests trivial or foolish claims is indeed scientific, but it is not good political science.

And, given the limits of our capacities for rigorous inference testing, I think we should be careful not to prompt researchers to abandon questions that we know are not amenable to randomized field experiments or credible large *n* data analyses or mathematically expressed formalization. To do so is to risk diminishing the contributions the discipline can make to improved understanding of important political topics in favor of what may well prove to be relatively minor and diminishing progress in strengthening the internal rigor of our formal models and our experimentally and statistically based inferential claims. Critics are also likely to assert that, by eschewing many clearly significant, controversial topics as unsuitable for scientific analysis, political science is implicitly endorsing status quo arrangements that it says it is unable to study. Even if that is not the intent, it may be the effect.

Furthermore, I believe the discipline needs to recommit itself more fully to the notion that the formation of substantively worthwhile hypotheses requires fairly substantial knowledge of politics, of sorts that cannot be obtained if we concentrate too exclusively on improving our techniques of statistical and formal modeling. Political scientists should always ask whether, in particular projects, they are best advised to strengthen confidence in their findings through statistical methods that will sometimes only affirm the obvious and at others be too problematic to add much credibility, or through more careful elaboration and defense of their interpretive frameworks and through nonquantitative modes of inference testing. This advice assumes what we know to be true: that we cannot practically or productively use all methods in all projects, so we must always make choices. I emphatically do not mean to suggest, however, that scholars must in principle commit themselves exclusively to one method at the expense of others. Because good hypothesis formation and rigorous inference testing *are both essential* to good political science, we should seek to improve our individual and collective abilities to pursue any and all methods that can assist us in doing better in any and all such work.

How might the contemporary profession of political science come to propagate, and to pursue, this broader vision of the challenges of doing good political science more successfully? I suggest that, in structuring graduate training, designing funding programs, and managing our general-purpose journals, political scientists should bear in mind the following points:

1. Though many political scientists believe that science requires infer-
    ence testing and that there is one unified inferential logic, all the
    methods political scientists use to engage in inference testing have
    significant limitations.

2. Many political scientists believe that political science needs sub-
    stantively important questions and interesting hypotheses as much
    as appropriate inference testing to be good political science.

3. Skill in generating good questions and hypotheses may require
    extensive knowledge of current and historical politics and of great
    scholarly works on politics, as well as knowledge of methods that
    involve deeper immersion in political phenomena than scholar-
    ship focused on formal and statistical methods sometimes reflects.

4. Many political scientists believe that in some projects the require-
    ments of inference testing sufficient to advance scientific knowl-
    edge can credibly be met without employing formal models or
    large n statistical analyses.

If we designed our curricula, structured major grant programs, made decisions on publications, and above all hired and promoted with these basic facts
of disciplinary life in mind, we would, I believe, not be so tilted toward identifying "good" political science with "mathematized" political science as I fear
that we are.

Still, I hope it is evident that none of these remarks is motivated by rejection
of the claim that inference testing is an essential dimension of political science.
Nor do I even oppose the more debatable claim that, in terms of methods of
inference testing, there is a pyramid, with many types of small n studies making up the base, appropriately structured statistical methods in the middle
(though not necessarily alone in the middle), and randomized experiments at
the top. My concern is that today, for understandable reasons, the discipline
seems to be telling its students and practitioners that only the statistical middle levels, and now possibly the experimental apex, really matter if they are to
master what it takes to do good political science.

That, surely, is a terrible mistake. The definition of good political science
must encompass more and must be even more demanding than this. It must
stress the importance of knowledgeably grounded, substantively significant
hypotheses and categorizations, not just inference testing. Such knowledge is
the true base on which good political science must be built. And a pyramid
that has no base cannot really have a point.

Notes

This chapter began as a "mini-essay" for the APSA's Task Force on Graduate Education, active during the 2002–03 academic year. I am grateful to the original Task
Force Chair, David Collier, for his comments on that essay.

1. Don Green and Alan Gerber have recently contended that randomized *field* experiments are most reliable of all, given the ineradicable distinctiveness of laboratory situations (Green and Gerber 2003).

2. See the National Science Foundation's Political Science Program "EITM Report," available at http://www.nsf.gov/sbe/ses/polisci/eitm_report/start.htm.

3. For analyses of the structures of graduate education and journal publication patterns, see Schwartz-Shea 2003; Bennett, Barth, and Rutherford 2003.

4. I am grateful to David Collier for calling this reference to my attention and for other constructive comments on the previous draft of this chapter.

5. I am grateful to Don Green for this example.

6. The logic of inference was, to be sure, still pervasively at work in the analysis: having formulated a hypothesis about the body of citizenship laws and rulings based on a partial sample, I had to demonstrate that similar patterns could be found in the remainder. And in regard to every statute and judicial decision analyzed, a categorization initially based on part of the "observables" in the legislative and judicial language and history had to be consistent with all my further observations about the statute or ruling. But throughout, the "action" occurred in the interpretive classifications. If one accepts them, the capacity of the data to support the descriptive inferences being made is transparent, and so far at least, uncontested.

References

Bennett, Andrew, Aharon Barth, and Ken Rutherford. 2003. "Do We Preach What We Practice? A Survey of Methods in Political Science Journals and Curricula." *PS: Political Science and Politics* 36: 373–78.

Green, Donald P., and Alan S. Gerber. 2003. "Reclaiming the Experimental Tradition in Political Science." In H. Milner and I. Katznelson, eds., *The State of the Discipline III.* Washington, DC: American Political Science Association.

King, Gary, Robert O. Keohane, and Sidney Verba. 1994. *Designing Social Inquiry: Scientific Inference in Qualitative Research.* Princeton, NJ: Princeton University Press.

Lijphart, Arend. 1971. "Comparative Politics and the Comparative Method." *American Political Science Review* 65: 682–93.

———. 1975. "The Comparable-Cases Strategy in Comparative Research." *Comparative Political Studies* 8: 169–71.

Ragin, Charles C. C. 2000. *Fuzzy-Set Social Science.* Chicago: University of Chicago Press.

Schwartz-Shea, Peregrine. 2003. "Is This the Curriculum We Want? Doctoral Requirements and Offerings in Methods and Methodology." *PS: Political Science and Politics* 36: 379–86.

Smith, Rogers M. 1997. *Civic Ideals: Conflicting Visions of Citizenship in U.S. History.* New Haven, CT: Yale University Press.

Tulis, Jeffrey K. 1987. *The Rhetorical Presidency.* Princeton, NJ: Princeton University Press.

CHAPTER 38

Perestroika, Politics, and the Profession

Targets and Tolerance

Robert Jervis

As the one who was president of the APSA during the year that Perestroika burst onto the scene, I am glad to have this opportunity to reflect on some of the issues this movement raised. I will do so under two headings: the target of many of the complaints, and the meaning of tolerance and diversity in a scholarly community. During my presidential year, friends often asked me how I was bearing up under the controversies. My reply was that as a student of international politics, I couldn't get too disturbed by any conflict in which people were not getting killed. Even by the milder standards of domestic political conflict, the disputes we have seen within the discipline, although heartfelt and significant, are of far less intensity and severity—and of fewer consequences—than we see within the normal realm of American politics. As far as I can tell, people have rarely stopped speaking to each other because they are on different sides of the issues, and most of the discussion has been carried out civilly. This is not a matter of self-congratulation or mere atmospherics, because it indicates that the degree of shared values and perceptions may be high, and it holds out the hope that different people and groups can learn from each other. The divisions within many other disciplines are much deeper. Literature departments are famously divided; history has seen the establishment of a national association that rivals the original one; and several anthropology departments have split into different units, one much closer to the sciences and the other to the humanities (unfortunately for us, social science seems to be the excluded middle). No one foresees or advocates such outcomes for political science.

I think part of the reason for the constructive—or at least nondestructive—way in which we have handled our conflicts is that we have learned something from studying politics. Most of us realize that conflict is an inevitable and often productive facet of any enterprise and is not a sign of pathology. Similarly, although not lacking in principles, political scientists generally understand the need for compromise. Although we may not be as politically skilled as those we study, most of us do realize that complete victories are unlikely, and indeed often unwise. This knowledge mutes our self-righteousness, at least at times, and can make it easier for us to work together despite considerable differences.

Perestroika's Grievances: The APSA, the *APSR,* and the Discipline

To talk about the grievances expressed by Perestroika is of course a simplification, because the movement is diverse. Nevertheless, I think it is fair to say that while some of its members did not fully realize this, their main objections were to the direction the discipline is taking, with the *American Political Science Review (APSR)* seen as both a symptom and a cause of this, and the activities of the APSA were tertiary. But at least at first, the association seemed to be Perestroika's main target, perhaps because it was within closer reach. The movement's major objection in this regard was the association's system of governance, and more specifically the lack of regular competitive elections and the underrepresentation of minorities, especially women. (Of course, it might be difficult to remedy both these ills simultaneously, as many Perestroikans understand.) During the year I was president, the APSA Council adopted guidelines for the Nominating Committee, declaring that ordinarily the president should not be of the same gender for more than two years in a row[1] and establishing a committee to consider the association's system of elections. The issues involved in the latter question are discussed in other chapters of this book, and here I would just like to note that I appointed to this committee only people who were both thoughtful and had no fixed views on the subject.

While some members felt that the association's leadership was dominated by an unrepresentative elite, it was less clear how they believed this was affecting the association's activities and what the critics wanted the association to do. Those who felt that the current governmental arrangements were appropriate believed that the APSA was largely a service organization, with the quite restricted role of publishing journals, holding a convention, serving departments and members by keeping them informed about what others were doing, and supporting the collective interests of the members of the discipline. Some Perestroikans felt that these roles were too limited and that the APSA should be more active in shaping the discipline and articulating political positions. The role of the association is obviously linked to many of the arguments for competitive elections. The Jacobson committee argued against such elections largely on the grounds that the APSA is a service organization; were the association to take a much more active role, there would be issues around which elections could be sensibly staged.

The *APSR*

I believe that a good deal of the unhappiness with the association was based on unhappiness with the *APSR.* This was not a new phenomenon. On entering graduate school over forty years ago, I heard my colleagues and professors complaining that the *Review* was unreadable, was overly specialized, and failed to represent the diversity of approaches used in the discipline. By the time I became president-elect, it was clear that the dissatisfaction had increased. One complaint was shared by almost all members of the discipline: because the *Review* published only research articles, most were of interest only to fellow specialists. So it is not surprising that many people say: "Why should I get the *Review* when there is rarely more than one article in an issue that I'm really interested in?" If there are four subfields to the discipline and, say, three approaches to each, and if I am interested only in the approach to my own sub-field that I use, I will indeed be lucky to find an article that suits me.

There is a real problem with running a discipline in the way the APSA runs it. Most members of the profession are not engaged in highly specialized research, and even those who are need to be informed about developments throughout political science. The *Review* is not designed to help us here. This problem, and the potential solution, came not from Perestroika but from the deliberations of the APSA's Strategic Planning Committee (SPC), appointed by my predecessor, Robert Keohane. As the SPC talked to rank-and-file members of the association, it became clear that we needed a publication that would educate us about what was going on throughout the discipline, that would pull together specialized lines of research, and that would examine broad and important questions that were not normally examined in any *APSR* article. This led to the formation of *Perspectives on Politics,* which is described by Jennifer Hochschild in her chapter of this volume.

The need for such a journal does not reflect shortcomings in the way the *Review* and its editors have carried out their task. But Perestroika and many other members of the discipline did feel that the *Review* had failed in not publishing articles that reflected the full range of methodologies and approaches used in the discipline and instead concentrated on highly quantitative and mathematical studies. There is little doubt that this description is—or at least was—accurate. Disagreement came over issues of diagnosis and responsibility. Many people felt that the review process was biased in favor of these approaches. Exactly how was rarely specified, but the suspicion was that while modeling or data-driven articles were sent to referees who shared the manuscript's approach, other submissions were sent to readers who would be more likely to be hostile. Put another way, the claim was that quantitative and mathematical referees dominated the process, reviewing articles of all types.[2] These arguments are hard to disprove without looking at detailed and confidential information about who has reviewed what manuscripts, but my own experience as a rejected author and as a referee for many articles (including heavily game-theoretic ones), what I know about the way most journals are run, and *Review* Editor Ada Finifter's rebuttal convince me that self-selection rather than bias is the main explanation, if not the only one.[3]

Some of the Perestroika communications blamed the association for the failings of the *Review.* But the links between the APSA and the *APSR* are quite attenuated. The Council appoints the editor (and now approves the editorial board as well), but after that has no role. The dissatisfaction of Perestroika and other members of the association did lead the selection committee for the new editor (of which I was a member) and the Council to place great weight on the need to break out of what we thought was the cycle of self-selection and unbalanced publications that had led to the *Review*'s not representing the range of research in the discipline. One reason we selected Lee Sigelman was that we believed he could convincingly reach out to people doing research of kinds that were rarely published in the *Review*, an expectation that I am happy to say has been borne out. While everyone, including past editors of the *Review*, knew of the problem, the more vocal objections by Perestroika usefully made it more salient to us and led us to place more weight on the criterion of reaching out than would have been the case otherwise. Once an editor and an editorial board have been selected, however, there is little the APSA can and should do to affect the *Review*'s content.

One of the main complaints about the *Review* was directed less at the contents of the journal per se and more at the *Review*'s function in the appointment and tenure decision-making processes at many institutions. Briefly put, members of Perestroika and others felt that departments and higher-level authorities were placing great weight on publication in the *APSR*. Indeed, at some institutions publishing there had become close to both a necessary and a sufficient condition for tenure. So it was imperative to change the *Review* in order to retain diversity in the profession. I fear that this description is quite accurate. But the responsibility—or blame, which I believe would not be inaccurate—should be properly attributed. The fault lies not with the *APSR*, but with the departments that use it incorrectly. Hiring and tenure should be based on a reading of a person's work, and while the outlets in which he or she publishes can be used as one measure of professional standing, it would be an abdication of professional responsibility to reach an appointment decision based on where a person's articles have been published rather than on what they say. Even those who have great faith in our ability to rank journals and in each journal's ability to select the best articles would agree that some less than excellent pieces appear in the best journals and that many superb pieces of scholarship are published in less prestigious outlets.

The Perestroikans certainly have a point, however. Even though the APSA and the *APSR* are not responsible for this sorry state of affairs, if departments and higher-level committees do reach personnel decisions on the basis of whether a candidate has published in the *Review*, it is vital for the association and the editor to ensure not only that the refereeing procedures are fair but that people who do all kinds of research feel that this is the case. Even if I am right that the previous problem was one of self-selection, as long as the *Review* is abused by being used as a gatekeeper, the effect will bias the field. This is why many of us felt it was so important that the new editor do all that was in his power to attract submissions from all parts of the discipline.

There may be two related ways in which the refereeing system works against many kinds of qualitative research that does not involve bias. First, there is often a greater degree of consensus in judging quantitative research. This means that referees are more likely to agree and, if it takes unanimity for a paper to be published, as appears to have been the case under some *APSR* editors, a higher proportion of these submissions will be accepted. Second, if a formal model or quantitative study is technically correct, referees are likely to recommend publication. This is not to say that no substantive contribution is necessary, but only that once the quite high hurdle of technical proficiency is surmounted, publication becomes more likely. This bias may be diminishing as referees come to routinely demand more and more checks for robustness and as the number of possible statistical tests increases, leading to more disagreements.

Perestroika, the Discipline, and Jobs

I believe the main source of Perestroikans' discontent is the trend in the discipline, which they correctly see as becoming more statistical and mathematical. They also see this as representing a narrowing of the discipline, but this judgment is a difficult one, involving as it does the breadth of research of different kinds. It is certainly true that much research in the style of work done fifty years ago has disappeared, and I believe this is a great loss. Could someone get tenure on the basis of a book like Neustadt's *Presidential Power?* This is not to say that the topics Neustadt dealt with are no longer addressed: Charles Cameron's *Veto Politics* does so. But instead of using case studies and narrative histories, he deploys quantitative data and formal models. Studies of Congress and individual representatives like those carried out by Richard Fenno are also a vanishing breed, although a wide range of institutional attributes are now being examined with multiple sources of data and models. Thus while it is true that certain kinds of studies have been abandoned, it would be hard to say that the range of research has been narrowed because the truncation has been accompanied by the growth of studies that were absent before.

Whether or not the discipline is narrower than it once was, the Perestroikans are certainly correct that it is different, and different in ways that they dislike. Political philosophy is less central than it was fifty years ago, normative and policy-related questions receive less attention, more theories and techniques are borrowed from economics and fewer from sociology and psychology. In American politics, books and articles without any quantification at all are rare. But the trends are not entirely in one direction. The importance of history is central to the thriving field of American political development; "interpretivist" scholars who borrow the sensibility of humanists, while still small in number, are no longer a marginal fringe; and in international relations, an increasing number of younger scholars combine formal models, quantitative analysis, traditional theories, and case studies.

But I do not think that the Perestroikans are wrong to worry about the future of the discipline from their perspective. I will discuss the question of tolerance and diversity later, but here I want to make two points. The first is obviously contentious and subjective: I believe that the discipline is excessively prone to fashions and fads. Of course the reply is that these represent considered judgments as to what subjects are most important and what approaches are most productive, but I am skeptical. But for whatever reason, it is clear that certain topics and approaches are more popular than others. To restrict myself to international politics, studies of nongovernmental organizations are more popular than analyses of armed forces; ethnic conflict is now of much greater interest than the crises of the cold war; and studies of international political economy are more likely to examine the domestic sources of policies than the existence and functioning of international regimes. Turning to approaches, political psychology remains marginal, the application of psychodynamics has become almost extinct, and close ethnographic studies of decision making are rare.

Everyone of course wants to be innovative, but this also means that studies that can be labeled "traditional" are seen as of limited value. It may be, of course, that the quantitative and formal studies are simply better than those that are traditional. There is no objective way to fully come to grips with this question, but from observing innumerable job candidates over more years than I care to remember I conclude that traditional scholars are at a disadvantage. That is, holding quality constant (obviously a personal evaluation on my part), quantitative scholars are more likely to get higher-prestige jobs. Inevitably, lacking any agreed-upon yardstick of excellence, this is a statement both about the job market and about my own judgment.

A second point is less disputable: hiring decisions both reflect and shape the discipline. They reflect it in that people decide among candidates not only on the basis of their own evaluations of the quality of the candidates' research, but also on their estimate of who will have the most impact on the discipline and who will be the most valued by the field. This creates obvious possibilities for self-fulfilling prophecies. Reflecting and shaping are intimately related processes. If many people or departments believe that a particular approach is or will be central to the discipline and hire people who use this type of approach, these skills and approaches will be strongly represented at major institutions and so will play a large role in constituting what the discipline will become. Although I may prefer the research of candidate A, I may favor B because I think others believe B's work makes more of a contribution. This does not mean that the decisions are arbitrary, let alone wrong. But it does remind us that what is seen as the best kind of work may not represent the independent judgments of large number of scholars, each giving his or her own opinions on the inherent value of the scholarship.

Of course individuals and departments do not always seek and reflect the judgments of others or mimic them. Rochester and Cal Tech gained great prestige and influence by becoming centers of formal analysis when this was widely regarded as problematic. Similarly, some universities today specialize in one or more of the nonquantitative approaches and a number of years from now may be seen as having produced many of the leaders of the field. Nevertheless, while international politics generally exhibits the dynamic of balancing against potential hegemons, academic life is more prone to bandwagoning.

A final claim of many Perestroikans seems to me less well founded. This is that political science has become increasingly divorced from important political issues and that the primary reason for this is the desire to become increasingly scientific. I think this description is by and large correct, but the causal attribution is not. At least in the international relations (IR) field, it is true that fewer scholars seek to address issues of policy and that "in-and-outers" are a vanishing breed. During and after World War II, it was not uncommon for major scholars to serve in the government for some years before returning to the campus. This is now rare, and few political scientists are central to the public dialogues on issues of the day.

There is something to the argument that the drive to be more scientific has led political scientists to study only those problems that lend themselves to this approach, which means that most issues relevant to policy are neglected. But this argument is not entirely convincing. If it were right, we would expect to see scholars outside of the scientific mainstream contributing heavily to policy debates, but this does not appear to be the case. Furthermore, economists participate in policy discussions and their findings are prominent in many government decisions, yet this discipline is dominated by quantitative data and formal models. In this light, it is not surprising that one of the topics of IR research that is most relevant to policy—arguments about the existence and cause of the ability of democratic states to settle their disputes with one another without resort to warfare—involves a great deal of quantitative research. A related issue is that neo-realism, often attacked for being excessively abstract and removed from the realm of foreign policy choices, in fact implied that the United States did not need to fight in Vietnam and points to the danger that the United States, now the world's only superpower, will expand its reach in a way that will harm both itself and the rest of the world. Nevertheless, I do believe that the hesitancy to look at what cannot be readily quantified or put in a formal model means that many important questions are put aside. It is also possible that a reluctance to go beyond what can be shown by hard data leads scholars to shy away from policy arguments, although this has not been the case in some areas, such as education policy, where strong claims rest on flimsy evidence.

A related argument is that highly quantitative or mathematical articles are impenetrable to those without highly specialized training and that the jargon involved diminishes the flow of information within the profession and between the scholars who have written these articles and the general public. There is something to this, and there are many articles in the *Review* that I cannot read. But authors often go to great pains to make their general arguments clear to those who cannot follow the details, many articles have had a great impact on a wide range of colleagues with very different levels of technical skill, and some scholars have written readily accessible versions of arguments that were originally developed in technical form.

If trying to be scientific does not constitute an insurmountable barrier to communication with others, it is even more obvious that the rejection of science does not necessarily make communication easy. Many articles in political theory make little sense to those in other subfields, and the writings of post-modernists who most vigorously reject the scientific model are written in what to most of us is a foreign language. It is particularly ironic that the latter group, and the humanists from whom they have learned, are strongly committed to social change and yet write in a way that sharply limits their audiences.

Diversity, Tolerance, and Respect

Central to Perestroika is the call for tolerance toward and indeed the encouragement of diverse approaches to the study of politics. I agree strongly, but the notions of tolerance and diversity need a closer examination.

To start with, political science is a discipline composed of embattled minorities. To many, formal theory seems to be a potential if not actual hegemon, to take a phrase in international politics. But the number of formal theorists is quite limited, and, far from dominating the APSA, this approach has had only one of its founders as APSA president. Since this approach has received not only its share of vigorous and legitimate criticisms, but an unusual degree of abuse as well, it is not paranoid for its proponents to call for tolerance of their approach.[4] Behaviorists, who were dominant a generation ago, see themselves derided as mere "number crunchers" and attacked by formal theorists from one direction and by interpretivists from another. Although still numerous, they can with some justice complain, "We ain't got no respect." People who study psychological processes and, even more, individual differences feel ignored when they are not being scorned. Political theorists believe that they are treated as serfs whereas they used to be royalty. Constructivists, although growing in number, claim to be misunderstood and oppressed even as their narratives appear in major outlets. Members of each subfield, furthermore, tend to believe that the other subfields are growing at the expense of theirs. Even when another subfield is not seen as the Other, it is rarely seen as welcoming and supporting.

In this context, many pleas for tolerance are really demands that one's own kind of work be respected. Thus it seems to me—although this may reflect my own bias if not paranoia—that the tolerance many constructivists trumpet does not extend to their views of competing analyses of international politics. Not only are they hesitant to see the extent to which the more empirical variants of this approach borrow heavily from social psychology, but their discussions of realism are often not only distorted, but contemptuous. Refusing to judge work within its own framework and to look for evidence and insights they might find enlightening, constructivists often provide only harsh reviews of books that do not employ their favored style.[5] Of course some people are more open-minded than others irrespective of their approach, but claims for the importance of tolerance should always be given greater weight when the person is defending points of view with which he or she disagrees than when it is a form of self-defense.

Four Forms of Tolerance

Tolerance can come in different forms and can operate through different motives. Four forms can be located, some more demanding than others. Probably the easiest is the willingness to help colleagues who are of a different persuasion by constructively commenting on their work, discussing ideas with them, and referring them to relevant sources of information. In doing this, we are trying to make alternative approaches work as well as possible. Although some of us may also harbor some hope of converting our benighted colleagues to our own point of view, at least we are not imposing it on them. It is also relatively easy to provide this kind of support to our students, although I once heard a colleague at another university tell a student who had asked for guidance to the literature that disagreed with the professor's perspective: "That work is terrible. I won't help you by pointing you to it."

A second form of tolerance is including works written from multiple perspectives in our reading lists. This is a bit more difficult, because for every article we think is misguided that we put on the list, we not only perhaps increase the chance of leading some students astray, but lose the opportunity to assign other material we think is of greater intrinsic value.[6]

The third form of tolerance is significantly harder to practice, at least for some people. This is to favorably review a book of a different persuasion or, even more difficult, to recommend such a manuscript for publication. Most of us would like to think that we can distinguish good from poor research no matter what its style. This is what we generally try to do when constructing a reading list: we want to use the best examples of realism, rational choice, and constructivism, for example. But when deciding whether to recommend publication, it is harder to separate the judgment of the particular manuscript from the genre it represents. Thus a leading quantitative scholar wrote a one-line review of a manuscript that was purely theoretical: "This is not appropriate social science and should not be published." At least he was explicit in showing that his rejection was based on the kind of work submitted; some referees purport to be taking a manuscript on its own terms when in fact their evaluations are based on whether it shares their perspective.

One reason tolerance is harder to come by in the refereeing of manuscripts is that the process is competitive in that only a limited number can be published. The pressures are even greater when it comes to decisions on whom to admit to graduate school and, even more so, on whom to hire. We all know how scarce these slots are, and the natural tendency for most people is to strongly prefer their own kind of scholars. While the intensity rarely approaches that of ethnic conflict, the process does share the same social-psychological processes that drive differing evaluations of members of one's own group and of outsiders. Of course it also shares with ethnic and many other political conflicts the centrality of power: to hire one of "them" means that "their" tribe will grow in number and influence at the expense of my own. We all fear domino effects and know of colleagues who voted against a particular candidate not because of faults in his or her research, but out of the concern that the person would not reciprocate the tolerance that would be expressed by a positive vote. Of course there is a real dilemma here, because if people who are tolerant are disproportionately concentrated in one intellectual perspective, this group will shrink over time as its members vote on the basis of the quality of work taken on its own terms while others are more sectarian. A related issue is that proponents of a rising school of thought are likely to claim support for their co-believers on the grounds of tolerance, but may adopt a very different stance toward the next generation of scholars doing work of a very different kind.

Motives for Tolerance

People can tolerate and even encourage diverse perspectives for a variety of reasons, moving from highly pragmatic to deeply principled. (These reasons roughly parallel many of the justifications for the role of free speech in an open society.) First, if reciprocated, tolerance can be an aspect of logrolling. Contrary to the logic discussed in the previous paragraph, I may agree to support a candidate who works from a different perspective than mine on the understanding or expectation that colleagues of that persuasion will support my candidate the next time. This way of behaving clashes with the model whereby each individual in a department exercises independent judgment on each candidate, but as students of politics we should recognize that logrolling not only reduces conflict, but can produce outcomes that support a general good.

A second rationale has more of an intellectual component. Although I believe that my own approach is the best one—why else would I have chosen it?—I may have some nagging doubts. Strong convictions are compatible with the belief that certainty is beyond our reach, that we cannot know what approaches will prove the most fruitful, that lines of inquiry that at first seem unpromising may blossom, and that what looks barbaric or incomprehensible today may yield great insight tomorrow. It follows that a department—and, even more so, the discipline as a whole—should hedge its bets and support a wide variety of forms of inquiry. Similarly, some people favor diversity in their own departments in order to present students with a variety of perspectives. While some professors hold up one approach as the one that all their students should adopt, others of us believe that students should be exposed to many approaches so they can decide which ones seem best and most suited to their individual talents and tastes. Furthermore, although a graduate program composed of students who are working in the same vein may gain the benefit of a critical mass, diversity not only broadens the students' education, but may lead to greater creativity as each person is prodded to examine the strengths, weaknesses, and assumptions of his or her own approach.

A third rationale sees intellectual diversity as a positive good rather than an insurance policy. The previous two rationales imply that there is in fact one best way to do political science, but that we do not know what it is. Here the argument is that our subject matter is so diverse and elusive and that all our methods and approaches have so many limitations that understanding is best pursued from multiple directions. Many IR scholars employ multiple techniques, and students of American politics have been applying quantitative methods to American political development, but there are sharp limits to how diverse any individual can be. Many of the techniques we use, either quantitative or qualitative, take extensive training to master, and one individual can no more master all of them than study all substantive questions. So some division of labor is required, and specialization and diversity not only will assist individual practitioners, who can learn about other approaches from colleagues even if they cannot use them, but will benefit the discipline as a whole. In this view, multiple or even incompatible perspectives are not only to be tolerated, but to be cultivated.

A more fundamental—but questionable—argument for diversity is based on the premise that there is no one right way to grasp political reality because there is no such thing as political reality, or at least not one political reality. Politics, like any other human endeavor, is created by the ways humans think about it and conduct it. Because these ways vary over time and space, there can never be a single stable way of understanding. Indeed, diverse studies of politics liberate us politically and facilitate, if not construct, political life in which individuals and groups can flourish.

Can There Be Too Much Tolerance?

All but the last defense of tolerance need to deal with the rebuttal that while we may not be sure what approach is right, experience, analysis, and evidence should allow us to reject some lines of inquiry. The claim that all approaches and ideas are created equal leaves us unable to make any judgments. Who is to say that the black magic approach to the study of politics should not be facilitated? The chemist who believed in the phlogiston theory would not get a job, and neither should we hire political scientists whose ideas we believe that theory and evidence have shown to be wrong.

Of course many Perestroikans reject the model of science, but even in the humanities certain approaches are discarded. Today no English department would hire a practitioner of "new criticism," for example. For better or for worse, the discipline has moved on. Indeed, I suspect that some of those who reject the scientific model would not hire quantitativists, formal modelers, or IR realists if they had the power to reject them.

In other words, a legitimate reply to the plea for tolerance is the claim that we can distinguish between productive approaches to the study of politics and dead ends. It is right to refuse to educate people in certain approaches or to appoint them because they are not contributing to our understanding of politics. Of course at this point the argument becomes circular, because there is no way to judge what in fact does contribute to our understanding of politics outside of a particular framework of understanding politics. These questions can be discussed, and occasionally people are convinced, but I do not see any way to escape the conclusion that the rejection of tolerance can be a highly principled stand. It simply will not do to dismiss those who take this position as narrow-minded, closed-minded, or true believers. These statements are in some sense correct, but they do not come to grips with the substantive argument that we can know that some approaches are well grounded and highly productive and that others are not.

Political Diversity

My discussion has followed the discipline in discussing tolerance and diversity in terms of methodologies and approaches.[7] I have put aside the topic of diversity on the dimensions of ethnicity and gender because it is familiar and I doubt if I could add much to the discussion. But I do want to mention another kind of diversity that is usually ignored. Even more than being a white male discipline, political science is composed of liberal Democrats.[8] I am happy to say that my own department is not entirely homogenous: we have always had a Republican on the faculty. I think occasionally we have had two, but no more. We do not discriminate against them, and many—well, a couple—of my best friends are Republicans, but we find few among our numbers. New York may be a hotbed of liberalism, but I do not think Columbia's experience is unusual.

Two replies come to mind. First, political diversity has increased with the rise of rational choice, because this approach, strongly influenced by microeconomics, is deeply skeptical of a large role for central authority. Thus many proponents of rational choice are libertarians and reject governmental solutions for problems and significant redistribution of income. This response is correct, but the number of libertarians is still small and rejects social conservatism. Second and more important, it can be argued that our politics do not play a role in our teaching and research. There are no Democratic and Republican questions to be asked, answers to be given, generalizations to be developed, or methodologies to be employed. Our political preferences and orientations are distinct from how we practice political science. There is something to this, but despite the fact that I am unable to provide evidence to the contrary, I remain deeply skeptical. Can it really be that our politics and our political science remain so compartmentalized? Most of us got into this business because we were fascinated by politics and held strong political views. As attractive as I now find abstract theories, they were not what first drew me to study politics. In the security studies field, the arguments that have been developed and the schools of thought that contend are not unrelated to deep involvement in policy questions and to the political preferences of the scholars, although these do not overlap with domestic political partisanship.[9] The proponents of the "democratic peace" thesis strongly believe in the benign effects of democracy, to take a related example. Are we to believe, then, that political science would be no different if the bulk of its practitioners were conservatives or Republicans? Perhaps the burden of proof rests on me to establish this proposition, but denying it is inconsistent with much that we know about how people and communities think.

Some evidence for my proposition is supplied by what the discipline has to say about the role of religion in political and public life. I think the answer is relatively little, despite the existence of the Religion and Politics section of the APSA. And that is the point. Religion is central to the lives of a great many Americans, perhaps a majority, has been a major source of political conflict, and obviously shapes developments within and among many countries. But it is not extensively studied, especially in the context of American politics. Is this entirely unrelated to what I believe to be the fact, that most political scientists are agnostics or atheists? As nonbelievers, we have trouble taking religion seriously, and indeed often are embarrassed by it. This is not a matter of any supposed conflict between science and religion; I do not see constructivists dealing more sympathetically with religion in the United States than quantitativists and formal modelers do. It is instead a reflection of our outlooks on the world and ourselves.

Respect

I serve as an external reviewer for one or two political science departments each year. All have their conflicts, problems, and deficiencies; some are able to handle them better than others. Unfortunately, it is not uncommon to find a department deeply divided, with factions formed along methodological, historical, or personal lines, with a great deal of hostility among the members. Tolstoy had it wrong, however: unhappy departments are alike in lacking mutual respect. Diverse departments are not necessarily deeply divided, and some departments that appear from the outside to be relatively homogenous are very troubled. In departments that manage their differences well, members tend to respect the work being done by their colleagues even when they feel that it is in some sense misguided. Departments become not only divided but embittered when members conclude that colleagues have contempt for their kind of scholarship.

Of course respect is an effect as well as a cause, and the causal arrow between it and a bitter department may run both ways, with the further possibility of third factors (most obviously, personalities) driving both. Just as telling squabbling children to "be nice" does little good, so telling members of unhappy departments to respect each other's research would be ineffective. But atmospheres, both good and bad, tend to perpetuate themselves as new members are socialized into prevailing mores and feuds gather momentum. Unfortunately, it is easier to transform a tolerant department into one characterized by irreconcilable differences than the reverse. Department members and the profession suffer from this, because it is hard for untenured members to thrive when they have to choose sides and difficult for even senior scholars to do their best work during a civil war. Doing political science should be fun, and it is a shame that it is not at many institutions. It is therefore to be hoped that the rise of the

Perestroika movement will contribute to productive discussions, healthy disagreements, and respectful treatment of alternative points of view.

Notes

1. This guideline was violated at the first possible moment with the selection of Margret Levi to follow two other female presidents. As far as I can tell, neither Perestroikans nor the women's caucus protested.

2. Gregory Kasza, "Rethinking *APSR* Review Policy," *PS: Political Science and Politics* 33 (December 2000): 737–41.

3. Ada Finifter, "*American Political Science Review* Editor's Report, 1999–2000," ibid., 931–28; Robert Jervis, "*APSR* a Reflection of Its Submission for Better and Worse," ibid., 738–39.

4. See, for example, Lisa Martin, "The Contributions of Rational Choice: A Defense of Pluralism," *International Security* 24 (Fall 1999): 74–83.

5. See, for example, Nicholas Onuf's review of Colin Elman and Miriam Fendius Elman, "Bridges and Boundaries: Historians, Political Scientists, and the Study of International Relations," *APSR* 96 (September 2002): 676; for comparison with a more generous review by a realist of a leading constructivist book see Dale Copeland, "The Constructivist Challenge to Structural Realism: A Review Essay," *International Security* 25 (Fall 2000): 187–212.

6. We could, of course, try to measure the diversity in reading lists, but a great deal would depend on the categories we would use, which would undoubtedly differ with the coder's own perspective. For one early study of this type see Hayward Alker Jr. and Thomas Biersteker, "The Dialectics of World Order: Notes for a Future Archeologist of International Savoir Faire," *International Studies Quarterly* 28 (June 1984): 121–42.

7. For another discussion see Susanne Rudolph, "In Defense of Diverse Forms of Knowledge," *PS: Politics and Political Science* 35 (June 2002): 193–98.

8. The latest survey is Daniel Klein and Charlotta Stern, "How Politically Diverse Are the Social Sciences and Humanities? Survey Evidence from Six Fields," forthcoming in *Academic Questions,* available at http://lsb.scu.edu/~dklein/survey/survey.htm; for older findings see Everett Carll Ladd Jr. and Seymour Martin Lipset, *The Divided Academy: Professors and Politics* (New York: McGraw-Hill, 1975).

9. For further discussion see Robert Jervis, "Security Studies: Ideas, Policy, and Politics," in Edward Mansfield and Richard Sisson, eds., *The Evolution of Political Knowledge: Democracy, Autonomy, and Conflict in Comparative and International Politics* (Columbus: Ohio State University Press, 2004), 100–126.

CHAPTER 39

Reforming the Discipline

Some Doubts

Peter J. Steinberger

The so-called Perestroika movement in political science embraces a variety of quite distinct claims: scholarly, sociological, and institutional. This seems not always to be well recognized. In the relevant literature—much of it in the form of evanescent messages, memoranda, and manifestos circulated through electronic mail—very different kinds of arguments addressing very different kinds of issues are frequently presented as if they weren't so very different at all. The result is a dense and often jumbled tissue of exhortation and explanation, accusation and analysis. Coming to grips with this material requires, at a minimum, an effort to tease out its various strands and to assess each of them more or less on its own terms.

Perestroikans have much to say about scholarly—primarily methodological—issues in political science. They are especially preoccupied with the role that mathematics plays, actually and prospectively, in the systematic analysis of political events. But they also have much to say about the social structure of the discipline itself. In particular, they worry deeply about the connection between intellectual orientation on the one hand and what might be called the quality or character of disciplinary culture on the other. Finally, they express very strong views about a range of institutions, including professional associations, learned journals, and academic departments within colleges and universities. In doing so they raise—whether intentionally or not—serious and extremely troubling questions about institutional and personal ethics.

When presented as an undifferentiated and intermingled package, these various claims pack a certain rhetorical punch. But when each is taken seriously on its own account, they turn out to be, collectively, far less compelling. I propose to look at some of these claims in detail, and thereby to raise some very real doubts about the cogency of the Perestroika project itself.

For the sake of convenience, I will focus primarily[1] on a single document, Gregory Kasza's essay in the September 2001 "Forum" section of *PS: Political Science and Politics* entitled "Perestroika: For an Ecumenical Science of Politics."[2] I have no reason to believe that this document has any special authority;

and as something like a letter to the editor, it certainly cannot be held to the same standards that one would expect of, say, a refereed article. But as a statement composed explicitly for publication, it is presumably free from the particular kind of looseness and sloppiness—often born of haste and enthusiasm —that one finds in a great many electronic communications (including "Mr. Perestroika's" own original message). And it seems to offer, albeit in abbreviated form, a reasonably representative and comprehensive overview of the Perestroika movement's central themes.

The Scholarly Argument

The Perestroika movement is concerned, perhaps above all, with the predominance in political science of so-called quantitative studies. Thus Kasza worries about "radical quantifiers" who, among other things, construct qualifying examinations for graduate students that focus heavily on "multiple regression, most-different-systems analysis, and the small-n problem." According to Kasza, the predominance of quantitative approaches results in a body of work that is, at once, uninteresting and unempirical. It is uninteresting in the sense of being "irrelevant to the normative and practical problems of real politics." It is unempirical insofar as it ignores—and presumably must ignore—"the political action of real, living human beings." As such, it examines "a nowhere politics" and "analyzes 'facts' out of context." It does not look at human beings "as they are." Rather, it transmogrifies political actors into "robots or abstractions, restricting their thoughts and actions for theoretical convenience." The result is a "narrow technicism"—excessively "mathematical," excessively "methodological," and profoundly innocent of the real world. We need dramatically to reorient the discipline of political science so that it comes to encompass and, indeed, to emphasize "qualitative research methods."

What Is "Qualitative"?

Countless books and articles have been written on the general topic of "qualitative research." A monograph series explicitly devoted to the subject, published by Sage, includes no fewer than thirty-five volumes. But while much of the literature covers a range of evidently standard topics—in-depth interviewing, participant observation, fieldwork, discourse analysis, document analysis, and the like—surprisingly little of it addresses conceptual questions in a truly satisfying way.[3]

Presumably qualitative studies are in some important sense nonquantitative. But what could this mean? Surely it doesn't mean the utter absence of numerical entities. Just as one can hardly read a newspaper story without quickly running into numbers, so too is this the case for social science, regardless of theoretical or methodological orientation. Numbers are hard to avoid. When we look at the world, we count; and when we report our observations, we add things up. We don't *always* do this, to be sure, but it would be the odd social-scientific study that didn't rely in some significant way on quantitative descriptions of some kind.

Perhaps, then, by "qualitative" we are really referring to studies that, though reliant on numbers, do not focus primarily on *relationships* among quantitative entities. They do not report—to put it crudely—correlations. But this too seems unlikely, for it's hard to imagine any serious investigation of social phenomena that does not propose, if only indirectly, important comparisons and analyses stated in terms of more or less, larger or smaller, frequent or infrequent, and the like. An ethnographer determines that certain kinds of things occur *more often* in certain situations than in others. The author of a case study finds that some factors played a *comparatively large* role in determining outcomes. A historian argues that one kind of group had a proportionately *greater* influence on the decision-making process. In all such cases, scholars are reporting patterns of co-variation, themselves described in terms of magnitudes; and magnitudes are quantities. Obviously not all magnitudes are measured in the same way, with the same presumed level of precision and accuracy. But they remain quantities nonetheless—more is a larger quantity than less— and any study that analyzes and compares them, however crudely, is in a nontrivial sense quantitative.

Of course at this point I will be accused of perversity. For surely the relevant domain is obvious to everyone: quantitative studies in political science are studies that measure magnitudes in a way that allows for (1) the simultaneous investigation of very large numbers of cases, often in the thousands, and (2) the analysis of such cases using a range of quite specific mathematical functions, often involving the tools of probability theory. "Quantitative" means, in short, "statistical." And if that's true, "qualitative" must mean something different from "statistical." The fact that case studies and other kinds of qualitative work often invoke magnitudes and numbers is a red herring, perhaps true, but trivial nonetheless. Indeed the sharp disparity between such studies on the one hand and statistically based research on the other is readily apparent to anyone who glances even casually at a recent issue of the *American Political Science Review* (*APSR*) and compares the highly mathematized material contained therein to the more traditional, narrative forms of political argument that one finds in, say, *Foreign Affairs*.

At least two things need to be said about this. First, many advocates of Perestroika are at least partly guilty of failing clearly to define what is meant by quantitative. Kasza himself embraces a typical confusion by uncritically conflating rational choice theory and research involving "large *n*" data sets. These are, at best, strange bedfellows. It's true that large *n* data sets are sometimes used to test hypotheses developed by so-called formal modelers. It's also true that rational choice theorists often use symbolic or numeric notation—equations —in presenting or summarizing arguments. Nonetheless, the differences between formal modelers and large *n* quantitative researchers would be difficult to overstate. Among other things, the phrase "rational choice theory"

refers, indeed, to a theory—or, rather, to a family of theories involving particular notions of how social and political activity occurs. As such, it is something that can in principle be examined in any number of ways: empirical or
logical, experimental or nonexperimental, large n or small n, and so on. The
phrase "large n quantitative research," on the other hand, refers not to a theory at all, but rather to a variety of analytic methods and techniques, each of
which can be applied in principle to a vast array of theories. Such techniques
are, in essence, theory-neutral. Thus very few claims made about rational
choice theory could in fact be transferred unproblematically to large n research, and vice versa. We are talking here of apples and oranges or, indeed, of
apples and, say, horses.

Second, and important, the ubiquity of magnitudes or quantitative entities, even if measured without great precision, raises the possibility that Perestroikans like Kasza are misinterpreting a difference of degree as a difference
of kind. After all, is a single case study anything other than an example of
"small n"—admittedly very small n—research, and hence no different from
large n research except for being, well, smaller? In principle, at least, small n
studies ask the same kinds of questions that large n studies ask. To be sure, they
may well pose those questions in a different way. They rely on different kinds
of evidence. They analyze a different type of data set. They look at certain
things in more detail and more depth, and as a consequence they generate a
different kind of research report. But such differences shouldn't be exaggerated.
For I would think that any case study in social science, just like any large n
study, could not but proceed in terms of (1) "variables" having some hypothe-
sized theoretical significance, (2) methods for "operationalizing" those variables, that is, obtaining evidence regarding the relative presence or absence—
the magnitude—of the factors in question, and (3) a protocol of some kind
designed to uncover "interactions" among them.[4]

A difference of degree is, to be sure, a difference. But I doubt that the kind of
sharp, seemingly ontological distinction that Kasza at least implicitly proposes
—a distinction between benighted, mathematically obsessed pedantry on the
one hand and enlightened, politically savvy scholarship on the other—can be
sustained. Indeed, it seems much more plausible to think of case studies primarily as exploratory exercises preliminary to, hence intimately connected
with, large n studies. In pursuing a single case, or a handful of cases, the
scholar seeks precisely the kind of evidence that would give rise to broad theories, and that would allow for the intelligent construction of large-scale data-
gathering procedures and hypothesis-testing protocols on the basis of which
those theories could be systematically evaluated.

Two Kinds of Empirical Inquiry

In at least one important respect, I have overstated the case. For I do believe
that certain kinds of empirical political research are, in fact, not like this at
all. There is, specifically, a sharp difference between studies that attempt to

explain why something happens and studies that attempt to explain what something means. This difference cuts across, and far outweighs, any putative differences between large n and small n studies. As such, it describes an extremely important categorical distinction—a difference of kind, not merely of degree—but one to which Perestroikans such as Kasza rarely advert.

Studies in the first category—studies that attempt to explain why something happens—are in the end investigations of cause and effect. They seek to account for some outcome by identifying the factors that brought it about. This is to say that they operate, explicitly or otherwise, in terms of independent and dependent (as well as intervening or conditioning) variables. An emphasis on cause and effect is precisely what makes an investigation (social-) scientific; and in this respect, it doesn't much matter whether the number of cases is immense or minuscule, whether the data are quantified with or without precision, whether the results are presented in tables and graphs and formulas or in prose narratives. In all such cases, the goal is the same: to posit some kind of causal connection among variables and to present evidence tending to confirm or disconfirm the existence of that connection.

Very different from this are studies that attempt to explain the meaning of an event or phenomenon. Here the goal is not to provide a causal analysis, but to describe how an incident or activity was understood by those who participated in it or how it should be understood by those who are observing it, if only from a distance. In a famous cartoon, two Martians are hovering in their spaceship above Yankee Stadium, watching a baseball game and taking notes. One says to the other: "I know how they're doing it, but I don't know why." Social actions are not simply physical motions; they are imbued with meaning, and can properly be comprehended only if that meaning is interpreted more or less correctly.

Characteristically, the interpretation of actions and events is the office—though certainly not the exclusive office—of the historian. Consider, for example, Herodotus's descriptions of Cyrus's ill-fated campaign against the Massagetae, of Spartan heroism at Thermopylae, of the strategic evacuation of Athens in 480. In each case, the account seems designed to explain not so much why the event happened as what it signified. Herodotus doesn't really tell us what caused the Spartans to hold their ground at Thermopylae. Rather he seeks to show what Thermopylae reveals about Spartan culture, about the differences between Greeks and Persians, about the nature of freedom and self-government, and so on. In proceeding along these lines, moreover, he appears to have established a model for much, if not all, subsequent historical inquiry. As Michael Oakeshott once put it, the primary goal of the historian is neither to describe an event, nor to explain its cause, but to render it an "intelligible occurrence."[5] Presumably the historian does this, at least in part, by placing the event in its proper context, that is, by describing the complex structure of proximate events that compose its setting or background. Thus the heroism of Thermopylae makes sense—it becomes fully intelligible—only when seen in the light of the extraordinary manifold of contemporaneous events that gave

Sparta in particular and Greece in general an identity, an import, a character, a meaning.

Insofar as political scientists pursue this kind of inquiry—and sometimes they do—they are functioning not as social scientists at all but as historians. That's no criticism. Ours is, by its nature, a derivative discipline, heavily reliant on methods and strategies developed primarily in other less unwieldy fields; and if a political scientist chooses to function as a kind of historian, who could complain about that?[6] To the degree, however, that political scientists have other interests—in particular, to the degree that they are interested not primarily in the intricacies of meaning or significance but in cause and effect—their approach will be different. It will be scientific rather than historical. And in this sense, the difference between "qualitative" and "quantitative" modes of inquiry—or, more properly, between highly mathematized and less mathematized approaches to questions of magnitude—is, I would argue, relatively unimportant.

It will be objected that social science itself cannot proceed unless it knows the nature—the meaning—of its objects of study. The interpretive protocols of the historical and humanistic disciplines are not separate or isolated endeavors, as I seem to have suggested, but are, to the contrary, necessary presuppositions of any intelligent inquiry into cause and effect. In fact, I myself believe this to be quite correct; but I also believe it to be, in the present context, trivially so. On the one hand, it's certainly true that inquiry into cause and effect—indeed, virtually any serious engagement with the world—cannot but reflect prior, often tacit understandings about how things really are. But while we can and should encourage the examination of such understandings, the necessary division of labor inherent in any intelligent activity means that much of the time they cannot function other than as premises or presuppositions. Any kind of causal analysis, whether involving ethnographic observation of a single case or statistical analysis of a large data set, inevitably invokes concepts, categories, and classifications the validity of which can only be, beyond a point, assumed. To deny this, to insist that only historical or, more generally, textual interpretation is legitimate, is simply to reject out of hand the possibility of rigorous causal analysis.

In this context, even the very basic and seemingly obvious methodological differences between a great deal of small n "interpretive" research on the one hand and large n "statistical" research on the other should not be overstated; and this suggests, in turn, that Kasza'a deep antipathy toward the "quantitative" and passionate preference for the "qualitative" is difficult to justify. We all know, for example, that many case studies rely on extended, open-ended interviews resulting in detailed and lengthy prose reports, while many large n studies rely on survey instruments involving short questions and fixed response categories. But is it implausible to suggest that survey questions are, in fact, little more than abbreviated, standardized versions of open-ended interview questions, and that fixed response categories are, in effect, highly condensed, shorthand versions of long answers? Note that responses to open-ended interviews are invariably "coded"—sometimes formally with precise numbers, sometimes informally through narrative summary—in terms of generalizable factors or variables that are either present or absent, strong or weak, frequent or infrequent, and so on.[7] It's true, to be sure, that abbreviation, standardization, and condensation should reflect, according to the canons, systematic protocols of theoretical specification, empirical pre-testing, analysis of reliability, and the like. But assuming that these protocols are pursued with care—admittedly a big assumption—it's not clear why a survey process could not in principle produce important and accurate evidence regarding the very same kinds of factors that open-ended surveys seek to investigate. Of course one would often lose at least some of the nuance or complexity that comes from sustained interaction with respondents. On the other hand, one would also gain a great deal in terms of consistency and replicability, along with the really quite extraordinary capacity to compare hundreds or thousands of cases. The more important point, however, is that for both kinds of study the basic strategy is essentially the same: to search for patterns of co-variation among discrete variables of theoretical interest. In this respect, the notion of a vast and deeply principled gulf between quantitative and qualitative, of the sort that Kasza suggests, seems hard to sustain.

The Proof of the Pudding

The most serious and compelling criticism of large n research is, remarkably enough, not mentioned at all by Kasza. This pertains to the problem of measurement. It is a fact, and an extremely important fact, that some factors or variables cannot plausibly be measured with the kind of precision—involving interval or ratio scales—to which large n research often aspires. Consider the quality of being "liberal." We can certainly agree, for example, that Justice David Souter is more liberal than Justice Clarence Thomas. We can, that is, easily enough specify an ordinal relationship between the two with respect to the degree or magnitude of their liberalism. Such a claim would be, moreover, a quantitative one: of the features associated with liberalism, Souter has more than Thomas. But it would be difficult or impossible to formulate that claim in terms of truly precise quantities. Exactly how much more liberal is Souter? Thirty percent more? Twice as much? Five times as much? Merely posing the question seems, at best, euphemistic. Of course one can always tabulate votes, identify voting pairs (e.g., Souter and Stevens), consider the ratings of interest groups (the American Civil Liberties Union, the Sierra Club, the American Conservative Union), and the like. But surely all of that would, in the end, beg the question. For if we measured Souter's liberalism by looking at how often he agreed with the ACLU, we would still have to determine, at a minimum, exactly how liberal the ACLU is, how the ACLU assesses various issues and cases in terms of salience, the extent to which Souter's written opinions or dissents—in virtue of their language and argumentation structure—speak directly to the ACLU's concerns, the extent to which a particular docket includes cases in which liberalism is really at stake, and so on. None of this would prevent us from making comparisons of more or less—even of much more and much less[8]—but claims of greater accuracy would be, at best, problematic. The characteristic of being liberal or of holding and espousing liberal views just doesn't seem to be precisely countable in the way that, say, votes or dollars or units of time are precisely countable.

The mismeasurement of social phenomena is a widespread feature of our world, and there can be no doubt that many large n studies are guilty of it. When it occurs, moreover, it can be an absolutely devastating problem. The claim to measure with precision things that cannot be so measured gives rise to all manner of deeply pernicious and profoundly misleading pseudo-science.[9] But it's not clear what this says about large n research per se. Specifically:

1. The opportunity to mismeasure or otherwise misinterpret data is hardly exclusive to large n research. In-depth interviewing, ethnographic study, participant observation, and related techniques are all obviously fraught with uncertainty and ambiguity. Indeed it's hard to see why anyone would think that such studies are *less* prone to error than large n studies.

2. It's important to note, moreover, that any respectable effort at large n research includes, as an internal and important part of its methodology, systematic protocols for assessing and improving the adequacy of its measures. I refer, for example, to the technical problem of "validity." Does an indicator really measure what it is supposed to be measuring? Of course invalidity can take many forms, and the attempt to measure with precision things that cannot be so measured is only one of them, though a particularly important one. The larger point, however, is that scholars engaged in research of any kind obviously need to think long and hard about the validity of their indicators. Now it's clear that large n researchers are, like small n researchers, trained to do precisely this; certainly all reputable textbooks on the subject belabor the point, as they should. But if it turns out that a scholar makes mistakes along these lines, those mistakes are and ought to be something that critics can identify. If, in other words, a large n study seeks to measure with precision factors that cannot be so measured, there is in principle nothing to prevent other scholars from showing in detail just how this is so, hence to raise the gravest doubts about the scholarly status of the study itself. Indeed this is precisely what one would want and expect them to do.

3. Ultimately, then, the proof of the pudding is in the eating. When a large n study produces strong results—for example, statistically significant coefficients of some kind—we cannot but conclude that *something* is going on. It may not be clear exactly what. Correlations can be spurious, and they can be misleading in many other ways;

survey questions can be poorly phrased, and data sets can be structurally biased; the opportunities for misinterpretation and over-interpretation are ever-present. But searching for mistakes of this kind is precisely what social scientists are supposed to do. It's an absolutely central part of the enterprise. The standard methods of large *n* research, presumably like those of any other scholarly approach, include—indeed profoundly depend upon—procedures for uncovering and correcting just such errors; and if those procedures are not followed scrupulously, other scholars (colleagues, readers, journal referees) are free to point this out. If, on the other hand, the research is done well, the results—those statistically significant co-efficients—have to be taken seriously. They count as evidence, potentially very strong evidence, and cannot be dismissed just because of the methodological tradition out of which they emerge.

Relevance

Kasza claims that quantitative studies are typically irrelevant in that they focus, and presumably must focus, on uninteresting and unimportant questions. Exactly why this should be, and what it has to do with primarily methodological issues, is not immediately clear. One can perhaps imagine how a particular analytic technique might encourage certain kinds of answers and discourage others; and one can perhaps also imagine how such a technique would lead us to ask our research questions in a particular way. But it is somewhat less easy to see why large *n* studies would have any intrinsic tendency to focus on questions either less or more interesting than those examined in other kinds of studies.

Of course what one person finds interesting, exciting, and deeply relevant is not necessarily another's cup of tea. But consider the following questions:

- How and why are levels of citizen political participation in the United States affected by the racial characteristics of officeholders?
- Does the election of African Americans to public office have any effect—positive or negative—on racial tension, racial sympathy, and racial tolerance in society, and if so why?
- Has increased partisan conflict among elites in the United States had any impact on the perceived importance of parties among ordinary voters, and if so why?
- Do democracies fare better or worse in international (primarily military) crises than other kinds of regimes, and if so why?
- Why do governments tend to adopt inefficient, rather than efficient, modes of income redistribution?
- Are smaller groups or organizations more successful in furthering their political interests than larger groups, and if so, why?

- To what extent does "party discipline" today account for voting behavior in the United States Congress?

These are among the questions addressed by articles published in the September 2001 issue of the *APSR,* exactly contemporaneous with the publication of Kasza's article in *PS.* A number of the articles employ statistical analyses of large data sets, while at least two of them operate within the formal rational choice tradition. I am certainly not prepared to claim that their conclusions are correct or even plausible; and again, I am not sure that we can decide in objective terms what is "interesting" per se and what is not. But it's hard to see why anyone would characterize the topics in question as intrinsically irrelevant or unimportant to the empirical study of politics and political behavior. Either they ask why individuals (whether elite or nonelite) do what they do in politics, or else they look at what those various doings produce. They approach such questions by examining a variety of phenomena—racial attitudes, partisan strife, governmental structure, organizational size—that don't seem obviously or self-evidently trivial or insignificant. Indeed some of them seem downright newsworthy. And it's certainly unclear why the questions that these studies address could not attract, in principle, the attention of scholars whose methodological predilections do not involve large *n* data sets. The topics, in other words, don't seem to presuppose, in and of themselves, any particular methodological orientation.

The Sociological Argument

According to Kasza, certain members of our profession—identified explicitly as "numbers crunchers"—aspire to form a "ruling coalition." They pursue a "hegemonic project" designed to "turn the study of politics into what Thomas Kuhn called a 'normal science.'" Presumably this normal science would exclude, or otherwise render marginal, approaches to political research that do not rely primarily on rational choice theory or large *n* data sets. In pursuing such a project, hegemonists seek, among other things, to monopolize journal space, manipulate graduate school curricula, undermine area studies, and "degrade political philosophy." More gravely, they try to "indoctrinate graduate students" and "enforce conformity." They thereby do enormous "harm" to the profession and, in particular, to young scholars. Indeed the prospective ruling coalition has "convinced many young people that they must sacrifice their intellectual integrity to enter this profession." Therefore, the entire endeavor "threatens academic freedom."

Normal Science

The idea of an oppressive, tyrannical normal science undermining the enlightened, liberating forces of revolutionary science has virtually no connection with anything that Thomas Kuhn has written. To the contrary. Normal science is, for him, normal indeed. It reflects the natural and salutary process of scientific inquiry at its best.

Kuhn could hardly be clearer. Normal science, operating internal to a prevailing paradigm, is absolutely "essential to the development of science."[10] Absent such a paradigm, scientific endeavor is a kind of "random activity" that produces, at best, an incoherent "morass" of findings, judgments, and claims (15–16). Kuhn mentions the writings of Pliny the Younger and Francis Bacon as examples of inquiry undertaken in the absence of a prevailing paradigm, and explicitly hesitates even to characterize their work as scientific (16). A science in its "maturity," on the other hand, is a normal science (11). Such a science is, to be sure, "esoteric" and highly technical, largely devoted—in Kuhn's famous imagery—to puzzle-solving and the activity of "mopping-up." But it is also "a highly cumulative enterprise," extremely successful in achieving "the steady extension of the scope and precision of scientific knowledge" (52; cf. 36). Indeed the "very best scientists" have concerned themselves primarily with the problems of "normal research" (34). The result is a scientific profession that has "solved problems that its members could scarcely have imagined and would never have undertaken without commitment to the paradigm" (25). In this sense, one can hardly overestimate the importance of Kuhn's claim that such solutions are always, at least in part, "permanent" (25).

As for revolutionary science, at least two things are worth noting. First, such a science absolutely and entirely depends on the development and maturation of normal science: "failure of existing rules is the prelude to a search for new ones" (68). It is not simply that revolutionary science needs something against which to rebel. The point is much stronger: scientific revolutions are unimaginable in the absence of a "crisis" involving the repeated failure of a prevailing paradigm. New paradigms arise out of the "awareness of anomaly, i.e., the recognition that nature has somehow violated the paradigm-induced expectations that govern normal science" (52). In this way, "research under a paradigm [is] a particularly effective way of inducing paradigm change" (52).

Second, the goal of revolutionary science is always, and can only be, the establishment of a new normal science. Scientific revolutions do not do away with paradigms or with the kind of puzzle-solving, mopping-up activities associated with them. To the contrary: "the decision to reject one paradigm is always simultaneously the decision to accept another" (77). That is to say, the "relatively sudden and unstructured event like the gestalt switch" that undermines normal science (122) creates, in and of itself, the basis for a new era of puzzle-solving and mopping-up, informed, of course, by a brand-new, previously unimagined "world view," that is, a new sense of how things in the world really are.

What all of this suggests is that, from a Kuhnian perspective, the claim that certain political scientists are seeking to establish a normal science is hardly surprising or alarming, and is very far from being an accusation. To the contrary: such individuals, qua scientists, are doing precisely what they should be doing. Indeed their attempt to establish a paradigm is, in Kuhn's terms, nothing other than a reflection of the discipline's relative maturity.

Political Science as Normal Science

Of course Kuhn may well be wrong. He may fail to appreciate the possibility of a pluralistic, multiparadigmatic science characterized by a multiplicity of incompatible theories and methods. Alternatively it may simply be that political science is, and can be, no science at all, hence that Kuhn's account, though accurate for many fields of study, is, in the instant case, literally irrelevant. Of course it is Kasza himself who invokes Kuhn, hence Kasza who insists on his relevance. But perhaps implicit in Kasza's criticism of the hegemonists is a criticism of Kuhn as well.

Now the question of normal science and present-day political science—that is, the question of whether the discipline is governed by a dominant paradigm, which is in turn a question about Kuhn's relevance—is a complicated one. But such a question cannot be answered unless we remember that, according to Kuhn, a paradigm is not a theory. At least in its first, "sociological" sense, it is something more akin to a "world view." A paradigm reflects the "entire constellation of beliefs, values, techniques, and so on shared by the members of a given community" (175). As such, it is apt to subsume a wide range of quite different and competing theories, along with a variety of methods or research protocols. Thus it seems doubtful that something like rational choice theory, as a theory, could be a Kuhnian paradigm in and of itself; it would be, at best, merely one possible manifestation of a much larger and more fundamental set of paradigmatic commitments. And so too for large n research; as a family of methods, it could not itself constitute anything close to a world view.

I would suggest, nonetheless, that political science today is indeed animated and governed by a distinctive and powerful paradigm. The discipline embodies a particular way of looking at things—an extraordinarily influential and historically distinctive structure of ontological belief. Professional political scientists, operating within academic institutions, share, wittingly or otherwise, a rather special and enormously important world view, and hence are very much engaged in something at least roughly akin to a Kuhnian normal science.

To be specific: contemporary political research characteristically is based on the notion that observable social behavior, including political behavior, reflects and is caused by underlying social structures. Such a notion is certainly not peculiar to the study of politics. It constitutes the intellectual foundation of contemporary behavioral science in general; and in this sense, political science is merely one branch of a larger scientific endeavor. As such, however, it reflects the fundamental and indeed rather astounding conviction that what individuals or groups do in politics is actually a result of deep-seated functional patterns and exigencies—whether material or cultural—of which the individuals and groups themselves are typically unaware. Political behavior is, in an important sense, epiphenomenal. It can be explained not primarily by examining conscious motivation and intention but rather by uncovering and explicating a hidden but profoundly influential substrate of social facts.

Such an idea is well captured in an old homily of the voting behavior literature: if you want to know why people voted the way they did, the very last thing you want to do is ask them, at least directly. For their behavior was undoubtedly a more or less unselfconscious expression of underlying social forces—demographic, interactive, social-psychological, cultural, and the like. One can understand political doings, and indeed political thoughts or "opinions," only by discovering the ways in which they reflect and instantiate a variety of fundamental and foundational structural imperatives that themselves compose, in effect, the essence of a particular social formation.

Certainly I'm saying nothing very surprising here. The point nonetheless deserves special emphasis, and for several different reasons. To begin with, the basic idea in question—the social-scientific perspective or paradigm—is itself fairly new. Vestiges of it can perhaps be found in any number of older works, for example, in the middle three books of Aristotle's *Politics,* in the *Germania* of Tacitus, in Machiavelli's *Discourses on Livy.* But the notion that social and political behavior can be systematically and rigorously—that is, scientifically— explained as the more or less direct effect of underlying and specifiable social-structural or ideational forces is, I believe, distinctively modern. It has its roots, arguably, in three great intellectual currents of the nineteenth century: economic, psychological, and sociological. The development of so-called bourgeois political economy was based on the astonishing insight that the choices made by buyers and sellers of commodities inevitably reflect fundamental laws of supply and demand, themselves embodied in and shaped by various (characteristically modern) organized systems of production and consumption. The invention of the psychological unconscious—glimpsed perhaps by Rousseau, encoded in the emergence of the novel as an important literary genre, and formalized in the metaphysical claims of modern psychoanalysis— conceived of everyday behavior as the superficial manifestation of dark, implicit, precognitive drives or impulses. The invention of sociology—primarily the work of Karl Marx, Max Weber, and above all Emile Durkheim—postulated a world of "social facts" interacting in complex, functional relations of cause and effect. Together these currents composed a substantially new way of looking at things, a distinctive paradigm or world view profoundly different from the ways in which previous ages had thought about politics, society, and human action.

Political science, as it has developed since its formal beginnings in the late nineteenth century, well reflects this paradigm in its several manifestations. Thus, for example, certain influential theories of political participation, including rational choice theory, embody one or another economic version of the paradigm, describing individual behavior largely as a matter of utility maximization constrained by deep-seated structural features of institutionalized decision contexts. Similarly, "behavioral" theories of voting behavior, influenced by the so-called Michigan school, pursue an explicitly psychological approach to the paradigm according to which the individual voter's choices are rooted in underlying, nonrational, affective responses to a specific set of symbols and images. Still other studies of voting behavior, inspired by the early sociologically oriented work of the so-called Columbia school, focus on the implicit social-structural and interactive causes of electoral choice. These various approaches are, of course, sharply distinct from one another, and their differences have produced a good deal of serious intellectual and scholarly debate and disagreement. But such debate and disagreement are, it seems to me, largely internal to a broader social-scientific paradigm involving conceptions and metaphysical commitments that would have been quite foreign to, say, Cicero or St. Augustine, to Thomas Aquinas or Dante, even to Thomas Hobbes or John Locke.[11]

The centrality of the social-scientific perspective or world view remains largely unacknowledged in the Perestroika literature, including Kasza's essay. As a result, the explicit call for a pluralistic and "democratic" political science seems at once gratuitous and irrelevant. It is gratuitous insofar as any discipline cannot but reflect a range of arguments—a plurality of distinct, sometimes incompatible claims and theories—the presence of which doesn't undermine but, to the contrary, actually reinforces the authority of the prevailing paradigm. Political science could never be as truly homogeneous as Kasza fears, or so it seems; the paradigm is inherently too generous. On the other hand, the demand for pluralism is irrelevant insofar as it disparages as hegemonic a project that cannot but be informed by an overarching sense of how the world is and that embraces, as a result, standards of judgment and scholarship thought to be legislative for everyone. The attempt to discover, and thence to propagate, the truth is endemic to the social-scientific enterprise; and in principle, any such attempt will inevitably seek to identify and to rule out—to marginalize—arguments and approaches that are judged wanting, at least according to the prevailing standards.

In this sense, then, several of Kasza's specific accusations seem especially perplexing. When Kasza claims that the hegemonists seek to "indoctrinate" graduate students, it's not immediately clear how this is different from the presumably benign and indeed absolutely necessary activity of training them. Don't we want our graduate students to be well versed in the discipline's prevailing paradigm? When Kasza deplores the attempt to monopolize journal space, it's not immediately clear how this is different from the effort to publish only the very best work, defined—as honestly and openly as possible —according to the established canons of a paradigm-based discipline. Shouldn't our top journals reflect, to the degree possible, the cutting edge, such as it may be? When Kasza complains about a ruling (and presumably undemocratic) coalition, it's not immediately clear how this is different from the identification of a group of scholars whose work is thought to be—again according to the discipline's constitutive standards—unusually accomplished and influential. There is, perhaps, an element of conservatism in all this, a certain resistance to change. But as Kuhn shows, that's in the very nature of a discipline interested in discovering or developing an account of how things in the world really are. It's not easy to imagine such a discipline that did not attempt to distinguish good scholarship from bad, hence one that did not seek to identify and recognize the very best scholars; and as an institutional matter, it's not easy to imagine such a discipline that did not accord to the opinions of those scholars a certain special weight.

The Institutional Argument

Kasza's article is sharply critical of important institutions in contemporary political science, and he proposes substantial and explicit institutional reforms. He emphasizes the need to change "hiring" practices in college and university departments so that they will better reflect "methodological pluralism." For the same reason, he insists on the need to reform the "curriculum" that is taught at these institutions, perhaps especially at the graduate level. He says that "we must revamp our professional associations" so that they will come to emphasize "political substance and catholicism with respect to methods and approaches." Perhaps most important, he seeks to change the editorial policies and, by necessary implication, editorial procedures of professional journals, and with the very same goal in mind. All of this is underwritten, moreover, by an accusation of unusual gravity: "to force conformity among us, some hard scientists have corrupted decision-making on hiring, promotion, curriculum, and publication."

Science and Politics

Kasza appears to believe that his institutional recommendations are in some way entailed by his scholarly and sociological criticisms. But even if those criticisms are correct—and I have tried to show that this is far from self-evident—it's not at all clear what that would mean institutionally. For at least in the first instance, scholarly arguments need to be pursued in scholarly rather than institutional or political terms.

If Perestroikans wish to show that mainstream political research is intellectually barren, scientifically unsound, and substantively irrelevant, presumably they ought to do so according to accepted or at least recognizable standards of scholarly or scientific judgment. The point is, again, Kuhnian. Scientific revolutions reflect more or less demonstrable—and demonstrated—failures of normal science. When the prevailing paradigm repeatedly produces and fails to explain anomalous results, the scientific community is inspired to search for better and perhaps entirely different approaches. In the instant case, if rational choice theorists or large n researchers consistently failed satisfactorily to account for political behavior, we should expect such failures to generate new and better ways of conceptualizing and measuring behavior, resulting in more accurate predictions and more persuasive explanations.

Kasza does point to one, though only one, substantial work along these lines, namely Donald Green and Ian Shapiro's fine study of rational choice theory.[12] That study does what it should do. It considers rational choice theory on its own terms and seeks to demonstrate—not merely to assert—its inherent flaws. It attempts to document the failures of the rational choice approach, and to show how those failures are rooted in the very logic of the theory. The trouble, however, is two-fold. First, Green and Shapiro's book, however useful, is far from the last word on the subject. It is an important part of what is, nonetheless, an ongoing dialogue, the conclusion of which is by no means certain.[13] Second, one finds in Kasza's article, and in the Perestroika literature generally, a paucity of similarly serious and systematic critiques. Too often, the barrenness of mainstream political science is merely assumed, not demonstrated. The scholarly and intellectual task of showing where and why large n studies, for example, have failed—and where and why other kinds of studies have succeeded in providing better results—has been pursued inadequately at best.

In this sense, the push to reform decision-making institutions—journals, academic departments, the APSA itself—seems both premature and inappropriate. Scholarly decisions about what to publish, what to study, and whom to appoint should be made on scholarly grounds. Case studies should be published only if they are judged publishable according to the very best scientific standards. The discipline should become more pluralistic only if we can explicitly show why doing so will deepen and enrich our understanding of politics. Hiring decisions should reflect only the kind of intellectual diversity that is warranted on intellectual grounds. To reform institutions in the absence of all this is to substitute politics for scholarship. It is to enshrine as scientific outcomes that may well have no scientific warrant but that instead reflect purely political motivations. It is indeed to propose a kind of intellectual revolution for no very clear intellectual reason. Kuhn himself suggests an analogy between political and scientific revolutions. But he also makes clear that an analogy is far from an identity. The Perestroika movement runs the risk of conflating political and scientific endeavor, hence of undermining the integrity of scholarly analysis and critique.[14]

Corruption

Everything I have just said would be trumped, of course, if it could be shown that the discipline's primary institutions have already been politicized along these lines. I take it that this is in part what Kasza has in mind when he accuses hard scientists of "corrupting" our learned journals, departments, and societies. Presumably my fears about Perestroika are already being realized by the so-called ruling coalition. Editorial decisions are made not on scholarly but on political grounds. Hiring decisions reflect not intellectual quality but illicit ideological prejudice and cronyism. Learned societies distribute rewards—material and honorific—for other than scientific reasons.

These are harsh accusations. To the degree that they are thought to reflect deep-seated structural exigencies—as in the underlying sociology of normal science—they call for the kind of scholarly engagement and critique that I have described earlier. But to the degree that they reflect darker claims of conscious or even unconscious prejudice and collusion, they are grave indeed. As such, they need to be formulated with special care and to be based only on the clearest and most compelling evidence.

While Kasza makes no effort to provide such evidence, David Pion-Berlin and Dan Cleary, in their contribution to the present volume, do. It seems doubtful, though, that the data they present are anywhere near sufficient to justify the serious and disturbing claims that they make. The data do pretty clearly demonstrate a certain methodological "imbalance" in the *APSR*. During the decade of the 1990s, nearly all of the published "empirical" articles employed either large n methods or rational choice theory. Beyond this, however, the data indicate absolutely nothing. Specifically, Tables 24.1–24.5 provide no evidence whatsoever about the cause of the imbalance. The data are purely descriptive; they include nothing that could properly be called an explanatory variable, except for Table 24.3's change-of-editorship variable, which turns out to have no predictive value. Pion-Berlin and Cleary claim to have discovered in their research "a historical editorial bias" that has "accumulated for decades," amounting to an ongoing pattern of "discriminatory practices" in which the journal has "systematically turned its back" on much of the discipline; a pattern, moreover, in which editors have relied—presumably intentionally—on "tighter-knit communities of methodologically like-minded scholars" with, apparently, an unreasonable "hostility and intolerance that raises serious doubts about their credibility as reviewers." But while the data are certainly *consistent* with such claims, they are exactly equally consistent with any number of quite different, far more benign, and no less plausible interpretations. Thus, for example, the authors downplay the importance of self-selection or nonsubmission, yet acknowledge that between August 1995 and August 2000 only 2 percent of *APSR* submissions were "qualitative empirical studies"—an astonishing figure given the supposedly "vast numbers of qualitative specialists" in the profession. Of course the data themselves say absolutely nothing about the quality of those submissions. Pion-Berlin and Cleary also downplay the rather extraordinary finding that fully one-fourth of all *APSR* articles are in political theory—a finding from which one might conclude that theorists, far from being "marginalized" as Kasza suggests, are actually sharply overrepresented in the discipline's major journal.[15] Perhaps most seriously, the data provide no evidence whatsoever to show that editors and referees have made decisions on anything other than honest scholarly grounds. To be sure, the data provide no exculpatory evidence either. But serious accusations and insinuations of unprofessional and unscholarly conduct carry with them very significant burdens of proof. In the instant case, I doubt that those burdens have been even approached, much less satisfied.

Pion-Berlin and Cleary do make one thing admirably clear: theirs is a starkly "political agenda." Again, this seems to me troubling. Politics is, at least at one level and on one plausible construal, the activity by which individuals and organizations with sharply different and competing interests—economic, moral, ideological, and the like—use a variety of resources to influence the decision-making process. The goal of the activity is comparative advantage, and the decision-making process is good to the degree that it is inclusive, responsive, and fair. Scholarship seems to me a very different kind of activity. It is, by definition, the dispassionate inquiry into how things in the world really are. The goal of such an activity is the attainment of truth, not comparative advantage, and the decision-making process is good to the degree that it reflects the very highest standards of evidence and argument. To confuse these two types of activity—and willfully to substitute one for the other—is to commit a kind of category error, the result of which is apt to be harmful to both politics and scholarship alike.

Notes

I am grateful to Paul Gronke, Albyn Jones, Brian Newman, and Marc Schneiberg for helpful comments on an earlier draft of this chapter.

1. Though not exclusively. See last section of this chapter.

2. *PS: Political Science and Politics* 34 (September 2001): 597–99.

3. For typical examples see Anselm Strauss and Juliet Corbin, *Basics of Qualitative Research: Grounded Theory Procedures and Techniques* (Newbury Park, CA: Sage Publications, 1990), 17–23; W. Lawrence Neuman, *Social Research Methods: Qualitative and Quantitative Approaches* (Boston: Allyn and Bacon, 1991), 321–23; and Norman K. Denzin and Yvonna S. Lincoln, *Handbook of Qualitative Research* (Thousand Oaks, CA: Sage Publications, 2000).

4. See, for example, Strauss and Corbin, *Basics of Qualitative Research,* 71, 100–102, 161–66. See also Neuman, *Social Research Methods,* 420–22.

5. Michael Oakeshott, *Rationalism in Politics* (London: Methuen, 1962), 157.

6. By the same token, historians who focus systematically on questions of cause and effect are engaged in a scientific endeavor—again, a perfectly acceptable choice, especially in a world where disciplinary boundaries are, and ought to be, permeable. Note, however, that the permeability of boundaries isn't the same as the elimination of boundaries or of the distinctions to which they conform.

7. Strauss and Corbin, *Basics of Qualitative Research,* 71–72.

8. For a representative recent example see Lee Epstein, Valerie Hoekstra, Jeffrey A. Segal, and Harold J. Spaeth, "Do Political Preferences Change? A Longitudinal Study of U.S. Supreme Court Justices," *Journal of Politics* 60 (August 1998): 801–18.

9. In the world of higher education alone, we have suffered from serious problems of mismeasurement in at least three areas: the obsession with so-called educational "assessment," whereby colleges and universities are forced by accrediting agencies to use "objective" quantitative indicators to measure that immensely complex and intricate thing we call student learning; the crude definition of scholastic "aptitude" in terms of essentially two numbers, one "verbal," the other

"mathematical"; and the *U.S. News & World Report* annual ranking of colleges and universities, a virtual paradigm of pseudo-scientific nonsense.

10. Thomas Kuhn, *The Structure of Scientific Revolutions* (Chicago: University of Chicago Press, 1970), 24. The numbers in parentheses in the text following this are page references to this volume.

11. The recent tradition of reading Hobbes in the light of rational choice theory, exemplified by Jean Hampton's *Hobbes and the Social Contract Tradition* (Cambridge: Cambridge University Press, 1986), is immensely insightful; but that's very different from saying that it describes what Hobbes himself explicitly had in mind.

12. Donald P. Green and Ian Shapiro, *Pathologies of Rational Choice Theory: A Critique of Applications in Political Science* (New Haven, CT: Yale University Press, 1994).

13. See, for example, the appreciative but also highly critical review by Kristen Renwick Monroe in *Political Theory* 25 (April 1997): 289–95.

14. It should be clear that in insisting on a strong distinction between science and politics I am by no means seeking to resurrect the myth of a value-free political science. That myth was exploded many years ago, perhaps most famously by Charles Taylor. But it is one thing to recognize the omnipresence of value as a potentially confounding factor, the influence of which scholars and scientists must strain both to acknowledge and to minimize, and quite another to celebrate value as the very life-blood of political action.

15. According to the APSA, only 17.5 percent of its members select political theory as one of their fields of interest; and it seems certain that many of these are not exclusively or even primarily theorists.

Further Reading

Because one of Perestroika's concerns has been graduate education, I asked the contributors to this volume to suggest possible readings too often overlooked in traditional methods courses, which tend to treat methodology as statistical. I have included the pieces suggested most frequently, along with commentary by the people who suggested each piece. The list is offered as suggestive and is intended to be supplementary, not comprehensive. It begins with pieces that provide a recent history of the discipline, because works that fill the gap between political theory (traditionally and perhaps narrowly understood) and political "science" are often omitted in graduate education. My thanks to the contributors, to members of the Perestroika list serve who submitted suggestions, and to David Easton for reminding me to note (1) the *Newsletter* of the APSA Organized Section on Qualitative Methods for its systematic and serious discussions about the use of qualitative methods and (2) the new summer training institute of the Arizona State University Consortium on Qualitative Methods (CQRM), a major communication mechanism for highlighting underlying systematic assumptions and methods to be found in the best kinds of qualitative research.

Recent History of the Discipline

Almond, Gabriel. 1966. "Political Theory and Political Science." *American Political Science Review (APSR)* 60 (4): 869–79. Following David Truman's presidential address to the APSA the previous year, Almond asserts a continuous arc of political-scientific development and attempts to move that project past behavioralism to the new "paradigm" of systems theory.

———. 1990. *A Discipline Divided: Schools and Sects in Political Science.* New York: Sage. Contains Almond's well-known "Separate Tables" essay arguing that political scientists do not talk across approaches anymore.

Dahl, Robert A. 1961. "The Behavioral Approach in Political Science: Epitaph for a Monument to a Successful Protest." *APSR* 55 (4): 63–72. Challenges the image of behavioralism as a monolithic movement; rather, he presents behavioralism as a "mood" or "scientific outlook" that successfully brought the study of politics new, rigorous methods and a concern for empirical analysis. Dahl saw behavioralism fading in the wake of its successes as its contributions were folded into the discipline's practices.

Easton, David. 1969. "The New Revolution in Political Science." *APSR* 63 (4): 105–61. Sketches outlines of a "post-behavioral" political science to meet the challenges of a new series of political crises in the United States and abroad (and, probably not coincidentally, the challenges of dissenters within the APSA). Easton calls for his colleagues to turn the advances of a science of politics to the pressing issues of war and civil unrest, to make the study of politics more "relevant" and "prescriptive."

Easton, David, and Raymond Seidelman, eds. 1993. *Discipline and History: Political Science in the United States.* Ann Arbor: University of Michigan Press. Central historical statements of the aims and scientific aspirations of American political science, coupled with short contemporary critical essays that review and compare these pieces in the history of the discipline.

Easton, David, John S. Dryzek, and Stephen T. Leonard, eds. 1995. *Political Science in History: Research Programs and Political Traditions.* Cambridge: Cambridge University Press. Recent critical, reflective essays that put the history of American political science in the context of other intellectual, social, and political trends.

Easton, David, John G. Gunnell, Raymond Seidelman, John Dryzek, and Stephen T. Leonard. 1990. "Controversy: Can Political Science History Be Neutral?" *APSR* 84 (2): 587–607.

Green, Philip, and Sanford Levinson, eds. 1970. *Power and Community: Dissenting Essays in Political Science.* New York: Pantheon. Essays by leading lights in and allies of the Caucus for a New Political Science that capture the range of the caucus's criticisms of behavioralism and other influences of positivism in the study of politics. Ancestor or precursor to the present volume.

Gunnell, John. 1993. *The Descent of Political Theory.* Chicago: University of Chicago Press. A treatment of the marginalization and eventual "dispersion" of political theory as it was split in American political science between an "empirical" theory and a "normative" philosophy. Gunnell argues that this resulted from the combination of the quest for a science of politics with the influence of the "Weimar conversation" over the relationship of liberalism and science in the modern world brought about by the influence of German universities at American political science's birth and of the émigrés or refugees from Nazi Germany in the 1940s.

Lindblom, Charles. 1990. *Inquiry and Change: The Troubled Attempt to Understand and Shape Society.* New Haven, CT: Yale University Press.

———. 1998. "Political Science in the 1940s and 1950s." *Dædalus* 126 (1): 225–52. Calls for a political science that moves away from a technocratic, social-control approach to society in favor of a political inquiry of data collection, critical observation, debates, and hard questions.

Monroe, Kristen Renwick, ed. 1997. *Contemporary Empirical Political Theory.* Berkeley: University of California Press. Traces the discipline's move from traditional political theory through behavioralism, rational choice, and postmodernism and links this to work in empirical political theory. Retrospectives by scholars who pioneered the field, including Gabriel Almond, David Easton, Murray Edelman, and Bill Riker, plus chapters on feminist theory, realist social theory, identity theory, policy models, and the possibility of value-free social science.

Purcell, Edward A. 1973. *The Crisis of Democratic Theory*. Lexington: University Press of Kentucky. Describes the controversy surrounding the newly developing descriptive and objective approaches to democratic theory, a controversy that emerged when critics in the late 1920s and the 1930s began to charge that such a value-free science of democracy would be unable to help protect a free democratic society against the threat of totalitarianism. Purcell concludes that postwar democratic theory addressed the gap between a normative commitment to democratic politics and a science of politics by building the outlines and presuppositions of American democratic institutions into their theoretical definitions and research programs.

Ricci, David. 1984. *The Tragedy of Political Science: Politics, Scholarship, and Democracy*. Berkeley: University of California Press. Argues that political science has failed in its aspirations to be a science of democracy because its three self-proclaimed goals—to promote democracy, to be scientific, and to improve public life and political institutions—are practically and conceptually incompatible.

Ross, Dorothy. 1991. *The Origins of American Social Science*. Cambridge: Cambridge University Press.

Seidelman, Raymond, with Edward J. Harpham. 1985. *Disenchanted Realists: Political Science and the American Crisis, 1885-1984*. Albany: State University of New York Press. The authors argue that the history of American political science's search for a "third tradition" between populism and elitism became corrupted over time as practitioners came gradually to confuse crises in politics with crises in political science. It is instructive to consider the Caucus for a New Political Science in the late 1960s and the present Perestroika movement in light of Seidelman and Harpham's argument.

Smith, Mark C. 1994. *Social Science in the Crucible: The American Debate over Objectivity and Purpose, 1918-1941*. Durham, NC: Duke University Press. Detailed treatments of Wesley Mitchell, Charles Merriam, Robert Lynd, Charles Beard, and Harold Lasswell and their struggles between moral purpose and scientific detachment in research, with the complicating factors of research funding, institutional politics, and political history as their context. Smith's description of the turbulent relationship between Beard the activist and Merriam the scientist —and the complications of their respective positions and arguments that each man's history presented—is both noteworthy and a story familiar to contemporary practitioners of political science.

Smith, Rogers M. 1998. "Still Blowing in the Wind: The American Quest for a Democratic, Scientific Political Science." *Dædalus* 126 (1): 253-87. A sharply written call for a "Socratic" political science.

Truman, David. 1965. "Disillusion and Regeneration: The Quest for a Discipline." *APSR* 59 (4): 865-73. Uses Kuhn's *The Structure of Scientific Revolutions* as the basis for arguing that political science, despite the advances of the behavioral movement, still needed (especially in the face of growing dissent in the profession) a paradigm that would allow it to become a disciplinary science proper.

Wolin, Sheldon S. 1969. "Political Theory as a Vocation." *APSR* 63 (4): 1062-82. Major criticism from the camp of political philosophers of the effects of behavioralism on the study of politics, and of unqualified notions of a science of politics or of society in general.

Methodology

Bayard de Volo, Lorraine, and Edward Schatz. 2004. "From the Inside Out: Ethnographic Methods in Political Research." *PS: Political Science and Politics* 38 (2): 267–71. Ethnographic methods have great utility in political research—whether research in the positivist or the interpretivist tradition—but they are rarely used by political scientists. This article covers their utility, making a call for their deeper incorporation into the discipline.

Berger, Peter L., and Thomas Luckmann. 1966. *The Social Construction of Reality.* New York: Anchor. Develops Schutzian phenomenology to the study of human action. A central source of the notion of "social constructionism" in social theory.

Bernstein, Richard J. 1976. *The Restructuring of Social and Political Theory.* New York: Harcourt Brace Jovanovich. An overview of early debates over the possibility of a science of politics, unsympathetic to the "positivist temper" of the social sciences. Bernstein believes a science of society (properly qualified) is possible, and explicates and teases out the implications of important contributions to the discipline's discussion about a science of politics, including, for example, David Easton's and David Truman's arguments.

Blyth, Mark, and Robin Varghese. 1999. "The State of the Discipline in American Political Science: Be Careful What You Wish For." *British Journal of Political Science and International Relations* 1 (3): 345–66. A genealogy of comparative politics from the 1960s to the present. A "how to get your head around the discipline" piece that argues that perennial concerns never really get resolved; they simply reappear in new language.

Brady, Henry E., and David Collier. 2004. *Rethinking Social Inquiry: Diverse Tools, Shared Standards.* New York: Rowman and Littlefield. A direct response to King, Keohane, and Verba (listed later).

Bulmer, Martin. 1986. "The Value of Qualitative Methods." In Martin, *Social Science and Social Policy.* Boston: Allen and Unwin, 180–203. An explication of the uses of qualitative methods.

Burrell, Gibson, and Gareth Morgan. 1979. *Sociological Paradigms and Organisational Analysis.* Exeter, NH: Heinemann. A treatment of a wide range of social theories, from positivism to interpretivism, including phenomenology, hermeneutics, symbolic interaction, and ethnomethodology.

Crick, Bernard. 1959. *The American Science of Politics.* Berkeley: University of California. An early systematic critical survey of the history of American political science. Questions the discipline's claims to scientific status—because few political scientists had any idea what a "science" really was—but finds early political science engaging nonetheless, because actual research had a good feel for politics and public life.

D'Amico, Robert. 1989. *Historicism and Knowledge.* New York: Routledge. D'Amico writes in the analytical tradition—with Marxist sympathies—but takes on claims that knowledge can be lifted from its historical context and attributed universality, and finds them all wanting, from Popper to Foucault.

Devault, Marjorie. 1990. "Talking and Listening from Women's Standpoint: Feminist Strategies for Interviewing and Analysis." *Social Problems* 37 (1): 96–116. A provocative article that asks the reader to think about how language and power affect what interviewees are (and are not) able to articulate.

Dupré, John. 1993. *The Disorder of Things: Metaphysical Foundations of the Disunity of Science.* Cambridge, MA: Harvard University Press.

Eagleton, Terry. 1991. Ideology: An Introduction. 1991. London: Verso. A Marxist exploration of the concept of ideology from the Enlightenment to postmodernism.

Elman, Colin, and Miriam Fendius Elman. 2002. "How Not to Be Lakatos Intolerant: Appraising Progress in IR Research." *International Studies Quarterly* 46 (2): 231–62.

Erlandson, David A., et al. 1993. *Doing Naturalistic Inquiry.* Newbury Park, CA: Sage. Tells how to develop alternative evaluative criteria to validity and reliability.

Friedman, Jeffrey. 1996. *The Rational Choice Controversy: Economic Models of Politics Reconsidered.* New Haven, CT: Yale University Press. A critical look at rational choice modeling.

Galison, Peter, and David J. Stump, ed. 1996. *The Disunity of Science: Boundaries, Context, and Power.* Stanford, CA: Stanford University Press. A volume on the variety (and therefore the pluralism) of "paradigms" that one finds in the hard sciences. See the chapters by Arthur Fine and John Dupré.

Gans, Herbert. 1976. "Personal Journal: B. On the Methods Used in This Study." In M. Patricia Golden, ed., *The Research Experience.* Itasca, IL: F. E. Peacock, 49–59. Discusses the differences between "observation" and "participation."

Geertz, Clifford. 1973. *The Interpretation of Cultures.* New York: Basic Books. Discusses the notion that social science should be about the study of meaning, providing "thick descriptions" of its subject matters.

Fine, Arthur. 1984. "The Natural Ontological Attitude." In Jarrett Leplin, ed., *Scientific Realism.* Berkeley: University of California Press. 1984, 83–107.

Flyvbjerg, Bent. 2001. *Making Social Science Matter: Why Social Inquiry Fails and How It Can Succeed Again.* New York: Cambridge University Press. Flyvbjerg uses Aristotle, Nietzsche, Foucault, and Bourdieu to demonstrate that what he calls a phronetic social science can offer a social science that would work within any contextualized setting to challenge power, especially as it is articulated in discourse.

———. 2004. "A Perestroikan Straw Man Answers Back: David Laitin and Phronetic Political Science." *Politics & Society* 32 (3): 398–416. Argues that political scientists should substitute *phronesis* for *episteme* to avoid emulating natural science, thus constructing social science that is strong where natural science is weak: in the reflexive analysis and discussion of values and interests aimed at praxis.

Green, Daniel, ed. 2002. *Constructivism and Comparative Politics.* New York: M. E. Sharpe. A volume whose first several chapters feature methodological discussions of use to scholars of comparative politics.

Green, Donald, and Ian Shapiro. 1994. *Pathologies of Rational Choice Theory: A Critique of Applications in Political Science.* New Haven, CT: Yale University Press. The first few chapters summarize the development of and assumptions underlying rational choice theory. The rest of the book is a strongly stated condemnation of applied work, with a focus on American political science.

Hawkesworth, M. E. 1988. *Theoretical Issues in Policy Analysis.* Albany: SUNY Press. Discusses positivist presuppositions and their critique and presents a set of case studies applying a post-positivist perspective.

Hesse, Mary. 1980. "Theory and Value in the Social Sciences." In C. Hookway and P. Pettit, eds., *Action and Interpretation.* Cambridge: Cambridge University Press, 1–16.

Hollinger, David A., and Charles Capper, eds. 1997. *The American Intellectual Tradition,* 3rd ed. Vols. 1 and 2. New York: Oxford University Press. Addresses key aspects of American political culture: liberty versus democracy, religion, war and imperialism, dissent and the cultural avant-garde, civil war and reform, and so on, and shows their relation to political science.

Horkheimer, Max, and Theodor W. Adorno. 1990. *Dialectic of Enlightenment.* Trans. John Cumming. New York: Continuum. A critique of modern culture and a founding text of the critical theory movement.

Johnson, James. 1993. "Is Talk Really Cheap? Prompting Conversation between Critical Theory and Rational Choice." *APSR* 87: 74–78.

King, G., Robert O. Keohane, and Sidney Verba. 1994. *Designing Social Inquiry.* Princeton, NJ: Princeton University Press. A classic statement, from the behavioral or rational choice perspective, of what methodology should be. Argues that qualitative research can and should be understood in the same terms as quantitative or aggregate research, and that social science research should follow the same rules for understanding causation, for drawing inferences, and for linking evidence to theory.

Klotz, Audie, and Cecelia Lynch. *Constructing Global Politics: Strategies for Research.* Forthcoming. Addresses the constructivist framework in international relations (IR): what it is, where it comes from, how it differs from other major IR paradigms, and how to use it. Organized around the concepts of structure, agency, interests, and identity, it discusses the stakes involved in a variety of specific methods used in constructivist work, from comparative case studies to genealogy to discourse analysis.

Kondo, Doreen. 1990. *Crafting Selves.* Chicago: University of Chicago Press. Tells how to do interpretive ethnography. The first chapter is a methodological primer on how to do reflexive social science.

Kuhn, Thomas. 1996. *The Structure of Scientific Revolutions.* Chicago: University of Chicago Press.

Lin, Ann Chih. 1998. "Bridging Positivist and Interpretivist Approaches to Qualitative Methods." *Policy Studies Journal* 26 (1): 162–80. Growing out of Gary King, Robert Keohane, and Sidney Verba's *Designing Social Inquiry: Scientific Inference in Qualitative Research* but moving beyond it, this article compares qualitative and quantitative approaches and shows how they can be used to complement each other

MacDonald, Susan Peck. 1989. "Data-Driven and Conceptually Driven Academic Discourse." *Written Communication* 6 (4): 411–35. Examines how research practices differ between the humanities and the social sciences.

MacIntyre, Alasdair. "Is a Science of Comparative Politics Possible?" In MacIntyre, *Against the Self-Images of the Age: Essays on Ideology and Philosophy.* Oxford: Blackwell, 1972, 260–79. Uses a novel hook—"There was once a man who aspired to be the author of the general theory of holes"—to demonstrate why one cannot study politics without addressing intentionality. Reprinted in (1) Philosophy, Politics, and Society, 4th series, ed. Peter Laslett, W. G. Runciman, and Quentin Skinner (Oxford: Blackwell, 1972), 8–26, and in (2) *The Philosophy of Social Explanation,* ed. Alan Ryan (Oxford: Oxford University Press, 1973), 171–88.

Matheson, S. 1988. "Why Triangulate?" *Educational Researcher* 17 (2): 13–17. Questions standard, positivist understandings of the concept of triangulation.

McKeown, Timothy J. 1999. "Case Studies and the Statistical Worldview: Review of Gary King, Robert O. Keohane, and Sydney Verba, *Designing Social Inquiry: Scientific Inference in Quantitative Research." International Organization* 53 (1): 161–90.

Monroe, Kristen Renwick, ed. 1991. *The Economic Approach to Politics: A Critical Reassessment of the Theory of Rational Action.* New York: HarperCollins. Critiques the assumptions underlying rational choice theory. Includes chapters by the founders of rational choice (Anthony Downs, Herb Simon, and Bill Riker) as well as by important critics. See also *Political Psychology* 16 (March 1995), a special issue titled "Political Economy and Political Psychology," which sets rational choice theory in the context of behavioral research and asks how rational choice has fared in attempting to fill in what behavioralism omitted.

———. 2004. *The Hand of Compassion.* Princeton, NJ: Princeton University Press. Illustrates how empirical political theory can yield insight into basic thinking about politics. An appendix on narrative details how interpretation of narrative interviews yields insight into the cognitive processes of others. The rest of the book shows how cognitive processes influence behavior—here the focus is on moral behavior—thus providing insight into the "little black box" left mysteriously empty in behavioral research.

Murphy, Jerome T. 1980. *Getting the Facts.* Santa Monica, CA: Goodyear. Discusses what makes research "scientific" even if it includes no numbers.

O'Neill, Barry. 1995. "Weak Models, Nil Hypotheses and Decorative Statistics: Review of Donald Green and Ian Shapiro's *Pathologies of Rational Choice Theory." Journal of Conflict Resolution* 39 (4): 731–48.

———. 1999. "Game Theory and Intangibles in International Relations." In O'Neill, *Honor, Symbols and War.* Ann Arbor: University of Michigan Press, 253–62.

Papa, M. J., M. A. Auwal, and A. Singhal. 1995. "Dialectic of Control and Emancipation in Organizing for Social Change: A Multi-Theoretical Study of the Grameen Bank in Bangladesh." *Communication Theory* 5: 189–223. Presents team research on the same topic using different paradigms and methodologies.

Parenti, Michael. 1974. "Reviewing the Reviewers: Ideological Bias in the *APSR* Book Section." *PS: Political Science and Politics* 7 (4): 370–74. An old and short piece, but edifying about the narrow conception within the discipline of what is legitimate and illegitimate political science. As relevant now as it was then.

Pierce, Jennifer. 1995. "Articulating the Self in Field Research." In Pierce, *Gender Trials: Emotional Lives in Contemporary Law Firms.* Berkeley: University of California Press, 189–214. An appendix analyzes the ways in which field researchers are simultaneously insiders and outsiders as a function of their own and others' multiple identities, and how these relationships affect research findings.

Polkinghorne, Donald. 1983. *Methodology for the Human Sciences.* Albany: SUNY Press. An overview of continental philosophies, situating them against positivism and explicating their application to the study of human action.

Putnam, Hilary. 1981. "Two Conceptions of Rationality." In Putnam, *Reason, Truth and History.* Cambridge: Cambridge University Press, 103–27. Argues that the two dominant social epistemologies—positivism and relativism—are self-refuting. Opens up the space for a "conventionalist" alternative and provides the underpinning of constructivism.

Rudolph, Susanne H., and Lloyd I. Rudolph. 1967. Introduction to *The Modernity of Tradition: Political Development in India.* Chicago: University of Chicago Press. Challenges the Eurocentrism of modernization theory. Addresses the problem of the "imperialism of categories" that can accompany comparative political studies when Western scholars turn to societies and polities outside the Atlantic community, to the world East and South of Istanbul. Especially relevant now as rational choice categories—via the new institutionalism—are being forced onto other societies with little regard for or understanding of local politics.

———. 2003. "Engaging Subjective Knowledge: How Amar Singh's Diary Narratives of and by the Self Help Explain Identity Politics." *Perspectives on Politics* 1 (4): 681–94.

Ryan, Alan. 1972. *The Philosophy of the Social Sciences.* New York: Pantheon. An overview of the question regarding whether there can be a science of society. Presents and critiques then-contemporary theories about what a science is, and the strongest arguments for and against a social science, including some central contributions from political thinkers, such as David Easton and Alasdair MacIntyre.

Schatz, Edward, and Irwin J. Schatz. 2003. "Medicine and Political Research: Parallel Lessons in Methodological Excess." *PS: Political Science and Politics* 36 (3): 417–22. Details the "evidence-based medicine" movement within medical research, arguing that it has led to methodological excesses similar to those within political science. Argues that if even medical research requires methodological pluralism, the same is doubly true for political research.

Schmidt, Mary R. 1993. "Grout: Alternative Kinds of Knowledge and Why They Are Ignored." *Public Administration Review* 53 (6): 525–30. Explores the relationship between power and knowledge using the case history of the collapse of a dam.

Schram, Sanford F. 2002. *Praxis for the Poor: Piven and Cloward and the Future of Social Science in Social Welfare.* New York: New York University Press. Includes examples of problem-driven, multimethodological research on issues of race, poverty, and welfare that illustrate that social science can play a meaningful role in politics.

———. 2004. "Beyond Paradigm: Resisting the Assimiliation of Phroentic Social Science." *Politics and Society* 32 (3): 417–33. Continues the Laitin-Schram debate and suggests how Perestroika could build on Flyvbjerg's insights to promote a "post-paradigmatic" social science.

———. 2005. "Contextualizing Racial Disparities under Welfare Reform: Toward a New Poverty Research." *Perspectives on Politics* 3 (2) (in press). Argues the need to move beyond the interpretive and normative limitations of conventional public policy research to address issues such as the role of race in welfare reform.

Shapiro, Ian. 1982. "Realism in the Study of the History of Ideas." *History of Political Thought* 3 (3): 535–78.

———. 1998. "Can the Rational Choice Approach Cope with Culture?" *PS: Political Science and Politics* 31 (1): 40–43.

———. 2005. *The Flight from Reality in the Human Sciences*. Princeton, NJ: Princeton University Press.

Shapiro, Ian, and Alexander Wendt. 1992. "The Difference That Realism Makes: Social Science and the Politics of Consent." *Politics and Society* 20 (2): 197–224.

Shotter, John. 1993. *Conversational Realities*. New York: Russell Sage. An exchange with scientific realists on how issues of ontology affect research practice.

———. 1993. *Cultural Politics of Everyday Life: Social Constructionism, Rhetoric and Knowledge of the Third Kind*. Toronto: University of Toronto Press and Taylor and Francis Group. One of the best explications of what a post-structural methodology looks like.

Steinmo, Sven, Kathleen Thelen, and Frank Longsreth, eds. 1992. *Structuring Politics: Historical Institutionalism in Comparative Analysis*. New York: Cambridge University Press. Highlights the methodological and theoretical foundations of the historical institutional approach and illustrates the potential of the approach to illuminate a broad range of issues, especially in comparative politics, such as how and why institutions change, how political ideas are filtered through institutional structures in the formation of specific policies, and how institutional structure can have unintended effects on the shaping of policy.

Thomas, George. Under review. "The Qualitative Foundations of Political Science: Moving Beyond KKV." Critiques work by David Collier and Charles Ragin and others as representatives of post–King-Keohane-Verba thinking.

Toulmin, Stephen. 2002. *Return to Reason*. Berkeley: University of California Press. Builds on philosophy of science, ordinary language philosophy, rhetoric, and the analysis of practical arts to offer a historically informed examination of the problem of scientism in the social sciences.

———. 2003 (1958). *The Uses of Argument*. New York: Cambridge University Press. Argues that the pragmatic criterion doesn't apply to the social sciences because there is no prior agreement on what it means for an explanation "to work." Social science is more like arguing a case before a jury.

Walt, Steven. 1999. "Rigor or Rigor Mortis? Rational Choice and Security Studies." *International Security* 23 (4): 5–48. Use with the responses to Walt by Lisa L. Martin, Emerson M. S. Niou and Peter Ordeshook, and Frank Zagare, and Walt's reply, in *International Security* 24 (Fall 1999): 74–130. Expresses IR's frustration with the banalities of rational choice. The responses are just as telling as to what really drives many arguments.

Wendt, Alexander, and Ian Shapiro. 1997. "The False Promise of Realist Social Theory." In Kristen Monroe, ed., Contemporary *Empirical Political Theory*. Berkeley: University of California Press, 166–87.

White, Hayden. 1973. *Metahistory: The Historical Imagination in Nineteenth-Century Europe*. Baltimore, MD: Johns Hopkins University Press. Shows how the persuasiveness of historical accounts rests on implicit narrative logic.

Yanow, Dvora. 2000. *Conducting Interpretive Policy Analysis*. Newbury Park, CA: Sage. Includes an overview of the issues in interpretive philosophies and methods for the study of the communication of meaning and a discussion of topics such as metaphor analysis, category analysis, and myth analysis.

———. 2003. *Constructing "Race" and "Ethnicity" in America: Category-Making in Public Policy and Administration*. Armonk, NY: M. E. Sharpe. An example of category analysis, focusing on race and ethnicity and the implementation of category-making and counting practices in birth or death tallies, crime reports, and other agency and policy acts, as well as at their use in academic research.

Yanow, Dvora, and Peregrine Schwartz-Shea. 2005. *Interpretation and Method: Empirical Research Methods and the Interpretive Turn.* Armonk, NY: M. E. Sharpe, forthcoming.

Weber, Max. 1949. *The Methodology of the Social Sciences.* New York: Simon and Schuster. A foundational expression of many methodological discussions of what constitutes a science of politics. The English translations of many of Weber's most important essays leave a lot to be desired.

Two Relevant Symposia

1995. "The Qualitative-Quantitative Disputation: Gary King, Robert O. Keohane, and Sidney Verba's *Designing Social Inquiry: Scientific Inference in Qualitative Research.*" *APSR* 89 (2): 454–82. Includes original debate on King, Keohane, and Verba's methodological perspectives, with articles by James A. Caporaso, David Collier, David Laitin, Ronald Rogowski, and Sidney Tarrow.

2004. "Two Paths to a Science of Politics." *Perspectives on Politics* 2 (2): 295–323. Offers direct engagement with Perestroikan issues. Includes an introduction by Henry Brady and articles by Rogers Smith and Jim Granato and Frank Scioli.

Contributors

Christopher H. Achen, professor of politics at Princeton University, has written on methodological issues in public opinion and voting, in public policy, and in international relations. Co-editor of two forthcoming volumes, *The European Union Decides* and *Voter Turnout in Multi-Level Systems,* Achen appears in this volume as the co-chair of an APSA committee and is not affiliated with Perestroika.

Martha Ackelsberg is professor of government at Smith College, where she teaches courses in urban politics, political theory, and feminist theory. Author of *Free Women of Spain: Anarchism and the Struggle for the Emancipation of Women* and articles on families, feminism, community politics, and social movements, Ackelsberg served on the APSA's Committee on the Status of Gays and Lesbians in the Profession, and chaired the Committee on the Status of Women in the Profession.

Hayward R. Alker is John A. McCone Professor of International Relations in the School of International Relations at the University of Southern California, where he recently helped design a PhD program in politics and international relations. Having first taught quantitative methodology courses at Yale and MIT, Alker now explores both naturalistic and humanistic philosophies of, and methodologies for, sociopolitical inquiry, often facilitated by computational representations and routines.

Leslie E. Anderson is associate professor of political science at the University of Florida. Her research interests include democracy, electoral studies, institutions, and the role of popular politics in developing democracies.

Samuel H. Beer, the Eaton Professor of the Science of Government emeritus at Harvard University, Beer is the first foreigner to be made a vice president of the Political Studies Association of the United Kingdom and in 2000 was the inaugural recipient of its Isaiah Berlin Award for Lifetime Achievement in the study of politics. President of the New England and the American Political

Science Associations, Beer received the APSA's Woodrow Wilson Prize for *British Politics in the Collectivist Age* and, through its Federalist Section, the Ten Year Achievement award for *To Make a Nation*.

Brian Caterino has taught at the University of Rochester, SUNY–Brockport, and the New School University. He holds an MA and a PhD in political science from the University of Toronto and also did graduate work in philosophy at Binghamton University.

Dan Cleary is a social science instructor at Abraham Lincoln High School in Riverside, California. As a graduate student at the University of California–Riverside, he served as Professor Pion-Berlin's research assistant on the project for this book.

John S. Dryzek is professor and head of the Social and Political Theory Program in the Research School of Social Sciences at Australian National University. He has taught in political science departments with an excess of hegemony (Ohio State), an excess of Perestroika (Melbourne), and a perfect balance (Oregon).

Kim Quaile Hill is a professor of political science at Texas A&M University and an editor of the *American Journal of Political Science*. His research seeks to advance theoretical understanding of democratic political processes, the roles of elites and the mass public in those processes, and policy making in democratic political systems.

Jennifer Hochschild is Henry LaBarre Jayne Professor of Government and professor of African and African American studies at Harvard University. A fellow of the American Academy of Arts and Sciences, former vice president of the American Political Science Association, member of the Board of Trustees of the Russell Sage Foundation, and member of the Board of Overseers of the General Social Survey, Hochschild served as the first editor of *Perspectives on Politics* and as co-chair of the Program Committee for the 1996 APSA convention.

Gary C. Jacobson is professor of political science at the University of California–San Diego, where he has taught since 1979. He received his AB from Stanford in 1966 and his PhD from Yale in 1972, and is a fellow of the American Academy of Arts and Sciences.

Robert Jervis, the Adlai E. Stevenson Professor of International Relations at Columbia University, is a past president of the American Political Science Association. A fellow of the American Academy of Arts and Sciences and the American Association for the Advancement of Science, Jervis specializes in international politics, with special emphasis on security policy, decision making, and theories of conflict and cooperation.

Gregory J. Kasza is professor of political science and East Asian languages and cultures at Indiana University. Author of *The State and the Mass Media in*

Japan, 1918–1945 and *The Conscription Society,* Kasza is finishing a comparative study of Japanese welfare policy.

Stuart J. Kaufman, professor of political science and international relations at the University of Delaware, is the author of *Modern Hatreds: The Symbolic Politics of Ethnic War,* which won the 2003 Grawemeyer Award. The winner of a Council on Foreign Relations International Affairs Fellowship for 1998–99, Kaufman spent 1999 working as director for Russian, Ukrainian, and Eurasian Affairs on the U.S. National Security Council staff.

Catarina Kinnvall is assistant professor in the Department of Political Science at Lund University, Sweden. Her most recent book is *Globalization and Democratization in Asia: The Construction of Identity* (edited with Kristina Jönsson).

David D. Laitin, the Watkins Professor of Political Science at Stanford University, is a specialist in comparative politics and political culture who combines formal and statistical methods with ethnographic fieldwork in Somalia, Yorubaland (Nigeria), Catalonia, and Estonia. Laitin was elected to the American Academy of Arts and Sciences in 1995, and his latest book is *Identity in Formation: The Russian-Speaking Populations in the Near Abroad.*

Jan E. Leighley, professor of political science at the University of Arizona, currently serves as editor, with Kim Quaile Hill, of the *American Journal of Political Science.* She received her PhD in 1988 from Washington University, St. Louis.

Theodore J. Lowi, the John L. Senior Professor of American Institutions at Cornell University, has written or edited a dozen books, including *The End of Liberalism* and *The Personal President—Power Invested, Promise Unfulfilled.* Winner of the Neustadt Prize for the best book on the presidency, Lowi is co-author of one of the leading American government texts, *American Government—Power and Purpose,* and a member of the American Academy of Arts and Sciences. He held the French-American Foundation's Chair of American Civilization in Paris, received the *Doctorat honoris causa* from the Fondation Nationale des Sciences Politiques of the University of Paris, and served as president of both the American and the International Political Science Associations.

Timothy W. Luke is University Distinguished Professor of Political Science at Virginia Polytechnic Institute and State University, where he serves as chair for the Government and International Affairs Program in the School of International and Public Affairs. With special interests in problems of international politics, environmental issues, cultural conflict, and political theory, Luke has most recently written *Museum Politics, Capitalism, Democracy, and Ecology: Departing from Marx,* and *The Politics of Cyberspace* (edited with Chris Toulouse).

Cecelia Lynch is associate professor of political science and international studies at the University of California–Irvine, where she directs the Center for

Global Peace and Conflict Studies. She is the author of *Beyond Appeasement: Interpreting Interwar Peace Movements in World Politics,* which was co-recipient of the Myrna Bernath Prize of the Society of Historians of American Foreign Relations, and won the Edgar J. Furniss Prize for the best first book on security from the Mershon Center at Ohio State University.

Maurice J. Meilleur is an academic advisor and adjunct professor of political science at the University of Illinois at Urbana–Champaign. He recently completed his PhD at Indiana University, Bloomington.

Kristen Renwick Monroe teaches at the University of California–Irvine, where she directs the UCI Interdisciplinary Center for the Scientific Study of Ethics and Morality. Best known as the author of the award-winning *The Heart of Altruism: Perceptions of a Common Humanity* and *The Hand of Compassion: Portraits of Moral Choice during the Holocaust,* Monroe is currently vice president of the International Society of Political Psychology, and is past vice president of both the American and the Midwest Political Science Associations.

David Pion-Berlin is professor of political science at the University of California–Riverside. A Latin Americanist known for his work on civil-military relations, military regimes, political repression, and human rights, Pion-Berlin has recently written *Civil-Military Relations in Latin America: New Analytical Perspectives* and *Through Corridors of Power: Institutions and Civil-Military Relations in Argentina.*

Marsha Pripstein Posusney, professor of political science at Bryant College and adjunct professor of international relations (research) at the Watson Institute for International Studies at Brown University, is an activist for electoral reform who has served on the advisory board of the Center for Voting and Democracy and the American Political Science Association Council. Her first book, *Labor and the State in Egypt: Workers, Unions and Economic Restructuring,* was co-winner of the Middle East Studies Association's Albert Hourani Prize.

Lloyd I. Rudolph is professor of political science emeritus at the University of Chicago, whose current research includes *Postmodern Gandhi and Other Essays on Gandhi at Home and in the World* (co-authored with Susanne Hoeber Rudolph) and *Experiencing the State* (co-edited with J. K. Jacobsen). Recent publications include the jointly authored *Reversing the Gaze: Amar Singh's Diary, A Colonial Subject's Narrative of Imperial India* and "Engaging Subjective Knowledge: How Amar Singh's Diary Narratives of and by the Self Help Explain Identity Politics," in *Perspectives on Politics.*

Susanne Hoeber Rudolph is the William Benton Distinguished Service Professor of Political Science emerita at the University of Chicago, a former president of the American Political Science Association, and author or co-author of eight books, among them *The Modernity of Tradition, In Pursuit of Lakshmi,* and *Reversing the Gaze.* Interested in comparative politics, synchronic and diachronic narratives of state formation, the political sociology of status groups, and transnational religion, Rudolph focuses her research on the Indian subcontinent.

Kamal Sadiq is a recent PhD recipient in political science from the University of Chicago and now teaches at the University of California–Irvine. A Smith Richardson fellow, Sadiq won the 2003 Ethnicity, Nationalism, and Migration Section Graduate Student Paper Award given by the International Studies Association for "Have Documents Will Travel: The Role of Documents in Illegal Immigration."

Elizabeth Sanders is professor of government at Cornell University. Her major publications include *Roots of Reform,* winner of the Greenstone Prize, and *The Regulation of Natural Gas 1938–1978,* winner of the Kammerer Prize.

Sanford F. Schram, member of the Graduate School of Social Work and Social Research at Bryn Mawr College, is active in policy deliberations regarding social welfare in the United States. He has testified before Congress on welfare reform, his research was used in the landmark Supreme Court case *Saenz v. Roe,* and his *Words of Welfare: The Poverty of Social Science and the Social Science of Poverty* won the Michael Harrington Award from the American Political Science Association.

Peregrine Schwartz-Shea is professor of political science at the University of Utah. Author of articles in the *American Political Science Review* and *Public Choice,* Schwartz-Shea now focuses on methodological and epistemological disciplinary practices and is completing *Interpretation and Method: Empirical Research Methods and the Interpretive Turn* with Dvora Yanow.

Joanna Vecchiarelli Scott is a professor at Eastern Michigan University. Author of *Hannah Arendt: Love and Saint Augustine* (with Judith Stark) and the forthcoming *Hannah Arendt Discovers America,* Scott has served on the Executive Committee of the Midwest Political Science Association and on the Nominating Committee, the Ethics Committee, and the Council of the American Political Science Association.

Ian Shapiro, William R. Kenan Jr. Professor and chairman of the Department of Political Science at Yale, is the author, most recently, of *The State Of Democratic Theory, The Moral Foundations of Politics,* and *Pathologies of Rational Choice Theory: A Critique of Applications in Political Science* (with Donald Green). Shapiro is a fellow of the American Academy of Arts and Sciences and has been a fellow of the Carnegie Corporation, the Guggenheim Foundation, and the Center for Advanced Study in the Behavioral Sciences in Palo Alto.

Lee Sigelman is a Columbian Distinguished Professor of Political Science at the George Washington University. A past president of the Midwest Political Science Association and former editor of *American Politics Quarterly,* Professor Sigelman is the current editor of the *American Political Science Review* and has research interests extending across various subfields of political science and into other social science disciplines.

Rogers M. Smith is the Christopher H. Browne Distinguished Professor of Political Science at the University of Pennsylvania, where he teaches American constitutional law and American political thought, with special interests in issues of citizenship and racial, gender, and class inequalities. Author of over eighty articles and author or co-author of five books, for his *Civic Ideals: Conflicting Visions of Citizenship in U.S. History* Smith received six "best book" awards from the American Political Science Association, the Organization of American Historians, the Social Science History Association, and the Association of American Publishers, and was a finalist for the 1998 Pulitzer Prize in History.

Peter J. Steinberger is Robert H. and Blanche Day Ellis Professor of Political Science and Humanities and dean of the faculty at Reed College. Best known for *Logic and Politics: Hegel's Philosophy of Right, The Concept of Political Judgment,* and *The Idea of the State,* Steinberger is currently working on a study of coherence and category error in contemporary politics.

Sven Steinmo is professor of political science at the University of Colorado at Boulder, where he works in political economy, comparative politics and policy, and American government. Director of the Tocqueville Initiative at the University of Colorado, Steinmo is the author of *Taxation and Democracy* and the editor of *Structuring Politics* and *Tax Policy.*

Dorian T. Warren has been an Erskine Peters Fellow in African-American Studies at Notre Dame and a Ford Foundation Pre-Doc and Dissertation fellow. At the University of Chicago Warren served as both a post-doctoral scholar in the Harris School of Public Policy and a visiting fellow at the Center for the Study of Race, Politics, and Culture. A former member of the Executive Councils of the National Conference of Black Political Scientists and the Working Class Studies Association, Warren specializes in the study of marginal groups in American politics, focusing on the political organization and mobilization of groups in response to ascriptive inequalities.

Dvora Yanow is a professor in the Department of Public Administration at California State University–Hayward. The recipient of the Best Book Prize of the American Society for Public Administration, Section for Public Administration Research, for *Constructing American "Race" and "Ethnicity": Category-Making in Public Policy and Administration,* Yanow is completing a book on empirical research methods and the "interpretive turn" with Peregrine Schwartz-Shea.

Index

Page numbers for entries in the notes are suffixed by an *n*.

Ackelsberg, Martha, 240, 282
agency, human, 15, 29, 55–57, 74–75, 232, 234, 433n, 478, 519; actors as culture-creating or culture-destroying, 8, 59
AJPS. See American Journal of Political Science
Alker, Hayward, 35, 357, 434, 446, 448, 547
Almond, Gabriel, 54, 476
American Journal of Political Science (AJPS), 293, 319–20; editorial biases, 342–45, 351–52
American Political Science Association, 278, 323–29, 330–34; Elections Review Committee, 238; as oligarchy, 45; problems, 9–11, 208, 536–8; relationship to perestroika, 1, 5, 265–67, 325–26, 466. *See also* elections, APSA; governance, APSA
American Political Science Review (APSR), 8, 51, 291–93, 297–98, 304, 331–32, 535–38; compared to standardized test, 294–95; editorial biases, 9–11, 13, 22, 208, 291–92, 301, 305–15, 318–20, 467; submissions, 46–47, 202, 292–93, 304–5, 325–29, 536–38, 564
Anderson, Leslie E., 356, 403, 417–18, 420
APSA. *See* American Political Science Association
APSR. See American Political Science Review
area studies, 18–19, 38, 474, 512
atomism, social, 139, 142

Barthes, Roland, 239, 268, 276
Bates, Robert, 127, 134n, 148, 159, 161

Beer, Samuel, 8, 53, 295, 466
behavioralism, 8, 23, 53–58, 316–17, 514–15
behavioral revolution, 8, 14–15, 47–49, 515; as consensus, 49
behavioral science, 48–49
Bender, Thomas, 30
Bensel, Richard, 170
Betts, Richard, 12, 20, 305
Bourdieu, Pierre, 109–10, 476–77, 485
Burke, Edmond, 268, 276

Calvert, Randall, 141–44
career benefits, 89, 227–28, 252, 356–57, 470–71, 484, 539; in Europe, 22, 35–39
case studies, 18–19, 108–9, 204, 308, 394, 525–29, 551. *See also* small *n* studies
Caterino, Brian, 15, 62–63
Caucus for New Political Science, 8, 14, 45–46, 251–52, 283, 468, 493, 502
causal reasoning, 17, 54–55, 58, 77, 552–54. *See also* modes of inquiry
classical economics as ideology, 50
classical realism, 23
Cleary, Dan, 47, 291–92, 294, 304, 421, 426–27, 564–65
Coase, Ronald, 231
Collingwood, R. G., 444–47
communicative action, 142–46; and hegemony, 517
comparative politics, 19, 131, 286, 313, 386–87, 525
comparative research, 64
constructivism, 24, 88, 156–58, 208–10
context, 119–20, 529–30